Windows® XP
GIGABOOK
FOR
DUMMIES®

by Peter Weverka
Mark Chambers, Greg Harvey, Woody Leonhard,
John Levine, Margaret Levine Young, Doug Lowe

D1419770

WILEY

Wiley Publishing, Inc.

Windows® XP GigaBook For Dummies®

Published by
Wiley Publishing, Inc.
111 River Street
Hoboken, NJ 07030-5774
www.wiley.com

Copyright © 2004 by Wiley Publishing, Inc., Indianapolis, Indiana

Published by Wiley Publishing, Inc., Indianapolis, Indiana

Published simultaneously in Canada

No part of this publication may be reproduced, stored in a retrieval system or transmitted in any form or by any means, electronic, mechanical, photocopying, recording, scanning or otherwise, except as permitted under Sections 107 or 108 of the 1976 United States Copyright Act, without either the prior written permission of the Publisher, or authorization through payment of the appropriate per-copy fee to the Copyright Clearance Center, 222 Rosewood Drive, Danvers, MA 01923, (978) 750-8400, fax (978) 646-8600. Requests to the Publisher for permission should be addressed to the Legal Department, Wiley Publishing, Inc., 10475 Crosspoint Blvd., Indianapolis, IN 46256, (317) 572-3447, fax (317) 572-4447, e-mail: permcoordinator@wiley.com.

Trademarks: Wiley, the Wiley Publishing logo, For Dummies, the Dummies Man logo, A Reference for the Rest of Us!, The Dummies Way, Dummies Daily, The Fun and Easy Way, Dummies.com, and related trade dress are trademarks or registered trademarks of John Wiley & Sons, Inc. and/or its affiliates in the United States and other countries, and may not be used without written permission. Windows XP is a registered trademark of Microsoft Corporation in the United States and/or other countries. All other trademarks are the property of their respective owners. Wiley Publishing, Inc., is not associated with any product or vendor mentioned in this book.

LIMIT OF LIABILITY/DISCLAIMER OF WARRANTY: THE PUBLISHER AND THE AUTHOR MAKE NO REPRESENTATIONS OR WARRANTIES WITH RESPECT TO THE ACCURACY OR COMPLETENESS OF THE CONTENTS OF THIS WORK AND SPECIFICALLY DISCLAIM ALL WARRANTIES, INCLUDING WITHOUT LIMITATION WARRANTIES OF FITNESS FOR A PARTICULAR PURPOSE. NO WARRANTY MAY BE CREATED OR EXTENDED BY SALES OR PROMOTIONAL MATERIALS. THE ADVICE AND STRATEGIES CONTAINED HEREIN MAY NOT BE SUITABLE FOR EVERY SITUATION. THIS WORK IS SOLD WITH THE UNDERSTANDING THAT THE PUBLISHER IS NOT ENGAGED IN RENDERING LEGAL, ACCOUNTING, OR OTHER PROFESSIONAL SERVICES. IF PROFESSIONAL ASSISTANCE IS REQUIRED, THE SERVICES OF A COMPETENT PROFESSIONAL PERSON SHOULD BE SOUGHT. NEITHER THE PUBLISHER NOR THE AUTHOR SHALL BE LIABLE FOR DAMAGES ARISING HEREFROM. THE FACT THAT AN ORGANIZATION OR WEBSITE IS REFERRED TO IN THIS WORK AS A CITATION AND/OR A POTENTIAL SOURCE OF FURTHER INFORMATION DOES NOT MEAN THAT THE AUTHOR OR THE PUBLISHER ENDORSES THE INFORMATION THE ORGANIZATION OR WEBSITE MAY PROVIDE OR RECOMMENDATIONS IT MAY MAKE. FURTHER, READERS SHOULD BE AWARE THAT INTERNET WEBSITES LISTED IN THIS WORK MAY HAVE CHANGED OR DISAPPEARED BETWEEN WHEN THIS WORK WAS WRITTEN AND WHEN IT IS READ.

For general information on our other products and services or to obtain technical support, please contact our Customer Care Department within the U.S. at 800-762-2974, outside the U.S. at 317-572-3993, or fax 317-572-4002.

Wiley also publishes its books in a variety of electronic formats. Some content that appears in print may not be available in electronic books.

Library of Congress Control Number: 2004101967

ISBN: 0-7645-6922-8

Manufactured in the United States of America

10 9 8 7 6 5 4 3 2 1

1B/RU/QU/QU/IN

WILEY

Acknowledgments

Wiley Publishing, Inc. gratefully acknowledges the contributions of these authors and contributing writers: Peter Weverka, Woody Leonhard, Mark L. Chambers, Greg Harvey, John Levine, Doug Lowe, and Margaret Levine Young.

We would like to thank Peter Weverka for editing this book, Jean Rogers for copy editing it, and Linda Morris for serving as project editor. Thanks as well go to Kerwin McKenzie for his technical edits, Richard T. Evans for his index, and Rich Tennant for the witty cartoons you will find in this book. Thanks are also due to the many page layout technicians, graphic artists, proofreaders, and others in Composition Services who worked to bring this book to fruition.

Peter Weverka wishes to thank Steve Hayes for the opportunity to work on this and other *For Dummies* books for Wiley Publishing, Inc.

Publisher's Acknowledgments

We're proud of this book; please send us your comments through our online registration form located at www.dummies.com/register/.

Some of the people who helped bring this book to market include the following:

Acquisitions, Editorial, and Media Development

Project Editor: Linda Morris

Acquisitions Editor: Steven Hayes

Copy Editor: Jean Rogers

Technical Editor: Kerwin McKenzie

Editorial Manager: Leah Cameron

Media Development Supervisor: Richard Graves

Editorial Assistant: Amanda Foxworth

Cartoons: Rich Tennant (www.the5thwave.com)

Production

Project Coordinator: Courtney MacIntyre

Layout and Graphics: Amanda Carter, Lauren Goddard, Lynsey Osborn, Jacque Schneider, Julie Trippetti

Proofreaders: Andy Hollandbeck, Carl W. Pierce, Christine Pingleton, Dwight Ramsey

Indexer: Richard T. Evans

Special Help: Joni Burns, Erin Zeltner

Publishing and Editorial for Technology Dummies

    Richard Swadley, Vice President and Executive Group Publisher

    Andy Cummings, Vice President and Publisher

    Mary C. Corder, Editorial Director

Publishing for Consumer Dummies

    Diane Graves Steele, Vice President and Publisher

    Joyce Pepple, Acquisitions Director

Composition Services

    Gerry Fahey, Vice President of Production Services

    Debbie Stailey, Director of Composition Services

Contents at a Glance

Table of Contents

xv

Introduction

This book is a general-purpose guide to computers. It takes on a variety of subjects — PCs, the Windows XP operating system, the Internet, and the Microsoft Office 2003 software suite. Don't look into this book to find out how computer stuff works. Look here to find out how you can make the most of the time you spend with your computer.

What's in This Book, Anyway?

This book is like four different books wrapped up in one convenient volume. It's jam-packed with tips, advice, shortcuts, and how-to's to help you squeeze the last drop of fun or profit from your computer. It's a reference book. It isn't meant to be read from start to finish. Dip into it when you need to solve a problem, you want to investigate a new use for your computer, or you want to find out if there is a better way to do a task. Here's a bare outline of the four parts of this book:

- ✦ **Book I: Windows XP:** Looks into the far and near corners of the Windows XP operating system, including how to customize Windows, manage files and folders, and use Windows as a multimedia device.

- ✦ **Book II: PCs and Peripherals:** Explores how to install and maintain your computer's hardware, make your PC double as a toy, and create a home network. You will also find advice here for using scanners, digital cameras, and other cool peripheral devices.

- ✦ **Book III: The Internet:** Explains how to surf the Internet, handle e-mail, and create Web pages, as well as chat online and download music files.

- ✦ **Book IV: Office 2003 and Money 2004:** Describes how to use these software programs in the Office 2003 suite: Word, Excel, PowerPoint, and Outlook. Book IV also explains how to manage your finances with Money 2004.

What Makes This Book Special

You are holding in your hands a computer book designed to make learning as easy and comfortable as possible. Besides the fact that this book is easy to read, it's different from other books about computers. Read on to see why.

Easy-to-look-up information

This book is a reference, and that means that readers have to be able to find instructions quickly. To that end, the authors that contributed to this book have taken great pains to make sure that the material in this book is well organized and easy to find. The descriptive headings help you find information quickly. The bulleted and numbered lists make following instructions simpler. The tables make options easier to understand.

The authors want you to be able to look down the page and see in a heading or list the name of the topic that concerns you and for you to be able to find instructions quickly. The contents of this book were organized such that you can find topics in a hurry.

A task-oriented approach

Most computer books describe what the software is, but this book explains how to complete tasks with the software. I assume that you came to this book because you want to know how to *do* something — print form letters, hook up a home network, build a Web site. You came to the right place. This book describes how to get tasks done.

A Greatest Hits Collection

The material in this book was culled from *For Dummies* books published by Wiley Publishing, Inc. You can think of this book as a kind of greatest hits collection of computer books. If you stumble upon a topic in this book that intrigues you and you want to know more about it, I suggest looking into one of the books from which this book was created:

✦ *Windows XP All-in-One Desk Reference For Dummies,* by Woody Leonhard.

✦ *PCs All-in-One Desk Reference For Dummies,* by Mark L. Chambers.

✦ *The Internet All-in-One Desk Reference For Dummies,* by Kelly Ewing, John Levine, Arnold Reinhold, Margaret Levine Young, Doug Lowe, Greg Harvey, Viraf Mohta, Jennifer Kaufeld, John Kaufeld, Peter Weverka, Brad Hill, and Lee Musick.

✦ *Office 2003 All-in-One Desk Reference For Dummies,* by Peter Weverka.

✦ *Windows XP Timesaving Techniques For Dummies*, by Woody Leonhard.

Foolish Assumptions

Please forgive me, but I made one or two foolish assumptions about you, the reader of this book. I assumed that

✦ You have a PC (not a Macintosh computer).

✦ You use a Windows operating system, preferably Windows XP. Book I explains how to use Windows XP, but all people who have the Windows operating system installed on their computers are invited to read this book. It serves for people who have Windows 95, Windows 98, and Windows NT, as well as Windows XP or higher.

✦ You have Microsoft Office 2003 installed on your computer. Book IV is devoted to Office.

✦ You are kind to foreign tourists and small animals.

Conventions Used in This Book

I want you to understand all the instructions in this book, and in that spirit, I've adopted a few conventions.

To show you how to step through command sequences, I use the ⇨ symbol. For example, you can choose File⇨Save to save a file. The ⇨ is just a shorthand method of saying, "From the File menu, choose Save."

 Yet another way to give a command is to click a toolbar button. Often when I tell you to click a toolbar button, you see a small illustration of the button in the margin of this book. The button shown here is the Save button, the one you can click to save a file in most programs.

Where you see boldface letters or numbers in this book, it means to type the letters or numbers. For example, "Enter **25** in the Percentage text box" means to do exactly that: Enter the number 25.

Icons Used in This Book

To help you get the most out of this book, I've placed icons here and there. Here's what the icons mean:

 Next to the Tip icon, you can find shortcuts and tricks of the trade to make your visit to Computerland more enjoyable.

 Where you see the Warning icon, tread softly and carefully. It means that you are about to do something that you may regret later.

 When I explain a juicy little fact that bears remembering, I mark it with a Remember icon. When you see this icon, prick up your ears. You will discover something that you need to remember throughout your adventures in Computerland.

 When I am forced to describe high-tech stuff, a Technical Stuff icon appears in the margin. You don't have to read what's beside the Technical Stuff icons if you don't want to, although these technical descriptions often help you understand how a software or hardware feature works.

Book I

Windows XP

Book 1: Windows XP

Chapter 1: Introducing Windows XP

In This Chapter

✓ **Figuring out where Windows XP fits into The Grand Scheme of Things**

✓ **Seeing what Windows can (and can't) do for you**

✓ **Perusing a brief history of Windows**

W indows XP is one of the most sophisticated computer programs ever made. It cost more money to develop and took more people to build than any computer program, ever. So why is it so blasted hard to use? Why doesn't it do what you want it to do the first time? For that matter, why do you need it at all? That's what this chapter is all about.

What Windows XP Does (And Doesn't)

Someday you'll get really, really mad at Windows. I guarantee it. When you feel like putting your fist through the computer screen, tossing your Windows XP CD in a bonfire, or hiring an expensive Windows expert to drive out the devils within (insist on a Microsoft Certified System Exorcist, of course), read through this section. It may help you understand why and how Windows has limitations. It also may help you communicate with the geeky rescue team that tries to bail you out, whether you rely on the store that sold you the PC, the smelly guy in the apartment downstairs, or your eight-year-old daughter's nerdy classmate.

Hardware and software

At the most fundamental level, all computer stuff comes in one of two flavors: either it's hardware, or it's software:

✦ **Hardware:** Anything you can touch — a computer screen, a mouse, a CD. Your PC is hardware. Kick the computer screen and your toe hurts. Drop the big box on the floor and it smashes into a gazillion pieces. That's hardware.

✦ **Software:** Everything else — e-mail messages, that letter to your Aunt Martha, pictures of your last vacation, programs like Microsoft Office. If you have a roll of film developed and put on a CD, the shiny, round CD is hardware — you can touch it — but the pictures themselves are software. Get the difference? Windows XP is software. You can't touch it.

When you first set up your PC, Windows had you click I Accept to a licensing agreement that's long enough to wrap around the Empire State Building. If you're curious about what you accepted, a printed copy of the End User License Agreement is in the box that your PC came in or in the

CD packaging (if you bought Windows XP separately from your computer). If you can't find your copy, choose Start⇨Help and Support. Type **eula** in the Search text box and press Enter.

When you bought your computer, you paid for a license to use one copy of Windows on the PC that you bought. The PC manufacturer paid Microsoft a royalty so that it could sell you Windows along with your PC. You may think that you got Windows from, say, Dell — indeed, you may have to contact Dell for technical support on Windows questions — but, in fact, Windows came from Microsoft.

Why do I have to run Windows?

The short answer: You *don't* have to run Windows. The PC you have is a dumb box. (You needed me to tell you that, eh?) In order to get the dumb box to do anything worthwhile, you need a computer program that takes control of the PC and makes it do things such as show Web pages on the screen, respond to mouse clicks, or print ransom notes. An *operating system* controls the dumb box and makes it do worthwhile things, in ways that mere humans can understand.

Without an operating system, the computer can sit in a corner and count to itself, or put profound messages on the screen, such as `Non-system disk or disk error. Insert system disk and press any key when ready.` If you want your computer to do more than that, though, you need an operating system.

Windows is not the only operating system in town. The single largest competitor to Windows is an operating system called Linux. Some people (I'm told) actually prefer Linux to Windows, and the debates between pro-Windows and pro-Linux camps can become rather heated. Suffice it to say that, oh, 99 percent of all individual PC users stick with Windows. You probably will, too.

A terminology survival kit

Some terms pop up so frequently that you'll find it worthwhile to memorize them, or at least understand where they come from. That way, you won't be caught flatfooted when your first-grader comes home and asks if he can download a program from the Internet.

A *program* is *software* (see preceding section) that works on a computer. Windows, the *operating system* (see preceding section), is a program. So are computer games, Microsoft Office, Microsoft Word (which is the word processor part of Office), Internet Explorer (the Web browser in Windows), the Windows Media Player, those nasty viruses you've heard about, that screen saver with splatting suicidal bungee-jumping cows, and so on.

A special kind of program called a *driver* makes specific pieces of hardware work with the operating system. For example, your computer's printer has a driver; your monitor has a driver; your mouse has a driver; Tiger Woods has a driver.

Sticking a program on your computer, and setting it up so that it works, is called *installing*.

When you crank up a program — that is, get it going on your computer — you can say you *started* it, *launched* it, *ran* it, or *executed* it. They all mean the same thing.

If the program quits the way it's supposed to, you can say it *stopped, finished, ended, exited,* or *terminated.* Again, all of these terms mean the same thing. If the program stops with some sort of weird error message, you can say it *crashed, died, cratered, croaked, went belly up, GPFed* (techspeak for "generated a General Protection Fault" — don't ask), or employ any of a dozen colorful but unprintable epithets. If the program just sits there and you can't get it to do anything, you can say the program *froze, hung, stopped responding,* or *went into a loop.*

A *bug* is something that doesn't work right. (A bug is not a virus! Viruses work right far too often.) Admiral Grace Hopper often repeated the story of a moth being found in a relay of an old Mark II computer. The moth was taped into the technician's log book on September 9, 1947, with the annotation "1545 Relay #70 Panel F (moth) in relay. First actual case of bug being found."

The people who invented all of this terminology think of the Internet as being some great blob in the sky — it's "up," as in "up in the sky." So if you send something from your computer to the Internet, you're *uploading.* If you take something off the Internet and put it on your computer, you're *downloading.*

And then you have *wizards.* Windows comes with lots of 'em. They guide you through complex procedures, moving one step at a time. Typically, wizards have three buttons on the bottom of each screen: Back, Next (or Finish), and Cancel (see Figure 1-1). Wizards remember what you've chosen as you go from step to step, making it easy to experiment a bit, change your mind, back up, and try a different setting without getting all the check boxes confused.

Figure 1-1:
The Add
Printer
Wizard
helps you
connect
printers to
your
computer.

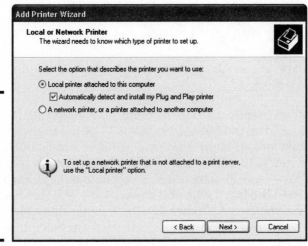

A brief history of booting

You probably know that the process of getting your computer started — from the time you hit the On button until the time the computer starts responding — is called *booting*, but do you know why? It's an old term, dating back to the dawn of computing history. When a computer starts, it has to bring in a teensy-tiny program that, in turn, brings in all the other programs that make the computer work. The process resembles pulling yourself up by your own bootstraps — the tiny program is called a bootstrap loader, whence *boot*. The name stuck.

Where We've Been

Unlike Windows ME (which is a barely warmed-over remake of Windows 98) and Windows 2000 (which should've been called Windows NT 5.0), Windows XP is quite different from anything that has come before. To understand why Windows XP works so differently, you need to understand the genetic cesspool from which it emerged.

Let's start at the beginning. Microsoft licensed the first PC operating system, called DOS, to IBM in late 1981. MS-DOS sold like hotcakes for a number of reasons, not the least of which is that it was the only game in town. None of this sissy graphical stuff; DOS demanded that you type, and type, and type again, in order to get anything done.

The rise of Windows

The 'Softies only started developing Windows in earnest when the company discovered that it needed an operating system to run Excel, its spreadsheet program. Windows 1.0 shipped in November 1985. It was slow, bloated, and unstable — some things never change, eh? — but if you wanted to run Excel, you had to have Windows.

Excel 2.0 and Windows 2.0 shipped in late 1987. This breathtaking, revolutionary new version of Windows let you overlap windows — place one window on top of another — and it took advantage of the PC/XT's advanced computer chip, the 80286. Version 2.1 (also called Windows 286) shipped in June 1988, and some people discovered that it spent more time working than crashing. My experience was, uh, somewhat different. Windows 286 came on a single diskette.

Do you have Macintosh friends who like to taunt you about the ways Microsoft "stole" ideas from the old Mac systems? The next time those revisionist historians start kicking sand in your face, make sure you set the record straight. The fact is that both Apple and Microsoft stole many of their ideas from Xerox — specifically the Star machine built at Xerox's Palo Alto Research Center in the late 1970s and early 1980s. The Star had a desktop with icons and overlapping windows. It used a mouse, supported "point-and-click" interactions, popped up menus, ran on dialog boxes, used an Ethernet network just like the one you swear at today, and introduced the laser printer.

Windows 3.0 arrived in May 1990, and the computer industry changed forever. Microsoft finally had a hit on its hands to rival the old MS-DOS. When
Windows 3.1 came along in April 1992, it rapidly became the most widely
used operating system in history. In October 1992, Windows for Workgroups
3.1 (which I loved to call "Windows for Warehouses") started rolling out,
with support for networking, shared files and printers, internal e-mail, and
other features you take for granted today. Some of the features worked.
Sporadically. A much better version, Workgroups for Windows 3.11, became
available in November 1993. It caught on in the corporate world.
Sporadically.

eNTer NT

At its heart, Windows 3.x was built on top of MS-DOS, and that caused all
sorts of headaches: DOS simply wasn't stable or versatile enough to make
Windows a rock-solid operating system. Bill Gates figured, all the way back
in 1988, that DOS would never be able to support an advanced version of
Windows, so he hired a guy named Dave Cutler to build a new version of
Windows from scratch. At the time, Dave led the team that built the VMS
operating system for Digital Equipment Corp's DEC computers.

When Dave's all-new version of Windows shipped five years later in August
1993, Windows NT 3.1 ("New Technology"; yes, the first version number was
3.1) greeted the market with a thud. It was awfully persnickety about the
kinds of hardware it would support, and it didn't play games worth squat.

NT and the "old" Windows

For the next eight years, two entirely different lineages of Windows
co-existed. The old DOS/Windows 3.1 branch became Windows 95 (shipped
in August 1995, "probably the last version of Windows based on DOS"),
Windows 98 (June 1998, "absolutely the last version of Windows based on
DOS, for sure"), and then Windows ME (Millennium Edition, September 2000,
"no, honest, this is really, really the last version of Windows based on DOS").

On the New Technology side of the fence, Windows NT 3.1 begat Windows
NT 3.5 (September 1994), which begat Windows NT 4.0 (August 1996). Many
companies still use Windows NT 3.51 and NT 4 for their servers — the
machines that anchor corporate networks. In February 2000, Microsoft
released Windows 2000, which confused the living daylights out of everybody: In spite of its name, Windows 2000 is the next version of Windows NT
and has nothing at all in common with Windows 98 or ME.

Microsoft made oodles of money milking the DOS-based Windows cash cow
and waited patiently while sales on the NT side gradually picked up.
Windows NT 5.0, er, 2000 still didn't play games worth squat, and some
hardware gave it heartburn, but Windows 2000 rapidly became the operating system of choice for most businesses and at least a few home users.

Merging the branches

Windows XP — in my opinion, the first must-have version of Windows since
Windows 95 — officially shipped in October 2001. Twenty years after

Microsoft tip-toed into the big time with MS-DOS, the Windows XP juggernaut blew away everything in sight.

Some people think that Windows XP (the XP stands for eXPerience, according to the marketing folks) represents a melding or blending of the two Windows lineages: a little ME here, a little 2000 there, with a side of 98 thrown in for good measure. Ain't so. Windows XP is 100 percent, bona fide NT. Period. Not one single part of Windows ME — or any of the other DOS-based Windows versions, for that matter, not to mention DOS itself — is in Windows XP. Not one.

That's good news and bad news. First, the good news: If you can get Windows XP to work at all on your old computer, or if you buy a new PC that's designed to use Windows XP, your new system will almost certainly be considerably more stable than it would be with Windows ME or any of its progenitors. The bad news: If you learned how to get around a problem in Windows ME (or 98 or 95), you may not be able to use the same tricks in Windows XP. The surface may look the same, but the plumbing is radically different.

Microsoft went to a lot of effort to make Windows XP look like Windows ME. But that similarity is only skin deep. Beneath the façade, Windows XP is a gussied up version of Windows NT/2000. Windows XP is *not* a descendant of Windows ME or Windows 98, even though it's marketed that way. Tricks that work in Windows ME or 98 may or may not work in Windows XP.

Chapter 2: Upgrading to Windows XP

In This Chapter

- ✔ Upgrading from an earlier version of Windows
- ✔ Activating Windows so you can use it
- ✔ Finding out what to do if something goes wrong

*I*f Windows XP wasn't preloaded on your computer, you may count yourself among the unlucky people who need to upgrade to Windows XP from an earlier version of Windows. This chapter tells you how to do that. It also tells you how to activate the product and scream bloody murder if something goes wrong.

Upgrading — A Brain Transplant

If your current machine runs Windows 98 or ME, you can upgrade to Windows XP by simply starting Windows, inserting the Windows XP CD into your CD drive, and following the instructions.

If you decide that Windows XP isn't your cup of tea, you can remove it and restore your old Windows 98 or ME system, intact. Here's how:

1. **Choose Start⇨Control Panel.**

2. **Click Add and Remove Programs.**

3. **Click Windows XP, and then click Add/Remove.**

4. **Pick the option to Uninstall Windows XP, and click Continue.**

If your current machine runs Windows NT 4 or Windows 2000, you can upgrade to Windows XP Professional directly with the CD. However, you will not be able to automatically uninstall Windows XP and reinstall NT 4 or 2000.

If your current machine runs Windows 95 or NT 3.*x*, you won't be able to upgrade. Your only option is to erase Windows from your hard drive (never a simple proposition) and perform a clean install from scratch (see the "Considering a clean install" section for sobering enlightenment). Chances are good that your Windows 95 or NT 3.*x* system isn't powerful enough to run Windows XP very well anyway. Far better to wait until you can afford a new PC with Windows XP preinstalled.

Windows Upgrade Advisor/Hardware Compatibility List

Microsoft keeps a master list of all hardware that's passed muster for Windows XP. The so-called Hardware Compatibility List (HCL to techies) contains the names of products that have received Microsoft's seal of approval. If you're thinking of upgrading your current computer to Windows XP or if you want to add new hardware to an existing PC, Windows XP compatibility is a bit, uh, important. You can browse through the list at www.microsoft.com/hcl/default.asp.

The hardware compatibility list must be taken with at least a small grain of salt. While it's true that hardware manufacturers sweat blood to meet Microsoft's stringent standards, the fact remains that any randomly chosen piece of hardware may refuse to behave itself, whether the cause is a conflict in another piece of hardware, in a lousy device driver, or the phase of the moon.

Before you upgrade an existing PC to Windows XP, you should check the machine to make sure there are no known problems. Microsoft distributes a program called the Windows XP Upgrade Advisor that reaches into the innermost parts of your PC and reports on potential problems with the upgrade. You can download the Windows XP Home Upgrade Advisor from www.microsoft.com/windowsxp/home/howtobuy/upgrading/advisor.asp. The Windows XP Professional advisor is at www.microsoft.com/windowsxp/pro/howtobuy/upgrading/advisor.asp. You may also find a copy of both advisors on a free CD at your friendly local computer shop.

Considering a clean install

Windows XP is an enormously complex program. In the best of all possible worlds, if you upgrade from your current version of Windows — be it 98, ME, NT 4, or 2000 — to Windows XP, the upgrade routines successfully grab all of your old settings, get rid of the extraneous garbage that's floating around on your old machine, and install a stable, pristine copy of Windows XP, ready for you to take around the block.

Unfortunately, the world is not a pretty place, and your hard drive probably looks like a bit-strewn sewer. Historically, Windows has been considerably less stable for upgraders than for those who perform a *clean install* — wiping out the contents of the hard drive and starting all over again. All the flotsam and jetsam left from an old version of Windows invariably mucks up the works with the new version.

A clean install is not for the faint of heart. No matter how hard you try, you will lose data, somewhere, somehow — it always happens, even to those of us masochists who have been running clean installs for a decade. If you value everything on your computer, go for the simple upgrade. If you want your PC to run smoothly, think about a clean install.

The following is my general procedure for a clean install on computers that can start from the CD drive, in very broad terms:

1. **Download and install Revelation from SnadBoy software at** www.
snadboy.com **(see Figure 2-1).**

Use Revelation for a few days (or weeks!) to retrieve any passwords that
you may have stashed away.

Figure 2-1:
SnadBoy's
Revelation
lets you see
passwords
that appear
as **** on
the screen.

2. **Make sure that you have current CDs for all the software that you
normally use.**

If the programs require passwords/installation keys, you need the passwords, too.

3. **Back up everything. Twice.**

If you have a Windows XP computer handy, and you can attach it to the
PC that you're upgrading through a network or a direct-connect cable,
you may want to try a Vulcan Mind Meld, er, the Windows XP Migration
Wizard. Use it to transfer all your files and settings over to the other PC,
temporarily. Follow the instructions in the next section, "Using the
Migration Wizard," to pick up the settings before you perform the
upgrade and stick them on the temporary machine. Then follow the
instructions again to move them from the temporary PC back to your
(freshly upgraded) original PC.

4. **Insert the Windows XP installation disk in the CD drive, and then
choose Start➪Shut Down to go through a full shutdown.**

Windows XP may offer to install itself while you're trying to shut down.
If it does, click Cancel. Power off the PC and wait at least a full minute.

5. **Turn the power on.**

If the PC is capable of starting ("booting") from the CD, you see a line on
the screen that says something like Press any key to boot from CD.
Press the Enter key.

6. **Go through the steps indicated by the installer to delete the primary
partition.**

That wipes out all the data on the hard drive.

7. **Pick your jaw up from the floor, kick yourself twice for being so obstinate, pat yourself on the back for starting out fresh, and follow through with the rest of the installation.**

   Windows XP does a good job of taking you through the steps. Just follow along. The only really tricky part of the installation: Windows XP has to restart your PC early in the installation process. When that happens, you'll probably get that `Press any key to boot from the CD` message again. This time — the second time you see the message — ignore it. Let Windows XP start itself from the hard drive.

Clean installs rate right up there with root canals and prostate exams. Nobody in their right mind will try one, unless they really want to make sure that Windows XP will run smoothly.

Using the Migration Wizard

Windows XP's Files and Settings Transfer Wizard (better known as the Migration Wizard) makes transferring certain kinds of settings and data files between two computers comparatively easy. It sounds great and works well, as long as you don't expect too much. You need to be aware of several limitations:

✦ The PC you're transferring files and settings "to" must be running Windows XP. If at all possible, it should be connected to the PC that you're transferring settings "from." The "from" PC can be running just about any version of Windows — Windows 95, 98, ME, NT 4, 2000, or XP.

The Files and Settings Transfer Wizard can send a humongous amount of data from one PC to another. You can schlep diskettes from one machine to another, if you have a few spare hours or days. Far better, though, is if you can get both PCs talking to each other on a network. Failing that, you can buy a special cable, called a Serial PC to PC Transfer Cable, that plugs into the serial slots on both PCs (the slots you may be using for printers). The wizard will work with any of 'em.

✦ The wizard can't install your old programs on your new PC. You have to do that yourself, manually, one at a time, generally from the original CDs that the programs came on.

If you use the Files and Settings Transfer Wizard but you don't install all of your old programs on your new PC, weird things may happen on the new PC. You may double-click on a file in Windows Explorer, for example, and have Windows XP say that it can't find the program associated with the file. Outlook may have trouble displaying a file attached to a message. Nothing earth-shattering will happen, mind you, but it can be annoying.

✦ The wizard picks up only data files and some Windows Registry entries. That means you can't expect it to pull across all of your passwords, and some copy protection schemes (on games, for example) may go haywire.

On the plus side, though, the Files and Settings Transfer Wizard doesn't pick up much of the garbage that seems to accumulate in every Windows PC, which means you can use it without fear of gumming up your new computer.

Here are the kinds of things you can expect to go across in a transfer:

✦ Data files from your Windows Desktop, the My Documents folder (including My Pictures and My Music, if you have those in the My Documents folder), and the Shared Desktop and Documents folders.

✦ Other files scattered around your hard disk(s), as long as Windows recognizes them as common data files.

The Files and Settings Transfer Wizard really chooses which files to transfer based on the filename extension. It looks for filename extensions that are commonly associated with data files, such as .doc or .jpg.

✦ Settings for Windows (desktop, screen savers, Taskbar options, and the like), Windows Explorer, Internet Explorer (including your list of Favorites), and Outlook Express.

✦ All of your Microsoft Office settings.

To use the Migration Wiz . . . er, the File and Settings Transfer Wizard:

1. **Make sure Windows XP is up and running on the "to" PC.**

Get your hardware installed, set up your users, and run Windows XP long enough to be familiar with it.

2. **Log on the "to" PC as the user who's supposed to receive all the files and settings from the "from" PC.**

If both the "to" and "from" PCs are connected to your network, choose Start⇨My Network Places or Start⇨My Computer to make sure that the network connection is up and kicking. If they aren't connected to the same network, get a Serial PC to PC Transfer Cable and attach it to the serial ports on both PCs.

3. **Choose Start⇨Files and Settings Transfer Wizard, if it's on the Start menu.**

If it isn't, choose Start⇨All Programs⇨Accessories⇨System Tools⇨Files and Settings Transfer Wizard.

4. **Follow the steps in the wizard (see Figure 2-2).**

The exact steps vary depending on the method you're using to transfer the data. If you have many large documents or picture files, plan on spending a few hours. If you're transferring by diskette, don't be surprised if it takes all day.

If you perform a scorched-earth clean install of Windows XP (see the preceding section), you can use the Files and Settings Transfer Wizard twice to drag most of your data (but none of your programs!) through the upgrade, even though you delete everything on your hard drive in the process of upgrading. All it takes is an intermediary machine running Windows XP that holds your settings while the old PC is wiped clean. For the first run of the Files and Settings Transfer Wizard, use the intermediary machine as the "to" machine. Then upgrade the old PC. Finally, run the Files and Settings Transfer Wizard again, this time using the intermediary machine as the "from" machine. Works like a champ.

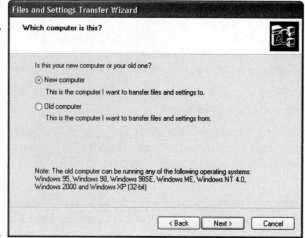

Figure 2-2:
The Files
and Settings
Transfer
Wizard can
send most
(but not all)
of your
important
information
from an
old PC to a
new one.

Product Activation

When you buy a copy of Windows XP in a shrink-wrapped box, you're allowed to install it on one — and *only* one — PC. When you buy a new PC with Windows XP preinstalled, Windows stays with the PC. You can't transfer Windows XP from the original, bundled machine to a different machine. Microsoft uses a technique called "BIOS locking" to make sure that the copy of Windows XP that ships with a PC stays tied to that specific PC, forever and ever.

There are some ifs, ands, and buts floating around, but in general, you can't copy Windows XP and pass around pirate CDs to your buddies or install a single copy on all the machines in your home. If you have three PCs, and you want to run Windows XP on all of them, you have to buy three copies of Windows XP, either in shrink-wrapped boxes or preinstalled on new machines.

Windows XP enforces this one-Windows-one-PC licensing requirement with a technique called *Windows Product Activation,* or WPA. Here's how WPA works:

1. **The Windows XP installer makes you type the unique 25-character code that's printed on the case of your Windows XP CD.**

   Later, the Product Activation program looks at various serial numbers inside your PC — the processor, network card, and disk drives, among others — mixes them together, and produces a second 25-character code that identifies your PC. Those 50 characters, taken together, are called the *Installation ID.*

2. **When you *activate* Windows XP (see Figure 2-3), you give Microsoft that 50-character Installation ID.**

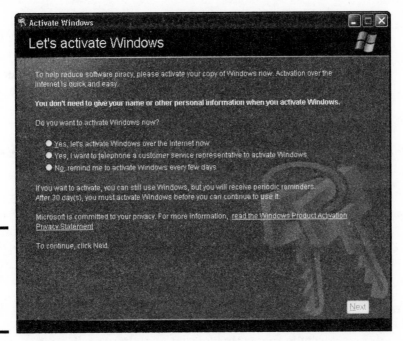

Figure 2-3:
The
Windows
Product
Activation
Wizard.

Microsoft checks to see whether anybody else has submitted the 25-character code from the case of the Windows XP CD.

- If nobody else has activated that 25-character code from the CD case, or if the 25-character code has been activated with that specific Installation ID (which means you activated this particular copy of Windows XP from the same PC twice), Microsoft sends back a 42-character *Confirmation ID*. Both the Installation ID and the Confirmation ID are stored on your PC.

- If that 25-character code has already been used on a different PC, though, you get a polite message on your machine saying, According to our records, the number of times that you can activate Windows with this product key has been exceeded. Please enter a different product key, and then click Retry. You're given further instructions for contacting Microsoft, if you feel the need.

3. **Every time Windows XP starts, it recalculates the 25-character code that's based on the various serial numbers inside your PC.**

   If the code matches the one that's stored on your PC, and the Confirmation ID is good, Windows takes off.

4. **On the other hand, if the recalculated 25-character code doesn't match your original code, pandemonium breaks loose.**

   Your hard drives start spinning at twice their normal speed, your keyboard gets short-circuited with your PC's power supply, and the local constabulary receives an urgent fax from Redmond with a preapproved no-knock search warrant. Okay, okay. I'm exaggerating a little bit. Here's what really happens:

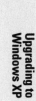

- If Windows decides that you've only made a few changes to your PC — replaced a hard drive, say, or even changed the motherboard — it lets you start Windows anyway.

- On the other hand, if Windows determines that you've made too many changes, it refuses to start and insists that you contact Microsoft for a new Confirmation ID. That starts the activation cycle all over again.

If you bought your PC with Windows XP preinstalled, it was activated before you ever got it.

If you bought and installed Windows XP yourself, though, the activation time clock takes over. From the day you install Windows XP, you have 30 days to activate it. Windows tries to get you to activate it while you're installing. Failing that, it continues to remind you, relentlessly, as the 30 days tick away. Reinstalling Windows XP won't bypass the activation requirement.

Activating via the Internet makes the whole process of generating, sending, and receiving ID codes invisible: All you know is that the process worked, and you can continue to use the software you bought. If you activate by telephone, though, you have to be sitting at your computer with your Windows XP installation CD handy. You get to read a bunch of numbers to the rep on the other end of the phone line, and she reads a bunch of numbers back to you so that you can type them into the WPA Wizard.

Surprisingly, Windows XP still works a little bit, even after the activation period has expired, and even though it won't start. For example, a modem attached to a PC that hasn't been activated can still dial out, if it's set up for Internet Connection Sharing.

As the Activation Wizard screens emphasize (see Figure 2-4), activation is not the same as registration. When you activate Windows XP, your computer sends Microsoft a 50-character Installation ID — *and nothing else*. When you register Windows XP, you send Microsoft your name, address, telephone number, and any other information that the screens can extract from you.

Activation is a given: You have to activate Windows XP or it dies. Registration, on the other hand, is entirely optional — and basically useless for Dummies everywhere. (What? You think Microsoft wants your mailing address to send you a product recall? A birthday card? Sheesh.) You have no reason in the world to register Windows XP. Don't do it.

Big companies with big bucks don't have to put up with Windows Product Activation. (One guess why.) Any company that buys Windows XP via a site license — that is, buys many copies at a time — gets a special version that doesn't require activation.

If you hear rumors on the Internet about a pirate version of Windows XP that magically bypasses Windows Product Activation, chances are very good that it's a corporate copy.

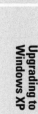

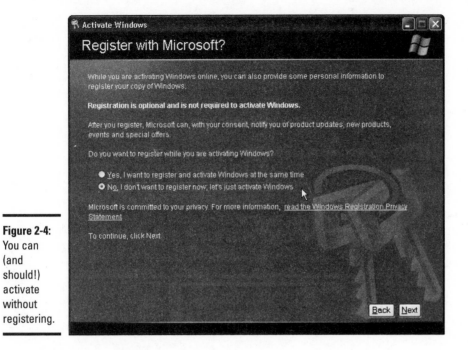

Figure 2-4:
You can
(and
should!)
activate
without
registering.

What if the Wheels Fall Off?

So what should you do if Windows XP dies?

✦ If you got Windows XP bundled with a new PC, scream bloody murder at the vendor who sold you the bleeping thing. Don't put up with any talk like "It's a software problem; Microsoft is at fault." If you bought Windows XP with a new PC, the company that sold you the machine has full responsibility for making it work right.

✦ If you upgraded from Windows 98 or SE to Windows XP, you can always uninstall Windows XP and go back to your old operating system, as unpalatable as that may seem.

✦ If you upgraded from Windows NT 4 or 2000 and you didn't go through a clean install, try that. You don't have much to lose, eh?

✦ If you've done a clean install and Windows XP still falls over and plays dead, man, you have my sympathies. Check with your hardware manufacturer and make sure you have the latest BIOS version installed. (Make sure you get an instruction book; changing the BIOS is remarkably easy, if you follow the instructions.) Hit the newsgroups online, or drop by the WOPR Lounge, www.wopr.com/lounge, to see if anybody there can lend a hand. If all else fails, admit defeat, and reinstall your old operating system. Again, life's too short.

Chapter 3: Finding Your Way around Windows XP

In This Chapter

- ✓ Finding your way around the desktop
- ✓ Making the mouse work your way
- ✓ Handling windows
- ✓ Looking at files and folders
- ✓ Taking a Windows XP tour

As soon as you log onto the computer, you're greeted with an enormous expanse of near-nothingness, cleverly painted with a pretty picture of a wheat field. Or is it Bill Gate's front yard? (Or if you bought a new PC with Windows XP preinstalled, you might see the PC manufacturer's logo on the screen.) In any case, you need to be well acquainted with the different parts of Windows XP before you can become a Windows Wiz. This chapter introduces you to Windows XP and gives you the lay of the land. It explains how to handle the mouse, what dialog boxes are, and what files and folders are. You also get a brief introduction to the many programs that are available by clicking the Start button.

The Desktop

Your Windows destiny, such as it is, unfolds on the computer's screen. The screen that Windows shows you every time you start is called the *desktop*, although it doesn't bear much resemblance to the top of a real desk. (Just try putting a pencil on it.) The first time you start Windows, your desktop looks something like the one in Figure 3-1.

Although the number and appearance of objects scattered on your computer monitor varies depending on who sold you the computer and what was included when you bought it, chances are pretty good that you have only a few pictures — they're called *icons* — sitting on the desktop. In Figure 3-1, one icon appears, the Recycle Bin icon, where Windows sticks everything you threw away.

 Your desktop probably looks different from the one in Figure 3-1. For one thing, you're bound to have a handful of icons sitting around. If you bought a new computer with Windows XP installed, chances are good that the manufacturer sold some desktop real estate to a software company or an Internet Service Provider. (Oh yeah, the AOLs and Nortons of the world compensate the Dells and Compaqs for services rendered. Don't you ever doubt it.) If you see an icon you don't like, right-click on it and choose Delete from the menu that appears. Good riddance to bad rubbish.

Where's Woodrow?

Programs sit behind here

The Windows taskbar

🏁 start

Figure 3-1: The bone-stock Windows XP Home desktop.

Yeah, yeah, I know. The terminology stinks: The Windows desktop doesn't look anything like your desktop. Mine, neither. And calling those little pictures "icons" seems a bit, uh, iconoclastic, given that real icons rate as exquisite *objets d'art,* rendered in paint on wood. The price of progress, I guess.

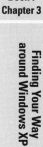

Stores deleted files

The current time, if
you set the clock right

System status
information

Recycle Bin

11:13 AM

When you get past the verdant fields rolling across your screen, the rest of
the desktop isn't very inspiring, although plenty of surprises await as you
begin clicking:

✦ **Windows taskbar:** Runs all along the bottom of the screen, keeps you posted on what your computer is doing — which computer programs are running, where you're visiting on the Internet, and almost anything else that requires your attention.

✦ **Notification area:** Also known to techies as the *system tray.* This area sits on top of the taskbar on the right side and tells you the time, but it also lets you know what Windows is doing behind the scenes. For example, if you're using a modem to connect to the Internet, little modem lights down here reassure you that the connection hasn't frozen. At least, that's the theory. Other tiny icons in the notification area may control your speaker volume or tell you if you're logged on to Windows Messenger.

✦ **Start button:** Located in the lower left of the desktop. This button gives you access to everything your computer can do. Click it and you see the Start menu — *menu* being geekspeak for a list of things that you can click. Look for all the details in the "Starting with the Start Button" section, later in this chapter.

The Windows desktop looks simple enough, but don't fool yourself: Underneath that calm exterior sits the most sophisticated computer program ever created. Hundreds of millions of dollars went into creating the illusion of simplicity — something to remember the next time you feel like kicking your computer and screaming at the Windows gods.

Mousing

Your computer's mouse serves as the primary way of interacting with Windows, but you already knew that. You can click on the left mouse button or the right mouse button, or you can roll the wheel down the middle (if you have one), and the mouse will do different things, depending on where you click or roll. But you already knew that, too.

You can interchange the action of the left and right mouse buttons — that is, you can tell Windows XP that it should treat the left mouse button as if it were the right button, and the right button as if it were the left. The swap comes in handy for some left-handers, but most southpaws I know (including my son) prefer to keep the buttons as-is, simply because it's easier to use other people's computers if your fingers are trained for the "normal" setting. To switch left and right mouse buttons, follow these steps:

1. **Choose Start⇨Control Panel⇨Printers and Other Hardware⇨Mouse.**

2. **Click the Buttons tab.**

3. **Select the check box (click the check box to place a check mark in it) called Switch Primary and Secondary Buttons.**

4. **Click OK.**

Making the mouse behave

Here are a few important rodent things you may not know:

✦ To move an item on the Windows desktop — a process called *dragging* — click the left button, move the mouse, and then release the button. On laptops with a touch pad, you can tie your fingers up in knots trying to replicate the click-move-release shuck 'n' jive. Chances are good that the touch pad recognizes a swift tap as the beginning of a drag. Check the documentation and practice a bit.

Windows has a feature called ClickLock that can come in handy if you have trouble holding down the left mouse button and moving the mouse at the same time — a common problem for laptop users who have fewer than three hands. When Windows uses ClickLock, you hold down the mouse button for a while (you can tell Windows exactly how long) and Windows "locks" the mouse button. To turn on ClickLock:

1. **Choose Start➪Control Panel➪Printers and Other Hardware➪ Mouse.**

2. **On the Buttons tab, select the check box called Turn on ClickLock.**

3. **Immediately click the Settings button and adjust the length of time you need to hold down the mouse button for ClickLock to kick in.**

Note that you can test the ClickLock time length setting by clicking next to Settings for ClickLock and dragging the box around.

✦ You can roll over items on the desktop too quickly! When you're spelunking around Windows XP trying to get a feel for what's happening, go slowly. The word for it is *hovering* — that's when you let the mouse pointer kind of sit in one place for a spell. You'll be surprised at how often Windows flashes information on the screen in response to hovering.

✦ Although almost everyone catches on to single-clicking, given a few tries, many people have trouble with double-clicking at first, and here's the reason why: Windows ain't that smart. If you click twice, Windows has to figure out if you wanted to make two single-clicks or one double-click — and that's surprisingly difficult. Windows watches as you click. You have to click twice, quickly, without moving the mouse in between clicks, for Windows to identify the two clicks as a double-click. If you have trouble getting Windows to recognize your double-clicks, you're probably moving the mouse just a bit too far between the clicks for a double-click to "take."

If you have consistent problems with Windows recognizing your double-clicks, try adjusting the double-click speed:

1. **Choose Start➪Control Panel➪Printers and Other Hardware➪ Mouse.**

2. **Click the Buttons tab.**

3. **Double-click the folder on the right side, as a test to see how much leeway Windows gives you.**

4. **Adjust the Double-click Speed slider as needed to suit your leisurely lifestyle.**

Inside the computer, programmers measure the movement of mice in units called *mickeys.* Nope, I'm not making this up. Move your mouse a short distance and it has traveled a few mickeys. Move it to Anaheim, and it's put on a lot of mickeys.

Pointers on pointers

When you move the mouse around on your desk, the *pointer* on the screen (see Table 3-1) moves around in concert. Click one of the mouse buttons while the pointer is sitting on something and it may (or may not) react.

Table 3-1	Standard Windows Mouse Pointers	
When a Pointer Looks Like This:	*It Means:*	*And Windows Is Trying to Tell You This:*
▸	Normal	The mouse is ready for action. Move it around the screen, and point and click to get work done.
☝	Hot	Windows has found a "hot" spot — a *hyperlink* in geekspeak — and if you click while this pointer is showing, you are transported to the linked location.
↕	Ready to resize	Hold down the left mouse button and move the mouse forward and backward on your desk ("up" and "down" as you're looking at the Windows desktop) to make a window taller or shorter.
↔	Ready to resize	Same as the preceding pointer, except it makes the selected window fatter or skinnier as you move the mouse left and right.
↖ ↗	Expand or shrink to fit	Click and drag on a window's corner, and the picture expands or shrinks to fit.
▸⧗	Kinda busy	You can keep doing whatever you're doing, but Windows may be a bit slow following along because it's working on something else. If Windows gets to be too slow to keep up with you, do yourself (and Windows) a favor and go grab a latte.
⧗	Out to lunch	Windows is really, really busy and doesn't want to be disturbed. You may be able to move the pointer around a bit, but you won't get much done.
+	Pick a pic	Windows expects you to draw or choose a part of a picture (for example, if you're selecting Uncle Ernie's head for cropping). When the pointer is like this, click in the upper-left corner of the picture, hold down the mouse button, and release it when you get to the lower right corner. Don't be too anal about it: When you're done selecting with this pointer, you always have an opportunity to use the resizing arrows to fix your mistakes.
✛	Move	Instead of resizing the selected area (see the preceding), if you see a four-headed arrow like this one, you know that Windows is going to move the entire selected area, all at once.
▸?	Help	Click on something to get help. If you don't want help, press Esc on the keyboard and the pointer returns to normal.

When a Pointer Looks Like This:	It Means:	And Windows Is Trying to Tell You This:
I	Text allowed	Click when the mouse pointer looks like an I-Beam and you can type text where you clicked.
Ø	No way	Windows shows you this pointer if you're trying to do something that can't be done — trying to move a printer into a word processing document, for example.

If Windows shows you one of its "busy" pointers, you go out to have a latte, and lunch, and run through a quick 18 holes, and come back only to discover that the busy pointer is still there, chances are pretty good that Windows is *hung*. (That's a technical term, okay? Don't laugh. You can also say that Windows *went belly up* or that it *crashed* or *froze* or *died* or *bit the big one*.) If Windows hangs, hold down the Ctrl key and, without letting go of it, press the Alt key and, without letting go of the preceding two, press the Del key. (That's called a *three-finger salute* or a *Vulcan Mind Meld* or, uh, several entirely unprintable things.) The Windows Task Manager appears, and you can (usually) use it to close down whatever is ailing Windows.

If you encounter one of the resizing pointers while working with a picture, remember that different programs use the resizing pointers differently: Some may cut off ("crop") parts of a picture as you resize it, while others may stretch or shrink the picture as you drag the mouse. Usually you can use some combination of the Shift and Ctrl keys to convince the program to behave itself: Hold down the Ctrl key while resizing, for example, and the program may start stretching the picture instead of cropping it. Experiment. If all else fails, you can always start over again.

The point where typed text gets inserted onto the screen is called the *insertion point* (more rocket science). Various word processors show the insertion point differently, but Word uses a solid vertical line. Don't be too surprised if some old cuss — yours truly included — calls the insertion point a "cursor." That's a throwback to the Cro-Magnon days when word processors worked more like typewriters, and the blinking cursor kept track of where text would go.

Using the right button

Windows XP allows you to right-click just about anywhere and choose from a list of actions to be performed on the item you've clicked. For example, you can right-click on a disk drive and choose to search the disk drive; you can right-click on a printer and make the printer stop printing. The choices that appear when you right-click on an item are called a *shortcut menu* (sometimes also called a *right-click menu* or a *context menu*). In Figure 3-2, you can see an example of the context menu that appears when you right-click on a blank portion of the Windows desktop.

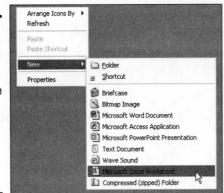

Figure 3-2: The right-click shortcut menu for the Windows desktop, with Microsoft Office installed.

Mice need to be cleaned! If you start having problems with a sluggish mouse — one that jumps, stalls, or doesn't move around the screen the way it should — you should immediately turn the beast upside down and clean it. If you see a rubber ball, pop the lid off, take out the ball, blow on it, and clean off the roller contacts inside (you may need a cotton swab and some isopropyl alcohol). Regardless of whether the mouse has a ball, the feet need to be cleaned from time to time — use your fingernail and scrape gently.

Windows

Most of the time that you spend working with Windows is spent working with, uh, windows. The kind with the little "w" — the rectangles that appear all over your screen. Each part of a window has a name and a specific function.

Many people spend most of their time on the computer working in Word 2003, which is the word processor in Office 2003 and the word processor used by Outlook 2003 for composing e-mail messages. You may have a copy of it on your machine. Look at Figure 3-3 for an overview of the components of the Word 2003 window, and what they represent.

A few details worth noting:

+ The window title appears both in the title bar — that is, the bar across the top of the window — and (usually) in the Windows taskbar, way down at the bottom of the screen. That makes it easy for you to identify which window is which and to switch among them by clicking on the taskbar.

+ Clicking the Minimize button makes the window disappear but leaves the title down in the Windows taskbar, so you can bring the window back with just a click.

+ Clicking the Restore button "restores" the size of the window. That is, if the window doesn't take up the whole screen and you click the restore button, it expands to take up the full screen. On the other hand, if the window is taking up the whole screen and you click on the restore button, it reduces in size to occupy a portion of the screen. I have no idea why that's called restoring.

✦ Clicking the Cancel button removes the screen entirely — even from the Windows taskbar — most commonly by shutting down the program that's using the window.

Many windows can be resized by clicking and dragging an edge or a corner. See the preceding section on "Mousing" for details.

Dialog Boxes

When the computer interacts with you — that is, when it has a question to ask, or when it needs more information in order to complete a task — it usually puts a *dialog box* on the screen. A dialog box is nothing more or less than a small window that requires your attention. Figure 3-4 shows a dialog box that illustrates how the various standard Windows components can be used to extract information from unsuspecting Dummies.

Each of the parts of a window has a name:

✦ **Title:** A dialog box's *title* appears at the top of the dialog box, but the title rarely appears in the Windows taskbar. This is one of the ways that a dialog box is different from a garden-variety window (see the preceding section): You can usually hop directly to a regular ol' window by clicking in the taskbar. To find a lost dialog box, you frequently have to hunt around.

Those "things" that appear on dialog boxes are called *controls*. (Sounds a whole lot better than "things," true?) Windows comes with many controls, and most of the controls you see from day to day are drawn from the standard control toolbox. Standard controls are a real boon to us Dummies because they work the same way, all the time, no matter where you are in Windows.

✦ **Cancel button:** The Cancel button almost always appears on a dialog box, but the other two buttons that you often see on a regular window — Restore and Minimize — rarely show up on dialog boxes. Clicking the Cancel button almost always makes the dialog box go away.

✦ **Tabs:** Those funny-looking index tabs (usually just called *tabs*) are supposed to remind you of filing tabs. Click on a tab, and you bring up a whole bunch of settings, which are usually related — at least, some programmer somewhere thought they were related.

You can usually hop from one part of a dialog box to the next by pressing the Tab key. Press Shift+Tab to move backwards. If you see an underlined letter in a dialog box — called an *accelerator key* — hold down the Alt key and press the letter, and you go directly to that location. In some dialog boxes, pressing Enter is the same as clicking OK (unless you've used the Tab key to move around). In other dialog boxes, though, pressing Enter doesn't do anything.

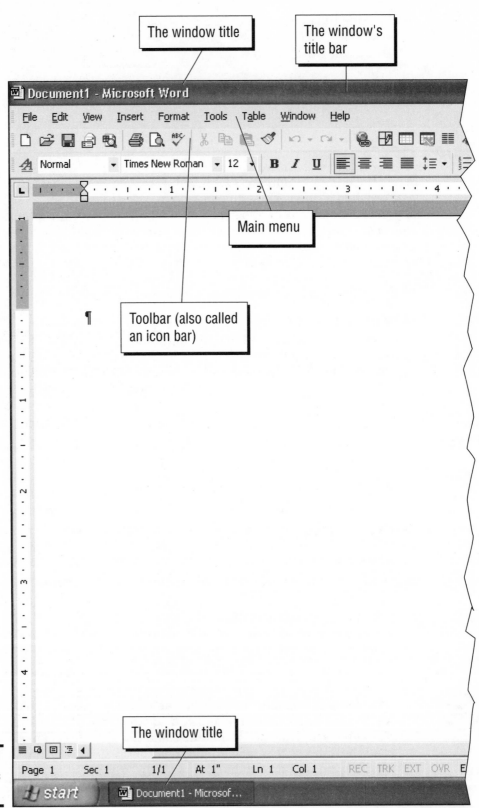

The window title

The window's title bar

Main menu

Toolbar (also called an icon bar)

The window title

Figure 3-3:
Word 2003's
window.

✦ **Spinners:** These are almost always placed right next to numbers, with the number hooked up so that it increases when you click the up arrow and decreases when you click the down arrow. Sometimes you can bypass the spinner entirely, select the number, delete it, and type whatever you want.

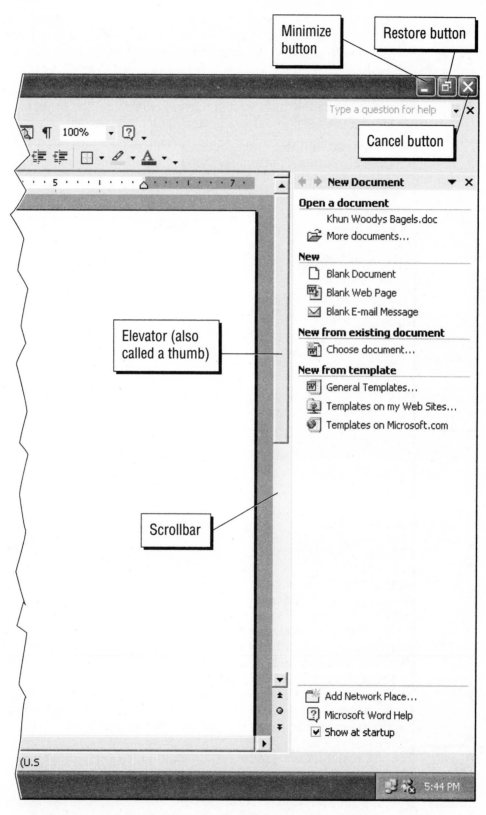

Minimize button

Restore button

Cancel button

Elevator (also called a thumb)

Scrollbar

- ✦ **Drop-down lists:** These lists come in two different flavors. With one
  kind, you're limited to the choices that appear in the drop-down list:
  If the item you want is in the list, you just pick it; if the item isn't there,
  you're up the ol' creek without a paddle. The other kind of drop-down

list lets you type in whatever you want if your choice doesn't appear in the list. Programmers hate that kind of drop-down list because it lets you do things like order anchovies and pepper sauce on your bagels.

+ **Check boxes:** *Check boxes* let you say "yes" or "no," independently, to a whole bunch of choices; if you see a bunch of check boxes, you can pick one or none or all of 'em. *Option buttons,* on the other hand, only let you choose one out of a group — no more, no less.

+ **Command buttons:** These buttons tell the dialog box to get on with it. Click a command button, and the dialog box does something.

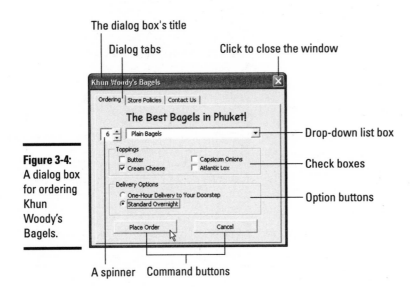

Figure 3-4: A dialog box for ordering Khun Woody's Bagels.

The dialog box's title

Dialog tabs

Click to close the window

Drop-down list box

Check boxes

Option buttons

A spinner   Command buttons

Files and Folders

"What's a file?" Man, I wish I had a nickel for every time I've been asked that question. A file is a, uh, thing. Yeah, that's it. A thing. A thing that has stuff inside of it. Why don't you ask me an easier question, like "what is a paragraph?" or "what is the meaning of life, the universe, and everything?"

A file is a fundamental chunk of stuff. Like most fundamental chunks of stuff (say, protons, or Congressional districts, or ear wax), any attempt at a definitive definition gets in the way of understanding the thing itself. Suffice it to say that a Word document is a file. An Excel workbook is a file. That photograph your cousin e-mailed you the other day is a file. Every track on Nine Inch Nails' latest CD is a file, but so is every track on every audio CD ever made. Trent Reznor isn't *that* special.

File and folder names can be very long, but they can't contain the following characters:

/ \ : * ? " < > |

Files can be huge. They can be tiny. They can even be empty, but don't short-circuit any gray cells on that observation.

Three things I know for sure about files:

✦ Every file has a name.

✦ Files — at least, files that aren't empty — contain bits, the 1s and 0s that computers use to represent reality (a tenuous concept under the best of circumstances).

✦ Windows lets you work with files — move them, copy them, create them, delete them, and group them together.

Folders hold files and other folders. Folders can be empty. A single folder can hold millions — yes, quite literally *millions* — of files and other folders.

Three things I know for sure about folders:

✦ Every folder has a name.

✦ Windows creates and keeps track of a whole bunch of folders, like

  • **A My Documents folder** for each user on the PC. That's where Windows and Microsoft Office usually put new documents that you create.

  • **My Pictures and My Music folders**, inside each user's My Documents folders. Windows — including the Media Player — tend to store your pictures and music files in these folders.

  • **A Shared Documents folder**, which includes Shared Pictures and Shared Music folders, to make it easy to share documents, pictures, and music with other people who use your PC or other people on a network, if you have one. For more info on sharing documents, see the section about sharing folders in Book I, Chapter 7.

✦ Windows lets you move, copy, create, delete, and put folders inside of other folders.

If you set them up right, folders can help you keep track of things. If you toss your files around higgledy-piggledy, no system of folders in the world will help.

To look at the files and folders on your machine that you're most likely to bump into, choose Start⇨My Documents. You see something like the list shown in Figure 3-5.

The picture of My Documents that you see in Figure 3-5 comes from a part of Windows called *Windows Explorer,* which can help keep your files and folders organized. Many of the things that you can do in Windows Explorer, you can also do elsewhere. For example, you can rename files in the File⇨Open dialog box in Word — but it's hard to beat the way Windows Explorer enables you to perform powerful actions quickly and easily. I talk about Windows Explorer in Book I, Chapter 7.

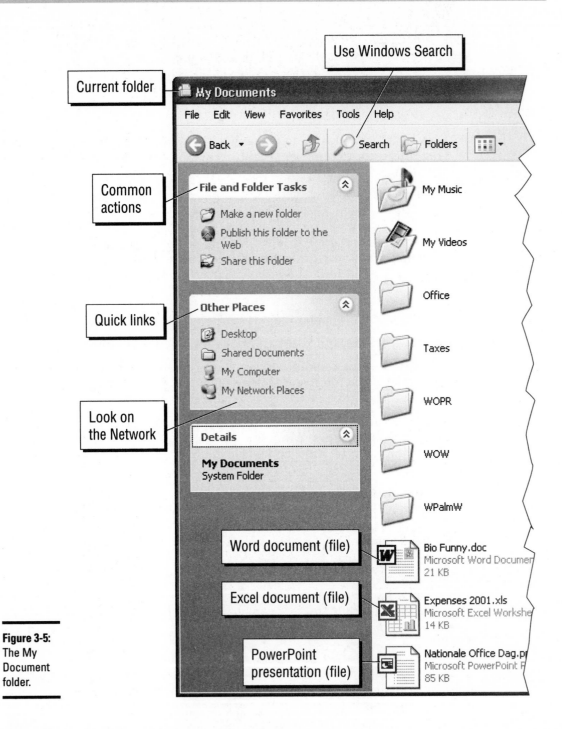

Figure 3-5:
The My Document folder.

Starting with the Start Button

Start Microsoft's subverting the Rolling Stones classic *Start Me Up* for advertising may be ancient history by now, but the royal road to Windows XP still starts at the Start button. Click it, and you get the Start menu, which looks something like the one shown in Figure 3-6.

The Start menu looks like it's etched in granite, but it isn't. You can change almost anything on it:

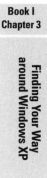

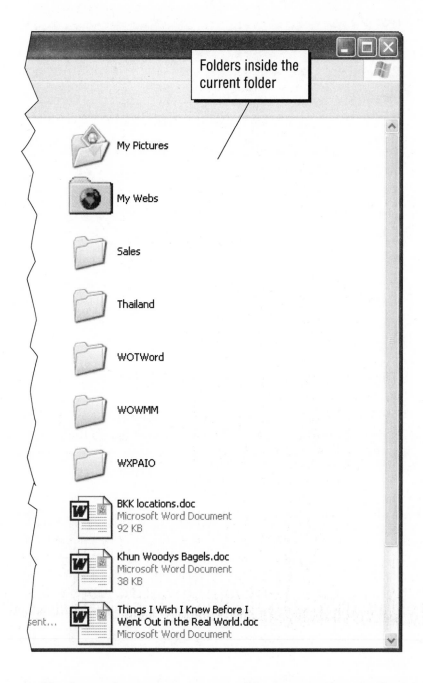

Folders inside the
current folder

My Pictures

My Webs

Sales

Thailand

WOTWord

WOWMM

WXPAIO

BKK locations.doc
Microsoft Word Document
92 KB

Khun Woodys Bagels.doc
Microsoft Word Document
38 KB

Things I Wish I Knew Before I
Went Out in the Real World.doc
Microsoft Word Document

✦ To change the name or picture of the current user, see Book I, Chapter 6.

✦ To remove a program from the "pinned" programs list or the recently
used programs list, right-click on it and from the shortcut menu that
appears, choose Remove from This List.

✦ To add a program to the "pinned" programs list, use Windows Explorer
to find the program (see Book I, Chapter 7), right-click on the program
and from the shortcut menu that appears, choose Pin to Start Menu.

Recently used programs

"Pinned" programs

Current user's name

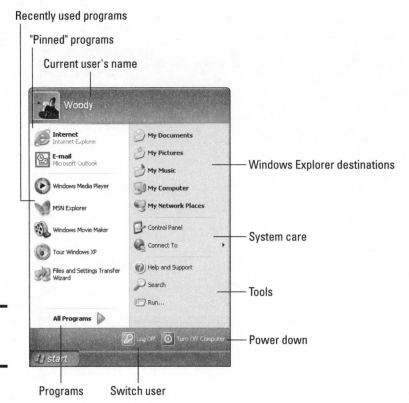

Windows Explorer destinations

System care

Tools

Figure 3-6:
The Start
menu.

Power down

Programs   Switch user

 If you bought a new computer with Windows XP installed, the people who make the computer may have sold one of the spots on the Start menu. Think of it as an electronic billboard on your desktop. Nope, I'm not exaggerating. I keep expecting to bump into a Windows XP machine with fly-out Start menu entries that read, oh, "Surveys have shown⇨Near and far⇨That people who drive like crazy⇨Are⇨Burma Shave." You can always delete those pesky Start menu billboards by right-clicking on them and choosing Remove from This List.

Don't expect a whole lot of consistency in the way adjacent Start menu items behave. You may expect that the recently used program part of the Start menu would list the programs you've used most recently. And it does. Sorta. Partly. Now and then. Microsoft stacks the deck, so MSN Explorer (which connects to Microsoft's for-pay MSN service) may stay on the list a whole lot longer than other programs. Some programs are more equal than others, eh?

Internet

Windows XP ships with Internet Explorer 6 (IE6), Microsoft's flagship Web browser. To bring up IE6, choose Start⇨Internet/Internet Explorer. The chapters in Book III describe how to surf the Internet with Internet Explorer.

Setting the time

Windows XP Home synchs the clock on your PC with the clock maintained at `time.windows.com` once a week. If your modem suddenly starts dialing the phone for no apparent reason, Windows is possibly trying to set its clock. Sometimes the clock doesn't get set — hey, stuff happens on the Internet. If you want to make Windows XP set your PC's clock:

1. **Double-click on the time on the Windows taskbar in the lower-right corner of the desktop.**

2. **Click the Internet Time tab. (Yes, it's true: In the future, everything will run on Internet time.)**

3. **Click Update Now.**

If that doesn't do the trick, follow the link on the Internet Time tab to look up the time synchronization topic in the Windows Help and Support Center.

If you're paranoid about allowing your PC to phone Uncle Bill once a week — `time.windows.com` is owned lock, stock, and barrel by Microsoft, natch — follow the preceding three steps, but before you click Update Now, choose the time server at `time.nist.gov`. That site is run by the National Institute of Standards and Technology, which is a division of the U.S. government. Of course, if you're *really* paranoid, you probably think that NIST is a small division of Microsoft's R&R organization, and that Bill G. talks to Martians on alternate Wednesdays, but I digress.

E-mail

Windows XP ships with a versatile e-mail program called Outlook Express. Outlook Express also handles *newsgroups,* the places on the Internet where people can freely exchange ideas, gossip, tips, and fertilizer. Choose Start➪E-mail/Outlook Express and it appears. Book III describes Outlook Express.

Media Player

Windows XP includes Microsoft's Media Player, a multi-faceted tool for playing, organizing, ripping, and burning audio and video files. Book I, Chapter 11 describes the Media Player in detail.

My Documents, Pictures, Music

Figure 3-5, earlier in this chapter, shows you the contents of my My Documents folder. (I guess that makes it a list of my My Documents documents, right?) Windows Explorer lets you look at your folders in various ways, called *views,* and you can switch from view to view depending on what you're trying to do, your mood, or the phase of the moon.

Within the My Documents folder sit two more folders that you can get to directly from the Start menu. If you choose Start➪My Pictures, the Windows Explorer appears with the My Pictures folder open. Choose View➪Filmstrip and your pictures look like the ones shown in Figure 3-7.

Double-click on a picture and it appears in the Windows Picture and Fax Viewer. At that point, you can easily zoom in and out on the picture, print it, copy it to a floppy, or even change the picture.

Pictures appear full-screen

Moves up one level

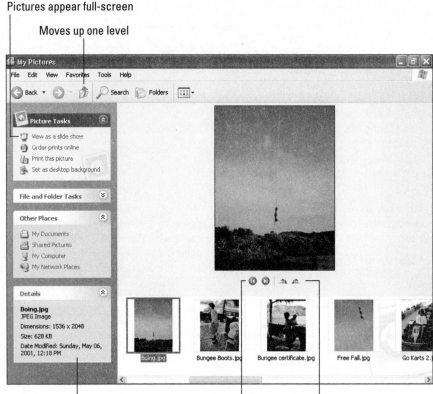

Figure 3-7:
My Pictures,
shown in
filmstrip
view.

Particulars on selected file   Previous/Next picture   Rotate

If you choose Start⇨My Music, and then choose View⇨Thumbnails, you see
the My Music folder, which appears with its own special set of actions in the
pane on the left.

If you use the Windows Media Player to rip audio CDs, it places all the
songs from a single CD into a folder, tucks each of those folders into a big
folder for each artist, and puts the artists' folders into My Music. The
covers appear, up to four on a folder, when you use Thumbnail view. The
Media Player is explored in Book I, Chapter 11.

My Recent Documents

Windows keeps track of documents as you open them, maintaining a list of
documents that you have opened most recently. Taking a leaf from the
"HUH?" School of Computer Design, Microsoft's Usability Lab decided that
Windows XP Professional users should see the list on the Start menu,
whereas Windows XP Home users should not. If you like, you can tell
Windows that you want to be able to get at that list. Here's how:

1. **Right-click Start and click Properties.**

2. **Click the Customize button.**

3. **Click the Advanced tab.**

4. **Select the List My Most Recently Opened Documents check box, and
   then click OK twice.**

When the Most Recently Opened Documents list is enabled, an entry called My Recent Documents appears on your Start menu. If you choose Start⇨My Recent Documents, Windows presents you with a list of the 15 documents that you opened most recently (see Figure 3-8). If you want to open a listed document again, pick it from the list, and Windows does the rest.

Take this list with a grain of salt. Windows doesn't always get all of the files listed correctly.

Figure 3-8:
The documents that you opened most recently can appear on your Start menu.

 If you want to wipe out the list of files that you've opened recently — hey, ain't nobody's business but your own — try this:

1. **Right-click Start and choose Properties.**

2. **Click the Customize button.**

3. **Click the Advanced tab.**

4. **Click Clear List, and then click OK twice.**

All of the entries in your My Recent Documents menu disappear.

My Computer

 Choose Start⇨My Computer, and Windows shows you the highest level of folders on your machine, in addition to a list of all the drives (see Figure 3-9). You can use this bird's-eye view to "drill down" to various nooks and crannies in your folders and in the folders of all the other people who use your PC.

For a traditional (that is, pre-Windows XP) view of the contents of your computer that enables you to easily navigate down to the lowest level, click the Folders icon. You see all of your folders and how they're interrelated in the pane on the left.

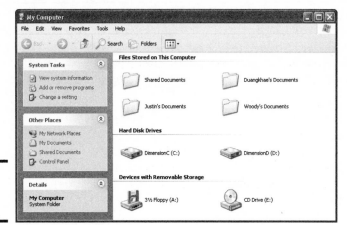

Figure 3-9:
My
Computer.

Control Panel

The inner workings of Windows XP reveal themselves inside the mysterious (and somewhat haughtily named) Control Panel. Choose Start⇨Control Panel to plug away at the innards (see Figure 3-10).

Makes Control Panel look like it did in Windows 98, ME, and 2000

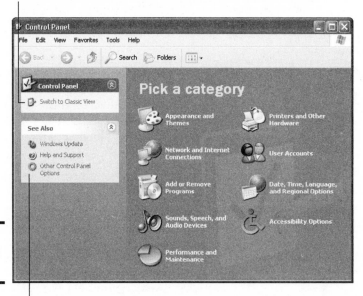

Figure 3-10:
The Control
Panel.

Outlook Express options are down here

The main components of the Control Panel are as follows:

✦ **Appearance and Themes:** Change what your desktop looks like — wallpaper, colors, mouse pointers, screen saver, icon size and spacing, and so on. Set screen resolution (for example, 1024 x 768 or 800 x 600) so that you can pack more information onto your screen — assuming your eyes can handle it. Make the Windows taskbar hide when you're not using it, and change the items on your Start menu. Change what Windows Explorer shows when you're looking at folders.

✦ **Printers and Other Hardware:** Add or remove printers and connect to other printers on your network. Troubleshoot printers. Set up and modify Windows faxing. Install, remove, and set the options for scanners and digital cameras. Control the options on mice, game controllers, joysticks, and keyboards. Set up dialing rules and other modem arcana.

If you use a modem for your Internet connection, Windows faxing may not do what you expect. You may have to disconnect from the Internet before you send or receive a fax, for example. Many people like J2 fax (www.j2.com) because it treats faxes like e-mail. Outbound faxes are converted to e-mail on your PC using J2's programs, and then they are sent to J2, which routes the fax to a local fax machine at your destination, thus bypassing long-distance telephone charges. Inbound faxes get delivered to your e-mail inbox.

✦ **Network and Internet Connections:** Set up a network. Configure Internet Explorer and its startup page, history files, cookies, AutoComplete, and so on. Set up Internet connections, particularly if you're sharing an Internet connection across a network, or if you have a cable modem or DSL.

✦ **User Accounts:** Add or remove users from the Windows welcome screen. Enable the "Guest" account (see Book I, Chapter 6 for more about adding users). Change account characteristics, such as the picture, password requirement, direct connection with .NET Passport, and so on.

✦ **Add or Remove Programs:** Add and remove specific features in some programs (most notably Windows XP).

✦ **Date, Time, Language, and Regional Options:** Set the time and date — although double-clicking the clock on the Windows taskbar is much simpler — or tell Windows to synchronize the clock automatically. Here you can also add support for complex languages (such as Thai) and right-to-left languages, and change how dates, times, currency, and numbers appear.

✦ **Sounds, Speech, and Audio Devices:** Control volume, muting, and so on, but those functions are usually better performed inside the Windows Media Player. You can also choose a Sound scheme, which is something like a desktop theme, except that it involves the pings and pongs you associate with Windows events (for example, the music that plays when Windows starts, or the cling! you hear when you try to click on something you shouldn't). Speech choices cover only text-to-speech output — the "Danger, Will Robinson!" voice you hear when the computer tries to read something out loud.

✦ **Accessibility Options:** Change settings to help you see the screen, use the keyboard or mouse, or have Windows flash part of your screen when the speaker would play a sound.

✦ **Performance and Maintenance:** Use an enormous array of tools for troubleshooting and adjusting your PC, and making it work when it doesn't want to. Unfortunately, it also includes all the tools you need to shoot yourself in the foot, consistently and reliably, day in and day out. Use this part of the Control Panel with discretion and respect.

Help and Support

Windows XP includes an online help system that's quite good in places, marginal in some areas, and very, uh, in tune with the Microsoft Party Line everywhere. To bring up the system, choose Start➪Help and Support.

Search

Windows XP jumbles an odd assortment of "searchables" in the Search feature. Choose Start➪Search and you see what I mean. I talk about Search extensively in Book I, Chapter 8.

Run

Harkening back to a kinder, gentler age, where you had to type (and type and type and type) to get anything done at a computer, the Run box lets you type program names and have Windows run the programs. It also recognizes Web addresses.

All Programs

Almost all of the programs on your computer are accessible through the All Programs menu. To see it, choose Start➪All Programs. Figure 3-11 shows you what the Games folder in All Programs looks like.

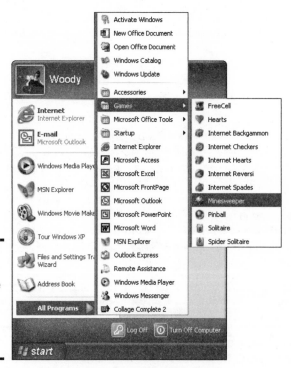

Figure 3-11: The Games folder in the Start Menu's All Programs menu.

Those right arrowheads that you can see to the right of Accessories, Games, Microsoft Office Tools, and Startup in Figure 3-11 simply indicate that you have more choices to make. You can let your mouse pointer hover over an arrowhead-endowed Start menu entry and the *pop-out menu* appears. Or if you're the impatient type, you can click on the menu entry to make the pop-out appear faster.

Are you an inveterate Windows 98/ME/NT/2000 user who misses her old Start menu — the single-column menu, with its little icons, that automatically tucked away menu items you didn't use very often? You can bring the old buzzard back to life, if you insist, and have it replace this new-fangled version of the Start menu. Here's how:

1. **Right-click Start and from the shortcut menu that appears, choose Properties.**

2. **Click the Start Menu tab.**

3. **Click the Classic Start Menu button, and then click OK.**

Personally, I prefer the new Start menu to the old one, but it's nice to know that you can go back to the classic version, if you like.

Organizing the contents of the All Programs menu is very easy:

✦ To copy or move an item on the All Programs menu to a different location on the All Programs menu, right-click it, drag it to the new location (you can navigate anywhere on the menu, even into the pop-out menus), release the right mouse button, and choose Copy or Move.

✦ To sort all of the items on the All Programs menu alphabetically (with folders sorting higher than programs), right-click on any folder or program and choose Sort by Name.

CHECK IT OUT

Arranging Multiple Windows Side-by-Side

There's a very quick and easy way to arrange multiple windows on your desktop. You can tile them side-by-side (vertically) or one-on-top (horizontally). Here's how:

1. Make sure both the windows are open and thus have icons that appear on the Windows taskbar.

2. On the taskbar, click one window's icon, hold down the Ctrl key, and click the other window's icon.

3. Right-click one of the selected icons and choose Tile Horizontally or Tile Vertically.

The selected windows are tiled.

Chapter 4: Personalizing Your Desktop

In This Chapter

↳ Getting the real story on how Windows puts together your desktop

↳ Taking control of each desktop level

↳ Finding out why you're better off ignoring some of the fancy stuff

↳ Discovering how to make your folders stand out

*I*t's your desktop. Do with it what you will. I've never bumped into a complete description of how the Windows desktop gets tossed together, so you Dummies go to the head of the class. You may think it'd be easy for a computer to slap windows on the screen, but it isn't. In fact, Windows XP uses seven separate layers to produce that Windows eXPerience — and you can take control of every piece. I show you how in this chapter.

I've also included a discussion of Desktop Themes, backgrounds in Windows Explorer, and custom pictures for folders. Pretty cool stuff, especially when you see CD album covers plastered on My Music folders.

Recognizing Desktop Levels

The Windows XP desktop — that is, the stuff you see on your computer screen — consists of seven layers (see Figure 4-1). For a quick change of pace, Desktop Themes change all seven layers, all at once. I talk about Desktop Themes later in this chapter in "Using Desktop Themes."

Here are the seven settings that control how Windows dishes up your desktop:

✦ At the very bottom, the Windows desktop has a *base color,* which is a solid color that you see only if you don't have a background or if your chosen background doesn't fill up the entire screen. Most people never see their Windows base color because the background usually covers it up. I tell you how to set the base color and all of the other Windows colors — for dialog boxes, the Taskbar, the works — in the section, "Setting Colors in Windows XP."

✦ Above the base color lives the Windows *background.* You may be familiar with the rolling hills background — the one Microsoft calls Bliss — because it's the one that ships with Windows XP.

The people who sold you your computer may have ditched Microsoft's Bliss background and replaced it with some sort of dorky ad or logo. I tell you how to get rid of the ad and replace it with a picture you want in the section called "Picking a Background."

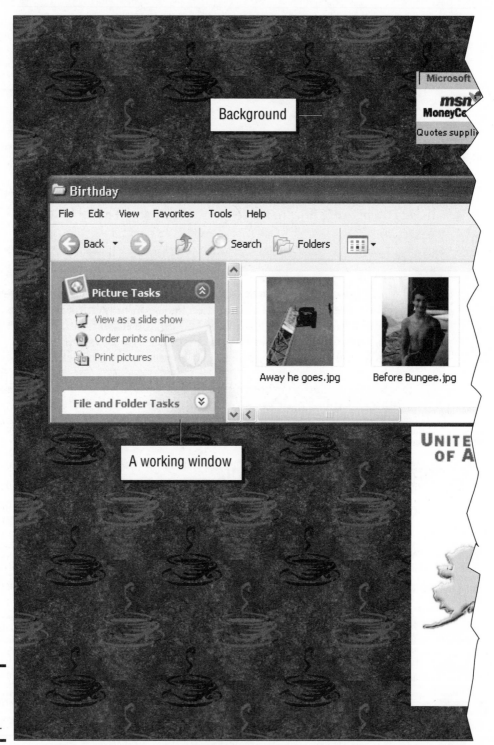

Figure 4-1:
The
Windows
XP desktop.

✦ On top of the background, Windows lets you put pictures, Web pages, and just about anything you can imagine. Microsoft even has a little stock ticker and weather map that you can download and stick in this layer. This is the so-called *Active Desktop* layer and, by and large, it's a disaster.

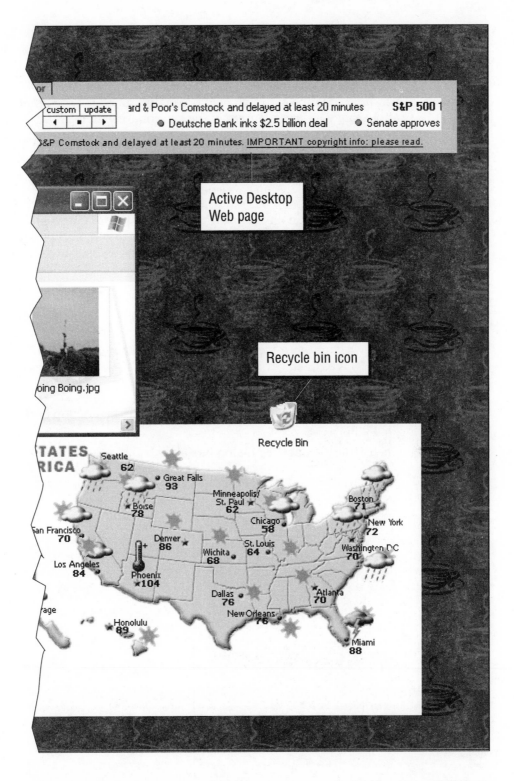

Active Desktop
Web page

Recycle bin icon

Recycle Bin

✦ Windows puts all of its desktop icons on top of the Active Desktop layer. Bone-stock Windows XP includes only one icon — the Recycle Bin. If you bought a PC with Windows XP preinstalled, chances are good that the manufacturer put lots of additional icons on the desktop, and you can easily get rid of them. I tell you how in the section, "Controlling Icons."

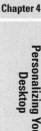

✦ Above the icons you (finally!) find the program windows — the ones that actually do work. You know, little things like Word, Excel, and the Media Player.

✦ Then you have the mouse, which lives in the layer above the program windows. If you want to change the picture used for the pointer, I talk about fancy mouse pointers in the section, "Changing Mouse Pointers."

✦ At the very top of the desktop food chain sits the screen saver. The screen saver kicks in only if you tell Windows that you want it to appear when your computer sits idle for a spell. I talk about that beast in the section called "Selecting Screen Savers."

If you have more than one user on your PC, each user can customize every single part of the seven layers to suit his or her tastes, and Windows XP remembers every setting, bringing it back when the user logs on. Much better than getting a life, isn't it?

Setting Colors in Windows XP

Windows XP ships with three designer color schemes: Blue (which you probably use), Olive Green (which looks just as bad as you might imagine) and silver (rather, uh, self-consciously techno-blah). To change color schemes:

1. **Right-click on any empty part of the Windows desktop and choose Properties.**

The Display Properties dialog box appears.

2. **Click the Appearance tab (see Figure 4-2).**

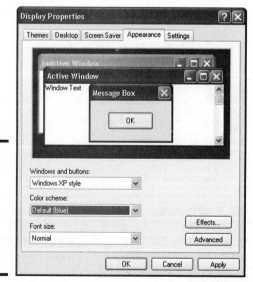

Figure 4-2: The three major Windows XP color schemes are accessible here.

3. **From the Color Scheme drop-down list, choose Default (blue), Olive Green, or Silver, and click OK.**

Windows changes the base color — that is, the color of the Windows desktop when no background appears or the background doesn't fit (see the section, "Picking a Background") — as well as the title bar color of all windows and dialog boxes, the color of the Windows Taskbar, menu highlight colors, and a dozen other colors, scattered in various places throughout Windows.

You aren't confined to Microsoft's three-color world. In fact, you can pick and choose many different Windows colors, individually, although some of them appear on-screen only if you tell Windows to use the Windows Classic Style of windows and buttons — the old-fashioned pre-XP style, where windows had squared off edges and OK buttons weren't so boldly sculpted.

To set the desktop's base color to white — regardless of whether you use Windows XP Style or Windows Classic Style windows and buttons — follow these steps:

1. Right-click on any empty part of the Windows desktop and choose Properties.

The Display Properties dialog box appears.

2. Click the Appearance tab (see Figure 4-2).

3. Click Advanced.

You see the Advanced Appearance dialog box shown in Figure 4-3.

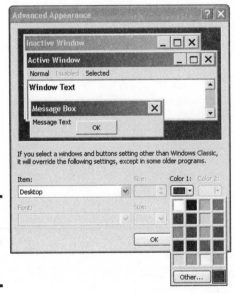

Figure 4-3:
Individual settings can be applied here.

4. Make sure that Desktop appears in the Item drop-down list; then click the down-arrow under Color 1 and click on the white color swatch in the upper-left corner.

5. Click OK twice.

Your desktop base color is now set to white, although you may have to change (or get rid of) your background in order to see it. I talk about strangling and axing the background in the next section. Stand back, Lizzie Borden.

Picking a Background

Windows XP, straight out of the box, ships with a picture of rolling verdant hills as the background. This background is peaceful and serene — Microsoft calls it "Bliss" — and it's booooooooring. If you bought a PC with Windows XP preinstalled, chances are very good that the manufacturer has replaced Bliss with a background of its own choosing — maybe the manufacturer's own logo or something a bit more subtle, like "Buy Wheaties." Don't laugh. The background is up for sale. PC manufacturers can include whatever they like.

There's nothing particularly magical about the background. In fact, Windows XP will put *any* picture on your desktop — big one, little one, ugly one, even a picture stolen straight off the Web. Here's how:

1. **Right-click on any empty part of the Windows desktop and choose Properties.**

The Display Properties dialog box appears.

2. **Click the Desktop tab (see Figure 4-4).**

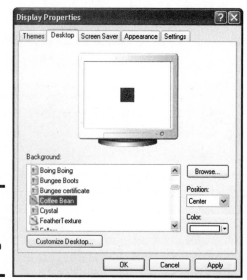

Figure 4-4:
Pick any picture on the Desktop tab.

In the Background box, Windows XP lists pictures from the Windows folder and the My Pictures folder. (It also lists Web pages — files with HTM or HTML as filename extensions — in both of those folders.) Windows ships with lots of pictures in the Windows folder.

3. **Scroll through the Background box and pick the picture you want.**

If you don't see the picture you're looking for — surprisingly, pictures in the Shared Pictures folder aren't included in this list, for example — click the Browse button and go find the picture. A preview of the picture appears in the little monitor screen on the dialog box.

4. **If your picture is too big to fit on the screen, you need to tell Windows how to shoehorn it into the available location.**

If your picture is too small to cover up the entire screen, you need to tell Windows what to do with the extra room. You do both in the Position drop-down list, as shown in Table 4-1.

Table 4-1	How Windows Resizes Desktop Pictures	
Position	*If the Picture Is Too Big*	*If the Picture Is Too Small*
Center	Windows carves a piece out of the middle of the picture and puts it on the screen.	Windows puts the picture in the center of the screen and fills the unoccupied part of the screen with the base color.*
Tile	Windows takes a suitably sized piece out of the upper-left corner of the picture and uses it as the background.	Windows puts one copy of the picture in the upper-left corner of the screen, and then "tiles" additional copies of the picture to fill up the remainder of the screen.
Stretch	Windows squishes the picture to fit the dimensions of the screen. If you're working with a photo, the effect is almost always horrible.	Windows stretches the picture so that it fits. Think Torquemada.

* See the discussion of base color in the section, "Setting Colors in Windows XP."

Selecting None for a background means that you don't want Windows XP to use a background at all: It should let the base color show through, unsullied.

5. **If you tell Windows to put your too-small picture in the Center of the screen in the Position box, you can use the Color box as a quick way to set the base color.**

6. **Click Apply.**

   Windows changes the background according to your specifications but leaves the Display Properties dialog box open so that you can change your mind.

7. **Click OK.**

   The Display Properties dialog box disappears.

Many people are mystified by the Color box on the Display Properties dialog box because it doesn't seem to do anything. In fact, Color kicks in only when you choose Center for the Position and when the picture you've chosen as a background is too small to occupy the entire screen.

Changing the base color in the Advanced Appearance dialog box (see Figure 4-3) also changes the color on the Desktop tab (refer to Figure 4-4) and vice versa.

Windows XP lets you right-click on a picture — a JPG or GIF file, regardless of whether you're using Windows Explorer or Internet Explorer — and choose Use as Desktop Background. When you do that, the picture appears as the background, with Position set to Stretch (if the picture is too big for the screen) or Tile (if the picture is not too big for the screen).

Controlling Icons

Windows XP, straight out of the box, ships with exactly one icon: the Recycle Bin. Microsoft found that most people appreciate a clean desktop, devoid of icons — but they also found that hiding the Recycle Bin confused the living daylights out of all of their guinea pigs (uh, Usability Lab Test Subjects). So Microsoft compromised by making the desktop squeaky-clean, except for the Recycle Bin: Bliss and a Recycle Bin. Who could ask for more?

If you bought a PC with Windows XP preloaded, you probably have so many icons on the desktop that you can't see straight. That desktop real estate is expensive, and the manufacturers get a pretty penny for dangling the right icons in your face. Know what? You can delete all of them, without feeling the least bit guilty. The worst you'll do is delete some shortcut to a manufacturer's tech support software, and if you really need to get to the program, the tech support rep on the telephone can tell you how to find it from the Start menu.

Windows XP gives you several simple tools for arranging icons on your desktop. If you right-click on any empty part of the desktop and choose Arrange Icons By, you see that you can do the following:

+ Sort icons by name, size, type (folders, documents, shortcuts, and so on), or the date that the icon was last modified.

+ *Auto Arrange* icons — that is, have Windows keep them arranged in an orderly fashion, with the first icon in the upper-left corner, the second one directly below the first one, the third below it, and so on.

+ If you don't want them arranged automatically, at least you can have Windows *Align to Grid,* so you can see all of them without one appearing directly on top of the other.

In general, you can remove an icon from the Windows desktop by right-clicking on it and choosing Delete, or by clicking on it once and pressing the Delete key. Unfortunately, PC manufacturers are wise to this trick, and they often disable the Delete function on icons that they want to remain on your desktop.

Some icons are hard-wired: If you put a Word document on your desktop, for example, the document inherits the icon of its associated application, Word. Same goes for Excel worksheets and text documents and recorded audio files.

Icons for shortcuts, however, can be changed at will. (I talk about shortcuts in Book I, Chapter 5.) To change an icon — that is, the picture — on a shortcut:

1. **Right-click on the shortcut.**

2. **Choose Properties.**

3. **In the Properties dialog box, click the Change Icon button.**

4. **Pick an icon from the offered list, or click Browse and go looking for icons.**

Windows abounds with icons. See Table 4-2 for some likely hunting grounds.

5. **Click OK twice and the icon will be changed.**

Table 4-2	Places to Look for Icons
Contents	*File*
Everything	c:\windows\system32\shell32.dll
Computers	c:\windows\explorer.exe
Communication	c:\windows\system32\hticons.dll
Household	c:\windows\system32\pifmgr.dll
Folders	c:\windows\system32\syncui.dll
Old programs	c:\windows\system32\moricons.dll

Lots and lots (and lots and lots) of icons are available on the Internet. Use your favorite search engine to find more icons.

Windows XP gives special treatment to five icons: the Recycle Bin (which can't be removed from the desktop unless you go into the Windows Registry with a blunt axe), My Documents, My Computer, My Network Places, and Internet Explorer. To control the appearance of those icons:

1. **Right-click on any open space on the desktop and choose Properties.**

2. **In the Display Properties dialog box, click the Desktop tab (refer to Figure 4-4), and then click Customize Desktop.**

3. **In the Desktop Items dialog box, click the General tab (see Figure 4-5).**

Figure 4-5:
Control
icons in the
Desktop
Items dialog
box.

4. **Select and/or deselect each of the four boxes — My Documents, My Computer, My Network Places, and Internet Explorer — depending on whether you want the associated icon to appear on the desktop.**

5. **To change an icon (that is, the picture itself), click on the icon and click the Change Icon button.**

Now you can look inside any files you want, looking for icons. Refer to Table 4-2 for some ideas.

6. **When you're done, click OK twice.**

Your new icons appear on the desktop.

Changing Mouse Pointers

Believe it or not, Microsoft has spent many thousands of person-hours honing its mouse pointers. The pointers you see in a standard Windows XP installation have been selected to give you the best visual "clues" possible, without being overly distracting. You can control your mouse pointer destiny in three different ways:

✦ By choosing a new Desktop Theme, which replaces all of your pointers, along with the background, screen saver, and virtually everything else that can be customized. I talk about Desktop Themes in the section called "Using Desktop Themes."

✦ By selecting and changing individual pointers — so you can turn, say, the Windows "I'm busy but not completely tied up" mouse pointer (which Windows calls Working In Background) into, oh, a dinosaur.

✦ By changing all of your pointers, wholesale, according to schemes that Microsoft has constructed.

To change individual pointers or to select from the prefab pointer schemes:

1. **Choose Start⇨Control Panel⇨Printers and Other Hardware⇨Mouse.**

2. **Click the Pointers tab (see Figure 4-6).**

3. **To change all the pointers at the same time, pick a new pointer scheme from the Scheme drop-down list.**

You can choose from purely functional sets of pointers (such as extra large pointers to use for presentations or pointers inverted to show solid black blobs) or fun sets (such as Conductor, Dinosaur, or Hands).

4. **If you want to bring back the original scheme, choose Windows Default (System Scheme), which is the one you started with.**

5. **To change an individual pointer, click on the pointer in the Customize box, and click Browse.**

Windows shows you all of the available pointers — which number in the hundreds. Choose the pointer you want, and click Open.

6. **If you want to change an individual pointer back to the original pointer for the particular scheme that you have chosen, click the pointer in the Customize box and click the Use Default button.**

7. **When you've settled on a set of pointers that appeals to you, click Save As, and give your new, custom scheme a name so that you can retrieve it at any time.**

8. **Click OK.**

Windows starts using the pointers you've chosen.

If the selected pointer is animated
the animation appears here

A Scheme replaces all pointers

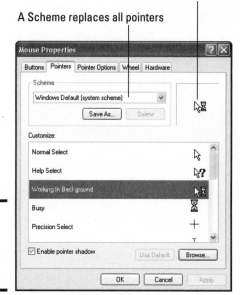

Figure 4-6:
Mouse
pointers
can all be
changed.

Selecting Screen Savers

Windows screen savers are absolutely, totally, utterly, 100% for fun. Ten years ago, screen savers served a real purpose — they kept monitors from "burning in" the phosphors in frequently used parts of the screen. Nowadays, monitors aren't nearly as prone to burn-in (or burn-out — would that were the case with humans!), and saving screens rates right up there with manufacturing buggy whips on the obsolescence scale. Still, screen savers are amusing. To select a screen saver:

1. **Right-click any empty part of the desktop and click Properties.**

2. **Click the Screen Saver tab.**

You see the dialog box shown in Figure 4-7.

Most of the settings are self-explanatory, but one can be a bit confusing: the check box in Figure 4-7 marked On Resume, Display Welcome Screen. That check box controls what happens when the computer "wakes up" after the screen saver has kicked in:

• If On Resume, Display Welcome Screen is checked, when the computer wakes up, it shows the Windows logon screen. If the user who was logged on has an account that requires a password, she will have to re-enter the password in order to get back into Windows.

• If On Resume, Display Welcome Screen is not checked, when the computer wakes up, it returns to the state it was in when the screen saver started. The user who was logged on remains logged on.

3. **When you're happy with your screen saver settings, click OK.**

Choose a screen saver

Options specific to the screen saver

Start the screen saver immediately

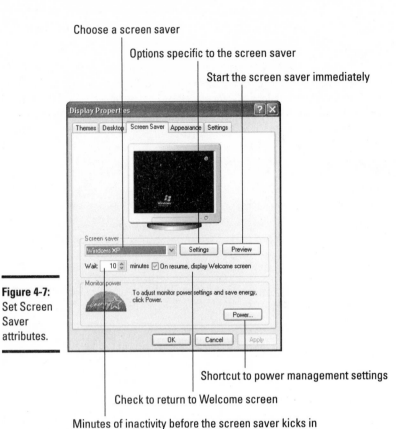

Figure 4-7:
Set Screen
Saver
attributes.

Shortcut to power management settings

Check to return to Welcome screen

Minutes of inactivity before the screen saver kicks in

In previous versions of Windows, bypassing the screen saver password protection scheme was relatively easy. Not so in Windows XP. If the On Resume, Display Welcome Screen box is checked, a potential cracker has to crack the Windows XP password itself — not an easy task.

If you want to get rid of your current screen saver, right-click an empty spot on the desktop, click Properties, click the Screen Saver tab, and click None in the Screen Saver drop-down list. Click OK, and your screen will no longer be saved.

Seeing Desktop Text

If the characters you see on the Windows screen aren't good enough, Windows XP includes several options for improving the legibility of text on your desktop. The five main options are as follows:

✦ Activate ClearType, which can make some text easier to read, especially on portable computers and flat panel displays.

✦ Have Windows show Large Fonts, which increases the size of the font used for icon labels, window titles, Windows Explorer text, and menus (but nothing else).

✦ Change the "dpi" setting, an arcane zoom setting that's poorly documented and best avoided, particularly because, once changed, the new zoom factor applies to everyone who uses the PC, in all of their applications.

Although you can find a few references to changing the dpi setting in the Windows XP Help and Support Center, only three people at Microsoft really understand the setting, and two of them are on sabbatical. (Okay, so I exaggerated a little bit. Not much.) Stay away from the dialog box (Display Properties⇨Advanced⇨General) and don't change the setting unless you're instructed to do so by someone who's willing to pay for all the therapy you'll need to cope with the aftermath.

✦ Use Magnification, which puts a strip on the screen that shows a highly magnified portion of the desktop.

✦ Try High Contrast, where Windows uses a coloring method that decreases details, but improves legibility, particularly at a distance, or for those with visual challenges.

Windows, per se, doesn't control as many of the font settings that you may imagine. For example, if you want to increase the size of the fonts in the Help and Support Center, Windows Large Fonts support doesn't do a thing. You have to bring up the Help and Support Center, click Options, and adjust the Font Size Used for Help setting.

Activating ClearType

Microsoft's ClearType technology uses a very strange color shading scheme — invented years ago — to make fonts look better on certain kinds of displays. If you choose to have Windows use ClearType, Windows employs the technology everywhere for showing text on the screen — on the Windows desktop, inside your spreadsheet program, even inside Internet Explorer. Conventional wisdom says that ClearType works great on portable computers and flat-panel monitors.

My UWD (Unconventional Wisdom for Dummies) says that ClearType helps a bit with the labels under icons and small amounts of text scattered here and there on a screen, but I'd rather hang my eyeballs out to dry than force them to stare at a word processing screen that's been "enhanced" with ClearType. Yes, ClearType works much better on flat panel displays than on traditional computer screens. No, I don't use it.

Here's how to turn on ClearType (it's buried pretty well):

1. **Right-click any empty location on the desktop and choose Properties.**

2. **Click on the Appearance tab, and then click Effects.**

3. **Select the Use the Following Method to Smooth Edges of Screen Fonts check box, and then choose ClearType from the drop-down list underneath (see Figure 4-8).**

4. **Click OK, and immediately start your word processor of choice. Work with it for a few minutes and see if you start getting a headache.**

If you do, head back to the Effects dialog box and turn ClearType off.

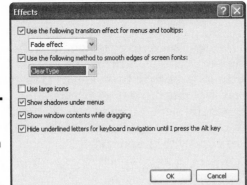

Figure 4-8:
Enable
ClearType in
the Effects
dialog box.

Showing large fonts

If you use the standard Windows Desktop Theme, you have an easy way to change the size of the fonts that Windows shows. Before you rush to your mouse, though, you should be aware of the limitations:

✦ The font size you select applies only to window title bars, labels for icons on the desktop, in Windows Explorer, and in menus. It doesn't change anything else.

✦ When you apply a new Desktop Theme (see "Using Desktop Themes" later in this chapter), your old font size settings are thrown away.

✦ Not all Desktop Themes support multiple font sizes. The only way to know for sure is to try to change the size and see whether it works.

To change to larger fonts:

1. **Right-click on any blank area on the desktop and choose Properties.**

2. **Click the Appearance tab.**

3. **Choose the font size you want in the Font Size drop-down list.**

Using magnification and high contrast

I won't belabor the point here, but two Accessibilities settings can come in handy, even if you don't normally think of Accessibility as a code name for "seeing text on the desktop." The Magnifier puts a magnified strip along the top of the screen, which follows your mouse as you move it. High Contrast uses a modified color scheme to increase legibility of text. To check out Magnification and High Contrast:

1. **Choose Start⇨Control Panel⇨Accessibility Options.**

2. **To work with High Contrast, choose Adjust the Contrast for Text and Colors on Your Screen under Pick a Task.**

3. **To start the Magnifier, choose Magnifier in the See Also section of the task pane.**

Using Desktop Themes

Windows XP Desktop Themes incorporate many settings in one easy-to-choose package. The themes revolve around specific topics that frequently (and refreshingly) have nothing to do with Windows — say, cars with carapaces, cavorting carnivores, or carnal caruncles. A theme includes six of the seven desktop levels I discuss in this chapter — a base color for the desktop, background, settings for fonts and colors of the working windows, pictures for the reserved Windows icons (Recycle Bin, My Documents, and so on), a set of mouse pointers, and a screen saver. A theme also includes a set of custom sounds that are associated with various Windows events. I've never seen a desktop theme that includes Active Desktop items. To bring in a new theme:

1. **Right-click any open spot on the desktop and choose Properties.**

2. **Click the Themes tab.**

3. **Choose a theme from the Themes box.**

When you bring in a theme, it replaces all seven of the desktop levels I discuss in this chapter, plus the sound scheme you may have had in place. The old background, icon pictures, mouse pointers, and screen savers all remain on your PC — the theme doesn't delete them — but if you want any of them back, you have to go through the customization steps you used earlier to reinstate them.

Customizing Folders

In some cases, Windows Explorer lets you change a folder's thumbnail by modifying the picture that's superimposed on a picture of a folder. You may have seen that startling capability if you used Windows Media Player to "rip" a CD — the cover art for the CD probably appeared on the folder that contains the CD. If you ripped more than one album by a single artist, chances are good up to four album covers appear on the folder that contains all of the albums.

To change the picture superimposed on a folder:

1. **Start Windows Explorer by choosing Start⇨My Documents; Start⇨My Pictures, My Music, My Computer, or My Network Places; or by running a search with Start⇨Search.**

2. **Navigate to the folder that you want to change.**

3. **Make sure that you're viewing thumbnails by choosing View⇨Thumbnails.**

   Superimposed pictures appear only in Thumbnail View.

4. **Right-click on the folder.**

5. **If you want Windows to scan all the picture files inside the folder (including album cover art inside music folders) and place the four most-recently modified pictures on top of the folder, choose Refresh Thumbnail.**

6. If you want to pick your own picture to superimpose on the folder, choose Properties and click the Customize tab.

You see the Properties dialog box shown in Figure 4-9.

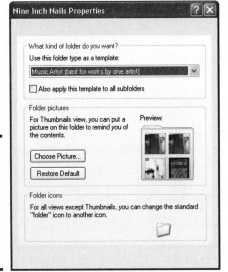

Figure 4-9: Choose the pictures to be superimposed on the folder in this dialog box.

If you can't see the Customize tab, chances are good that you're trying to change the picture on a shortcut folder. Unfortunately, Windows won't let you change the picture superimposed on a shortcut folder.

7. Click the Choose Picture button and choose any picture file — it need not be inside the indicated folder.

8. Click OK and the chosen picture will now appear superimposed on the folder while in Windows Explorer.

Although Windows can put up to four pictures on top of a folder, you are allowed to put only one on top.

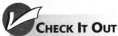

Cleaning Up Old Icons

Your desktop is a great place to park things for short periods of time, but a lousy place for organizing anything long-term. Start by cleaning up the mess that's there right now:

1. Right-click an empty location on the desktop and choose Properties; in the Display Properties dialog box that appears, click the Desktop tab.

2. Click the Customize Desktop button.

You see the Desktop Items dialog box. Don't believe what you read about

Desktop Cleanup, by the way. The straight story follows.

3. Click the Clean Desktop Now button.

The Desktop Cleanup Wizard appears.

4. Click Next.

The Desktop Cleanup Wizard scans only for shortcuts. It doesn't even look at other kinds of files or folders (or zipped/compressed folders). Follow this procedure all the way to the end to move all your unused, or rarely used, desktop items.

The Desktop Cleanup Wizard presents the
results of its scan.

5. **Review the shortcuts with check marks
    next to them, and feel free to check any
    shortcuts that you don't expect to use in
    the near future.**

6. **Click Next and then click Finish.**

    All the shortcuts you checked are shuffled
    to a folder on the desktop called Unused
    Desktop Shortcuts.

7. **Click OK twice to clear out the dialog
    boxes.**

Some of the Date Last Used entries in the
Desktop Cleanup Wizard are just plain wrong. For
example, I found that shortcuts to MP3 files with
the name "Shortcut to . . ." didn't appear on this
list, although they had been opened multiple
times by Windows Media Player 8. Shortcuts to
Web pages also failed to appear.

Chapter 5: Organizing Your Windows XP Interface

In This Chapter

✔ Harnessing the power of the Windows Start menu

✔ Creating shortcuts to open files and programs

✔ Getting at your most recently used documents quickly

✔ Starting your favorite programs with just a click

✔ Making workhorse programs start automatically

*W*indows XP contains an enormous variety of self-help tools that can make your working (and playing!) day go faster. As you get more comfortable with the Windows inner world, you will find shortcuts and simplifications that really do make a difference. This chapter shows you how to take off the training wheels.

Customizing the Start Menu

I gave you a brief overview of the Start menu in Book I, Chapter 3. In this chapter, I show you the beast in far greater detail.

Your screen may not look exactly like the one shown in Figure 5-1. If you bought your PC with Windows XP preinstalled, chances are very good that the PC manufacturer stuck some programs on the Start menu that didn't originate with Microsoft. If you want to take control of your Start menu, follow the steps in this chapter to get rid of the stuff you don't want or need. It's your Start menu. You won't break anything. Take the, uh, bull by the horns. In order to change the Start menu for everyone who uses your computer, you need to be a designated Administrator. Find out more about becoming an Administrator in Book I, Chapter 6.

Genesis of the Start menu

Although the Start menu looks like it sprang fully formed from the head of some malevolent Windows god, in fact Windows creates the left side of the Start menu on the fly, every time you click the Start button. That's why your computer takes a little while between the time you click Start and the time you see the Start menu on the screen. Here's where the various pieces come from, looking from top to bottom:

✦ The name and picture at the top are taken from the Windows sign on screen.

✦ You can *pin* a program to the upper-left corner of the Start menu. Once pinned, it stays there until you remove it. Unfortunately, you can't pin a file. I go into details in the next section of this chapter.

✦ The *recently used programs* list maintained by Windows goes in the lower left. Although you have a little bit of control over this list, Windows stacks the deck, loading its favorite programs first, whether you use them or not. Most of the time, you'll probably let Windows play with it — after you've learned how to unstack the deck. I talk about the way Windows maintains this list in the section, "Reclaiming most recently used programs."

✦ Down at the bottom, *All Programs* actually connects to two folders on your hard drive. This is the part of the Start menu that was designed by Microsoft to be easy to modify. You can add fly-out menus and change and delete items to your heart's content — all of which is really pretty easy.

Although you can make many little changes to the items on the right side of the Start menu (see "Making minor tweaks to the Start menu") — and you should definitely spend a few minutes deciding whether any of the changes are worthwhile for you — the one big change on the right side is the inclusion of a Most Recently Used Documents list. Some people love it. Some people hate it. Read "Showing recent documents" and decide for yourself.

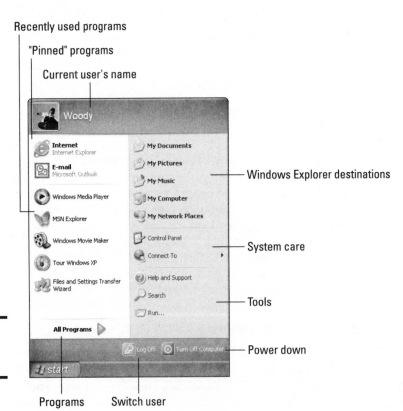

Recently used programs

"Pinned" programs

Current user's name

Woody

Internet — Internet Explorer
E-mail — Microsoft Outlook
Windows Media Player
MSN Explorer
Windows Movie Maker
Tour Windows XP
Files and Settings Transfer Wizard

My Documents
My Pictures
My Music
My Computer
My Network Places

Control Panel
Connect To
Help and Support
Search
Run...

All Programs

Log Off | Turn Off Computer

start

Windows Explorer destinations

System care

Tools

Power down

Figure 5-1: The Start menu.

Programs   Switch user

Pinning to the Start menu

Do you have one or two programs that run your life? Yeah. Me, too. Word and Outlook. I use them day in and day out. I dream in Word. Sad but true. Windows XP enables you to easily put programs of your choice way up at the top, in the upper-left corner of the Start menu. That's the high-rent district, the place my mouse gravitates to every time I click Start.

I don't know why, but Microsoft calls this "pinning" — kind of a wimpy name for the most powerful feature on the Start menu, eh? If you have Office 2003 on your computer, chances are good that the Office installer pinned Outlook 2003 on your Start menu as your e-mail program. Here's how you pin Word 2003 (the word processing program from Microsoft Office 2003) on your Start menu. The procedure for any other program works similarly:

1. **Both Word 2003 and Outlook 2003 are on the All Programs menu, so pinning them is easy. Choose Start⇨All Programs; then right-click on the program and choose Pin To Start Menu.**

   If you pin a program on the Start menu by right-clicking on it and choosing Pin to Start Menu, Windows creates a second entry in the Start menu for the pinned copy. Your original — the program you right-clicked on — stays where it was. You can also drag and drop a program from anywhere in Windows onto the pinned list.

   When the program gets pinned, it appears at the bottom of the pinned pile — which is to say, below your Web browser and e-mail program. You can left-click on the program and drag it to any other spot in the pinned list that you like.

2. **Right-click on the program and choose Rename; then give the program a name that you can live with.**

   If you pin a program on the Start menu by right-clicking on it and choosing Pin to Start Menu, both the original Start menu entry and the new pinned entry are linked. If you change the name on one (right-click and choose Rename), the other copy is changed as well.

You can remove any program in the pinned part of the Start menu. If you right-click either of the built-in pinned programs (marked Internet and E-mail) and choose Remove From This List, the program is removed. If you right-click any other pinned programs (presumably ones that you put up in the high-rent district, or ones that your computer's manufacturer so graciously added to the list), choose Unpin from Start Menu and the item goes away.

Note that unpinning a program removes it from only the pinned list in the upper-left corner of the Start menu. The program itself stays right where it is. So do any other shortcuts to the program, whether they're elsewhere on the Start menu or somewhere else in your computer, such as on your desktop.

Reclaiming most recently used programs

Directly above the Start button, in the lower-left corner of the Start menu, you find a list of the programs that you've used most recently. This list is really handy: It is updated dynamically as you use programs, so you always have a very good chance of seeing the program you need right there on the list.

When you run a program that's pinned to the upper-left corner of the Start menu (see the preceding section), it doesn't count: The most recently used list includes only programs that aren't up at the top of the Start menu. At least, that's the theory. In fact, the most recently used counter that controls what shows up in the most recently used programs box isn't quite kosher. If you play with the list for a while, you discover that the programs higher up in the list tend to stay on the list longer — whether you've used them or not. So Windows Media Player and MSN Explorer tend to hang around a whole lot longer than the Files and Settings Transfer Wizard (which you would expect), and many programs that you happen to run (which you probably wouldn't expect).

Fortunately, you can easily get rid of all the built-in most recently used programs and start out with a clean slate:

1. **Right-click on the Start button and choose Properties.**

2. **On the Start menu tab, make sure that Start menu is checked, and click Customize.**

3. **On the General tab, in the middle of the Customize Start Menu dialog box (see Figure 5-2), click the Clear List button.**

Figure 5-2: Control the most recently used program list from here.

4. **While you're here, consider switching to smaller icons — which puts more programs on the Start menu in a smaller slice of real estate, although they'll be smaller and thus harder to hit with your mouse — and adding to the Number of Programs on the Start menu.**

The Windows Customize Start Menu dialog box says that you can set the Number of Programs on Start menu (refer to Figure 5-2). That isn't true. In fact, the number shown is actually the number of programs that appear in the most recently used box, in the lower-left corner of the Start menu.

5. **Click OK twice, and your most recently used program list starts to reflect the programs that, uh, you have most recently used.**

Windows maintains the most recently used program list on its own: You cannot drag and drop items on the list. You can, however, remove programs from the list. Just right-click on an offending program and choose Remove From This List.

Showing recent documents

Some people love the recent documents feature. Most people hate it. That's why Microsoft turned it off in the final, shipping version of Windows XP. In most normal circumstances — with well-behaved programs that don't crash — Windows keeps track of which documents you've opened. You can have Windows show a list of those documents on the Start menu, just under My Documents (see Figure 5-3).

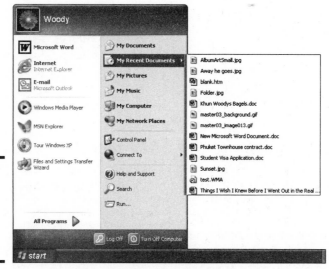

Figure 5-3:
The My Recent Documents fly-out menu.

Folks who like the feature appreciate being able to retrieve documents quickly and easily, without spelunking for the program that created them: Click on a Word document in the My Recent Documents folder, and Word comes to life, with the document open and ready to rumble.

Folks who hate the feature would just as soon open the application and use the application's most recently opened file list (typically on the File menu) to retrieve their documents. Some of the curmudgeons — present company definitely included — don't particularly want to leave (yet another) record of what they've been doing lying around for prying eyes. To turn on My Recent Documents:

1. **Right-click Start and choose Properties.**

2. **On the Start Menu tab, make sure Start Menu is checked, and click Customize.**

3. **On the Advanced tab, select the List My Most Recently Opened Documents check box (see Figure 5-4).**

Note that you can return to this location to clear out the list. But clearing the list here does *not* clear similar lists in your applications, such as Word or Internet Explorer. For those, you have to refer to the application itself.

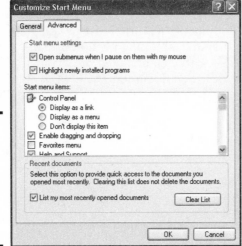

Figure 5-4:
Enable My
Recent
Documents
in the
Customize
Start Menu
dialog box.

Making minor tweaks to the Start menu

You can make a number of additional changes to the Start menu. Some of
them are actually useful, particularly if you go into your computer fairly frequently to jiggle things. To tweak:

1. **Right-click Start and choose Properties.**

2. **On the Start Menu tab, make sure Start Menu is checked, and click
Customize.**

3. **Click the Advanced tab and select the features you want to enable,
based on the following list. Click OK twice.**

The following six Start menu items can be turned into fly-out menus:

✦ **Control Panel:** This item can show all of the "classic applets" (read: all
of the individual Control Panel applications) in a fly-out menu. That's
the Display As a Menu option in the Start Menu Items list.

✦ **Favorites:** This item creates a menu that can appear above My Computer,
with Favorites (primarily from Internet Explorer) listed on a fly-out menu.
To show Favorites, select the Favorites check box in the Start Menu
Items list.

✦ **My Computer:** This item can have its own fly-out menu, listing your
drives, as well as the Control Panel (which now appears twice on the
Start menu), My Documents (again), and Shared Documents. Enable the
fly-out menu by selecting the Display As a Menu option in the Start
Menu Items list.

✦ **My Documents, My Music, and My Pictures:** These items can all have
their own fly-out menus listing files and folders in each. Select the
Display As a Menu check box on the relevant Start Menu Items list.

If you're an inveterate twiddler (or twiddler-in-training), in the Start Menu
Items list, select the System Administrative Tools/Display on the All Programs
Menu check box. The programs there will keep you occupied for years.

Creating Your Own Shortcuts

Sometimes, life's easier with shortcuts. (As long as the shortcuts work, anyway.) So, too, in the Windows XP realm, where shortcuts point to things that can be started. You may set up a shortcut to Word and put it on your desktop. Double-click on the Word shortcut, and Word starts, the same way as if you chose Start⇨All Programs⇨Microsoft Word.

You can set up shortcuts that point to the following:

✦ Programs of any kind

✦ Web addresses such as `www.woodyswatch.com/signup`

✦ Documents, spreadsheets, databases, PowerPoint presentations, and anything else that can be started in Windows Explorer by double-clicking on it

✦ Specific chunks of text inside documents, spreadsheets, databases, presentations, and so on (they're called *scraps*)

✦ Folders (including the weird folders that are inside electronic cameras), even the Fonts folder and others that you may not think of

✦ Drives (hard disks, floppies, CDs, Jaz drives, the works)

✦ Other computers on your network, and drives and folders on those computers

✦ Printers (including printers on other computers on your network), scanners, cameras, and other pieces of hardware

✦ Dial-up network connections

Shortcuts can do many amazing things. For example, you can set up a short-cut to a specific network printer on your desktop. Then, if you want to print a file on that printer, just drag the file onto the shortcut. Windows XP takes care of all the details. There are many different ways to create shortcuts.

Say you use the Windows calculator all the time, and you want to put a short-cut to the Windows calculator on your desktop. Here's an easy way to do it:

1. **Right-click any blank spot on the desktop.**

2. **Choose New⇨Shortcut.**

The Create Shortcut Wizard appears (see Figure 5-5).

3. **Click Browse.**

4. **In the Browse for Folder dialog box, click My Computer, click the C: drive, click Windows, and then click System32.**

Scroll way down to `calc.exe`.

5. **Click `calc.exe` and click OK.**

6. **Click Next; type a good, descriptive name like Calculator; and click Finish.**

Figure 5-5:
Use the
Create
Shortcut
Wizard to
put a
shortcut
to the
Windows
Calculator
on your
desktop.

Any time you double-click the Windows Calculator shortcut on your desktop, the Calculator comes to life. You can use a similar procedure for setting up shortcuts to any file, folder, program, or document on your computer or any networked computer.

Often, the hardest part about setting up a shortcut is finding the program that you want the shortcut to refer to. In the preceding example, you saw how the Windows Calculator is located in the system32 folder, which in turn sits inside the Windows folder (techie shorthand is `C:\Windows\system32`). Many other Windows programs are in the system32 folder. If you're looking for the Microsoft Office XP programs, they're probably in `C:\Program Files\Microsoft Office\Office10`, while Office 2000 programs are most likely in `C:\Program Files\Microsoft Office\Office`. The Fonts folder sits in `C:\Windows`. In general, if you're looking for programs, your best bet is to look in the Program Files folder first and then in the Windows folder.

You have many other ways to skin the shortcat . . . uh, skin the shortcut cat. When you're working in Windows Explorer, you can right-click many types of files and folders, drag them to new locations — other folders, the desktop, even the Start menu or the Quick Launch Toolbar — release the mouse button, and choose Create Shortcuts Here.

Quick Launch Toolbar

Windows XP Professional turns on the Windows XP Quick Launch Toolbar automatically. Some people, however, don't care to see the Quick Launch toolbar crowding their taskbar. To those people, and to people who want to customize the Quick Launch toolbar, I dedicate the next few pages of this book.

Activating

Windows XP's Quick Launch Toolbar is a little tray of icons that sits next to the Start button, where you can stick shortcuts to start all of your favorite programs (see Figure 5-6). It's one of the handiest features in Windows — and if you are running Windows XP Home, you may not even know that it exists.

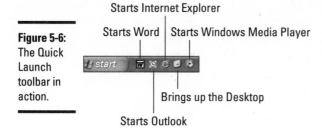

Figure 5-6:
The Quick
Launch
toolbar in
action.

Starts Internet Explorer

Starts Word   Starts Windows Media Player

Brings up the Desktop

Starts Outlook

To start the Quick Launch Toolbar, right-click on any open spot down on the Windows taskbar and choose Toolbars⇨Quick Launch. That's all there is to it. Your initial Quick Launch Toolbar includes icons for Internet Explorer, the desktop, and the Windows Media Player.

Customizing

Adding your own icons to the Quick Launch Toolbar is very simple, too, but you immediately run into problems trying to squeeze more icons into that teensy-tiny space. Here's how to avoid the problem in the first place:

1. **Make sure the Quick Launch Toolbar is showing (right-click any open spot down on the Windows taskbar and choose Toolbars⇨Quick Launch).**

2. **Unlock the taskbar so that you can increase the size of the Quick Launch Toolbar.**

   To do so, right-click any open spot on the Windows taskbar, and uncheck the line marked Lock the Taskbar. Windows shows two small drag handles, one to the left and one to the right of the Quick Launch Toolbar.

3. **Grab the drag handle on the right and stretch it out (to the right) a bit.**

4. **Find a program that you want to put in the Quick Launch Toolbar.**

   For example, if you have Microsoft Office installed and you want to put Word down there, choose Start⇨All Programs, and look for Microsoft Word.

5. **Right-click on the program, and drag it down to the Quick Launch Toolbar.**

   You see a big, black I-Beam in the Quick Launch Toolbar that indicates where the icon will go. When you release the icon, choose Copy Here.

   When you drag icons to the Quick Launch Toolbar, right-click and choose Copy Here, so that the original program shortcut stays intact. If you left-click (or right-click and choose Move Here), the shortcut gets moved.

6. **Drag as many icons to the Quick Launch Toolbar as you like. When you're done, butt the right drag handle up against the rightmost icon, and then right-click on the Windows taskbar and choose Lock Toolbar.**

You have more "play" with the Quick Launch Toolbar's resizing drag handles than you think. Try squishing the Quick Launch Toolbar by setting the right drag handle on top of the rightmost icon, and then lock the Toolbar. When you choose Lock Toolbar, chances are good that all of the icons appear anyway. It never hurts to tighten things up a bit, so Windows can use as much of the taskbar as possible.

Customizing the Windows Taskbar

If you have more than one program running, the fastest way to switch from one program to another is via the Windows taskbar, shown in Figure 5-7. With a few small exceptions, each running program carves out a chunk of space on the Windows taskbar. If more than one copy of a program is running (not an unusual state of affairs for Windows Explorer, among others) or if a program has more than one file open (common in Word, for example) and Windows runs low on real estate in the taskbar area, the chunks are grouped together, with the number of open documents in front of the program name.

Figure 5-7:
The
Windows
taskbar.

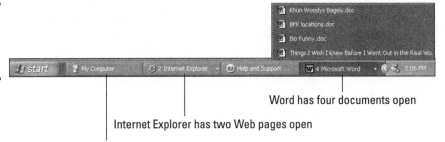

Word has four documents open

Internet Explorer has two Web pages open

Windows Explorer is looking at My Computer

If you click on the button marked 4 Microsoft Word (as shown in Figure 5-7), for example, you see a list of the four documents that Word currently has open. Click on one of those documents, and Word comes up, loaded for bear.

The Windows taskbar has many tricks up its sleeve, but it has one capability that you're likely to need. *Auto-Hide* lets the taskbar shrink down to a thin line until you bump your mouse way down at the bottom of the screen. As soon as your mouse hits bottom, the taskbar pops up. Here's how you teach the taskbar to Auto-Hide:

1. **Right-click an empty part of the taskbar.**

Usually the area immediately to the right of the Start button is a good place.

2. **Choose Properties.**

The Taskbar tab should be visible.

3. **Select the Auto-Hide the Taskbar check box, and then click OK.**

If you don't want to hunt around for the mouse — or if your mouse has suddenly gone out to lunch — Windows XP has a feature called Coolswitch that lets you switch among running programs, while (insert your best W.C. Fields impression here) your fingers never leave your hands . . . er, your fingers never leave the keyboard. Wink, wink. Just hold down the Alt key and press Tab. When you get to the program you want, release the Alt key. Bang.

Custom Startup

Do you start a specific program just about every time you crank up Windows? Maybe you want to get the Windows Media Player going every time Windows wakes up. A friend of mine always starts the Windows Calculator. Of course, he's a hopeless drudge, so don't let him influence you. You can easily tell Windows XP that you want to run a specific program every time Windows starts. You just have to put the program in the \Startup folder.

Say you want to start the Windows Calculator every time anybody logs on to Windows. You can make that happen if you put a shortcut to the Calculator into the All Users \Startup folder, like this:

1. **Right-click on the Start button and choose Explore All Users.**

2. **Double-click your way down to the Startup folder (**C:\Documents and Settings\All Users\Start Menu\Programs\Startup**).**

3. **Go back to the Start button, and choose Start➪All Programs➪ Accessories.**

4. **Right-click on the Calculator and drag it to the \Startup folder. When you release the Calculator, choose Copy Here.**

   You see a shortcut to the Calculator go into the \Startup folder (see Figure 5-8).

Figure 5-8: Put a shortcut to the Calculator in the \Startup folder, and it starts every time Windows does.

You're done. The next time anyone logs on to Windows, the Calculator will start.

If you want the Calculator to start for just one user, you need to put a short-cut to the calculator in that user's \Startup folder. The easy way: Have that user log on, right-click the Start button and choose Explore. Then follow Steps 2 through 5 in the preceding list.

Chapter 6: Setting Up Personal Accounts

In This Chapter

✔ Understanding how logons work

✔ Adding users

✔ Logging off

This chapter explains strategies for sharing a computer among two or more people. If you play your cards right, you can set up Windows XP so that each person who uses your computer gets to make his or her own settings. Peace will prevail. All will be well in your household.

Controlling Who Gets On

Windows XP assumes that, sooner or later, more than one person will want to work on your PC. All sorts of problems crop up when several people share a PC. I get my screen set up just right, with all my icons right where I can find them, and then my son comes along and plasters the desktop with a shot of Alpha Centauri. He puts together a killer teen Media Player playlist, and "accidentally" deletes my Grateful Dead list in the process. It's worse than sharing a TV remote.

Windows helps keep peace in the family — and in the office — by requiring people to *log on*. The process of logging on (also called *signing on*) lets Windows keep track of each person's settings: You tell Windows who you are, and Windows lets you play in your own sandbox.

Having personal settings that activate when you log on to Windows XP isn't heavy-duty security, at least in the Home version of Windows XP. (Windows XP Professional beefs up security substantially, but makes you jump through many more hoops.) In Windows XP Home, your settings can get clobbered, and your files deleted, if someone else tries hard enough. But as long as everybody sharing the PC cooperates, the XP logon method works pretty darn well.

Getting a warm welcome: The Welcome screen

When it's ready to get started, Windows XP greets you with a *Welcome screen* — variously called a "Logon screen" or a "Signon screen" as well — like the one shown in Figure 6-1. The screen lists all the users who have been signed up to use the computer. It may also show a catch-all user called "Guest." (I guess that sounds better than "Other" or "Hey, you!")

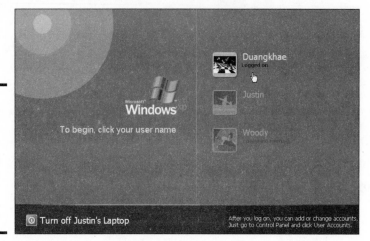

Figure 6-1:
The Welcome screen helps keep users from bumping into one another.

You can set up a Guest account to grant very limited capabilities to anyone who hasn't been formally set up on that specific PC. (I explain how to set up the Guest account and new users in the next section, "Adding users.") Of course, nothing prevents a guest — friend, foe, or mother-in-law — from clicking on one of the other icons and logging on under an assumed identity: Windows XP Home relies on the gentlemanly conduct of all participants to keep its settings straight. And if you can't rely on gentlemanly conduct, you need to set up a password. I talk about how you do that in the section, "Changing user settings."

Adding users

After you log on by clicking your name on the Welcome screen, you can add more users quite easily. Here's how:

1. Choose Start⇨Control Panel⇨User Accounts.

You see the User Accounts dialog box, as shown in Figure 6-2.

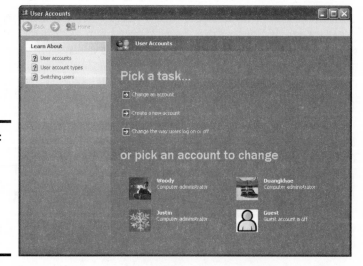

Figure 6-2:
Perform all kinds of maintenance in the User Accounts screen.

2. Click the task marked Create a New Account.

3. Enter a name.

You're done. Rocket science.

The name now appears on the Welcome screen.

A note on account names — you can give a new account just about any name you like: first name, last name, nickname, titles, abbreviations. No sweat. Even weird punctuation marks make it past the Windows censors: The name "All your base@!^" works fine.

To make the Guest account available on your computer, click Guest Account on the User Accounts screen (refer to Figure 6-2). Then click Turn On the Guest Account.

Changing user settings

If you pick an account from the User Account screen, which you bring up by choosing Start⇨Control Panel⇨User Accounts, Windows immediately presents you with five options. (See Figure 6-3.) Click on any of these options to begin the chosen task. Here's what the options entail:

Gives the user a new picture ID

Changes the user's name

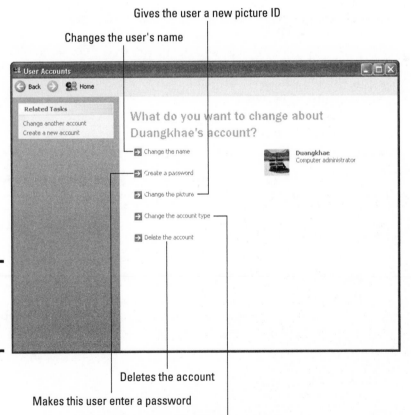

Figure 6-3:
Maintain
another
individual's
account.

Deletes the account

Makes this user enter a password

Lets you put on user restrictions

✦ **Change the name:** Modifies the name displayed on the Welcome screen and at the very top of the Start menu, while leaving all other settings intact. Use this option if you want to change the name on the account only — for example, if "Bill" suddenly wants to be called "William."

✦ **Create a password:** Requires users to enter a password whenever they start Windows. They can't get past the Welcome screen (using their own account) without it. This is a weird setting because you can change it for other people — you can force "Bill" to use a password when none was required before. Worse, you specify the initial password when you set up an account this way, so Bill would have to pry the password out of you before he can log on.

Passwords are cAse SenSitive — you must enter the password, capitals and all, precisely the way it was originally typed. If you can't get the computer to recognize your password, make sure the Caps Lock key is off. That's the number one source of logon frustration.

If you decide to put a password on your account, take a couple of minutes to run the Forgotten Password Wizard (choose Start⇨Help and Support and type **forgotten password wizard**). This nifty little program creates a diskette that you can use to unlock your password and get into your account, even if your precocious seven-year-old daughter changed it to MXYPLFTFFT. You have to run the wizard just once; the diskette it creates will always unlock your account.

✦ **Change the picture:** Changes the picture that appears next to the user's name on the Welcome screen, the Start menu, and in the User Accounts areas. You can choose a picture from any of the common file types: GIF, BMP, JPG, or PNG. Windows offers a couple dozen pictures to choose from, but you can reach out and grab any picture, anywhere. If you pick a big picture, Windows automatically scales it to size.

✦ **Change the account type:** Lets you change accounts from Computer Administrator to Limited and back again. The implications are somewhat complex; I talk about them in the next section.

✦ **Delete the account:** Allows you to deep-six the account, if you're that bold (or mad, in all senses of the term). Windows offers to keep copies of the deleted account's My Documents folder and Desktop, but warns you quite sternly and correctly that if you snuff the account, you take along all the e-mail messages, Internet Favorites, and other settings that belong to the user. Definitely not a good way to make friends.

Okay, I fibbed — you can't make all of those changes to other peoples' accounts if you're a lowly Limited user. In fact, you must be a designated Computer Administrator before Windows grants you such power. But therein lies a different, mottled story, which I relate to you in the next section.

Using account types

All Windows XP Home users can be divided into two groups: the haves and the have-nots. The haves are called *Computer Administrators*. The have-nots are called *Limited*. That's it. "Limited." Kinda makes your toes curl just to think about it.

A Limited user, running his or her Limited account, can only do, uh, limited things:

✦ Run programs that are installed on the computer (but he can't install new programs)

✦ Use hardware that's installed on the computer (but he can't install new hardware)

✦ Create and use documents/pictures/sounds in his My Documents/My Pictures/My Music folders, as well as in the PC's shared folders

✦ Change his password or switch back and forth between requiring a password for his account and not requiring one

✦ Change the picture that appears next to his name on the Welcome screen and the Start menu

On the other hand, Computer Administrators can change anything, anywhere, at any time, with the sole exception of getting into folders marked Private. Computer Administrators can even change other users' passwords — a good thing to remember if you ever forget your password.

In order to mark a folder as Private — and thus keep other users from getting into it — you must be using the Windows NT file system, known as *NTFS*. If Windows XP was installed on your computer when you bought it, chances are good that it's using NTFS. If you upgraded from Windows 98 or ME to Windows XP Home, though, there's a very big chance you aren't using NTFS. Book I, Chapter 7 shows you how to find out if you're using NTFS, and how to mark a folder as Private if it's possible.

When you install Windows XP Home, every account that's set up is considered a Computer Administrator account. That's why other people can make Windows suddenly require you to enter a password: Everybody is an Administrator.

Avoiding Microsoft Passport

On the surface, *Microsoft Passport* dazzles as a wonderful idea: a central location where you can put all the consumer-related information you'll need to interact with vendors over the Web, not to mention chat with other people using Windows Messenger, download stock prices, customize weather predictions, send and receive e-mail using Microsoft's own Hotmail e-mail service, open a bank account, trade stock, and on and on.

If you choose Start⇨Control Panel⇨User Accounts and then select your own account in the User Account screen, you have the option of signing up for Microsoft Passport — or linking your local PC to your existing Passport — as shown in Figure 6-4.

Here's the downside of Microsoft Passport: *How much do you trust Microsoft to protect your privacy?* That seems to be the root question when any discussion of Microsoft Passport hits the ether. Most people don't trust Microsoft much farther than they can throw a cow. With a tractor and two barns attached.

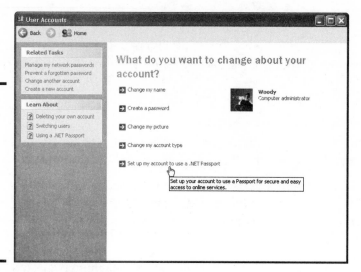

Figure 6-4:
When you bring up your account, you have the choice of hitching up to Microsoft Passport.

On the face of it, the Passport seems innocuous: Type in your name, pick an ID and a password, and suddenly all of these wonderful features become available. Beneath the surface, though, you have to realize that Microsoft holds the keys to all of the Passport data. If you trust Microsoft (and, personally, in this case, I do), the only real problem with Passport is a growing sense of Big Brother's imminent arrival. If you don't trust Microsoft, you'd be a fool to hand over your personal information — even something as simple as a list of your favorite stocks.

On the third hand, if you don't sign up for Passport, you can't use Windows Messenger for instant chatting, can't use Hotmail for e-mail on the Web, can't ask someone to take over the controls at your computer and help you with Remote Assistance, can't put Microsoft's neat stock ticker on your Windows desktop, and on and on.

What's a person to do? Many folks strike a balance between privacy and convenience by getting a Passport, but being very vigilant about the kinds of information they hand over to Microsoft's ever-expanding database. You may find that a workable solution, too. Just be aware that Passport data collection can be a two-way street: If you use a Passport to get onto a site, there's a chance that the site will send gathered information back to Microsoft. I don't mean to make you paranoid, but almost anything that you enter on any Web page hooked up to Passport could end up sitting in a Microsoft database.

At any rate, if you want to sign up for Microsoft Passport and have your account on your PC linked to that big MS Passport logbook in the sky, follow these steps:

1. **Choose Start⇨Control Panel⇨User Accounts.**

2. **Choose your own account.**

3. **Click Set Up My Account to Use a .NET Passport.**

   You are transported to Microsoft's Web site, where you can consummate the relationship.

Deleting yourself

AHA! I bet you saw it. Did you compare Figure 6-3 to Figure 6-4? Bonus
Dummies Merit Points if you noticed the subtle difference. (One hundred
Dummies Merit Points are redeemable for one Severe Bragging Right at any
local Dummies store. Tell 'em I sent ya.)

You can't delete your own account.

Windows has to protect itself. Every PC must have at least one user signed
up as Computer Administrator. If Windows XP lost all of its Administrators,
no one would be around to add new users or change existing ones, much
less to install programs or hardware, right? Although you and I could probably think of a few dozen ways to ensure that a PC always has at least one
Computer Administrator, Microsoft has chosen a rather straightforward
approach. First, you can't turn yourself into a Limited user if you're the only
Computer Administrator left. Second, you can't delete your own account.

Betwixt the two of those requirements, Windows XP is assured of always
having a minimum of one Computer Administrator available at its beck
and call.

Logoff

Last things last, I always say. Windows XP Home allows you to have more
than one person logged on to a PC simultaneously. That's very convenient
if, say, you're working on the family PC checking Billy's homework when you
hear the cat screaming bloody murder in the kitchen, and your wife wants
to put digital pictures from the family vacation in the Shared Pictures folder
while you run off to check the microwave.

The ability to have more than one user logged onto a PC simultaneously is
called *Fast User Switching,* and it has advantages and disadvantages:

✦ **On the plus side:** Fast User Switching lets you keep all of your programs
   going while somebody else pops onto the machine for a quick jaunt on
   the keyboard. When they're done, they can log off, and you can pick up
   precisely where you left off before you got bumped.

✦ **On the minus side:** All of the idle programs left sitting around by the
   inactive ("bumped") user can bog things down for the active user. You
   can avoid the overhead by logging off before the new user logs on.

If you want to disable Fast User Switching, choose Start➪Control Panel and
click User Accounts. At the bottom of the Pick a Task list, click Change the
Way Users Log On or Off. Then clear the check box marked Use Fast User
Switching.

If you've used Windows for any time at all, you have undoubtedly discovered that you have to click Start in order to stop. That's one of the hallmark
wonders of the modern Windows world, an oxymoron codified in code.

You probably won't be surprised to find out that you have to click Start in order to log off or switch users. Simply choose Start⇨Log Off, and then click Switch User or Log Off.

To further confuse matters, many computers — especially portables — can go into *Hibernate* or *Standby* mode (variously called Suspend, or Suspend to File, or any of a handful of out-to-lunch synonyms). The primary differences between the two modes are as follows:

✦ In Standby mode, the PC shuts off the monitor and hard disks but keeps everything in memory so it can "wake up" quickly.

✦ In Hibernate mode, the PC shuts off the monitor and hard disks and shuffles a copy of everything in memory to the hard drive before going night-night. It takes longer to wake up from Hibernate mode because the contents of memory have to be pulled in from the hard drive.

If your portable runs out of power while in Standby mode, you're up the creek without a paddle. If it's in Hibernate mode (and Hibernate mode is working properly — not always a given!), running out of juice poses no problem at all: Plug the PC back into the wall and it comes out of Hibernate mode, brings its memory back from the hard drive, and picks up where you left off.

Not all computers support Standby mode or Hibernate mode. Some older computers don't handle either mode. Other computers can do both. If you have a choice, the guidelines are quite simple:

✦ If there's any chance that your PC will run out of power while in Standby mode, don't use it. Hibernate instead.

✦ If you have to bring your machine back up quickly (say, for a presentation, or to take sporadic notes), use Standby mode.

To go into Standby or Hibernate mode, choose Start⇨Turn Off Computer. You see a dialog box with the recommended mode as your first option (see Figures 6-5 and 6-6).

Figure 6-5: Go into standby mode.

If your PC supports both Standby and Hibernate modes, hold down the Shift key while the Turn Off Computer dialog box is on the screen. Windows obliges by changing back and forth between Standby and Hibernate.

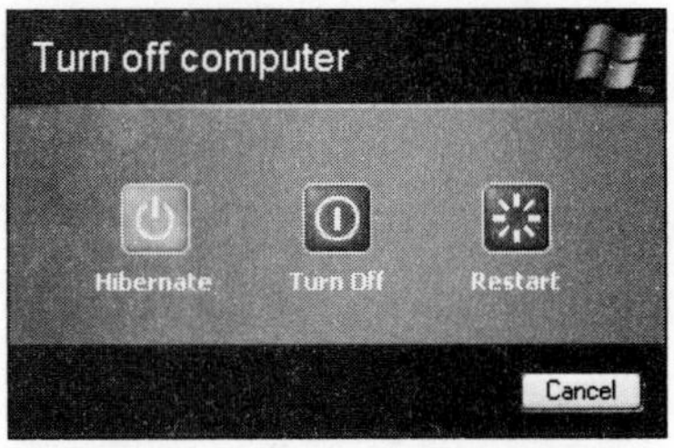

Turn off computer

Hibernate   Turn Off   Restart

Cancel

Figure 6-6:
Or use
Hibernate
mode.

You should always turn your computer off the "official" way, by choosing
Start⇨Turn Off Computer⇨Turn Off. If you just flip the power switch off,
Windows can accidentally zap files and leave them unusable. Windows
needs time to make sure that everything is in order before turning the lights
off. Make sure it gets the time it needs by using the official method for shutting down.

Chapter 7: Managing Files and Folders

In This Chapter

✔ Getting around in Windows Explorer

✔ Selecting and creating files and folders

✔ Viewing files in different ways

✔ Sharing folders with others

✔ Recovering a file or folder you deleted

*F*iles and folders are the heart and soul of a computer. This chapter explains everything a mere mortal needs to know about handling files and folders. It explains how to create, name, select, and delete them. It describes the different ways to view folders, share them with others, and even privatize them to keep snoops and future biographers at bay. Finally, this chapter tells how to recover a file or folder you deleted accidentally.

Using Windows Explorer

Computer geeks refer to the way Windows interacts with people as the *human interface.* As far as I'm concerned, that jargon's more than a little presumptuous. We poor, downtrodden Windows victims should refer to people-machine interactions as the *stupid computer interface.* About time to put the horse before the cart, sez I.

Now that we have the terminology turned right-side-out, you can easily understand where Windows Explorer fits into the Grand Scheme of WinThings. Windows Explorer lies at the center of the stupid computer interface. When you want to work with Windows — ask it where it stuck your wedding pictures, show it how to mangle your files, tell it (literally) where to go — you usually use Windows Explorer.

If you choose Start⇨My Documents or Start⇨My Computer or Start⇨My Pictures or My Music or My Network Places, Windows Explorer jumps to your command like an automated bird dog, pointing at whatever location you selected. When you run a search with Start⇨Search, Windows Explorer takes the reins.

Windows Explorer takes a snapshot of your hard drive and presents that snapshot to you. If the contents of the disk change, the snapshot is not automatically updated, which can be a real problem. Say you're using Windows Explorer to leaf through the files in My Documents. You suddenly realize that you need to write a letter to your Aunt Emma, so you start Word and write the letter, saving it in My Documents. If you switch back to Windows Explorer, you may not be able to see the letter to Aunt Emma: The snapshot may not be updated. Disconcerting. To force Windows Explorer to update its snapshot, you can close it down and start it again, or you can press F5.

The following are some Windows Explorer high points:

✦ **The name of the current folder appears in the title bar.** If you click once on a file or folder, details for the selected file or folder appear in the Details box in the lower-left corner. If you double-click on a folder, it becomes the current folder. If you double-click on a document, it opens. (For example, if you double-click on a Word document, Windows fires up Word and has it start with the document open and ready for work.)

✦ **Almost any actions that you want to perform on files or folders show up in the File and Folder Tasks list in the upper-left corner of Windows Explorer.** Provided you know the secret, that is! You have to click once on a folder to select it before the list of folder actions becomes visible; and you have to click once on a file to select it before you can see the list of file actions. So if you're trying to copy a file, and you don't see Copy File in the list of File and Folder Tasks, click the file you want to copy first. When you do, Copy This File shows up in the list of Tasks.

✦ **You can open as many copies of Windows Explorer as you like.** That can be very helpful if you're scatterbrained like me . . . er, if you like to multi-task, and want to look in several places at once. Simply choose Start⇨My Documents (or My Computer, whatever), and a totally independent copy of Windows Explorer appears, ready for your finagling.

Creating Files and Folders

Usually, you create new files and folders when you're using a program; you make new Word documents when you're using Word, say, or come up with a new folder to hold all of your offshore banking spreadsheets when you're using Excel. Programs usually have the tools for making new files and folders tucked away in the File⇨Save and File⇨Save As dialog boxes. Click around a bit and you'll find them. But you can also create a new file or folder directly in My Documents quite easily, without going to the hassle of cranking up a 900-pound gorilla of a program:

1. **Move to the location where you want to put the new file or folder.**

For example, if you want to stick a new folder called Revisionist Techno Grunge in your My Music folder, choose Start⇨My Documents and double-click on the My Music folder. (If you want to show off, you could just choose Start⇨My Music, which does the same thing.)

2. **Right-click a blank spot in your chosen location.**

By "blank" I mean "don't right-click on an existing file or folder," okay? If you want the new folder or file to appear on the desktop, right-click any empty spot on the desktop.

3. **Choose New (see Figure 7-1) and pick the kind of file you want to create.**

If you want a new folder, click Folder.

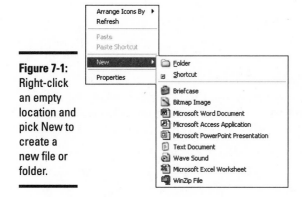

Figure 7-1:
Right-click an empty location and pick New to create a new file or folder.

4. **Windows creates the new file or folder and leaves it with the name highlighted, so that you can rename it by simply typing.**

Creating new folders is fast and easy. If you choose Start⇨My Music, right-click an empty location in the My Music folder, choose New⇨Folder, immediately type **Revisionist Techno Grunge**, and hit Enter, you become the proud owner of a new folder called Revisionist Techno Grunge, located inside the My Music folder.

Selecting Files and Folders

Before you can copy, move, or delete files or folders, you have to select them. As Figure 7-2 shows, Windows Explorer and My Computer offer a bunch of different methods for selecting multiple files and folders:

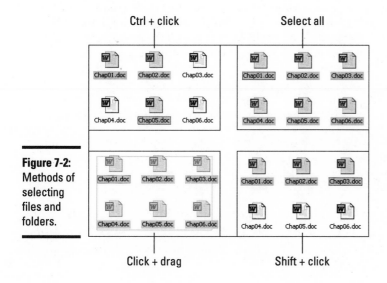

Figure 7-2:
Methods of selecting files and folders.

✦ **Selecting various items:** Hold down the Ctrl key and click the files or folders one at a time.

✦ **Selecting neighboring items:** Click the first file or folder and, holding down the Shift key, click the last.

✦ **Selecting a group of items:** Click a blank space in the window and drag to lasso the items and form a box around the group.

✦ **Selecting all the items:** Choose Edit⇨Select All or press Ctrl+A. Suppose you want to remove one or two items after you've selected them all. In that case, Ctrl+click the ones you want to remove.

✦ **Selecting all but one or two items:** Click the items you *don't* want and then choose Edit⇨Invert Selection. This is a great technique to use when you want to select all but one or two items in a folder with many items.

Some views are better than others when the time comes to select files. The Shift+click method, for example, works best in List and Details view. The Click+drag method works best in Tiles and Icons view. Later in this chapter, "Different Ways of Viewing Folders and Files" explains how to change views in My Computer and Windows Explorer.

Modifying Files and Folders

Modifying files and folders is easy — rename them, delete them, move or copy them — if you remember the trick: Click once and wait.

The whole world's in a rush. When I'm learning something new, I tend to try a lot of different things all at once, and that plays havoc on computers. They're only human, ya know? When it comes to working with files and folders, it's important that you wait for the computer to catch up with you. In particular, when you're trying to rename, move, copy or delete a file, *click once and wait* while the computer figures out what you can do and shows you the legal choices in the File and Folder Tasks area.

If you double-click on a file, Windows interprets your action as an attempt to open the file and start working on it. Double-click on a Word document, for example, and Word springs to life with the document loaded, ready to rumble.

Click once and wait is, far and away, the easiest way to rename, move, copy, delete, e-mail, or print a file. It's also the least error-prone, because you can see what you're doing, step by step.

Different Ways of Viewing Folders and Files

By opening the View menu in Windows Explorer or My Computer and making a choice, you can see files and folders in different ways. Figure 7-3, for example, shows the My Documents folder in Details view. Following are the views you can choose from:

Choose your View here

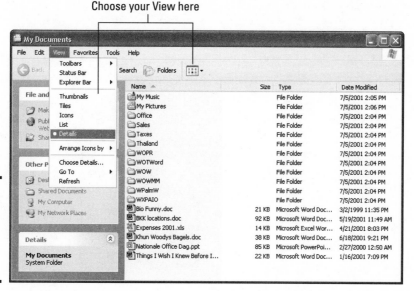

Figure 7-3:
The My
Documents
folder in
Details
view.

◆ **Thumbnails:** Shows small versions (called *thumbnails*) of graphics files, along with a few surprises: tiny pictures of the first slide in PowerPoint presentations, small pictures of enclosed graphic files on file folders, even album cover art on identified My Music albums.

◆ **Tiles:** Gives large icons but makes no attempt to show you a small version of picture files. Documents are identified by what application "owns" them and how big they are.

◆ **Icons:** Trims down the large size of the Tiles but sacrifices document details.

◆ **List:** Simply lists filenames. This view is a good choice for looking at folders with lots and lots of files.

◆ **Details:** Shows filenames, sizes, and types. In most folders, the Details list also includes the date when the file was created, but for music and pictures, artist names and titles appear. In Details view, you can sort the list of files by clicking on one of the column headings — name, size, and so on. You can right-click on one of the column headings and click More to change what the view shows (get rid of Type, for example, and replace it with Author).

◆ **Filmstrip:** Shows thumbnails of pictures across the bottom of the screen, with a Play button below the selected picture, as shown in Figure 7-4. (This view is available only in picture folders.)

Pictures appear full-screen

Moves up one level

Figure 7-4:
The My
Pictures
folder in
Filmstrip
view.

Particulars on selected file   Previous/Next picture   Rotate

Sharing Folders

Sharing is good, right? Your mom taught you to share, didn't she? Everything you need to know about sharing you learned in kindergarten — like how you can share your favorite crayon with your best friend and get back a gnarled blob of stunted wax, covered in mysterious goo.

Windows XP Home supports four kinds of sharing. Unfortunately, "sharing" means different things in different contexts, and the devil (as you surely know by now) can be in Windows' details. Here's a quick guide to the four kinds of sharing that you find lurking in various parts of Windows, how to make them work, and what they really entail.

Sharing on one computer

The simplest form of sharing is with other people who use your computer: They log on with a user name that's different from yours, and you want them to be able to get a specific file or folder. In fact, in Windows XP Home, just about anybody can get to any of your files, at any time. Sharing with other people on your computer is more about making it easy for them to find the files they need, as opposed to preventing them from seeing files that they shouldn't see. Thus, I think of this simple approach to sharing as "sticking your file or folder in a place where other people may think to look for it." It's all about location, location, location.

Windows has a folder called Shared Documents that looks and acts a lot like My Documents. Inside Shared Documents, for example, you find folders called Shared Music and Shared Pictures. The Shared Documents folder has three cool but minor characteristics that make it a special place:

✦ Windows Explorer makes it easy to get to the Shared Documents folder with a link to Shared Documents in the Other Places box on the left side of the screen. A Shared Music link shows up on the left when you're in My Music. A Shared Pictures appears in My Pictures, too.

✦ The Shared Documents folder is shared across your network (if you have one).

✦ Limited users, such as the Guest account, can get into the Shared Documents folder but not into other My Documents folders (Book I, Chapter 6 explains accounts).

Aside from those three minor points, the only real advantage to putting a file or folder in Shared Documents is the location: People may think to look there when they go rooting around looking for stuff.

To put a file or folder in the Shared Documents folder — and thus make it "shared" in this sense of the term — you have to physically move it. The following is the easiest way to do that:

1. **Bring up Windows Explorer (choose, say, Start⇨My Documents), and click on the files and/or folders that you want to put in the Shared Documents folder.**

2. **In the File and Folder Tasks box on the left, choose Move this file or Move this folder.**

3. **In the Move Items dialog box (see Figure 7-5), pick a location in or under the Shared Documents folder where you want the chosen files and/or folders to go, and then click Move.**

The Windows XP documentation suggests that you click and drag the file(s) and/or folder(s) that you want to share to the Shared Documents folder in the Other Places box on the left of the Windows Explorer screen. I strongly recommend that you *not* follow those instructions. Dropping the files in the wrong "Other" place is too easy. More than that, using drag and drop gives you no opportunity to see any folders that may be sitting underneath the Shared Documents folder. That's a sure way to stack tons of unrelated files in one messy folder. It's also an invitation to disaster — or at least massive confusion — if Windows encounters duplicated folder names.

After you move the file or folder, you may have a hard time finding it! For example, if you use Word to create a document and then you move the document to the Shared Documents folder, Word isn't notified that the file has been moved. In Word, if you choose File and then click the name of the document, Word won't be able to find it. Ditto if you use Word's Task Pane to try to open the document. The only way you can open the document is via the File⇨Open dialog box.

Click here   Select the file(s) and/or folder(s) you want to share

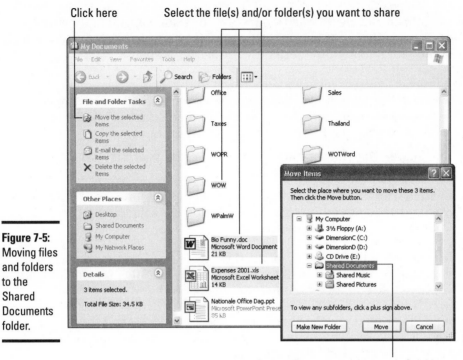

Figure 7-5:
Moving files
and folders
to the
Shared
Documents
folder.

Navigate to the Shared Documents folder, and click Move

Sneak-in-any-time-you-like sharing

The Windows Shared Documents approach to sharing files on a single computer works, but it really doesn't do much, particularly in Windows XP Home
where any user (except a Limited user; see Book I, Chapter 6) can get into
any folder (except those marked Private) with a couple of clicks.

Unless you take very specific steps to make a folder private, any file you put
on a computer running Windows XP Home is immediately and easily available to anyone who can stumble up to the mouse. Other people who use
your computer may take a gander inside the Shared Documents folder to
find what they're looking for, but Shared Documents is only a convenient
dumping ground. There's no security, no privacy, no way, no how.

Sharing on your network

This is real sharing. Windows XP lets you identify specific folders (or entire
disk drives) that are to be shared with other people on your network. You
can also tell Windows whether those other people should be able to only
read the files in the folders, or whether they should also be allowed to change
the files.

Windows XP does not allow you to share individual files across a network.
You can either share a folder (which may include other folders and certainly
includes files), or you can share an entire drive. But single files won't work.

With Windows XP Home, the sharing choices are quite straightforward: A folder (or drive) is either shared or it isn't. A shared folder (or drive) can be read-only or read-write. That's it. Anybody on the network can get at a shared folder or drive. There's no additional authorization, no secret password, no clandestine handshake, no list of who can get in and who can't.

In Windows XP Professional, security options are legion — and chances are very good that you have little choice about security settings. That's why there are network administrators, eh?

Windows sets up the Shared Documents folder, detailed in the preceding two sections, for network sharing. So any files or folders that you move into the Shared Documents folder are "automagically" shared across the network — you needn't lift a finger.

If you don't mind lifting a finger once or twice, you can easily share a folder on your network:

1. **Bring up Windows Explorer (for example, choose Start⇨My Documents) and find the folder you want to share.**

2. **Right-click on the folder that you want to share and choose Sharing and Security.**

3. **In the folder's Properties dialog box (see Figure 7-6), select the Share This Folder on the Network check box.**

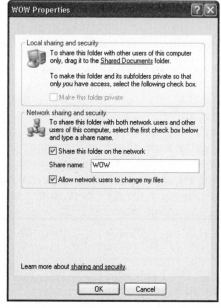

Figure 7-6:
Share a folder called WOW by using the Properties dialog box.

4. **Type a name that other people on the network will find enlightening.**

   Officially, that name is known as a *share name,* but any ol' moniker will work.

5. **If you want to give read-write access to every Tom, Dick, and Harry who can get on the network, select the Allow Network Users to Change My Files check box.**

Click OK, and the shared folder becomes accessible from all the computers on your network. For example, if I choose Start⇨My Network Places on a computer connected to the computer that holds the newly shared folder, Windows Explorer lets me get into that folder.

When you share a folder on your network, all of the files and folders inside the shared folder are shared, too.

Sharing an entire drive

The process for sharing an entire drive is only slightly more difficult, but considerably more intimidating, than sharing a folder:

1. **Choose Start⇨My Computer to bring up My Computer in Windows Explorer.**

2. **Right-click the drive that you want to share.**

   Note that you can share CD drives, diskette drives, and just about any kind of drive.

3. **Choose Sharing and Security.**

   Windows responds with a rather odd statement: `To protect your com-puter from unauthorized access, sharing the root of a drive is not recommended. If you understand the risk but still want to share the root of the drive, click here.` (Bafflegab alert: The *root* of a drive is the whole drive, including all the folders on the drive.)

Setting up an entire drive for sharing (by right-clicking the drive choosing Sharing and Security) elicits a message from Windows about "the risk" of sharing an entire drive. Somewhat predictably, I've never found an explanation of "the risk" or its presumably dire consequences in any Windows documentation. Suffice it to say that granting access to an entire drive lets anybody on your network get at everything on the drive. If you're sharing your C: drive, granting access to the drive probably includes the Windows folder (which contains Windows itself), the Program Files folders (which contain most of the programs on your computer), settings for everybody on the computer — the whole enchilada.

4. **Click "If you understand the risk but still want to share the root of the drive, click here."**

5. **Select the Share This Folder on the Network check box. Type a name for the drive that's intelligible to other people.**

   If you want to give everyone on the network write access, select the Allow Network Users to Change My Files check box. Click OK and the drive becomes accessible from anywhere on the network.

When sharing CD drives, Jaz drives, and even diskette drives, including a description of the drive in the share name is often a good idea. That way, you know what the drive can handle before you try to use it, so you won't find yourself frustrated by repeated attempts to, oh, transfer your 2.3 MB resume to a 1.44 MB diskette.

Recycling Files and Folders

 When you delete a file, it doesn't go to that Big Bit Bucket in the Sky. An intermediate step exists between deletion and the Big Bit Bucket. It's called *purgatory* — oops. Wait a sec. Wrong book. (*Existentialism For Dummies*, anybody?) Let me try that again. Ahem. The step between deletion and the Big Bit Bucket is called the Recycle Bin.

When you delete a file or folder on your hard drive — whether by selecting the file or folder in Windows Explorer and pushing the Delete key, or by right-clicking and choosing Delete — Windows doesn't actually delete anything. It marks the file or folder as being deleted but, other than that, doesn't touch it at all. If you ever accidentally delete a file or a folder, you can easily recover the "deleted" file from the Recycle Bin.

To rummage around in the Recycle Bin, and possibly bring a file back to life, double-click the Recycle Bin icon on the Windows desktop. Windows Explorer takes you to the Recycle Bin, as shown in Figure 7-7.

Figure 7-7:
The Recycle Bin, where all good files go when they kick the bucket.

To restore a file or folder (sometimes Windows calls it "undeleting"), click on the file or folder, and then click Restore This Item in the Recycle Bin Tasks box in the upper-left corner. You can select a bunch of files or folders by holding down the Ctrl key as you click.

To reclaim the space being used by the files and folders in the Recycle Bin, click Empty the Recycle Bin in the Recycle Bin Tasks box. Windows asks if you really, really want to get rid of those files permanently. If you say yes, they're gone. Kaput. You can never get them back again.

Files and folders on floppy drives and on network drives really are deleted when you delete them. The Recycle Bin doesn't work on floppies or on drives attached to other computers on your network.

Chapter 8: Locating Stuff with Windows XP

In This Chapter

✔ Constructing a search query

✔ Searching for files of different kinds

✔ Using wildcards in searches

✔ Best ways to search your computer

Computers store lots and lots of stuff. As long as you're churning out the stuff, life goes along pretty easily. Sooner or later, though, the time comes when you have to find some stuff — the right stuff — and that's when the stuff hits the fan. Windows XP includes a powerful search feature with a cute name — Search Companion — and a cloying mascot, a mutt called Rover. This chapter explains how to make Rover sit up, heel, fetch, and . . . play dead.

Introducing the Search Companion

If you choose Start⇨Search, you bring the Search Companion to life, with Rover (see Figure 8-1) sitting ever-so-patiently at the bottom of the pane, tail wagging, waiting to help you fetch whatever you like. (The end of this chapter explains how to make Rover disappear.)

If the Search Companion screen shown in Figure 8-1 looks familiar, it should. In fact, Search Companion is a pane inside Windows Explorer. You can see the striking similarities as shown in Figure 8-2.

Very few options

All do basically the same thing

Recognize Windows Explorer? The folder that holds the file

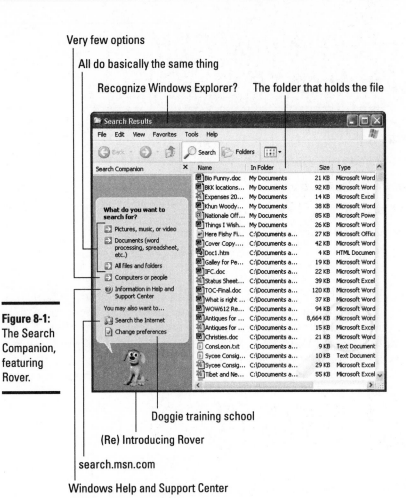

Figure 8-1:
The Search
Companion,
featuring
Rover.

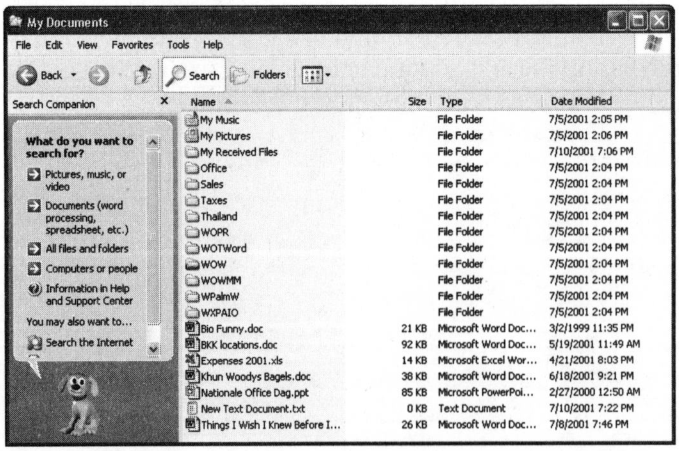

Doggie training school

(Re) Introducing Rover

search.msn.com

Windows Help and Support Center

Figure 8-2:
Click the
Search icon
in Windows
Explorer and
the Search
Companion
appears.

What you can find

When you bring up the Search Companion by choosing Start⇨Search (refer to Figure 8-1) or clicking the Search icon in any Windows Explorer window (refer to Figure 8-2), Rover offers to search for the following:

✦ **Pictures, music, or video:** Choosing this option leads Rover (see Figure 8-3) to ask whether you want to limit your search to Pictures and Photos, Music, and/or Video. You can check as many check boxes as you like; if you don't check any, Windows assumes that you want to check them all. Windows then runs a full search (as described in "Looking for Files and Folders," later in this chapter) but narrows down the search to files with specific filename extensions, as shown in Table 8-1.

Figure 8-3: Narrowing down the search based on filename extensions.

Note that the contents of the file don't matter: Windows XP doesn't look inside the file to see if it contains, oh, a JPEG image, for example. The Search Companion cares about only the filename extension.

✦ **Documents (word processing, spreadsheet, and so on):** Like the Pictures, Music, or Video option, choosing Documents leads to a full search, limited to the specific filename extensions shown in Table 8-1.

✦ **All files and folders:** This leads to the full search described in the section, "Looking for Files and Folders."

✦ **Computers or people:** The computer side of this search (assuming you leave the computer name box empty) is identical to choosing Start⇨My Network Places and clicking View Workgroup Computers.

The people side of the search leads to your Outlook Express (not Outlook) address book. From there, you can also use OE's crude interface to look in the Bigfoot, VeriSign, or WhoWhere directories.

Don't bother using Start⇨Search to find people on the Internet. As of this writing, two of the three options don't work very well: The VeriSign directory is very tiny, and the Bigfoot directory automatically redirects to AT&T's AnyWho lookup site. If you're serious about finding somebody on the Web, use one of the standard search engines: www.anywho.com works well, as do people.yahoo.com and www.whowhere.lycos.com.

✦ **Information in Help and Support Center:** This option opens up the Help and Support Center, precisely the same as if you had chosen Start➪Help and Support Center.

Table 8-1	Filename Extensions in Search
Choose This Type of File	*And Windows Limits the Search to Files Common with These Filename Extensions**
Pictures and Photos	ANI, ART, BIT, BMP, CDR, CGM, CMP, DIB, EPS, GIF, JPG, TIF, PCX, PNG, PS, WMF
Music	AIF, AIFF, ASF, CDA, FAR, MID, MP3, RAM, RMI, WAV, WMA
Video	ASF, ASX, AVI, MMM, MPG
Documents	ASC, ASP, AW, CHI, CHT, DBF, DOC, DOT, HTM, HTML, MDB, MSG, OBD, PDD, POT, PPS, PPT, PUB, RTF, SAM, TIF, TXT, WRI, XLA, XLL, XLS, XLT

* This list is far from exhaustive; yes, TIF appears in two lists

What you can't find

Surprisingly, Windows XP Search Companion doesn't search Outlook or Outlook Express e-mail messages unless you turn on the Indexing Service. If you want to look for text in a message, or even a message Subject line, Windows XP can't do it.

Phrasing a search query

You have two different, almost mutually exclusive, ways to ask a computer to look things up:

✦ **Keyword searches:** These searches take the words you specify and look for those words. In some cases, keyword searches can be augmented by *qualifiers* like AND or NOT. So you may have the Search Companion look for files with the names **blue or dolphin**, and you get back a list of files with either *blue* or *dolphin,* or both, in their names.

✦ **Natural language searches:** These searches, on the other hand, expect you to ask a question in the form of a question (with apologies to Alex Trebek). Thus, you might ask your computer, **What color are dolphins?** and get back a list of Web sites that discuss dolphins' colors.

Windows XP's Search Companion combines both search methods, but in a very specific way. If you're looking for Web sites, you're expected to ask a question — that is, Windows uses a natural language search approach when going out to the Internet. For everything else, you should type only keywords. It's an odd dichotomy that you may find irritating, or confusing, or both.

Looking for Files and Folders

Maybe you need to find all of the handouts you typed for your Porcine Prevaricators seminar. Maybe you remember that you have a recipe with tarragon in it, but you can't remember where in the world you put it. Maybe you accidentally moved or deleted all of the pictures of your trip to Cancun, or Windows Media Player suddenly can't find your MP3s of the 1974 Grateful Dead tour. Good. You're in the right place.

People generally go looking for files or folders on their computers for one of two reasons. Perhaps they vaguely remember that they used to have something — maybe a Christmas letter, a product description, or a great joke — and now they can't remember where they put it. Or they have been playing around with Windows Explorer, and whatever they thought was sitting in a specific place isn't there any more.

In either case, the solution is to make Windows XP do the work and go searching for your lost files or folders.

If you choose Start⇨Search, the Search Companion dog Rover (refer to Figure 8-1) gives you a chance to narrow down your search, in advance, by choosing Pictures, Music or Video, or Documents. If you know in advance what kind of file you're looking for, those choices can hone in on specific file types (refer to Table 8-1). If you don't know exactly what you're looking for, though, it's just as easy to go straight to the full-fledged search — the choice marked All Files and Folders.

Can you remember what's in the file you're looking for? Can you remember at least part of the file's name? Nine times out of ten, that's all you need. The best approach to performing a simple search depends on whether you know for an absolute, dead-certain fact what kind of file you're dealing with. Here's how it works, in the best of all possible worlds.

Searching for pictures, music, or video

Here's what to do if you know for an absolute, dead-certain fact that the file you want is a picture, photo, music file, and/or video:

1. **Choose Start⇨Search.**

   You see Rover (refer to Figure 8-1) or something like him (or, if you're lucky, nothing at all!).

2. **Click Pictures, Music, or Video.**

   You see the Search pane (refer to Figure 8-3).

3. **Select the kind of file you're looking for.**

   If you know anything at all about the file, type it in the box marked All or Part of the File Name. Windows is a whole lot smarter than this dialog box would have you believe. For example, if you search for Music files and you type **Ludwig** in the box, Windows will find Beethoven's 9th Symphony, even though Ludwig doesn't appear in the filename. Try it. You'll see.

All of the advanced search options described in the section "Digging Deeper with Advanced Searches" are available by choosing Use Advanced Search Options.

4. If you don't find the file you want, crank up the Windows Media Player and see whether you can find it from there.

Searching for a document

Here's what to do if you are absolutely, completely certain that the file you want is a document — which is to say a text file (with the `.txt` filename extension), Word document (`.doc`), Excel workbook (`.xls`), PowerPoint presentation (`.ppt` or `.pps`), or one of the other documents listed in Table 8-1:

1. Choose Start➪Search.

2. Click Documents (Word Processing, Spreadsheet, and so on).

You see the dialog box shown in Figure 8-4.

Figure 8-4:
Telling Rover to search for documents.

3. Tell Rover how to narrow down the search.

If you can remember the last time that the document was modified — not created, or opened, but changed — click the appropriate button. There's no wiggle-room. If you select the Within the Last Week check box, and you last modified the file eight days ago, it won't show up in the search.

If you can remember any part of the filename, type it in the box. The Search Companion matches any file with a name that includes the characters you've typed. (See Table 8-2.)

Table 8-2	Simple Filename Matches	
Type This	*And You Will Match*	*But You Will Not Match*
a	`a.xls`	`b.xls`
bug	`bed bug.txt`	`abu ghanim.txt`
add	`madden.ppt`	`dad.ppt`
wood	`woody.doc`	`woo.doc`

Search Companion recognizes the key words OR and AND. If you type **new or recent** in the All or Part of the File Name box, Rover brings back files such as new pictures.jpg and recent songs.mp3. If you type two words in the All or Part of the File Name box, Rover assumes you mean AND.

The search for filenames is quite literal, and filename extensions are included if you have Windows show filename extensions. So if you show filename extensions and search for the characters txt, you see all of your .txt text files.

All of the advanced search options described in the section "Digging Deeper with Advanced Searches" are available by choosing Use Advanced Search Options.

4. **If you don't find the file you want, try the option called Change File Name or Keywords. This option enables you to easily switch over to searching for text inside the documents.**

Searching for All Files and Folders

If you aren't absolutely, totally, utterly certain that you want to find a picture, photo, music file, video, or document, it's best to tell Rover to fetch everything matching your criteria, and sift through the results yourself. Here's how:

1. **Choose Start⇨Search.**

2. **Click All Files and Folders, and go for a full-fledged search.**

When you do, you get the search dialog box shown in Figure 8-5.

Figure 8-5:
The full-
fledged
search.

3. **Help Rover find your file.**

The filename part of the search is identical to the details I discussed in Table 8-2. If you have filename extensions showing, and you type **.doc** in this box, for example, you get a list of all the .doc files.

The A Word or Phrase in the File box jumps through some interesting hoops. If you type a single word, Search Companion looks for that word, of course. If you type a phrase like **back in a minute**, Search Companion looks for that precise phrase, with spaces and punctuation exactly the way you specify.

Search Companion also looks for information attached to a file — information you may not see if you open the file. It's called *metadata,* and I gave you an example of a metadata search earlier when I said that Search would find Beethoven's 9th if you looked for Ludwig. Media files usually have metadata attached to them with information about the content. Microsoft Office documents always have metadata attached to them. You can see Office metadata by bringing up the Office application (such as Word, Excel, or PowerPoint) and choosing File⇨Properties. The file's metadata appears on the tabs marked Summary and Custom.

The Look In box lets you pick the starting point of the search. If you want to search your entire network (a process that could take many hours!), click the down-arrow and choose Browse⇨My Network Places⇨Entire Network.

4. **Click Search and the Companion returns the names of files that match all of your criteria. (In geek terms, they're "ANDed" together.)**

If you tell Rover that you want to see files with **woody** in all or part of the filename, with the phrase **blew it again** in the file, Search Companion returns only files with names that match AND contain the indicated phrase. So a file named `woodrow.doc` containing the phrase *blew it again* wouldn't make the cut. Nor would a file called `woody.txt` with the text *blewit agin.*

That's the lowdown on simple searches. Much more power awaits, in the rest of this chapter.

Using Wildcards

Windows XP's Search Companion lets you use *wildcards,* symbols that substitute for letters. The easiest way to describe a wildcard is with an example. ? is the single-letter wildcard. If you tell Rover to look for files named **d?g.txt**, the mutt dutifully retrieves `dog.txt` and `dug.txt` (if you have files with those names), but it doesn't retrieve `drag.txt` or `ding.txt`. The ? matches one — and only one — character in the filename.

Search Companion recognizes two wildcards. ? matches a single character, and * matches multiple (zero or more) characters. (See Table 8-3.)

Table 8-3	Wildcards for Filenames	
This	*Matches This*	*But Not This*
d?g.txt	dog.txt, dug.txt	drag.txt, ding.txt
ne*w.mp3	new.mp3, neosow.mp3	ne.mp3, new.doc

Wildcards work with only file and folder names. The A Word or Phrase in the File box does *not* recognize wildcards.

Digging Deeper with Advanced Searches

The full-fledged search dialog box (refer to Figure 8-5) has three buttons: When Was It Modified?, What Size Is It?, and More Advanced Options. If you click on the (inappropriately named) When Was It Modified? button, you have a chance to specify when the file you're looking for was last changed (in computerese, *modified* means changed). As you can see in Figure 8-6, though, you aren't limited to the modified date. In fact, Search Companion searches for files based on the date that they were created or last opened ("accessed" in computer lingo) as well.

Figure 8-6: Narrow your search based on the date that the file was last changed, created, or opened.

If you click on the What Size Is It? button, Search Companion lets you pick the file size. In my experience, people are amazed at how big files get, so if you use this option, allow yourself lots of breathing room on the high side.

Finally, the More Advanced Options selection (see Figure 8-7) holds six possibilities:

Figure 8-7: A hodge-podge of additional Search criteria.

107

✦ Type of File lists all of the filename extensions that your computer recognizes, except that you don't get to see the filename extensions; you have to make do with the hokey names. If you have Microsoft Office installed, the list of Types starting with "Microsoft" goes on forever (my list includes one called Microsoft FrontPage Dont Publish — an all-time classic). If you know the filename extension that you're looking for, this is the worst place to tell Search Companion what kind of file you want. Type the filename extension in the All or Part of the File Name box (for example, ***.mpeg** or ***.ani**).

✦ Select the Search System Folders check box, and Search Companion looks in the Windows, Documents and Settings, and Program Files folders.

✦ Select the Search Hidden Files and Folders check box, and Search Companion looks in any files or folders that are marked Hidden.

Hidden files and folders aren't really hidden. They're just marked a certain way so that Windows Explorer won't show them — unless you tell Windows Explorer to show hidden files and folders. To hide a file or folder, choose Start⇨My Documents to start Windows Explorer. Right-click on the file or folder, and click Properties. At the bottom of the Properties dialog box, in the Attributes area, select the Hidden check box. Now your file or folder is hidden from view.

✦ The Search Subfolders box tells Search Companion that you want to look in the folder specified in the Look In box, as well as in all folders inside of the Look In folder. You almost always want to have this check box selected.

✦ In spite of what you read in other books, the Case Sensitive box has nothing to do with filenames. If you check this box, Search Companion matches the case of the text you type in the A Word or Phrase in the File box. So if you type **Blue Mango** in the box and check this box, Search Companion looks for **Blue Mango** text inside files, but passes on both **blue Mango** and **BLUE mango**.

Filenames are never case sensitive. Ever. My Documents and my documents always refer to the same folder.

✦ Search Tape Backup applies only if you are using Windows XP's Backup feature.

If you've managed to read to this point, you're probably serious about searching. Good on ya, as they say Down Under. If you want the Search Companion to cut to the chase, and stop bothering you with the "helping" screens that divert you to searching for specific kinds of files, do this:

1. **Choose Start⇨Search and bring up Rover and the Search Companion (refer to Figure 8-1).**

2. **Click Change Preferences.**

3. **Click Change Files and Folders Search Behavior.**

4. **Click Advanced — Includes Options to Manually Enter Search Criteria. Recommended for Advanced Users Only.**

After you change to Advanced, the Search Companion always starts, ready for a full-fledged search (refer to Figure 8-5).

Saving a Search

Do you find yourself repeating the same searches, over and over again? Maybe you need to look in BearShare's Download folder to see if those MP3s have finally arrived. Or you want to look at a list of invoices for your number-one customer. Only a real dummy would do the same thing over and over again when the computer can do the work. A *For Dummies* dummy, on the other hand, knows that he or she can save and reuse searches 'til the cows come home. If he or she reads this book, anyway.

Here's how you save and reuse a search:

1. **Choose Start⇨Search to bring up the Search Companion.**

2. **Set up your search.**

In Figure 8-8, for example, I've instructed Rover to fetch all the MP3 files in the My Music folder that are less than a week old.

Figure 8-8:
To save and reuse a search, set up a search the way you want it, and then run the search.

3. **Click Search and run the search.**

This is the trick. It doesn't matter whether or not you really want to run the search. You have to, if you're going to save the search to use in the future.

4. **Choose File⇨Save Search.**

Windows XP offers to save a file called `Files named @.mp3.fnd` or something equally obtuse.

5. **Navigate to a convenient location (if you put the search on your Desktop, it'll always be handy); give the search a more descriptive name, if you like; and click Save.**

6. **Any time you want to run the saved search, double-click on the `.FND` file and click Search. Voilà!**

Nixing the Mutt

Rover is Windows' anointed Search Companion. You might think that having Rover around slows down your searches. He (she? it?) won't. The animation itself doesn't slow down your computer. But the distraction might cause you to waste time. Take Rover, change him, or leave him, with impunity. The Rover overhead is sorely overstated. Say that ten times fast.

To change Rover to another Companion (or get rid of him completely), follow these steps:

1. **Click Start⇨Search.**

2. **Click Change Preferences.**

3. **If you replace Rover, click With a Different Character. If you want to get rid of Rover and don't want another character to replace him, click Without an Animated Screen Character.**

   If you decide to replace Rover, step through the Rogue's Gallery by clicking the Back and Next buttons.

4. **Click OK.**

Chapter 9: Adding and Removing Software

In This Chapter

✔ Installing and removing a computer program

✔ Weighing when to use the program's installer

✔ Adding and removing parts of Windows XP

*O*nce upon a time, a chapter like this about adding and removing software programs would have required many tedious explanations and hard-to-follow directions. Count yourself lucky to be living in the 21st century. Microsoft has done a good job of making it easy to add and remove software as well as add and remove different parts of the Windows XP operating system. This short chapter explains precisely what to do.

Installing and Removing Programs

Windows XP includes a one-stop shopping point for adding and removing programs. To get to it, choose Start➪Control Panel➪Add or Remove Programs. You see the Add or Remove Programs dialog box, as shown in Figure 9-1.

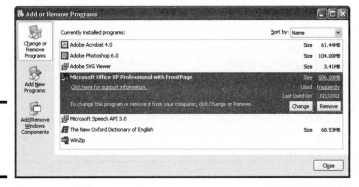

Figure 9-1: Add or remove programs.

When Windows talks about changing programs, it isn't talking about making minor twiddles — this isn't the place to go if you want Microsoft Word to stop showing you rulers, for example. Add or Remove Programs is designed to activate or deactivate big chunks of a program — graft on a new arm or lop off an unused head (of which there are many, particularly in Office). If you look at Figure 9-2, you can see the kind of grand scale I'm talking about: In Add or Remove Programs, you may tell Excel that you want to use its Analysis Pack for financial analysis. Similarly, you may use Add or Remove Programs to completely obliterate Office's Speech Recognition capabilities. That's the kind of large-scale capability I'm talking about.

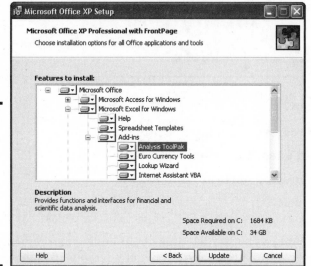

Figure 9-2:
The Office
XP Setup
dialog box,
as seen
from the
Windows
Add or
Remove
Programs.

Windows XP itself doesn't do much in Add or Remove Programs. The main function of Windows is as a gathering point: Well-behaved programs, when they're installed, are supposed to stick their uninstallers in Add or Remove Programs. That way, you have one centralized place to look when you want to get rid of a program. Microsoft doesn't write the uninstallers that Add or Remove Programs runs; if you have a gripe about a program's uninstaller, you need to talk to the company that made the program.

Lessons from the School of Hard Knocks

Several school-of-hard-knocks comments pertain to adding and removing programs:

✦ In practice, you never use Add or Remove Programs to add programs. If you want to install a program, do what savvy Dummies always do: Put the CD in the CD drive and follow the instructions. It's a whole lot easier that way.

✦ You rarely use Add or Remove Programs to remove parts of a program. Either you try to add features in a program that you forgot to include when you originally installed the program — most commonly with Office — or you want to delete a program entirely, to wipe its sorry tail off your hard drive.

Why sweat the small stuff? When you install a program, install all of it. Even Office XP, in all its bloated glory, only takes up 500MB if you install every single far-out filter and truculent template. With hard drives so cheap they're likely candidates for landfill, it never pays to cut back on installed features to save a few megabytes.

✦ Many uninstallers, for reasons known only to their company's programmers — I won't mention Adobe by name — require you to insert the program's CD into your CD drive before you uninstall the program. That's like requiring you to show your dog's vaccination records before you kick it out of the house.

When you start a program's uninstaller, you're at the mercy of the uninstaller and the programmers who wrote it. Windows doesn't even enter into the picture.

Installing and Removing Parts of Windows

Most people never use big parts of Windows XP. Some parts are made with very specific functions in mind and, with two exceptions, the average Person on the Street rarely encounters the requisite specific situations. Thank heaven. The two exceptions? Fax support and automatic backup in Windows. Neither gets installed unless you make the trek to retrieve it.

Windows support for faxing has never been great. Although it's theoretically possible for you to get the Windows fax application working, one great Achilles' heel hampers you: If you have just one modem and it's connected to the Internet, you can't use it to send or receive faxes! Funny how Microsoft glosses over that detail, eh?

The smartest Dummies I know don't try to use Windows for faxing. Instead, they have a standalone fax machine (connected to its own telephone line, of course), or they use a fax service such as J2 Messenger (www.j2.com). J2's software lets you send faxes as easily as you print: Choose File⇨Print⇨Send with J2 Messenger, and the program turns your fax into an e-mail message. When you send the message to J2 headquarters — along with all your other e-mail — it's routed to a location close to the recipient, converted into a fax and then actually faxed for you, generally at a fraction of the cost for a long-distance phone call. J2 also offers inbound fax delivery: Your correspondent sends a fax to a specific phone number, the fax is converted to e-mail, and the e-mail is sent to you — all within a matter of seconds.

If the preceding caveat hasn't warned you off, here's how you install the Windows fax software. The same general procedure works for installing other obscure parts of Windows:

1. **Choose Start⇨Control Panel⇨Add or Remove Programs to bring up Add or Remove Programs.**

2. **Click Add/Remove Windows Components to bring up the Windows Components Wizard (see Figure 9-3).**

3. **Find the component that you want to add.**

   In this case, because you're trying to add fax support, select the Fax Services check box. In general, you may have to click on a likely sounding component, and then click the Details button to see which subcomponents are available.

4. **Insert the Windows XP CD so that Windows can pull the component off the CD and install it on your PC.**

   You may be required to restart Windows. In any case, by the time the wizard is done, your new component should be available and ready to use.

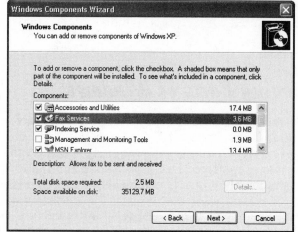

Figure 9-3:
Install
unusual
Windows
compo-
nents in Add
or Remove
Programs.

If you performed a typical installation of Windows XP Home, the following list covers the components that you installed and have available:

✦ All the Accessories and Utilities are installed.

✦ Fax Services aren't installed. Follow the instructions above to install Windows faxing, but make sure you understand the limitations.

✦ Indexing Service is installed.

✦ The only Management and Monitoring Tools available are for an obscure Internet network management standard called SNMP, or Simple Network Management Protocol. You can look up SNMP in the Windows Help and Support Center, but if you need to look it up, you probably don't need it.

✦ Internet Explorer and MSN Explorer are installed. You can get rid of them here, if you really want to.

If you read the fine print, you'll discover that Add/Remove Windows Components isn't really offering to remove Internet Explorer. This option, ahem, "Adds or removes access to Internet Explorer from the Start menu and the Desktop." In other words, you can get rid of the shortcut to IE from the Start menu (Windows XP, as it ships in plain-vanilla systems, doesn't have a shortcut to IE on the Desktop) using this option. Not exactly what you expected, eh?

✦ Under Networking Services, you can add three subcomponents — RIP Listener, which works with NetWare's Router Information Protocol Version 1; Simple TCP/IP Services, an obscure group that includes Quote of the Day; and Universal Plug and Play support, which comes into question only if you have UPnP devices installed. (Confusingly, UPnP isn't related to Plug 'n Play, the industry-wide standard for identifying hardware.)

✦ Other Network File and Print Services includes support for only UNIX (and Linux) computers to print on printers connected to your PC.

✦ The software to automatically Update Root Certificates (digital security certificates for Microsoft products) is installed and running.

CHECK IT OUT

Updating a Driver

Microsoft has a driver certification program that reviews drivers to see if they function properly. (A *driver* is software that connects programs to computer hardware.) The certification program is a voluntary (and expensive) service conducted by the Windows Hardware Quality Labs (WHQL) that aim to improve the stability of Windows XP drivers. If a specific driver passes muster, Microsoft allows the manufacturer to distribute it as a certified (or so-called *signed*) driver. *Unsigned* drivers trigger warning messages when they're installed. Signed drivers install with a couple of clicks.

Windows XP always sets a System Restore check point before installing an unsigned driver — that is, a driver that hasn't been specifically tested and blessed by Microsoft's WHQL team. Unfortunately, Windows XP doesn't automatically set a System Restore point prior to installing a signed driver. Call me a Luddite, but even with WHQL certification, I want the extra safety net that a System Restore Point provides. You should insist on having one, too.

Most kinds of drivers can be *rolled back* like they were never installed. Printer drivers aren't afforded that protection. If you install a printer driver, you absolutely must have a System Restore Point — and it's safest to create one yourself. Here's how to safely update a driver:

1. **Click Start⇨All Programs⇨Accessories⇨ System Tools⇨System Restore.**

    The System Restore Wizard appears.

2. **Click the Create a Restore Point option, and then click Next.**

The wizard asks for a name for the Restore Point.

3. **Type a name that will make sense to you a week from now to identify the Restore Point, and then click the Create button.**

    The wizard takes awhile to create the Restore Point, and then notifies you that it's complete.

4. **Click Close (X) to exit the System Restore Wizard.**

5. **In the Windows Update site, click the Add button to add the driver to your "shopping cart," and then click the Review and Install Updates button.**

    Follow the instructions to remove any updates that you don't want. I suggest installing driver updates all by themselves, one at a time, so that you can trap any problems as quickly as possible.

6. **Click the Install Now button.**

    Downloading a big driver can take a long time, even over a fast Internet connection. Relax.

    The installer kicks in immediately after the download finishes. You may be asked to restart Windows.

7. **Test, test, test.**

    If there's a problem with the driver, you want to find out about it now, not three weeks from now.

Chapter 10: Maintaining Your Windows XP System

In This Chapter

✔ Getting the latest version of Windows XP

✔ Using the different utility programs

✔ Scheduling boring things so that your computer does them automatically

✔ Storing more and spending less with Zips

*I*nto every Windows XP's life a little rain must fall. Or something like that. More than half a million people tested Windows XP: real people, not Microsoft internal "testers." That's the main reason why Windows XP has a well-deserved reputation for working pretty darn well on almost all computers. Still, Windows XP is a computer program, not a Cracker Jack toy, and it's going to have problems. The trick lies in making sure you don't have problems, too.

This chapter takes you through all of the important tools you have at hand to make Windows XP do what you need to do, to head off problems, and to solve problems as they (inevitably!) occur.

Keeping Up-to-Date

One of the first times you start Windows XP, a little balloon appears in the notification area (the box on the lower right of the screen, where the clock sits) telling you "Stay current with automatic updates/Click here to learn how to keep your computer up-to-date automatically with important downloads from Windows Update."

Understanding Windows Update

Windows XP has many reasons to be so insistent in its desire to phone home and update itself. Windows Update helps you do the following:

✦ Avoid lockups and dodge other weird Windows gremlins by retrieving and installing the latest versions of various Windows programs, particularly drivers.

Drivers are computer programs that make specific parts of your computer work. You have a driver for your keyboard, mouse, modem, printer, USB port, camera, and on and on. Drivers are notorious for causing grief: In my experience, if Windows locks up on you, you have at least a 50/50 chance that a driver did the dirty work.

✦ **Keep up with the latest security patches.** Windows 98/ME had its share of security problems, but Windows XP introduced an entire genre of viruses, worms, and attack methods that the guys in black hats have only begun to exploit.

✦ **Find more help.** Microsoft continually refines (and in some cases improves) its Help system. Windows Update ensures that you have the latest Help files installed and ready to go the next time you dive into the Help and Support Center.

All of this benefit comes at no price: There's no charge (although you do have to be connected to the Internet); you needn't register your copy of Windows to take advantage of Windows Update; and no information about your machine is sent to Microsoft when you use it, aside from the obvious catalog of Windows components necessary for Update to do its job.

Setting up automatic updates

Here's how to start working with automatic update:

1. **If you want to change your Windows Update settings, you have to be an Administrator.**

   If you're running Windows XP Home (and using anything other than a Guest account), chances are very good that you are already an Administrator, and you don't have to worry about it. If you're running Windows XP Professional, you probably aren't an Administrator, unless you've convinced your company's network administrators to induct you into the club.

2. **Start the Windows Update Wizard by clicking the "Stay current with automatic updates" balloon.**

   You see a screen that looks something like the one shown in Figure 10-1.

Figure 10-1:
The
Windows
Update
Wizard.

3. **Tell Windows whether you want to have updates applied automatically or whether you want to look over the update candidates before (and after!) they're applied to your machine.**

I strongly recommend that you tell Windows that you want to review changes to your system before they're applied. Why? Because Microsoft has a long history of releasing updates that don't quite work right. In rare instances, you'll want to download and install an update immediately — if a major virus or worm starts making its way across the Internet, for example, and your machine is in its path. In most cases, though, you can afford to wait a week or two before changing major components on your machine, which gives you time to hear loud screams from other users.

4. Click Finish.

Windows connects to the Internet, following your instructions to look for the latest updates. If any updates are found, an icon appears in your notification area (near the clock).

Choose Start⇨Control Panel⇨Performance and Maintenance⇨System and look at the Automatic Updates tab to change the update approach at any time.

Performing the update

Unless you turn off Windows Update completely, each time you log on to the Internet, Windows checks to see whether any new versions of Windows files, drivers, Help files, and so on are available specifically for your computer. If new versions are available and you've told Windows to notify you and let you select updates, you see an icon in the notification area (near the clock) with a balloon message that says, "New updates are available from Windows Update. Click here to review these items and begin downloading."

During the automatic updating process, you may be asked (several times) whether you want to allow Windows to download and install certain Windows components that handle the updating itself. It's a classic chicken-and-egg situation: You need these components in order to do the updating, but Windows can't automatically pull them down unless you give your permission. Say OK when asked about installing the components, if you want automatic update to work, uh, automatically.

Here's how the automatic update works, if you chose to review updates:

1. Choose Start⇨Help and Support, and under the Pick a Task heading, click Keep Your Computer Up-To-Date with Windows Update.

You see the Windows Update screen shown in Figure 10-2.

2. Click Scan for Updates.

Windows compares its database of available updates to the components installed on your machine and tells you what's available.

You can bypass Steps 1 and 2 by simply going to the Windows Update Web site, `www.windowsupdate.Microsoft.com`. If you click on the balloon in the notification area that says "New updates are available from Windows Update. Click here to review these items and begin downloading," you end up in Step 3. The final result is the same.

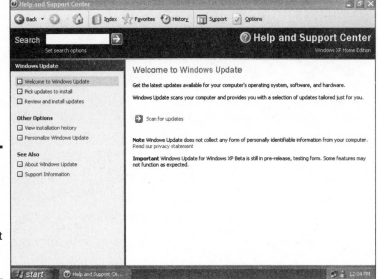

Figure 10-2:
Windows
scans your
machine
and finds
updates that
are specific
to your PC.

3. Click Review and Install Updates.

You see a list of available updates. If you don't want to install a particular update, click Remove. If you want to install an optional add-on, click Add.

Don't worry. Any Windows XP updates that you choose to Remove from the automatic updating machinery can be resurrected at a later date.

4. Windows downloads and installs the software you've selected.

You may be required to Accept a licensing agreement. You'll probably be required to restart your computer. But in the end, the updates almost always go smoothly.

Installing old updates

Like bad pennies that won't go away, Windows XP continues to bug — er, I mean *bother* — you about old updates that you've declined: The old updates appear on the Pick Updates to Install list for a long time. Follow these steps to banish certain updates, so that they never darken your door again:

1. **Bring up the Windows Update screen. (Choose Start⇨Help and Support, and under the Pick a Task heading, click Keep Your Computer Up-To-Date with Windows Update.)**

2. **Click Personalize Windows Update.**

3. **Select the Display the Option to Hide Individual Updates check box.**

Doing so puts a check box next to every offered update, which effectively hides the update from all further searches on your machine.

4. **If you change your mind and want Windows to show you all the pending updates, choose Start⇨Control Panel⇨Performance and Maintenance⇨System. Then, on the Automatic Updates tab, click Restore Declined Updates.**

Performing Periodic Maintenance

Drives die at the worst possible moment. A drive that's starting to get flaky can display all sorts of strange symptoms: Everything from long, long pauses when you're trying to open a file to completely inexplicable crashes and other errors in Windows itself.

Windows XP comes with a grab-bag of utilities designed to help you keep your hard drives in top shape. One of them runs automatically every time your system shuts down unexpectedly, like when the dog finally bites through the power cord: The next time you start your system, Windows scans your hard drives to see whether any pieces of files were left hanging around.

You can spend a lot of time futzing around with your hard drives and their care and feeding if you want, but as far as I'm concerned, just three utilities suffice and they are explained here. You have to be a designated Administrator (see Book I, Chapter 6) to get them to work.

Running an error check

If a drive starts acting weird — for example, you get errors when trying to open a file, or Windows crashes in unpredictable ways — run the Windows error-checking routines:

If you're an old hand at Windows — or an even older hand at DOS — you probably recognize this as the venerable CHKDSK routine, in somewhat fancier clothing.

1. **Choose Start⇨My Computer.**

2. **Right-click the drive that's malfunctioning and click Properties.**

3. **On the Tools tab, click the Check Now button.**

The Check Disk dialog box appears (see Figure 10-3).

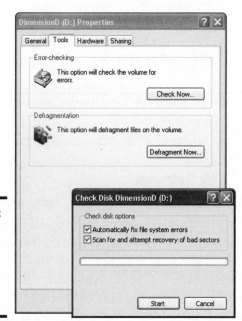

Figure 10-3:
Use Check Disk to perform a complete surface scan.

4. **In most circumstances, you want to select the Scan For and Attempt Recovery of Bad Sectors check box and click Start.**

   If you don't want to sit and wait and wait (and wait) for Windows to finish, you probably want to select the Automatically Fix File System Errors check box, too.

As long as you aren't using any files on the disk that Windows is scanning, Windows performs the scan on the spot and reports back on what it finds. If you are using files on the disk, however, Windows asks whether you want to schedule a scan to run the next time you restart your machine. If you say yes, you have to turn the computer off and then turn it back on again before Windows runs the scan. (Note that merely logging off isn't sufficient.)

Scheduling Cleanups

In addition to running an error check from time to time, I use the Windows Task Scheduler to periodically go through and remove temporary files that I don't need with a utility called Cleanup. I tell you how to do that in the section, "Scheduling Task Scheduler," later in this chapter.

Defragmenting a drive

Every week or so (or whenever I'm thinking about it), I run the Windows Disk Defragmenter on all my hard drives. This is quite different from the Check Disk routine (refer to Figure 10-3), which concentrates on the surface of the hard drive and whether it has been corrupted. Files become *fragmented* — scattered in pieces all over a hard drive — when Windows dynamically creates and deletes files. Having many fragmented files on a hard drive tends to slow down processing because Windows has to jump all over a disk to reassemble a file when you ask for it. Windows Disk Defragmenter focuses on putting the pieces of files back together, in contiguous slots, so that Windows doesn't have to scamper all over the disk to read an entire file. To run the Defragmenter, follow these steps:

1. **Choose Start➪All Programs➪Accessories➪System Tools➪Disk Defragmenter.**

   Alternatively, you can navigate to the drive in question, right-click it, click Properties, click Tools, and click the Defragment Now button (refer to Figure 10-3).

2. **Click the drive that you want to work on, and then click Analyze.**

   Windows XP checks to be sure that the files are put together properly, and then it advises you about whether a defragmentation run is worthwhile (see Figure 10-4).

3. **To run the defragmenter, click Defragment.**

4. **Break out that novel you've always wanted to read. This can take a long, long time.**

   While Windows is defragmenting, it keeps you posted on its progress at the bottom of the Disk Defragmenter dialog box, but don't be surprised if the "percent complete" figure freezes for a while and then jumps inexplicably.

Use those three tools regularly — Chkdsk, Cleanup, and Disk Defragmenter — and your disks will thank you. Profusely.

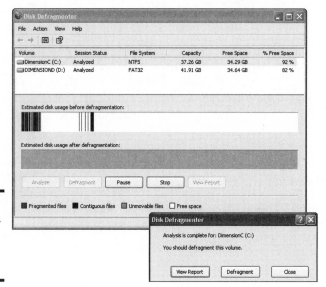

Figure 10-4:
The Defrag-
menter's
Analyze
phase.

Backing Up and Restoring

Windows XP Professional comes with a very thorough (and very complex) backup and restore capability called Automated System Recovery, or ASR. The Backup part of ASR works through a Wizard. The Restore part can kick in, at your command, when you re-boot the computer — even if your system was so thoroughly messed up you had to replace the hard drive.

If you think you're going to click a couple of times and get automatic back-ups from Windows XP, you're in for a very rude awakening. While working with ASR isn't as complex as, say, setting up and maintaining a Big Corporate client/server Network, mastering ASR will certainly take you more than a day, assuming you already have a Ph.D. in Computer Science. Check the Windows XP Help and Support Center for the topic ASR and you'll see why.

Earlier versions of Windows let you boot your PC with a special diskette called an Emergency Repair Disk (or Emergency Boot Disk in very early versions). Windows XP doesn't have an ERD. All of the functions of the old ERP have been subsumed by ASR. Yes, that means you can't boot to Windows XP directly from diskette any more.

If you're using Windows XP Professional and you need automatic backups through your Big Corporate Network (you probably do!), and your network isn't already set up to handle backups, your only realistic choice is to bring in somebody who knows ASR and have them configure it for you. Usually, the designated stuckee is your favorite whipping boy, the Network Administrator. ASR kinda goes hand in hand with other Big Corporate Network chores.

What if you're using Windows XP Home? Ah, have I got a gotcha for you. Back in the weeks leading up to Windows XP's release, Microsoft announced that it would ship ASR and its Backup subsystem with Windows XP

Professional, but would *not* include any sort of automatic backup with Windows XP Home. That brought a hailstorm of criticism from two different perspectives: the "Windows XP Home users need backup just as much as Windows XP Professional users" contingency and the "Windows has always had a backup routine even if nobody ever used it" contingency. Both contingencies won.

Microsoft does, indeed, ship ASR Backup with Windows XP Home — if you know where to find it. Except, uh, well, er, there's no ASR Restore to go along with it. That makes Windows XP Home's Backup just about as useful as a Ferrari Testarossa with no wheels. Or a transmission, engine, seats, or brakes.

If you really, really want to install ASR Backup (better known as NTBackup) in Windows XP Home, even though there's no built-in Restore, put the Windows XP Home CD in a convenient drive and wait for the Welcome to Microsoft Windows XP screen. Choose Browse this CD⇨Valueadd⇨MSFT⇨NTBACKUP. Make sure you read (and understand!) the warning in the file `readme.txt` before running the installer.

Scheduling Task Scheduler

Windows XP has a built-in scheduler that runs just about any program according to any schedule you specify — daily, weekly, monthly, middle of the night, on alternate blue moons. The scheduler comes in handy in two very different situations:

✦ When you always want to do something at the same time of day. Perhaps you always want to dial up the Internet at 6:15 every morning, so that your machine is connected by the time you drag your sorry tail into your desk chair. Or maybe you want to run a PowerPoint presentation every morning at 7:30, so that your boss hears the tell-tale sounds as she walks by your cubicle. (And who said Dummies aren't Devious?)

✦ When you want to make sure that the computer performs some mundane maintenance job when it won't interfere with your work time. Thus, you may schedule disk cleanups every weekday at 2:00 in the afternoon, because you know you'll always be propped up in the mop closet taking a snooze.

Any discussion of scheduled tasks immediately conjures up the old question, "Should I leave my computer running all night, or should I turn it off?" The fact is, nobody knows which is better. You can find plenty of arguments on both sides of the fence. Suffice it to say that your computer has to be on (or suspended) for a scheduled task to run, so you may have to leave your computer on at least one night a week (or a month) to get the maintenance work done.

You find absolutely no debate about one "should I leave it on" question, though. Everybody in the know agrees that running a full surface scan of your hard drive daily is a bad idea. A full scan simply inflicts too much wear and tear on the hard drive's arms. It's kind of like forcing yourself to fly every morning, just to keep your shoulders in shape.

One of the most important uses of the Task Scheduler is driving a Windows file cleanup program called, imaginatively, Cleanup. Here's how to get Cleanup scheduled — and how to use Scheduler in general:

1. **Choose Start⇨All Programs⇨Accessories⇨System Tools⇨Scheduled Tasks to get the Scheduler going.**

You see the (odd) Windows Explorer window.

2. **Double-click the icon marked Add Scheduled Task.**

The Scheduled Task Wizard appears with a frou-frou introductory screen.

3. **Click Next.**

You see a list of some available programs, as shown in Figure 10-5.

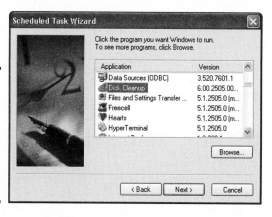

Figure 10-5:
The scheduled regular Disk Cleanup runs; choose Disk Cleanup.

Does the list in Figure 10-5 look like an odd assortment of programs? It is. The Scheduled Task Wizard takes all the programs listed on the Start menu, alphabetizes them, and throws them all in this list. Literally. If you want to schedule a program that isn't on the Start menu, you have to click the Browse button.

4. **In this example, assume that you want to schedule regular Disk Cleanup runs, so click Disk Cleanup, and then click Next.**

You can tell Windows how frequently you want to run Disk Cleanup.

5. **Click Next again, and you can set the exact schedule — which days, what times.**

6. **Click Next again, and the Scheduled Task Wizard asks you to provide security information.**

This is an important screen because it reinforces the point that you aren't given any special security privileges just because you're scheduling a program. The program runs only if you have the authority to make it run (see Book I, Chapter 6.)

7. **In the very last step, you can set Advanced Properties for the scheduled task.**

The advanced properties include telling Windows XP what to do if the task takes a very long time to complete; whether the task should go into hibernation if something else happens on the computer (presumably you're awake in the wee hours, banging out an assignment); and whether Windows should wake up the computer if it's hibernating or run the task if the PC is using batteries at the time.

The Windows Disk Cleanup program has a handful of settings that you may want to twiddle (see Figure 10-6). The System Schedule Wizard doesn't have any way to allow you to pick and choose your options for a scheduled program. The solution? Run Disk Cleanup once by hand (choose Start➪All Programs➪Accessories➪System Tools➪Disk Cleanup). Disk Cleanup remembers the settings that you applied when you ran it manually, and it uses those settings every time you run it with the Scheduler. Many other Windows programs work the same way.

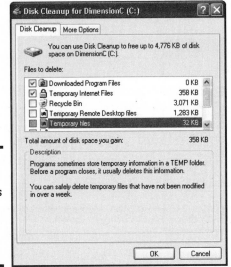

Figure 10-6:
Disk
Cleanup lets
you choose
what kinds
of files will
be deleted.

Zipping and Compression

Windows XP supports two very different kinds of file *compression*. The distinction is confusing but important, so bear with me. File compression reduces the size of a file by cleverly taking out parts of the contents of the file that aren't needed, storing only the minimum amount of information necessary to reconstitute the file — *extract* it — into its full, original form. A certain amount of overhead is involved, because the computer has to take the time to squeeze extraneous information out of a file before storing it, and then the computer takes more time to restore the file to its original state when someone needs the file. But compression can reduce file sizes enormously. A compressed file often takes up half its original space — even less, in many cases.

How does compression work? That depends on the compression method you use. In one kind of compression, known as Huffman encoding, letters that occur frequently in a file (say, the letter *e* in a word processing document) are massaged so that they take up only a little bit of room in the file, while letters that occur less frequently (say, *x*) are allowed to occupy lots of space. Instead of allocating eight 1's and 0's for every letter in a document, say, some letters may take up only two 1's and 0's, while others could take up 15. The net result, overall, is a big reduction in file size. It's complicated, and the mathematics involved gets quite interesting.

Windows XP's two file compression techniques are as follows:

✦ Files can be compressed and placed in a "Compressed (zipped) Folder," with an icon to match.

✦ Files, folders, or even entire drives can be compressed using NTFS's built-in compression capabilities.

Here's where things get complicated. NTFS compression is built into the file system: You can use it only on NTFS drives, and the compression doesn't persist when you move (or copy) the file off the drive. Think of NTFS compression as a capability inherent to the disk drive itself. That isn't really the case — Windows XP does all the sleight-of-hand behind the scenes — but the concept will help you remember NTFS compression's limitations and quirks.

Although Microsoft would have you believe that Compressed (zipped) Folder compression is based on folders, it isn't. A Compressed (zipped) Folder is really a file — *not* a folder — but it's a special kind of file called a Zip file. If you've ever encountered Zip files on the Internet (they have a file-name extension of .ZIP and they're frequently manipulated with programs such as WinZip, www.winzip.com), you know exactly what I'm talking about. Zip files contain one or more compressed files, and they use the most common kind of compression found on the Internet. Think of Compressed (zipped) Folders as being Zip files, and if you have even a nodding acquaintance with ZIPs, you'll immediately understand the limitations and quirks of Compressed (zipped) Folders. Microsoft calls them Folders because that's supposed to be easier for users to understand. You be the judge.

Table 10-1 shows a quick comparison of NTFS compression and Zip compression.

Table 10-1	NTFS Compression versus Compressed (Zipped) Folders Compression
NTFS	*ZIP*
Think of NTFS compression as a feature of the hard disk itself.	Zip technology works on any file, regardless of where it is stored.
The minute you move an NTFS-compressed file off an NTFS drive — by, say, sending a file as an e-mail attachment — the file is uncompressed automatically, and you can't do anything about it: You'll send a big, uncompressed file.	You can move a Compressed (zipped) Folder (actually a Zip file, with a .ZIP filename extension) anywhere, and it stays compressed. If you send a Zip file as an e-mail attachment, it goes over the ether as a compressed file. The person receiving the file can view it directly in Windows XP, or he or she can use a product such as WinZip to see it.

(continued)

Table 10-1 *(continued)*

NTFS	ZIP
A lot of overhead is associated with NTFS compression: Windows has to compress and decompress those files on the fly, and that sucks up processing power.	Very little overhead is associated with Zip files. Many programs (for example, anti-virus programs) read Zip files directly.
NTFS compression is great if you're running out of room on an NTFS formatted drive.	Compressed (zipped) Folders (that is to say, Zip files) are in a near-universal form that can be used just about anywhere.
You have to have Administrator privileges in order to use NTFS compression.	You can create, copy, or move Zip files just like any other files, with the same security restrictions.
You can use NTFS compression on entire drives, folders, or single files. They cannot be password protected.	You can Zip files or folders, and they can be password protected.

If you try to compress the drive that contains your Windows folder, you won't be able to compress the files that are currently in use by Windows.

To use NTFS compression on an entire drive, follow these steps:

1. **Make sure that you are a full-fledged Administrator (see Book I, Chapter 6).**

2. **Choose Start⇨My Computer and right-click the drive that you want to compress. Click Properties and click on the General tab (see Figure 10-7).**

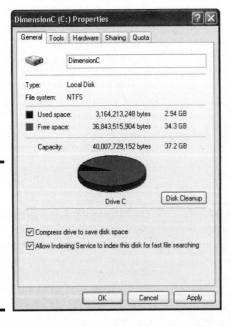

Figure 10-7: NFTS Compression is available only on drives formatted for NTFS.

3. **If the drive is formatted with NTFS, you see a check box saying Compress Drive to Save Disk Space. Select this check box.**

4. Click OK.

Windows asks you to confirm that you want to compress the entire drive. Windows takes some time to compress the drive — in some cases, the estimated time is measured in days. Good luck.

To use NTFS compression on a folder or single file, follow these steps:

1. Make sure that you are a full-fledged Administrator (see Book I, Chapter 6).

2. Navigate to the folder or file you want to compress (for example, choose Start⇨My Documents or Start⇨My Computer). Right-click on the file or folder you want to compress. Click Properties and click the Advanced button on the General tab.

The Advanced Properties dialog box appears (see Figure 10-8).

Figure 10-8: The Advanced Properties dialog box.

3. Select the Compress Contents to Save Disk Space check box and click OK.

To uncompress a file or folder, go back into the Advanced Properties dialog box (right-click the file or folder, click Properties, and then click Advanced) and deselect the Compress Contents to Save Disk Space check box.

To use Zip compression, er, Compressed (zipped) Folders, you must first create a Zip file, er, a Compressed (zipped) Folder. Here's how:

1. Choose Start⇨My Documents to navigate to the folder that you want to contain your new Zip file.

2. Right-click in any convenient empty location within the window and choose New⇨Compressed (Zipped) Folder.

Windows responds by creating a new Zip file, with a `.ZIP` filename extension, and placing it in the current folder.

The new file is just like any other file — you can rename it, copy it, move it, delete it, send it as an e-mail attachment, save it on the Internet, or do anything else to it that you can do to a file. (That's because it *is* a file.)

3. **To add a file to your Compressed (zipped) Folder, simply drag it onto the zipped folder icon.**

4. **To copy a file from your Zip file (uh, folder), double-click the zipped folder icon, and treat the file the same way you would treat any regular file.**

5. **To copy all of the files out of your Zip file (folder), click Extract All Files in the Folder Tasks Pane.**

   You see the Windows XP Compressed (zipped) Folders Extraction Wizard, which guides you through the steps.

The Compressed (zipped) Folders Extraction Wizard places all the copied files into a new folder with the same name as the Zip file — which confuses the living bewilickers out of everybody. Unless you give the extracted folder a different name from the original Compressed (zipped) Folder, you end up with two folders with precisely the same name sitting on your desktop. Do yourself a huge favor and feed the wizard a different folder name while you're extracting the files.

Chapter 11: Jammin' with Windows Media Player

In This Chapter

✔ Media Guide: The world-wide program schedule

✔ What's playing now?

✔ Copying music from a CD

✔ The Media Library: Where your music is kept

✔ Radio Tuner

✔ Copying music to a CD or digital audio player

Windows Media Player (or WMP) sucks you in from the moment you start it. As Windows XP's built-in boom box, it plays CDs, of course, but it also lets you play, organize, and generally enjoy any kind of music stored on your computer, whether the tunes came from CDs, the Internet, or your buddy down the hall. It also plays video and lets you tune into the nascent Internet radio market. If you have a CD writer, Windows Media Player creates CDs that contain any combination of tracks you want. If you have a digital audio player, WMP copies music to the player, so that you can hip and/or hop, as circumstances dictate, wherever you go.

 Windows Media Player is useful to you only if your computer has a sound card and a headphone or a set of speakers. The little speaker inside the box that goes "beep" when you start the computer won't cut the mustard. If your computer doesn't have sound hardware, you have to get some or forget about using Windows Media Player.

Starting with the Media Guide

To start Windows Media Player, choose Start⇨All Programs⇨Accessories⇨ Entertainment⇨Windows Media Player. (If you have run WMP recently, it's in the Start menu's short list, and you can much more easily choose Start⇨ Windows Media Player.) Click the Media Guide button on the left side of the WMP window. The application now should look something like the version shown in Figure 11-1.

The Media Guide hooks into www.WindowsMedia.com, which is owned and operated by — you guessed it — a little company in Redmond, Washington that also makes PC operating systems. The www.WindowsMedia.com site features clips from new music and videos, entertainment news, and other information that may interest users of WMP. Many of the pages have links that allow you to buy the products described.

To control WMP
To see menu
Recommended download speeds
To minimize and close windows

Figure 11-1: Windows Media Player looks like this when it starts.

Playing with Now Playing

The first control button on the left edge of WMP is named Now Playing. When you click it, WMP displays the Media Playlist, as shown in Figure 11-2. The right side of the window displays a *playlist,* which is just a sequence of tracks. The left side displays details of the first track. When the track is playing, the area below the details shows either a picture of the album cover or a psychedelic *visualization* of the music.

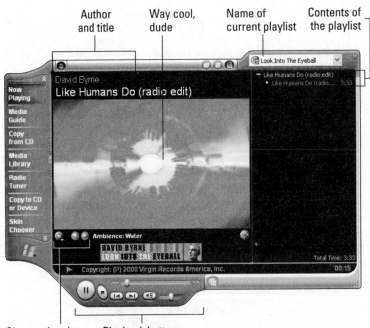

Author and title
Way cool, dude
Name of current playlist
Contents of the playlist

Figure 11-2: The Media Playlist display.

Change the picture   Playback buttons

To select a different playlist, choose one from the drop-down list of playlist names. When you do, WMP behaves just as a CD player does when you put in a CD: It starts playing the first track, then it plays the second one, and so on until it reaches the end. To select a different track from the current playlist, double-click the track down in the list of playlist contents.

The buttons along the bottom of the window control Now Playing. They work similarly to the buttons on a conventional CD player.

Playing a CD

Want to play a CD? That's hard, too. Here's how:

1. **Take the CD out of its plastic case, if it's in one.**

2. **Wipe the pizza stains off the shiny side (don't worry about the other side).**

3. **Stick the CD in the PC's drive and close it.**

If WMP isn't running already, it starts all by itself. Then you wait a few seconds (well, quite a few seconds, especially if you're afflicted with a slow Internet connection), and WMP starts playing the first track. To WMP, the CD *is* a playlist. The tracks on the CD appear in the playlist area on the right side of the window. Look at the drop-down list of playlists in the upper-right corner of the window; the name of the CD appears as the selected item.

Changing the graphic area

The three buttons below the graphic area, er, visualizations screen, change its contents:

✦ Click the first button to display a list of options. The first option is Album Art. The others are different groups of abstract visualizations of the music.

✦ Click the second button to cycle through the selected group of visualizations backward.

✦ Click the third button to cycle through it forward. (These buttons disappear when you select Album Art. You only get one Album Art per album.)

Changing the size of the window

In its initial form, WMP occupies a substantial chunk of real estate on the Desktop. To make it smaller, drag a corner of the window to the desired location, as you do with any other window. But note that when the menu bar is not visible, the only corner you can drag is the lower-right one.

When you make the window small, the window may not have enough room for all of the buttons that run down the left side. Use the double arrows above and below the buttons to scroll them so that you can reach them all.

Copying from a CD

Click the Copy From CD button on the left edge of the WMP screen to copy tracks from a CD to your computer. If the CD is already in your PC when you click Copy From CD, WMP simply presents a list of tracks, like the display shown in Figure 11-3.

Figure 11-3:
The Copy
from CD
display.

If you select Copy From CD first and then insert the CD, WMP automatically starts playing the first track. Click the Stop button at the bottom of the window to make it stop or, if you remember, hold down the Shift key when Windows starts reading the CD. The Shift key tells Windows "don't try to run this CD, or play these songs; I just want to look at what's on the stupid CD."

See the column of check boxes down the left side of the track list? They indicate which tracks are selected for copying to your computer.

✦ To copy all of the tracks, just leave the check boxes alone.

✦ To exclude a few tracks, clear those tracks' check boxes.

✦ To copy only a few tracks, clear the check box at the top of the column, level with the column titles. This clears the whole track list. Now select the check boxes for the tracks that you want to copy.

Copying a track takes a significant fraction of the track's play time. Select just a few tracks so that you can see how the copying process works, without having to wait all day.

When you've chosen the tracks that you want to transfer to your PC, click the Copy Music button. (It's above the playlist, roughly in the middle of the screen.) Watch the track list's Copy Status column; it shows your computer's progress as it copies the selected tracks.

Where can you find the copied music in your computer? In a playlist, of course. WMP creates a new playlist with the same name as the album and puts the copied tracks in it. If you switch to Now Playing and look at the playlist drop-down list, you see the CD's title with a playlist icon next to it (see Figure 11-4). That's where your copied tracks live.

Figure 11-4:
The newly copied CD's playlist.

 The music itself is stored in the My Music folder. WMP makes a folder for each artist, and inside the artist's folder, it makes a sub-folder for each album. The music tracks go into the album's folder. If you use the Copy From CD command, WMP stores all the associated information — track titles, album cover art, artist — along with the music. That's handy because WMP can pick up the info from the files and folders when it needs to, without having to run to www.WindowsMedia.com.

Organizing Your Media Library

WMP uses the Media Library to organize sound tracks. When you understand how the Media Library works, you'll be able to organize your music just the way you want. WMP constructs the Media Library on the fly, using all the entries in your My Music folder and the shared My Music folder for the PC, if one exists.

Leafing through the Media Library

Click the Media Library button to display the Media Library. WMP displays a window split into left and right panes, with the Media Library's structure on the left and the contents of the selected item on the right, as shown in Figure 11-5.

Figure 11-5:
My Media Library.

The Media Library is organized into folders, just like the Windows XP file system. Unlike the file system, the Media Library has a fixed set of folders:

✦ **Audio:** Contains audio tracks, such as those you have copied from CDs.

  • **All Audio:** Contains all of the sound tracks in the Media Library.

  • **Album:** Contains all of the albums in the Media Library. An album is "in" the Media Library if you have copied at least one track from that album with the Copy from CD operation. Click the plus sign next to Album to expand Album into a list of albums. Click an album to display that album's tracks in the right pane.

  • **Artist:** Contains all of the artists known to have tracks in the Media Library. Click the plus sign next to Artist to display a list of artists under the Artist folder. Select an artist to display tracks known to be by that artist.

  • **Genre:** This item works just like Artist, except that it organizes tracks by genre (rock, classical, and so on) instead of by artist.

✦ **Video:** Video recordings, discussed in Book I, Chapter 12.

  • **All Clips:** Contains all of the video clips in the Media Library.

  • **Author:** Contains authors who have video clips in the Media Library. This item works just like the Artist subfolder in the Audio folder: You can expand the item into a list of authors by clicking the plus sign, and you can select an author to display a list of that author's video clips.

✦ **My Playlists:** Playlists that you create or that come with Windows XP. Click the plus sign to expand the item into a list of playlists, and select a playlist to see the audio tracks or video clips it contains.

✦ **Radio Tuner Presets:** Lists streaming audio providers on the Web that you have stored as *presets* (see "Radio Tuner," later in this chapter).

✦ **Deleted Items:** Items you have deleted from the other folders. Deleted Items serves the same function that the Recycle Bin does for files: It lets you restore a deleted item if you change your mind.

Finding the tracks you want

The Media Library folders are powerful tools for keeping your recordings organized because they offer so many different ways of looking at the same information. Want to know what albums contain recordings by a given artist? That artist's entry in the Artist folder tells you. Want to look at one of those albums to see what else is on it? The album's entry in the Album folder tells you.

Sorting

You can sort a list in the right pane by the contents of any column. For example, click the All Audio folder to display a list of all of your audio tracks. Now click the heading of the Artist column to sort the list of tracks by artist. Click the heading of the Album column to sort the list by album.

Click a heading twice in a row to sort the list backwards on that column. If your collection of recordings is large, sorting the list in different ways can help you find items you want.

Searching

You can search the Media Library for items that have certain words in their titles or for artist names, album names, or genres. When your collection of recordings becomes too large to inspect easily, this is a convenient way to find things in it.

To search the Media Library, click the Search button, located just above the panes of the window. WMP displays the Search Media Library dialog box, as shown in Figure 11-6. Enter a word that appears in at least one track title, artist name, or album name in the Media Library. Click the Search button. WMP searches the library and displays a larger version of the same dialog box.

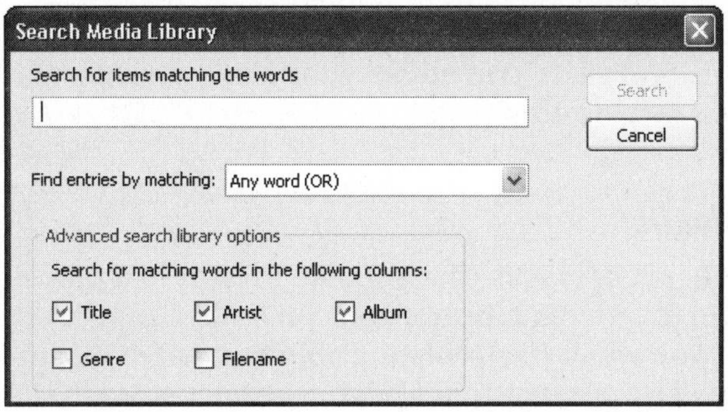

Figure 11-6:
The Search
Media
Library
dialog box.

Click the View Results button to close the Search Media Library dialog box. Notice that a new playlist is named Search Results; it's selected, and it contains, logically enough, the tracks that were found in the search. Figure 11-7 shows such a result list.

Figure 11-7:
The Search
Results
playlist.

The Search Results playlist is just like any other playlist, except that the contents of the list — the matching tracks — are changed every time a search is run. You can keep a Search Results playlist around for a long time.

Playing tracks in the Media Library

You can play a track directly from the Media Library. Just select the track and click the Start button at the bottom of the WMP window. You can even play a group of tracks by selecting the group. To play all of the songs by a given artist, for example, select that artist under the Artist folder and click Start.

Managing playlists

Er, maybe that should be *mangling* playlists. WMP gives you all sorts of control over which songs you hear, and it does so through playlists. Did you ever want to rearrange the order of the songs on the Beatles' *White Album*? My son just about croaked when he found out he could burn a CD that plays *Oops... I Did It Again* immediately after Eminem's homage *Oops... The Real Slim Shady Did It Again.* You've got the power. Hmmm. That's a catchy tag line, isn't it? Media Library lets you create your own playlists, and you can modify them to your heart's content.

Creating a new playlist

If you have a favorite set of tracks that you like to hear in a particular order, and the tracks are in the Media Library, you can build a playlist that gives you precisely what you want. It's like being able to create your own custom CD. In fact, you can use a playlist to make your own custom CD. Nothing to it. The section "Copy to CD or Device" explains how.

To make your own playlist, click the New Playlist button on the left side of the Media Library window. WMP opens a dialog box that prompts you to name the new playlist (see Figure 11-8). Enter a name for the list and click OK. If you look at the drop-down list of playlist names above the right pane of the window, your new playlist is there. That's how hard it is to create a new playlist.

Figure 11-8:
Enter the new playlist name.

Adding a track to a playlist

In the Media Library, you can add a track to any playlist, at any time:

1. **Select any folder or folder item that contains that track, so that the track appears in the right pane of the window.**

138

2. **Click the track to select it.**

3. **Click the Add to Playlist button (which is next to the New Playlist button, in the upper left).**

   WMP displays a drop-down list of playlists.

4. **Click the playlist that you want.**

   If you have a lot of playlists, WMP displays only the first few of them in the drop-down list. If the one you want isn't there, click the last list item, Additional Playlists. This opens a scrolling list of all playlists. Click the one you want, and then click OK.

5. **WMP adds the track to the playlist and closes the scrolling list.**

You can add the same track to any number of playlists. Just go through the preceding steps again, this time specifying a different playlist.

You can even add a track to a playlist from a different playlist, using the same procedure. Pick the playlist with the desired track on the left. Click the track on the right, and click Add to Playlist. Voilà.

Renaming and deleting playlists

To delete a playlist, right-click the playlist and click the Delete command from the resulting menu, as shown in Figure 11-9. Or you can just select the playlist and press the Delete key. A deleted playlist goes into the big digital bit bucket in the sky. Actually, it goes into the Media Library's Deleted Items folder. To get it back, display the contents of that folder; then right-click the playlist and click the Restore command.

Figure 11-9: How to delete a playlist.

To change a playlist's name, right-click the playlist and click the Rename command from the resulting menu.

Deleting tracks from the Media Library

If you've been reading about the Media Library, you know that no matter how many playlists a track is added to, the Media Library still contains just one copy of the track. The reverse is just as true: even if you delete a track from every playlist that contains it, the Media Library still contains one copy of the track. It's possible to delete a track from the Media Library, though. You can do this in a couple of ways:

✦ Select the All Audio folder, or an appropriate item under the Album, Artist, or Genre folder, so that the track appears in the right pane of the window. Then right-click the track and click the Delete From Library command. Or, select the track and press the Delete key.

✦ Select a playlist that contains the track. Then right-click the track and click the Delete From Library command. (In this case, pressing the Delete key does not work; it simply deletes the track from the playlist.)

Take care not to delete a track from the Media Library when you intend to delete it only from a playlist. When you right-click a track in a playlist, the Delete From Library command and the Delete From Playlist command are right next to each other! It's easy to choose the wrong one.

Radio Tuner

Microsoft controls the appearance of the WMP Radio Tuner from its bunkers located thirteen stories below ground level at a secret location underneath a heavily fortified parking lot on 156th Street in Redmond, Washington. Okay, okay. That's not quite accurate. Still, Microsoft can change the appearance and the function of the Radio Tuner at any moment, simply by changing a Web site. That means the detailed instructions and screen shots that you see here may or may not reflect what you actually get when you crank up the Radio Tuner. If you're having a hard time getting the radio to work, follow along here because the functions that you need to perform — setting preset lists, picking channels, and so on — will be the same, no matter what whim strikes the fancy of the Windows Media Web designers this week.

Many Web sites offer *streaming audio,* which is essentially broadcast sound (radio) over the Internet. Many AM and FM radio stations offer their own programming through their own Web sites. Other organizations provide streaming audio that isn't available over the air waves at all. WMP lets you listen to all of these.

If you click the Radio Tuner button on the left side of the screen, and you're connected to the Web, WMP presents the display shown in Figure 11-10. The Radio Tuner doesn't look much like a conventional radio, but you control it in a very similar way. The right half of the window does the job of a radio's tuning dial. It lets you find *stations* (streaming audio sources) through a search service provided by Microsoft's Windows Media Web site, www. WindowsMedia.com. The left half of the window lets you set up and select your favorite stations more easily, like a radio's preset buttons.

Figure 11-10:
The Radio
Tuner
display.

Listening to a station

The simplest way to tune in to a station is to select it from one of the lists of presets in the left half of the window. There are three lists there, titled Featured Stations, My Stations, and Recently Played Stations. Initially, only the Featured Stations list is displayed.

You can see more information about a station by clicking either its name or the double arrowhead to the right of the name. The Radio Tuner expands that station's listing. To tune in to this station, click the Play or the green arrowhead next to it. (You can also click the green arrowhead next to the station's name, whether you display the station information first or not.) Wait a few seconds (well, actually, quite a few seconds, particularly if you have a slow Internet connection), and WMP starts playing the station.

At least, WMP starts playing the station if everything goes right. Streaming audio is still an immature medium, though, and many things may go wrong. For example, the Web site that provides the station that you chose may be out of order or may have gone "off the air."

The first few times you try to tune in a new station you're liable to get a message box that asks whether you want to install a "codec," a "Java Virtual Machine," or some other arcane nonsense. Don't be scared by "Security Warning." This type of message is normal, and is not as dangerous as it appears.

Saving a station in the Media Library

You can save a station setting in the Media Library along with your sound recordings, as well as in a preset list. When a station setting is in the Media Library, you can include it in playlists.

To store a station in the Media Library, make sure that WMP's menu bar is visible. (*Remember:* If it is not visible, click the round button in the upper edge of the frame, near the upper-left corner.) Tune in the station by whichever means you prefer. Then choose File⇨Add to Media Library. This command opens a submenu; select Add Currently Playing Track.

After you add a station to the Media Library, you can select the Media Library tab and see the station in the All Audio folder.

Copy to CD or Device

If your computer has a CD writer, you can copy sound recordings from the Media Library directly to CDs. If you own a digital audio player that is compatible with Windows XP, you can copy sound recordings from the Media Library to your player. In either case, you can't copy live feeds such as programs from radio stations. Such programs are broadcast for listening only, so recording them would often violate the intellectual property rights of the radio station or of others.

You also can't copy files that use certain recording techniques, indicated by a file's extension. As of this writing, the only types of files that you can copy to a CD are Windows Media files (.wma extension), MP3 files (.mp3), and Wave sound files (.wav).

Understanding CD-Rs and CD-RWs

There are two types of writeable CDs:

✦ *CD-R* is short for *CD read*. This is a CD that you can write once. After a CD-R has been written, you cannot add to it or erase it. A CD-R writer can write only CD-Rs. A CD-RW writer generally can write either CD-Rs or CD-RWs.

✦ *CD-RW* is short for *CD read-write*. This is a CD that you can erase and rewrite many times.

You generally can play a CD-R on a conventional CD player or on a computer's CD-ROM drive (or a CD-R drive, or a CD-RW drive). As a rule, only a computer's CD-ROM drive can play a CD-RW.

WMP cannot add data to a partially recorded CD-RW. Before you can reuse a CD-RW, you must erase it, like this:

1. **Put the CD-RW in the CD writer.**

2. **Choose Start➪My Computer.**

3. **Select the CD writer.**

4. **Click Erase CD-RW.**

Burning a CD

In this section, "CD" refers to both CD-Rs and CD-RWs. The process of writing data to a CD is called *burning*. WMP enables you to burn a CD very, very easily. Here's how:

1. **Choose Start➪Windows Media Player to start Windows Media Player.**

(If for some reason WMP isn't visible when you click Start, use Start➪All Programs➪Windows Media Player.)

2. Click the Copy to CD or Device button.

WMP displays the window shown in Figure 11-11. The left pane of the window, Music to Copy, shows the tracks currently available to copy to the CD.

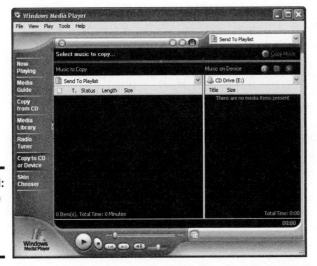

Figure 11-11:
The Copy to CD or Device window.

3. If the left pane is not empty, select all of the tracks and delete them.

This deletes the tracks only from the window — not from the Media Library. The right pane of the window, Music on Device, shows the device to which Windows Media Play is set to copy, and what is on the device. Your CD writer should be shown in the drop-down list at the top of the pane.

4. If your CD writer is not shown in the list, click the drop-down list and select it.

5. Select the tracks that you want to copy to the CD. Start by clicking the Media Library tab.

6. To copy an individual track, display the track that you want in the right pane of the window. Then right-click the track and click Copy to Audio CD.

WMP returns to the Copy to CD or Device window and displays the track in the Music to Copy pane.

7. To copy another track, return to the Media Library and do it again.

8. To copy several tracks at once from a playlist, display the contents of the playlist in the Media Library's right pane. Select the tracks with either Shift+click or Ctrl+click, and then right-click any one of the selected tracks and choose Copy to Audio CD.

9. After you collect all of the tracks that you want to copy to the CD, consider the order of the tracks.

WMP records them on the CD in the order that they appear in the Music to Copy pane. If that isn't what you want, drag each track to the desired position.

If you see a track in the Music to Copy pane that you don't want to copy, you can delete it from the pane, or you can clear the check box to its left. Only items whose check boxes are selected will be copied.

10. **Put a blank CD in the CD writer and close the door.**

   Wait a few seconds, and the message Copy . . . to drive appears above the Music to Copy pane.

11. **Look at each track's status, shown in the Status column.**

   All statuses should say "Ready to copy." If some say "Will not fit," the total play time of the tracks is greater than the recording capacity of the disc. If you write the CD anyway, the tracks that will not fit will not be copied to it. You probably want to remove some tracks so that the whole list will fit.

12. **Click the Copy Music button, above the Music on Device pane, to begin the copying operation.**

   WMP makes two passes through the list of tracks to copy. In the first pass, it prepares each track for copying and changes the track's status from "Ready to copy" to "Converted." In the second pass, it writes the tracks to the CD and changes each track's status to "Copying to CD" and then to "Complete" when it is done.

13. **When the last track's status changes to "Complete," the CD is done, and WMP ejects it from the drive.**

The copying process takes a substantial fraction of the time it would take to play the copied tracks, the exact time depending on the speed of your CD writer.

It is best not to use your computer for other tasks while writing a CD. If another task's activity prevents WMP from writing a continuous stream of data, the CD will be spoiled.

When you copy an entire playlist to the Music to Copy pane in this way, you are copying the playlist itself — not the tracks in the playlist. If you then delete a track from the Music to Copy pane, that track will be deleted from the playlist!

Copying to a digital audio player

The "Device" in "Copy to CD or Device" refers to a digital audio player: one of those nifty little gadgets that you can carry around with you and use to play music out of electronic memory. People will forgive you if you call it an MP3 player. The folks at Microsoft call it that. Here's how to get your tunes onto your MP3 player:

1. **Attach your player to one of your computer's USB ports and turn it on.**

2. **Select WMP's Copy to CD or Device tab.**

3. **If your player is not selected in the Music on Device pane's drop-down list, click the list and select it.**

If you click the list and don't see your device there, a couple of things could be wrong:

✦ WMP may not have noticed that you have attached the player to the computer. To fix this problem, quit and restart WMP.

✦ Windows XP may not support your particular player. To fix this problem, you may need a new bank account.

The rest of the copying process is essentially the same as burning a CD, which I discussed in the preceding section: Build a list of tracks in the Music to Copy pane, click the Copy Music button, and wait for the process to complete.

Some differences in the process reflect differences between a digital audio player and a CD writer:

✦ You can add tracks to a digital audio player that already has tracks stored on it.

✦ You can delete tracks from your digital audio player. To delete a track, click the track and then click the button labeled with an "X" at the top of the Music on Device pane.

Chapter 12: Lights! Action! Windows Movie Maker

In This Chapter

✔ **Recording and editing video**

✔ **Bringing in narration and background sounds**

✔ **Organizing your clips**

Windows Movie Maker brings a full-featured video-editing workshop to your PC. You can use it to create anything from a few seconds of action — say, to dress up an e-mail message — to a full-length documentary about your kid's first birthday party. Get the sound synchronization right, and you could even toss together a decent music video, sell it to Hollywood, and turn into an overnight sensation. Just remember where you got the idea, huh?

Windows Movie Maker isn't going to drive George Lucas out of business any time soon, and it's definitely still an "in progress" application. You don't want to bet your company or your reputation on it. But for casual stitching together of home movies, it works great.

What You Need to Create Movies

Moviemaking requires a lot of hardware. Obviously, you need some type of video camera. But you need a lot of computer, too. Microsoft recommends the following as a minimum:

✦ A 300 MHz Pentium II or equivalent

✦ At least 64MB of RAM

✦ A sound card or equivalent hardware on your computer's main board

✦ At least 2GB of free space on the hard drive

Depending on the type of video camera you have, you may also need a special kind of video card to pull recorded video into your computer. If you're going with a full-fledged digital video camera, with direct feed into your PC, plan on using at least a 600 MHz Pentium, with 128MB of memory, and acres (and acres) of free hard drive space. Video goes through disk space like Orville Redenbacher goes through corn.

Introducing Windows Movie Maker

Windows Movie Maker doesn't look much like other Microsoft applications: It's specially built for the task at hand and doesn't make many bones about that fact. If you start Windows Movie Maker (choose Start⊅All Programs⊅ Accessories⊅Windows Movie Maker), you see the window shown in Figure 12-1.

Take a moment to become familiar with the parts of the window. The central part is divided into three panes. The one on the left shows collections of movie clips. A *collection* is a group of related movie clips with a name. You can use collections to organize your movie clips, much as you use folders to organize other types of files. The middle pane is called the *collection pane*. If one of the collections is selected (if there is a *current collection*), the collection pane shows the clips stored in it. You can play movie clips in the right pane, which is called the *monitor*.

Below the three panes is the *workspace*. As you assemble movie clips into a whole movie, this area displays the state of your work and lets you control it.

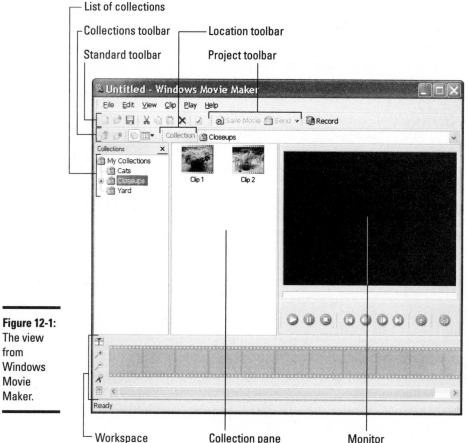

List of collections

Collections toolbar Location toolbar

Standard toolbar Project toolbar

Figure 12-1:
The view
from
Windows
Movie
Maker.

Workspace Collection pane Monitor

Up at the top of the window, you see a menu bar, and below it are a couple of toolbars. The upper toolbar controls the operation of Windows Movie Maker. The small lower toolbar controls the appearance of the left and middle panes. The most useful button in the lower toolbar is the one on the right, which controls the appearance of the collection pane.

Recording and Editing Video

Before you can edit video, you must get it into your computer. If you want to reuse (and slice and dice) existing video, head for the Web: Any MPEG or AVI file can import directly into Windows Movie Maker. If you want to work on your own video, in videospeak, you must *capture* it. That can get complicated, because capturing video may require additional hardware, and the procedure you use depends to some extent on what hardware you use.

Choosing a camera

Video hardware comes in four major types:

✦ **Analog video camera:** This is the traditional type of video camera. Its recordings are essentially of the same quality as regular TV. You capture the video with an analog video capture card — the type of card that you can use to display TV on your computer.

✦ **Digital video camera:** This type of video camera produces the highest-quality results. To capture digital video without loss of quality, you must connect the camera to an *IEEE 1394* card (also called a *FireWire* card) installed in your computer. You can use an analog video capture card instead, but you lose some of the digital video quality.

✦ **Video cassette recorder (VCR):** You can capture video from a VCR by cabling its Video Out connector to your analog video capture card. You can capture either recorded video or live TV.

✦ **Internet camera (Webcam):** Capturing video from an Internet camera requires no additional hardware. Just plug the camera into your computer's USB port, let Windows XP install the appropriate driver, and get to work.

If your Internet camera has a built-in microphone, Windows Movie Maker can capture both image and sound from it. If not, you must have a separate microphone in order to capture sound. Plug the microphone into your computer's microphone input jack.

Recording video

Windows Movie Maker makes recording video a snap:

1. **Plug in the camera.**

If you're capturing video from a recording, connect the camera or VCR to your computer and prepare it to play back the recording. If you're recording from an Internet camera, make sure that the camera is plugged in and pointed at something interesting.

2. Click the Record button in Windows Movie Maker's Project toolbar.

Windows Movie Maker opens the Record dialog box, as shown in Figure 12-2. The controls in the left half of the dialog box determine what Windows Movie Maker will record. The Record drop-down list lets you record video and audio together, video only, or audio only.

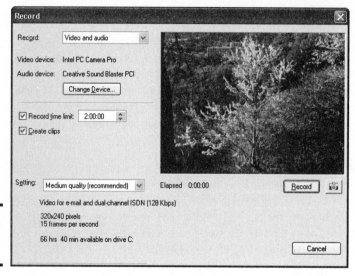

Figure 12-2:
The Record dialog box.

3. For now, select Video and Audio.

Video only and audio only are useful for recording an image and sound track separately.

4. Video Device and Audio Device, listed near the top of the Record dialog box, show the devices from which Windows Movie Maker is set to record. If these are not the right devices, click the Change Device button to change them, and then click OK.

This button opens the Change Device dialog box. The Video and Audio drop-down lists choose the devices through which your computer captures video and audio. The Line list selects the type of source that originates the audio signal. In most cases, Windows Movie Maker sets Line correctly when you select the audio capture device. The Change Device dialog box closes and you return to the Record dialog box (refer to Figure 12-2).

5. To record, click the Record button.

Windows Movie Maker may take a few seconds to get started. When it does, the Record button is relabeled Stop and the elapsed time starts counting. The image being recorded is shown in the Record dialog box's monitor window.

6. If you're recording from a video tape in a camera or VCR, roll the tape as soon as Windows Movie Maker starts recording. Record enough material to include at least a few different shots.

If you're recording from an Internet camera, quickly cover and uncover the lens with your hand a few times. (I'll explain why in a moment. For now, just *do* it!)

7. When you're ready to stop recording, click Stop.

Windows Movie Maker opens a Save dialog box that prompts you to enter a name for the material you've just recorded.

8. Enter a name and click Save.

Windows Movie Maker saves the material and closes both the Save dialog box and the Record dialog box. Look at the left pane in Windows Movie Maker's main window: the pane that lists collections. You see a new collection with the name you entered in the Save dialog box. This collection contains the video you just recorded.

9. Click the collection that you just recorded to display its contents in the collection pane.

You should see several clips named Clip 1, Clip 2, and so on. These contain the individual shots from the recorded video. If you recorded from an Internet camera, they contain the "shots" you created by covering the lens with your hand.

How does Windows Movie Maker know where one shot ends and another begins? It looks for a complete change in the image between two consecutive frames of the recording. Whenever it observes that, it closes the video clip that it was recording and starts a new one. This separates your recording into smaller, logically divided segments.

Look back at the Record dialog box in Figure 12-2. See the check box labeled Create Clips? That check box controls the behavior you just saw. If you clear that check box, Windows Movie Maker stores an entire recording in one clip.

Assembling a movie

A *project* is a file that contains your work on a movie. In effect, a project *is* a movie, either completed or in development. A *clip* is a piece of a movie. In the preceding section, I showed you how to create clips with a camera or VCR. When the clips are ready, you assemble the clips to create a project. Here's how to put together a project, er, a movie:

1. Choose File⇨New⇨Project.

This menu selection creates a new project, which means that it starts a new movie.

2. Choose a clip from one of your collections and drag it to the workspace at the bottom of the window.

An image of the clip appears at the beginning of the workspace.

3. Drag one or two more clips to the unoccupied part of the workspace.

An image of each one appears in the workspace. The workspace now looks like the one shown in Figure 12-3.

You can insert a clip between two existing clips. Just drag it into the workspace at the boundary between the two clips.

Figure 12-3:
The
workspace
with some
clips.

4. **When a clip is in the workspace, you can move it to a different position. Click the clip, drag it to the place where you want to insert it, and release.**

When you need to move a clip a long way, dragging can be clumsy and error-prone; cutting and pasting is more convenient. To cut and paste, right-click the clip that you want to move and choose the Cut command. Then right-click the clip *before which* you want to place this clip, and click the Paste command.

To delete a clip from the workspace, right-click the clip and choose the Delete command.

5. **To save your project, choose File⇨Save.**

The first time you save a project, Windows Movie Maker opens a Save dialog box to let you give the project a name. Congratulations. You're well on your way to becoming a film legend.

Playing a clip or a movie

Have you wondered how you're supposed to tell which clip is which from the tiny images in the collection pane? It's actually easy because you can see what's in any clip by playing it in the monitor.

To play a clip, select it either in the collection pane or in the workspace. Then click the Play button under the monitor. When you've seen enough, click the Pause button to stop the playback. (See Figure 12-4.)

As you play a clip, the pointer on the *seek bar* moves across the bar to show how far the monitor has progressed through the clip. The number near the monitor's lower-right corner shows the elapsed play time to the nearest 0.01 second.

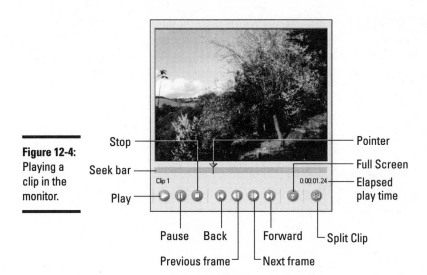

Figure 12-4:
Playing a
clip in the
monitor.

The other buttons below the monitor are as follows:

✦ **Stop:** Stops playing the clip and deselects the clip.

✦ **Back:** Selects the preceding clip.

✦ **Previous Frame:** Positions the monitor to the previous frame (use after Pause).

✦ **Next Frame:** Positions the monitor to the next frame (use after Pause).

✦ **Forward:** Selects the following clip.

✦ **Full Screen:** Expands the monitor to fill the whole screen. The seek bar and control buttons are not visible. While in full screen, you can control the monitor with these keys (they work in the normal display mode, too):

  • **Play or Pause:** Space bar

  • **Stop:** Period key

  • **Back:** Ctrl+Alt+Left Arrow

  • **Previous Frame:** Alt+Left Arrow

  • **Next Frame:** Alt+Right Arrow

  • **Forward:** Ctrl+Alt+Right Arrow

  • **Leave Full Screen Mode:** Esc

  • **Split Clip:** Ctrl+Shift+S

✦ **Split Clip:** Splits a clip in two (see "Splitting and combining clips").

You can also play your entire movie on the monitor. Choose Play⇨Play Entire Storyboard/Timeline.

Viewing storyboard and timeline

The storyboard and the timeline are two different ways of viewing a movie. The *storyboard* view represents each clip in the movie with a thumbnail image, as shown in Figure 12-5. Storyboard view is useful for assembling and rearranging clips. The *timeline* view represents each clip with a thumbnail image set in a space whose width is proportional to the clip's length, as shown in Figure 12-6. A timeline above the thumbnails helps you judge the playing time of each clip. Timeline view is useful for trimming the beginnings and ends of clips.

Figure 12-5:
The storyboard view of the workspace.

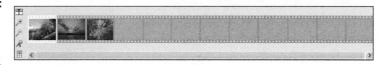

Figure 12-6:
The timeline view of the workspace.

To switch between the storyboard and timeline views, click the topmost icon in the group of five icons to the left of the workspace.

Trimming a clip

Windows Movie Maker lets you *trim* individual clips — hack away pieces at the beginning or end of the clip — to make it shorter. You can trim a clip in either storyboard or timeline view, but in most cases you want to do it in timeline view because the workspace shows what you're doing. To trim either end of a clip, follow these steps:

1. **Select the clip in the workspace.**

The first frame of the clip appears in the monitor.

2. **Move the monitor's seek bar to the point where you want to trim the clip. You can choose from several ways to do this:**

- Click the Play button, and then click the Pause button when the clip reaches the right point.

- Drag the seek bar's pointer to the right position. The monitor displays the frame at the spot in the clip where you release the pointer.

- Click the Previous Frame and Next Frame buttons to move the pointer (and the monitor) backward and forward one frame at a time.

3. **When the seek bar's pointer is correctly positioned, choose Clip⇨Set Start Trim Point to trim the start of the clip to that point. Choose Clip⇨Set End Trim Point to trim the end of the clip to that point.**

When you trim a clip, the remaining part expands to fill the entire seek bar. If the workspace is in timeline view, the clip contracts in the timeline so that only the trimmed part is shown.

4. **If you trim too much from a clip, choose the Clip menu's Clear Trim Points command to display the entire clip again and start over.**

If you drag a clip from the collection pane to the workspace and trim it, and then you drag the same clip into the workspace again, the second copy is *not* trimmed. You can trim it differently if you want to.

Try another way to trim a clip: In timeline view, drag the clip's *trim handles* to the points where you want to trim. Figure 12-7 shows the trim handles.

Left trim handle   Right trim handle

Figure 12-7:
A clip in timeline view, with trim handles.

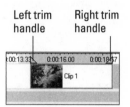

The monitor display and the seek bar's pointer track each trim handle as you drag it. Hold the mouse button down until you're sure you have the handle in the right spot.

If you trim a clip too far, choose Clip➪Clear Trim Points. This moves the trim points back to the beginning and end of the clip, and you can start over.

The timeline view's trim handles give you a more precise remedy. Drag either trim handle outward (away from the clip) to move the corresponding trim point back toward the start or end of the clip. You can drag a handle as far as it will go, or just a little way.

When you undo trimming by dragging a trim handle, the clip is left *overlapping* the adjacent clip. If you leave the clips in this state, the overlapping parts of the clips are superimposed when you play the movie. (See "Fading," coming up next.) To remove the overlap, drag the right overlapping clip to the right. Any clips to the right of that one move along with it.

To see more detail in the timeline view, click the *zoom in* icon. To see a larger span of time in less detail, click *zoom out*.

Fading

A *fade* is a transition where one clip fades out while the next one fades in. To create a fade, the workspace must be in timeline view. Select the second clip (the one that will fade in) and drag it to the left so that it partially overlaps the first clip (which will fade out). The amount of overlap determines the length of the fade.

To plan a fade, study the two clips and use the monitor's time display to find the points where you want the fade to start and end. After you trim the two clips appropriately, use the workspace's timeline to judge the proper amount of overlap.

Splitting and combining clips

You can split or combine clips in two ways: In the workspace and in the collection pane. When you split or combine clips in the workspace, the effect is similar to trimming a clip: Only that use of the clip is affected. When you split or combine clips in the collection pane, you actually split or combine the files that store the clips. This affects all projects that use the clips, now or in the future.

Splitting a clip in the workspace is useful if you want to insert a still picture or another clip in the middle of a clip. Combining clips in the workspace is not as common as splitting a clip, but it is possible if you want to do it.

Splitting/combining clips in the workspace

To split a clip in the workspace, follow these steps:

1. **Click the clip you want to split.**

2. **Set the monitor's seek bar pointer to the position where you want the split to occur.**

3. **Click the monitor's Split button.**

   The first part of the clip retains the clip's name. The second part becomes a new clip with same name followed by a number in parentheses. For example, if you split a clip named *Blowing out the candles,* the first part retains that name, and the second part becomes a new clip named *Blowing out the candles (1).*

These clip names have meaning only in the workspace; the clip in the collection is not affected.

To combine two or more consecutive clips in the workspace, hold down the Shift key and click the first and last of the clips. Then right-click any of the selected clips and click the Combine command.

Splitting/combining clips in the collection pane

Splitting and combining clips in the collection pane is useful for organizing your clips. For example, you may need to split a clip because Windows Movie Maker failed to start a new clip between shots when recording. You may need to combine clips because Windows Movie Maker started a new clip where a new shot did not begin. To split a clip in the collection pane, select the clip in that pane. Move the seek bar's pointer to the split point that you want, and click the monitor's Split button. To combine clips in the collection pane, select the clips in the collection pane, right-click, and select the Combine command.

You can combine clips only if they were recorded consecutively or were previously split from a single clip.

Finishing the movie

After you edit a movie to your satisfaction, you probably want to show it to other people. Windows Movie Maker stores the movie as a project that can be watched only in Windows Movie Maker. If you want your friends to be able to view it, either they have to run Windows Movie Maker, or you have to convert the movie into a form that other folks can use. The .WMV extension (for *Windows Media Video*) works well with the Windows Media Player, and Windows Movie Maker uses WMV format as its "final" recording format of choice.

To let others view your movie, follow these steps:

1. **Choose File⇨Save Movie.**

Windows Movie Maker opens the Save Movie dialog box shown in Figure 12-8.

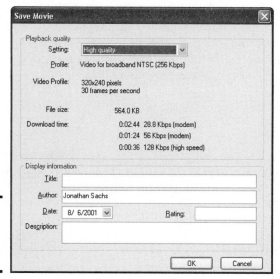

Figure 12-8:
The Save Movie dialog box.

2. **Choose the quality setting most appropriate for this movie.**

Higher quality makes the movie file larger, which may be a problem if you plan to write the movie to a CD, send it in e-mail, or put it on a Web site.

Profile describes the uses appropriate for each quality setting. File Size shows how much space your movie will occupy if saved with the selected quality setting.

3. **Fill in the display information to describe your movie.**

When Windows Media Player lists your movie in its Media Library, it displays the information you enter here.

4. **Click OK.**

Windows Movie Maker opens a Save dialog box to let you choose a name and location for the movie file.

By default, a movie has the name of its project file (with the file extension .WMV) and is saved in the My Videos folder. You can name it whatever you want and save it wherever you want.

I recommend saving movies to some folder other than My Videos. Otherwise, they are hard to distinguish from your clips, which are also stored in the My Videos folder and also use the file extension .WMV.

5. Click Save.

Windows Movie Maker displays a progress bar while it saves the movie to the file. After the file is saved, Windows Movie Maker opens a dialog box that asks whether you want to watch the movie now.

6. If you click Yes, Windows Media Player opens and plays the movie.

Anyone running Windows can view the movie later by double-clicking on the file. This starts Windows Media Player and plays the movie.

To add a movie file to Windows Media Player's Media Library, choose File⇨Add to Media Library⇨Add File. Windows Media Player opens a file choosing dialog box. Select the movie file that you want to add to the Media Library and click the Open button. Now the movie appears in the Media Library's Video folder under both All Clips and Author (provided you filled in the author's name when you created the movie file).

Using Sound Clips

You can record narration (or any other type of sound clip) for use in your movies. Windows Movie Maker stores the sound clip on your hard drive as a .WAV file and inserts it in the current collection. When it is in a collection, you can add it to the workspace much as you add a video clip or a still picture.

Recording a sound clip

Choose from two techniques for recording a sound clip. One is used specifically for narration, which has to be synchronized with the movie. The other is more convenient for recording background sound and other types of material where synchronization isn't as crucial. To record a narration, follow these steps:

1. Open the project in which you want to use the recording and select the collection to which you want to add it.

2. When you're ready to record, choose File⇨Record Narration.

Windows Movie Maker opens the Record Narration Track dialog box, as shown in Figure 12-9.

3. Device and Line display the device and line through which Windows Movie Maker will record. If you need to change them, click the Change button. Use the Record Level slider to set the recording level.

If the video clips have a sound track of their own and you don't want to be distracted by it, select the Mute Video Soundtrack check box.

Figure 12-9:
The Record
Narration
Track dialog
box.

4. **Click the Record button to start recording.**

   Windows Movie Maker plays the movie as you record so that you can synchronize your narration with it.

5. **When you're done, click the Stop button (which replaces the Record button while you're recording).**

   Windows Movie Maker opens a Save dialog box. Choose a filename and location for the recording and click the Save button. Windows Movie Maker saves the file and adds it to the current collection. After Windows Movie Maker saves the file, it returns to the Record dialog box.

6. **You can make another recording or click Cancel to close the dialog box.**

You can't synchronize narration with a single clip selected in the workspace. To get the same effect, create a separate project that contains the clip, and synchronize the narration to it.

Material other than narration usually doesn't have to be recorded to synchronize with the movie. Such material can be recorded just like video:

1. **Click the toolbar's Record button to open the Record dialog box.**

2. **Use the Record drop-down list to select Audio Only.**

3. **Click the Change Device button if necessary to select the input device and line for your computer's audio input.**

   Normally, the device should be your sound card, and the line should be Mic Volume for a microphone; Line In for a radio, tape deck, or other external device; or CD Audio for your computer's CD-ROM drive.

4. **Proceed as you would to record video and audio.**

   Windows saves your sound clip in a Windows Media Audio (.WMA) file.

Adding a sound clip to a movie

To add a sound clip to a movie, drag the sound clip from the current collection to the appropriate point in the workspace. This is essentially the same operation as adding a video clip, but note the following differences:

✦ Sound clips are visible only in timeline view and can be added or managed only in timeline view.

✦ Sound clips appear below video clips, as shown in Figure 12-10.

✦ You can't leave spaces between video clips in the timeline, but you can leave spaces between sound clips. This lets you set each sound clip's exact position relative to the movie's video clips.

Figure 12-10:
Sound clips are shown below video clips in the workspace.

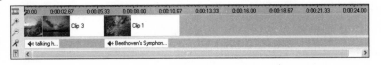

You can play a sound clip by selecting it and clicking the monitor's Play button, just as you would play a video clip. You also can trim a sound clip the same way you would trim a video clip. Click the sound clip, and then use the monitor or the trim handles in the workspace's timeline.

Organizing Your Clips

When you make movies, you tend to accumulate a lot of clips. A single project may use dozens or even hundreds of them. It's important to organize your clips so that you can find them easily. Whenever you record a clip, add descriptive information to it. Here's how to attach descriptive information to a clip:

1. **In Windows Movie Maker, right-click the clip and click the Properties command.**

Windows Movie Maker opens the Properties dialog box shown in Figure 12-11.

Figure 12-11:
A clip's Properties dialog box.

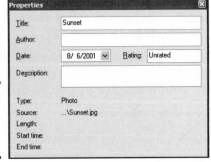

2. **Replace the clip's default title with something descriptive and fill in the other fields as appropriate.**

3. **When you're done, close the Properties dialog box by clicking its Close button or pressing the Esc key. (This dialog box has no OK button.)**

The collections that Windows Movie Maker creates when you record clips are rarely useful for organizing them. Create additional collections to support the type of organization that suits your needs, and then move your clips into them. After you have emptied a collection that Windows Movie Maker created for you, you may delete it.

To create a new top-level collection, follow these steps:

1. **Click the My Collections icon in Windows Movie Maker's collection list.**

2. **Choose File⇨New⇨Collection.**

   This creates a new collection named New Collection.

3. **Type an appropriate name to replace New Collection and press the Enter key.**

Windows Movie Maker lets you put collections inside other collections, just as the Windows file system lets you put folders inside other folders. To put collection X inside collection Y, drag the icon for X on top of the icon for Y. To create a new collection inside collection Z, select collection Z, and then create the new collection.

Although Windows Movie Maker lets you put clips and collections in other collections, that type of organization is not represented on your hard drive by files and folders in other folders. All of the clip files created by Windows Movie Maker go in the My Videos or My Audios folder; when you import clips, you may put them anywhere. Collections are represented not by folders, but by data in a special collections file that Windows Movie Maker maintains.

If the collections file is damaged, Windows Movie Maker "loses" some or all of your collections and clips. The clips may be right where they always were, but Windows Movie Maker can't find them. I had a lot of problems working with the collections backup feature and strongly suggest that you not rely on it for anything important. Your clips are safe — they're sitting in files that you can see and copy and store wherever you like. Your projects are safe, too. But, until Microsoft gets its act together, don't bet the farm on your collections. They may disappear on you one day.

Chapter 13: Working with Digital Pictures

*W*indows XP stands light years ahead of Microsoft's earlier operating systems in its ability to handle images. Most of its capabilities aren't really new, but Windows XP makes many things easy that used to require a lot of technical knowledge and a lot of work.

In this chapter, you discover everything you need to know to choose a camera, hook it up with your PC, and move pictures from the camera to the PC, where you can store, edit, and print them, with just a couple of clicks.

Choosing a Camera

Before you can have fun with your images, of course, you need to get them into your computer. The following are several ways to do that:

✦ You can use a *conventional camera* to record images on film and then request the film processor to return the images to you on computer media. When I talk about conventional cameras in this book, I'm talking about the kind that produce images on regular, ol' everyday film. Silver halide.

✦ You can use a *digital camera* like the one shown in Figure 13-1 to record images in electronic memory and then transfer them into your computer. When I talk about digital cameras in this book, I mean a camera that produces images as files, one image at a time, and stores the files inside the camera.

✦ You can use an *Internet camera* (a "Webcam") to feed live images directly into your computer and capture them as either still frames or movie clips. When I talk about Internet cameras here, I'm talking about the ones that have to be tethered to a computer. They have no capability to store images.

✦ You can use an analog or digital *video camera* (a "camcorder") to record movie clips on tape and then feed them into your computer from the camera or from a playback device. When I talk about video cameras in this book, I'm talking about the kind that internally store moving images.

Figure 13-1: The 5.24 megapixel DSC-F707 Cybershot® from Sony. Photo courtesy of Sony Electronics, Inc.

Strictly speaking, Internet cameras are digital cameras. So are many video cameras. Then again, strictly speaking, Dummies are smart. But I digress.

Understanding digital cameras

You use a digital camera just like a conventional one, but it records images in electronic memory, not on film. Instead of sending a roll of film to be processed and printed, you simply copy the images into your computer. Then you can erase the camera's memory and use it again.

Digital cameras have sorted themselves roughly into four categories:

✦ **Point-and-shoot cameras:** The simplest and least expensive type. Most point-and-shoot cameras have inexpensive lenses, often made of plastic, and often with no means of adjusting the focus. They're good for casual photography and for taking pictures to use on your personal Web site.

✦ **Advanced viewfinder cameras:** More capable than point-and-shoots, and more expensive. Their design is essentially the same, but they have more features and use higher quality parts. For example, advanced viewfinder cameras have more sophisticated all-glass lenses and generally focus the lens automatically.

✦ **Zoom-lens reflex (ZLR) cameras:** These cameras have a zoom lens that is permanently attached. The viewfinder's image is formed by the same lens that takes the picture, rather than by a separate optical system. Because these cameras are designed for advanced amateur photographers and professionals, they tend to offer better quality and more features than advanced viewfinder cameras.

✦ **Single-lens reflex (SLR) cameras:** The most capable kind. And the most expensive. These cameras work like the ZLR cameras, but they feature interchangeable lenses. Many of them are based on conventional SLR cameras, adapted to use digital imaging instead of film.

This brief summary should give you a good idea of which type of camera is most appropriate for you, but it doesn't begin to cover the variety of features that camera makers have developed. Becoming a fully informed buyer in this market takes weeks of research.

TIP

Unless you enjoy learning obscure technical details, seek advice from a well-informed friend or a retailer whom you trust.

Resolution

A digital camera forms its image on a sensor that contains a square grid of tiny light-sensing areas called *pixels. Resolution* refers to the number of pixels the sensor has. The more pixels, the more detail the camera can record. The more detail, the larger a print you can make without the individual pixels becoming noticeable.

Here's a good rule to remember: A sensor with about 1 million pixels is good for a 5" x 7" print. At 2 million pixels, you can make a good 8" x 10" print. At 3 million pixels, you can make an 11" x 14" print.

Having more resolution than you need gives you leeway to crop out the unimportant parts of an image and still get a good quality print. Those extra pixels cost money, of course.

Zoom lens

A *zoom lens* lets you vary the angle of view that your camera takes in by increasing or decreasing the lens's magnification. Most advanced viewfinder cameras have this feature, as do all ZLRs and SLRs. The better ones cover a wider range. Most point-and-shoot cameras do not have a zoom lens.

The zoom lens feature is also known as *optical zoom.* Many cameras offer *digital zoom,* which simply enlarges an image by making each pixel bigger. Digital zoom isn't very useful. You can get the same result by enlarging the final image.

Focusing

Many point-and-shoot cameras have a lens with one or a few fixed focus settings that give reasonably good results over a range of distances. If you're looking at a camera with one setting for close-ups and another for general shots, you are dealing with a fixed-focus camera.

Better cameras adjust the focus automatically — they *auto-focus* — to give the sharpest result at any distance. Auto-focusing cameras generally can be held closer to the subject than fixed-focus ones, sometimes down to a few inches, which can be useful if you want to photograph small objects like flowers or coins.

As an added feature, some advanced cameras let you deal with special photo situations — where the auto-focus just doesn't work very well — by adjusting the focus manually. Typically, auto-focus has problems when the subject of the shot isn't at the middle of the picture; when the subject is very bright, very dark, or low-contrast; when you're taking the picture through glass or water; or when you want to emphasize a small part of a picture by giving it the sharpest focus — a small flower standing quite some distance in front of a face, for example.

Exposure control and flash

All digital cameras adjust the exposure automatically to suit different light levels. The better ones have more sophisticated circuits that produce good results under a wider range of conditions. Better cameras also give you some control over exposure, either by taking a picture that's lighter or darker than what the camera thinks is ideal, or by allowing you to set the exposure controls (the aperture and shutter speed, for those technically inclined) yourself.

Many cameras have a built-in electronic flash that fires automatically when needed. Better cameras have more powerful and flexible flashes, and offer you various types of control. You may be able to turn off the built-in flash and attach a separate electronic flash of your choice, for example.

Digital cameras are notorious for overly powerful or utterly wimpy flash systems — and far too frequently the same flash is too powerful under one set of lighting conditions and doesn't work worth squat under slightly different conditions. If you're willing to schlep around a standalone flash unit (called an *external flash*), look for a camera that has a *synchro-flash terminal* — a place to plug in and control a standalone flash. Using an external flash with simple techniques like bouncing (aiming the flash at a white ceiling or wall) can make a world of difference in the quality of your pictures, and in most cases the camera does all the work.

Image storage and transfer

Really inexpensive cameras store images in built-in memory. When the memory is full, you must transfer the images to your computer to make room for more. If you're at the Grand Canyon and your computer is at home, this can be, uh, awkward.

Better cameras use removable memory media, often shaped like little cards. When one memory card fills up, you just pull it out and insert a new one. Different cameras use different types of memory cards; all of them work about equally well.

Most recent cameras have a USB interface for transferring images to your computer. USB is easy and fast, but the whole setup can be clumsy, especially if you want to plug your camera into the wall outlet to avoid draining the batteries during file transfers.

If you buy a camera that uses memory cards, spend an extra $40 or so for a card reader that plugs into your computer's USB port. You can then slide the camera's memory card into the reader and treat it like any other disk drive. Or you can plug the camera's memory card into the reader, then plug the reader into a USB port or PCMCIA slot, and Windows XP will identify it immediately.

Plugging your camera's memory card into a USB or PCMCIA reader virtually eliminates compatibility problems (see the next section). More than that, you don't have to worry about the dog tripping over the camera's power cord or USB cable, knocking the camera off your desk. I know. My Beagle broke my Nikon Coolpix that way, and it cost hundreds of dollars to get it fixed. Blecch!

Compatibility

Windows XP provides direct support for many digital cameras, but not for all of them. If you happen to own a camera that Windows XP doesn't support, it's not a big deal; you may have to use the application provided with the camera to move pictures onto your PC, instead of the Scanner and Camera Wizard built in to Windows XP itself. If you're buying a new camera, though, direct support in Windows XP is a feature you should consider.

Look and feel

Yeah, cameras have look and feel, just like computer applications do. And it's important. The best camera in the world won't do you much good if you can't use it easily. If you're always pushing controls the wrong way, or you can't quite find a comfortable way to hold the camera when you're taking a shot, that camera isn't for you.

It's always wise to try out a camera in a quiet, unpressured environment before you buy it. And in case you miss something important, buy from a dealer who will let you exchange your purchase if you change your mind. For these reasons, buying from a reputable local dealer can be a good move, even if a discounter on the Web offers you a better price.

Using conventional cameras

If you don't want to buy a digital camera, you can take pictures with a conventional film camera and have the photofinisher digitize them. The photofinisher may return the digitized images to you on a CD-ROM or may post them on a secure Web site from which you can download them.

If you're a casual picture taker, this approach lets you get your pictures online without buying a new camera. If you're an advanced user, it may be attractive because the best film cameras still produce better results than the best digital cameras. By having the photofinisher do the digitizing, you get the best of both worlds: digital images for their ease-of-use, and negatives/positives for the highest quality results.

On the other hand, digitizing with a photofinisher is relatively slow, because you have to wait for the film to be processed. It is expensive, because you have to pay for film, processing, and digitizing. And you may have to change photofinishers to get the service.

Plugging Internet cameras

An Internet camera (also called a *Web camera* or *Webcam*) is like a little video camera designed to work only while attached to a computer. All Internet cameras nowadays come with USB interfaces.

Some people use Internet cameras to publish a continuous live video feed through a Web site. Popular feeds include pictures of fish in a tank, waves on a shore, burglars breaking into houses, and . . . uh, let's just leave it at that. Other popular uses are video conferencing and recording still pictures or short movie clips to include in e-mail.

Internet cameras are generally less expensive than digital picture-taking cameras, but are also more limited because they only work when plugged into an operating computer. Their resolution is low: typically 320 x 240 pixels (about 77,000 pixels, compared to 1 million pixels for a typical point-and-shoot camera). The better ones can go up to 640 x 480 pixels (about 300,000 pixels). The lens, image quality, and color accuracy are adequate for the camera's intended purpose, but may be poorer than a point-and-shoot camera.

If you want to get images into your computer quickly and easily, and you don't need high quality, an Internet camera may be just the thing for you. They're pretty darn cheap, to boot.

Consult the Windows XP hardware compatibility list before you buy an Internet camera. Windows XP may be unable to work with a camera that is not on the list. See the section "Compatibility" earlier in this chapter, for details.

If you have a video camera, you can transfer its recordings onto your computer. Depending on the type of camera you have, you may need additional hardware to connect the camera.

A video camera is an ideal tool for recording video that you will edit with Windows Movie Maker. It is less suitable for capturing still images. A video camera's resolution is much less than that of a comparable digital camera.

Moving Images to Your Computer

How you transfer images to your computer depends on the type of camera you're using. If you're using a conventional camera and your images were scanned by the photofinisher, transferring images is easy: Simply put the CD-ROM in a handy CD drive and copy the files, or go to the photofinisher's Web site and follow its directions. Rocket science.

If you're using a video camera, the procedure depends on the type of camera and interface you use. There are so many different permutations and combinations, I won't try to cover them all here. If you're looking for answers, start with the camera manufacturer's Web site. See Table 13-1.

Table 13-1	Major Camera Manufacturers' Web Sites
Manufacturer	*U.S. Web Site*
Canon	www.canon.com
Intel	www.intel.com
Kodak	www.kodak.com
Logitech	www.Logitech.com
Minolta	www.minolta.com
Nikon	www.nikon.com
Olympus	www.olympus.com
Panasonic	www.panasonic.com
Philips	www.Philips.com
Sony	www.sony.com

You can use any one of three procedures to bring images from digital cameras and Internet cameras into your PC:

✦ With Internet cameras and digital cameras supported by Windows XP, the Windows XP Scanner and Camera Wizard is the simplest way.

✦ With any digital camera, you can use the file transfer application provided with that camera.

✦ With any digital camera that uses memory cards, you can transfer images by putting the card — most likely a SmartMedia or CompactFlash card — in a memory card reader.

Use the Scanner and Camera Wizard to transfer images stored in the memory of a digital camera to your PC or to capture still images from an Internet camera:

1. **Plug the camera into the appropriate port on your computer.**

If it's a digital camera, turn it on. You may have to move the camera's controls to some particular setting; consult the camera's instructions for transferring images.

2. **The Windows Scanner and Camera Wizard may start automatically at this point. If it doesn't, choose Start⇨My Pictures to display the contents of the My Pictures folder in Windows Explorer.**

When you start Windows Explorer this particular way, it displays some special *task lists* in its left pane, as shown in Figure 13-2.

Figure 13-2:
The
Windows
Explorer
with task
lists.

3. **From the Picture Tasks list, choose Get Pictures from Camera or Scanner.**

This opens the Select Device dialog box. Select the icon that represents your camera, and then click OK. The wizard displays a welcome box.

4. **Click Next to display the dialog box shown in Figure 13-3.**

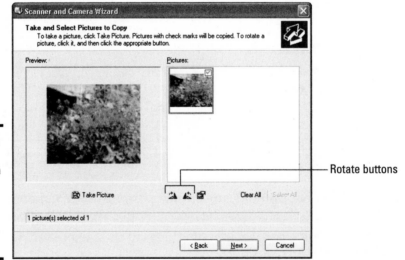

Figure 13-3:
Scanner
and Camera
Wizard,
Take and
Select
Pictures to
Copy.

If you're connected to an Internet camera, the Preview panel shows the live image captured by the camera. Each time you click the Take Picture button, the wizard captures a still image. The images appear in the Pictures panel.

If you're connected to a digital camera, the process is very similar, but the Pictures panel shows the pictures stored in the camera's memory.

If any of the pictures are not right-side up, you can rotate them. Click a picture to select it, and then click one of the "rotate" buttons under the Pictures pane to rotate the picture a quarter turn right, a quarter turn left, or a half turn.

Notice the small check box above each picture. Select the check boxes for the pictures that you want to save and/or clear them for the pictures you don't want to save. You can use the Clear All and Save All buttons for convenience.

5. **Click Next.**

The wizard displays the next dialog box.

6. **In the Type a Name field, enter the name you want to give the first picture you're saving.**

If you're saving several pictures, the wizard gives each one a unique name. For example, if the name you enter is "head shots" and you're saving three pictures, the wizard names the pictures "head shots," "head shots 001," and "head shots 002."

The wizard automatically stores the pictures in the My Pictures folder, in a subfolder with the name you entered. If you entered "head shots," for example, it stores the pictures in My Pictures\head shots. If you want a different folder, you can choose one with the Browse button or the Choose a Place drop-down list.

Notice the Delete Pictures from My Device after Copying Them check box. If you're using a digital camera, selecting this check box deletes the pictures from the camera's memory. It deletes only the pictures that it transferred — that is, the ones you selected in the wizard's previous box.

If you're using an Internet camera, the camera has no memory, but the wizard gets the same result by keeping copies of the pictures itself. If you don't select the check box, the next time you use the wizard, the pictures you saved will still be in the Pictures pane. If you do select the check box, the next time you use the wizard, the pictures you saved will not be there.

7. **Click Next.**

The wizard copies the pictures to the folder you chose and displays the next dialog box.

8. **Click the option button for the operation you want to perform next. Then click Next.**

The wizard displays a "farewell" screen.

If you don't want to publish pictures or order prints now, you can still do those things at a later time.

9. **Click Finish.**

The wizard closes itself and opens a Windows Explorer window showing the folder in which you just saved your pictures.

If Windows XP doesn't recognize your camera, the least-hassle alternative, by far, is a memory card reader. These cheap little devices plug into your computer's PCMCIA card slot or USB port. Simply stick your camera's memory card (probably a SmartCard or a Compact Flash card) into the card reader, and Windows XP thinks you have a new hard drive. Files on the camera's memory card are treated just like any picture files in Windows.

You may also want to try the software that shipped with the camera to transfer images from the camera to your PC. Most digital cameras come with such an application. Install the application and follow its instructions. Good luck.

If Windows XP *does* support your camera directly, you may still want to take a look at the camera's file-transfer application anyway. Many of these applications have additional functions that Windows XP does not provide, such as remotely setting some of the camera's controls.

Printing Pictures

Windows XP provides several ways to print photos and other images. If you have a photo-quality printer, you can use Windows XP's Photo Printing Wizard to print pictures from the My Pictures folder.

Printing with the wizard

To use the Photo Printing Wizard:

1. **Choose Start⇨My Pictures.**

This opens a copy of Windows Explorer with the My Pictures folder in the right pane and task list commands in the left pane.

2. **Select the picture you want to print, and then click the wizard's Print This Picture command.**

This starts the Photo Printing Wizard. The wizard displays a "welcome" page. Ho hum.

3. **Click Next.**

The wizard displays thumbnails of the pictures in the folder, as shown in Figure 13-4. Above each picture is a check box. The picture you selected has its check box checked, indicating that this picture will be printed. You can select additional pictures to make the wizard print more than one at a time.

Figure 13-4:
Photo
Printing
Wizard,
Picture
Selection.

4. Click Next.

The wizard displays a panel of printing options. This panel lets you select the printer to use (if you have more than one printer). The Printing Preferences button opens a dialog box that lets you set options such as the type of paper you're printing on, the level of print quality you want, and whether to print in black-and-white or color. The options displayed depend on the type of printer you have.

5. Click Next.

The wizard displays a page that lets you select a layout and set the number of times to print each picture (see Figure 13-5).

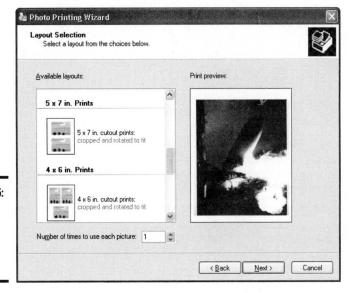

Figure 13-5:
Photo
Printing
Wizard,
Layout
Selection.

You can choose among a full-page layout (one print per page) and several options that put two or more smaller pictures on a page. The latter options are useful if you selected several images or told the wizard to print a picture more than once.

6. Click Next.

The wizard displays a panel with a progress bar while it prints and then displays a panel that says it is finished.

7. Click Finish to close the wizard.

The Windows Explorer View menu lets you select several different views of your pictures. The Thumbnails view and the Filmstrip view are particularly useful. Try both to see which you prefer.

The plain old Details view is not quite so plain in the My Pictures folder. It displays some additional information that you may find useful: the date each picture was taken, if recorded, and the dimensions of the picture in pixels.

When your pictures are in the My Pictures folder, you can organize them any way you want. For example, you can put them in one folder for "Vacations," one for "The Kids," one for "Blackmail" (just kidding), and so forth. You can create two or more levels of folders if you want. As long as you keep your folders inside the My Pictures folder, they inherit the My Pictures folder's task lists, and they show the same additional information in the Details view.

Advanced printing software

The Photo Printing Wizard is okay for making an unmodified print of an entire picture. But suppose you want to print just part of a family portrait to omit the rude gesture one of your kids was making? Or suppose the light in your back yard made Aunt Gertrude's face look a little green, and you want to make the color balance more flattering? Want to chop your ex's head off? It's easier than you think.

The wizard can't do those things, but many commercial photo printing programs can. If you're interested in capabilities like these, look into programs like Adobe Photoshop (the professional's choice), Microsoft Picture-It, PaintShop Pro, MGI Software's PhotoSuite, and Ulead PhotoImpact. See Table 13-2 for some URL listings.

Table 13-2	Commercial Photo Printing Programs
Program	*URL*
Photoshop	`www.adobe.com/products/photoshop/main.html`
Picture-It	`http://pictureitproducts.msn.com/default.asp`
PaintShop Pro	`www.jasc.com`
PhotoSuite	`www.photosuite.com`
Ulead PhotoImpact	`www.ulead.com/pi/runme.htm`

Troubleshooting

Here are some suggestions to try if you have a problem with one of the procedures described in this chapter:

✦ *I plugged my camera into the computer, but the Scanner and Camera Wizard doesn't believe it's there.*

Be sure the cable is secure at both ends, the camera is turned on, and its batteries are charged.

If your camera's controls must be set a certain way to permit a transfer, be sure they are set.

If you haven't used this camera with Windows XP before, be sure it's on the Windows XP hardware compatibility list. If it isn't, install and use the file transfer application provided with the camera.

✦ *I displayed the My Pictures folder in Windows Explorer, but the left pane doesn't show the Picture Tasks list — just the usual map of my folders.*

Exit Windows Explorer and start it again directly from the Start menu. (Choose Start⇨My Pictures.) This is the easiest way to make it display the Picture Tasks list.

✦ *My pictures look pretty good on the screen, but when I print them they look awful.*

The quality of many color inkjet printers leaves a lot to be desired, but here are some things you can do that may help:

- Use the highest quality settings available: Superior will produce a much better image than Normal.

- Use an appropriate paper. Paper formulated for printing photos on inkjet printers is best. Any coated (glossy) paper is likely to work better than ordinary printer paper. Photo-quality paper produces the best results of all.

- Be sure you have a photo printer. Many older color inkjet printers are designed for printing things like business charts, with large areas of solid color. They can't handle the subtle gradations of a photograph very well.

✦ *This is fascinating, and I want more information about one of the topics you discussed.*

See the answer to the next question.

✦ *I'm totally confused!*

Lots of information about digital photography is available on the Internet.

One good place to start looking is www.zdnet.com. Enter a topic like "digital camera" in the Search dialog box and see what the site comes up with. For easy-to-read background information, look for the "Quick Start guides."

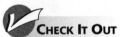

CHECK IT OUT

Burning Pictures on a CD

Do you have about a hundred gajillion pictures on your PC eating up hard drive space? Yeah. I thought so. If you have a CD-R, CD-RW, DVD-R or DVD-RW drive, burning those pictures onto a CD, where they'll last for decades (maybe even centuries), is very easy. A CD will certainly last longer than your hard drive. Burning pictures couldn't be simpler:

1. **Make sure that your CD-R, CD-RW, DVD-R, or DVD-RW drive is installed and working.**

2. **Start Windows Explorer. (Just click, say, Start⇨My Pictures or Start⇨My Computer.)**

3. **Navigate to the pictures you want to burn to CD.**

If you're in a picture or photo album folder, Copy to CD appears on the Picture Tasks list.

4. **Select the picture(s) you want to burn; click Copy to CD on the Picture Tasks list. If Copy To CD doesn't appear on the list, right-click one of the selected files (or folders) and choose Send To⇨CD Drive.**

A small CD icon appears in the Notification Area, next to the clock.

5. **Keep moving around Windows, gathering pictures that you want to burn.**

In spite of what the Picture Task list and right-click menu say, Windows actually copies the files you select to a staging area — a place on your hard drive that holds files temporarily, before you burn them to CD.

CONTINUED

6. **When you're done gathering files, click Start⇨My Computer⇨your CD burner drive (whichever drive letter that is).**

   Windows shows you the contents of the CD's staging area.

7. **Put a recordable CD in your CD burner and click Write These Files to CD.**

   The CD Writing Wizard appears.

8. **Type the name you want to be burned on the CD; click Next.**

   If you've chosen too much data — too many pictures — the wizard alerts you.

9. **If you have too many pictures selected, don't do anything with the wizard. Instead, go back to the staging area and start deleting files or folders (right-click and click Delete) until you're under the size limit.**

   Don't worry — you aren't deleting the pictures. You're just removing them from the staging area. Unfortunately, neither the wizard nor Windows offers you much help: They give you no handy list of folder sizes or suggestions for what to trim. You're pretty much on your own, although you can right-click a folder and choose Properties to see the folder's size.

10. **When you think that you've deleted enough files or folders, go back to the wizard, click Retry Writing the Files to CD Now, and then click Next.**

   If you still have too many pictures selected, you'll get the warning again. Sooner or later, you'll have your picture collection trimmed down to the point where it will fit on the CD. At that point, the wizard starts writing files to the CD. Depending on the speed of your burner, it can take 20 minutes or more to burn a full CD.

11. **When the wizard finishes, click Finish.**

   The wizard removes all the files from the staging area.

12. **Immediately try looking at the pictures on the CD.**

   Chances are very good that they'll all be in excellent shape.

Book II

PCs and Peripherals

The 5th Wave   By Rich Tennant

@RICHTENNANT

INTENSE BUT UNINFORMED AUDIOPHILE
BILLY WIGGINS ENJOYS HIS CUSTOM
BURNED CD COLLECTION OF DIAL UP
MODEM WARBLES

Book II: PCs and Peripherals

Chapter 1: Starting with the Basics

In This Chapter

✓ Defining hardware, software, and peripherals

✓ Identifying the common components of all PCs

✓ Comparing laptop and desktop PCs

✓ Understanding RAM and your PC's CPU

✓ Defining the operating system

This chapter tackles the basic questions, such as what components make up your PC and why you need an operating system. You'll discover more about the specific parts of your PC that determine how fast it is, as well as the pros and cons of choosing a laptop over a desktop PC.

If you're a hardware technician or a PC power user, you might decide to eschew these basic concepts and move on . . . and that's okay. But if you're new to the world of personal computers or you're going to buy your first PC, this chapter is a great place to start. In fact, you'd be amazed by the number of folks who have owned a PC for a year or two and still don't know some of the terms that you'll read here!

Defining Basic Terms

A wise man once said, "Never jump into anything before defining your terms." Before you venture further, commit these terms to memory, and you'll have taken a giant first step toward becoming a PC power user.

There's no reason to walk around with this stuff tattooed on your arm; you certainly don't need to know these technicalities just to check your e-mail or use Microsoft Word. However, when you grow more knowledgeable about Windows and your PC, you'll find that these terms crop up in your computer conversations more and more often.

Hardware

In the PC world, *hardware* is any piece of circuitry or any component of your computer that has a physical structure. For example, your computer's monitor is a piece of hardware, as is your PC's floppy disk drive. Even those components that you normally can't see or touch — the ones that are buried inside your case — are considered hardware, too, like your PC's motherboard and power supply. (And yes, your computer's case is technically a piece of hardware as well, although it's not electrical.)

Figure 1-1 illustrates a common piece of hardware — in this case, a video card with an Accelerated Graphics Port (AGP) connector.

Figure 1-1:
Hardware
like this
video card
is, well,
hard.

Software

The flip side of the PC coin is the software that you use. *Software* refers to any program that you run, whether it resides on your hard drive, a floppy disk, a CD-ROM, or somewhere on a network.

When you hear folks discussing a software *upgrade, patch,* or *update,* they're talking about (you guessed it) yet another piece of software! However, the upgrade/patch/update program isn't designed to be run more than once; rather, its job is to apply the latest features, bug fixes, and data files to a piece of software that's already installed and running on your PC, updating it to a new *version.* (Virtually all software developers refer to successive versions of their software, such as *Version 1.5* or *Version 3;* the later the version, the more features that the software includes.)

And software might be cheap!

You'll probably encounter two other types of "ware": freeware and shareware. *Freeware* is a program that's either been released into the public domain — in which case the author generally releases the programming code needed to modify it or maintains the rights to it — but you can still use it for free.

Shareware, on the other hand, is not free: You get to try it before you buy it; if you like it, you send your payment directly to the author. Because there's no middleperson (you won't catch me using a sexist term) and you're not paying for an expensive box or advertising, shareware is usually far cheaper than a similar commercial program.

Before using freeware or shareware, check to make sure that the author offers regular updates. When you work for peanuts, you're not going to be able to afford a Quality Assurance department or comprehensive beta testing!

Two other types of "ware" have emerged on the scene in the past few years: *spyware* and *adware.* These insidious software programs load themselves surreptitiously on your computer and tell advertisers and companies where you surf on the Internet.

Typically, think of software as an application that you buy or download, such as Microsoft Works or Windows Media Player, shown in Figure 1-2. However, the term *software* actually applies to any program, including Windows itself and the driver programs that accompany the hardware that you buy. Unfortunately, computer viruses are software as well.

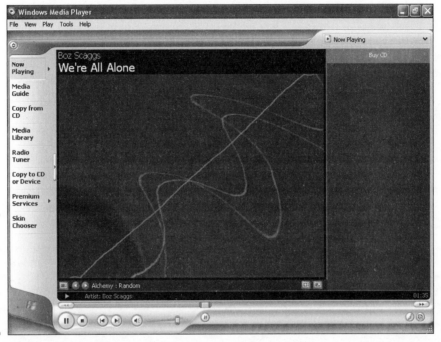

Figure 1-2: Listen to the latest MP3s with software from Microsoft.

From time to time, you might see the word *firmware* in a magazine or on a hardware manufacturer's Web site. *Firmware* is the software instructions that you find stored in the internal memory or the internal brain of a piece of hardware, so it's not quite software, and it's not quite hardware. For example, your CD or DVD recorder has a firmware chip inside that controls the mundane tasks required to burn a disc. Generally, you won't have to fool with firmware, but a manufacturer might release a firmware upgrade to fix bugs that have cropped up with a piece of hardware (or even to add new features). To upgrade firmware, you run a software utility program supplied by the manufacturer.

Peripherals

Peripherals comprise things that reside outside your PC's case, which can include all sorts of optional hardware. Examples include

✦ Printers

✦ External CD recorders, such as the model shown in Figure 1-3, and hard drives

✦ Web cams

✦ Graphics tablets

✦ Joysticks and other game controllers

✦ Network hardware such as Internet-sharing devices

✦ Scanners and digital cameras

Figure 1-3: This particular CD recording peripheral enjoys sunshine and clean air.

The three pieces of external hardware that are found on every PC — your monitor, keyboard, and your mouse (or trackball or touchpad) — are generally *not* considered peripherals because they're required to operate your PC. Call 'em hardware instead.

Peripherals connect to your computer via the ports that are built into the back (and often the front) of your PC. Book II, Chapter 3 goes into more detail about ports. Any PC power user worthy of the name will be able to identify any common port on a computer on sight. (If you're a hardware technician, you can identify them in the dark by feel.)

The Common Components of a Desktop PC

"Aw, crikey . . . look what we have here, mates! This little beaut is a PC — step back now, mind ya, for if one of these digital guys goes bonkers, it'll spread itself all over yer bloomin' desktop!"

Although a PC is hardly a crocodile, your system can grow like one — and it can become just as unwieldy and tough to move. Turn your attention to the components that you'll find equipped on just about any PC that you buy (or assemble) these days.

The computer

The computer itself is housed in a case, which protects all the internal parts from damage. (Unfortunately, dust will still find its way inside, which is why you should remove the case at least once a year and blow all that dust out by using a can of compressed air.)

Techs refer to your PC by any of the following names:

✦ Box

✦ CPU (meet your PC's actual *CPU* — which is a single integrated chip — later in this chapter)

✦ Chassis

✦ $*Q(#*$*!% (reserved for special occasions)

Consider thy form factor

Not all PCs are created equal; several different form factors are available. (Geez, yet another two-dollar word for a fifty-cent concept.) A *form factor* determines the height and "spread" of your computer, depending on the case. (In the original days of the IBM PC, all computer cases were designed to straddle your desk, parallel to the floor; however, folks soon realized that a PC takes up far less room if it stands vertically.)

Book II
Chapter 1

Starting with the Basics

Your desktop PC's case can look like any of the following:

✦ **The standard tower machine:** Because a tower case like the one in Figure 1-4 gives you the largest number of expansion bays and room for multiple fans, it's the case favored by PC power users and network administrators. Tower cases are often placed on the floor because they are sometimes too tall for your computer desk.

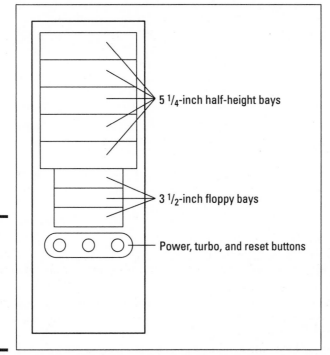

5 ¼-inch half-height bays

3 ½-inch floppy bays

Power, turbo, and reset buttons

Figure 1-4: No tower in Middle Earth can compete with the tower PC case.

✦ **The mini-tower machine:** The standard case offered with most PCs, the mini-tower is simply a shorter version of a tower case. The mini-tower is suitable for home and standard office workstation use.

✦ **The lunchbox and pizza box machines:** These are the smallest PC cases of all, built for those areas where space is at a premium (or you know ahead of time that expansion won't be required in the future). These machines are often used in larger corporate offices, hospitals, banks, and the like. Figure 1-5 shows a pizza box case, which sits flat on your desktop rather than standing upright.

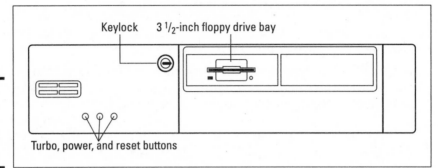

Figure 1-5: It's a lean, mean pizza box machine.

Keylock   3 ½-inch floppy drive bay

Turbo, power, and reset buttons

Custom colors are great (for a while, anyway)

You might be interested in buying a PC with a special color scheme. Typically, these machines are black or brushed aluminum, but they are also available in every color of the rainbow as well. (The fancy neon green and Florida orange are especially nice.)

Personally, I think these works of art are fun, but I will caution you up front: Finding a neon green CD-ROM drive in any store — online or otherwise — is more difficult than getting a teenage girl off the telephone. Therefore, you might find it difficult to maintain that exotic color scheme when you start upgrading your hardware because most of the civilized world uses PCs that are off-white or beige. Black computers are also easy to match because black is the next most popular color scheme.

Of course, if you're a Macintosh owner, all bets are off . . . but that's another book entirely.

The monitor

Today's monitors come in two different varieties:

✦ **The traditional CRT monitor:** The cathode ray tube (CRT) monitor is big, brassy, and less expensive to buy than a liquid crystal display (LCD) monitor, but it uses more electricity, gets hot while you use it, and emits all sorts of radiation. (Nothing harmful, mind you, but it's there all the same.) Because CRT monitors use older technology that's similar to a TV set, they're bulky, but they're also significantly cheaper than an LCD monitor, especially at larger screen sizes such as 19 or 21 inches. Most CRT monitors are flat-screen models; older designs with curved screens tended to distort the image that you see.

✦ **The LCD monitor:** LCD monitors — also called *flat-panel monitors* — share the same technology as laptop computer screens, so they're very thin and use much, much less electricity than a CRT monitor. (Many are even designed to hang on the wall.) LCD screens emit neither heat nor radiation. In fact, the only downside to an LCD monitor is the price. Though prices are coming down for LCD monitors, they still cost significantly more than traditional CRT monitors.

Either type of monitor is fine for a home or office environment, but (naturally) I recommend an LCD monitor if you can afford one. The larger the monitor size, the easier it's likely to be on your eyes, and the more windows and documents that you can stuff on your desktop at once.

The keyboard and mouse

Keyboards are rather mundane. Virtually all today's models have the Windows-specific keys that will help any PC power user — but I still have a suggestion or two:

✦ **Consider an ergonomic keyboard.** That cool, curved appearance that makes ergonomic keyboards such as the Microsoft Natural Keyboard Elite stand out in a crowd isn't just for looks. You'll find that you can type longer, faster, and with less strain on your wrists if you use an ergonomic keyboard, as shown in Figure 1-6.

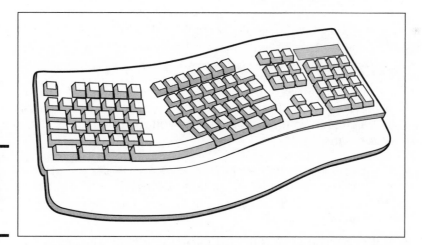

Figure 1-6:
Ergonomic keyboards are user friendly.

✦ **Keyboard tasks are easier with one-touch buttons.** Many keyboards on the market today — and most that ship with today's systems — feature one-touch keys that you press to automatically launch your e-mail program or Web browser, print a document, or mute your computer's audio. Even if you don't use the standard functions for these keys, they can generally be reprogrammed to work with other applications. For example, I've reprogrammed the Print key on my server's keyboard (which isn't connected to a printer) to run my network management application instead.

On the other side of the coin, most PC power users will eventually find themselves looking for a different mouse or pointing device; the standard equipment mouse rarely gets the job done unless you're buying a more expensive system that comes with a premium mouse. Mouse-y features to consider include the following:

✦ **Cordless mice:** These mice are sans tails — instead, they use a built-in infrared (IR) emitter to communicate with a separate base station, which in turn connects to your PC. The base station often acts as a battery charger when you're not using your PC. Many folks find these mice liberating because there's no tail to drag around and because you can place the mouse farther away from the computer.

✦ **Optical operation:** Optical mice advantages include no mouse ball to clean, far fewer moving parts, and better control — no wonder that optical pointing devices are so popular! If you're still using a mouse with a ball, jettison it and pick up an optical mouse.

✦ **Multiple buttons:** Of course, any self-respecting PC mouse has two buttons, but most of the new offerings include a programmable third button and a scroll wheel, which you use to scroll the contents of a page just by turning the wheel with your fingertip. (For example, I have the middle button programmed as a double-click.)

✦ **Trackballs and touchpads:** Many tech types swear by these alternatives to the traditional mouse. To use a *trackball,* which is kind of like a giant stationary mouse turned on its back, you move the ball with your thumb or the tips of your fingers. With a touchpad (like what's found on many laptops), you move the tip of your finger across a pressure-sensitive pad.

Speakers

Today's multimedia PCs are just as attractive to an audiophile as a traditional stereo system. If you think that you're limited to two desktop speakers and a chintzy volume knob, I invite you to contemplate the latest in PC speaker technology:

✦ **Flat-panel speakers:** Like LCD screens are to CRT monitors, so are flat-panel speakers to older PC speakers. Most flat-panel speakers are less than half of an inch thick yet provide the same power and punch as their older brethren.

✦ **Dolby Surround sound:** I get into more detail about high-fidelity PC audio in Book II, Chapter 15. For now, suffice it to say that with the right sound card and multiple speakers, your PC can equal the clarity and realism of a home theater system. And consider this: What home theater system will let you play the latest 3-D games?

✦ **Universal Serial Bus (USB) digital connections:** For the ultimate in sound quality, today's best digital speakers connect to your system through the USB port — you can say goodbye to old-fashioned analog forever.

Desktop PCs versus Laptop PCs

"So should I buy a desktop or a laptop PC?" Naturally, if the portability of a laptop PC is a requirement for you — if your job or your lifestyle demands

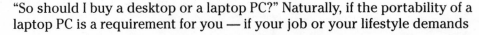

plenty of travel every year — you really have no choice but a laptop computer. Luckily, today's laptops are virtually as powerful as desktop PCs, so you no longer have to feel like a second-class citizen, even when it comes to features such as high-resolution graphics, larger hard drives, and CD/DVD recording, which used to be very expensive options in the laptop world.

However, if you're sitting on the fence and portability is a lesser requirement, I generally recommend a desktop system for the following three reasons:

✦ **Laptops aren't as expandable as desktops.** Although you can hang plenty of peripherals off a modern laptop (using USB and FireWire ports), desktops are just plain easier to expand and upgrade (especially the processor and your graphics card, which are practically impossible to swap on a laptop).

✦ **Laptops are much more expensive.** My friend, you'll pay dearly for that portability. So if you don't need it, jump to the desktop side of the fence. It's as simple as that.

✦ **Laptops cost much more to repair.** If the sound card fails in your desktop, you can replace it yourself with a new, relatively inexpensive adapter card. However, if the sound hardware fails in your laptop, it's time to pull out your wallet because you can't fix it yourself, and the entire motherboard inside the unit will probably need to be replaced. (Remember, part of that portability stems from the fact that laptop manufacturers tend to put all the graphics and video hardware on the motherboard to save space.)

Luckily, most of Book II is still valuable to laptop owners. Just ignore the parts about upgrading the components that you can't reach.

RAM and Processors: The Keys to Performance

When you hear PC owners talking about the speed and performance of their computers, they're typically talking about one of three different components (or all of these components together, as a group):

✦ **Your system memory, or random access memory (RAM):** The more memory that your PC has and the faster that memory is, the better your PC will perform — especially Windows, which enjoys memory like a hog enjoys slops. I tell you more about slops — sorry, I mean memory — in Book II, Chapter 11.

✦ **The central processing unit (CPU):** Most of today's PCs use either an Intel Pentium 4 or its cheaper and slower cousin, the Celeron. The other popular processor is the AMD Athlon XP, along with its cheaper and slower cousin, the Duron. The speed of your processor is measured in either megahertz (MHz) or gigahertz (GHz), with 1 GHz equaling 1000 MHz. The faster the speed of your processor, the faster your PC will perform. (I go into this big-time in Book II, Chapter 12.)

✦ **The graphics processing unit (GPU):** This is the chipset used on your video card. The better the chipset, the faster and the more realistic 3-D graphics that your PC can produce. For the skinny on graphics cards, visit Book II, Chapter 15.

To display what type of processor your PC uses, its speed, and how much RAM your PC has, right-click My Computer and then choose Properties from the shortcut menu that appears. A dialog box appears, similar to the one shown in Figure 1-7, with these interesting facts: the operating system, who the computer belongs to, the type of processor and its speed, and the amount of RAM in the computer.

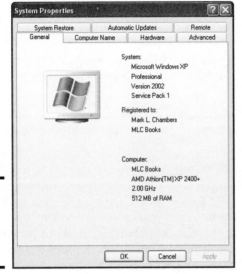

Figure 1-7:
Displaying your system's properties.

Your Friend, Your Operating System

Windows, which is your PC's *operating system,* is the program that you run in order to

+ Navigate through the files on your hard drive.

+ Run other programs.

+ Listen to music, view pictures, or watch movies.

+ Copy, move, and delete things, and much more.

Actually, Windows is composed of hundreds of smaller programs, but you'll rarely notice anything else running. Instead, Windows presents a cohesive and relatively easy-to-use interface to the world. (The tech word *interface* simply means the design of the screen and the controls that you see when you're using software.)

I should mention, however, that Windows isn't the only operating system that runs on a PC. For example, you can run Unix, Linux, BeOS, OS/2 Warp, or even good old-fashioned DOS. To be honest, your PC couldn't care less — but it's a good bet that many of the programs that you want to run are designed for Windows, and much of the hardware you add to your PC either won't work or will be harder to configure if you use another operating system. Therefore, I heartily suggest that you stick with Windows XP: The various flavors of Windows are the choice of the vast majority of PC owners.

Chapter 2: Additional Toys Your PC Will Enjoy

In This Chapter

↙ **Comparing printers**

↙ **Adding a scanner to your system**

↙ **Upgrading your input devices**

↙ **Adding a game controller**

↙ **Introducing digital cameras and digital video (DV) camcorders**

↙ **Adding new storage to your system**

↙ **Protecting your PC with a surge protector or an uninterruptible power supply (UPS)**

You've bought your PC — congratulations! — or you've decided to finally turn on that totem pole of a desktop computer that you've been looking at for the last six months. Here's a friendly warning for you: Serious computing requires serious peripherals. In other words, those PC owners who are hoping to get the maximum return and explore the maximum power of their computers will need additional stuff (*peripherals,* as you can read in Book II, Chapter 1) that connects to your PC to take care of a specific job. Printers are a good example; a PC certainly won't produce hard copy by itself.

In Book II, Chapter 1, I discuss hardware and software. This chapter is designed as both a showcase and an introduction to PC peripherals that will familiarize you with the most popular additional toys for your computer. Some of these devices are covered in great detail later on — for example, scanners have all of Book II, Chapter 5 to themselves — and others are covered primarily right here.

One warning: This chapter can be hazardous to your wallet or purse.

Printers

The first stop in the world of peripherals is the most common (and most folks would say the most useful) device of all: the system *printer,* which allows your PC to produce hard copies of documents, artwork, and photographs.

Inkjet versus laser printers

In the digital days of yore — in other words, more than six years ago — making a choice between an inkjet and a laser printer was ridiculously easy. After all, laser printers were prohibitively expensive, and they couldn't print in color. Therefore, every home PC owner picked up an inkjet printer and got on with his or her life. These days, however, the line between inkjet and laser printers has blurred, so here's a list of the advantages of each so that you can shop with the right type of printer in mind.

Laser printer advantages

Today's monochrome laser printers start at around $200–$300, which is still mind-bendingly weird for an old hardware hacker like me who still remembers the days when the *absolute* cheapest (and likely refurbished) laser printer that you could find would set you back $1,500–$2,000. Advantages of the laser printer include

✦ **Speed:** A laser printer can turn out pages more quickly than an inkjet printer.

✦ **Low cost:** Over time, toner costs for a laser printer will total far less per page than refilling/replacing inkjet printer cartridges.

✦ **Quiet operation:** A laser printer is generally quieter than low-cost inkjet printers — which is a big deal in a quiet office, where the printer usually occupies a central location.

✦ **Best quality text:** No inkjet printer — no matter how much you pay for it — will ever turn out black text and line graphics as crisp as a laser printer.

Also, if you can afford the $1,000 for a color laser printer, you'll find that it offers better quality color output than most low-cost inkjet printers. With these advantages in mind, pick a monochrome laser printer if most of the pages that you'll print will be text and if color isn't a requirement. You'll be glad that you chose that laser model after you've gone three months without changing a single toner cartridge!

The monochrome laser printer shown in Figure 2-1 can produce 12 pages per minute without blinking an eye. (If it had one.)

Figure 2-1:
Invest in a low-cost mono-chrome laser printer for document printing.

Inkjet printer advantages

Inkjet printers are still cheaper than laser printers. You can find an acceptable color inkjet printer for under $100 anywhere on the planet, and they're still the color printing solution for the home PC owner. Other advantages include

✦ **Versatility:** A color inkjet can print on many types of media, including glossy photo paper, craft paper, and T-shirt transfers.

✦ **Smaller size:** This saves you space on your desktop.

✦ **Larger paper sizes:** If you spend more, you can add a large-format inkjet printer to your system that can print 11-x-17-inch or larger items.

The inkjet printer in Figure 2-2 costs less than $300 yet includes both Ethernet and Universal Serial Bus (USB) connections. It can print laser-quality black text at seven pages per minute and photo-quality color images at five pages per minute. You can even set this model to print on both sides of the paper.

Figure 2-2:
This inkjet printer produces stunning photo-quality color.

Photo printers

Photo printers are specifically designed to create photographs that rival any 35mm film print. They either use the best quality inkjet technology, or they rely on dye-sublimation (dye-sub) technology (also called *thermal wax* printing). A *dye-sub printer* transfers heated solid dye from a ribbon to specially coated paper, producing the same continuous tones that you see in a photograph produced from a negative. Photo printers can often accept memory cards from digital cameras directly, so you don't need a PC to print your digital photographs.

Although a number of different sizes of photo printers are on the market, most are smaller than typical inkjet printers. (They can't use standard 8.5-x-11-inch paper, and they can't print black text, which makes an inkjet printer far more versatile.) Both photo and inkjet printers can produce borderless images (just like a film print), but a true dye-sublimation photo printer is far slower than an inkjet, and the special paper and dye ribbon that it requires make it much more expensive over the long haul.

If you're a serious amateur or professional digital photographer, a photo printer is worth the expense. For a typical home PC owner, however, a standard color inkjet printer is the better path to take.

Label printers

Before I move on, I'd like to discuss a popular new class of printers — the personal *label printer,* like the DYMO LabelWriter 330 Turbo that I use (www.dymo.com). As shown in Figure 2-3, these printers might look a little like toys — they're not much bigger than the label tape that they use — but I've found that a label printer is worth twice its weight in gold.

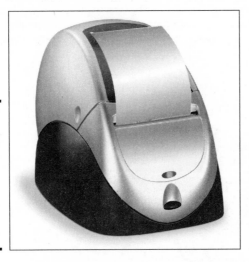

Figure 2-3: A personal label printer is a convenient tool for printing all types of labels.

For example, the LabelWriter 330 Turbo can produce all these materials with aplomb:

+ **Address and shipping labels,** complete with your logo
+ **ID badges**
+ **CD and DVD labels**
+ **Bar codes and U.S. mail codes**
+ **File folder labels**
+ **Floppy disk labels** (for those who still use floppy disks, anyway)
+ **VHS tape and cassette labels**

When you design your labels, the software that ships with the LabelWriter 330 Turbo gives you control over fonts, time and date stamping, line drawings, and even thumbnail photographs. You can rotate and mirror text or set up bar coding with ease. Plus, you get the capability to print labels directly from applications such as Outlook, Word, ACT!, and QuickBooks.

Just as valuable as the output, however, is the sheer convenience that you get from one of these printers! A label printer frees you from the hassle of designing and preparing labels on your inkjet or laser printer, and you don't have to hunt for your label sheets every time that you need to print a new batch. (Anyone who's fought tooth and nail to align and print a bar code or address labels on a standard laser printer knows just what I mean.)

The LabelWriter 330 Turbo uses a USB connection and sells for about $130–$200 online.

Scanners

Scanners are interesting beasts — and man, you get a lot of bang for your buck! In fact, a perfectly serviceable USB scanner, as shown in Figure 2-4, is waiting for you at your local Maze O' Wires store for under $100, and it can do all of the following:

✦ **Produce digital images from magazine and book pages, photographs, and just about any other printed material.** These images can later be edited to your heart's content, sent as an e-mail attachment, or recorded to CD or DVD.

Figure 2-4:
This scanner can bring all sorts of printed material to your PC monitor.

✦ **Read text from a printed document into your word processor.** This trick is called *Optical Character Recognition* (OCR) and can save you hours of typing.

✦ **Produce images that you can fax with your PC's fax/modem.**

✦ **Produce images from transparencies or slides (with the right attachment).**

✦ **Create copies of a document (in concert with your printer).**

Plus, prices on the better scanners have been dropping for some time now. For example, the ScanMaker 4900 from Microtek (www.microtek.com) is priced under $200, yet it scans at a quality that five years ago would have cost you more than $500. This scanner contains seven one-touch buttons on its front. You can e-mail, copy, or even create PDFs from the original — or even run your OCR software with a single punch of a button. *Sassy!*

Specialized scanners are designed especially for things such as bar codes and business cards. A unique favorite of mine is a digital, hand-held pen scanner (see one in Figure 2-5) with which you can re-create what you draw or write on special sheets of paper in the included notebook and a special type of self-adhesive notes. I use the Logitech io (www.logitech.com). No more stuffing napkins with scribbles all over them into your jacket pocket after lunch! You can also use the io to enter appointments and To Do data into Microsoft Outlook or Lotus Notes and also flag information that should be automatically entered into an e-mail message when you connect the pen to your PC. (It uses a USB connection.) If you're like me — constantly moving back and forth between old-fashioned pen and paper one minute and a mouse and Adobe Illustrator the next — you'll find that the io is worth every penny of the $200 that you'll pay for it.

Figure 2-5:
A digital pen is a specialized scanner.

Keyboards, Tablets, and Pointing Things

Gotta have 'em. Using a PC without an input device is . . . well, I guess it's like playing ping-pong without paddles. In this section, I discuss the upgrades that you can make to your PC's existing keyboard and mouse. (Although they're technically not peripherals, as I mention in Book II, Chapter 1, some of these hardware devices are too cool not to cover.)

Tickling keys wirelessly

Mr. Bill (Gates, that is) has remodeled the hoary PC keyboard in his own fashion, adding extra keys that make it easier to control Windows. If you're using a PC built in the last few years, you'll already have these keys handy. I mention a few keyboard features to look for in the previous chapter of this book, such as ergonomic keyboards that can help reduce the strain of typing on your wrists. But what if you want to relax in a better chair several feet away from that big-screen monitor?

Enter the wireless keyboard, which is the perfect complement to a wireless mouse or trackball. The wireless keyboard shown in Figure 2-6 is a combination of both a wireless keyboard and wireless mouse that use the Bluetooth short-range wireless network technology I cover in Book II, Chapter 18. This keyboard is festooned with no less than 11 one-button hotkeys and even includes a set of audio CD player controls for listening to your music.

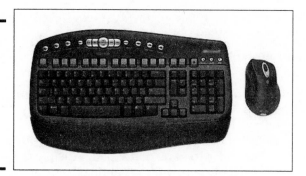

Figure 2-6: This wireless keyboard/ mouse combo is the nomad's dream.

Putting a tablet to work

If you're a graphic artist, a professional photographer, or someone who wants to paint or draw freehand, consider a *graphics tablet* (shown in Figure 2-7), which allows you to draw or make notes with a stylus in the familiar old-fashioned method. Like an ergonomic keyboard, a tablet can also help ease the strain on your wrist.

Figure 2-7: A graphics tablet makes drawing a breeze.

"But what about the fine control I get with paper or canvas?" you may ask. No problem! Today's tablets can recognize thousands of different levels of pressure. Some can even detect the angle of the stylus, allowing you to tilt your virtual brush in graphics applications like Photoshop and Painter for special effects with watercolor, chalk, and pencil filters.

A typical tablet like the Intuos2 from Wacom (www.wacom.com) has no batteries or cords on the stylus, and it even comes with its own mouse. The tablet uses a USB connection to your PC, and it sells for about $350 on the Web — that's the 6-x-8-inch model. (The 9-x-12-inch model is about $100 more.)

Repeat after me: Buy a trackball!

I can't work with a traditional mouse any longer — I'm now firmly set in the trackball camp. A trackball offers a number of benefits:

✦ **Compact:** Trackballs require far less space on your desktop because just the trackball moves (instead of the entire device).

✦ **Control:** Many folks find that using a trackball provides a finer level of cursor control.

✦ **Cleanliness:** A trackball stays cleaner than a mouse. (Even optical mice get dirtier than trackballs.)

Figure 2-8 illustrates a trackball mouse that you control with your thumb; other trackballs use the first finger to control the ball. This particular model uses either a USB or PS/2 connection to your PC and sells for about $35 online.

Figure 2-8:
A trackball is much more efficient than the traditional mouse.

Big-Time Game Controllers

Ah, do you remember the old Atari joysticks that ushered in the age of the video game (and the Atari personal computers after that)? A plastic tube, a base with a single red button, and a cord . . . what more could you possibly want, right?

Because modern game players want a lot more than one button, witness the arrival of the game controller (which I think has a much grander sound than just a *joystick*). For example, check out the controller shown in Figure 2-9 — does that look like an old-fashioned joystick to you? In fact, this model is more like a combination of a mini-keyboard and a gamepad (reflecting the current complexity of PC games, which rely as much on the keyboard as the pointing device that you're using). Your entire hand fits on top of the controller, much like a trackball, and your fingers use the keys while your thumb operates the gamepad directional control. (You can also use this controller along with your regular mouse or trackball.) This model, which sells for about $30 online, can even be programmed to fit your preferences for each individual game that you play. Sweet!

Another popular feature of today's game controllers is *force feedback,* where the controller actually rumbles or provides resistance to your hand that matches the action onscreen, such as a steering wheel that gets tougher to turn in curves or a joystick that shakes each time that your WWII fighter is hit by enemy fire.

Figure 2-9:
It's a bird, it's a plane . . . no, it's the latest in PC game controllers!

Consider the Microsoft Sidewinder Force Feedback steering wheel, which has the same optical tracking mechanism as today's optical mice and track-balls. It even has its own onboard processor, which keeps track of what's happening within the game and activates the wheel's internal motors to provide the matching feedback. (Naturally, it also has programmable buttons. What a surprise.) Anyway, you get the steering wheel and a set of pedals to boot for about $100, making you the hit of your NASCAR crowd!

Video and Digital Cameras

Images and full-motion video have traditionally been based on film (which retains an image when exposed to light) or magnetic tape. That whole approach, however, is now strictly '90s . . . and very early '90s to boot. Today's digital cameras and digital video camcorders have heavy-duty advantages over film cameras and tape camcorders:

✦ **No processing at Wal-Mart is required.** Your digital images can be downloaded directly to your PC.

✦ **Editing is easy, using programs like Adobe Photoshop and Paint Shop Pro (for digital images) and Adobe Premiere (for video).**

✦ **No film rolls to buy.** Instead, you simply delete images from your digital camera after they're downloaded to your PC.

✦ **Your images and videos can be saved to a CD or DVD for permanent storage.**

✦ **Images can be sent via e-mail or displayed on your Web page.**

✦ **You can create your own DVD movies from your video clips.**

A specialized model of DV camcorder (about the size of a baseball) is designed especially to sit atop your desktop PC: a Web cam. Folks use them to send digital video over the Internet, to add a video signal to their Web pages, or to record simple movies from their chair. Web cams have been in use as Internet videoconferencing tools for years now; most are under $100; and they use either a FireWire or USB cable connection to your PC.

Figure 2-10 illustrates a typical digital camera, which looks and operates much like its film counterpart. Figure 2-11 shows a camcorder, ready to record straight to digital video, which you can transfer over a FireWire connection to your PC.

Figure 2-10: The image maker of the new millennium: the digital camera.

Figure 2-11: With a digital camcorder, you can record your footage on a DVD.

For the skinny on digital cameras, see Book II, Chapter 9. And for a look at how the video clips that you take with your DV camcorder can be turned into movies, see Book II, Chapter 7.

External Drives

Next, consider how simple it is to add fast storage — or the ability to record your own CDs and DVDs — to today's PCs. If you're the least bit nervous about digging inside your PC's innards in order to add more hard drive space, you'll be pleased to know that it's easy to connect a fast external hard drive to your system . . . providing that you have the FireWire or USB 2.0 ports available on your PC. (If you're not familiar with these high-speed connections, fear not: I launch into a complete discussion of both of these in Book II, Chapter 14.)

In fact, not every form of external storage even needs a cable. Read on to see what I mean.

Portable hard drives and CD/DVD recorders

Forget the huge external hard drives of just five years ago. Those doorstops have been replaced by slim, trim models (see Figure 2-12) that run faster and are more reliable and yet are no bigger than a pack of playing cards. At current prices, you can pick up an external 40GB hard drive for about $350 that is a mere one inch thick and shock resistant, yet can connect effortlessly to PCs with either FireWire or USB 2.0 ports.

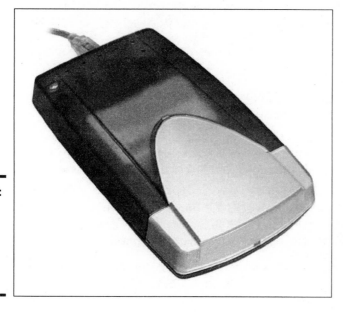

Figure 2-12:
This external 40GB drive means mobile storage.

On the CD and DVD recording scene, you'll find four major types of drives:

+ **CD-R/CD-RW drives:** Can store around 700MB on a CD

+ **DVD-R/DVD-RW drives:** Can store 4.7GB on a DVD

+ **DVD-RAM drives:** Can store 9.4GB on a double-sided DVD

+ **DVD+R/DVD+RW drives:** Can store 4.7GB on a DVD

The *RW* in the drive moniker stands for *rewriteable,* meaning that you can reuse a CD-RW, DVD-RW, or DVD+RW over and over. All these recorders can produce audio CDs and standard data CD/DVDs, but only the drives that can record the DVD-R and DVD+R formats are likely to create a DVD movie that can be played in your standalone DVD player. Unfortunately, the rewriteable DVD-RW and DVD+RW standards aren't compatible with each other, and they're not compatible with most standalone DVD players, either; you'll have to watch your discs on your PC. (Insert sound of palm slapping forehead here.)

The current morass that is the DVD standards battle is too complex to go into in this chapter. If you'd like the full story about what works with what and how to record any type of disc under the sun (audio, video, data, and even a mix), I can heartily recommend Mark L. Chambers' *CD & DVD Recording For Dummies,* 2nd Edition, by Wiley Publishing, Inc. (It'll keep your library consistent, too.)

Backup drives

Backup drives used to mean inexpensive, slow-running tape drives — however, today's typical 60GB and 80GB drives are simply too humongous for such tapes to be worth much anymore. Heck, I remember when everyone backed up to floppy disks, and now even the highest-priced digital audio tape (DAT) drives are losing ground fast in the backup storage world.

Instead, you now have three choices to pick from when backing up your system:

✦ **DVD recorders,** especially DVD-RAM drives, which can store over 9GB per double-sided disc.

✦ **Online backups,** using a commercial Internet backup service. (This is really only a viable solution if you're using a broadband connection to the Internet; backing up a big hard drive takes too long over a pokey 56K modem.)

✦ **External FireWire and USB 2.0 backup hard drives** like the 200GB Maxtor Personal Storage 5000DV (www.maxtor.com), which allows you to start a full, automated backup of your system by pressing the button on the front of the drive.

The Maxtor unit isn't cheap at $450, but how much are your documents and files worth? No matter what backup method you use, I strongly urge you to do your duty as your PC's guardian and *back up your system!*

USB flash drives

The final storage toy is a little something different: the *USB flash drive,* which is a keychain-sized unit that needs no batteries and has no moving parts! Instead, it uses the same method that digital cameras use to store images. Your files are stored on memory cards (either removable cards or built-in memory inside the unit). Most USB drives now range anywhere from 16MB to 256MB of storage, and after you plug them into your PC's USB port, they look just like any external hard drive (or a whomping huge floppy disk), but they can be unplugged and carried with you in your pocket. These drives don't need any extra software — Windows XP recognizes them instantly — so they make a great "digital wallet."

Figure 2-13 illustrates a 128MB flash drive that sells for about $50 online. It even includes a write-protect switch so that you can safeguard your data from being accidentally erased.

Figure 2-13:
Carry
128MB in
your pocket
with a USB
flash drive.

Surge Protectors and UPS Units

You know, one clear sign of a PC power user is at the end of the PC's power cord. True power users will use either a surge protector or a UPS to safeguard their system. However, I always make sure that I stress the following fact when I'm talking about surge protectors and UPS units: Neither will be able to protect your PC from a direct lightning hit on your home or office wiring! (That's just too much current for any commercial surge device to handle.)

Otherwise, using both a surge protector and a UPS will help guard against less serious power surges, and both will provide additional AC sockets for your rapidly growing system. If you can afford to spend $200–$300, the UPS is the better choice because of the following reasons:

✦ **Safety nets:** A UPS provides a number of extra minutes of AC power if your home or office experiences a power failure — generally enough so that you can close any documents that you're working on (like that Great American Novel that you've been slaving over for 20 years) and then shut down your PC normally.

✦ **Auto shutdowns:** More expensive UPS models can actually shut down your PC automatically in case of a power failure.

✦ **Current cleaners:** Most UPS units filter the AC current to smooth out brownouts and noise interference from other electronic devices.

✦ **Audible alerts:** Some UPS units sound an alarm whenever a power failure or significant brownout occurs.

The number of minutes that your UPS will last during a power failure depends on the power rating of the battery. Don't forget, however, that a honking big cathode ray tube (CRT) monitor will use much more power than the PC itself, so you should allow for it when deciding on which UPS to buy.

If you're using a dialup or digital subscriber line (DSL) modem connection, make sure that you get a surge protector or UPS that will also protect your modem from electrical surges — that juice can travel just as easily across a phone line as across your power line.

CHECK IT OUT

Pulling Out Stuck Diskettes and CDs

As your floppy drive gets older, it starts eating diskettes. The cause of the problem isn't the drive, per se. The real problem is the piece of metal on the diskette that slides away, revealing the recording surface. If your drive gets a bit dirty, it probably has a hard time putting that slider back in place — and that's why the diskette won't come out.

There's a tool that's absolutely perfect for pulling stuck diskettes out of sticky drives. It's called a *stamp tong*. Any kid with a stamp collection will be able to show you: Philatelists use tongs so they don't leave dirt and oil from their fingers on their stamps. There's a good picture of one at www.globalstamps.com/tongs.htm. When a diskette gets stuck, you have to work the stamp tong down into the drive deep enough to release the pressure on the metal slider:

1. **Shut down Windows and turn off the computer.**

2. **Push open the drive cover with your finger.**

3. **Work the stamp tong back and forth until you feel the diskette ease out.**

While getting a diskette out of a floppy drive is hard, removing a stuck CD is almost always very easy:

1. **Shut down Windows and turn off the computer.**

2. **Take a paper clip and unbend it.**

3. **Stick the tip of the paper clip in the little hole at the front of the CD drive.**

   No, I'm not talking about the speaker jack. There's a little hole that's just big enough for the end of a paper clip. Look harder.

   That's all it takes.

Chapter 3: Connectors, Ports, and Sundry Openings

In This Chapter

✔ Connecting USB devices

✔ Connecting FireWire devices

✔ Putting the antique serial port to rest

✔ Recognizing the PC parallel port

✔ Connecting your monitors

✔ Locating the jacks and ports on your sound card

✔ Connecting your mouse and keyboard

*I*n the beginning (okay, last century), there was the serial port and the parallel port — who would have needed anything else? If you could afford a printer back then, it was connected to the parallel port, and your modem (or perhaps your mouse) was hooked to your serial port. End of story.

Today's typical PC sprouts those same two ports. And although you can still use them with a printer, modem, and even a mouse, you'll also find a number of relatively new connectors that greatly expand the range of peripherals that you can add to your system. In this chapter, I help you make sense of the various ports and sundry openings that you'll find on the back of your PC.

Using USB Stuff

The first port on the tour is rapidly becoming the most important standard PC connector. A Universal Serial Bus (USB) port (see Figure 3-1) allows you to connect all sorts of peripherals, and it's even becoming popular for connecting keyboards and mice. Intel is responsible for this most versatile of ports.

A USB connection is the cat's pajamas because

✦ **It's Plug and Play.** You don't even need to reboot your PC after you connect a USB device because Windows automatically recognizes the connection, and you can start using your USB peripheral immediately.

✦ **One port supports dozens of devices.** A single USB port can support up to 127 different devices, either connected in a daisy-chain configuration or by using a USB hub. I doubt that you have that many connections to handle.

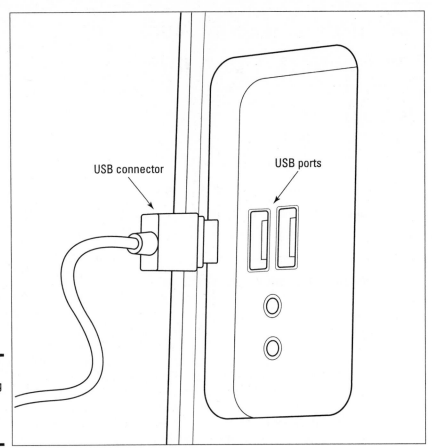

USB connector

USB ports

Figure 3-1:
The docking
procedure
for a USB
port.

+ **It's relatively fast.** The two current standards for USB devices are the older USB 1.1 standard (which still delivers data transfer speeds that are many times that of a traditional serial port) and the USB 2.0 standard (which is the fastest connection currently available for the PC).

I discuss USB connections in greater detail in Book II, Chapter 14; for now, just remember that any device with a USB port connection is a better choice over the same device with a serial port or parallel port connection.

Riding in the Fast Lane with FireWire

Until recently, the FireWire port (often referred to by its more official name, IEEE 1394) was the fastest port on any personal computer and has therefore become the standard for digital video (DV) camcorders and high-resolution scanners — both of which produce honking big files that need to be transferred to your computer as quickly as possible. Believe it or not, Apple Computer is the proud parent of FireWire.

Back off, SCSI!

Many hardware technicians and techno-wizards are familiar with Small Computer System Interface (SCSI) connectors. *SCSI* was the original high-speed, daisy-chaining technology that allowed you to add a string of multiple devices *(a SCSI chain)* both inside and outside your PC's case. Even today, SCSI internal hard drives are some of the fastest on the market.

However, external SCSI devices are somewhat scary: A SCSI chain is much harder than USB 2.0 or FireWire to configure. In fact, entire chapters are devoted to it in some older books. External SCSI devices aren't Plug and Play, and an external SCSI peripheral is much slower when it comes to transferring data than the newer USB/FireWire technologies.

For these reasons, I advise even PC power users to give SCSI the cold shoulder when considering an external device unless your PC already has SCSI hardware, and you're experienced with configuring SCSI hardware. Take my word for it; you'll be glad you did.

The original FireWire standard has now been overtaken in raw speed by USB 2.0, but because FireWire has been around far longer, it's in no danger of disappearing any time soon. In fact, I personally would pick FireWire over USB 2.0 every time because none of my current crop of digital gear will recognize USB 2.0.

Unlike USB ports — which are included with every PC today — FireWire ports are generally available as optional equipment, so make certain that you have a FireWire port before spending the big bucks on that new DV camcorder. (Of course, you can always buy an adapter card to add FireWire ports to your computer.) Like USB, FireWire is also a Plug-and-Play connection; a FireWire port can support 63 devices (using a daisy-chaining technique).

Find more information about FireWire in Book II, Chapter 14, where I introduce the new FireWire 800 standard, which ups the ante in the port speed race, churning an incredible 800 Mbps (or twice as fast as the original FireWire)!

Your Antique Serial Port

Okay, perhaps the serial port isn't *antique,* but it is one-half of the original Dynamic Duo that first appeared with the premiere of the IBM PC.

Today, most peripherals have jumped the serial ship and joined the USB bunch. However, you can still find the following serial devices from time to time (usually used, and probably on eBay):

✦ Modems

✦ Game controllers (especially the more complex joysticks)

✦ Digital cameras

✦ Personal digital assistant (PDA) docks for Palm and Pocket PC units

Serial devices aren't Plug and Play, so you'll have to reboot your PC before Windows will recognize a serial device. Also, serial devices — especially modems — might require additional manual configuration inside Windows, such as editing files with Notepad and turning off certain port features. All in all, go USB. Everyone else is, and it's a good thing.

The Once-Renowned Parallel Port

Ah, I remember those days . . . the early 1980s, when the parallel port was truly the Queen of the PC Connections. Printers were hideously expensive peripherals that only a doctor, lawyer, or Supreme Court Justice could afford. And if you did have a printer, it was connected to your PC's parallel port with all the pomp, grace, and grandeur of the RMS Queen Elizabeth II. (Perhaps I need more Diet Coke.)

Figure 3-2 illustrates the standard PC parallel port as it appears today. Unlike the serial port, the parallel port is still somewhat useful today; a large number of parallel port printers are still manufactured, and the parallel port is also used with other peripherals such as Zip drives and scanners (usually with older PCs without USB support).

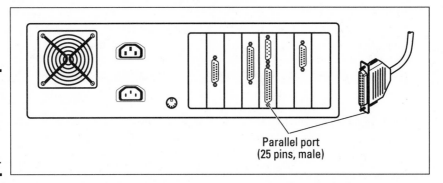

Figure 3-2:
A grand old dame of the PC world, the 25-pin parallel port.

Parallel port
(25 pins, male)

I'm sorry to report, however, that the parallel port's days are numbered. The popularity of the USB port as a printer connection has doomed the parallel port to obsolescence, and we can wave goodbye to her with a wistful smile.

Many laptops feature an infrared port (commonly called an *IrDA* port, short for *Infrared Data Association*) that can be used to communicate with devices such as PDAs and other laptops. Windows provides full support for an infrared connection. However, these ports don't do diddly-squat if the external peripheral that you're trying to communicate with doesn't have its own IrDA port — and not many do, so you won't be able to use this whiz-bang technology with many devices.

Meet Your Video Port

At last, a port that's been around for many years and still rocks! Yes, friends and neighbors, today's video cards still use the same 15-pin, D-SUB video port that originally appeared with the IBM Video Graphics Array (VGA) specification. However, another new face is on the block: the 29-pin, *DVI-I port,* which is used to connect digital flat-panel (liquid crystal display [LCD]) monitors. Figure 3-3 shows a typical video card that offers both ports onboard.

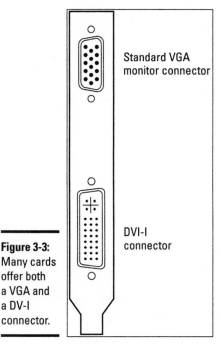

Figure 3-3: Many cards offer both a VGA and a DV-I connector.

Standard VGA monitor connector

DVI-I connector

If you're wondering, virtually every card that has both of these video ports can actually use two monitors at once (either showing an *expanded* desktop, where your mouse moves seamlessly from one monitor to the other, or two separate and discrete desktops).

In a pinch, a DVI-VGA adapter allows you to use the DVI-I port to connect a standard cathode ray tube (CRT) monitor, so you can use two analog monitors instead.

Audio Connectors You'll Likely Need

Today's speakers connect to your PC's sound card in one of three ways:

✦ **Through standard analog Line-Out/Speaker jacks on the card:** These are the familiar audio jacks that you'll find on the card itself, just like the headphone jacks on your MP3 player or boom box. Most PC speakers use these jacks, shown in Figure 3-4.

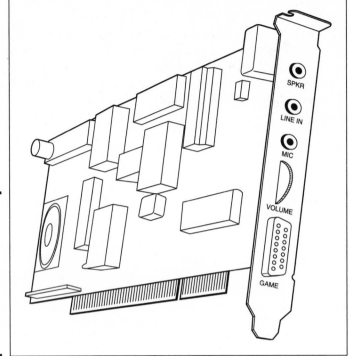

Figure 3-4:
The business end of a typical PC sound card, with speaker jack and game port.

✦ **Through standard analog RCA jacks on the card:** Some cards also include the RCA jacks that most folks associate with a stereo system or a VCR. These jacks are more convenient than the Line-Out/Speaker jacks because you don't need a miniplug-to-RCA adapter to use your stereo system with your PC's audio output.

✦ **Through the USB port:** Surprise! It's our new-old friend making another appearance. This time, your speakers can use any USB port on your system for a digital audio connection — analog gets tossed out the door, and audiophiles can wax enthusiastic about their pristine digital sound.

You'll also find a PC game port on most audio cards, allowing you to connect a joystick or other game controller. The game port is going the way of the dodo (thanks once again, as you can guess, to USB game controllers), but they're still quite common on today's sound cards.

Keyboard and Mouse Ports on Parade

The final stop on the port tour is the ubiquitous PS/2 keyboard/joystick port. Figure 3-5 illustrates the plug that fits in these ports. Each port is typically color coded and marked with an icon to indicate which piece of hardware gets connected where.

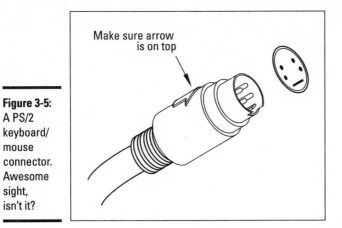

Make sure arrow
is on top

Figure 3-5:
A PS/2
keyboard/
mouse
connector.
Awesome
sight,
isn't it?

I hate to bring it up, but at the risk of sounding like a broken record, many
PC hardware manufacturers are turning to USB keyboards and USB mice.
(See why I stress just how important USB is to the modern PC?) In this case,
however, I see no real advantage to using a USB keyboard or mouse over a
PS/2 keyboard or mouse because the latter really don't require any configu-
ration, and they're not constantly being unplugged and reconnected.

Chapter 4: Maintaining Your Hardware

In This Chapter

✔ **Moving your PC the right way**

✔ **Dusting your PC**

✔ **Keeping cables under control**

✔ **Cleaning your monitor and scanner**

✔ **Freshening your mouse and keyboard**

✔ **Practicing printer maintenance**

*W*ith the right credit card balance, anyone can buy a supercharged $2,500 PC — but maintaining that expensive equipment is another kettle of fish altogether. Although your PC's case might appear to be a closed environment, those fans draw in dust while they're cooling things down . . . and what about peripherals, such as your printer and scanner, which are always more exposed to dust, dirt, and contaminants? The only PC that I've encountered that doesn't need regular maintenance is the model that you can buy in *The Sims*.

In this chapter, I cover the basic cleaning and maintenance necessary to keep your hardware in top shape — long enough for it to become a seriously outdated antique! (And that's coming from the proud owner of two antique RadioShack computers and three antique Atari computers.)

When Should I Move My PC?

Counter to popular myth, even a desktop PC can go mobile whenever it wants. Of course, you won't be stowing it with your other carry-on items on a plane, but if you've been challenged to a LAN game at someone's apartment or you're moving to a new home, you'll find that your PC actually enjoys chaperoned trips. (Rather like a dog, without the tongue out the window.)

Here are the guidelines that you should follow when moving your PC:

✦ **Never move your PC until it's completely powered down.** In this case, *move* means any movement whatsoever (even nudging your PC's case a few inches across your desktop).

✦ **Never move your desktop PC if it is running.** (Even laptop computers shouldn't be jolted or jerked around while they're running.) Many PCs have only a handful of moving parts, such as fans, CD/DVD recorders, and hard drives — but brother, any movement while the latter two are still spinning carries the possibility that you can shorten the drive's operational life. Always give your PC at least ten seconds after it shuts down before you pick it up.

✦ **Never set your PC upright in a seat or the floor of your car**. We've all seen the videos of crash test dummies . . . and your beloved digital friend doesn't have a car seat in case you come to a sudden stop. You can actually use seatbelts to secure your PC in a vehicle, but I think it's just easier to lay your PC's case down flat on the floor of your vehicle. The same also goes for your monitor, which is also dangerous (for itself and your head) when airborne for short distances.

✦ **Use a towel if necessary.** If your PC has to ride on top of a surface that might scratch your case, wrap your PC in a towel or blanket to protect its finish.

Avoiding Dust Bunnies

Think I'm kidding? Dust bunnies are real — and they seem to reproduce as fast as their namesakes, too. Thanks to your trusty can of techno-nerd compressed air, however, you can banish that dust from your PC and get back to work or play.

Here's a checklist of what to do:

✦ **Open and dust your PC at least once a year.** Consider it a birthday present for your computer. Unscrew or unlatch your PC's case and use your compressed air (available at any office supply store) to blow any accumulated dust from the motherboard, adapter cards, and cables. If allowed to accumulate, that dust can act as a comfy heat-retaining blanket over your PC's circuitry, and overheated components have a significantly shorter lifespan. (For proof, check out the fans at the back of your PC's case and the fan on top of the processor. Heat is the enemy.)

✦ **Remove dust that's settled on the fan blades.** Speaking of fans, use your compressed air to get rid of any additional dust on fan blades and within air intake holes. In order to properly ventilate and cool your PC, these openings need to be free of dust bunnies.

✦ **Wipe down your PC's case and your monitor with a clean, dry cloth every few months.** You should never use any household solvents to clean your PC's case or monitor, but antistatic cleaning solutions and cloths are made just for cleaning computer hardware, which you can find at your local computer shop or office supply store.

Are you facing a stain that won't come off your PC's case, even when you use an antistatic cleaning cloth? Then try my secret weapon: Armor All protectant (which you've probably been using on your car's rubber and vinyl for years!). Apply a small amount of Armor All directly on the stain and try again.

✦ **Avoid eating around your PC.** I know; it's difficult not to snack while you're on the Internet, but at least be diligent about cleaning up afterwards and never park anything liquid anywhere near your computer!

✦ **Keep your workspace clean and open.** Surrounding your PC with papers and knickknacks might optimize your desktop space (or at least help you feel more human around an inhuman boss), but you'll be contributing to the accumulation of dust inside your computer. And, in the worst case, you'll actually be blocking the flow of air. I try to leave at least six inches of free space around the base of my PC at all times.

If your PC must be located in a dusty environment, consider an air cleaner and ionizer unit. I use one in my office, and I find significantly less dust to clean from my PC every year.

Watching Your Cables

With the popularity of external Universal Serial Bus (USB) and FireWire peripherals these days, the forest of cables sprouting from the back of your PC can look like Medusa on a bad hair day. Normally, this isn't a problem . . . until you decide to move your PC, or you want to repair or upgrade an internal component. Talk about the Gordian knot!

Here's a list of tips for keeping your cables under control:

✦ **Use ties to combine and route cables.** I'm a big fan of the reusable Velcro cable tie strips that you can find at your local office supply store. With these ties, you can easily combine cables that are heading in the same direction into a more manageable group. You can also fasten these cable ties to the underside of your desk or behind furniture to keep network and power cables hidden and out of danger.

✦ **Label your cables!** Sure, you can tell the source and destination of some cables at a glance — for example, network cables are pretty easy to spot — but what about your USB printer and scanner, which both use the same type of cable? If you must move your PC or unplug cables regularly, avoid the ritual of tracking each cable to its source by doing what techs and computer shops do: Use a label machine to identify the tip of each cable with the peripheral name.

✦ **Tighten those connectors.** "Gee, my monitor was working last night. What gives?" If you didn't use the knobs on either side of the video cable connector to tighten things down, small shifts in position over time could make cables work loose.

✦ **Check your cables for damage periodically.** I have a cat. Do you have a cat? How about a dog? If so, don't be surprised to find a chewed cable one morning . . . and pray that it isn't a power cable. (I keep all animals away from my office for this reason — not to mention the mess that a shedding dog can leave around your PC.) Of course, cables can also be damaged by bending or stretching them, so I recommend checking each cable at least once a year; I combine this ritual with my PC's yearly cleaning.

Cleaning Monitors and Scanners

Most PC owners are aware that they should keep the glass surfaces of their monitor and scanner clean — but beware, because you can do more harm than good if you don't know what you're doing. Here are the guidelines that I recommend you follow when working with monitor and scanner glass:

+ **Abrasives are taboo!** Even some household glass cleaners — which you might think could be trusted — can scratch the glass in your monitor or flatbed scanner when used with a rag or paper towel. With a scanner, small scratches can mean real trouble because a scratch can easily show up in your images at higher resolutions. Therefore, I recommend that you use only a dry, soft photographer's lens cloth (which won't scratch) or lens cloths with alcohol that are made specifically for monitors and scanners.

+ **Never spray liquids onto a flatbed scanner**. If liquid gets under the glass and into the body of the scanner, you could end up with condensation on the inside of the scanner when you use it. Again, a dry, photographer's lens cloth is a good choice . . . or premoistened lens cloths, which don't carry enough alcohol to do any harm. (I launch into scanners full-scale in Book II, Chapter 5.)

+ **Monitors should never be opened.** Never take the cover off a cathode ray tube (CRT) monitor, even if it needs cleaning. Why? Well, your PC's monitor is one of the two components of your system that carry enough voltage to seriously hurt you (the other being your PC's power supply). If your monitor needs to be serviced or cleaned on the inside, take it to your local computer shop. (Find more about monitors in Book II, Chapter 1.)

+ **Use a cover for your scanner.** Scanners are somewhat different from most external peripherals. They don't generate any heat while they're on (unlike an external hard drive), and most of us only use a scanner once or twice a week. Therefore, your scanner is a perfect candidate for a cover that will keep it clean . . . and, by no small coincidence, you'll find such covers at your local office supply store.

Cleaning Your Mouse and Keyboard

"Natasha, why we must clean Moose and Squirrel?" (Sorry, I couldn't help it.) Mice and keyboards get *grimy — fast —* because your PC's keyboard and pointing device are constantly in use, and they get pawed by human hands. (Of course, you could always wear surgical gloves, but what about your kids?)

Never fear. Here's a list of guidelines that will help you keep your pointing device and keyboard clean and working:

+ **Do the Keyboard Shake!** No, it's not a new dance craze, but it is the best method of cleaning accumulated gunk from your keyboard, and I recommend doing this at least once a month. Turn your keyboard upside down and shake it vigorously back and forth; prepare to be amazed (or grossed out, especially if the whole family uses your PC).

✦ **Buy an optical mouse or trackball. (You'll thank me.)** If you're still using an old-style mouse with a ball — how very '80s — clean it once a month as well. Unscrew the retaining ring on the bottom, remove the mouse ball, and use a cotton-tipped swab dipped in tape-cleaning alcohol (which is 90+ proof and will leave no residue) to clean the rollers inside. Also, make sure that your mousepad is clean and dust-free, and you'll prolong the life of your rodent. (Book II, Chapter 1 talks trackball.)

An optical mouse or trackball doesn't need to be cleaned anywhere near as often (if ever) — that's why I keep crowing about them.

✦ **Find yet another use for your compressed air.** Your keyboard can collect debris that can't be shaken free. If so, using compressed air will likely blow it free (unless it's alive and well dug-in, but I haven't encountered anything like that in my travels so far).

Book II
Chapter 4

Maintaining Your Hardware

Cleaning and Maintaining Your Printer

Time to consider a peripheral that not only needs cleaning but can also contribute mightily to its own mess. If you've ever had to clean up spilled laser printer toner, I think you know what I mean. Printers have all the necessary features that make them prime targets for regular maintenance:

✦ They're open to the outside world.

✦ They're stuffed full of complex moving parts.

✦ They're constantly running out of ink or toner.

✦ They act as a magnet for dust.

In this section, I show you how to clean and maintain yon printing instrument. Consider this section as the maintenance highlights from *HP Printer Handbook,* 2nd Edition, by Mark Chambers (Wiley).

Cleaning laser printers

Your laser printer contains a mortal enemy — *toner,* that insidious stuff that seems to have a diabolical mind of its own. Luckily, most cartridges are at least partially sealed, and only older models of laser printers can produce a really nasty Three Mile Island-level spill. If any toner escapes, however, you'll quickly find that it's a very fine powder that's sensitive to static charges and that immediately heads to every corner of your printer. Those nooks and crannies can be a real pain to clean. And because toner can permanently stain clothing and carpet — *and* it's harmful to pets and kids — you should be doubly careful to keep toner inside the cartridge where it belongs.

Therefore, please take the time to completely read the instructions for your specific laser printer before you install that first toner cartridge. Also avoid shaking the cartridge unless the manufacturer recommends a particular motion to help distribute the toner evenly.

If you do spill toner, head to your local office supply store for toner clean-up cloths. These handy wipes contain a chemical that attracts toner and keeps it on the cloth. Oh, and don't use warm or hot water to wash toner off your hands — toner can literally melt and adhere to your skin!

Never attempt to clean the interior of your laser printer while it's on! Laser technology uses very high temperatures to bond toner to paper, so you could be subject to serious burns if you're not careful. I always make sure that a laser printer has been off for at least 30 minutes before I clean or service it.

Although you should follow the specific instructions for your brand and model of laser printer while cleaning the interior, here's a list of the parts that are generally covered in a good cleaning:

✦ **Corona wires:** These wires (see Figure 4-1) transfer a static charge to the paper to attract toner, but if they get dusty, you'll immediately see spotting and degraded print quality in your printed documents. Most manufacturers advise that you use a clean, dry cotton swab to gently wipe the wires. You should find the wires close to the paper rollers inside your printer. (Look for labels added by the manufacturer that point to them and also check your printer's manual if necessary.)

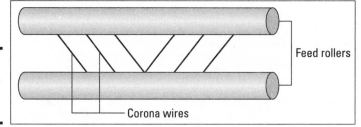

Figure 4-1: In this case, a Corona is not a beer.

Feed rollers

Corona wires

✦ **Toner guard:** These felt pads trap excess toner before it gets on your documents. You might receive a new toner guard set with each cartridge, but in a pinch, you can probably remove the pads from your printer and rub them on a clean cloth to remove that built-up toner.

✦ **Paper feed rollers:** Use a cotton swab soaked in alcohol to clean the buildup from your paper rollers, as shown so artistically in Figure 4-2.

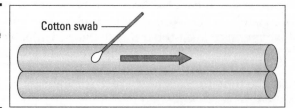

Figure 4-2: Cleaning the paper-feed rollers can make a big difference.

Cotton swab

✦ **Fan vent:** Yep, your laser printer has its own fan — remember the intense heat that I mention a few paragraphs ago? And just like the fan cleaning that I recommended for your PC, it's a good idea to use compressed air to blow any dust from the fan and the ventilation grill.

I highly recommend using the laser printer cleaning sheets that you can find at your local office supply store. These papers are treated to remove dust and excess toner from the printer's paper path, which you normally wouldn't be able to clean. Plus, they're very easy to use: You just run them through the printer as if they were regular sheets of paper. If your printer resides in a dusty or smoky room, these sheets are worth their weight in gold.

Changing inkjet cartridges

Here are two methods of determining when you need to change the cartridges in your inkjet printer:

✦ **The automatic route:** Most inkjet printers on the market today have on-screen alerts that appear when the ink level of the cartridge is low. Or, like you see in Figure 4-3, your printer might actually be able to display the amount of ink remaining in a cartridge. (A very valuable trick, indeed, especially for students with term papers looming in the near future.)

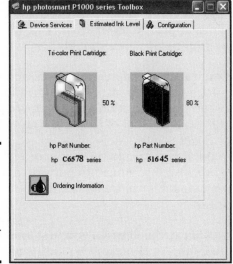

Figure 4-3:
Checking
the ink
levels on a
late-model
inkjet printer
is a cinch.

✦ **The "Man, I can barely read this page!" method:** If you have an older inkjet printer, you might not receive any warning at all about the ink levels in your cartridges — but when they're empty, pardner, you'll know.

After you know that you need to change your cartridges, however, the general procedure is the same for virtually every inkjet printer that I've ever encountered:

1. **Open the top of your printer.**

This will cause most printer models to politely center the carriage to provide you with access to the cartridges.

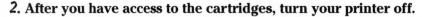

2. After you have access to the cartridges, turn your printer off.

Never try to change the cartridges in a printer that's still powered on! (Your fingers will thank me.)

3. Lift or turn the latches holding the ink cartridge in place.

Most inkjet printers have at least two cartridges — one for black and one for color — so make sure that you're working with the right cartridge before you remove it.

4. Remove the used cartridge and consider refilling it.

I discuss the pros and cons of refilling cartridges later in this chapter.

5. Load the new cartridge and fasten the latch to hold it down.

6. Turn your printer back on and close the lid.

Calibrating your printer

This maintenance task is reserved only for inkjet printer owners. (My, aren't we lucky?) *Calibration* refers to the proper alignment of the inkjet cartridge nozzles to both the paper and each other; without a properly calibrated printer, your print quality will degrade over time. This is usually the problem when folks complain that lines appear fuzzy in artwork or when colored areas in printed images start or stop before they should.

If you hear a professional photographer or graphic artist talk about *color calibration,* that's something completely different; color calibration is the process of color matching between the colors that appear on your monitor and the colors produced by your printer. Most of us will never need that level of precise color, and most inkjet printers now allow you to make changes to the hue and saturation of your prints by simply dragging a slider in a printer's Properties dialog box. But if you need to perform a full color calibration, check your printer's manual for more information about using Windows color profiles.

Your printer will automatically calibrate itself when you first load a new cartridge, so I recommend that you calibrate either three months after installing a new cartridge or when you notice that your print quality is suffering . . . whichever comes first. (Of course, the time period will vary according to how often you use your printer and the length of your average printed document.)

Although each brand (and sometimes each model) of printer has different onscreen controls for calibrating output, you should be able to access them from the printer's Properties dialog box. Follow these steps in Windows XP:

1. Choose Start⇨Printers and Faxes (or Start⇨Settings⇨Printers and Faxes, depending on how your Start menu is configured).

You see the available printers on your system, as shown in Figure 4-4.

2. Right-click the printer that you want to calibrate and then choose Properties from the shortcut menu that appears.

A dialog box somewhat similar to Figure 4-5 appears.

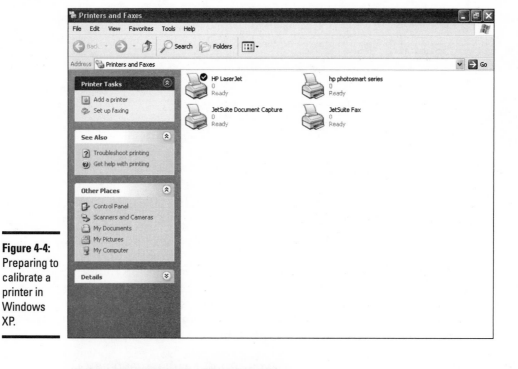

Figure 4-4:
Preparing to
calibrate a
printer in
Windows
XP.

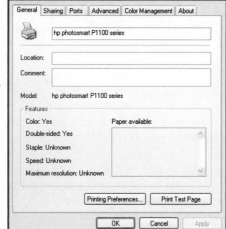

Figure 4-5:
The
Properties
dialog box
for a typical
Hewlett-
Packard
inkjet
printer.

3. **If the printer's calibration function isn't visible from the General tab, you might have to search for it on the Advanced tab. You can try clicking the Printing Preferences button as well — in my case, I have to do that and also click the Services tab.**

If it still fails to appear, check your printer manual for the location of the calibration controls; some printer manufacturers provide a separate application that you can run to display your maintenance toolbox.

Figure 4-6 illustrates the calibration dialog box for my HP printer.

4. **Run the calibration. (In my case, I click the Calibrate button.)**

The process takes under a minute and uses a single sheet of paper.

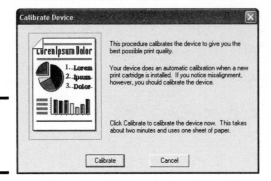

Figure 4-6:
Ready to
calibrate,
Captain!

Cleaning inkjet cartridges

Here's yet another fun task limited to just inkjet owners. I usually clean my inkjet cartridge nozzles about once every three months or whenever the output from my printer suddenly starts showing streaks of horizontal white lines. (As you've probably guessed, the nozzles control the placement and amount of each droplet of ink.) The good news is that you won't need a bucket and a scrub brush for this chore; instead, your printer can take care of cleaning its own cartridges (with your approval, of course).

A new inkjet cartridge provides your printer with a brand-new set of nozzles, so you should restart that three-month period when you change cartridges. However, if you refill an inkjet cartridge — which I discuss in the next section — you should clean the cartridge nozzles immediately after the refilled cartridge has been reinstalled.

Like the calibration controls that I discuss in the preceding section, the location of your printer's cartridge cleaning controls is very likely buried somewhere within its Properties dialog box, or it's available when you run the maintenance program supplied by your printer manufacturer. To display the Properties dialog box for your printer, follow the procedure that I cover earlier.

Figure 4-7 illustrates the cleaning controls for my HP inkjet printer. I just click the Clean button, wait about a minute, and I'm done.

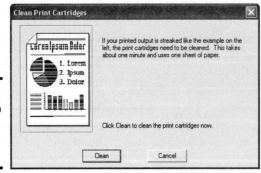

Figure 4-7:
Preparing to
clean my
inkjet
nozzles.

Should you refill used inkjet cartridges?

I'll be honest with you: I don't refill inkjet cartridges, and I don't recommend that you do, either. The only real advantage to refilling cartridges is the money that you save over buying a new cartridge. As a fellow inkjet owner myself, I feel your pain when you're standing in the checkout line at Wal-Mart with a $40 cartridge in your hand.

However, here are the reasons why I buy new cartridges — consider these the facts that you *won't* see when that refill kit TV commercial appears for the umpteenth time:

✦ **You'll probably get messy.** Even if you're experienced at refilling an ink cartridge, there's a good chance that you'll end up with a toxic spill. Make sure that you cover your work surface with a plastic sheet and don't wear anything formal.

✦ **You get substandard ink.** One of the reasons why ink refills are cheaper is that the quality of the ink used in the refill kits is usually never as good as the ink in a new cartridge. That second-rate ink can cause color changes or uneven coverage and might also end up taking longer to dry (resulting in Smear City).

✦ **You're reusing the nozzles.** I mention cleaning cartridge nozzles in the previous section. Unfortunately, those nozzles are not meant to be reused, and refilling a cartridge can result in clogs. You'll have to clean your cartridges far more often, and the quality of your printer's output might drop appreciably over time when you use a refilled cartridge.

Thus my decision and my recommendation — let someone else suffer below-par print quality by refilling used cartridges.

CHECK IT OUT

Cleaning CDs and the Keyboard

If you don't have a CD cleaning kit handy, how do you do clean a CD? The answer: Take your CD into the shower with you. Use a little bit of hand soap, lathered in your hands, lightly applied to the shiny side of the CD. When you get out of the shower, use a soft, clean towel and wipe the shiny side from the middle of the CD toward the outside. Works like a champ — on eyeglasses, too.

Have you ever spilled a latte on your keyboard? Don't panic. Turn the keyboard upside down. Let it sit that way for a few hours. Then take the screws off the back of the keyboard and pop off as much of the plastic as you can — but *leave the keys attached*. Using a washcloth that's been slightly moistened, clean up as much of the spilled junk as you can. Pull out a handful of cotton swabs and, using rubbing alcohol, dig into the nooks and crannies. Then reassemble the keyboard and give it a go.

**Book II
Chapter 4**

Maintaining Your
Hardware

Chapter 5: Scanning with Gusto

In This Chapter

- Understanding scanner technology
- Shopping for a flatbed scanner
- Acquiring an image
- Rotating and cropping your scans
- Converting and saving scanned images
- Guidelines to follow while scanning
- Handling copyrighted material

A scanner might rank as one of the most versatile pieces of hardware that you can slap onto your PC. With an investment of anywhere from $100 to $400, you can add the ability to copy and fax printed documents (with a modem and printer, of course), create digital images from all sorts of materials, and even use Optical Character Recognition (OCR) to read text from documents directly into your PC's word processing application.

What's inexpensive isn't always easy to use, however. You'll have to choose from different types of scanners that use different types of connections to your PC — and to produce the best results, you need at least an introduction to the basics of scanning. You also need the skinny on cleaning a scanner, deciding on an image format, and handling copyrighted material.

In this chapter, I provide you with an introduction to the basics of scanning. Consider these recommendations, tips, and tricks as a quick-start guide from *Scanners For Dummies* by Mark Chambers (published by Wiley Publishing, Inc.). If scanning catches your fancy and you decide to delve deeper, you may want to add that volume to your home or office library. (By the way, if you're planning to copy your face — or any other body part — you don't need to read this chapter. Just visit your local copy center or stay a little late at the office . . . um, and be discreet.)

What Happens Inside a Scanner?

I can't say that it's Party Central inside your scanner; in fact, most popular scanners on the market today actually have very few moving parts, so the entire device is rather boring compared with a CD recorder. Plus, you don't really have to know how your scanner does its job to use one, so you can skip to the next section with a clear conscience.

Still with me? Then read on to discover how this magic box can turn a printed document into a digital image. Check out Figure 5-1. Here's how it works:

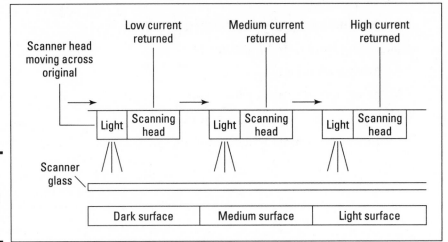

Figure 5-1:
A scanner captures an image, line by line.

1. The scanner's *sensor* (an array of photosensitive cells) moves one line across the material that you're scanning. (In some scanners, the material actually moves past a fixed sensor; this gets important pretty soon.) The sensor is paired with a strong light source that illuminates whatever you're scanning.

2. As the sensor moves past the original, each cell sends a level of current corresponding to one dot (a *pixel*) of the reflected light from the material. For example, scanning the white part of a printed page results in a far different signal than scanning the black text on the same page.

3. Your scanner's electronic brain (tiny as it is) collects all the signals from each pixel, resulting in a digital picture of one line of the original.

4. The scanner sends the data from the scanned line to your PC.

5. The sensor (or the material) advances one line, and the entire process begins again at Step 1.

I often compare this process with taking a digital photograph of each line of your document and then laboriously pasting those separate images together in an image-editing program. Luckily, you don't have to do the hard work: Your PC collects each line sent by the scanner and builds the document for you, usually while you watch. Technology is grand that way.

Your Friend, the Flatbed

Figure 5-2 illustrates a flatbed scanner preparing to do its duty; note that the top lifts up, just like a copy machine. The sensor head moves in a flatbed scanner while the material that you're scanning remains motionless on top of the scanning glass. (In a second, you'll discover why a motionless original is a good thing.)

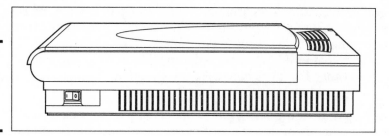

Figure 5-2:
Nothing pleases like a flatbed scanner.

Comparatively, with a sheetfed scanner, the material that you're scanning moves through a system of rollers while the sensor remains stationary. Printer manufacturers typically use sheetfed scanning hardware in all-in-one or *multifunction devices,* which combine the functionality of a printer, a scanner, a fax machine, and a copy machine in one svelte case. Gotta be honest, though — I don't recommend sheetfed scanners. And before all you owners of sheetfed scanners out there in PC Land begin reaching critical mass and flooding my e-mail inbox, let me attest to the one major advantage to sheetfed scanners like the one that you see in Figure 5-3: They do take up far less space. (I know this from personal experience because I have both sheetfed and flatbed scanners in my office.)

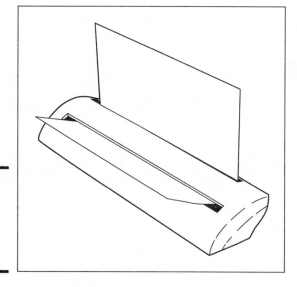

Figure 5-3:
A sheetfed scanner looks like a fax machine.

"Okay, I'll byte: If I can save valuable desktop space with a sheetfed scanner, why are you such a die-hard supporter of flatbed models?" Good question: Here are the top three reasons why you should pick a flatbed scanner:

✦ **They deliver a better quality scan:** Because the original material remains fixed in a flatbed (compared with the moving original in a sheetfed), you have less chance of shifting, allowing a flatbed to deliver a better scan with more detail.

+ **They're versatile:** If an original can fit on top of the flatbed's glass, you can scan it — pages from a book, very small items such as business cards, or even items such as clothing. With a sheetfed scanner, you're limited to paper documents, and you have to use a clear plastic sleeve to hold those business cards. (Many sheetfed scanners won't accept small items at all.)

+ **They have fewer moving parts:** Sheetfed scanners can easily jam if the original document doesn't feed correctly — and I've found them less reliable over the long run than flatbed models because sheetfed scanners require more cleaning and adjustment.

For you sheetfed scanner owners out there: Keep those documents as pristine as possible — meaning no torn edges, no staples, and no antique documents that could suddenly decide to decompose inside the hard-to-reach areas of your all-in-one unit.

If you've already invested in a sheetfed model, don't despair; there's no reason to scrap your hardware. However, you'll have to limit yourself somewhat in your material . . . unless, of course, you don't mind cutting pages out of books and magazines to scan them.

Here are other specialized types of scanners:

+ **Negative scanners:** These expensive models are especially designed to produce the best possible scans from film negatives. They do nothing else, so versatility isn't their claim to fame.

+ **Business card scanners:** Again, the name says it all. These portable scanners capture images and information from standard-size business cards. They're often used in conjunction with laptop computers or palmtop computers.

+ **Pen:** A pen scanner captures only a single line of text at once, but they're easy to carry around and can be used with a laptop computer and OCR software to read text from documents into a word processing application.

Popular Scanner Features

Here's a list of the minimum features that I typically recommend for home or home office use when you're shopping for a flatbed scanner:

+ **An optical resolution of at least 600 x 1200:** Without delving too deeply into the details of scanner *resolution* — the number of pixels that your scanner can capture — you should reject any scanner that offers less than 600 x 1200 dots per inch (dpi). Note that you should be checking the *optical* (also often called *raw*) resolution and not any resolution figure that's *enhanced* or *interpolated.* Those are just fancy words that indicate that the scanner's software is adding extra dots in the image.

I call 'em *faux pixels* because they aren't actually read from the original. Just ignore any enhanced or interpolated resolution figures when shopping for a scanner.

✦ **Single-pass operation:** If a scanner can capture all the color data that it needs in one pass, it takes less time (and introduces less room for registration error) than a scanner that must make three passes across the same original. 'Nuff said.

✦ **One-button operation:** Most of today's scanners offer one or more buttons that can automatically take care of common tasks. For example, one button might scan the original and create an e-mail message with the scanned image as an attachment, and another might scan the original and automatically print a copy on your system printer. I'm all about convenience.

✦ **A minimum of 36-bit color:** The higher the bit value, the more colors that your scanner can capture. Ignore any scanner that can't produce at least 36-bit color; most of today's scanners can produce up to 42-bit color.

✦ **A transparency adapter:** Whether it's optional or included with the scanner, the ability to add a transparency adapter allows you to scan film negatives and slides with much better results.

✦ **USB or FireWire connection:** Although a number of the most inexpensive scanners still offer parallel port connections (which share the parallel port with your printer), steer clear of them. Instead, I strongly recommend that you choose a scanner that uses either a Universal Serial Bus (USB) connection (good) or a USB 2.0 or FireWire connection (much better). Of course, your PC will need the prerequisite ports, as I explain in Chapter 3 of Book II. These Plug-and-Play ports are much faster than a parallel connection.

Basic Scanning with Paint Shop Pro

Scanner manufacturers ship a bewildering number of different capture (or *acquisition*) programs with their hardware, so there's no one proper way to scan an original. However, scanners that comply with the TWAIN standard can be controlled from within popular image editors such as Photoshop or Paint Shop Pro. (*TWAIN*, for you acronym nuts, stands for nothing . . . some people say it stands for Technology Without An Interesting Name.) Devices that are TWAIN compatible are operating system-independent — that is, interchangeable between Windows and Macintosh. Any TWAIN-compatible hardware device can work with any TWAIN-compatible image editor or software application . . . pretty *sassy*, no?

Acquiring the image

In this section, I demonstrate how to use a typical USB Hewlett-Packard scanner within Paint Shop Pro, which is my favorite image editor. If you follow along with this procedure, you'll end up with an image that you can edit within

Paint Shop Pro, convert to another format, or simply save to your hard drive. (I can heartily recommend Paint Shop Pro for its Big Three features: It's much, much cheaper than Photoshop, almost as powerful, and much easier to use!)

Assuming that you have Paint Shop Pro installed on your computer, follow these steps:

1. Double-click the Paint Shop Pro icon on your desktop or choose Start➪Programs➪Jasc Software➪Paint Shop Pro.

The main program window shown in Figure 5-4 appears.

2. Choose File➪Import➪TWAIN.

3. From the pop-up menu that appears, choose Select Source to select which TWAIN source you're using to capture the image.

The Select Source dialog box that you see in Figure 5-5 appears.

4. Highlight the TWAIN entry for your scanner (in my case, it's HP PrecisionScan LT 3.0), and then click the Select button.

Paint Shop Pro can also acquire images from most digital cameras. (I told you that this was a great program, didn't I?) From the Import menu, choose TWAIN, choose Digital Camera from the pop-up menu that appears, and then click Access. In Book II, Chapter 9, I demonstrate how to acquire images using the Windows XP Camera Wizard, but if you grow as enamored of Paint Shop Pro as I am, you might prefer to use Paint Shop Pro to download your photographs as well.

Figure 5-4:
The Paint Shop Pro main window.

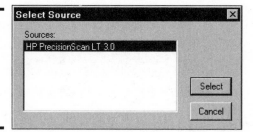

Figure 5-5:
Select your
scanner
from the
Select
Source
dialog box.

5. **Choose File⇨Import⇨TWAIN⇨Acquire.**

At this point, Paint Shop Pro invokes the scanner's TWAIN driver, so if
you're using another brand of scanner, the resulting dialog box will look
different; however, the same controls should be available if you explore
a bit.

6. **Click the Start a New Scan button.**

Your scanner should rumble to life, and eventually the Acquire dialog
will produce a thumbnail image of the original, as shown in Figure 5-6.

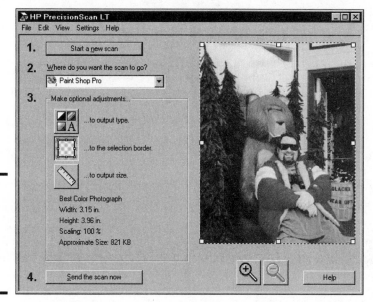

Figure 5-6:
Use the
thumbnail
image to
resize the
picture
area.

7. **If you're satisfied with the dimensions of the image and the automatic
settings chosen by your scanning software, click the Send the Scan
Now button.**

The result appears as a new image within Paint Shop Pro, as shown in
Figure 5-7, ready for you to edit and experiment with to your heart's
content.

Book II
Chapter 5

Scanning with Gusto

Figure 5-7:
The finished scan appears in Paint Shop Pro.

However, if you need to fine-tune the image before sending it to Paint Shop Pro in Step 7, here are the common settings that you can change in most scanner drivers, along with what you'll accomplish (with my scanner driver, you click the icon buttons under Step 3):

+ **Output type:** This setting controls what type of image file that the scan will produce. Typically, you'll want a color photograph in 24-bit (or 16.7 million) colors, but other choices might include a Web image at 256 colors, a grayscale image, a black-and-white drawing, or simple text (that's been optimized for reading with an OCR program).

+ **Image boundaries:** Use this feature to click and drag the boundaries of the scanned image. For example, I recommend moving the scanned image border inside any extraneous material on the edges of the original, such as text that surrounds a picture that you want from a magazine page. By reducing the size of the actual scan, your image file is smaller, and the scanner takes less time to do its job — plus, you'll eliminate the need to crop that extraneous part of the image later within Paint Shop Pro.

+ **Image scale:** Figure 5-8 illustrates the scale options for my HP scanner. Note that I can use the original image size, or I can scale the scanned image by a specified percentage. Also, I can set the width or height of the scanned image in inches, and the software automatically calculates the proper proportion change for the other dimension.

+ **dpi (or resolution):** A setting of 150 dpi is usually fine for scanning photographs or documents, but if you're planning on enlarging an image with a lot of detail, you might want to specify a higher resolution. However, this will significantly increase the size of the finished image file.

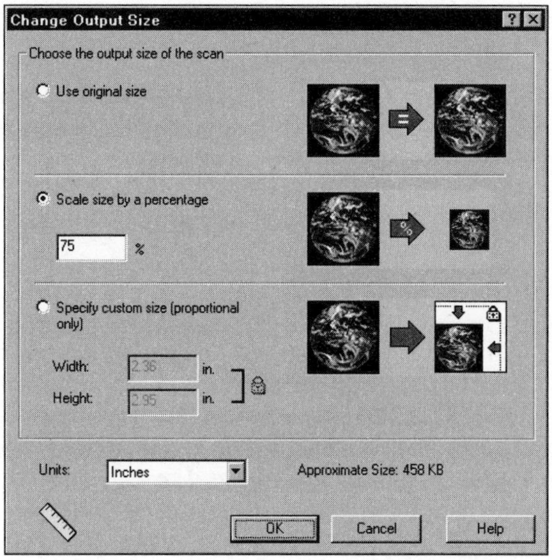

Figure 5-8:
Adjust the
size of the
scanned
image.

Rotating and cropping images

After the scanned image is safely in Paint Shop Pro or Photoshop, you're free to have fun — fixing problems big and small, removing portions of the image that you don't want, or even zooming in to view and change individual pixels.

Although a complete discussion of image editing is far too in-depth of a subject for this chapter — in fact, you can find dozens of books on Paint Shop Pro and Photoshop on the shelves, including the step-by-step coverage of image editing in *Scanners For Dummies* — I'd like to cover the two most common procedures that are required for most scanned images:

✦ **Rotation:** An image that's literally standing on end or displays upside-down needs to be *rotated* (turned).

✦ **Cropping:** An image with too much extraneous background needs to be *cropped* (trimmed). Cropping an image can significantly cut down its file size.

To rotate an image that you've scanned so that it displays in the proper orientation, follow these steps:

1. **Scan an image into Paint Shop Pro.**

Read how in the previous section.

2. **Choose Image⇨Rotate to display the Rotate dialog box, as shown in Figure 5-9.**

Figure 5-9:
Rotate an
image from
here.

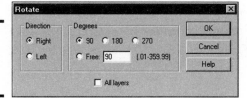

3. **Select either the Left or the Right radio button to specify the direction of rotation.**

4. **Select a Degrees radio button to rotate the image (usually either 90 or 180 degrees) or select the Free radio button and then enter a specific amount of rotation in its accompanying text field.**

5. **Click OK to rotate the image.**

To crop a scanned image, follow these steps:

1. **Click the geometric selection tool — it looks like a dotted rectangle — on the left toolbar.**

2. **Click in the top-left corner of the image area that you want to keep; then, while holding the mouse button down, drag the selection rectangle to the lower-right corner of the desired area.**

3. **Release the mouse button to select the area.**

   Paint Shop Pro indicates the area you've selected with an animated dotted line, as shown in Figure 5-10.

4. **Choose Image⇨Crop to Selection to remove everything outside the selection box; see the results in Figure 5-11.**

If you make a mistake, you can always choose Edit⇨Undo to cancel the last action that you performed.

The geometric selection tool

Figure 5-10: Select an area of an image before cropping it.

Figure 5-11:
The image is
cropped.

Converting and saving the image

When you're finished editing your image, your new work of art is ready to
be saved to disk. That takes me to discussing another feature of Paint Shop
Pro: the ability to convert the existing image format into a format that might
be more suited to your needs.

Think of a format as the structure of the image file — which, after all, is a
data file just like the programs that you run and the documents that you
save. The format is the method by which the image data is organized within
the file. I'm not going to go into a huge discussion of the different formats in
this section; rather, I just indicate which formats are better for certain applications and which ones you should avoid for those same applications.

You want to consider converting an image that you've scanned because

✦ **Some formats can save space.** The winner in this first category is definitely the JPEG (or JPG) image format, which is a file compression
format that can save you several megabytes over image formats such as
Windows bitmap (BMP) and uncompressed TIFF.

✦ **Some formats maintain image quality.** The reason why JPEG images
are so small is that they use a form of compression (rather like that
used in Zip files) to crunch the file size down to a minimum.
Unfortunately, that compression can result in degradation of the image
over time; each time that you open, edit, and save a JPEG file, it can lose
a tiny bit of detail. If archival image quality is your aim, throw file size
limitations to the wind and use BMP or uncompressed TIFF; they're
huge in size, but they preserve image quality no matter how often you
open them.

✦ **Some operating systems prefer certain formats.** Naturally, those folks on the Mac and Linux side of the fence might have problems loading and using an image in Windows (BMP) format. For compatibility reasons, consider saving your image in TIFF format, which is well supported on just about every computer in use today.

✦ **Some formats are better suited for the Web.** Virtually all Web pages use JPEG and GIF images, which are the common formats recognized by all browsers. GIF images are well suited for smaller graphics, such as buttons and animated banners, but JPEG images are better for inline graphics and full-size images that are designed to be downloaded.

Okay, now that you know whether your image needs converting, follow these steps to save (and optionally convert) your image within Paint Shop Pro:

1. **Choose File⇨Save As to display the Save As dialog box.**

2. **To convert the image to another format, click the Save as Type drop-down list and select the desired format.**

3. **Type a filename in the File Name text box.**

4. **Some formats allow you to choose additional settings — click the Options button to display them.**

For example, Figure 5-12 shows the settings that you can change for JPEG images within Paint Shop Pro. Generally, I recommend sticking with the defaults, but if you need these advanced options, make your changes and then click OK, which will return you to the Save As dialog box.

5. **Click the Save button.**

Figure 5-12:
Change advanced settings for a JPEG image.

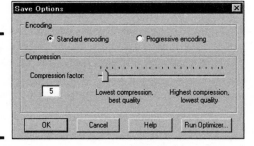

Scanning Do's and Don'ts

Today's scanning software helps to make the scanning process easier than it was just three or four years ago, but here are a number of tried-and-true guidelines that you should follow for the best results from your hardware. Here's a cheat sheet of rules that every scanner owner should follow:

✦ **Don't place heavy objects on your scanner's glass.** Believe it or not, I've heard horror stories of people trying to scan bricks and rocks — usually trying to capture a particular color or pattern for an e-mail attachment or a Web graphic. Besides the possibility of a cracked or a broken scanner glass, rough or pointed objects can cause scratches that will show up in your images.

Don't forget that paper clips and staples are public enemy number one for your scanner. Please remove them before you place your original!

✦ **Do work with the largest possible original.** The larger the original, the better quality image that you're likely to get. (Sure, you can scan a postage stamp, but use a higher dpi setting so that you have enough pixels to enlarge the image later.)

✦ **Do clean your scanner glass with the right material.** Never spray glass cleaner directly on the glass: Too much liquid on the glass can leak under the surface, causing condensation later. Instead, use a soft photographer's lens cloth or a monitor wipe premoistened with alcohol, which evaporates quickly. I clean my scanner glass at least once a week.

✦ **Do add as much RAM to your PC as you can afford.** The more memory that you add, the easier and faster your PC can handle larger scans. Remember that some of those scanned images might end up being 40 or 50MB in size. Also, any image editor will perform much better with additional memory. If you're using Photoshop or Paint Shop Pro on a regular basis, I recommend a minimum of 256MB of RAM. Memory, my friend, is cheap.

✦ **Don't overwrite your original scan.** If you're experimenting with a scanned image — for example, if you're applying filters or changing the color balance for an artistic effect — keep the original as is and save a copy with your changes. After you've applied changes in an image editor and saved those changes, you usually can't backtrack to the quality of the original image.

✦ **Do keep your scanner drivers up-to-date.** Like other hardware devices that I mention throughout this book, check your scanner manufacturer's Web site often for updates to your scanning software and for Windows drivers.

✦ **Don't use outdated or specialized image formats.** PC owners should avoid Microsoft Paint (MSP) images. (I like to call these little-known and less-recognized formats by a single collective acronym — WIF, which stands for *Weird Image Format*.) My point is simple: By using one of the major image formats (TIFF, JPEG, BMP, or GIF), you give others a better chance to load and work with your scanned images.

Those Irritating (Or Invaluable) Copyrights

Of course, copyrights aren't so doggone irritating if you happen to be the creator of a work of digital art (whether it be a photograph, a painting, or a poem). As an author, I'm personally all for copyrights. However, as a scanner owner, you might find yourself walking a legal tightrope without a pole when you decide to include scanned material in your own documents.

Like I said, I'm an author — not a lawyer! (I do know some great lawyer jokes, but that's not the same as a law degree.) Therefore, before I describe some of the common myths about copyright law, let me say that you should *always* consult with a knowledgeable copyright lawyer. These guidelines are here to help, but they're not a substitute for bona fide legal advice.

With that well-worded disclaimer in mind, here is a selection of the most common fallacies concerning copyrighted material:

✦ **"I got it off the Internet, so it must be public domain."** Wrong. It doesn't matter where you got a creative work — from the Internet, a publication, or even off the wall of a subway tunnel. If you use anything that you didn't create completely by yourself, you need permission from the author.

✦ **"I added a line and some shading to this scanned image, so now it's mine."** Embellishing an original work does *not* make it yours. (After all, I can add an extra line of lyrics to any Beatles song that you can name, but that doesn't give me the copyright to "Eight Days a Week.")

✦ **"This photograph didn't carry a copyright mark, so the scan is my original work."** Nope. An original work, whether a document, a photograph, or a scribble on a napkin, doesn't need any mark (although a copyright mark does reinforce your copyright claim). In the legal world, a copyright is bestowed automatically in most cases as soon as the creator completes the work.

✦ **"This is a not-for-profit project, so I can include this artwork."** This might be true, but only if you're using a clip art collection or royalty-free photograph archive that gives you specific rights to use intellectual property in your work. Otherwise, it doesn't matter whether your work is for profit or nonprofit — a copyright applies to the original work in either case.

✦ **"Why, the very act of scanning this photograph gives me the copyright."** I don't hear this one often. Evidently, by creating a digital copy, these folks think that they can magically acquire the copyright. (Sound of palm slapping forehead.) Why didn't I think of that before? Oh, yes, now I remember — it's not true. Simply changing the form of a work doesn't release the creator's copyright.

✦ **"This artwork was drawn a hundred years ago — the copyright doesn't apply to me."** Before you assume that a copyright has expired on a work, check with a copyright lawyer. Descendents of the original copyright owner might now own the rights to the work.

Adding a Copyright Line

If you'd like to add a copyright line to the work that you've scanned, Paint Shop Pro can help you out there as well. Run the program and follow these steps:

1. **Choose File⇨Open to display the familiar Windows Open dialog box.**

2. **Navigate to the location of the scanned image file, click it to highlight the file name, and then click the Open button.**

3. **Click the text icon on the left toolbar (it looks like a capital letter A).**

4. **Click the cursor in the area of the image where you want the mark to appear.**

   Paint Shop Pro displays the Text Entry dialog box, as shown in Figure 5-13.

5. **To select a new font, click the Name drop-down list.**

   From the Text Entry dialog box, you can also change the size of the text as well as its color and characteristics (such as bold, italics, and underlining).

6. **After the font in the Sample Text display appears as you want, click within the Enter Text Here box and type the text of your copyright line.**

   A typical copyright mark reads like this: **Copyright (c) [*year*] by [*name*], All Rights Reserved**. (Naturally, you'll want to substitute the current year and your name where I've indicated.)

7. **Save the new image under a new filename by choosing File⇨Save As and entering a filename in the Save As dialog box that appears.**

Book II
Chapter 5

Scanning with Gusto

Figure 5-13: Select the font characteristics for a copyright line.

Text tool

CHECK IT OUT

Burning a Slideshow on a CD

If you have a CD filled with pictures, you can plop that CD into any computer that has Windows XP on it and use all of the many Windows XP features to look at the pictures, copy them, and so on. In particular, it's easy to view all of the pictures in a folder as a slideshow — just open the folder in Windows Explorer and choose View⇨As Slideshow.

But what about your friends who don't have Windows XP? If you send the CD to people who don't have Windows XP installed, they can open the files, or (on most versions of Windows) view thumbnails of the pics. But they'll have a devil of a time watching the pictures as a slideshow — a feature that older versions of Windows simply don't have.

Fortunately, if you have the foresight, you can burn the CD as a slideshow — one that will run on any version of Windows. This technique is quick, efficient, and surprisingly easy to perform after you figure out what to do.

To burn a slideshow to a CD, follow these steps:

1. **Start Internet Explorer and go to** www.microsoft.com/windowsxp/ pro/downloads/powertoys.asp.

2. **Download the file listed as** Slideshow.exe.

   This is more complicated than it should be. The main PowerToys page identifies this particular PowerToy as the CD Slideshow Generator. The program listed for download on that page is called Slideshow.exe, but when you download it, you discover that the file is really called SlideshowPowertoySetup. exe. **Argh.**

3. **After** SlideshowPowertoySetup.exe **is downloaded, run it.**

   Windows steps you through a very simple installation wizard. The CD Slideshow Generator isn't a separate, standalone program. Instead, it works by inserting itself as an extra step in the CD Writing Wizard.

4. **Gather the pictures you want to burn on the CD and click the Copy from CD button to start the CD Writing Wizard.**

5. **Click Next on the first screen of the CD Writing Wizard.**

   You see a new option to add a picture viewer to the CD.

6. **Click Yes, Add A Picture Viewer; then click Next.**

   The CD Slideshow Generator adds three files to the CD being burned.

7. **Burn the pictures onto the CD.**

8. **After you're finished creating the CD Slideshow, test the CD by putting it into a machine that's running an earlier version of Windows.**

   A slideshow appears along with a very simple set of control buttons in the upper-left corner. The slideshow runs all by itself if you don't push any buttons or click anything on-screen. However, you can use the control buttons or arrow keys in the obvious way to move from picture to picture.

Chapter 6: Dude, MP3 Rocks!

In This Chapter

- Understanding the MP3 format
- Ripping MP3 files from an audio CD
- Playing MP3 files
- Downloading MP3 music to your MP3 player
- Comparing other audio formats with MP3
- Burning audio CDs from MP3 files

*C*an you name one or two truly revolutionary technologies that have arrived in the last ten years? Perhaps CD-ROMs and DVD-ROMs, mobile telephones, or the *Jerry Springer Show?* (Okay, that last one was a deliberate attempt at humor.) Anyway, historians often claim that no person can accurately point to a world-changing technology in his or her lifetime because we just don't have the perspective to recognize its importance when it happens. Well, guess what? MP3 is here in your lifetime; it absolutely rocks; and my friend, it is *indeed* one of those revolutionary technologies.

To be honest, that's not really such an earth-shattering prediction . . . in fact, it's already happening! In this chapter, I tell you what's so incredibly cool about MP3 digital music, how you can create your own MP3s, and — here's the spoiler — why the recording industry would love to stop you from using MP3 files altogether. (Yes, MP3 is legal when used correctly. Sorry, Big Brother Music.)

An MP3 Primer

First off, what is a furshlugginer MP3, anyway? Things can get real technical real fast here, and that's not what this book is about — therefore, here's my definition of the MP3 process for Normal Human Beings: When you create (or *rip*) an MP3 (short for MPEG-1 Layer 3) file, you're capturing (or *sampling*) an analog sound recording and saving that audio in digital form.

Clear as mud? Here's another way to think of it: MP3 files store music and audio in the same fashion that music is stored on an audio CD — as a string of *binary* characters. It's all zeroes and ones, but your PC — and Macs, and MP3 players, and even many personal electronic devices such as personal digital assistants (PDAs) and portable stereos — can decode that binary information and re-create it as the original analog signal.

Note that just about any CD-ROM drive — including the read-only variety — can rip tracks, so you don't need a CD or DVD recorder to do the job. The process is technically called *digital audio extraction,* but you and I call it *ripping.*

Here are more parallels between audio CDs and MP3 files:

✦ A typical MP3 file corresponds to a single track on an audio CD (which makes sense because virtually all MP3s are ripped directly from audio CDs).

✦ MP3 files offer the same — or even better — audio quality than audio CDs.

✦ Like the tracks on an audio CD, MP3 files can contain information about the song title and artist.

✦ Like the music on an audio CD, the quality of an MP3 recording stays pristine no matter how many copies of that MP3 file you make. Because it's digital, there's no degradation when you make additional copies of an MP3.

✦ A series of MP3 files can be recorded (or burned) onto a blank CD-R, creating a new audio CD. You can even burn MP3 files from many different CDs to produce your own compilation discs.

Because an MP3 file is just another data file to your PC, you can do many of the same things with an MP3 file that you can do with other digital media files (such as an image from your digital camera). For example, you can

✦ **Send 'em:** Send smaller MP3s as e-mail attachments.

✦ **Download 'em:** Allow MP3 files to be downloaded from your Web site or File Transfer Protocol (FTP) server.

✦ **Save 'em:** Save MP3 files to removable media such as Zip disks, CDs and DVDs, and Universal Serial Bus (USB) Flash drives.

Of course, this very portability is a double-edged sword because it makes MP3 music easy to copy — which, under copyright law, is another synonym for *steal.* I discuss what you can and can't legally do with your MP3 files at the end of the chapter.

The audio quality of an MP3 file is determined by the *bit rate* at which it is sampled. The higher the bit rate, the better the sound file (and the larger the size of the physical MP3 file itself, which makes sense). Table 6-1 lists some of the common bit rates for different types of MP3 files — anything over 128 Kbps is actually better than the quality of audio CD tracks.

Table 6-1		Bit Rates for MP3 Files		
Audio Books	*FM Stereo Quality*	*Near-CD Quality*	*Audio CD Quality*	*Audiophile Quality*
48 Kbps	64 Kbps	96 Kbps	128 Kbps	160/192/256/320 Kbps

Ripping Your Own MP3 Files

To demonstrate just how easy it is to rip MP3 files from an existing audio CD, I'll choose an audio CD from my collection at random — hmmm, how about the Chairman of the Board, Frank Sinatra, and his classic album *Come Fly with Me* — and then extract a set of MP3 files that I can listen to with my Apple iPod MP3 player.

For this demonstration, I'll use my favorite software for ripping MP3 files on the PC: MUSICMATCH Jukebox 7.5, from MUSICMATCH (www.musicmatch.com). You can download the basic version of Jukebox for free from the company's Web site or upgrade to the Pro version for a mere $20.

Here's the first inkling of the copyright controversy, which I wade into at the end of this chapter: You can only legally rip MP3 files from audio CDs that you've bought for yourself! By ripping songs from a friend's CD — or even an audio CD that you borrowed from the public library — you're violating copyright law. (In this case, I own this audio CD, so I can legally create MP3 files from it for my own personal use. However, I can't give those MP3 files to anyone else, or I'm in violation of copyright law.)

Now that Perry Mason has had his say, follow these steps to create your own MP3 files from an audio CD:

1. **Choose Start➪All Programs➪Musicmatch➪Musicmatch Jukebox to run the program, which displays the main window that you see in Figure 6-1.**

Book II
Chapter 6

Dude, MP3 Rocks!

Figure 6-1:
The familiar curvaceous line of MUSIC-MATCH Jukebox.

2. **Load the audio CD into your drive.**

Jukebox displays the track names in the playlist pane, shown at the right in Figure 6-2, and begins to play the CD. Because I don't want to listen to the disc right now, I click the Stop button (which sports a square shape) on the program's control panel.

Figure 6-2:
Jukebox can automatically play an audio CD.

3. **Before you extract any tracks, you must configure the MP3 settings within Jukebox.**

    a. **Click the Options menu.**

    b. **Choose Recorder.**

    c. **Click Settings to display the Settings dialog box shown in Figure 6-3.**

    In this case, I want my MP3 tracks for my iPod player, so I want CD-quality music. Typically, this will be your best choice as well, unless you need the smallest possible MP3 file sizes (use 8 Kbps) or you're ripping something like an audio book.

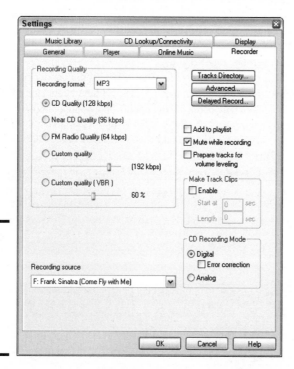

Figure 6-3: Always configure (or check) your MP3 settings before you rip.

4. **Click the Recording Format drop-down list box and choose MP3; then select the CD Quality (128 Kbps) radio button.**

    If you want to listen to the tracks while you rip 'em, deselect the Mute while Recording check box. Click OK to save any changes that you've made and return to Jukebox.

    If you have more than one CD or DVD-ROM drive in your PC, check to make sure that the Recording Source is set to the proper drive before you leave the Settings dialog box.

5. **To start the actual ripping process, click the Record button on the control panel (bottom left); like a VCR or cassette recorder, it has a red dot on it.**

TIP

Don't click the Record button *under the track list* (bottom right), which burns a CD with the contents of the list. (You don't need to record a disc that you already have!) Jukebox displays the Recorder pane that you see in Figure 6-4, complete with the track names already listed.

Figure 6-4:
The Recorder pane appears when you're ready to rip.

6. **Select the tracks that you want to rip.**

   By default, Jukebox automatically rips all the tracks on the disc, so they're all checked. If you don't want to rip a track, just deselect the check box next to the track title. Note that you can click the None button to remove all the checks, which makes it easier to rip only one or two tracks from an entire CD.

7. **Let the ripping begin! Click the red Record button on the Recorder pane, and then sit back and watch the progress for each track, as shown in Figure 6-5.**

   The completed MP3 files are placed in a separate folder within your My Music folder, complete with the artist name and album title.

Figure 6-5:
Keep an eye on the progress of your rip.

Listening to Your Stuff

After you're riding the digital wave of the future and you've ripped a number of MP3 files, you're ready to enjoy them. Here are a number of different ways to listen to MP3s on your PC, using both MUSICMATCH Jukebox and the built-in MP3 support in Windows XP:

✦ **Double-click an MP3 file in Explorer.** Double-clicking an MP3 file loads the program associated with MP3 audio on your system. By default, this is Windows Media Player, but if you've installed another MP3 player — such as Jukebox, or the great freeware media player Winamp (www. winamp.com, shown in Figure 6-6) — Windows will play the file with that program instead.

✦ **Right-click an MP3 file and then choose Play from the shortcut menu that appears.**

✦ **Run an MP3 player application such as MUSICMATCH Jukebox.**

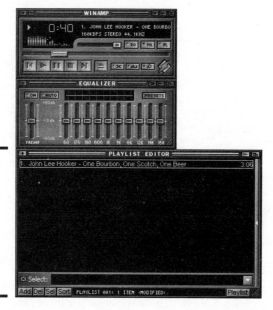

Figure 6-6:
The freeware program Winamp, hard at work playing MP3 files.

If Windows XP is using the wrong application to play MP3 files — for example, if you want Windows Media Player to run when you double-click an MP3 file — it's time to change the association for the file. Right-click the MP3 file and choose Open With from the menu that appears; then click Choose Program to display the Open With dialog box. Click the application with which you want to play your MP3 files, make sure that the Always Use the Selected Program to Open This Kind of File check box is selected, and then click OK.

If you're using Jukebox, follow these steps to listen to one or more MP3 files:

1. **Choose Start➪All Programs➪Musicmatch➪Musicmatch Jukebox to run the program.**

2. **Click and drag the desired MP3 files from an Explorer window and drop them in the Jukebox playlist pane.**

If you select multiple MP3 files, they're played in order.

3. **To skip to the previous and next tracks, click the Previous and Next buttons on the Jukebox control panel — huge surprise there, right?**

MP3s are easy to pause while you're retrieving your toaster pastry from the toaster. Just click the Pause button to pause the audio and click it again to restart the playback.

Jukebox remembers the songs that you added to your playlist, so if you want to start over with a clean slate, click the Clear button at the bottom of the playlist. Also note that you can repeat the playlist by clicking the Repeat button. To save a playlist for future use, click the Options menu, choose Playlist, and then click Save Playlist — you can open the playlist file later by pressing Ctrl+O.

Downloading to an MP3 Player

Here's yet another significantly cool thing that Jukebox can do for you: It can download MP3 files to your personal MP3 player for your portable listening pleasure. For example, I use my iPod, which has 5GB of storage, a built-in 5-hour battery, and a very fast FireWire connection. (Although PC owners might not like it, the iPod is another masterpiece of design from our friends at Apple Computer, www.apple.com. Luckily, it works on the PC as well, when using MUSICMATCH Jukebox.) I can heartily recommend this sweet machine as the best MP3 player on the market today.

To use a supported MP3 player with Jukebox, you must first download the proper device plug-in from the MUSICMATCH Web site. This process is easy because Jukebox takes care of it automatically. After the plug-in is in place, follow the steps in the previous section to add MP3 tracks to your playlist (or to load an existing playlist).

To download the songs in your current playlist to your MP3 player, follow these steps:

1. **Plug your MP3 player into the USB or FireWire port.**

   Windows should automatically recognize that you've plugged the device in.

2. **Choose File⇨Send to Portable Device.**

   The Portable Device Manager window that you see in Figure 6-7 displays.

3. **If you want to rearrange any of the tracks before downloading them, click the track title that you want to move and then drag it to its new location in the window.**

   You can also click the Add button to add extra MP3 files, or you can click the Remove button to delete the selected track from the MP3 player playlist. (Note that this will not delete the MP3 file from your hard drive, just from the playlist. Whew.)

4. **After the Portable Device Manager playlist is just the way that you want it, click the Attached Portable Devices folder in the left pane of the window and then click your MP3 player to select it.**

5. **Click the Sync button to copy the songs to your MP3 player.**

6. **After the copying process is complete, click the Eject button, unplug your player, and jam!**

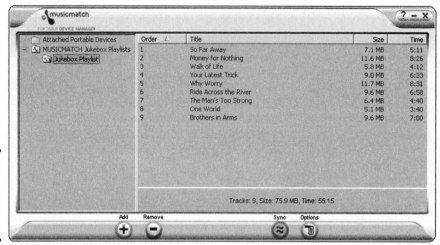

Figure 6-7:
Preparing to
download
MP3 files to
my iPod.

Using Other Sound Formats

I would be remiss if I didn't mention some of the other sampled sound formats out there on the Internet (and sometimes swapped between PC owners). However, the MP3 format is now so popular for music that these other formats have been reduced to storing Windows sound effects and such. Some sound editors can convert audio between different formats, but if you're working with music, you can't lose with MP3.

I got the music in me — illegally?

"Okay, everything that I've read in this chapter is cool beyond belief — now, what's this you're telling me? My MP3 collection might be *illegal?*" It's possible . . . it all depends on where you obtained the original audio CDs! Here's the rule: If you didn't buy the audio CD and you don't own it, you can't legally rip any audio. Period.

The reasoning behind this copyright law is similar to the law governing the duplication of computer programs, where only the owner is generally allowed to copy a piece of commercial software. By law, any copy of a program that you make is to be used for backup purposes; you can't give that copy to anyone else, and it can't be loaded on anyone else's PC.

Likewise, you can create all the MP3 files from your own audio CDs that you like, and you can listen to them with your personal MP3 player — but you can't give those MP3 files to anyone else. You also can't distribute them over the Web or Internet newsgroups, and you can't give one of your *Best of Slim Whitman* compilation CDs to your friend.

Music publishers are considering a number of different copy protection schemes that can help safeguard audio CDs from wanton ripping. Only the future will determine just how successful these schemes will be. You know how tricky those hackers can be, and it's likely that any copy protection will be broken sooner or later.

Of course, not everyone follows these rules to the letter. As a matter of fact, I don't know any folks who spend their nights tossing and turning because they ripped tracks from *Johnny Cash at Folsom Prison.* However, it's my duty to make sure that you know the legal ramifications of The Rip Thing. End of story.

WAV format

Microsoft's Windows Audio/Video (WAV) audio format is the standard format used by Windows for playing sound effects, and it's also used in games and on the Web. Your browser should recognize and play WAV audio files like a familiar old friend. Although WAV files can be recorded at audio CD quality — and therefore can be used to record music — MP3 files offer the same (or better) quality and are much smaller in comparison. All current versions of Windows include a simple sound recorder that can capture WAV files by using a microphone plugged into your PC.

WMA format

Not to be outdone by MP3, Microsoft has recently been pushing the WMA format (short for *Windows Media Audio*) as a real contender for the Best Digital Audio Format crown. Indeed, WMA files are as high in quality as MP3 files, and WMA audio can be recorded in multichannel 5.1 Surround sound. However, I don't see the challenger from Redmond usurping MP3 anytime soon. For once, I think that the open standard is stronger than any proprietary standard that Microsoft will attempt to enforce. For example, many current MP3 players won't recognize or support WMA tracks — and portable MP3 players sure don't need Surround sound.

AU format

The Audio Unix (AU) format was introduced by Sun Microsystems, so (as you would expect) it's a popular standard for systems running Unix and Linux. AU audio files are typically lower quality than MP3 files, but they're even smaller in size, making them popular on many Web sites. Luckily, both Internet Explorer and Netscape Navigator can play AU files with ease.

AIFF format

Apple once used the Audio Interchange File Format (AIFF) sound file format as standard equipment within its operating systems, including music files. However, these days the Cupertino Crew has switched wholeheartedly and completely to MP3, so AIFF has already started down the road once taken by the dinosaurs. (Mac OS 9 and Mac OS X still recognize AIFF files for sound effects, but that's about it.) Although AIFF files can be recorded at CD quality, they're simply huge, so don't expect to find them on the Web or on your personal MP3 player.

MIDI format

Musical Instrument Digital Interface (MIDI) files aren't actually digital audio but instead are directions on how to play a song — kind of like how a program is a set of directions that tells your computer how to accomplish a task. Your PC or a MIDI instrument (like a MIDI keyboard) can read a MIDI file and play the song back. As you might guess, however, MIDI music really doesn't sound like the digitally sampled sound that you'll get from an MP3 or WMA file. I discuss MIDI support when I cover upgrading your sound card in Book II, Chapter 15.

Burning Audio CDs from MP3 Files

Return with me to the multitalented MUSICMATCH Jukebox so that I can demonstrate how to burn your own audio CDs from your MP3 collection. The resulting disc is a perfect match for any home or car CD player and can also be played in your PC's CD or DVD drive. (Both the free version and the Plus version of Jukebox can burn CDs, but here I describe how to record a disc by using the Plus version.)

To record an audio CD from MP3 files, follow these steps:

1. **Build your playlist within Jukebox as you normally would.**

2. **When you've added all the tracks that you want to record, click the Burn button at the bottom of the Playlist pane.**

Jukebox displays the Burner Plus window that you see in Figure 6-8.

Figure 6-8:
Arrange
MP3 tracks
before
burning
them to an
audio CD.

3. **Like the Portable Device Manager window that I describe earlier (see the section, "Downloading to an MP3 Player"), you can rearrange the order of the tracks on your audio CD by clicking the desired track title and then dragging it to its new location in the window.**

To add more songs, click the Add button; to remove the selected track from the disc layout, click the Remove button.

This does not delete the offending MP3 file from your hard drive.

The Burner Plus window keeps track of the percentage of space that you've used with the current playlist as well as the remaining time left on the disc layout (measured in seconds). You can use these totals to determine how many additional tracks you can squeeze onto your CD.

4. Make sure that the first button next to the disc name is selected.

This button, which carries a musical note icon, specifies that you want to record an audio CD (rather than an MP3 CD or a data CD).

5. Load a blank CD-R into your recorder.

Only certain audio CD players can read a CD-RW (rewriteable disc), so always use write-once CD-R media for true compatibility with all audio CD players.

6. Click the Burn button on the Burner Plus window, sit back, and relax while your new disc is recorded.

Chapter 7: Making Movies with Your PC

In This Chapter

✔ Importing video clips

✔ Assembling a movie

✔ Adding transitions

✔ Using special effects

✔ Adding a soundtrack

✔ Using titles

✔ Previewing your movie

✔ Saving and recording the finished film

*H*ave you long harbored the urge to make your own film? You pick the subject — from your kid's kindergarten graduation to a science fiction action flick worthy of Arnold himself. You edit your footage, add professional-looking transitions and special effects, and even set the mood with a custom soundtrack recorded on your aunt's antique Hammond organ. Ladies and gentlemen, this is the definition of *sweet* — and it's all made possible by your PC. (For the full effect, buy a canvas director's chair and a megaphone.)

In this chapter, I demonstrate how you can use footage from your digital video (DV) camcorder — or, with the right equipment, even the footage that you've recorded on tape — to produce your own film. Your finished work of visual art can be saved to a CD-R or DVD-R or stored on your hard drive for use on your Web pages.

Getting the Lowdown on ArcSoft's ShowBiz

My filmmaking tool of choice is ShowBiz, which is a popular, entry-level $79 video editor from ArcSoft (`www.arcsoft.com`), as shown in Figure 7-1. ShowBiz has far more features than Windows Movie Maker (which ships with Windows XP Home and Professional Editions), and I find it easier to use. The program runs on Windows 98 SE/Me/2000, too.

After you install ShowBiz, you can run it from the Start menu by choosing Start⇨All Programs⇨ArcSoft⇨ShowBiz.

Figure 7-1:
ArcSoft
ShowBiz
makes it
easy to edit
your movies.

Take a moment to examine the ShowBiz main window, and you see the four major controls that you use to edit movies:

✦ **Media library:** Consider this collection your treasure chest of things that you can add to your film. Movies can contain any mix of items from these four categories: media (includes video clips, still images, and audio), transitions (effects that occur between the clips and images), special effects, and text.

✦ **Player window:** It sounds self-explanatory, and (for a change) it actually is. The Player window allows you to play back and view your movie within ShowBiz while you're working on it.

✦ **Storyboard strip:** If you're familiar with the concept of *storyboarding* in cinematography — where sketches of scenes are arranged to create a paper mock-up of the film — you've probably already guessed that you use this strip to add items from the Media library list. And you'd be right. These media clips, audio clips, and effects are the building blocks of your finished movie.

✦ **Timeline strip:** Click the Timeline tab at the top of the Storyboard strip, and voilà! — you switch to the Timeline strip, where you can trim or expand the length of effects and transitions. The Timeline strip is also the control that you use to add and edit the soundtrack for your movie.

Rounding Up Clips and Images

A video editor like ShowBiz allows you to use raw footage, or video *clips,* transferred to your hard drive from a DV camcorder (or downloaded from the Web, or taken from a royalty-free video clip collection). You can also import digital photographs and use them anywhere you like within your movie — even directly from your scanner or your digital camera.

However, throwing together a hodgepodge of unorganized clips is (to say the least) not particularly creative or satisfying. (Imagine trying to build *Star Wars* by using clips from *Gone With the Wind,* and you'll see what I mean.) Before you build your first work of cinematic art, you must import your own video and still images into one or more *albums,* which is the name that ShowBiz gives to each of those tabbed sections within your Media library. Each item in an album is actually a link to a file on your hard drive.

To import video clips or images that are saved to your hard drive, follow these steps:

1. **Click the Media tab at the top of the Media library.**

2. **Click the Add button that appears under the list (which, strangely enough, bears a book with an arrow).**

3. **From the Open dialog box that appears, navigate to the location of the video, photograph, or sound effect that you want to add, click the file name to select it, and then click the Open button.**

4. **Click New Album in the drop-down list or click an existing album to import into an existing album.**

   You can create a new album — ShowBiz won't allow you to add items to the *Sample album,* which contains preloaded ShowBiz clips — or add the item to an existing album using the oddly unnamed drop-down list box located beneath the library tabs.

   Some types of media albums have advanced settings for the items that they contain; if you're presented with a dialog box like this, you can make any changes you like or simply click OK to keep the current settings. ShowBiz displays the new album (if you created one) or adds the item to the existing album that you chose.

To display thumbnails of album items, click the Album view mode button at the upper-right of the Media library. This toggles the thumbnail feature on and off. To rename an album, click the album name to select it, type a new name in the drop-down list box, and then press Enter.

ShowBiz allows you to sort an album in many different ways, such as by size or date. Just click the Sort button (which sports a capital A and Z conjoined with an arrow), choose the desired sort order, and then click OK. Sorting makes it easier to locate a specific item in an overstuffed album.

Besides the method I describe earlier, here are three other easy ways to import items:

✦ **By downloading them:** ArcSoft offers registered users the opportunity to download new media items from the ArcSoft Web site. These freebies include new transitions, still images, audio clips, and sample video clips.

✦ **By capturing video and audio:** If you have a video capture board or a FireWire port on your PC, you can capture video from your VCR or camcorder. Hook up your video source, click the Capture button in the Movie section of the ShowBiz window, and then click the Record button (the button with the red dot) to save the video (or just the audio component) to a new album within the library. (For information on connecting your video hardware, refer to the user manual for your video capture card and camcorder.)

✦ **By acquiring images from your scanner or camera:** If your scanner or digital camera is TWAIN compatible — and just about every decent model is — connect your hardware and then click the Acquire button (which bears a tiny digital camera and scanner) to import items directly. ShowBiz will prompt you to select the image source from the available TWAIN-compatible hardware devices. Again, the process varies according to the hardware that you're using, but if you're experienced with scanning or downloading images, you'll be in familiar waters.

Building Your First Movie

You import all the pieces of your new film — video, photographs, and audio effects — and you arrange them into orderly albums, ready for use in ShowBiz. Now it's time to grab your megaphone and start creating. You'll start by adding items on the linear Storyboard strip, which you use to literally assemble your movie, moving from left to right on the strip.

I recommend mapping out the general flow of the film on paper — even as a simple list of scenes, titles, and images — before you start creating it. However, ShowBiz makes editing so easy that many folks can simply build a film on the fly, following their inspiration where it takes them. Go figure.

Anyway, when you're ready for the real work, follow these steps:

1. **Start ShowBiz by choosing Start⇨All Programs⇨ArcSoft⇨ShowBiz. Or, if you're already using the program, click the New button (under the Project menu).**

2. **To add either a video clip or an image, click the Media tab in the library to view the corresponding type of items; if you've built multiple albums, you can switch between them by clicking the drop-down list arrow next to the album name.**

If you need help identifying an item, view any item in the Player window before you add it to the strip by right-clicking on the element in the list and then choosing Preview Media from the shortcut menu that appears.

3. **To include an item, add it to the strip in either of two ways:**

- Click and drag the item from the library directly to the storyboard.

  or

- Click the item in the library to select it and then click the Add Media button at the bottom of the library.

ShowBiz adds the item to the next open media square on the strip. Figure 7-2 illustrates a video clip that I added as the first scene in my film.

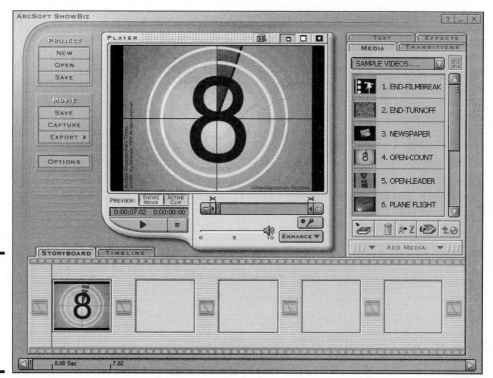

Figure 7-2:
I've added a video clip to the beginning of the storyboard.

When you have multiple items on the storyboard, you can change the order in which they appear on the strip by clicking and dragging an item from one media square to the desired media square.

4. **Delete any item that you've added to the strip by right-clicking the item on the strip and then choosing Delete from the shortcut menu that appears.**

Decided that you don't need that (somewhat disturbing) image of Uncle Milton feeding the family dog? No problem! I wholeheartedly agree.

5. **To trash everything that you've added to the strip and start over, right-click any item on the strip and then choose Delete All Videos and Images from the shortcut menu that appears.**

Remember: All Hollywood directors occasionally throw temper tantrums.

To display the properties of an item on the Storyboard strip — for example, the format of a video clip or its location on your hard drive — right-click the item in the strip and choose Properties from the shortcut menu that appears. Figure 7-3 illustrates the file information for a video clip on my storyboard.

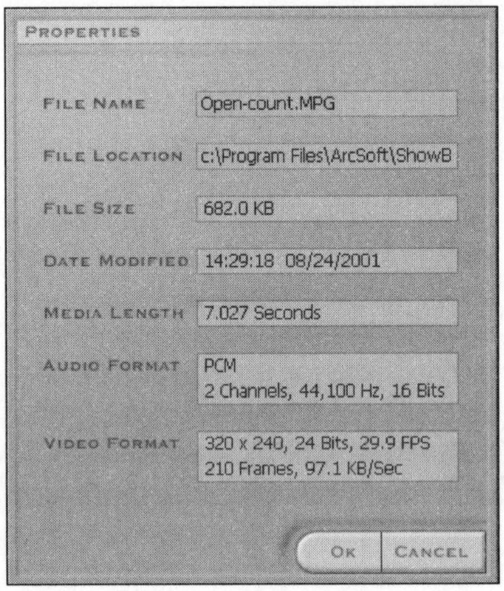

Figure 7-3:
Check properties for a video clip here.

PROPERTIES	
FILE NAME	Open-count.MPG
FILE LOCATION	c:\Program Files\ArcSoft\ShowB
FILE SIZE	682.0 KB
DATE MODIFIED	14:29:18 08/24/2001
MEDIA LENGTH	7.027 Seconds
AUDIO FORMAT	PCM 2 Channels, 44,100 Hz, 16 Bits
VIDEO FORMAT	320 x 240, 24 Bits, 29.9 FPS 210 Frames, 97.1 KB/Sec

OK   CANCEL

Adding Transitions without Breaking a Sweat

Imagine a film that cuts directly from scene-to-scene with no fade-ins, fade-outs, dissolves, or wipes. These are all types of *transitions* — and without transitions, your movie will end up moving at a frantic pace. (I call it *jarring the audience;* most horror films are shot with few transitions.) Of course, this might be your intention with some projects, but it's not likely to be your goal with most films that you make. In this section, I demonstrate how to add transitions to your film.

Transitions can be placed on the Storyboard strip only after you've added at least one video clip or still image. After the strip contains at least one item, follow these steps:

1. **Click the Transitions tab in the library to display the list of transitions. (Click the Album drop-down list to select a different category of transition effects.)**

ShowBiz has a cool feature to help you decide which transition you want to use: Rest your mouse pointer on top of a transition in the list for a few moments, and the item actually animates to demonstrate how the transition will appear onscreen.

2. **After you choose the perfect transition for this point in your film, click the desired transition entry in the media list to select it.**

3. **Click the Add Transition button (below the library) to copy the transition into the next open transition square on the strip.**

The effect is placed in front of the clip. *Note:* Transition squares are smaller than media squares, and they're marked with a filmstrip icon with a diagonal cut. Figure 7-4 illustrates the list of wipe transitions in the library list.

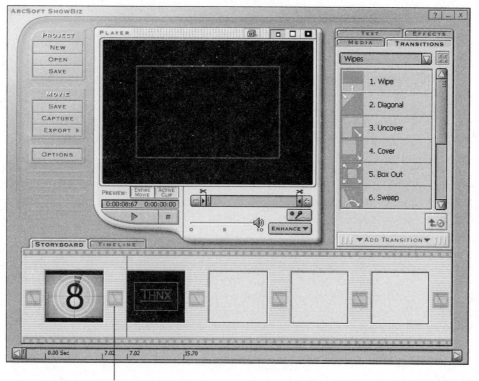

Figure 7-4:
Add
transitions
to tie your
clips
together.

This icon indicates a transition.

4. **To delete a transition that you've added to the strip, right-click the transition square on the strip and then choose Delete from the shortcut menu that appears.**

   Or, to get really radical, choose Delete All Transitions — from the same shortcut menu — to remove all the transitions in your film with one fell swoop.

   To add the same transition throughout your movie, right-click any transition square on the strip and choose Apply Transition to All. (You can even add a different transition between all the items by right-clicking and choosing Random Transition to All. However, I personally don't use this feature because I think it generates a very haphazard film. Think *Monty Python's Flying Circus* . . . without the humor.)

 As you experiment with transitions, you'll begin to understand where your movie needs them to link scenes and still images together, as well as where you can simply cut from one item to the next. Remember, one of the cardinal rules of filmmaking is to maintain the focus of your audience on your message: Too many transitions are distracting.

Adding Special Effects without Paying George Lucas

I haven't mentioned the Timeline strip yet because the first step of movie making is to edit the clips and still images in your movie and add transitions (all of which is taken care of on the Storyboard strip). After you finish these tasks, click the Timeline tab to switch to the display that you see in Figure 7-5. From here, you can add special effects, incorporate a soundtrack and text titles, and then modify the starting and ending points for each.

Note that the Timeline strip also has four smaller mini-strips (bottom-left of Figure 7-5). The upper two, Text and Effects, allow you to edit the text and special effects that you add; the lower two, Audio 1 and Audio 2, allow you to edit the two audio tracks you can add to your movie. (I discuss each of these in the sections to come.)

To refresh your memory on what's happening in your film at any point on the timeline, rest your mouse pointer over the desired spot for a moment, and ShowBiz displays a ToolTip that tells you the name of the transition, clip, or still image that you added previously on the Storyboard strip.

When most of us think about special effects in the movies, *Star Wars* and *Harry Potter* come to mind: lightsabers, flying brooms, and invisibility cloaks. (I really, *really* want one of those.) However, in the world of video editing, an *effect* is a special visual appearance that you add to the video. For example, ShowBiz allows you to

✦ Flip your movie's alignment (horizontally or vertically)

✦ Add virtual raindrops or flames

✦ Display your movie on the side of a blimp

✦ Turn a video clip into a neon sign

Figure 7-5: Add the bells and whistles in the Timeline strip.

Maybe these effects aren't appropriate for your sister's wedding video, but when the subject of your movie is fun and games or when you want to create a new film noir masterpiece in stark black-and-white, effects are just the ticket. (Horrible pun intended.)

Because ShowBiz is an entry-level (and hence relatively low-powered) video editor, you can have only one effect active at a time, but you can place multiple consecutive effects throughout your movie.

To experiment with effects, follow these steps:

1. **Switch to the Timeline strip display and click the Effects tab in the library to check out the available effects.**

Again, you can choose another album of effects by clicking the Album drop-down list box.

2. **Click the desired effect in the list to highlight it.**

3. **Click the Add Effect button (bottom of the Media list).**

This copies the selected effect into the next open block on the Effects row, located above the Timeline strip (see Figure 7-6).

4. **To determine where your new effect will start and end during the movie, hover your mouse pointer over the beginning or ending edge of an effect block in the Effects row and then click and drag the edge.**

To move the entire effect to another spot, simply click and drag the effect block up or down the row to the desired spot.

Book II
Chapter 7

Making Movies
with Your PC

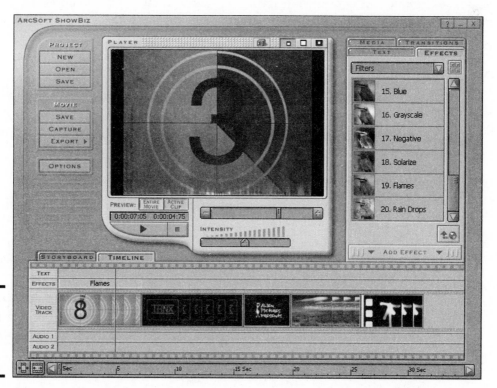

Figure 7-6: Heat things up with the Flame effect.

Naturally, you can toggle back and forth between the Storyboard strip and the Timeline strip as you work. In fact, one of the things that I enjoy most about video editing is the freedom to try new things. With just a few clicks of the mouse, you can add and delete clips, tinker with the effects, and just generally monkey around with timings and placement until you get precisely the film you want. How about them apples, Mr. Hitchcock?

Adding Sound

What movie is complete without a stirring soundtrack? For example, would the zombies in *Return of the Living Dead* have been anywhere near as scary without that punk rock playing in the background? Or how about the signature scary chord every time you saw any body part from the monster in *Creature from the Black Lagoon?* With ShowBiz, you can add two audio tracks to your film; typically, I use one for the soundtrack and a second one for any additional narration or sound effects that weren't recorded with the video clips.

If a video clip already contains audio, you don't have to add anything. (In fact, most of the sample video clips provided with ShowBiz already have their own audio.) However, you can still overlay — or, as videoheads call it, *dub* — extra music or sound effects, which will play along with the audio from the clip.

In addition to the sample audio provided with ShowBiz, the program also accepts audio in MP3 and Microsoft WAV formats, and you can add your audio tracks to the library in the same manner as video clips and still photographs.

To add a soundtrack, follow these steps:

1. **Switch to the Timeline strip display, click the Media tab in the library, and then choose either the Sample Audio album or an album of audio that you've added yourself.**

   Click the Album drop-down list box to choose another album.

2. **Click the desired audio entry in the list to select it.**

3. **Click the Add Media button to add the selected audio.**

   It will appear in the next open block on the Audio 1 or the Audio 2 row below the Timeline strip.

   Just like when adding an effect, each audio clip appears as a block. ShowBiz adds the audio block to the Audio 1 row until that row is filled, and then the clip is added to the Audio 2 row.

4. **To move an audio block to another point within your film, click and drag the block to where you want it.**

   Unlike an effect, however, you can't extend or condense the length of an audio clip by dragging the beginning and ending points.

You've Just Gotta Have Titles!

In movie jargon, *titles* can be anything from the opening titles of your film to the ending credits. With ShowBiz, you can open your film with impressive titles that fill the screen, or you can thank your brother for being Best Boy, Grip, or Gaffer. (I have no earthly idea what those exalted individuals do, but they must be pretty important.)

To add titles, you can use either of two methods (or mix both methods in one film):

✦ **Add a text item from the library:** With the built-in animated text formatting provided by ShowBiz, you can impress your audience with your powerful message. (This is the easier method, but you're restricted to the text formats provided by ShowBiz.)

✦ **Insert a still image, which you've created, from the library:** If you need a specific title to match your exact specifications — for example, something incorporating a company logo — create a digital image with Photoshop or another image-editing program and then add the image to your library. A title that you build yourself outside of ShowBiz is added to a media square just like a video clip, so follow the steps in the earlier section, "Building Your First Movie."

Book II
Chapter 7

Making Movies
with Your PC

To create and add a text item, follow these steps:

1. **Click the Text tab in the library.**

Feel free to click the Album drop-down list box to choose different categories of text effects.

2. **Click the desired entry in the album list to select just the right text effect.**

3. **Click the Add Text button to add the text effect into the next open block on the Text row (above the Timeline strip).**

For most of the text effects, ShowBiz will display a Text settings panel like the one illustrated in Figure 7-7. In addition to typing the text for the effect, you'll typically be able to choose a font type, the size and color of the letters, and even niceties such as shadows, blurring, and the intensity (or opacity) of the letters.

4. **After you type the text and set the type options, click any other block on the Timeline strip to return to your work.**

Text blocks can be adjusted and moved just like the visual effects: Simply click and drag the beginning and ending edges of the text block, or click the block and drag it to a new location.

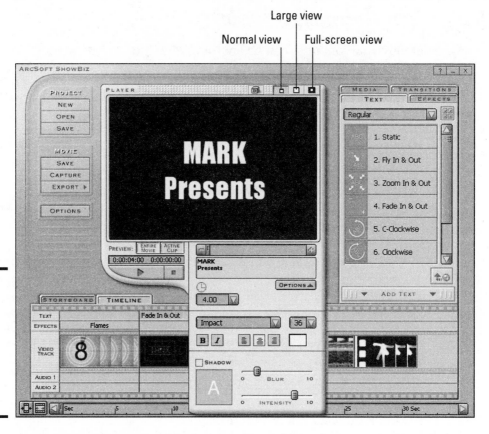

Figure 7-7:
Would you give your film anything less than 36-point titles? I think not.

Previewing Your Oscar-Winning Work

Okay, I know you're itching to see what your next masterpiece looks like. Lucky for you, ShowBiz allows you to preview your work any time. Of course, your Storyboard strip must contain at least one video clip or still image, or you'll have nothing to preview. These are the two different Preview modes:

✦ **Preview the current clip:** To see how a single clip or image will look, click the desired media square on the Storyboard strip to select it and then click the Active Clip button (which appears under the Player window). Click the familiar Play control — the right-pointing triangle — to start the preview.

✦ **Preview the complete movie:** To view the entire film from beginning to end, click the Entire Movie button under the Player window and then click the Play button. Like most other video editors, ShowBiz must apply the effects that you've selected before the film can be shown. This process is *rendering,* and it can lead to a considerable wait on older PCs. (This is the reason why professional video editors crave the most powerful personal computers on the market . . . otherwise, they tend to keel over from sheer boredom while the rendering drags on.)

ShowBiz generally has to render your effects any time that you preview a film if you've changed anything. Therefore, I advise that you save a full-length preview until you've finished as much of your effects work as possible.

When you click Play, ShowBiz displays a yellow line across the Timeline or Storyboard strip to show you the current point in the film, which comes in handy when you need to check the synchronization of different elements in your film with one another, such as effects, titles, or audio. The program also displays the total duration of the selected clip (or the entire movie) as well as the elapsed time.

The other controls under the Player window operate much like they do in Microsoft's Windows Media Player. To stop the preview, click the Stop button (it's the button with the yellow square); to pause the film at the current point, click the Play button again. You can also reposition the preview at any point within your film by clicking and dragging the slider underneath the Player window.

 For a larger preview, toggle the Player window into expanded mode with the three View buttons at the top-right corner of the Player window. You can choose between Normal view (the default), Large, and Full-screen.

Saving and Burning before Traveling to Cannes

I think that Cannes is somewhere in France . . . or perhaps Belgium. Anyway, it's a big thing among filmmaking legends like you and me, so you'll want at least one copy of your finished masterwork to carry along with you. Luckily, ShowBiz allows you to save your films or even record them to a disc — both of which I cover in this last section.

 You can always save your work in progress. To save a project that you're working on to your hard drive for later, click the Project button in the upper-left corner of the ShowBiz window and choose Save. Windows opens the familiar Save As dialog box, where you can specify a location and a filename.

After your project is completed, here are two methods that you can use to produce a finished movie.

Creating a digital video file on your hard drive

If you simply want to watch your film on your PC monitor — without necessarily burning it to a CD or DVD — this is the best option. Just don't forget that it can take several hundred megabytes or more of space to store a single movie. Follow these steps:

1. **Click Save (located in the Movie group at the upper-left of the window).**

ShowBiz displays the Save dialog box that you see in Figure 7-8.

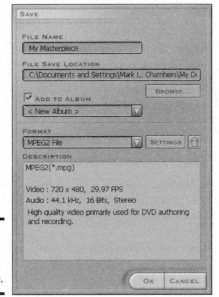

Figure 7-8:
Save your
master-
pieces here.

2. **Type a filename and click the Browse button to specify a location where the video file will be stored.**

   If you select the Add to Album check box, your movie becomes a clip that you can use in future projects; just click the Album drop-down list box to specify the destination album. (Why re-edit that chariot race over and over? Turn it into stock footage!)

3. **Click the Format drop-down list box to choose the format (MPEG1, MPEG2, QuickTime MOV, or Windows AVI format).**

   I usually choose either MPEG2 (which is the most common format and can be readily viewed on Mac OS and Linux) or Windows AVI (which is limited to PCs, but any machine running Windows 98 or later can view your movie).

4. **Click the Settings button to specify options such as the frame size and audio quality.**

   The Format dialog box opens. Check out the settings for MPEG-2. Naturally, your movie's file size will grow if you choose larger frame sizes, higher frame rates, and the better audio and video quality settings.

   After these settings are correct, click Save to return to the Save dialog box.

5. **Click OK to create the DV file.**

ShowBiz allows you to save your film as a video e-mail file, which is small enough to attach to an e-mail message and send to anyone running Windows. This is guaranteed to amaze and delight your Dad, who will think you've been hobnobbing with Bill Gates.

Recording your own CD or DVD

For me, this is the neatest option of all. You can walk up to that smug know-it-all at your local video store and boast that you have the world's only video CD copy of *My Family Reunion Bloopers 2004!* (Heck, tell him you'll be happy to burn him a copy for a small fee.)

To record your movie on a CD or DVD, follow these steps:

1. **Rest your tired mouse pointer atop the Export button in the Movie group and choose CD/DVD from the menu that appears.**

ShowBiz snaps to attention and displays the Make CD dialog box that you see in Figure 7-9.

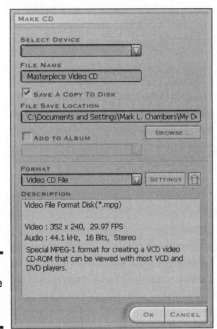

Figure 7-9:
Houston, we are go to burn!

2. **If ShowBiz recognizes a CD recording application on your system, click the Select Device drop-down list and select your CD or DVD recorder.**

If your drive doesn't appear, don't panic — that means that ShowBiz doesn't recognize any compatible recording programs. Instead, select the Save a Copy to Disk check box to enable it. Then type a filename, click the Browse button to specify a location where the video file will be stored, and record it manually later with your CD recording software.

3. **To save your movie as a clip in the library album that you specify, select the Add to Album check box.**

4. Click the Format drop-down list to choose the type of disc that you want to burn.

The most compatible choice (and the one I use most often) is Video CD File, which can be played on virtually any DVD player and on most PCs as well.

5. Click the Settings button to select the proper quality settings for the film.

The Format dialog box opens.

The default settings for the Video CD and DVD formats are optimized for those specific media types, so leave these settings alone unless you're sure of what you're doing. (Repeat after me: "Defaults are usually good things.")

6. Click Save to apply any changes and to return to the Make CD dialog box.

7. Click OK.

ShowBiz automatically cranks up your CD-burning software to handle the rest of the job.

If you're going to create a DVD, make sure that you use the DVD File format, which results in a much higher-quality MPEG-2 image. (As you might expect, you won't be able to burn this monster video to a mere CD, so most of us will stick to the Video CD File format.)

If you're feeling somewhat lost inside your CD recording software, I can heartily recommend a sister book in the *For Dummies* series that can answer your burning questions. (Sorry, that pun was uncalled for, and my editors should have removed it.) Anyway, *CD & DVD Recording For Dummies,* 2nd Edition, by Mark Chambers, can walk you through all the tricks that your faithful CD or DVD recorder can perform. You'll be creating all sorts of audio, data, and video CDs in no time . . . with aplomb, too. (I *think* that's a good thing.)

Chapter 8: I Can Make My Own DVDs?

In This Chapter

✔ Creating a menu

✔ Selecting a style

✔ Trimming your clips to fit

✔ Previewing your DVD menu

✔ Recording a finished DVD video

You know, as a PC owner — and a dedicated movie fan with my own digital video (DV) camcorder — I honestly can't think of a current technology in the world of personal computers that's more exciting than burning my own DVD videos! That's why I chose the title for this chapter: DVD recording is new enough and sounds so much like rocket science that even many PC power users don't know much about it. (Another large cross section of PC owners knows that recording DVDs is possible on a PC but thinks that it's too complex or far too expensive.)

With the recent drop in the price of DVD-R drives — and the availability of easy-to-use DVD authoring software like MyDVD 4 — recording your own DVD videos is now kid's stuff. Trust me: You *can* do this, and it won't cost you an arm and a leg. Your DVD videos will have professional-looking menus, and they'll run on standard DVD players. But instead of watching Arnold Schwarzenegger, you'll be watching your family at Walt Disney World. (And unlike those old tapes, your DVD home movies will never wear out!)

MyDVD 4 can also create video CDs with MyDVD, which means that the program even accommodates those of us with antique CD-RW drives. Note, though, that a video CD has much less storage space than a DVD, so your movies must be much shorter (usually about an hour). Also, the video quality of a video CD is nowhere near as good as that of a DVD. Therefore, I eschew video CDs in this chapter and concentrate on recording DVDs by using existing video clips and multimedia files from your hard drive.

Welcome to MyDVD

As you can tell, I'm a big fan of MyDVD 4, from Sonic Solutions (www.sonic.com); for about $80, you can produce truly professional-looking DVD movies on your own PC. To begin your foray into the world of *Digital Versatile Discs* (or whatever the heck *DVD* means — check out the nearby sidebar), either double-click the MyDVD icon on your desktop or choose Start➪All Programs➪Sonic➪MyDVD➪Start MyDVD. The program displays a combination welcome screen and wizard.

From the opening wizard, you can choose to

✦ **Create a new MyDVD project or edit an existing project.**

✦ **Transfer video Direct-to-DVD.**

✦ **Edit an existing DVD and then re-record it.**

✦ **Run the MyDVD tutorial, which is HyperText Markup Language (HTML)-based (and launches Internet Explorer).**

✦ **Display the MyDVD Help system.**

To bypass the wizard screen entirely and jump to the MyDVD main window, select the Don't Show This Window Again check box.

Speaking of the MyDVD main window, click Create or Modify a DVD-Video Project to begin your first project. Figure 8-1 illustrates the program's main window.

Of the slew of different DVD formats out there, only one is compatible with virtually all DVD players: That's *DVD-R,* the record-once version of the DVD-RW (rewriteable disc). If you burn a DVD project on a DVD-RW, DVD+R, or DVD+RW, it might not run on your DVD player. Or, even worse, it might run fine on yours but be completely useless on your Aunt Betty's machine. *+R/RW* and *-R/RW* are different formats, too, and they're not compatible! The only way to be completely sure that a DVD produced by your recorder will work on a particular DVD player is to actually try it!

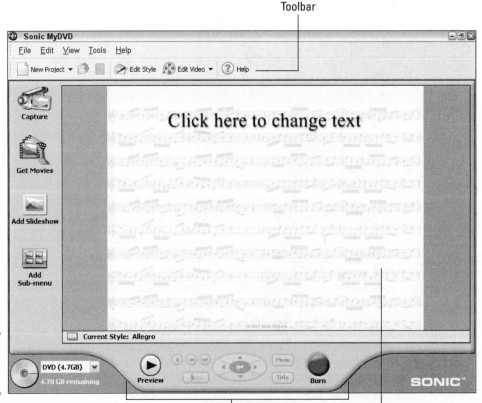

Toolbar

Figure 8-1:
Your DVD
wonderland.

DVD remote control panel   Content window

I *should* know what DVD stands for . . .

. . . and the rest of the civilized world is still scratching its head as well. Normally, I'm pretty sure about what an abbreviation stands for, but in this case, I have two choices!

When the DVD standards were being developed, everyone agreed that the recordable version of the new disc would be useful for all sorts of neat things — not just for storing video, but for backups, data, superior audio, and anything else that a PC owner could think of with 4.7GB of free space handy. Therefore, everyone proudly agreed that the new standard should be called DVD, short for *Digital Versatile Disc*. Everyone went home and celebrated.

However, it took three or four years for recordable DVD technology to arrive at a price point that regular folks could afford. And by that time, *DVD* had

become firmly entrenched in people's minds as a video storage medium. (After all, DVD movies caught on like wildfire — there was none of that VHS-versus-beta waffling that the 30-something crowd remembers.)

During that same time, everyone without a DVD standards book handy took one look at the abbreviation and exclaimed, "That's got to mean *Digital Video Disc*, right?" Now, even most computer books and Web sites claim that Digital Video Disc is the original meaning!

That leaves us with one of the most interesting abbreviations this side of TWAIN (Technology Without An Interesting Name). And whether you side with the original translation or the popular meaning, everyone still agrees that DVD technology is the cat's meow. (You can still celebrate if you like.)

Menus 'R Easy!

DVD authoring programs allow you to build a menu system that can be controlled by a DVD player's remote control; the person viewing your disc will press buttons to select from the menu choices that you've laid out. After you build the menu framework, you essentially connect your video clips to the menu system. MyDVD also enables you to add screens with still photos from your digital camera or scanner. I always think of an art gallery, where the walls provide a backdrop for the paintings (and where those silly little rope fences are supposed to guide you to the proper place). (Personally, I jump right over the fences — which is why I'm barred from visiting any art galleries in my town.)

In the past, DVD authoring software was a confusing nest of weird-looking arrows, funky technical terms, and configuration settings that would give a Mensa member a splitting headache — but applications like MyDVD (and iDVD in the Mac world) have revolutionized how you construct a DVD video.

The default style used in MyDVD is Allegro, which has a musical feel to it. A MyDVD *style* is a combination of a menu background, a button appearance, and a font format. (More on this in the next section.)

In this example, I show you how to build a menu system with a video clip, a submenu, and a still image slideshow. Follow these steps:

1. **First, change the menu title to something more appropriate than** `Click here to change text` **(refer to Figure 8-1).**

Okay, it's catchy and instructive, but I doubt Uncle Milton would be impressed.

    a. **Click the title, which opens a text editing box.**

    b. **Type the new title for your disc menu and then press Enter to save it.**

2. **Add your first video clip to your menu.**

    a. **Click the Get Movies button in the toolbar at the left of the window (or press Ctrl+G).**

    MyDVD displays a standard Open dialog box.

    b. **Navigate to a specific clip on your hard drive and double-click it to load it.**

    This displays your first menu button, as shown in Figure 8-2, with the clip filename as the default button label.

MyDVD can accept all three of the Big Three digital video formats: AVI, MOV, and MPEG. Therefore, you don't have to convert your video clips from one format to another before you use them in your projects.

3. **If you wish, change the title on the button to something more appealing.**

    a. **Click the text under the clip button.**

    MyDVD opens a text editing box.

    b. **Type the new label for the button and then press Enter to save it.**

Figure 8-2: Add video clips to your library.

Menu button

Disc space remaining

You just created your first menu! (A little rudimentary, of course, but you could actually save the project and record it at this point.) By the way, keep an eye on the disc-shaped graph in the lower-left corner of the MyDVD window. When you add menus, photos, and video clips, it's updated to show how much space is available on a disc (and how much space remains on a typical 4.7GB recordable DVD).

If you're going to record your project onto a video CD, click the drop-down list next to the disc graph to switch between different DVD format capacities.

You can now add a submenu to your DVD menu. A *submenu* is a branch command that takes you to another menu level under the top-level menu. I use submenus for organizing different clips and images by date or subject. For example, you could create a single DVD with clips from an entire year and then add submenus for vacation video clips, Christmas videos, and school clips.

Book II
Chapter 8

I Can Make My Own DVDs?

To create a submenu, just follow this yellow brick road:

1. **Click the Add Sub-menu button on the left toolbar to create the Untitled Menu button that you see in Figure 8-3.**

   Note: The default icon for the submenu is different from a video clip button, which uses a frame from the clip itself.

A submenu button

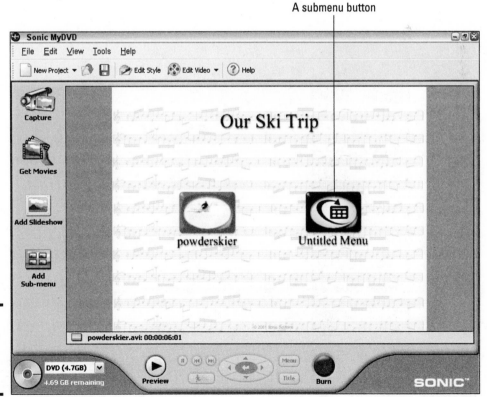

Figure 8-3:
A submenu button in its natural habitat.

2. **To change the label on the submenu button to something appropriate, click the text under the submenu button, type the new label for the button, and then press Enter to save it.**

Look at the structure of the submenu screen. Double-click the submenu button to display it (see the results in Figure 8-4). MyDVD always adds two new navigation buttons to the bottom of the new screen:

- **Home:** Clicking this takes you back to the main Title screen of the menu.

- **Previous:** Clicking this takes you back to the previous menu screen, which is handy for when a submenu appears within another submenu.

These buttons also work while you're creating the menu; just double-click a navigation button to use it. (After all, you need a way to move between menu screens.)

Other than the Home and Previous buttons, a submenu works just like the top-level Title menu. You can add another video clip by clicking the Get Movies button (as I demonstrate earlier) or the Add Slideshow button or even add another menu level with another submenu. However, note this one thing that you can do with a submenu that you can't do to the Title menu screen: *A submenu can be deleted.* (This makes sense because your project always needs a Title menu.) To delete a submenu, display it, right-click the menu background, and then choose Delete Menu from the shortcut menu that appears.

Figure 8-4:
An empty submenu screen.

Home   Previous

Deleting a submenu also deletes any buttons (and the corresponding content) that might still be on the submenu. For this reason, MyDVD will prompt you for deletion confirmation. To verify that you want to delete everything on the current menu from your project, click OK. (Note, however, that deleting a submenu doesn't permanently delete any video clips that were on it from your hard drive. That would be the very definition of A Bad Thing.)

Speaking of deleting items, you can also delete any button that you've added to a menu by right-clicking it and then choosing Delete Button from the shortcut menu that appears. Again, deleting a button is like deleting a menu: You remove everything that was linked to the button — so MyDVD again prompts you for confirmation, just to make sure.

To add a slideshow to your submenu, walk this way:

1. **Click the Add Slideshow button (left side of the main screen).**

MyDVD opens the Create Slideshow dialog box that you see in Figure 8-5.

2. **Click the Get Pictures button (left side) to display the Open dialog box. There, select one or more pictures from your hard drive for your slideshow and then click the Open button, which displays the images in the filmstrip.**

At the bottom of this screen, check out how MyDVD keeps track of how much space the show takes on the DVD as well as the length of the show.

3. **To choose a specific picture as the slideshow button image, click the desired image in the filmstrip and then click the Button Image button on the left toolbar.**

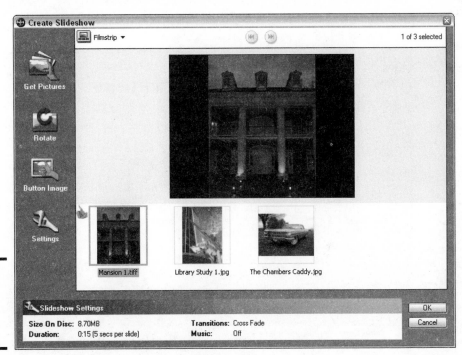

Figure 8-5: Choose photos for your slideshow.

4. **To control the delay for each image and choose an audio soundtrack (in MP3 or WAV format), click the Settings button, which displays the Slideshow Settings dialog box.**

5. **Click the Advanced tab to choose an optional transition that will appear between slides.**

6. **After you add all the photos that you want to your slideshow film-strip, click OK to save your changes and return to the submenu screen.**

   Figure 8-6 shows the slideshow button (Untitled Slideshow) on the submenu. (You'll probably want to change the label on the slideshow button as well. Just click the text, type in a new name, and then press Enter.)

You've finished your menu system — in a minimum of short steps, no less! Press Ctrl+S to save the project, enter a filename when MyDVD prompts you, and then click Save to store your masterwork on your hard drive.

Changing the Look of Your Menus

At this point, you might be satisfied with the results of your work. If so, you're ready to move to the next section. However, what if your video clips and photo slideshow have nothing to do with music? At this point, it's time to dump Allegro (no offense) and choose a menu style more fitting for the content of your disc. MyDVD includes special styles for holidays and all sorts of events, as well as themes based on colors.

Figure 8-6: Your completed submenu.

You can switch styles at any time during the development of your DVD menu. Generally, I wait until the end because I can see the entire effect with the fonts, colors, and button borders on the different elements in my project.

To choose a new style, follow these steps:

1. **Click the Edit Style button in the top toolbar.**

This displays the Edit Style dialog box that you see in Figure 8-7. Here, you can choose from two different types of menu styles. By default, MyDVD uses nonanimated graphics.

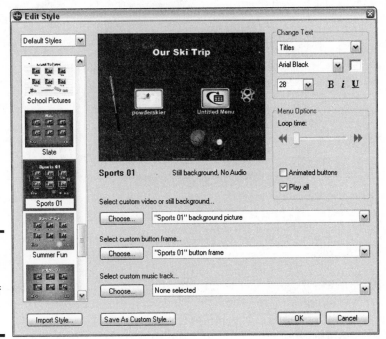

Figure 8-7: Change the style to fit the mood of your DVD content.

2. **To use an animated style, choose Motion Styles from the drop-down list box at the upper-left of the Edit Style dialog box.**

3. **Click the style that you want from the scrolling list at the left of the dialog box.**

The preview window is automatically updated with the new style.

To use the new style as it is, click OK. Figure 8-8 illustrates the menu system that uses the Sports 01 style. You can also use the options on the Edit Style dialog box to choose a favorite background picture, button frame, or background music track for your style. And, in turn, if you want to use it for future MyDVD projects, you can click the Save As Custom Style button to create a new style under the name you provide. (For instance, I create new styles with my own background pictures and save them for later.)

To pick a photo (or a video clip) of your own as a background, click the Choose button next to the Select Custom Video or Still Background drop-down list box in the Edit Style dialog box (refer to Figure 8-7).

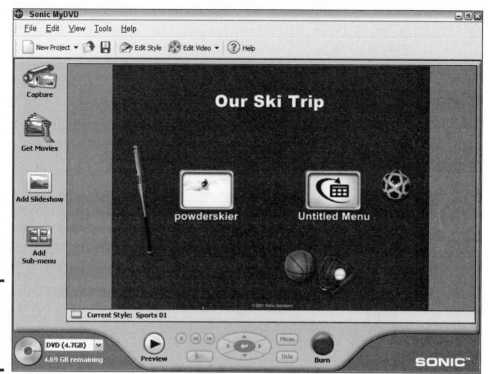

Figure 8-8:
Now you're ready for that soccer footage.

Trimming Movies with Panache

Unfortunately, it's rare that a video clip will begin or end precisely where you want; most clips have extraneous stuff that needs to be trimmed away. Instead of loading your clips in a full-blown video editor like Adobe Premiere — which is a much more powerful and ponderous program than you need for this simple task — MyDVD gives you the ability to trim the beginning and ending of your clips from within the program. Truly *sassy!*

This great feature even goes one better: It doesn't actually remove any material from your video clips, so you don't have to spend any time saving or converting them (which can take minutes, even on the fastest PC). Instead, the MyDVD trim process only marks the beginning and ending points that you choose for a clip, leaving the original digital video file untouched on your hard drive.

To trim a clip, follow these steps:

1. **Navigate through the menus that you've created until you find the menu screen with the video that you need to trim.**

2. **To begin trimming the clip, double-click it.**

MyDVD displays the Trimming dialog box, as shown in Figure 8-9. Three thumbnail frames show you the start of the clip, the frame used as the button image, and the ending of the clip.

Figure 8-9:
Just a trim,
please.

Drag the slider where you
want the clip to begin.

Drag the slider where you
want the clip to end.

Drag to change the button image.

3. **Click and drag the green slider (which corresponds to the Start Frame) to the desired location where you want the clip to begin.**

   MyDVD automatically updates the Start Frame preview to show you the new starting frame.

   You can also click the slider that you want to move and press the left- and right-arrow keys to move backward and forward one frame at a time.

4. **Click and drag the red End Frame slider to the desired location where the clip should end.**

   You can use the updated End Frame preview image to gauge where you are in the clip.

5. **To choose a different frame for the image that will appear on the video button, click the thumbs-up marker and drag it until you see the desired frame in the Button Image preview image.**

   This is a great feature when your video starts with a black screen.

6. **When you're done trimming, click OK to set the markers and return to the menu screen.**

   If you'd rather start over and try again, click Reset and follow these steps anew.

Trimming a video clip is different from actually editing the video. But if you happen to have both MyDVD and ArcSoft ShowBiz installed on your PC, you can click the Edit Video button in the top toolbar to edit your video clips. In fact, MyDVD automatically launches ShowBiz, which I conveniently cover in Book II, Chapter 7.

277

Time to Preview

Would a Hollywood studio release a movie these days without a trailer? Not very likely . . . and MyDVD allows you to preview your disc before you burn it. I'm all for avoiding the possibility of wasting a recordable DVD because something was wrong with my videos or my menu system. In Preview mode, MyDVD will display your project just as it will appear in a DVD player. You even get a virtual remote control that you can use to test out your menu system.

To enter Preview mode at any time, click the Preview button on the bottom of the screen (or press Ctrl+P). Your menu system appears exactly as it will on-screen, and the remote control pad (which is normally disabled) is ready to use, as shown in Figure 8-10. Click any button to simulate the press of that button on your DVD player's remote control.

Click the Title button to display the Title menu, and click the Menu button to display the last menu that you used.

After you've checked each button and function on your menu, click the Stop button on the remote control to exit Preview mode. You can then make any changes that you need to make to your menu, or you can record your project to disc.

Figure 8-10: Preview your work before you record the disc.

A simulated remote control

Dig that crazy safe zone!

Did you know that your TV has a safe zone? Well, at least it does to a video editor. The *safe zone* refers to the actual height and width dimensions of the TV signal that's displayed by an NTSC (or North American Standard) television. An NTSC signal is somewhat larger than the television screen. That additional border helps prevent you from seeing any distortion at the edges of your picture, but it also means that you could conceivably chop off part of the background or a video clip.

To verify that your movies look good in the safe zone before you record them, use MyDVD's safe zone border. The program displays a rectangle that marks the boundary of the safe zone. To turn on the safe zone border, choose View⇨Show TV Safe Zone. To turn it off, choose the menu item again.

Now if they could only invent a gadget to edit out that reality-TV trash that they show these days.

Burning Your DVD and Celebrating Afterwards

Here it is — the moment that you've been waiting for with such anticipation! But before you decide to spend a disc on your project, I should mention that MyDVD can actually create two different types of DVD videos:

✦ **A standard DVD video:** This is a physical DVD-R that can be loaded in a DVD player.

✦ **A DVD volume:** If you select this method of recording a DVD, the files aren't actually burned to a disc. Instead, MyDVD records them to a separate folder on your hard drive, where you can either record them later or view them with a software DVD player like Sonic's CinePlayer. (This is a great option if you're working on a laptop and you're using an external FireWire or USB 2.0 DVD recorder, but you don't happen to have the recorder handy. You can save the project as a DVD volume and burn it later when you get back to your home or office.)

To burn a DVD video from your project, follow these steps:

1. **Load a blank disc into your recorder.**

2. **Click the Burn button on the remote control pad on the bottom of the MyDVD window (or press Ctrl+D).**

MyDVD prompts you to save the project.

3. **Click Yes, type a filename, and then click Save.**

The program displays the Make Disc Setup dialog box that you see in Figure 8-11.

Figure 8-11: Preparing to burn a DVD video.

4. If you have more than one recorder on your system, click the Device drop-down list to choose which drive will be used.

5. Click in the Copies text box and type the number of copies that you want to make.

I recommend leaving the Write Speed setting at Auto; that way, your DVD recorder can record at a slower speed if the DVD media that you're using doesn't support full-speed burning.

6. Click OK and sit back to watch your recorder do the work.

To save a DVD volume, follow these steps:

1. Choose Tools⇨Make DVD Folder.

MyDVD displays the Browse for Folder dialog box.

2. Click the location where the DVD volume folder should be stored.

3. Click OK to begin creating the DVD volume.

Chapter 9: I'm Okay, You're a Digital Camera

In This Chapter

- ✓ Understanding digital camera technology
- ✓ Evaluating the advantages of digital photography
- ✓ Buying extras (besides your camera)
- ✓ Composing photographs for better results
- ✓ Organizing your images
- ✓ Downloading your images

I'll be the first to assure you that I'm no Ansel Adams, yet I've been capturing moments and memories on film for most of my life now, and I've slowly worked my way into what most folks would deem semiprofessional photography. (That means I can shoot a decent portrait, I take on a commission from time-to-time, and I have a reasonably well-stuffed camera bag.)

Does that mean I'm loaded down with expensive 35mm cameras and a dozen different varieties of film? Definitely not! I've never been darkroom material, and film photography no longer excites me. These days, I work entirely with *digital* cameras, which don't use traditional film at all. Why digital? My entire portfolio of digital photos — which would easily fill up a dozen traditional bound photo albums — fits comfortably on a 700MB CD-ROM. I can display those photographs on practically any PC or print hard copies that are almost impossible to tell from film prints. I don't spend a dime on film processing, either — and when you take 10 to 20 images a day, that savings really adds up.

I'd like to spend this chapter introducing you to the world of digital photography. You'll discover how a digital camera works, why it's better in many respects than a film camera, and how to move images that you've taken from your camera to your PC. If you're interested in shooting better pictures, I'll also cover a number of well-worn basic rules used by professional photographers all over the world. You also discover how to download your images from your digital camera (by using the features that are built into Windows XP) and how to catalog your photographs (thus making it easier to locate a specific image).

If you're hungry for a much more comprehensive, in-depth look at digital photography (after you finish this appetizer of a chapter), you'll find the *Digital Photography Handbook* by Mark Chambers (published by Wiley Publishing, Inc.) to be a valuable guide. Plus, it's a full-color book — the pictures look much better in living color!

How Does a Digital Camera Work?

A common misconception surrounds today's digital cameras: Because they don't use film and because they produce pictures as data files, many folks think that digital cameras must use a radically different method of capturing an image. Actually, your family film camera and that power-hungry, battery-munching digital camera that you got for Christmas are remarkably similar in most respects.

As you see in Figure 9-1, a film camera has a shutter that opens for a set amount of time (usually a fraction of a second), admitting light into the body of the camera through at least one lens. (Of course, that lens can be adjusted to bring other objects at other distances into focus, or different lenses can be tacked on.) Figure 9-2 illustrates (up to this point, anyway) that your film camera and its digital brethren work exactly the same.

Figure 9-1:
A film camera captures your image on light-sensitive material.

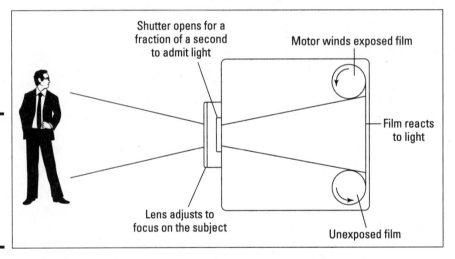

Figure 9-2:
In a digital camera, the light triggers a set of photosensitive scanners.

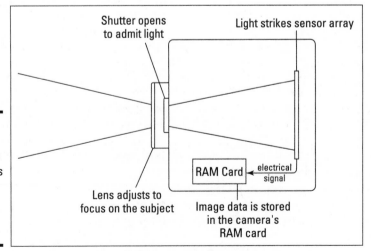

The big difference is the method that each of these two types of cameras uses to record that incoming light. To wit:

✦ **A film camera** uses a strip of light-sensitive celluloid coated with silver halide, which retains the image. The film must later be developed, and the negatives/positives that are produced can be used (reproduced, usually on photographic paper) to make copies of the photograph.

✦ **A digital camera**, on the other hand, uses a grid (or *array*) of photo-sensitive sensors to record the incoming pattern of light. Each sensor returns an electrical current when it's struck by the incoming light. Because the amount of current returned varies with the amount of light, your camera's electronic innards can combine the different current levels into a composite pattern of data that represents the incoming light: in other words, an image, in the form of a binary file.

If you've read some other books on CD recording and scanning, you already know about *binary,* which is the common language shared by all computers. Although your eye can't see any image in the midst of all those ones and zeros, your computer can display them as a photograph — and print the image, if you like, or send it to your Aunt Harriet in Boise as an e-mail attachment.

"Wait a second: How does the image file get to my computer?" That's a very good question because naturally, no one wants to carry a PC (or even a laptop) around just to shoot a photograph. Your digital camera stores the image file until you can *transfer* (download) it to your computer. Different types of cameras use different methods of storing the image files:

✦ **RAM cards:** *Random access memory (RAM) cards* (the most common storage method) are removable memory cards that function much like the memory modules used by your computer. In fact, some cards are actually interchangeable with personal digital assistants (PDAs) and palmtop PCs. The most popular types of media include CompactFlash (www.sandisk.com), SmartMedia (www.microtech.com), and Memory Stick (www.sony.com) cards, generally ranging from 8 megabytes (MB) to 256MB or 512MB of storage. When the card is full of images, you either download the images from the card to free up space, or you can eject it and put in a spare empty card.

✦ **Hard drives:** Yep, you read right; some cameras have their own onboard hard drives, and others use tiny removable hard drives that are roughly the same size as a RAM card. Naturally, these little beauties can easily store a gigabyte (GB) or more of your images. (Geez, I'm old enough to remember when a full-sized computer hard drive couldn't store that much.)

✦ **Floppy drives:** Some digital cameras use floppies to store photos. (Guess what? I don't like those cameras.) If your camera uses floppies, make doggone sure that you get your images backed up to your computer's hard drive as soon as possible. Because of the larger images produced by today's cameras, floppy-based digital cameras are rapidly disappearing from the market.

✦ **CD-RW drives:** Here's the ultimate: A camera that can burn your digital photographs directly onto a CD-R or CD-RW! Although these cameras can be a little bulkier than models that use RAM cards, this just plain *rocks.* As you might expect, you'll pay a premium price for one of these jewels.

If you're wondering approximately how many images you can fit onto a specific RAM card, remember that most of today's 2- to 3-megapixel cameras produce images ranging from 1.5 to 2MB at their highest quality mode.

The Pros and Cons of Digital Photography

I mention earlier in this chapter that I've switched completely from my 35mm single lens reflex (SLR) cameras to a (rapidly expanding) collection of digital cameras. However, there's a lot more to like about the digital revolution than just cutting the expenses of film and processing. Other advantages include the following:

✦ **Digital prints are versatile.** The digital photographs that you take can be enclosed in e-mail messages, burned as CD-ROM slide shows, or displayed as your PC's Windows desktop and screensaver. Of course, you can also print them; and with today's special inkjet papers, your images can end up on things like greeting cards and T-shirt transfers.

If you're interested in producing prints from your digital photographs in the shortest time possible, check out one of the latest inkjet printers that can directly accept memory cards from your digital camera. Heck, with one of these inkjet marvels, you don't need a PC. Some of these printers can even rotate and resize images as well.

✦ **Look, Ma, no developing!** With a digital camera, you have practically instant access to your photographs. Save yourself the trip to the photo store — even a one-hour photo lab can't match the five minutes that it takes to connect your camera to your PC (with a Universal Serial Bus [USB] or FireWire cable) and download your images to your hard drive. (And you'll also avoid the ravages of a misaligned development machine or a clumsy operator.)

✦ **Easy editing with your PC.** Imagine everything that can go wrong with a picture: a bad exposure, a case of red eye, or perhaps a tree sprouting from someone's head. With a digital photograph, you can reduce or eliminate these problems altogether; with the proper editing, a bad picture becomes mediocre, and a good picture can become a work of art. *Bonus:* After the images are on your PC, you can edit or print them immediately.

✦ **Manage your photographs on location.** Imagine being able to review a shot as soon as it's taken. With a traditional film camera, you're stuck with what you've taken, and you won't see the results until that roll of film has been developed. A digital camera, however, gives you the freedom to actually manage your images. For example, you can view each image on a memory card and delete the ones that you don't need to free up space. Using the camera's liquid crystal diode (LCD) screen also allows you to review a photograph as soon as you've taken it. Don't like the way a particular photograph turned out? If you review each shot as soon as you've snapped it — which I always do — you can try to retake most pictures immediately! (Of course, this feature won't help you if the UFO has already zipped over the horizon, but it's darned handy on vacation.)

Many digital cameras on the market these days can also do double-duty as simple video camcorders — at least for 30, 60, or 120 seconds — using a feature called *movie mode.* Some cameras can even record audio along with the video; the amount of time that you can record depends on the amount of storage available, so a digital camera with a 128MB memory card can capture many more seconds of video than a camera with only a 16MB memory card.

However, all is not perfect in the digital world . . . not yet, at least. Film cameras aren't doomed to share the fate of the dinosaurs because traditional film photography still has these advantages over digital photography:

✦ **Film cameras are still less expensive.** Although digital cameras have dropped considerably in price over the last few years, film cameras still provide better resolution and image quality for a lower initial price. In fact, at the time of this writing, any inexpensive film camera under $100 can still take a better photograph than a $300 digital camera. Of course, if you're willing to spend more, you'll narrow the quality gap . . . but not for long. While digital camera prices continue to drop, an average digital camera will eventually be able to take a shot that's as good as a film camera.

How can you tell which digital cameras produce better images? While shopping for a digital camera, keep the camera's *megapixel rating* in mind — that's the number of *pixels* (or individual dots) in an image that the camera can capture. The higher the megapixel value, the better the image quality, the more expensive the camera, and the larger the photographs that you can print.

As a rule, a 2-megapixel camera is suitable for most casual photography, but amateur photographers will prefer at least a 3-megapixel camera. Cameras in the 4- to 5-megapixel range can match a typical 35mm camera in quality.

✦ **Film cameras are better at capturing motion.** Most consumer digital cameras in the 2- and 3-megapixel range still have trouble taking shots of subjects in motion, such as sporting events. (This is because of the longer delay required for those photosensitive sensors to capture the image.) Today's more expensive, higher-megapixel cameras are much better at *motion* (stop action) photography.

✦ **Man, do those digital cameras use the juice!** Unlike a film camera, a digital camera relies on battery power for *everything,* including that power-hungry LCD display. If you're in the middle of shooting a wedding and you haven't packed a spare set of batteries, you have my condolences. A film camera is far less demanding on its batteries.

✦ **You need those ports.** If your PC doesn't have USB ports (or, for a more expensive camera, FireWire ports) handy, you'll have to add an adapter card that provides the correct type of port for your camera.

As you might have already guessed, many photographers have chosen to carry both traditional film and digital cameras, which allows them to use whatever best fits the circumstances (depending on the subject and the level of control that they need on location). For me, the long-term savings and convenience of my digital cameras — and the ability to review my photographs as soon as they're taken — makes them the better choice.

So what can you do with digital photographs? A heck of a lot more than a film print, that's for sure (at least on your PC and in the online world)! Common fun that you can have with a digital image includes

✦ **Printing 'em.** Today's inkjet printers can produce a hard copy on all sorts of media (everything from plain paper to blank business cards and CD/DVD labels), but naturally you'll get the best results on those expensive sheets of glossy photo paper.

✦ **Using them on your personal or business Web site.** Jazz up your Web pages with images from your camera.

✦ **Sending them as e-mail attachments.** I get a big kick out of sending photos through e-mail! As long as you add a total of less than 2MB of images to an e-mail message, the recipient should receive them with no problem. (And then the attached files can be viewed, printed, or saved to the recipient's hard drive.)

✦ **Creating slide shows.** Check your camera's software documentation to see whether you can create a slide show on your hard drive (or on a CD-ROM) to show off your digital photographs.

✦ **Using them in crafts projects.** Plaster your digital photographs on T-shirt transfers, buttons, greeting cards, and all sorts of crafts.

Digital Camera Extras to Covet

No one gets a pizza with just sauce, and the extras are important in photography, too. If you'll be taking a large number of photographs or you're interested in producing the best results from your camera, consider adding these extras to your camera bag.

External card readers

As I mention earlier, the majority of modern digital cameras connect to your computer via a USB cable to transfer pictures. The downside to this is that you can't take more shots until the downloading process is complete. If you're in a hurry or if convenience is important, buy an external card reader that takes care of the downloading chores for you. Simply pop the card into the reader (which in turn connects to your PC's USB port), load a backup memory card into your camera, and you're ready to return to the action.

External card readers are also the best solution if you have an older digital camera that connects to your PC's serial port. Because a serial connection is as slow as watching paint dry, you can speed things up considerably by ejecting the memory card from your camera and pushing those pictures to your PC through a much faster USB connection. An external reader is cheap, too, usually running less than $50.

Rechargeable batteries

Gotta have 'em. I'm not kidding. You'll literally end up declaring bankruptcy if you use your digital camera often with single-use batteries. For example, one of my older 2.1-megapixel cameras can totally exhaust four AA alkaline batteries after one session of 20 photographs.

Here are the three major types of rechargeable batteries to choose from:

✦ **Nickel-cadmium (NiCad):** *NiCad* batteries are the cheapest and are available in standard sizes, but they drain quickly and take longer to recharge.

✦ **Nickel-metal-hydride (NiMH):** NiMH rechargeable batteries provide the middle of the road between higher cost and longer life; they take less time to recharge than NiCad batteries, and they last longer, but they're not as expensive as LIon batteries.

✦ **Lithium-ion (LIon):** These are the best batteries available. They provide more sustained power over a longer period than either of the other types, but they're the most expensive, and they're hard to find in standard sizes. Your camera might need an adapter to use them.

Just as you would an extra memory card, I recommend carrying a spare set of charged batteries in your camera bag. The Boy Scouts are right on this one: Be Prepared.

Lenses

Like their film brethren, most medium-priced and higher-end digital cameras can use external (add-on) lenses. Although your digital camera is likely to have several zoom levels (both digital and optical), photographers use a number of specialized lenses in specific situations. For example, consider these common extra lenses:

✦ **Telephoto:** Using a *telephoto* lens provides you with tremendous, long-distance magnification, but you don't have to be James Bond or a tabloid *paparazzo* to use one. For example, wildlife and sports photographers use telephoto lenses to capture subjects from a distance. (Referees tend to get surly when you stray on the field just to photograph the quarterback.)

✦ **Macro:** These lenses are especially designed for extreme close-up work; with a *macro* lens, you can capture images at a distance of a few inches. (They're great for making an engagement ring look much, much bigger.)

✦ **Wide-angle:** A *wide-angle* lens can capture a larger area — what photographers call the *field of view* — at the expense of detail. These lenses are often used for scenic or architectural photographs.

Don't forget a decent lens cap and a photographer's lens cleaning cloth to help prevent scratches on those expensive lenses!

Tripods

When most people think of tripods, they think of unwieldy, 5-foot-tall gantries suitable for launching the Saturn V. Yes, some tripods do meet those requirements, but they're absolutely required for low light, time-lapse, and professional portrait photography.

My camera bag also stows two other platforms that are much smaller:

✦ **Mini-tripod:** My Ambico mini-tripod can hold my cameras anywhere from 2 inches to 4 inches above the table. I use it in concert with my macro lens for shooting my scale models from a realistic perspective.

✦ **Monopod:** My collapsible monopod (which looks just like a walking stick) can hold the camera steady for quick shots on just about any surface. It also works great when you trip over exposed roots in the forest . . . but you didn't hear me admit to that.

Although a tripod isn't a requirement for the casual photographer, you'll find yourself wishing for one quickly if you move to more serious amateur photography. They sell tripods at Wal-Mart for a reason.

The Lazybone's Guide to Composing Photographs

If you'd like to remain firmly in the point-and-shoot casual photography crowd, you can comfortably skip any discussion of *composition* — that's the process (most call it an art) of aligning your subject and compensating for the available light at your location. Composition isn't a requirement for simple snapshots, but if you're going to create true visual art, you need the time to prepare your subject, your viewing angle, and your lighting.

In fact, what if I told you that composing a shot can result in less cropping and editing time on your computer — and that you'll end up taking better photographs? If you follow the tips that I provide in this section, I can just about guarantee that you'll discover at least one FRP in every set of images that you download! (*FRP*, coined by a favorite instructor that I had in journalism school, means First-Rate Photo — the kind of photograph that you'll be proud to display on your wall.) The example photographs in this chapter are taken from my personal FRP collection.

And despite what you might have heard about composing photographs, it only takes a few seconds before each shot to make a difference. Take it from me — with practice, you'll compose your shots automatically.

The Rule of Thirds

The *Rule of Thirds* is the foundation of good composition for most photographers. Applying this guideline helps draw the eye toward multiple subjects or to the focus of interest while maintaining balance within the frame. To use the Rule of Thirds, simply split the frame in your viewfinder into nine equal areas, as shown in Figure 9-3, "Time Tunnel." Align your subject(s) and the surroundings (where possible) along either

✦ A line crossing the frame

or

✦ One of the intersections where two lines meet

The Rule of Thirds works exceptionally well when taking photographs of landscapes or architecture, as you can see in Figure 9-4. This photograph, "View from Hoover Dam," uses the rule to draw the viewer's eye along the river until it disappears around the bend.

Figure 9-3:
Divide your photograph by the rule of thirds.

**Book II
Chapter 9**

**I'm Okay, You're a
Digital Camera**

Figure 9-4:
The movement of water flows closely along one line and ends at an intersection.

That's all there is to it. If you take a moment to examine the composition of the photographs in your favorite magazines, you'll see this time-tested classic rule followed over and over.

The Rule of Asymmetry

The second rule of composition often used in photography, the *Rule of Asymmetry,* presents the subject against a number of minor subjects as well as the background. Asymmetrical composition revolves around a relationship that you build between the major subject and either one or more minor subjects or the background itself. Following this rule, you merge different combinations of the three basic shapes — the square, the circle, and the triangle — to form a new outline or contour.

To illustrate, take the still life in Figure 9-5, "Cultures." Here I mix a light circular shape (the instrument) with strong rectangles (the skis). I find that an asymmetrical composition works better when you feature a sharp contrast level between light and dark elements or between strong color patterns and shadows.

Figure 9-5: Add interest with a classic asymmetrical composition.

I always make it a point to experiment with different camera angles — for instance, moving to the side or below the subject, as in "Warbird" (see Figure 9-6). Of course, sometimes you won't have the luxury of extra time to try something different, but I think that you'll like the results. (And remember, you're not wasting any film.)

Using lighting creatively

Before I finish this quick tour through photo composition, turn your attention to lighting. Virtually every digital camera made these days has an automatic flash feature, and this is usually a good thing to use. However, if your camera allows you to disable the flash, you'll take better photographs in many different situations.

Figure 9-6: Experiment with unusual camera angles.

Here's a list of exposure do's and don'ts for those who want to compose with light:

✦ **Do** make use of existing light when possible, if you can disable your camera's flash. Natural lighting can really make the photo.

✦ **Don't** attempt to photograph your subject through a sheet of glass or plastic if you're using a flash. Also, don't pose your subject against a reflective background — you'll create *hotspots* or flash reflections.

✦ **Do** use a tripod (or brace your camera if possible) when taking photographs without flash (which requires a longer exposure time to capture the image).

✦ **Don't** use a flash if your subject is illuminated internally or with spotlights, such as a neon sign or a statue at night.

✦ **Do** use an image editor — such as Photoshop or Paint Shop Pro — to enhance the contrast for underexposed shots. You can also change the hue and saturation levels for the colors in a photograph with your image editor. In Book II, Chapter 5, I cover some of the basics within Paint Shop Pro (like cropping and rotating images, converting images to different formats, and saving them to disk).

Shadows can add a tremendous visual impact, as shown in my photograph "French Quarter Staircase" in Figure 9-7. In this case, I needed no additional light, but I'm not above using an isolated spot *flood* (light source) to cast the shadow effect that I want. Even a flashlight can do the job in a pinch.

Figure 9-7:
Remember that shadows can be your friend.

Organizing Your Pictures

If you'd rather not stare at a meaningless collection of filenames, here are some tricks that you can use to help you locate a photograph that you stored on your hard drive or a CD-ROM full of images. First, organize your photos into folders based on the date, location, or subject of your photographs. Also, use the long filename support in Windows XP to better describe your photograph. After all, it's easier to visualize `Goats Grazing Outside Nepalese Village.jpg` than `nepgoats.jpg`.

To take your organization a step further, use an image-cataloging program such as Media Center Pro from Jasc Software (`www.jasc.com`). This great application not only handles images but sound files and video clips as well. The contents of your photo collection are shown as *thumbnails* (small images), making it easier to spot the photograph that you're looking for. Plus, Media Center Pro can create a slide show from your images, and you can export pictures to the Web with the HyperText Markup Language (HTML) pages that the program creates. At $30 for the downloadable version, Media Center Pro is an invaluable tool for any amateur (or professional) photographer.

Downloading Your Images

Before you launch into the downloading process, make sure you've taken care of those dull prerequisites:

✦ Make sure that you've installed any software that came with your digital camera or card reader; this ensures that any USB or FireWire drivers are installed before you connect.

✦ Connect the cable that came with your camera (or your external card reader) to the corresponding port on your PC . . . which is very likely your PC's USB port. If you're using a card reader, eject the memory card from your camera and load it into the slot in the card reader (as shown in the card reader's documentation). For more details on ports, visit Book II, Chapter 3.

✦ If you're connecting your digital camera directly to your PC and it has an AC adapter, make sure that you plug the camera into the AC adapter first; this can save you an hour of recharge time!

Although most digital cameras come with their own software, Windows XP has its own built-in wizard for downloading images. (If your camera comes with its own downloading software, it's a better idea to use that program instead, but at least Windows XP can likely do the job alone in a pinch.) If your camera or card reader is supported within Windows XP (check the manufacturer's Web site or the specifications on the side of the box) and you're not using your camera or card reader's software, you'll see the Scanner and Camera Wizard screen when you plug in the USB cable from your camera.

To complete the download process using the wizard, follow these steps:

1. **In the welcome wizard screen, click Next to advance to the second screen, as illustrated in Figure 9-8.**

   By default, the wizard copies all the images from your camera.

2. **To leave an image on the camera without transferring it to your PC, click the check box next to the image to clear it.**

   Click the Clear All button to deselect all the images, which comes in handy when you just want to select one or two pictures to download.

Figure 9-8:
Select and
rotate
images
before
they're
transferred.

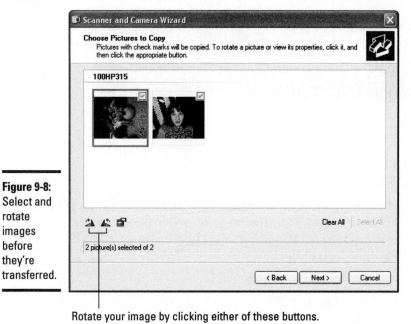

Rotate your image by clicking either of these buttons.

3. **To rotate an image, click the desired photograph to highlight it and then click either of the rotation buttons below the thumbnails.**

4. **After you select the images that you want to transfer and you rotate any shots that need attention, click Next to continue.**

5. **In the next wizard window, type a descriptive name and then choose a destination folder or drive where the images will be saved.**

   • **Name:** Windows XP uses this name as the basis for the image. In this example, the filenames will be `Fun Photos 001.jpg`, `Fun Photos 002.jpg`, and so on.

   • **Destination:** If you want to use a location that you've used before, click the drop-down list box, and the wizard displays it. To choose a new location, click the Browse button, navigate to the desired spot on your system, and then click OK.

6. **To delete the images from your camera after they've been successfully transferred to your PC, select the Delete Pictures from My Device after Copying Them check box.**

7. **Click Next to begin the transfer.**

   The wizard displays the progress window that you see in Figure 9-9.

   As soon as the transfer is complete, the next wizard screen appears.

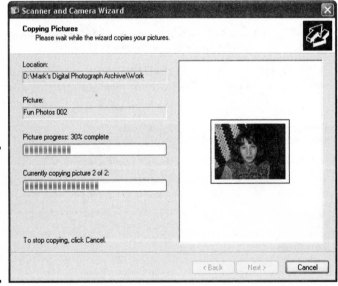

Figure 9-9: Watch the progress of your photographs from camera to PC.

8. **After the images have been transferred, you can choose to publish them to a Web site that you choose or to order prints of your photographs from a photo printing Web site. If you simply want to transfer the photographs, select the Nothing radio button.**

9. **After you make this choice, click Next.**

10. **In the final wizard screen that appears, click the Finish button to return to Windows XP, and then unplug your camera from your PC.**

CHECK IT OUT

Recovering Deleted Pictures on Your Camera

Tell me whether this has ever happened to you . . . I just pressed the wrong button on my digital camera and deleted all the pictures I'd stored. I thought I had selected just one file, but my not-so-nimble fingers were working in preprogrammed mode, far faster than my brain. The net result: an entire compact flash memory card wiped out. Surprisingly, unless your camera manufacturer specifically has a program set up to do it, the fastest, easiest, best way to undelete files on your digital camera is through your PC.

Lots and lots of programs on the market claim to resurrect dearly departed digital image files from your camera. I'm sure most of them work (although I've bumped into several that don't, at least on my cameras). But I've only hit one company that has the guts to let you download its software and use it to bring back two pictures for free. If you want to undelete more, you have to pay $30 for the program. But the two-shot demo version of File Rescue Plus doesn't cost a thing. It's cost-effective and saves time, too. Hard to beat.

Here's how to test drive File Rescue Plus:

1. **Start Internet Explorer and go to** www. softwareshelf.com.

2. **Click Downloads.**

3. **Fill out the information form, making sure that you choose File Rescue Plus as the Product Download.**

4. **Click Submit.**

5. **Follow the directions to download** FileRescuePlusDemo.exe.

6. **After the download has finished, double-click** FileRescuePlusDemo.exe.

   Follow the short installation wizard.

7. **Connect the camera that contained the recently deceased picture(s).**

8. **Choose Start➪All Programs➪Software Shelf➪File Rescue Plus to start File Rescue Plus.**

   The program asks about the File Scan mode.

9. **Click Picture Rescue; then click OK.**

   File Rescue Plus asks you which drive to scan.

10. **If you aren't sure which drive to use, click Start➪My Computer and look for your camera.**

11. **Choose the drive that corresponds to your digital camera, and then click OK.**

   Fire Rescue Plus wants to know if the drive has been reformatted. Not likely.

12. **Click Partition (Drive) Has Not Been Reformatted, and then click OK.**

   Fire Rescue Plus offers to show you thumbnails of the deleted files.

13. **Click Show Me a Thumbnail of the Pictures Available to Be Recovered; then click OK.**

   The first time I saw this happening, I could hardly believe my eyes. Fire Rescue Plus goes into the camera, reconstructs the deleted files, and then presents them to you. This process takes a while, so be patient.

14. **Click the file (or files) you want to undelete; then click the icon on the main Toolbar that looks like a computer monitor with a life preserver in front of it. (I'm tempted to talk about computers as boat anchors, but never mind.)**

   Fire Rescue Plus asks you where you want to put the reconstructed file. If you put the recovered file back in the camera, you may overwrite a different deleted picture in the process. Only save restored pics back to the camera if you want to keep them on the camera.

15. **Pick a location on your PC, give the file a name, and click Save.**

   The file is reconstituted and put in the location you choose. You can verify that the picture is alive and well by using Windows Explorer. Chances are good that you can see the picture by using the camera's controls as well.

Chapter 10: Determining What to Upgrade

In This Chapter

✔ Knowing when to upgrade your CPU and motherboard

✔ Figuring out whether you need additional memory

✔ Determining whether you need extra ports

✔ Considering a hard drive upgrade

✔ Evaluating a CD/DVD recorder or a tape backup drive

✔ Deciding on audio and video improvements

My father always said, "Son, never take a long trip without a road map handy." This is why our old family Plymouth had six metric tons of paper maps for every state in the Union stuffed into the glove compartment, ready to be pulled out just in case we went astray. (Now I just visit Yahoo! and use the Maps service — progress marches on.)

Consider this introductory chapter a road map to upgrading your PC: What you can do, what you should add or replace, and what your benefits will be after the dust has cleared. After you read this PC upgrade primer, you'll be able to easily determine what you need to upgrade, and you can jump to the proper chapter in Book II, Part III to find the specifics.

One note before you jump in: Upgrading your PC is not a difficult job! All it requires is

✦ The courage to remove your computer's case. (Believe me, you'll get used to it.)

✦ The ability to follow step-by-step instructions.

✦ Basic skills with a screwdriver.

With that in mind, read on to determine what you need to turn your PC back into a hot rod.

Making Performance Upgrades: CPU, Motherboard, and Memory

I've cordoned off these first upgrades into a separate category that I call *performance upgrades;* that is, they give your PC an overall performance boost that affects all the programs that you run, including Windows XP.

Upgrading your CPU and motherboard

A *central processing unit* (CPU) is the brain of your PC. A significant upgrade to your CPU usually results in more than just replacing the CPU chip itself. For example, if you decide to upgrade from a Pentium III computer to a Pentium 4, your PC's motherboard will probably need to be replaced as well. The *motherboard* is the largest circuit board in your computer's case — it holds the CPU, memory, and all the rest of the electronics — so this is probably one of the most technically demanding upgrades that you can make.

Naturally, replacing your computer's brain with the next generation of chip will result in faster performance. How much faster depends on the speed of the chip — which is usually specified in megahertz (MHz) or gigahertz (GHz) and whether you're skipping a generation. For example:

✦ Upgrading from a Pentium 4 1.5 GHz processor to a Pentium 4 1.7 GHz processor will result in a speed increase. And because the chip generation remains the same, you'll probably be able to use your current motherboard. However, the performance increase might not actually be significant enough to be noticeable in many of your programs . . . you're not really advancing very far.

✦ On the other hand, upgrading from an 800 MHz Pentium III processor to that same Pentium 4 1.7 GHz will change your plodding plowhorse into Shadowfax (the uber-stallion from Tolkien's *The Lord of the Rings*). Not only are you installing a CPU that's much faster, but you're also upgrading from Pentium III technology to Pentium 4 technology — and the tasks that you perform now will finish in a fraction of the time.

Anything less is a waste of time and effort (unless the CPU fairy dropped a new chip on your pillow for free).

Adding memory

I'll be honest — adding memory (random access memory, or RAM) is my favorite performance upgrade, and I recommend adding memory far more often than I recommend upgrading a CPU/motherboard combo. Here's why:

✦ **Memory packs performance punch.** Any PC tech will tell you that dollar for dollar, adding additional memory results in a far more significant performance boost than simply upgrading your processor by a few megahertz. Windows will use every bit of that additional memory (bad techno-nerd pun intended there), and everything that your PC does will be faster.

✦ **Memory is cheap.** I'm talkin' really, *really* cheap. Most folks can now afford to max out their memory capacity. (The total that you can add is dependent upon your motherboard, so check with the PC manufacturer or the specifications for your motherboard to determine the maximum amount of memory that you can add.)

✦ **Memory is easy to install.** Compared with upgrading a motherboard and CPU, adding memory is one of the simplest upgrade tasks that you can perform in the bowels of your machine. Add additional memory to your PC before embarking on a CPU and motherboard upgrade.

Expansion Upgrades: USB 2.0 and FireWire

Consider adding ports onto an older PC — what I call *expansion upgrades*. Although adding or upgrading ports won't speed up your computer, you'll be able to connect a wider range of external devices — and those devices are likely to run faster, transferring data to and from your PC at many times the rate of your pokey old serial and parallel ports.

Like the RAM upgrade that I discuss earlier in this chapter, adding Universal Serial Bus (USB) or FireWire ports to your PC is a relatively easy upgrade. All this involves is removing the cover from your PC and adding an adapter card to one of the open slots on your motherboard. Remember, this is how that original cadre of IBM engineers — the ones who designed the architecture of the first PCs — intended for you to add functionality to your computer, so it's practically a walk in the park.

Because I discuss USB 2.0 and FireWire ports earlier (see Book II, Chapter 3), here I just reiterate the major differences and what each type of port will do for you:

Book II
Chapter 10

Determining What
to Upgrade

✦ **USB 2.0:** This is the faster version of the USB port, with blazing speed and the ability to connect to older USB 1.*x* hardware. Unless you're using an external FireWire drive, digital camera, or digital video (DV) camcorder, USB 2.0 is the best choice for adding state-of-the-art, modern portage (ports for scanners, external hard drives, CD/DVD recorders, fax machines, printers, and the like) to your PC.

✦ **FireWire:** If you'd like to upgrade your PC for use with your DV camcorder — or if you're interested in adding a fast external hard drive or DVD recorder — FireWire is your port of choice. Also, FireWire periph-erals are usually easy to share with Mac owners because every modern Mac made within the last two or three years has at least one FireWire port.

If you already have USB or FireWire ports on your PC and you've simply run out of connections — for example, you have two USB ports, and you're using one for your printer and one for your Web cam — you don't need to add yet another set of ports. Instead, you just need a nifty little device called a USB or FireWire *hub,* which plugs into one of those ports and turns it into four or eight additional ports! (Think of the familiar AC extension cord, which plugs into one of your wall power sockets and allows you to plug in three or four cords.)

Making Storage Upgrades: Internal and External Drives

Why limit yourself to that sorry patch of digital real estate that originally shipped with your PC? I'm talking about your hard drive, a tape backup unit, or perhaps a slower, older CD recorder. Upgrading these devices is a *storage upgrade* because you use these devices to permanently store (or record) data for later use.

Hard drives and CD/DVD recorders are both constantly dropping in price (and adding extra capacity and features), which is fortuitous because today's operating systems and applications tend to take up more and more hard drive space. Therefore, it's only natural that most serious PC users will eventually decide to add a second drive (or replace their existing drive with a new unit).

Adding a hard drive

The vast majority of today's PCs use Integrated Drive Electronics (IDE) hard drives, which can be mounted internally (within your PC's case) or externally (by connecting to a USB or FireWire port).

Here's how to tell which type of drive you should choose:

✦ **Internal:** Choose an internal drive if you don't mind opening up your PC's case and installing a new drive. (I show you how in Book II, Chapter 8.) Internal drives are significantly cheaper than external drives, and they're somewhat faster than even an external FireWire or USB 2.0 drive. Finally, you won't use any more of your precious desktop space.

✦ **External:** Choose an external drive if you'd rather not open your computer, or if you have no available hard drive bays left in your computer's case. (Don't laugh — techno-types can fill up even the largest tower case with all sorts of devices.) External hard drives can be shared among computers that have the same ports, and you can simply unplug an external drive and carry it with you. (How's that for security?)

Adding a recorder or a tape drive

CD/DVD recorders and backup tape drives have been around for years now, but only with the advent of USB and FireWire have they become attractive to the PC power user. In years past, hardware manufacturers had to depend on the PC's parallel port to connect these peripherals. (If you had *real* money, you could get an external Small Computer System Interface [SCSI] drive, but I recommend avoiding SCSI altogether; read why when I describe SCSI hardware in the sidebar, "Just let SCSI fade away . . ." elsewhere in this chapter.) The PC's parallel port was never designed for high-speed data transfer, so parallel port drives were as slow as your Aunt Gertrude in her '53 Pontiac.

However, today's FireWire and USB 2.0 drives are almost as blazing fast as their internal brethren! Therefore, as long as you have a USB 2.0 or FireWire port, you now have the same choice that I describe with hard drives: Either stick it in your machine or leave it outside: It'll work like a charm either way.

One final word about today's tape backup drives: They're beginning to disappear from the PC landscape because today's recordable DVD formats can hold 4.7GB (or even more) on a single disc — and DVD recorders are faster and more reliable than most tape drives. Therefore, before you invest in a hideously expensive Digital Audio Tape (DAT) backup drive, consider buying a (comparatively) inexpensive rewriteable DVD drive instead and use that for your backups.

Just let SCSI fade away . . .

Officially, the acronym SCSI stands for *Small Computer Systems Interface*, but for most PC owners, it used to stand for *waking nightmare*. Before the arrival of FireWire and USB, a SCSI adapter card was the only way that you could add fast external devices to your PC. In fact, you can add multiple SCSI peripherals to the same card, like a SCSI scanner and a SCSI CD recorder. Unfortunately, SCSI hardware has always been more expensive. SCSI devices were also once notoriously difficult to configure, and even today's SCSI implementation — which offers more automated setup features — is nowhere near as reliable and easy to install as either FireWire or USB 2.0. (Forget Plug and Play — the running gag is that SCSI is *Run and Hide* or *Plug and Pray*.)

Both FireWire and USB 2.0 ports can handle more external devices than a SCSI port, and they can transfer data at speeds that are fast enough to allow SCSI to fade into the archaic computing past. Take the word of a graying techno-Gandalf here: You're better off without SCSI, good buddy.

Making Sound and Video Upgrades: Sound and Video Cards

To finish my road map of PC upgrades, consider the hottest video and audio cards on the market today. There are more reasons than just gaming to add or upgrade your PC's eyes and ears: For example, maybe you'd like to move up to a sound card with Dolby Surround sound support or perhaps a video card with video capture capability. Like the addition of USB and FireWire ports, these upgrades are pretty simple: Just take the case off your PC, remove your current sound or video adapter card, and plug the replacement card in its place.

Before I jump into a discussion of these cards, I should note that some of today's motherboards have their sound (and/or video) hardware on the motherboard instead of on separate adapter cards. If you have a motherboard with either a built-in video card or sound card, you should be able to disable the onboard hardware so that you can add your upgrade card. Typically, you must either display your PC's Basic Input/Output System (BIOS) and disable the onboard hardware from there, or you need to move a jumper on the motherboard. Read your motherboard user manual to discover which avenue to take.

Sound cards on parade

A number of specialized sound cards are available for the discriminating audio connoisseur — which, no doubt, you are. Consider these gems:

✦ **An MP3 card:** If you're an MP3 wizard with a hard drive's worth of MP3 digital audio files, you'll appreciate one of these specialized audio cards. An MP3 card contains a hardware encoder/decoder, which speeds up your PC's *ripping* (another name for the process of creating MP3 digital audio files from existing audio CDs) and MP3 playing performance. With one of these cards (which typically run about $100–$150), you can listen to (or rip) the Talking Heads while using Photoshop, and the sound quality stays just as good.

✦ **A 24-bit card:** For the absolute best in audio reproduction, a card such as the Audigy 2 from Creative Labs can produce 24-bit audio (that's 192 KHz for you audioheads), which is far superior to the sound produced by virtually all audio CD players. The fact that these cards can also support DVD audio and carry a built-in FireWire port is just the whipped cream and cherry on the sundae. Expect to pay a prime price for one of these cards, usually in the $200 range.

✦ **A Surround sound card:** These cards are specifically designed for 3-D environmental audio within games as well as full support for Dolby Surround sound as you watch DVD movies on your PC. Naturally, you'll need more than two mundane speakers from Wal-Mart to enjoy the full effect — which is why a premium set of speakers is usually included with these cards. Again, look for these cards to set you back around $200.

Deciding which video card is right for you

When you think about upgrading a video card, please do not — I repeat, *do not* — just think "gamers only." A number of specialized video cards are on the market that have nothing to do with games. (Okay, I admit it . . . gamers like myself do indeed love video cards.) Here's a cross section of what's available:

✦ **A gamer's card:** The latest 3-D video cards (equipped with GeForce4 and Radeon chipsets, from NVIDIA and ATI, respectively) simply kick serious tail no matter whether your favorite games involve mowing down Nazis, building a civilization one stone at a time, or matching wits with your computer over a chess board. If you haven't seen the realistic 3-D figures that these cards can produce, visit the Maze o' Wires store at your local mall and ask a salesperson to crank up the latest game. Of course, Windows XP will display ho-hum applications faster with one of these cards as well. Many 3-D gaming cards also offer dual monitor support so that you can run two monitors side-by-side for a really big desktop.

 These high-end 3-D cards run tremendously hot — after all, they're practically separate computers themselves — so they usually have their own fan on the card itself. However, if you're planning on installing the card in an older PC, I recommend having at least two fans installed in your case — that's one for the power supply (which is standard equipment) and at least one auxiliary fan (to help circulate air to all those hot components).

✦ **An MPEG card:** These cards are specifically designed for encoding and decoding Motion Picture Experts Group (MPEG) digital video (usually from a DVD, but hardware MPEG support is also very useful for doing serious video editing on your PC). Like the MP3 card that I describe in the previous section on audio cards, the idea is simple: Let the card do the video grunt work instead of your PC's processor, and everyone is happier.

✦ **A capture card:** This popular video upgrade card allows you to capture an incoming analog video signal and convert it to digital video. For example, you can connect your VCR or older analog VHS-C camcorder into the card, convert the signal to digital video, and then record CD or DVD backups of your home movies. I've even seen these cards used to capture footage from Xbox games — if you can display it on your TV, you should be able to capture it with one of these toys.

Chapter 11: Adding RAM to Your Hot Rod

In This Chapter

✔ Determining what type of memory you need

✔ Understanding the myth behind "minimum RAM"

✔ Installing additional memory

*W*hat's not to like about a memory upgrade? As I discuss in the previous chapter, the dinero required for extra random access memory (RAM) is a mere pittance compared with a new CPU (or CPU and motherboard combination). Plus, RAM is easy to install, requiring only that you remove your PC's case and plug in the modules. Your PC should recognize additional RAM immediately, with no silly drivers required. Also, additional RAM will make everything run faster in Windows . . . both the applications that you run and the operating system itself.

Maybe you're saying, "But there's *got* to be a hitch *somewhere*." True: The problem is that you have so many different types of RAM modules to choose from. Therefore, read through this chapter before you buy your RAM modules and keep these pages handy when you upgrade.

Figuring Out What Type of Memory You Need

To begin a primer on memory, review the different types of RAM available for PCs made within the last five years or so.

One tip before I begin: If you're considering installing a new motherboard and CPU on an older PC, you might want to double-check to make sure that the new motherboard will still use the same RAM type and speed as your current motherboard. (To check, visit the manufacturer's Web sites to compare the specifications for your existing motherboard and the new toy, or you can refer to the documentation for both motherboards.) If not, the RAM that you add now won't do you any good when you upgrade your motherboard. If you have your eye on a significant motherboard/CPU swap in the near future, I definitely recommend that you upgrade the motherboard, CPU, *and* RAM all at the same time. For example, the memory modules that work with your older Pentium III PC aren't likely to work with a fast Pentium 4 motherboard. In cases like this, I recommend simply ordering a *populated* motherboard, which comes complete with a preinstalled CPU and the amount of RAM that you specify.

The different types of RAM commonly used on PCs are

✦ **Rambus dynamic random access memory (RDRAM):** These modules are very expensive, but they're the fastest memory modules available on the market today, with access speeds up to 1200 MHz at the time of this writing. If your PC uses RDRAM, it's really cooking already, so you probably won't be upgrading for a speed increase anytime soon. (More likely, you're preparing to add more memory to your existing RDRAM motherboard.)

✦ **Double Data Rate (DDR):** These modules are the fastest standard 168-pin Dual Inline Memory Module (DIMM) available; they're commonly used on today's Pentium 4 and Athlon computers that run Windows XP. The *double* in the DDR name is significant because a DDR module effectively doubles the speed of the module (compared with older synchronous DRAM [SDRAM] memory). Also, DDR memory is assigned a speed rating as part of the name, so it's commonly listed as DDR266 or PC2100 (for the 133 MHz speed versions) and DDR333 or PC2700 (for the 166 MHz version). As you might guess, the faster the access speed, the better the performance. The speed rating that you should choose is determined by the memory speeds that your motherboard supports. DDR memory modules have one notch on the connector and two notches on each side of the module.

✦ **SDRAM (sometimes called *SyncDRAM*):** These modules take the form of standard 168-pin DIMMs. These modules are standard equipment for most Pentium III and some older Pentium 4 machines. SyncDRAM runs at an access speed of 133 MHz, and it's the most common memory type used for PCs these days. SDRAM memory modules have two notches in the bottom and only one notch on each side.

✦ **Extended Data Output (EDO):** These modules take the form of 72-pin Single Inline Memory Modules (SIMMs), and they are used in older Pentium motherboards. Typically, you must add SIMM memory in pairs.

If you're planning on adding memory to a motherboard that uses EDO modules, I strongly urge you to instead upgrade the Big Three — motherboard, CPU, and memory. (I don't intend to offend, but I'll be blunt: Your PC is so far behind the performance of today's models that it just isn't worth adding EDO memory to your older motherboard. Plus, EDO memory is now much harder to find and is actually getting more expensive over time. Just chalk that up to the price of running antique hardware.)

Here are two methods to determine what type of memory modules your current motherboard requires and what memory speeds it can handle:

✦ **Check the specifications:** Refer to the motherboard manual. Or, if you purchased your PC from a manufacturer, check the documentation that accompanied the computer. If you didn't get any manuals with a used PC, visit the company's Web site for memory compatibility information or specifications. This is definitely the preferred method because you won't have to open your PC's case until you're ready to install the new RAM modules.

✦ **Check the existing modules:** If you can't find any documentation, specifications, or data on the Web concerning your PC's RAM modules, it's time to remove the case from your computer. (For more details on removing the cover, see the step-by-step procedure at the end of this chapter.) Look for the memory slots on your motherboard; DDR modules look like Figure 11-1. (*Note:* You might have more than one module already installed on your PC.) Your RAM modules might have a descriptive label (which will allow you to read the specifics without actually taking anything out); however, it's more likely that you'll have to remove one and take it to your local computer shop. Use the instructions later in this chapter to remove a module; then protect the module in an empty CD-ROM jewel case when you take it for identification. The good techs should be able to tell you what type and speed of memory you're using when presented with the module.

Figure 11-1:
A DDR
DIMM,
caught in
the open.

Deciding How Much RAM Is Enough

Every motherboard has a maximum amount of memory that it can support. You can install the maximum amount by filling up all the motherboard's memory banks (sockets) with modules of the right type. Whenever possible, buy RAM modules of the same brand, at the same time, and from the same dealer.

This will ensure that you are spared any compatibility problems when you install the modules. (Theoretically, any RAM module of the same type and speed should work with any other brand of RAM, but I date back to the earlier days of PCs when using memory chips from different manufacturers would result in errors and a locked computer.) In fact, I still hear tales of compatibility problems, even in our new, improved, fresher-smelling world.

However, not everyone can afford to take a PC's memory to the max — even with today's prices, buying a gigabyte of RAM modules can set you back. Therefore, the following table illustrates my recommendations for the minimum amount of RAM that you'll need to run the different versions of the Windows operating system comfortably on your PC. (By *comfortably,* I mean my opinion of decent performance, perhaps with a copy of Microsoft Word running. Of course, memory-hungry applications such as Adobe Photoshop will only run their best with plenty of memory elbow room to spare, so I'd consider this the bare minimum.)

Windows 98	*Windows NT*	*Windows Me*	*Windows 2000*	*Windows XP*
64MB	64MB	128MB	128MB	256MB

You might notice that my recommendations sometimes don't jibe with Brother Bill's — that's because the folks in Redmond literally mean *the least you can get away with* when mentioning minimum memory requirements. With 24MB of RAM, Windows 98 is slower to awaken than my kids on a school day. Personally, I actually like to *use* my computer and not wait half an hour for a scanned image to load.

Installing Extra RAM

Ready to install your new RAM upgrade? Follow these steps to install a typical SDRAM or DDR module:

1. **Cover your work surface with several sheets of newspaper (to protect your case).**

2. **Unplug your PC and place it on top of the newspaper.**

3. **Remove the PC's case.**

   Most PC cases are held on with two or three screws; just remove the screws and slide the case off. (Don't forget to stash those screws in a safe place.) Other cases are hinged, often with a lock. If you're unsure how to remove your PC's case, check the manual that accompanied your computer.

4. **Touch the metal chassis of your case to dissipate any static electricity on your body.**

   An electrical charge can send your new RAM modules to Frisco . . . permanently.

5. **Locate the DIMM slots.**

   Check the motherboard manual, which should have a schematic that will help you locate the slots. Typically, the RAM modules are found close to the CPU, in the center or one corner of the motherboard.

6. **Turn your PC's chassis so that the DIMM slots are facing you (as shown in Figure 11-2) and make sure that the two levers on the side of the socket are extended.**

Figure 11-2:
Align a DDR module with its socket.

Note that the notches cut into the connectors on the bottom of the memory module match the spacers in the sockets themselves, so you can't install your modules the wrong way. (Smart thinking there.)

7. **Align the connector on the bottom of the module with the socket and push down with a light pressure to seat the module.**

8. While you push down, the two levers at each side of the socket should move toward the center, as shown in Figure 11-3, until they click in place.

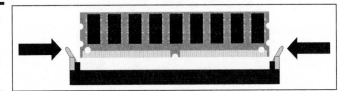

Figure 11-3: Hey, those levers just clicked into place!

After you correctly install the module, the two levers should be tightly flush against the sides of the memory module to hold it securely.

9. Slide the cover back on your PC and secure it.

10. Move your PC back to its place of honor and plug it in.

11. Restart your computer and prepare to enjoy a faster PC!

Chapter 12: Scotty, I Need More Power!

In This Chapter

✓ Evaluating your need for a CPU/motherboard upgrade

✓ Shopping for features

✓ Installing a CPU/motherboard upgrade

Upgrading your central processing unit (CPU)/motherboard — the Big One — is the most costly and the most complex upgrade that you can make to your PC. In this chapter, I discuss what you should look for in a CPU and a motherboard . . . and the very real possibility that you shouldn't upgrade this combo at all. (Hey, I'm always open minded, upfront, and cutting edge.)

If you do decide to upgrade, take heart. You'll find the proper step-by-step procedure in this chapter.

Hey, Do I Need to Do This?

Before you read another sentence of this chapter, remember this: Postpone a CPU/motherboard upgrade as long as possible. I know that sounds a little silly, considering that there are several pages of perfectly good tips and procedures remaining in this chapter, but I stand by my maxim. Here are four good reasons:

✦ **A CPU/motherboard combo is one of the most expensive upgrades that you can make to your computer.** First consider upgrading random access memory (RAM) and your video card. Adding RAM and a faster video card is (usually) cheaper than upgrading a CPU/motherboard combo. And depending on the types of applications that you run, the RAM/video card upgrade might actually provide a better performance boost than using a new CPU and motherboard. (*Side benefit:* The longer that you postpone a CPU/motherboard upgrade, the more of a performance jump that you'll get when you finally do take the plunge.)

✦ **A CPU/motherboard combo is one of the most difficult upgrades to install.** To facilitate this upgrade, you're going to have to take out every adapter card and unhook every wire and possibly even disassemble parts of your case — then do it all again in reverse. (That's what we techies call "putting it back together." My Dad used to tell me I'd have to eat anything left over after fixing the family car, so I got very careful very quickly about assembly.)

Which is better: Intel or AMD?

Chip choice time. Intel and AMD are the two leading processor manufacturers. I can honestly say that both the Pentium 4 (Intel) and the Athlon XP (AMD) are great processors, so let price and the chip speed be your guide. Just make sure that you get the right CPU for your motherboard because every motherboard is specifically designed for one brand of CPU. In general, AMD processors are less expensive than Intel processors of the same performance level.

✦ **A CPU/motherboard combo has dependencies.** Hmm . . . strange term here, so let me explain. You see, no matter how fast your new motherboard and CPU combo might be, it will still depend on your existing adapter cards — including video, sound, modem, and port cards — to take care of putting video on your monitor, sound in your speakers, and Internet data in your browser (respectively). Therefore, if you upgrade to a blazing fast CPU/motherboard combination but you're still using a five-year-old video card, your 3-D games might still end up as slow as Aunt Harriet in her Plymouth Volare.

✦ **You might have to scrap your existing memory modules and power supply**. Along the lines of the previous reason, using a new CPU/motherboard combo might force you to dump all the memory modules that you've been collecting over the last few years as well as that low-rated power supply. You can sell 'em on eBay, of course, but don't expect a whopping amount back.

With these reasons in mind, I recommend that you upgrade your motherboard and CPU only when you've exhausted the other possibilities — upgrading RAM or your video card, for example. I'm not saying that you shouldn't eventually put a new heart and brain in your PC. Just don't resort to major surgery until it's really necessary.

Selecting a New Motherboard

Keep these guidelines in mind while shopping for a new motherboard to match your CPU of choice:

✦ **Determine what type of motherboard fits in your PC's case.** Virtually all PCs manufactured in the last few years use ATX cases and ATX motherboards, but it never hurts to make sure. Older cases might use AT or Baby AT motherboards. If you need help with classifying your case, take it to your local computer shop and have a technician tell you.

✦ **FSB means Front Side Bus.** The higher the bus speed on your new motherboard, the better the performance — and the more expensive the RAM modules. (At higher bus speeds, more data is sent to the CPU at one time, and the data arrives there faster; from an efficiency and performance standpoint, this is a Good Thing.) Most CPUs will work with a range of bus speeds.

✦ **Shop for the best controllers.** Today's motherboards have onboard hard drive controllers that vary widely in performance, so make sure that you compare the controller's rated speeds and supported hard drives when shopping for a motherboard.

✦ **Consider onboard FireWire, Universal Serial Bus (USB) 2.0, and network hardware.** Why force yourself to add a separate adapter card later when you can buy a motherboard with networking, FireWire, and USB 2.0 ports built in?

✦ **RAM capacity is important.** Check what type of RAM is supported and the maximum amount of RAM that the motherboard can accept. (For more information about the RAM types on the market today, check the previous chapter.)

I *highly* recommend that you buy one of the package deals — a CPU already installed on the motherboard of your choice — offered by most PC Web stores. This will simplify both your shopping (you're guaranteed to buy a motherboard and CPU that work together well) and your installation. Trust me!

Installing a Motherboard and CPU

Before you decide to launch into a motherboard/CPU swap, carefully read over the following procedure and then visit the nearest bathroom. (No, I don't expect you to be sick; I want you to stand in front of the mirror.) Look yourself in the eye and ask yourself honestly, "Can I do this? If I can do this, do I really *want* to do this?"

If your answer is a confident "Yes," by all means continue with your upgrade, and may you have the wind always at your back.

If, however, your answer is an uncomfortable "Maybe," don't forget that you can always take your PC to a local computer shop and have the techs there install your new hardware for you. This is the only spot in all of Book II where I even consider the option of professional installation. Of course, anything in this book can be professionally installed, but a CPU/motherboard combo is often more difficult and more of a hassle for the typical PC owner than any other upgrade.

With that said — and if you're still reading on — then get to work!

Installing an Athlon XP or Pentium 4 CPU

If you didn't buy a combo motherboard with the CPU already installed, follow these steps to install your processor before you install the motherboard:

1. **Touch a metal surface.**

Static is bad. You know the drill.

2. **Locate the CPU socket on your motherboard — it's the largest socket on the planet, with several dozen pins.**

Check the motherboard manual if you have a problem finding it.

The CPU socket is also called a ZIF (short for *Zero Insertion Force*) socket, which means that you can quickly install and remove the CPU without undue pressure on the chip (and with as little danger of bending the CPU pins as possible). The little lever clamps the CPU firmly to the motherboard, as you will see.

Pay close attention to the markings on your new CPU. "What markings?" Well, cast your eyes on Figure 12-1, which illustrates different types of markings on both CPUs and sockets. Look for a stubby corner, a tiny groove, or a dot or triangle on one corner of the chip — that marked corner will match up with the socket's marked corner. If you can't locate the marked corner, your motherboard and CPU manuals will identify them for you.

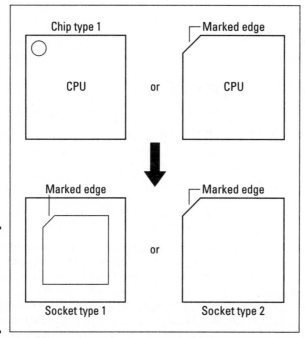

Figure 12-1: Match marked corners on the CPU and sockets.

3. **Raise the ZIF lever on the side of the socket to unlock the socket.**

4. **Align the CPU chip on top of the socket, matching marked corners and double-checking your pin placement from the side of the chip.**

5. **Use your fingertips to gently press down evenly on the edges of the chip.**

   The chip should settle in until the pins aren't visible from the side.

   Do not force your CPU! If it doesn't comfortably settle into place, put it down and retreat to the comfort of your motherboard and CPU manuals. Breaking the pins on your CPU will turn it into an extremely expensive, nonfunctioning brooch.

6. **Lower the ZIF lever on the side of the socket to lock the CPU in place.**

7. **Clamp the fan on top of the processor.**

Note: You might need to apply a special glue or compound between the fan plate and the processor before you install the fan.

8. **If your CPU fan has a separate power cable, plug it into the proper connector on the motherboard.**

   The location of the CPU fan plug will be listed in your motherboard manual.

Relax. Breathe deeply. Congratulations!

Installing your motherboard

Time to put that granddaddy of all circuit boards inside your case. Grab your screwdriver and follow these steps:

1. **Unplug your PC and move it onto your work surface.**

2. **Remove the cover from the case.**

   Keep the screws handy, naturally.

3. **Work that anti-static magic by touching your PC's metal chassis.**

4. **Unscrew and remove all the adapter cards, placing them on top of a handy sheet of nearby newspaper.**

5. **Unplug all cables leading to your motherboard.**

   Note: You might also have to remove sections of your case as well as all internal devices such as hard drives, CD/DVD drives, and your floppy drive. (I told you this was going to be a bear, didn't I?) Because all cases are designed differently, this might take a little investigation on your part.

6. **After the motherboard is completely uncovered, remove all the screws and nonconductive washers holding down the motherboard and put them in a bowl, keeping them separate from any other screws.**

   Carefully note the location of the screw holes and any plastic spacers securing the old motherboard to the case before you remove them. This will save time later. If necessary, grab a piece of paper and a pencil and sketch a quick drawing of which holes you should use when installing the new motherboard.

7. **Reach into your PC's case and gently work the old motherboard free.**

   Take the time to make sure that you don't scratch the surface of your motherboard on exposed metal or sharp edges. A deep-enough scratch can ruin the delicate circuitry etched into the surface of the board.

8. **After the old motherboard is clear, put it in the anti-static pouch that protected your new board, and start wondering who will buy it. (If any plastic spacers were attached, remove them and put them with your motherboard screws.)**

9. **Holding the new motherboard by the edges, carefully place it inside the case to align it. Keep the memory modules and CPU side facing up and toward you, ensuring that the adapter card slots line up with the slots in your case (see Figure 12-2).**

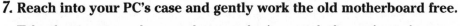

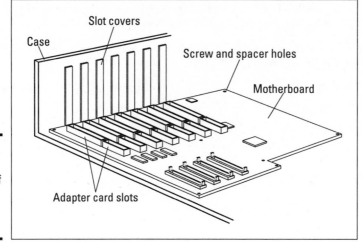

Figure 12-2:
Check the
alignment of
your new
mother-
board.

Labels in figure: Slot covers, Case, Screw and spacer holes, Motherboard, Adapter card slots

10. **Check to determine which screw holes in your motherboard line up with which screw holes in your case.**

    Note that your case will likely use three or four screws to actually hold the board, but other spots on the board might need to be supported by those plastic spacers; the spacers slide under metal grooves in the case.

11. **If you need to add spacers, remove the new motherboard from the case and push the spacers through the holes from the bottom of the board until they snap into place, as shown in Figure 12-3.**

12. **If you had to remove your motherboard in Step 11, slide it back into the case (making sure that all the plastic spacers are correctly positioned).**

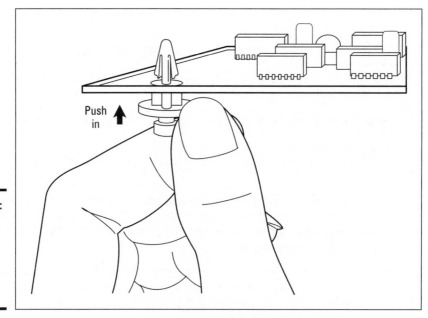

Push
in

Figure 12-3:
Add
spacers,
if needed,
to the new
mother-
board.

13. Check each corner of the motherboard to make sure that it's separated from the metal of the case and doesn't wobble.

14. Secure the motherboard with the screws and washers from Step 6, being careful not to overtighten them.

15. Plug the power cables, hard drive, floppy cables, and case control cables back into the new motherboard.

   Because every motherboard is different, you'll have to rely on your motherboard manual to locate what goes where. (This is why I've never tossed a motherboard manual in the trash.)

16. Reinstall any drives or case chassis parts that you had to remove in Step 5.

17. Reinstall your adapter cards, connecting any cables that you had to remove back to their original location.

18. After you double-check every connection, replace the cover on your case.

19. Plug your PC back in and boogie.

   It is now appropriate to book a vacation to Disneyland.

Chapter 13: Adding Hard Drive Territory to Your System

In This Chapter

✔ Understanding virtual memory

✔ Selecting the proper drive

✔ Choosing an internal or external drive

✔ Adding a second internal drive

*H*ere is what I call the *Elbow Room Hypothesis:* Both mankind and his computer tools will expand to fill whatever room they're given. If you're bent on becoming a PC power user, I can assure you — in fact, I can downright *guarantee* you — that the largest hard drive that you can buy today will eventually be filled in the future. As you discover in this chapter, even Windows XP demands a chunk of hard drive territory . . . both when you install it and when it's running.

Hence the explosion in hard drive capacities over the last five years or so. I'm old enough to remember when a 1GB drive was an unheard-of dream. Heck, I still have the first hard drive that I ever owned: a huge RadioShack 15MB (yes, you read right, *fifteen megabyte*) Disk System that I used with my TRS-80 Model IV. (Oh, did I mention that those 15 megabytes of storage cost me over $1,000 in 1983 and that the drive is about the size of a typical modern PC case?) I use it as a combination monitor stand, conversation piece, and possible proof of past visits by extraterrestrials.

Luckily, you can upgrade your PC's hard drive with ease either by connecting an external drive or by upgrading your current internal hard drive. Alternatively, you can simply cast yourself to the four winds with abandon and keep your current internal drive and add a second drive. This chapter is your road map.

The Tale of Virtual Memory

"Wait a furshlugginer minute here — you cover memory upgrades in Book II, Chapter 11. Why bring it up now?" Good question, and the answer lies in the fact that the pseudo-RAM called *virtual memory* actually exists on your hard drive rather than as memory modules on your motherboard.

Now that you're totally confused, here's the explanation: Today's modern operating systems (meaning Windows XP and 2000, Mac OS 9 and OS X, Unix, and Linux) all use a trick called *virtual memory* to feed your applications the memory that they need. Suppose that your PC has only 64MB of random access memory (RAM) installed, but you've just run Photoshop and demanded that it load a 30MB high-resolution digital image. If Windows XP were limited to using only your computer's *physical* RAM (the memory modules that you've installed on your PC's motherboard), you'd be up a creek because Windows XP requires a minimum of around 24MB of memory itself, and Photoshop takes a significant chunk of memory to run. And on top of all that, you're loading 30MB of data, too! With the size of today's documents and the amount of RAM needed by memory-hungry mega-applications, your 64MB PC literally can't do its job. And don't forget, you're probably running more than one application at once. What's a computer to do?

As you can see in Figure 13-1, Windows turns to your hard drive for help. It uses a portion of the empty space on your hard drive to temporarily hold the data that would otherwise be held in your computer's memory. In this case, our hardworking silicon warrior uses 64MB of hard drive space, so the total memory available within Windows (using both 64MB of physical memory and 64MB of virtual memory) is now 128MB, providing more elbow room to work with. Your programs actually don't know that they're using virtual memory — Windows takes care of everything behind the scenes, so Photoshop thinks that you have 128MB of physical memory.

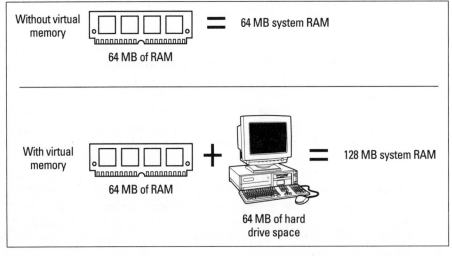

Figure 13-1: Windows XP creates memory space from the free space on your hard drive.

Now that you understand how virtual memory works, commit this to heart: Always leave enough empty hard drive space for Windows to use as virtual memory!

How much is enough? I try to leave at least 1 or 2GB free on the C: drive at all times on my Windows XP machines. A PC that runs out of hard drive space is a terrible thing to see; applications will start to lock up, you might lose any changes that you've made to open files, and Windows will begin displaying pitiful error messages begging you to close some of your open application windows (or even restart).

Also, note that virtual memory is always — and I mean *always* — slower than true physical memory. After all, that data has to be written to and read from your hard drive instead of super-fast memory modules. This is why I'm such a proponent of adding as much RAM to your PC as possible because

the more memory that you add, the less likely that Windows XP will need to resort to virtual memory.

PC techs call your computer's use of virtual memory *drive thrashing* because Windows must constantly write to, read from, and erase data from your hard drive. When you run out of physical memory, the hard drive activity light never seems to go out. And yes, if you're wondering, all that activity will shorten the life of your hard drive.

Recognizing a Well-Dressed Hard Drive

When you decide to take the plunge and add storage space, reading this section helps you shop by separating the good specifications from the gobbledygook.

Today's PCs use Enhanced Integrated Drive Electronics (EIDE) hard drives. Although a PC can use an internal Small Computer Systems Interface (SCSI) hard drive, anyone using expensive and complex SCSI hardware is already a PC power user and can probably skip this chapter without a second glance.

Book II
Chapter 13

Adding Hard Drive Territory to Your System

Size definitely does matter

Virtually all EIDE drives on the market today are 3½-inch format, meaning that they can fit within a typical floppy drive/hard drive combo bay within your computer's case. Unfortunately, some mini-tower cases have only one or two of these 3½-inch bays.

Therefore, if you're planning on parking that 3½-inch drive within a much larger 5¼-inch bay — the kind used with CD- and DVD-ROM drives — you'll need a metal framework called a *drive cage kit*. In effect, the hard drive is mounted into the drive cage, which in turn is mounted in the PC's 5¼-inch bay. Most drives don't come with a drive cage kit, so you'll need to buy one at your computer shop. (They usually run about $10.)

How fast is your access?

When you see a drive's *access* (or *seek*) time listed, that's the amount of time in milliseconds (ms) that it takes the drive to read or write data. Naturally, a lower access time is desirable — and usually somewhat more expensive. Drives with access times below 10 ms are usually at the top of their price range, especially when the drive in question has a higher revolutions per minute (rpm) rating.

What does rpm have to do with hard drives?

In the world of personal computers, just like in the world of the Indy 500, the abbreviation *rpm* means *revolutions per minute*. (However, I'm counting the revolutions that the magnetic disk platter turns inside the drive.) And, with a refreshing constancy, a higher rpm hard drive means better performance, just like a beefier engine's rpm's mean greater speed in auto racing.

Most of today's IDE drives fall into one of two rpm ranges:

✦ **5,400 rpm:** These drives are standard equipment on most older PCs and can also be found on low-cost Pentium 4 computers. As reliable as vanilla ice cream, one of these drives will get the job done . . . but don't expect whipped cream and a cherry.

✦ **7,200 rpm:** These faster drives are found on today's high-performance PCs. 7,200 rpm drives used to be 10–20 percent more expensive than their slower brethren, but lately, the cost on these faster drives has dropped to about the same price point.

I heartily recommend that you select a 7,200 rpm drive when upgrading any Athlon or Pentium 4 computer. The significantly faster read/write performance on one of these drives will pep up your entire system.

Internal versus External Storage

I address the idea of internal and external peripherals in a number of places elsewhere in Book II, so I won't go into a crazy amount of detail here. Suffice it to say that I recommend using an internal hard drive whenever

✦ You don't need to share the drive among multiple computers or take it with you while traveling.

✦ Your PC has an additional open drive bay, or you're willing to upgrade the existing drive.

✦ You want to save money.

As you might expect, with those criteria, I usually push internal hard drives on both my unsuspecting consulting customers and myself as well. Figure 13-2 shows the curvaceous rear end of a typical modern hard drive. (Well, at least it *looks* curvaceous to a techno-nerd like myself.)

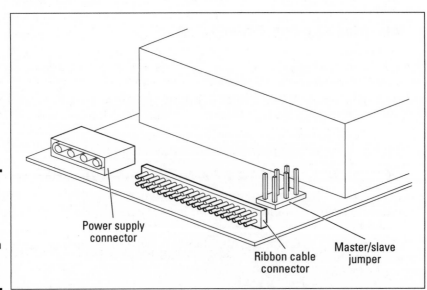

Figure 13-2:
You need all the connectors that fit on an EIDE hard drive.

Power supply connector

Ribbon cable connector

Master/slave jumper

Don't get me wrong — external drives are neat toys. However, they cost significantly more than their internal counterparts, and you'll lose some of your precious desk space accommodating them. Most external drives also have their own power cord, meaning that you have to pull yet another AC wall socket out of your magician's hat. If you really do need an external drive and you want to save yourself the hassle, consider a drive that's powered over a Universal Serial Bus (USB) or FireWire connection, which means no additional power cable worries.

If someone tries to give you a USB 1.*x* hard drive — or, heaven forbid, if you're thinking of buying a used USB 1.*x* hard drive — I beg you *not* to do it! The first generation of USB drives were ridiculously slow. In other words, your kids are likely to graduate from college before you finish transferring a single gigabyte's worth of data from that drive to your PC. Keep a safe distance from that tired drive and call your local antique hardware shelter.

Adding a Second Internal Hard Drive

For most current PC owners, the easiest method of adding more hard drive space is to add a second hard drive to your system. I cite three very good reasons for this:

✦ **No backup is required.** Of course, *you should be backing up your current hard drive anyway.* (If not, shut this book immediately and back up your drive!) Adding a second drive eliminates the setup that you'd have to perform if you upgraded your current drive because you won't have to restore the current contents of your old drive to the new drive.

✦ **Most PCs have at least one open drive bay.** Unless your computer is already stuffed to the gills, you should have enough room to add a second hard drive. If it *is* stuffed to the gills, you'll either have to upgrade the current drive or add an external FireWire or USB 2.0 drive.

✦ **It's like . . . well . . . more for less.** Rather than replace your existing 30GB drive with a 60GB drive — and end up with only 30GB more room — I always find it more attractive to leave the original drive as is and add that second drive, resulting in the full 60GB that you paid for. (***Remember:*** You *will* eventually use that space. Trust me.)

Are you girded and ready for battle? Then follow this procedure to add a second internal hard drive to your current system:

1. **Cover your work surface with several sheets of newspaper.**

2. **Unplug your PC and place it on top of the newspaper.**

3. **Remove the case screws and slide the case off, putting the screws aside in a bowl or cup.**

If you're unsure how to remove your PC's case, check the manual that accompanied your computer.

4. **Touch the metal chassis of the computer to dissipate any static electricity.**

5. **Verify the jumper settings on the back of your original drive, as shown in Figure 13-3. If necessary, change the existing drive to *multiple drives, master unit* (or just *master*) by moving the jumper to the indicated pins.**

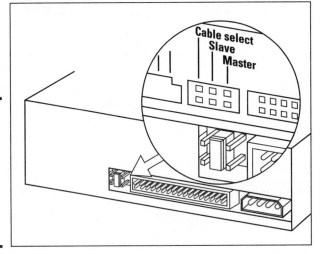

Figure 13-3: Change jumper settings on an EIDE drive when installing a second hard dive.

If you haven't encountered *jumpers* yet, they're the tiny plastic and metal shunts that you use to configure hard drives and CD/DVD drives.

Your jumper configuration will probably be different than Figure 13-3. Most hard drive manufacturers now print the jumper settings on the top of a hard drive. If the settings aren't printed on the drive, you can refer to the drive's manual or visit the manufacturer's Web site and look up the settings there. If all this seems a little exotic, the terms are really not risqué; *master* means *primary* (and if you have at least one drive, there must be a master device), and *slave* means *secondary*. Other than that, the devices are treated the same way by your PC.

6. **Set the jumpers on the back of the new drive for *multiple drives, slave unit* (often listed as just *slave* unit).**

7. **If your new drive needs a drive cage to fit into the desired bay, use the screws supplied by the drive manufacturer to attach the cage rails onto both sides of your drive.**

For more on drive cage kits, see the earlier section, "Size definitely does matter."

8. **Slide the drive into the selected bay from the front of the case, making sure that the end with the connectors goes in first and that the exposed circuitry of the drive is on the bottom.**

9. **Slide the hard drive back and forth in the drive bay until the screw holes in the side of the bay are aligned with the screw holes on the side of the drive (or the drive cage rails).**

10. **Tighten the drive down to the side of the bay with the screws that came with the drive (or your cage kit), as illustrated in Figure 13-4.**

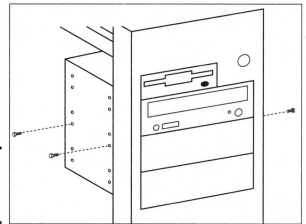

Figure 13-4:
Secure your
new friend
in place.

11. **Choose an unused power connector and plug it in, making sure that
the connector is firmly seated (see Figure 13-5).**

Joyfully, there's only one way to connect a power cable to a hard drive:
the right way.

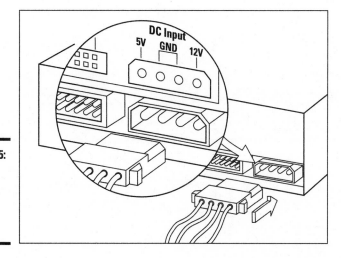

Figure 13-5:
A drive
without
power is
a paper-
weight.

12. **Plug the other connector from the hard drive cable into the back of
the drive and make sure that the cable is firmly seated.**

Note that both hard drives will use the same cable, so you might need
to unplug the original drive from the cable and switch connectors. Don't
worry: It doesn't matter which connector goes to which drive as long as
the jumpers are correctly set.

Check for a blocked hole in the cable connector, which should align
with a missing pin on the drive's connector. This alignment trick, called
keying, helps ensure that you're installing the cable right-side up.
However, don't panic if the cable isn't keyed: Remember that the wire
with the red or black marking on the cable is always Wire 1 and that it
should align with Pin 1 on the drive's connector (see Figure 13-6).

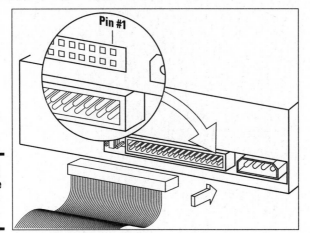

Pin #1

Figure 13-6:
Connect the
drive to the
data cable.

13. Replace the cover on your PC and tighten its screws.

14. Plug your PC back in and turn it on.

15. Run the drive formatting utility that accompanied your new drive to prepare it for use.

Chapter 14: Partying with USB, FireWire, and Hubs

In This Chapter

✔ Comparing USB 1.*x* with USB 2.0

✔ Using FireWire for high-end fun

✔ Extending your system with a hub

✔ Adding a USB or FireWire card

In the days of the early IBM PCs, practically every device that you added was *internal* (located within the computer's case). Because so few peripherals existed that you could add to your system, this really wasn't a problem. Naturally, the parallel port took care of the printer (if you could afford one), and as the modem grew in importance, it took up residence with the serial port.

Today, however, PC cases are shrinking. When it comes to size, I can't tell the difference between many new desktops and my kid's PlayStation 2. Less internal room means more need for external stuff. Also, because of the huge increase in the number of portable devices that you can add to your computer, those toys are naturally designed to be external, such as digital cameras, MP3 players, and the like. The days of the PC as a monolith are over.

So what's a poor CPU to do? Enter the two star ports of the digital age: Universal Serial Bus (USB) and FireWire. Talk about *sassy:* They're fast, offer Plug-and-Play convenience, and won't hassle you with arcane errors or strange settings. Plus, you can use them to connect practically everything but the kitchen sink to your computer simultaneously. In this section, I share the joy as we party with these two ports together.

Comparing USB Ports

You might think that all USB ports are the same, but they're not. In the beginning, only USB 1.*x* was available. Sure, USB 1.*x* was a fine little port (easy to use and requiring no configuration) but only a few times faster than an old-fashioned serial connection. To be honest, a FireWire device will wipe the floor with the first generation of USB devices when it comes to speed. Two or three years ago, the list of peripherals that really required 400 Mbps of transfer speed was limited to digital video (DV) camcorders and external audio/visual (AV) hard drives used by video professionals. Today, that list has expanded.

To illustrate:

✦ **Digital cameras** that produce images with bigger file sizes.

✦ **High-resolution scanners** that need to churn out images with 200MB of pixels.

✦ **External CD and DVD recorders that require a high-speed connection.** USB 1.*x* external CD recorders are limited to about 4X speed (and don't even dream of recording a DVD over a USB 1.*x* connection).

✦ **MP3 players,** including my favorite, Apple's iPod, which was the first MP3 player to use a FireWire connection.

Check out Table 14-1 to see just what a dramatic lead FireWire offered in connection speed.

Table 14-1	Comparing Speeds of Popular PC Ports	
Port	*Year Appeared on PCs*	*Transfer Speed (in Megabits/Second)*
PC serial	1981	Less than 1 Mbps
PC parallel	1981	1 Mbps
USB (version 1.1)	1996	12 Mbps
FireWire 400 (version A)	1996	400 Mbps
USB (version 2.0)	2001	480 Mbps
FireWire 800 (version B)	2003	800 Mbps

Enter USB 2.0, the latest specification. This new generation of port ups the ante, delivering 480 Mbps, which handily tops the original FireWire specification, version A. It's backward compatible with older 1.1 devices, so you won't have to start all over with your USB hardware, but naturally, only those peripherals that support the new 2.0 standard can take advantage of the warp speed increase.

1 Vote for FireWire

Even with the new 2.0 USB specification, I'm still a FireWire kinda guy, and not just because it has a cooler name. Here's why:

✦ **Device support:** FireWire has been around since 1996 on most DV equipment, so it's a well-recognized standard. On the other hand, USB 2.0 has only been around for about two years, so don't expect to see a high-speed USB port on an older DV camcorder.

✦ **Control over connection:** Ignore the engineer-speak. Basically, this feature allows you to control your FireWire device from your PC. For example, if you have a DV camcorder with a FireWire (or *IEEE 1394,* which is the techie name for FireWire) port, you can control your camcorder from your keyboard or with your mouse. Just click Play within your editing software, and your camera jumps into action just as if you had pressed the Play button on the DV camcorder itself. Although USB can send a basic signal or two to the device (for instance, a command to erase an image from your digital camera), it's nowhere near as sophisticated as the control over connection possible with a FireWire connection.

✦ **Mac and PC compatibility:** The current crop of Macs does not offer USB 2.0 ports; you get USB 1.1 ports. However, every single Mac leaving Cupertino (or wherever they're manufactured) comes equipped with at least one FireWire port. This compatibility allows me to pull my DVD recorder from my PC and plug it right into my Mac. (I prefer life without hassles.)

"Hey, Gladys, the external USB drive isn't getting any power. And I've got it plugged in and everything!" Of course, that drive might not be plugged in to the wall socket for AC power — an easy troubleshooting task — but if you're using a USB device that's powered through the USB port itself, the problem might be more insidious. Some USB ports don't provide the full power support called for by the USB standard because they're designed only for connecting mice, keyboards, and joysticks. Therefore, try plugging that USB drive into another PC's USB port to see whether it wakes up.

Or Do You Just Need a Hub?

A technician friend of mine has a great T-shirt with the logo *Got Ports?* If your PC already has FireWire or USB ports but they're already all taken, you don't need to install an adapter card to provide your computer with additional portage. (Of course, you could eject one of those devices and unplug it each time when you want to connect your digital camera, but that probably involves turning your PC around and navigating through the nest of cables on the back.)

PC power users eschew such hassles. Instead, buy a *hub,* which is a splitter box that turns one USB or FireWire port into multiple ports. (Don't get a USB/FireWire hub confused with a network hub, which is an entirely different beast altogether.) Although using a hub fills a port, you'll gain four, six, or eight ports in the bargain (depending on the hub), and everything stays as convenient and Plug-and-Play as before. (Engineering that's both simple and *sassy.*)

Don't forget to check whether some of your USB/FireWire devices have daisy-chaining ports on the back that will allow you to connect another device. You can tell that a device is designed for daisy-chaining by checking whether it sports two of the same type of port (like a scanner that has two USB ports). If so, you should be able to daisy-chain additional devices. A series of daisy-chained devices will likely help you avoid buying a USB or FireWire hub because everything is still linked to one physical USB or FireWire port on the back of your PC.

By using these methods, you can theoretically plug 63 devices into one FireWire port and 127 devices into one USB port. Heck, not even James Bond can stack gadgets that high!

Installing a Port Card

Here's where the original modular design of the IBM PC (all those many, many moons ago) comes in handy. If your computer didn't come with USB 2.0 or FireWire ports, you'll find that adding new ports to your PC is as simple as plugging in an adapter card into a slot at the back of your motherboard. A typical FireWire/USB 2.0 combo card costs around $100 and gives you two USB and two FireWire ports. Follow these steps to do it once the right way:

1. **Cover your work surface with several sheets of newspaper.**

2. **Unplug your PC and place it on top of the newspaper.**

3. **Remove the case screws and slide the case off, putting the screws aside in a bowl or cup.**

   If you're unsure how to remove your PC's case, check the manual that accompanied your computer.

4. **To dissipate any static electricity, touch a metal surface before you handle your new adapter card or touch any circuitry inside the case.**

   Yes, I know I keep haranguing you about static electricity — but it's important. I typically touch the metal chassis of the computer.

5. **Locate an adapter card slot of the proper length at the back of your computer case.**

   This should be a Peripheral Component Interconnect (PCI) slot, which is the standard adapter card connector in today's PCs.

6. **Remove the screw and the metal slot cover at the back of the case, as shown in Figure 14-1.**

   Because you won't need them again, put these in your spare parts box.

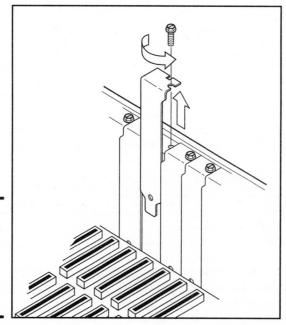

Figure 14-1: Remove the slot cover and screw before installing a new card.

7. **Pick up your port card by the top corners and line up the connector on the bottom of the card with the slot on the motherboard.**

   The card's metal bracket should align with the open area created when you remove the slot cover from the back of your PC.

   Never try to force a connector into a slot that's smaller! Older 8-bit cards have smaller connectors, and they won't accept a PCI card.

8. **After the connector is aligned correctly (as shown in Figure 14-2), apply even pressure to the top of the card and push it down into the slot until the bracket is resting against the case.**

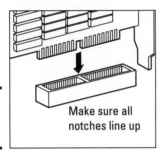

Figure 14-2:
Alignment!
Alignment!

Make sure all notches line up

9. **Place the screw in the corresponding hole in the bracket and tighten it down.**

10. **Place the cover back on your PC and replace the screws that you saved from Step 3.**

11. **Plug your PC back in and turn it on.**

12. **Run the installation disc that came with your port card or load the driver disc when prompted by Windows XP.**

Chapter 15: Pumping Up Your Sound and Video

In This Chapter

✓ Selecting a sound card

✓ Upgrading your video card

✓ Installing your new toys

*T*echnology has advanced so much that at last we've reached the point where the personal computer lives up to all that personal entertainment hoopla. You know, the idea that your PC is at the center of your gaming, audio, and TV environment. Or, as I've been putting it for the last couple of years: One box to rule them all and in the den to find them.

However, putting your PC at the center of your digital lifestyle is a bit difficult if you're still stuck with a subpar sound card, or if your computer's video card is more than a year or two old. Look at what you're missing out on: Closing your eyes and enjoying Dolby Surround sound with better-than-CD quality audio, watching TV with TiVo-style control on your PC's crystal-clear monitor, and playing games where you can behead a super-realistic, 3-D orc with extreme prejudice. This, ladies and gentlemen, is a good time to be alive! If your system needs an audio/visual upgrade, you'll find what you need to know right here.

Sound Card Features to Covet

The first stop on your audio-visual upgrade tour is your PC's sound card (naturally). Shoppers, in this section, I show you what to look for when comparing sound cards.

3-D spatial imaging

Most PC owners think of 3-D sound as a pure gamer's feature, but nothing could be further from the truth. Sure, today's games are even more fun when you can use your ears as well as your eyes to locate your enemy, but 3-D sound comes in handy when you're listening to audio CDs or playing digital audio files from your hard drive. With audio files and music, 3-D spatial imaging can add an auditorium or concert hall effect, where the stereo separation is enhanced.

Surround sound support

With a Dolby Surround sound card and the right speakers, your PC can deliver Dolby Surround sound while you're listening to audio CDs or watching DVD movies on your PC. (For me, the biggest hassle wasn't the extra cost or upgrading my PC's sound card: It was finding the space for all five speakers around my already crowded computer desk!)

High-end Surround sound cards such as the Sound Blaster Audigy 2 from Creative Labs can deliver Dolby Digital 6.1 Surround sound, 24-bit/192 KHz audio playback (which is far superior in quality than even a commercial audio CD), and 3-D imaging for your games — and all for about $120 from most Web stores. In fact, this card even has an optional, front panel control that you can add to an empty drive bay, so you don't have to move your PC to plug in all your speakers and other external sound hardware. Life is truly good.

Figure 15-1 illustrates an old friend to any PC audiophile: A *subwoofer* not only adds realistic, deep subsonic bass to your music but to your games as well. Whether you're experiencing the thumping bass of techno music, the grinding of tank treads, or launching a Hellfire missile, a subwoofer provides the necessary sonic punch. Most subwoofers should be placed on the floor where the vibration isn't a factor.

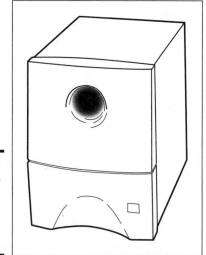

Figure 15-1:
All hail your subwoofer, king of the PC speaker system.

MP3 hardware support

Although I discuss MP3 files in detail in Book II, Chapter 6, I want to mention them again here because anyone who's heavily into MP3 digital audio will really appreciate a sound card with built-in MP3 hardware encoding and digital effects. That MP3 hardware feature relieves your PC's processor from the job of ripping and playing MP3 files so that you can rip music while you edit a digital photograph in Photoshop with nary a drop in performance. No stuttering audio or long delays, especially on older PCs.

Many hardware MP3 sound cards also allow you to introduce the same concert hall environmental effect that I mention earlier to the MP3 files that you create . . . now your garage band can claim to have played Carnegie Hall.

Game and FireWire ports

Many sound cards are equipped with a little something extra: a FireWire port or an IBM game port like the one shown in Figure 15-2, which was once a dear friend of any PC game player (because it used to be the only way to hook up most joysticks and external game controllers). Lately, most PC controllers have switched to the Universal Serial Bus (USB) port, but it's still a plus for a sound card to include a game port. Older game peripherals — like many joysticks and flight throttles — won't work with USB, so it's a legacy thing. (Book II, Chapter 14 delivers the goods on FireWire.)

MIDI ports

Before I move on, I have to address musicians and their Musical Instrument Digital Interface (MIDI) ports. A sound card with standard MIDI ports allows you to connect synthesizers and many different electronic musical instruments, such as drums and keyboards, to your computer. With a MIDI instrument connected, your computer can play MIDI music files on the instrument, or you can play the instrument and record the music as a MIDI file on your computer.

Note, however, that most of today's sound cards can play MIDI music files without attaching an instrument, so it's not necessary to buy a card with built-in MIDI ports just to play MIDI music files.

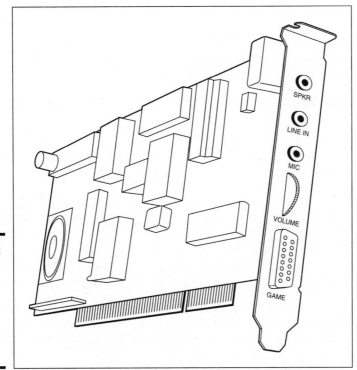

Figure 15-2:
Gamers,
take note:
You get a
free port
with most
sound
cards.

Shopping for a Monster Graphics Card

Having a terrific graphics card isn't all about blasting aliens to kingdom come. A fast 3-D video card can speed up the display of digital video and even Windows XP itself. In this section, I clue you in on what to look for when considering a video card upgrade.

Pray, what slot do you need?

Although today's video cards look like any other typical adapter cards, they actually fit in either of two types of motherboard slots:

✦ **Accelerated Graphics Port (AGP):** The fastest video cards for today's Athlon and Pentium 4 computers use a dedicated AGP slot; no other adapter cards will fit into this slot. (Refer to your motherboard or PC manual to make sure that you have an AGP slot before you buy an AGP video card.) AGP video cards provide the best performance, but they're usually a bit more expensive than their Peripheral Component Interconnect (PCI) counterparts.

✦ **PCI:** These video cards fit into a standard PCI card slot, so they work with just about any PC motherboard currently available. However, you'll encounter a performance hit when you use a PCI video card; if your motherboard has an AGP slot available, I strongly recommend that you use an AGP video card instead.

Rate the performance of a particular card while you're shopping by checking on the box or the manufacturer's Web site for benchmark results that you can use to compare with other cards. Try the popular benchmark program 3DMark 2001 SE ($40, from www.futuremark.com). You can also run Quake III or Unreal Tournament 2003 and compare the maximum frames-per-second that the card can display (the higher the frame rate, the better). You can also find up-to-date reviews of the latest cards and video chipsets at Tom's Hardware on the Web at www.tomshardware.com.

Exploring the differences between chipsets

Short trip. There really aren't any differences between *chipsets,* which are the separate Graphics Processing Unit (GPU) "brain" that powers today's top 3-D video cards. Allow me to explain. The two major players in the PC video card chipset battle are

✦ **NVIDIA:** The cutting-edge crew at NVIDIA (www.nvidia.com) has produced some of the fastest video cards for the PC in recent years, including the classics RIVA TNT and TNT2 as well as the GeForce/GeForce2/GeForce3 series. The latest NVIDIA chipset, the NVIDIA GeForce4, is just plain awesome. In fact, very few games or 3-D applications on today's software market can actually push a GeForce4 card to its limit. (I know because I have a GeForce4 TI4200.)

✦ **ATI:** ATI Technologies (www.ati.com) has been producing popular video chipsets for a decade now, including its Rage line. Typically, ATI video cards are somewhat cheaper than NVIDIA cards, and many mother-board manufacturers build ATI video hardware directly onto their products. Lately, ATI's new Radeon 9700-series chipset has been a big winner with performance that even tops the latest GeForce4 cards.

And here's the payoff — the latest offerings from either of these companies will deliver more performance than PC gamers are likely to need for at least a year. In fact, I've been told recently by my friends at NVIDIA that they're appealing directly to the PC game development community, attempting to help develop games that actually use all the hardware power featured on the cards. (Ah, for once . . . hardware that doesn't suddenly turn outdated in six months. *Awesome.*)

Other video card features that you'll want

Naturally, you can evaluate more than just chipsets and connectors when comparing video cards. Keep an eye out for these features and specifications while you shop.

Onboard random access memory (RAM): Like your motherboard, your video card carries its own supply of memory. Today's cards typically include anywhere from 32–128MB of memory. Again, the general rule is to buy a card with as much onboard RAM as possible. More RAM equals higher resolutions with more colors on-screen.

Driver and standards support: Any PC video card should fully support the Microsoft DirectX video standards — currently at DirectX 9.0. Gamers will also appreciate robust *OpenGL* support (an open video standard that's becoming very popular in 3-D action games). Support for these standards should be listed on the box.

Maximum resolution: The higher the resolution that a card can produce, the more that your monitor can display at once — and not just in games, but documents, digital photographs, and your Windows desktop. For example, I like to write manuscripts at a resolution of 1152 x 864 instead of 1024 x 768 because I can see more of the page in Microsoft Word without scrolling. Today's cards can reach truly epic resolutions, such as 2048 x 1536; personally, however, I don't work at such stratospheric resolutions often because a few hours of work usually leaves me with eyestrain (and possibly a headache as well).

The maximum resolution that you can display on your system is also dependent upon the monitor that you're using. Therefore, if you upgrade to the latest video card but you're still using an old clunker of a monitor with a maximum resolution of 1024 x 768, you're stuck there. (Time to invest in a new display.) For more about your monitor, see Book II, Chapter 1.

Video capture and TV output: A card with these features can create digital video footage from an analog TV signal (that's the *video capture* part) and transfer the image that you see on your monitor to a TV, VCR, or camcorder (that's the *TV output* part). If you need to produce a VHS tape with images from your PC, or if you want to create video CDs or DVDs from your home movies on VHS tape, spend a little extra on a video capture/TV output card. For example, the ATI All-in-Wonder Radeon 8500 has both of these features built in.

TV tuner: A card with a built-in TV tuner can actually turn your PC into a TV set, including the ability to pause and replay programs on the fly (like how a TiVo unit works with a regular TV). You can use a traditional antenna or connect the card to your cable or satellite system. Just don't let your boss know that the new video card that the company bought gives you the ability to watch your favorite soaps in a window on your desktop . . . you're supposed to be working.

Multiple monitor support: Many of today's video cards allow you to connect two monitors to one card. You can either choose to see two separate desktops, or you can opt to make the two monitors into a seamless desktop. Imagine the size of your Windows workspace when it's spread across two displays!

MPEG hardware support: Finally, I come to digital video — which, as you can read about in earlier chapters of Book II, is typically stored in either MPEG, AVI, or MOV formats, with the most popular being the MPEG format. Without the *compression* that these video formats offer (which shrinks the digital video file in size), you'd never get a full-length movie on a single DVD. Although your PC can use software to *encode* (create a compressed MPEG file) and *decode* (read a compressed MPEG file) MPEG files on your hard drive or a DVD, a video card with built-in encoding and decoding features can really speed up the process. This hardware support is particularly valuable if you're going to do serious video editing on your PC because you'll cut down the amount of time required to save your movies to your hard drive.

Installing Sound and Video Cards

Installing a sound card or video card is much like adding any other adapter card to your PC. If you're installing a sound card, make sure that you connect the audio cable from your CD-ROM/DVD-ROM drive (Step 5); if you're installing a video card, make sure that you pick the right AGP or PCI slot (Step 7).

Follow these steps:

1. **Cover your work surface with several sheets of newspaper.**

2. **Unplug your PC and place it on top of the newspaper.**

3. **Remove the screws on the back of the case and slide the case off, saving the screws for later.**

4. **To dissipate static electricity, touch a metal surface before handling any cards or touching your PC's motherboard.**

   For example, touch the PC's metal chassis — I shudder to think of what I'll do if anyone develops a fiberglass computer case.

5. If you're installing a new sound card, check for a thin audio cable connected from your old sound card to your CD-ROM or DVD-ROM drive; if you find one, disconnect the cable from the old sound card.

6. Remove the screw holding the adapter card that you're upgrading and pull upward to remove it.

Don't forget to put the screw in your spare parts box and put the old adapter card in an anti-static bag for safekeeping. (I use the bag left behind by the new card.)

Some AGP card slots have plastic tabs that act as a locking mechanism. Just bend the tab gently with your finger, and you should be able to remove the existing AGP card.

7. Locate the adapter card slot that matches the card that you're installing.

An AGP video card can fit only in a dedicated AGP slot, but a PCI video adapter or sound card should fit in any open slot. Naturally, if the upgrade card uses the same type of slot as the card that it's replacing, use the empty slot that you've just opened up.

8. Pick up the adapter card by the top corners and line up the bottom connector on the card with the slot on the motherboard, making sure that the card's metal bracket aligns properly with the opening in the back of the PC.

9. After the card is aligned, apply even pressure to the top of the card and push it down into the slot.

10. Place the screw in the corresponding hole in the bracket and tighten it down.

11. If you're installing a sound card and you disconnected a CD-ROM/DVD-ROM audio cable from the old card, reconnect the cable from your drive to the new card.

Check the manual for the card to determine where the CD/DVD audio connector is located; this is a standard connector, so it should be easy to track down.

12. Place the cover back on your PC and replace the screws that you saved from Step 3.

13. Plug your PC back in and turn it on.

14. Run the installation disc that came with your upgrade card or load the driver disc when prompted by Windows.

**Book II
Chapter 15**

**Pumping Up Your
Sound and Video**

Chapter 16: Do I Really Need a Network?

In This Chapter

- Evaluating the advantages of a network
- Connecting to other computers and devices
- Selecting networking hardware and software that you might need

Networking is neat: The ability to copy or edit a document that's on another computer halfway down the hall is invaluable in a business environment. (And that includes a home office like mine, where six computers are constantly vying for my attention. Although they're only a few feet apart, moving 2GB worth of data between them would be no small feat without a common network connection.)

However, not everyone with multiple computers actually needs a network — and that's what this introductory chapter will help you determine. Here, I cover what a network can do for you, what hardware and software you'll need, and how much work will be involved. Later chapters in Book II will fill in the blanks, but after you read this introduction, you'll know whether a network is worth your effort.

Discovering the Advantages of a Network

If you've never used a network to link multiple computers, you might not realize what applications are network ready. Here's a quick list of the most common uses for a network.

File transfer

There's no faster method of moving files between computers than a network connection. And network file transfers are *transparent* to the person making the transfer, meaning that you don't have to do anything special to transfer files between computers on a network. You can just drag and drop files as usual or use your favorite file management application to copy or move files between computers on the network, and Windows acts like you'd expect. I like the Total Commander file management tool, as shown in Figure 16-1. To try out this great piece of shareware, visit www.ghisler.com. With Total Commander, it's a cinch to compare the contents of two different drives or folders, and the list display format can pack the maximum number of file names possible onto your monitor. Copying or moving files betwixt the panes is as simple as selecting and clicking a button.

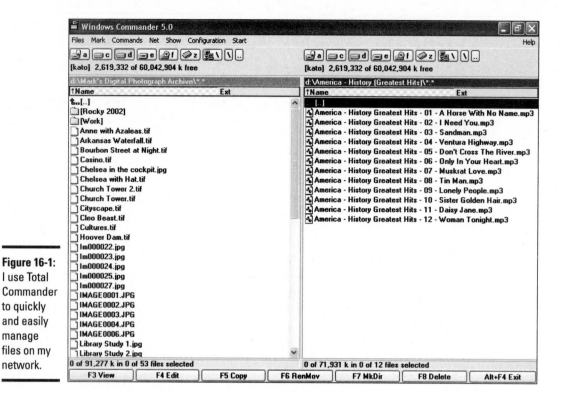

Figure 16-1:
I use Total Commander to quickly and easily manage files on my network.

However, you certainly don't want just *anyone* transferring files to and from your PC — or, for that matter, even accessing your PC over the network at all. To help preserve security, Windows XP makes certain that only the users and PCs with the proper rights can transfer files over your network.

Sharing that there Internet

Another popular networking advantage is the ability for one computer to share a single Internet connection with all the other computers on a network. Typically, this works best with a broadband connection technology like a digital subscriber line (DSL) or cable, but it's possible with a dialup connection as well.

The two methods of sharing a connection are

✦ **Through software:** You can use the built-in Internet Sharing within Windows XP.

✦ **Through hardware:** You can add an Internet sharing device (such as a network hub or switch), which usually comes with other features such as a built-in firewall.

I cover both of these methods later in Book II, Chapter 19.

One word: Games!

What's that you're saying, bunkie? You're tired of predictable computer opponents in your favorite games? Giant walking robots in Microsoft's Mechwarrior 4 that you can handle in your sleep? How about timid enemy monsters that won't attack you or ambush your character in Impossible Creatures (as shown in Figure 16-2)?

Figure 16-2:
One of my
favorite
multiplayer
network
games,
Impossible
Creatures,
from
Microsoft.

Well, forget those lazy tactics because in network *multiplayer mode,* you'll be fighting real human beings — the treacherous, backstabbing kind (which, oddly enough, usually turn out to be your best friends). I try to attend *LAN parties* whenever possible — that's the term for a get-together where multiplayer games are the featured attraction. Your host might have all the PCs and network hardware necessary for 8 or 16 people, but I usually bring my desktop or laptop computer so that I can sit down and plug in with a minimum of effort.

Shared documents and applications

Of course, a document that's handed from person to person on a floppy or Zip disk is technically shared, but is that really a convenient method of working on a document together? (To this day, PC hardware technicians and software developers call this kind of floppy-based transfer a *sneaker-net.*) Anyway, forget wearing out your shoe leather just to hand off a document for the next person's comments — today's office workgroup relies on the company network to share documents and common applications, the *right* way!

After you network your computers, any PC on your network can copy or open a document on another computer *if* the owner of the PC being accessed has been granted the proper rights to that file or to the folder where it's stored. For example, if you have a Word document that others need to edit but you'd like to keep it on your hard drive, you can move that document to a shared folder. Others on the network can open the document within Word from their computers, just as if it were on their local machine.

And if that's not *sassy* enough, consider the fact that Bob over in accounting (or your daughter in her bedroom) might be using an application that you don't have. If that application has been written for network use, you can run it on your computer remotely over the network! Such a program is a *shared application,* and I think that they're the neatest things since sliced cheese.

Read the details on both shared documents and shared applications in Book II, Chapter 17.

What Can I Connect To?

A surprising number of objects on the planet have network ports or wireless network cards. Here's a list of the network-savvy stuff that I've used in the past:

✦ **Other PCs:** The most common connection on a Windows network is to other PCs — some of which are standard desktop and notebook PCs, and others are specialized network *servers* that perform only one task (like a *file server,* which is used like a mega-hard drive that everyone on the network can access).

✦ **Macintosh and Linux computers:** Your network need not be a snobby Windows-only country club; invite the neighbors to join in! Macs running Mac OS X version 10.2 (Jaguar) or later can plug right in, as can those Linux folks with the beards and suspenders. Of course, you won't be able to run a Mac program on a PC, but — and this is a winner — many applications are available in versions for both operating systems, and they can share the same document! The best example is Microsoft Office, which is available in both Mac and PC versions. Word and Excel on both operating systems can open and edit the same Office documents.

Speaking of Mac OS X 10.2 Jaguar, I recommend the *Mac OS X All-in-One Desk Reference For Dummies* by Mark Chambers (published by Wiley Publishing, Inc.). And, yes, I really do own both PCs and Macs, and I take advantage of what both operating systems have to offer on my same office network. Anyway, if you find this tome helpful and you know a Mac owner who's using Jaguar, please drop 'em a line and recommend the MOSXAIODRFD! (Now how's *that* for an abbreviation?)

✦ **Personal digital assistants (PDAs):** With the right adapter, your Palm Pilot or Pocket PC can join in the fun.

✦ **Shared network hardware:** Some shared hardware actually resides within a PC on the network (like an internal hard drive or CD-ROM drive that you've selected to be "visible" and accessible on the network), and other network hardware works as stand-alone units (like an Internet sharing device, which is a box by itself).

✦ **Network printers:** Finally, a shared network printer can be connected to a PC on the network. Or, if you have enough pocket change, you can buy a stand-alone network printer that actually has its own network card.

Of course, this list is incomplete because it's constantly growing, but suffice it to say that a network usually includes more than just a smattering of desktop and laptop PCs.

What Hardware Do I Need?

The hardware basics that you'll need for a simple network include

+ **A network adapter card or PC Card:** Each computer on your network will require either a network adapter card (for desktops) or a PC Card (for a laptop). These cards can accept either a wired connection or a wireless connection.

+ **A network hub or switch:** I describe these black boxes in depth in Book II, Chapter 17. For now, I'll just say that they allow you to connect multiple computers onto the same network. Some hubs and switches are wireless, so no cables are necessary.

+ **Cabling:** If you're not going the wireless route, you need an Ethernet cable for each computer that you add to the network. Again, more on this in the next chapter.

The hardware that I list here would be used in a standard Ethernet network, but remember that other types of network technologies might use your home's AC wiring or telephone jacks (which I cover in Book II, Chapter 18). You can also network two computers by using special Universal Serial Bus (USB) and FireWire cables, but these are no substitute for the convenience and compatibility of an Ethernet network; they're simply for transferring files in a single session.

You might be able to pick up all these hardware toys in a single box — *a network kit* — which is a great choice for a home or small office network with four or fewer PCs. (Plus the documentation is typically pretty well written.)

Book II
Chapter 16

Do I Really Need
a Network?

What Software Do I Need?

Actually, if each of your PCs will be running any version of Windows 98 or later, you have all the operating system software that you need for a home network. (Thanks, Microsoft!) However, you might also need

+ **Drivers for your network adapter card or PC Card:** The manufacturer of your network card will provide you with the drivers that Windows will need during installation, but don't forget to check the manufacturer's Web site for updated drivers.

+ **Network management software:** Although not necessary for a simple network, the administrator of a larger network (I consider a network of ten or more computers to be a larger network) will likely buy extra software to monitor network traffic and optimize network hardware.

+ **Network-ready applications:** As I mention earlier in this chapter, network applications might include productivity suites (such as Microsoft Office), fax software, and workgroup applications (such as Lotus Notes) that provide a common calendar and e-mail system.

To Network or Not to Network . . .

So that's the scoop. If you have more than one desktop within your home or office and you need to share files, applications, and an Internet connection between them on a regular basis, you can buy a network kit for $75 to $100 that comes complete with everything that you need.

If, on the other hand, you have only two computers and you don't exchange information very often between them (or if you don't need to share an Internet connection), you might consider a simple USB or FireWire transfer cable.

Chapter 17: Ethernet to the Rescue

In This Chapter

- ✔ **Understanding how Ethernet works**
- ✔ **Gathering the various pieces o' hardware**
- ✔ **Configuring Windows XP for your network**
- ✔ **Putting shared folders to work**
- ✔ **Configuring a network printer**
- ✔ **Connecting a hub to the Internet**
- ✔ **Troubleshooting your network**

*T*his is it, my friend: The chapter with the bravado and the chutzpah to actually show you how to set up a home or small office network in Windows XP! Setting up a network gives you many advantages, including saving money by sharing resources (such as printers and an Internet connection) and the added convenience of file sharing.

You'll find that a *working* network — note that I stress the word *working* — quickly becomes as essential as Tabasco sauce (or insert name of your favorite condiment here). By the way, if you find that word *working* to be more elusive than you first expected, I include a section at the end of this chapter that highlights common problems experienced by folks running their own network . . . as well as several possible solutions for each, of course.

After your network is purring as smoothly as the proverbial kitten, you'll walk proudly to the closest person on the planet and proclaim proudly, "I am . . . a *network administrator!*" (Feel free to throw confetti or have a T-shirt made. If you like, send me an e-mail message at `ohmyitworks@mlcbooks.com`, and we can celebrate together.)

A Quickie Ethernet Primer

No, don't close the book! Of all the supposed techno-wizard technologies connected with PCs, Ethernet networking is the easiest to master. Windows XP has come a long way in taming the home networking beast. Sure, you used to need a gold medal in the Tech Olympics to install a small home network, but that was in the days of DOS and Windows 3.1. We've come a long way, baby.

In fact, Ethernet has been around since the days of stone-tipped spears. The first widely used network structure, it's still the most popular structure for homes and offices with around 25 PCs or less. Sure, faster networking designs exist these days, but old faithful Ethernet is also the cheapest to set up and maintain, and it's directly supported within all flavors of Windows.

So how does Ethernet work? Surprisingly, it's much like ham radio. A PC that wants to share data (as in moving or copying a file, or sending and receiving stuff from the Internet) actually broadcasts that data across the network cabling in discrete bursts called *packets*. Each packet is marked with an address — much like how an e-mail message always has a To address — of the receiving computer.

When the PC with the matching address receives the packet across the network (along with tons of other packets bound for other locations), it processes it; other computers simply ignore any packets that aren't addressed to them. Figure 17-1 represents an Ethernet network at its best.

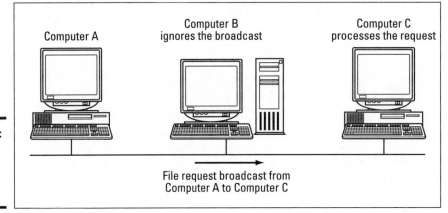

Figure 17-1: The basics of an Ethernet network.

This sounds just nifty, but here's the catch: If two computers on your network try to broadcast packets at the same time, a network *collision* occurs, and everything stops until one computer successfully gets its data across the network. Collisions slow down the transfer of data, and that's why Ethernet networks are slower than other types of networks. (Of course, you'll see far fewer conflicts with fewer machines, so if you have only four PCs on your network, you'll typically get great performance. It's only when 25 PCs are all trying to talk to each other at once that conflicts start slowing things down dramatically.)

The first step when installing a small network is to create a chart that lists which computers need to be connected and where they are, plus the approximate distances between all the players. Because of the limitations on the size of this chapter, I can't provide you with a complete discussion of how to plan the cabling for your network — that's a book in itself. In fact, that book is *Home Networking For Dummies,* 2nd Edition, written by Kathy Ivens and published by Wiley Publishing, Inc., which expands on all the basics that I mention in this chapter.

Hardware That You'll Need

Another advantage of Ethernet networks is their simplicity. You won't need a degree in Advanced Thakamology to install your network, and you can put four PCs in a simple Ethernet network for under $75 if you buy a kit.

In this section, I discuss the basic hardware requirements of any small Ethernet network.

Cables

In books that I've written that cover Ethernet networking, I discuss two different kinds of cabling that connect computer to computer (or connect a computer to a network device):

✦ **Coaxial (coax) cable:** This is the same type of cable used to connect your TV to your cable box. Coax is thick stuff and not easily routed or hidden. Also, each end of a coax Ethernet network must have a terminator to mark the end of the network circuit, which is a hassle (a small one, granted, but a hassle nonetheless).

✦ **Twisted pair cable:** Twisted pair cable looks almost exactly like telephone wire or the cable that runs between your PC's dial-up modem and the telephone wall jack. It's easier to hide and much easier to route. (Figure 17-2 illustrates the connector — an RJ-45 connector — for a twisted pair cable.) The one downside to using a twisted pair Ethernet network is that you need a *hub,* which acts as a central connection point. (See how it's used in Figure 17-3.) However, hubs are cheap these days, and twisted pair cabling is much cheaper overall than coaxial cable.

Figure 17-2: Most network techs think the RJ-45 connector is rather attractive.

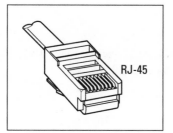

RJ-45

I used to cover coax cabling, but in this book, I cover only twisted pair cabling. It's by far the cheapest and the easiest to install, which makes it the most popular standard . . . and that explains why Ethernet networks that use coaxial cabling are rapidly disappearing from the face of the globe. In fact, you'll have to go out of your way to find a late-model network interface card (NIC) that has a coax connector on it. (As the MCP said so eloquently and frequently in the classic movie *Tron,* END OF LINE.)

If you'd rather eschew cables altogether — well, almost altogether — consider a wireless network. Although it's a bit slower, you'll have freedom of movement undreamed of by the wired crowd. (Plus, alternate wired networks can use your home or office's existing telephone or AC power lines. No, really!) I cover all these marvels of wireless (or almost wireless) networking in Book II, Chapter 18.

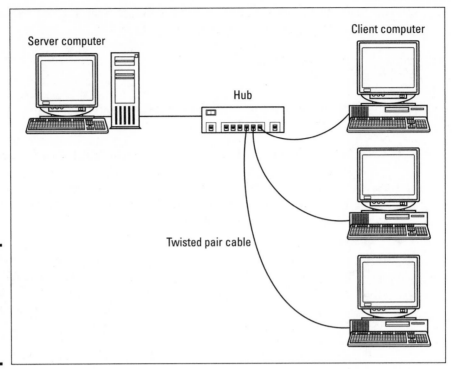

Figure 17-3:
The hands-down favorite is a twisted pair Ethernet network.

Hubs

As I mention earlier, a *hub* is essentially just an overgrown connection box, linking (via cabling) each computer on your network to all the other network computers and peripherals (like a printer). However, you need either a hub or a switch for a twisted pair network. There's not much need to include a picture of a hub in this chapter. Imagine the most boring, nondescript box that you can, add a few lights and several RJ-45 jacks, and you've got a hub. At least they're cheap — how much you'll pay depends upon how many ports the hub provides (typically 4, 8, or 16 ports), ranging from about $50 to about $300.

NICs

You need a *network interface card* (NIC) for each computer on your network. If your desktop PC doesn't have a built-in NIC, an internal adapter card is probably the best choice, but installing a NIC doesn't necessarily have to involve opening your PC's case. You can get a Personal Computer Memory Card International Association (PCMCIA; or PC Card) NIC for your laptop, and other network adapters can be connected through a Universal Serial Bus (USB) port. However, you might not actually need to buy a separate NIC for your PC because most PCs now include a built-in network connector. (Check your PC's manual or look for a port labeled *Ethernet 10/100* or *Network* on the back of the computer.)

NICs are rated by the speed of the network. Most home networks will use a *10/100 NIC* (meaning that your network can operate at either 10 Mbps or

100 Mbps), which will set you back about $40 to $50. The third speed, called *Gigabit Ethernet,* runs at a whopping 1000 Mbps, but you probably won't need such throughput. (Gigabit hardware is also as expensive as a meeting with a good lawyer, which is another reason why it's not a big hit with the home networking crowd.)

When shopping for your card, check the manufacturer's Web site and verify what drivers the card uses. The card should support Windows 98, ME, NT, 2000, and XP. (For me, the value of a NIC is in direct proportion to its compatibility.) Also, check how often those drivers are updated; two-year-old drivers are not a good sign. In general, most manufacturers display certification statements (both on the box and on the company's Web site) that guarantee that a NIC will work with specific operating systems.

Switches

A *switch* is kind of like a super-hub. In fact, a switch looks like a slightly bigger hub, but it's about as visually interesting as a shoebox. On the inside, however, a switch is a mighty leap in performance because a switch prevents those dastardly collisions that I discuss earlier in this chapter. In effect, a switch narrows the broadcast of a packet to only the PC that needs it, so it's much more intelligent than a simple hub.

A switch really isn't that much more expensive than a hub, but a switch is only really necessary if you have more than four computers on your network or if the PCs on your network are constantly using network resources. This is why most switches are equipped with eight ports. A typical switch costs about $200.

Heck, let's buy a kit!

Ah, now you're thinkin' smart! I always recommend that those folks installing a network from scratch buy a kit rather than trying to cobble together the components I describe in the previous section. Kits are much more convenient, and the various components are guaranteed to work together.

A typical kit comes with

✦ Two or four NICs

✦ Premade cables

✦ A hub or switch

✦ The drivers for the NICs

✦ Complete instructions, an installation program, and diagnostic software

As an example of an Ethernet starter kit, I often recommend the D-Link Network Kit in a Box, which includes two NICs, a four-port hub, cabling, drivers, and even a few network games to try out. (Because we all know what networks are *really* for.) You can buy the Kit in a Box directly at the D-Link Web site (www.dlink.com) for a mere $70 or so.

Doing the Cable Dance

You have far fewer hassles when installing a twisted pair network as opposed to a coaxial network, as I mention earlier in this chapter. But even considering that the cables are easier to handle, I still have a number of time-tested recommendations that I can make from experience:

✦ **Always draft someone to help.** If you're wiring a small office, enlist the help of a steadfast friend (as a gopher, general cable handyperson, and sympathetic ear).

✦ **Always buy premade cables!** Building a cable yourself is like cutting a diamond yourself — it can be done, but you'd better be experienced or you'll ruin a perfectly good . . . well . . . length of cable. Plus, first-timers can very easily create a cable that appears to be correct but doesn't work or that introduces all sorts of spurious problems later on that will be practically impossible to track down. (Can you say *electrical short?* I knew you could.) Instead, do what I do (and everyone else who's already built one or two small networks does as well). Walk into your local computer store or online Web shop and buy premade cables in the lengths that you need.

✦ **Always buy extra cables.** Having a few spares never hurts. Hey, they're cheap. And buying cables that are at least a foot or two longer than what you think you're going to need is a wise idea.

✦ **Always test a cable before installing it.** Of course, you can buy a twisted pair cable tester (usually called a *remote cable tester*), but for those with a life other than networking, simply connect the cable between your hub (or switch) and a laptop to check it.

✦ **Always consider pets!** Does Fluffy spend time in your home office unattended? Then prepare for the likelihood of chewed network cabling. (This can *really* test the relationship between pet and person.) To avoid such moments, use cable ties and anchors to run your Ethernet cabling underneath desktops and above the floor level whenever possible.

✦ **Always avoid exposed cable.** Make sure that your cables are well out of reach of clumsy feet. Also, never cover a cable with tape or a rug where it can become a victim of foot traffic. The stress on the connectors and the wear from contact will destroy even the best cable over time and will likely result in eventual network errors.

Don't forget that your hub or switch is a powered device, so it needs to be located close to an AC outlet.

Configuring Windows XP for Your Network

After the NICs have been installed, the cabling is in place, and everything's plugged in, you're ready to flip that big *Frankenstein*-style leaf switch and start networking — and that's done from within Windows XP. In this section, I discuss what every home "network administrator" should know.

Ah, sweet DHCP

You know, very few acronyms in the computer world make me genuinely smile every time that I see them. There's TWAIN *(technology without an interesting name),* of course, and BBS *(Bulletin Board System).* But in networking, folks hold a fond spot in their hearts for DHCP, which stands for *Dynamic Host Configuration Protocol.*

What's so uplifting about a networking standard? It's the *Dynamic* part. You see, DHCP was developed to automatically assign Internet Protocol (IP) addresses to the computers on your network. A computer's *IP address* is that address that I mention at the beginning of the chapter: It's a unique number that identifies that particular PC on the network.

In days of yore, whoever set up a network had to keep track of which IP addresses were assigned to which computers. If a number was assigned twice, all hell broke loose (at least on those two machines). A device with DHCP — such as an Internet sharing device or a PC that's acting as an Internet connection server — automatically assigns a number whenever needed.

If you're already using an Internet sharing device (such as a cable modem or digital subscriber line [DSL] Internet router that has DHCP built in) or a switch with DHCP built in and a connection port for your modem, you need to follow the steps provided in that device's manual. That's because you don't need a PC to act as the DHCP host for your network. I cover Internet connection sharing in Book II, Chapter 19.

Setting up the host

To set up a network under Windows XP by using DHCP and a shared Internet connection — where your dial-up modem or DSL/cable modem connects directly to the PC — you need to run the Network Setup Wizard on that PC. (That lucky computer becomes your Internet host, providing the DHCP functionality for your network.)

If your host PC is currently using a NIC to connect to a DSL or cable modem (as most do) and the hub *won't* accept a direct connection to your modem, you need a second NIC installed in that computer so that you can connect it to the hub! (Take a break and read the section titled, "Using a Standard Hub with a Cable or DSL Modem," toward the end of this chapter before you proceed any farther. Things get explained there.)

Ready to go? Follow these steps:

1. **Choose Start⇨All Programs⇨Accessories⇨Communications⇨Network Setup Wizard, which displays the wizard welcome screen.**

2. **Take a moment to connect to the Internet (if you're not using a broadband always-on connection), and then click Next to continue.**

The wizard displays a checklist screen to make sure that all hardware has been installed, connected, and turned on. ("Now, Rochester, have you installed the network hardware like I asked?")

3. Click Next to get with the program.

The next wizard screen, as shown in Figure 17-4, prompts you for the configuration that you're using to connect to the Internet.

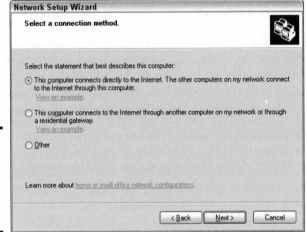

Figure 17-4:
Select your
Internet
connection
configura-
tion here.

4. In this case, you should select the This Computer Connects Directly to the Internet radio button, and then click Next to continue.

5. The wizard prompts you to select the network adapter that's support-ing your Internet connection (or, if you're using a dialup modem, the modem itself) — and the program takes the best shot at what it thinks is the likely choice (see Figure 17-5). After you make your choice, click Next to continue.

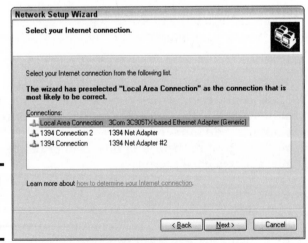

Figure 17-5:
Choose the
Internet
connection.

Note that if your PC has FireWire (IEEE 1394) ports, these are also listed because you can set up a FireWire network with the right hardware and cabling.

6. **Type a description and name for the host PC, as shown in Figure 17-6, and then click Next to continue.**

If your Internet service provider (ISP) requires a specific computer name, use that here. Check your ISP's documentation to make sure.

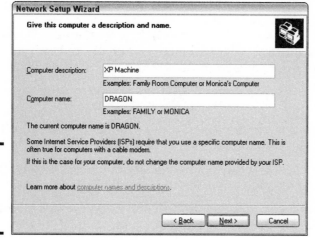

Figure 17-6:
Your new
network
host needs
a name.

7. **Name your network (or, in Microsoft-speak, your *workgroup*), and then click Next to continue.**

I recommend that you enter something unique. Jot down this name because it will be important later on.

Let's do this! The wizard displays a screen with your settings so that you can verify the proceedings.

8. **Click Next and sit back while Windows XP works its magic.**

9. **As a final step, the wizard offers you the chance to create a network setup disk (suitable for client PCs that aren't running Windows XP).**

- If you choose to create the disk, you need a single, blank floppy disk handy. Select Create a Network Setup Disk.

- Otherwise, just select the Just Finish the Wizard option, and then click Next to continue.

10. **Click Finish to exit the wizard.**

Setting up the clients

After the host has been configured, it's ready to accept connections from the other computers on your network. However, you also have to configure each of those PCs as network clients. Yep, that's where the buzzphrase *client/server* comes from. The good news is that you'll be using your friend the Network Setup Wizard again, and the process is pretty similar.

Again, make sure that the host computer is connected to the Internet, and then follow these steps on each PC running Windows XP that needs to join the network crowd:

1. **Choose Start⇨All Programs⇨Accessories⇨Communications⇨Network Setup Wizard to start the wizard, and then click Next to continue.**

   If the client PC is running an older version of Windows, you can load the Network Setup Disk that you created on the host PC at the end of the previous procedure. Open Windows Explorer, navigate to the floppy disk, double-click NETSETUP.EXE to start things going, and then follow the on-screen instructions.

   You're graced with the same doggone Before You Continue screen, warning you of dire consequences if you haven't connected everything, turned everything on, and connected to the Internet via the host PC.

2. **Because you've already done all that, smile smugly, and then click Next.**

3. **Select the network adapter that's going to connect this client PC to your network, and then click Next to continue.**

   Because most client PCs have only one Ethernet adapter, this should be a cinch, and the wizard should already have the correct choice selected.

4. **Time to choose a network description and name for this client PC, like you did for the host. When you're done, click Next to continue.**

5. **Here's where you need to enter the workgroup name that you chose for the host PC (see Step 7 in the previous section). Make sure that it's spelled exactly the same, and then click Next to continue.**

   The wizard again displays the settings verification screen.

6. **Click Next to make Windows XP configure your client machine.**

7. **Select the Just Finish the Wizard option, and then click Next to continue.**

8. **Click Finish to exit the wizard and have Windows XP reboot your client PC.**

   When it completes the boot process, the added client PC should be a member of your network family.

Browsing the neighborhood

After you set up your network, you can easily see which other PCs are available. Windows XP power users call this activity *browsing* your network, where you saunter around, admiring what's connected. Choose Start⇨My Network Places, and then click View Workgroup Computers to display each of the PCs in your networked surroundings, as shown in Figure 17-7.

Whoops! I can hear all sorts of irate Windows XP faithful growling in irritation. "What's that in your My Network Places window? Is that a . . . (gasp) *Macintosh* that I see there?" That's right. As long as other computers conform to standard Ethernet protocols and they've been recognized by the host PC (or DHCP device), they'll show up as well. (This includes PCs running Linux, Macs running Mac OS 9 or Mac OS X, and Unix machines.)

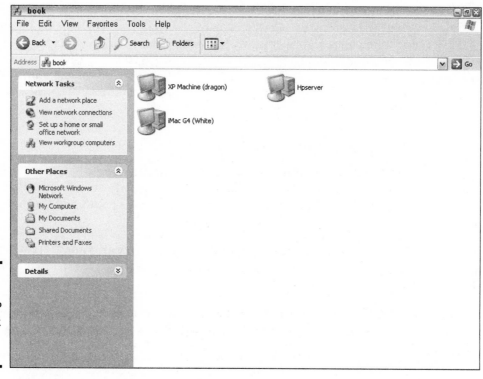

Figure 17-7:
The
Windows XP
My Network
Places
window.

"Wait! Where's Boopsie?" Well, if the client PC that you named *Boopsie* has been turned on *after* you opened the My Network Places window, it won't show up. To see it, choose View➪Refresh, which will rescan the network and update the window's contents. (And whatever moved you to name a PC *Boopsie,* anyway?)

To display which folders and devices are available on each computer, simply double-click the computer icon to open it up. Note that you might be greeted by a login dialog box, like the one that you see in Figure 17-8; I get this because I've set up my iMac as a secure system, and I have to supply my username and password to my Mac OS X account. (If you set up your clients with the procedure above, you shouldn't require a login to access their stuff . . . unless, of course, that computer's user has specifically configured Windows XP to require a login.)

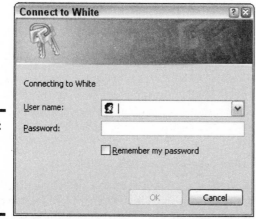

Figure 17-8:
A closed
system
requires a
network
login.

Windows XP automatically adds shared folders and printers and displays them in the My Network Places window. However, you can also manually add a new location to your My Network Places window. Display the taskbar (if necessary) and click Add a Network Place to run the Network Place Wizard, which will guide you through the steps. Or you can simply create a shortcut by dragging a network folder or URL address to the My Network Places window.

Sharing folders and documents

"So what precisely controls what I can and can't see when browsing the network?" Now you've entered The Sharing Zone, where time and space have no meaning. What *does* matter are the shared files and folders that you've set up on each computer in your network.

Sharing something across the network allows other computers to see it when browsing. (Note that network sharing is very different from sharing a local file among users of the same PC.)

By default, Windows XP takes the safe and conservative approach: Nothing is shared across a network until specifically set. (To be honest, I like it that way instead of defaulting to a completely open machine.) However, you can share a folder and all its contents by following these steps:

1. **Double-click My Computer (the icon on your desktop) to open the Explorer window; then navigate to the folder's location.**

2. **Right-click the folder and choose Sharing and Security from the shortcut menu that appears to display the settings that you see in Figure 17-9.**

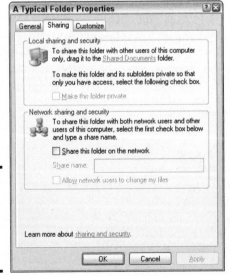

Figure 17-9: Select a folder as a shared network folder here.

3. **Select the Share This Folder on the Network check box.**

Windows XP provides a default share name based on the folder name, but you can type a new name if you like (less than 24 characters, please). I usually add the PC's network name so that I know which

Really Important Cool Stuff folder I'm actually looking at. The share name must be 12 characters or less for PCs running Windows 98/ME/NT that need to access the folder. Also, periods and exclamation points are allowed in the share name.

4. **Decide whether you want anyone on the network to be able to edit, delete, or rename the files in this folder.**

   If so, select the Allow Network Users to Change My Files check box to enable it. If this check box remains disabled, others can open any documents or files in this folder, but they can't make changes. (To do that, they must copy the file to their own computer and edit their local copy.)

5. **Click OK to close the dialog box.**

   You'll note that the icon for a shared folder is different from a standard folder. Windows tacks on an open hand, so it's easy to tell which folders on your system are shared.

You can also share a drive in the same fashion, but Windows XP cautions against it — and so do I. It's much better to assign just one shared folder on your drive.

When you share a folder, you place everything in that folder on the network. Therefore, if there's even one item (either a document or a subfolder) that you don't want to distribute with others inside a folder, do not share that folder!

After a folder is share enabled, its contents can be opened, moved, or copied either from Windows Explorer or from the File Open/Save/Browse dialog boxes that are common throughout Windows XP and your applications. (This assumes that the client user has the proper access level, as you can discover in the previous procedure.) That's the neat thing: Everything works normally across the network by using the same functionality.

Printing across the Network

Although sharing an Internet connection is one of the prime advantages of using a network these days, one other resource has been shared across networks now for decades: the network printer. (Read all about Internet connection sharing in Book II, Chapter 19.) And any printer connected to any PC on your network can be used by any other PC, which is a real boon when your office has only one large-format inkjet and only one color laser printer.

You can follow one of four avenues for network printing:

✦ **Hook up the printer to a PC so that it acts as a printer server.** As long as the printer only receives moderate use and it's in an open area, this option can work. (If the PC is in a private office, don't even think about it. You'll drive the occupant smackers.)

✦ **Set up a separate PC as a simple print server.** This is the traditional solution for high-traffic printers that need a central location. The client PC is basically just a doorman, existing only to queue print jobs for the connected printer. Expensive, but efficient.

✦ **Buy a network printer box.** These standalone devices are essentially Ethernet cards with a slightly more intelligent brain, and they provide the same functionality as a print server.

✦ **Buy a printer with onboard Ethernet network support.** Sure, they're more expensive, but a network-ready printer is the most elegant solution of all.

If you choose one of the latter two — either a network printer box or a network-ready printer — you'll have to follow the manufacturer's specific instructions to set things up. However, if you decide to use a client PC to provide printing services, you can follow these steps to set things up in Windows XP:

1. **Set up the printer normally under Windows XP and make sure that it's working properly.**

2. **Choose Start⇨Printers and Faxes to display the Printers and Faxes window that you see in Figure 17-10.**

3. **Right-click the printer that you want to share and choose Sharing from the shortcut menu that appears to display the Properties dialog box with the Sharing tab active (see Figure 17-11).**

4. **Select the Share This Printer radio button.**

Windows XP creates a default share name for the printer, but it might not be descriptive enough (especially in a larger building with many identical printers). Feel free to edit it.

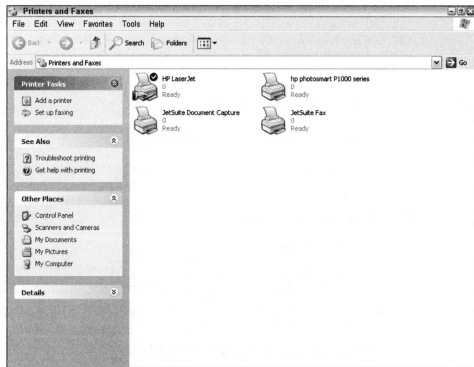

Figure 17-10: Enable printer sharing from the Printer and Faxes window.

Figure 17-11:
Sharing my HP inkjet printer, for the good of all.

5. **Windows XP offers a feature called *shared printer drivers,* in which you can install the drivers for other PCs on the network that might be using different versions of Windows besides Windows XP.**

   a. **If you want to make printer drivers available for these folks (which, believe me, will make things easier for both you and them), click the Additional Drivers button, which displays the dialog box that you see in Figure 17-12.**

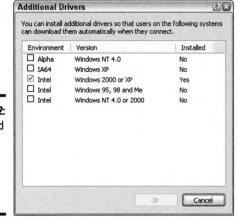

Figure 17-12:
With shared printer drivers, everyone can join in the fun.

   b. **Select the check boxes next to the other operating systems that might access this printer and click OK.**

   You'll need the manufacturer's driver CD-ROM when prompted by Windows XP. Or, if you're really hot stuff, you can download the latest drivers to your hard drive, expand (or unzip them), and browse to that location instead.

By the way, don't select the IA64/Windows XP check box unless someone on your network is running a computer that uses Intel's 64-bit chip. This environment is not required for regular PCs running standard Windows XP. That's taken care of by the Intel/Windows 2000 or XP check box, which is selected by default.

6. **Click OK to close the dialog box.**

   The icon for a shared printer (like a shared folder) is different; look for the open palm icon. (A reminder to cross it with additional funds, perhaps?)

Now any computer on the network can connect to the shared printer, but of course, it has to be added to each client first. You can do this by running the Add a Printer Wizard (which appears in the task pane on PCs running Windows XP when you open the Printers and Faxes window). When prompted, make sure that you choose to install a network printer, and then use the Browse function to allow Windows XP to locate the printer on the network for you.

Using a Standard Hub with a Cable or DSL Modem

I discuss Internet sharing devices earlier in this chapter, and they're covered in detail in Book II, Chapter 19. Many have built-in hubs or switches, virtually all of them have DHCP support, and they have ports that allow a direct connection to your cable or DSL modem. That's great: In fact, as I mention earlier, you won't even need a host PC in that case. Feel free to prance about.

But what if your hub *doesn't* have a connection point (typically called a wide area network [WAN] port, or an uplink port) for your DSL or cable modem? That's the situation that I mention earlier, where your host PC will need two NICs, and you will have to set it up as a host PC.

To do this, connect your hardware and cables so that

✦ The cable or DSL modem is connected to one of the NICs on the host PC. (It should already be configured this way, so no big deal.)

✦ The other NIC on the host PC is connected to one of the ports on the hub.

✦ The client PCs on the network are connected to the hub.

Now follow the procedure that I provide earlier for setting up the host PC and the client PCs, and all should function like butter.

Troubleshooting Your Network

I sure hope you're reading this section for fun . . . or because you thirst for knowledge, or just to be thorough. Why? Well, unfortunately, a misbehaving network can leave even the best techs with a four-bell headache. Your network is a mass of differing hardware, software, and data, all of which must work well in concert before you can send or receive a single packet.

Windows XP does the best job that it can to automate the process; and if you've bought a networking kit, you can pretty much assume that everything will be compatible. But if you have one bad cable or one faulty NIC driver, your state-of-the-art network becomes a family of dead cables and a little box with no lights. (Sounds like my last attempt at outdoor Christmas decorations.)

In this section, I provide the most common solutions to the most common problems.

Windows XP doesn't recognize my NIC

Man, talk about starting with a problem from step one! That's my kind of luck as well. Anyway, here are the possible problems and fixes:

✦ **An incompatible driver:** NIC drivers are legendary for their fickle behavior. Unlike some printers that allow you to use the same driver for both Windows 98 and 2000, or for Windows 2000 and XP, a network interface card simply demands the proper driver, or it won't work. Period. Reinstall the driver from the manufacturer's media (making sure that you select the right operating system version). If that doesn't work (and you still have access to the Internet on another computer), download the manufacturer's latest driver for your operating system from the company's Web site. (To download a driver, you will need to have access to another, working PC, and you might need a formatted floppy to install it.) And oh, by the way: You might actually have to uninstall the NIC and reinstall it to reload the driver. Such fun.

✦ **A faulty NIC:** This is a definite possibility. If you have a NIC that you know is working, replace the misbehaving card (along with its drivers) to see whether the problem is solved.

✦ **A hardware conflict:** This is quite rare under Windows XP, but it can still happen (and if your client PCs are running Windows 98 or ME, conflicts can crop up much more often). Use Device Manager to check whether Windows is having problems getting everyone to play nicely together.

No lights show up on my network card(s) or hub

This is classic stuff. Not the most comforting thing to hear, but then again, it's good to know that others have been here before you. (To be precise, me. I used to handle network problem calls at a major hospital.) Anyway, a lack of lights indicates that you're not getting a signal, which suggests a number of possible hardware problems:

✦ **Your cable is faulty.** An improperly made cable can short, causing everything to come to a crashing halt. This is a likely cause if all the other client PCs have illuminated signal lights, and the hub's lights are lit as well. (If the computer store sold you a special type of cable called a *crossover* cable, march right back and demand a standard twisted pair cable; crossover cables are meant to hook two computers together directly via their network ports. Unfortunately, it's hard to tell the difference with just your eye unless you see the word *crossover* printed on the cable.)

✦ **Your NIC or hub is faulty.** If either has gone off the deep end, they need to be replaced. If other client PCs are working, you can remove a working NIC from one of them and use it to test your hub.

✦ **Your hub isn't powered on.** (Whoops . . . no need for embarrassment.) A hub needs AC power to operate.

✦ **You're using the WAN/uplink port.** This is a special port on your hub, as I explain in "Using a Standard Hub with a Cable or DSL Modem"; it won't work for a client PC connection.

Nothing shows up when I browse

Just plain nasty. If everything seemed to go well when you set up your host PC and your client PCs, but you still come up empty when you browse, here are the possibilities (and my recommended troubleshooting tips):

✦ **Client PCs are powered down.** Simple, but effective. Boot up a client PC and refresh the My Network Places window by choosing View⇨Refresh. The client should now be visible.

✦ **A piece of hardware is faulty.** I use this term because any piece of your networking hardware might be experiencing problems, and you wouldn't be able to browse. See what I mean about the four-bell headache? Anyway, make sure that all your NICs and your hub have lighted activity/ signal lights.

✦ **No network resources are shared.** Remember, Windows XP doesn't share diddly by default, so when you first browse your My Network Places window, it's likely to be absolutely blank. However, click the View Workgroup Computers link in the window's taskbar to see whether the client PCs don't show up.

✦ **Workgroup names are mismatched.** As I declare earlier in this chapter, if you don't assign the exact same workgroup name to the host PC and every client PC on the network, those network packets are "walking around in different neighborhoods," as an old boss of mine used to say. Check to make sure that everyone has joined the same party.

I can't connect (or print) to a shared printer

I saved the best for last because this problem is usually much easier to solve (apart from the obvious, such as running out of paper, ink, or toner). Try these stress relievers:

✦ **The printer is powered down.** I wish I had a dime for every time that someone complained that they couldn't connect to Fred's printer, only to find that Fred was out of the office . . . and (ahem) his PC (and the specific printer in question) was turned off. (D'oh! Sound of hand slapping forehead.)

✦ **The printer isn't actually shared.** Yep, you guessed it; this is the other hot potato. Make sure that the shared printer hasn't been disabled (either by accident or on purpose).

✦ **You have faulty NIC or cables.** Again, check the NIC for the PC that's connected to the printer. The easiest thing to do is to see whether you can browse or work with shared files on that PC. If not, there's a good chance that either the NIC or the twisted pair cable is giving you problems.

✦ **The printer has been placed offline.** Some older laser printers have an Online/Offline button. If a printer like this is offline, the printer goes comatose and won't respond.

CHECK IT OUT

Finding Your Computer's IP Address

Sometimes you can't tell exactly which computer on a network has what address. You can walk around to each computer, choose Start⇨Control Panel⇨Network and Internet Connections⇨Network Connections, click the network connection, and read the IP address in the lower-left corner of the screen. But it can be a real pain in the neck to run around to all the computers, clicking and checking. There's an easier way, if you know the name of the computer whose IP address you want to check:

1. **Choose Start⇨All Programs⇨ Accessories⇨Command Prompt.**

You see the DOS command prompt. Uh, I mean the Windows Command Line Interface.

2. **At the C: prompt, type** `ping` **and the name of the computer (for example,** `ping` `thinkpad`**).**

If all is well, the local IP address for the computer appears — repeatedly. Yes, you can even ping your own computer. That's the fastest, easiest (and most reliable) way to verify its IP address. For help with cable modems, see `support.` `microsoft.com/?kbid=310089`. For the mother of all peer-to-peer networking diagnosis techniques, visit `support.` `microsoft.com/?kbid=308007`.

Chapter 18: Going Wireless

In This Chapter

↙ **Comparing wireless and wired networks**

↙ **Comparing wireless standards**

↙ **Using existing telephone and AC wiring**

↙ **Ensuring security on your wireless network**

↙ **Making a wireless connection in Windows XP**

*W*elcome to the future: A world where network cables are on display in museums, and your PCs can wirelessly access your home or office network from 100 feet away. Fast, convenient, and (most of all) as secure as a wired network, the wireless network of years to come will even bring other types of devices under its umbrella such as cellular phones, palmtop PCs, and personal digital assistants (PDAs), just to name a few.

Hang on a second . . . now that I think about it, all that stuff is available now! Wireless networks are rapidly overtaking traditional wired networks in homes and small offices. Even companies with extensive wired networks have added access points (APs) for the laptop crowd, just to be hip.

In this chapter, I show you how wireless networking works, what's available, and how you can set up a wireless network in Windows XP.

Understanding Wireless Networking

In a sense, wireless networking isn't as revolutionary as you might think. In fact, it operates in the same manner as the standard wired Ethernet configuration that I discuss in the preceding chapter, complete with packets, collisions, and all the hoo-hah that you read about networking. Of course, the method of transmitting and receiving packets is different when you're using wireless networking; instead of being sent over a wire, the packets are broadcasted through the air like a radio signal.

(However, you can't use your wireless network hardware to run a pirate radio station. Sorry about that, matey.)

How does wireless compare with wired?

Other than the transmission method, here are the only three major differences between a wired network and its wireless sibling:

✦ **Wireless connections are slower.** This is the big 'un as well as the major reason why most larger networks still depend on wired Ethernet for the bulk of their connections. Even the fastest current wireless technology can only pump data at 54 Mbps, but any run-of-the-mill wired network can easily deliver 100 Mbps; heck, the fastest wired networks can hit gigabit (1000 Mbps) speeds! In fact, they can use fiber optic cabling instead of plain copper wire cabling to hit their top speeds; recently, a group of researchers used fiber optic connections to transfer the same amount of data stored in 2 DVD movies in less than 60 seconds.

✦ **Wireless hardware is more expensive.** Depending on the standard supported by your wireless hardware — more on standards in the next section — you'll pay up to twice as much for wireless hardware as you would for 10/100 Mbps wired hardware.

✦ **Wireless networks require no hubs or switches.** Most wireless base stations and APs can provide connections for up to 253 simultaneous users, so a larger wireless network (with 50 PCs or more) requires far less hardware and upkeep than a wired network that can handle the same number of computers.

Would you like to impress your network administrator? Of course . . . wouldn't we all? (If you run your own home or small office network, you can impress a PC hardware technician instead.) Use the techno-nerd buzzwords for network transmission technologies and refer to your wireless network as an *unguided* network — as opposed to a *guided,* or wired, network.

Naturally, you can add a *wireless access point* — or, as it's commonly called, a *WAP* — to your wired network, which will give you the best of both worlds. Figure 18-1 illustrates a WAP device, which brings 802.11b wireless connectivity to an existing wired network; this baby runs about $75. Most WAP units actually require two physical connections: one to your wired Ethernet network (naturally) and a Universal Serial Bus (USB) connection to the computer that will control it. You can also share your Internet connection with a dual router, which has both wired and wireless hardware built in (as I discuss in Book II, Chapter 19).

Figure 18-1: A typical WAP for your LAN.

The standards involved

Like any other evolving PC technology, wireless networking suffers from competition between different standards — some are compatible with others, and some are not. Readers of my other books are already acquainted with my overwhelming love for strange names and obfuscating acronyms in the PC world . . . NOT. Unfortunately, wireless networking has a handful of the most confusing names in the entire PC world, so make sure that you have a bottle of aspirin handy.

Here, in one easy-to-consume section, is the lowdown on the different wireless standards, as well as which you should consider and which you should eschew.

Book II
Chapter 18

The current standard: 802.11b

Commonly called Wi-Fi (short for *Wireless Fidelity*), the first 802.11b wireless base station (named the AirPort) was introduced by Apple Computer in 1999 — a fact that the good folks at Cupertino have been gloating over ever since. Wi-Fi supports a maximum transfer rate of 11 Mbps, which is just a little faster than the slowest 10 Mbps wired Ethernet standard in common use.

Distance is important in the wireless world, of course. It's one thing to be able to use your laptop on your network from across the room and another thing entirely to use it in your backyard. 802.11b devices are rated at a maximum distance of 300 feet from the base station, but that figure is about as realistic as an African wildebeest wearing a hula skirt appearing in your living room. This idea of "theoretical top speed" also applies to high-speed dialup modems, which practically never deliver the top speed that the manufacturer lists on the box. By experience, I can tell you that you can count on 150 feet — and even less if a number of intervening walls stand between you and your network, or if you're a victim of interference.

A word about USB wireless connections

You can connect a desktop PC to a wireless network without using any internal adapter card at all. Just use a *USB wireless adapter,* which uses a USB connection to your PC as a path for wireless network data packets. Hey, that USB is really amazing, isn't it? (Note that this toy isn't the same as a simple USB cable network, which allows PCs to share files and printers over USB cabling.) The remote PC gets all the benefits of a wireless Ethernet connection.

As you can read in Book II, Chapter 14, USB 1.1 ports can transfer a maximum of 12 Mbps, so they work just fine with 802.11b hardware. However, you'd have to turn to a FireWire or USB 2.0 wireless adapter to deliver the 54 Mbps top speed of an

802.11a or 802.11g connection. (Personally, I think that both FireWire and USB 2.0 are examples of tremendous overkill in this scenario. After all, you're moving 54 Mbps over a cable that can reach as high as 480 Mbps! However, USB 1.1 won't cut it at 54 Mbps, so what's a poor PC owner to do?)

Anyway, an external USB wireless adapter is a great way to add "temporary wireless" to a PC in your home or office. Many of these external adapters can also be used to make a printer a stand-alone wireless device, so you can place your printer in a central location that's convenient to everyone.

Going Wireless

Oh, didn't I mention the interference? 802.11b networking uses the 2.4 GHz broadcasting spectrum, which unfortunately is now being used by a regular horde of devices, including cellular phones, cordless phones, Bluetooth devices (which I cover in a bit), and even microwave ovens. Therefore, 802.11b wireless networks can slow down significantly because of interference from other devices. It's not likely that your entire wireless network will shut down completely, but you will *definitely* be able to tell when your teenage daughter is using your cordless phone.

The misfit: 802.11a

Why is 802.11a such a misfit, and why did I list it after 802.11b? Well, you're going to love this:

✦ **The numbering is wrong.** Believe it or not, 802.11a is a more recent standard. (Can someone please explain to me why this select group of engineers decided to number successive standards in *reverse* order?)

✦ **It has a shorter range.** Although it's officially rated at 150 feet under perfect conditions, in the real world, 802.11a can only reach a distance of 60–70 feet — your wireless world shrinks even further.

✦ **It doesn't play well with others.** 802.11a is completely incompatible with both 802.11b and 802.11g, so you're effectively limited to 802.11a equipment. (And there's not all that much out there.)

So why did folks develop 802.11a, anyway? It has two advantages:

✦ **It's speedy.** 802.11a was the first speed demon in wireless networking, delivering up to 54 Mbps (over five times as fast as 802.11b).

✦ **It uses a different broadcasting spectrum.** 802.11a uses the 5 GHz spectrum, which prevents it from working in the 2.4 GHz range needed by 802.11b (hence the incompatibility). Because there's a lot less activity around most homes and offices in the 5 GHz spectrum, you get less interference and a better chance of achieving the best reception.

Here's a bit of trivia that no person should be without: 802.11b networking uses a modulation scheme called *Direct Sequence Spread Spectrum* (DSSS). On the other hand, 802.11a networks use the *Orthogonal Frequency Division Multiplexing* scheme (OFDM). Why the heck is this important? Well, DSSS uses less power than OFDM, so — yes, there's actually a point — 802.11b networking hardware uses less power than 802.11a hardware, and that translates into longer battery life for your laptop if you use a 802.11b Wi-Fi card while you're traveling.

The darling child: 802.11g

I know you're probably thinking to yourself, "Self, I sure wish someone would get off their duff and produce a standard that's both compatible with 802.11b and provides speeds as fast as 802.11a." Good news; your wish has been heard! The latest wireless standard 802.11g does precisely that, combining the best of both worlds. If you (or your company) have already invested in 802.11b wireless hardware, you can continue to use it on an 802.11g network. Naturally, you won't get 54 Mbps, but at least it'll work at 11 Mbps. New 802.11g hardware will transfer packets at that magic 54 Mbps.

The downside? Aw, geez, we're back to the 2.4 GHz spectrum again, so once again, your buddy in the next cubicle who loves microwave popcorn is going to introduce interference. It just goes to show that nothing's perfect . . . except, perhaps, a 1964 Cadillac two-door coupe.

The strangely named: Bluetooth

Okay, now here's a wireless standard name that sounds like some scriptwriter or concept artist in Hollywood was working overtime . . . but at least it does break the 802.11*x* mold. Unlike the other three standards, Bluetooth is not designed for full-scale wireless Ethernet networking. Instead, it was developed in 1995 as a specialized wireless technology for short distances to be used with cell phones, PDAs, laptops, palmtops, printers, and other external devices. The maximum distance for a Bluetooth network is about 30 feet.

The Bluetooth wave is even supposed to reach household appliances, like your TV and your stereo system. I'm sure there's a Bluetooth toaster out there. If you've seen it, drop me a line at mark@mlcbooks.com and tell me all about it.

Anyway, unlike the other standards that I discuss here, Bluetooth requires very little power to use (befitting its design, which concentrates on battery-operated devices). It's also painfully slow compared with 802.11b — only about 1 Mbps — but that's not supposed to affect the small fry as much as it would your desktop PC. No base station is required for Bluetooth communications between devices. For example, after your laptop gets within 30 feet of your cell phone, they can update each other's telephone number directories. Eerie.

Oh, and Bluetooth also uses the — you guessed it — 2.4 GHz spectrum, so it will actually conflict with existing 802.11b and 802.11g networks! (The airwaves are getting so overpopulated that tin cans and string are starting to look attractive again.)

Table 18-1 sums up each of the four wireless networking standards.

Table 18-1	Wireless Standards on Parade		
Standard	*Transfer Speed*	*Maximum Distance*	*Compatibility*
802.11b	11 Mbps	300 feet	802.11g
802.11a	54 Mbps	150 feet	None
802.11g	54 Mbps	150 feet	802.11b
Bluetooth	1 Mbps	30 feet	None

I should note here that you can buy an external wireless antenna for your base station or WAP. An 802.11b directional antenna is typically about $40 or $50, and it can boost your existing signal quality as well as extend the range of your wireless network into every nook and cranny of your home or office. Check your station/WAP to see whether it can accept an external antenna.

AC and phone line networking

Although wireless hardware has become very popular over the last four years, here's another alternative to a traditional wired network: You can also build a network by using either the existing AC power wiring (a *power line* network) or the telephone wiring (a *phone line* network) in your home.

If running packets across your AC power lines sounds a little dangerous, let me put your fears to rest: Both of these alternative wired networks have been around for several years now — longer, in fact, than 802.11b — and they're perfectly safe. (If you're wondering, you can continue to use your telephone or your AC appliances with no changes.) The advantages of an alternative wired network over a wired or wireless network are clear:

✦ **No wires — at least, no Cat 5 cables:** Your home or office is already set up with all the "cabling" you need, and you likely have "ports" in every room.

✦ **Better security than a wireless network:** Although a wireless network can be made quite secure — I cover how to do this in the next section — you're still beaming a signal that can be picked up outside in the street. On the other hand, the network packets transferred over a phone line or an AC network stay within the building and are practically impossible for anyone outside to intercept.

✦ **Very easy to install:** A wireless network might be the easiest to install, but a phone line or an AC network is still much easier to set up than a traditional wired network.

So why aren't phone line and power line networks more popular? Unfortunately, compared with wireless, both of these network solutions leave much to be desired:

✦ **They're slower than wireless.** Both the latest phone line standard (from HomePNA, at www.homepna.org) and the HomePlug power line standard (www.homeplug.org) deliver approximately 10 Mbps. An 802.11g network will wipe the floor with either alternative wired network when it comes to raw file transfer speed.

✦ **They're less convenient than wireless.** Even though you don't have to string Ethernet cabling all over your office, your networked PCs and peripherals are still tied down to certain areas (either around your telephone jacks or your AC power sockets). A wireless connection works wherever you are as long as you're in range.

✦ **You can connect fewer computers.** A wireless network can accept twice as many users (or stand-alone network devices) as either a phone line or power line network.

When readers ask me to recommend a network solution for their home or small office, I almost always recommend either a traditional wired (Cat 5) network (for the fastest speeds and the best security) or a wireless network (which offers convenience and easy installation). The drawbacks of phone line and power line networks (along with the explosive popularity of wireless hardware) will likely doom them to gradual extinction.

Ensuring Security on Your Wireless Network

If you're adding a wireless network to your home or office, security should be your first consideration before you send a single packet over the airwaves. First, for those who are currently shopping for wireless hardware, let me list the standards that you should look for:

✦ **Do the WEP.** WEP is blissfully short for *Wired Equivalency Privacy*. It's a form of encryption that acts as your main defense against outside intrusion, as shown in Figure 18-2. Without the proper *key* (or, in human jargon, the proper *password*), a hacker is faced with a decoding job. That's not a hard job because hacker applications are available that will help the bad guys decode WEP, but at least it's a first level of defense. WEP is supported in wireless hardware at several different levels, ranging from 40-bit encryption (a rather weak implementation that might as well be called Diet Protection) to 256-bit (Armor Plated Protection). The 128-bit WEP standard is the most common these days, and it does a creditable job of keeping your data secure. Choose hardware that supports the 128-bit WEP standard whenever possible, and make sure that WEP is enabled.

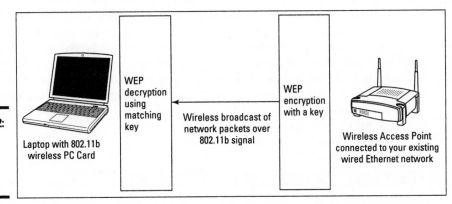

Figure 18-2: WEP in action. Thrilling, isn't it?

Laptop with 802.11b wireless PC Card

WEP decryption using matching key

Wireless broadcast of network packets over 802.11b signal

WEP encryption with a key

Wireless Access Point connected to your existing wired Ethernet network

Make your WEP key as long as allowed by your hardware and also use the same common sense that you use when choosing your Internet passwords. Keys should be completely random. Don't use your middle name or your Social Security number, and remember to mix both letters and numbers together.

✦ **LEAP for security.** Man, these acronyms are such a delight. (If you need an aspirin, I'll understand.) *Lightweight Extensible Authentication Protocol* (LEAP) is also an encryption protocol, but unlike WEP, the key is automatically changed periodically while you're connected, which turns a hacking job from a difficult proposition into a nearly impossible feat. You can specify the time delay before the key changes . . . five minutes ought to do it. (Big grin.) Hardware that offers LEAP is much more expensive than the run-of-the-mill WEP hardware, but for those who need the best possible wireless security, it's the best that you can get.

After you configure your wireless network, here are the security guidelines I recommend that you should follow:

✦ **Use Virtual Private Networking (VPN) for extra security.** As you can read in the next chapter of this book, VPN is a hard nut for an outsider to crack. When security is all important, set up a VPN session (as I demonstrate in Book II, Chapter 19).

✦ **Secure your SSID.** I know that sounds weird, but your *SSID* is your *Service Set Identifier* — essentially, the name for your WAP or base station. Change your SSID immediately when you install your wireless base station or access point, making sure that you've configured your system so that your SSID is not broadcast to the outside world. (This means that you have to configure your wireless connections manually — your WAP or base station won't show up automatically when your PC is in range.) Determining your SSID is the first step in hacking your wireless network. I guarantee that it'll be practically impossible for an outsider to guess that your SSID is *Bullwinkle007* (or something similar).

✦ **Change your access point/base station password.** Naturally, you also don't want anyone to be able to guess the password that secures your wireless access point or base station, so change that hardware password to something unique.

If anyone asks you to jump in his vehicle for a bit of *war driving,* you'll understand why wireless security is so important. The term refers to hackers who rig up their cars with a laptop PC, equipped with a wireless network card and a cheap omnidirectional antenna, and then drive around neighborhoods in their town looking for unsecured wireless networks. When such an example of easy pickings is found, the hacker can use any broadband connection that's hooked up to that network (read that as *free Internet connection*), or — much worse — haul away copies of the files and documents found on that network.

Using Wireless Hardware in Windows XP

After you install your wireless base station or WAP, you're ready to configure your PC for use on your network.

Preparing to install

Before you begin the installation of an internal adapter card, make sure that

✦ **You've read the manual.** Even if you've already installed an adapter card in your PC, take a few minutes to check the documentation that shipped with the card. A maxim to live by: It's better to know about a "gotcha" before you install.

✦ **You've gathered the Big Four.** That means a Phillips screwdriver, a plastic bowl to hold any spare parts, a good light source, and some sort of static-free cover for your work surface. (Newspaper always works well if I'm away from my workbench.)

✦ **You've grounded yourself.** After you've removed the cover from your PC, I highly recommend touching the metal chassis of your computer to dissipate any static electricity that's stowing away on your body before it can cause damage to the card.

Installation tricks

All manufacturers of wireless adapter cards (for desktops) and wireless PC Cards (for laptops) include their own installation and setup programs — which, under Windows XP, also create the necessary wireless connection automatically — so I won't go into the gory details here. However, here are some suggestions that I can give you that will help with the installation, no matter what type of card you're using:

✦ **Choose between ad hoc and infrastructure.** You might be prompted to choose between ad hoc and infrastructure mode. In most cases, you want to choose *infrastructure* mode (where your laptop and PC workstations connect by using a base station or wireless access point) instead of *ad hoc* (where the devices actually talk directly to each other on a specific channel number that you determine, just like the CB radio days of old, without a base station or WAP). Figures 18-3 and 18-4 illustrate how ad hoc and infrastructure modes work. ***Note:*** If you're trying to connect your wireless device to your existing wired network, you must use infrastructure mode.

**Book II
Chapter 18**

Going Wireless

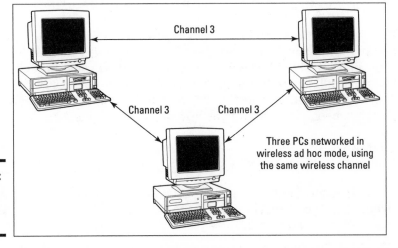

Channel 3

Channel 3   Channel 3

Three PCs networked in wireless ad hoc mode, using the same wireless channel

Figure 18-3: An ad hoc networking layout.

✦ **Check your WEP encryption.** When prompted for WEP information, use the highest level that the PC Card supports. WEP is designed to automatically fall back to the encryption level used by your base station or WAP.

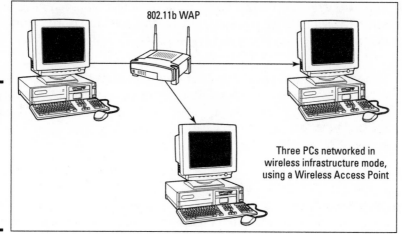

Figure 18-4:
Connecting your wired network with an infrastructure configuration.

802.11b WAP

Three PCs networked in wireless infrastructure mode, using a Wireless Access Point

✦ **Check your SSID.** You need an SSID that matches the SSID used by your base station or WAP. *Remember:* Change it to the unique value that you used on your base station or WAP. For the best security, *don't* use the default SSID!

✦ **Keep your drivers current.** I sound like a broken record, but check for the latest drivers from the manufacturer's Web site every time that you install new hardware . . . and that includes wireless networking hardware.

Making the connection

You have two methods of connecting to your wireless network in infrastructure mode: the easy way (where your base station or WAP broadcasts its SSID for public use) and the harder way (where you've turned off the SSID broadcast feature for greater security, which I mention earlier in this chapter).

The easy way? Just plug your wireless network card into your laptop, and Windows XP will automatically search for and connect to your network. If you're using a desktop PC with a wireless card, this same process occurs when you first log in to Windows XP. (See? I told you it was easy.) Windows XP displays a notification icon in the taskbar letting you know that the connection has been made, as well as how strong the signal is.

If you're smart and keep your SSID close to the chest, follow these steps to do things the slightly harder way:

1. **Choose Start⇨Connect To, right-click the Wireless Network Connection icon, and then click View Available Wireless Networks from the shortcut menu that appears.**

   Windows XP displays the Connect to Wireless Network dialog box.

2. **Click the Advanced button.**

   The Properties dialog box opens.

3. **Click the Add button in the Properties dialog box.**

4. **Type the matching SSID value from your base station or WAP in the Network Name (SSID) text box, and then select the Data Encryption (WEP Enabled) check box (if necessary).**

If you've set your own WEP key, select the This Key is Provided for Me Automatically check box, and then type the key in the Network Key text box. Click the Key Length drop-down list and choose the proper key length. (It's okay to use an automatically generated key, but your base station or WAP is likely to choose a shorter key than you can assign manually.)

5. **Make sure that the This Is a Computer-to-Computer (Ad Hoc) Network check box is deselected.**

6. **Click OK to close the dialog box.**

This adds the network to your Preferred Networks list.

7. **Click OK again to return to your Windows XP desktop, which should initiate the connection.**

**Book II
Chapter 18**

Going Wireless

Chapter 19: Sharing Your Internet Connection

In This Chapter

✓ Understanding the advantages of connection sharing

✓ Sharing your connection using Windows XP

✓ Using a wired hardware sharing device

✓ Using a wireless hardware sharing device

✓ Putting Network Address Translation (NAT) to work for you

✓ Setting up Virtual Private Networking (VPN) in Windows XP

A high-speed Internet connection is a thing of beauty, especially when it's shared with everyone in your home or office over your network. After your network is set up and running smoothly, consider whether you want to share that connection through hardware or software as well as what sort of security you'll need to protect everyone on your network.

In this chapter, I discuss all the possibilities — including the whiz-bang Virtual Private Networking (VPN) feature — and show you how to set up Internet connection sharing within Windows XP.

Why Share Your Internet Connection?

"Don't I need a separate Internet connection for each PC on my network?" Actually, you've just answered your own question: That network that you've installed allows for all sorts of data communications between PCs, including the ability to plug in to a shared connection.

I should note here that it is indeed technically possible to share a dialup Internet connection by using the software connection-sharing feature in Windows XP. However, I don't think that you'll be satisfied with the results. (Sorry, that dialup connection won't provide enough horsepower to adequately handle more than one computer.) Therefore, I'm going to assume for the rest of this chapter that you're already using either a digital subscriber line (DSL) or a cable modem Internet connection.

Here's a list of advantages that help explain why Internet connection sharing — whether through a program or a dedicated hardware device — is so doggone popular these days:

✦ **It's cheap.** As long as your Internet service provider (ISP) allows you to share your broadband DSL or cable modem connection, you'll save a bundle over the cost of adding completely separate connections for multiple machines in your home or office. (Naturally, this is the major advantage.)

✦ **It's convenient.** With a shared Internet connection, other PCs on your network are easy to configure, and each is content as a sleeping cat. Each PC on your network operates just as if it were directly connected to your DSL or cable modem.

✦ **It offers centralized security.** With a *firewall* in place — either running on the PC (if you're sharing through software) or on the device itself (if you're sharing through hardware) — you can protect the Internet activity on all the PCs on your network at one time.

✦ **It's efficient.** Most folks whom I talk to are surprised that a shared Internet connection is so fast — even when multiple computers on your network are charging down the Information Superhighway at the same time.

A connection shared through a dedicated hardware device, however, will always be faster than a connection shared through software. Keep that in mind.

Speaking of convenience and efficiency, I should also mention that many hardware sharing devices also double as Ethernet hubs or switches. This allows you to build your entire home or office network around one central piece of hardware rather than using a separate hub and a PC running a software sharing program.

Sharing through Software in Windows XP

If you decide to use the built-in Internet connection sharing (ICS) feature of Windows XP, first double-check that you already have everything in this list:

✦ **A working Ethernet network.**

✦ **A working broadband Internet connection to one of the PCs on your network.** Okay, you can use ICS with a dialup connection as well, but everything will be much faster with a DSL or cable connection.

✦ **An installed copy of Windows XP on the PC that's connected to the Internet.** This PC will also need two network cards installed — one that leads to the network hub, and one that leads to the cable or DSL modem. Because many flavors of network cards exist (using many different connections, like USB, PC Card, and the more traditional internal adapter card), follow the installation instructions provided by the card manufacturer to add both cards to your PC.

Everything shipshape? Good. Follow these steps to share that existing Internet connection with the other computers on your network:

1. **Choose Start⇨Connect To, and then right-click the connection that you want to share and choose Properties.**

The An Example ISP Properties dialog box appears.

2. **Click the Advanced tab to display the settings that you see in Figure 19-1.**

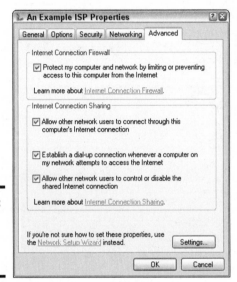

Figure 19-1:
Set up ICS within Windows XP.

3. **Select the Allow Other Network Users to Connect through This Computer's Internet connection check box.**

- If you are sharing a dialup connection, I recommend enabling automatically dialing. If necessary, select the Establish a Dial-up Connection Whenever a Computer on My Network Attempts to Access the Internet check box. (Keep in mind, however, that this can wreak havoc on a voice call.)

- To allow other network users to control the shared connection — as in disconnecting it — then select the Allow Other Network Users to Control or Disable the Shared Internet Connection check box.

4. **Click OK to save your changes and return to the Windows XP desktop.**

Windows XP indicates that a connection is shared by adding a friendly looking cupped hand under the connection icon.

Figure 19-2 illustrates how things will work after you're done. Of course, your IP addresses will be different from those in the figure, but it should help you understand how everything will fly.

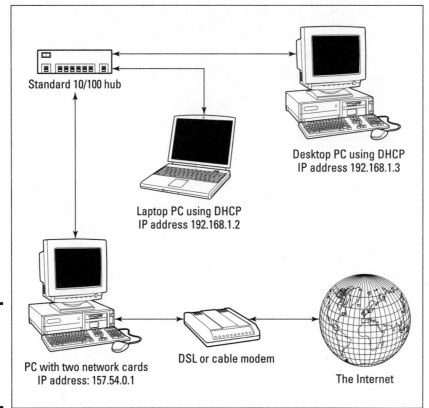

Figure 19-2:
A shared Internet connection using software.

Standard 10/100 hub

Desktop PC using DHCP
IP address 192.168.1.3

Laptop PC using DHCP
IP address 192.168.1.2

PC with two network cards
IP address: 157.54.0.1

DSL or cable modem

The Internet

Sharing through Hardware

As I mention earlier, I personally think that a hardware sharing device is somewhat preferable to sharing a connection through software. For example, with a software solution

✦ You end up with at least one PC on your network that must always remain on if anyone wants to use the Internet.

✦ You'll notice a significant slowdown on the sharing PC when several other PCs are using the Internet.

✦ You still need a hub, switch, or wireless base station.

With a hardware device, all the PCs on your network can concentrate on their own work, eliminating the need to leave a PC running constantly as an "Internet server." (After all, a PC that's capable of running Windows XP at a decent clip is an expensive resource compared with an investment of $50–$100 on a hardware sharing device.)

In this section, I familiarize you with the two different types of hardware sharing devices.

Wired sharing devices

For those PC owners who either already have a traditional wired Ethernet network — or those who are considering building one — a device like the combination switch-firewall-DHCP-server-sharing-thing that you see in Figure 19-3 is the perfect solution to Internet connection sharing. (*Dynamic Host Configuration Protocol,* or DHCP, is a feature that allows your hardware sharing device to automatically configure IP addresses on your network. If all that sounds like an alien language, visit Book II Chapter 17, where I wax enthusiastic about DHCP.)

Figure 19-3: An Internet connection router.

Perhaps I should be a little more specific in my description. (Not even Google will return much if you search for *switch-firewall-DHCP-server-sharing-thing.*) The illustrated device is actually a cable/DSL router with a four-port switch.

For an idea of why hardware sharing is so popular, look at what you get — in one small tidy box — selling online for a mere $50:

✦ A built-in, four-port Ethernet 10/100 switch into which you can plug four PCs (to start with) directly into the router for an instant Ethernet network. (For more information about network speeds, see Book II, Chapter 17.)

✦ A direct-connect port for your DSL or cable modem, which can also be used as a wide area network (WAN) connection to hook the device to an existing external network.

✦ A DHCP server, providing near-automatic network configuration for the PCs hooked into the device.

✦ The ability to block certain Internet traffic (both coming in and going out) as well as the ability to lock out individual PCs from Internet access.

✦ An easy-to-use, Web-based configuration screen, which can be used on any PC connected to the router. Figure 19-4 illustrates the Web configuration screen from my router.

✦ Built-in NAT functionality. (I dive into NAT in the next section.)

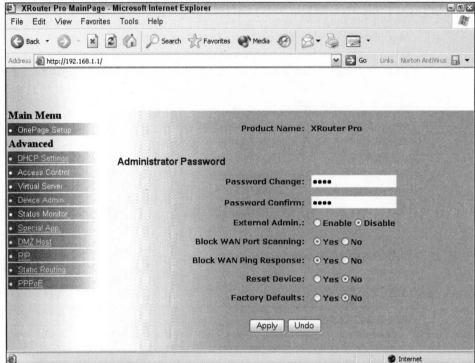

Figure 19-4:
Most
Internet
sharing
devices
can be
configured
with a Web
browser.

Pretty neat, huh? Remember, this device is used in tandem with your existing cable or DSL modem, which is typically included by your ISP as part of your Internet subscription (but you might be paying more because you're renting the modem).

I should also note that you can get a similar device with all these features *and* a built-in DSL or cable modem. Because you won't be charged a monthly rental for a modem, you can thumb your nose at your ISP and save money in the long run. (Please avoid mentioning my name when you gleefully return your modem to your ISP.)

Naturally, the setup procedure for each device on the market is different, but here's a sample of what's in store when you take your new Internet sharing router out of the box:

1. **If you're currently running a typical stand-alone network switch or hub, you can either unplug all the existing computers and put them on the new box, or you can connect the WAN port from the existing hub into one of the ports on the Internet sharing device.**

The device manual will tell you how to take care of the latter method.

If you're setting up a new network, naturally, you'll just connect each Ethernet cable directly to the sharing device.

2. **Plug the power supply from the sharing device into your AC socket.**

3. **Configure one of the PCs on your new network with the default network settings provided by the device manufacturer.**

4. **Run Internet Explorer on the PC that you configured in the last step and use the Web-based configuration utility to finish configuring the device.**

That's it! If you're running a typical home or home office network, you'll likely keep the default settings for everything. For an idea of just what kind of power you can wield over your network as you share your Internet connection, take a gander at the sidebar titled, "What the Sam Hill does *that* mean?" Luckily, you probably won't have to use any of those optional settings, but it's good to know that they're there.

Wireless sharing devices

Most folks think that sharing an Internet connection over a wireless network must be harder to set up than a traditional wired network — and that it's likely to be a tremendous security risk as well. I'm happy to tell you that both preconceptions are wrong. Wireless connection sharing with a hardware device is as simple to set up as the wired device that I discuss in the preceding section. And, with the settings that I discuss in Book II, Chapter 18, you'll make it very difficult (if not impossible) for someone to hack his way to your network or your Internet connection.

What the Sam Hill does *that* mean?

When you're shopping for a wired or wireless Internet sharing device, you'll find that the side of the box mentions a number of nifty security features that seem to have been named by a very depressed engineer (who didn't speak much English either). Allow me to translate for you:

Static routing: A feature that enables you to set up a preset network path between the device and an Internet host, which is likely to be an external network. Without static routing, you might not be able to use Virtual Private Networking (VPN), which I discuss at the end of this chapter.

Dynamic routing: Basically, the reverse of static routing — and it's a great feature for those who are constantly yanking PCs, servers, and network hardware off the network and plugging stuff back in at other locations. With dynamic routing, the sharing device automatically compensates and adjusts for changes made to the *topology* (whoops, I meant *layout*) of your network.

Port forwarding: If you're running an e-mail, Web, or File Transfer Protocol (FTP) server on your network, you can set the router to automatically divert any incoming traffic of that type — HyperText Transfer Protocol (HTTP) for the Web server, for example — directly to the server PC.

IP filtering: This is the feature that allows you to block certain users or PCs from Internet access. It's also a good feature to have when you're using VPN.

WAN blocking: This sounds like something that happens in a nuclear reactor, doesn't it? Luckily, this feature just prevents other PCs on the Internet from *pinging* (scanning) for your network, so it's a good idea to leave this one on. It's generally a good thing to be invisible to other computers on the Internet.

Demilitarized Zone (DMZ) host: Finally, here's a feature that's designed just for us Internet gamers: You can set up your router with a special set of "holes" to "reveal" your PC to others on the Internet when you're connecting to an Internet game server (or if you're hosting your own server). Without a DMZ, your router's NAT firewall would likely block your PC from communicating with others (as I explain later in this chapter), and you wouldn't be able to join or create an Internet gaming battleground. Anyone for a fragfest in Unreal Tournament 2003?

As an example of a truly versatile all-in-one Internet sharing device, check out the device shown in Figure 19-5. It's got the antenna that marks it as a wireless switch, but what you don't see is that it also sports four 10/100 Ethernet ports on the back for your old-fashioned wired network. Yep, you guessed it, this is just plain neat: It can accommodate multiple 802.11b wireless connections *and* four wired connections, all at the same time! (The somewhat spaghetti-fied world of wireless networking is covered in depth in Book II, Chapter 18.)

As you might expect, the cost on this puppy (about $200 online) is much higher than the wired-only device (see the preceding section). Another factor is the speed of the wireless connection; as you can read in Book II, Chapter 18, you'll pay much more for the speed of an 802.11g device. (And yes, if you've decided to opt for a wireless-only network, you can find a cheaper wireless sharing device that doesn't include any of those silly "antique" wired ports.) Wireless adapter cards (including the USB and PC Card varieties) are much more expensive than standard wired adapter cards, too.

As I mention in Book II, Chapter 18, don't forget to demand a wireless sharing device that offers 128-bit Wired Equivalent Privacy (WEP) private encryption. Anything less, and your wireless network will be much easier for outsiders to hack.

Figure 19-5: Is it wired? Is it wireless? This sharing device is both!

Why You Need NAT

Okay, I know I've been harping about NAT (short for *Network Address Translation*) on and off for several pages now. You know that it's important, but what does it actually *do?* Well, check out Figure 19-6. If your Internet sharing device (or your Internet sharing software) supports NAT, a number of different PCs — each with a different Internet Protocol (IP) address — are masked behind the single IP address that's assigned to your cable or DSL modem by your ISP. No one can tell what individual IP addresses are used behind your NAT device.

In order to hack a PC on your system, someone on the outside (meaning elsewhere on the Internet) has to know the IP address of an individual computer on your system, and NAT prevents the intruder from learning just that. Instead, the only IP address that's visible is the modem/Internet-sharing device itself. Plus, a NAT blocks the most common weapon in the hacker arsenal: probing "port sniffers" that hunt for open, unprotected ports across the Internet.

Note that NAT isn't a complete firewall in and of itself. But when your connection-sharing hardware or software uses NAT in conjunction with a commercial firewall program such as Norton Personal Firewall (www. symantec.com), you've effectively shut the door on Internet intruders!

By the way, the built-in Windows XP firewall has NAT built in, naturally.

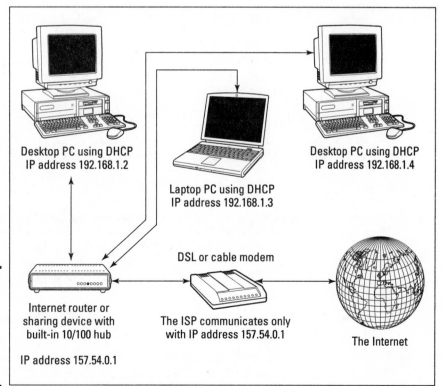

Figure 19-6: With NAT on the job, individual PCs on your network are invisible.

Desktop PC using DHCP
IP address 192.168.1.2

Laptop PC using DHCP
IP address 192.168.1.3

Desktop PC using DHCP
IP address 192.168.1.4

DSL or cable modem

Internet router or sharing device with built-in 10/100 hub

IP address 157.54.0.1

The ISP communicates only with IP address 157.54.0.1

The Internet

The Magic of Virtual Private Networking

Imagine if you could take your networking one step further. Instead of wires or even a wireless network, what if you could create a secure network connection over the Internet into your private network itself? You'd be able to enjoy the benefits of using your private office network anywhere in the world . . . as long as an Internet connection was handy.

Such is the reality of Virtual Private Networking — and the emphasis, of course, is on the words *private* and *secure*. (It's one thing to have access to your files from across the country, but giving that same access to an interested hacker is another thing entirely.) Your data is protected by encryption when it passes over the Internet, so for all intents and purposes, your connection is as well protected as a correctly configured wireless network.

VPN places you squarely back into the realm of client/server networking, where the VPN *client* is the PC that you're using remotely and the VPN *server* is the machine on the network that you're connecting to. (If you're unsure whether your office network is set up for VPN, ask that dashing system administrator.)

In this section, I demonstrate how to set up your laptop PC (or a remote desktop) as a VPN client under Windows XP, with the following assumptions (based upon how VPN is used most often in real-world situations):

✦ You're using either

- A broadband connection to the Internet

or

- Another company's network Internet connection

VPN over a dialup connection is the definition of the word *frustrating*, and I don't recommend it.

✦ Your network administrator has provided you the IP address of the VPN server.

✦ You'll use your regular network username and password to log in.

Follow these steps to create and use a VPN connection:

1. **Choose Start⇨All Programs⇨Accessories⇨Communications⇨New Connection Wizard, and then click Next on the first wizard screen.**

The wizard displays the options shown in Figure 19-7.

2. **Select the Connect to the Network at My Workplace radio button and click Next to continue.**

3. **Select the Virtual Private Network connection radio button and click Next to continue.**

4. **Type a descriptive name that will help you keep track of the connection, such as *MLC Books VPN Client*, and then click Next.**

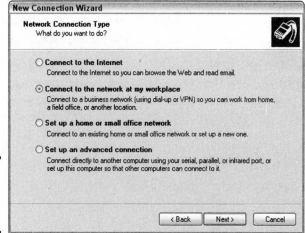

Figure 19-7:
Build a VPN
client the
wizard way.

5. **On the wizard screen that you see in Figure 19-8, type the VPN server address provided by your network administrator (such as 157.54.0.1), and then click Next to continue.**

    Note that this can also be in the form of a host name in good ol' English (like *mlcbooks.com*).

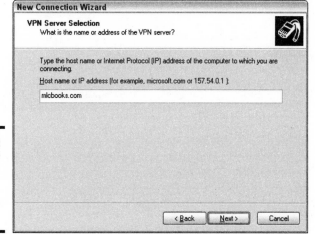

Figure 19-8:
Enter the IP
address or
host name
for a VPN
server.

6. **If you'd like to add a desktop shortcut for your new VPN connection, select the Add a Shortcut to This Connection to My Desktop check box.**

7. **Click Finish.**

    Windows XP creates the connection.

If you need to make changes to your VPN connection properties — for example, if your network administrator gets all high and mighty and changes the IP address of the VPN server — choose Start⇨Connect To. Right-click your VPN connection and choose Properties from the shortcut menu that appears, which will display the VPN Client Properties dialog box. From here, you can make any necessary changes.

When you're ready to use your VPN connection — and you're hooked up to the Internet during your travels — double-click the VPN connection shortcut on your desktop or choose Start⇨Connect To and choose the VPN entry.

Windows XP will prompt you for your username and password via the Connect VPN Client dialog box that you see in Figure 19-9. As always, I'm a bit paranoid about enabling the Save This User Name and Password for the Following Users check box because anyone using your (unattended) computer could simply log on as you. Click the Connect button to begin your VPN session, and you'll find that you can now access all the network resources that you're accustomed to on your office PC. *Now* tell me that technology ain't grand!

Figure 19-9:
Making
the VPN
connection.

Book III

The Internet

The 5th Wave   By Rich Tennant

INTERNET ACCESS
.50¢ - Min.

Book III: The Internet

Chapter 1: Hooking Up with the Right Service

In This Chapter

✔ **Choosing an Internet service provider**

✔ **Deciding between a broadband or dial-up connection**

✔ **Choosing an ISP for hosting a Web site**

*T*his short chapter is for people who want to jump aboard the Internet but haven't chosen an ISP yet. ISP stands for Internet service provider. You will need one of those to surf the Internet and send and receive e-mail. This chapter also gets you up to speed on speedy broadband connections and slower dial-up connections. It also explains how to go about finding a company to host your Web site, in case you want to create a Web site of your own.

Selecting an Internet Service Provider (ISP)

If you intend to surf the Internet, send and receive e-mail, or create a Web site for the Internet, your first task is to choose an Internet service provider (ISP). An ISP is a company that provides customers access to the Internet, e-mail services, and, in some cases, the opportunity to post Web sites. You've probably heard of popular ISPs such as America Online, MSN, and Earthlink. There are some 5,000 ISPs in the United States. How do you choose which one is right for you?

Here are some considerations to make as you choose an ISP:

✦ **What is the monthly service charge?** Monthly service charges range from $15 to $30 for people who use dial-up modems, to $50 or more per month for a fast DSL, cable modem, or T1 connection. (These connections are explained under "Broadband or Dial-Up?" later in the chapter.)

✦ **What is the set-up fee?** Most ISPs charge a one-time set-up or enrollment fee. Depending on how many ISPs are located in your area and how stiff the competition among ISPs is, fees vary from no charge at all to $40.

✦ **Can I dial in without having to call a long-distance number?** If you connect to the Internet by modem, the modem in your computer calls the ISP's computers. If that telephone call is a long-distance call, going on the Internet becomes an expensive proposition because you have to pay long-distance rates each time you go on the Internet. National ISPs such as those run by the major telephone companies offer regional phone numbers that you can call no matter where you travel. If you travel a lot and have to connect a laptop computer to the Internet from various cities and regions, consider signing on with an ISP that offers what are called "points of presence," or simply POPs, the regional telephone numbers you can dial to connect to an ISP.

✦ **How many hours of monthly online time are included in the monthly fee?** Nowadays, most ISPs charge a flat monthly rate to go online for as many hours as you want. Still, find out if the ISP whose services you are considering charges a flat rate or a by-the-hour rate. That way, you will know what to expect from your first bill.

✦ **How much storage space am I allowed for the Web pages I want to post on the Internet?** Some ISPs offer their subscribers the opportunity to post Web sites at no extra charge; others charge an additional fee to subscribers who want to post their Web sites on the Internet. Most ISPs allow from 1 to 2MB to as much as 50MB of file storage space.

✦ **Do you have spam-blocking and virus protection?** Some ISPs have built-in software that screens out spam, the Internet equivalent of junk mail. Some ISPs screen all files for viruses as well. On the face of it, spam-blocking seems like a good deal, but some spam-blocking software is not sophisticated and merely blocks certain kinds of files, such as .exe (executable) files, or files that are larger than a certain number of megabytes. You might legitimately receive these kinds of files from co-workers, in which case spam-blocking is not for you.

✦ **Do you have a length-of-service contract?** Anybody who has a cell phone knows that length-of-service contracts can be a real burden. Under these contracts, you have to sign on for a year. If the service doesn't suit you, you can't quit the service during the first year without paying a fee. If an ISP you are considering requires you to sign a length-of-service contract, make sure you investigate the ISP, especially its billing policies, before you put your name on the dotted line.

✦ **Do you offer technical help?** Typically, ISPs that charge a low monthly rate do not offer very much technical assistance to customers, but even if you go with an expensive ISP, find out how long the company takes to reply to e-mail queries for technical assistance. Find out as well if the ISP maintains a 24-hour telephone line that you can call if you need technical assistance. By the way, queries as to what to do about smoke coming from a modem should be directed to the local fire department, which is obliged to respond faster than an ISP.

Broadband or Dial-Up?

A *broadband connection* is an Internet connection that is always on and is capable of transmitting data very quickly. Broadband services can be delivered over the telephone lines, by way of a private network, by way of a cable modem, or in a wireless network. A *dial-up connection* is one that literally dials a telephone number whenever you connect with the Internet. This type of connection operates over the telephone lines. The only advantage of a dial-up connection over a broadband connection is the cost. At $20 to $25 per month, dial-up service costs half as much as broadband service. The broadband service is much, much faster. In fact, if you've surfed the Internet using a broadband service, it's hard to go back to the slower dial-up method. What's more, you can talk on the telephone while you surf the Internet if you have broadband service. With a dial-up connection, the phone line is occupied, so you can't make a phone call while you're online, nor can anyone call you.

A *modem* (the term stands for modulator/demodulator) is a hardware device for connecting a computer to the Internet. Data transmission rates for Internet connections are measured in megabits per second (Mbps) or kilobits per second (Kbps). Table 1-1 describes the different Internet connections. The first two entries in the table are dial-up connections; the others are broadband.

Table 1-1		Internet Connection Choices
Modem	*Speed*	*Description*
Internal	28.8–56 Kbps	The modem is plugged into the motherboard of the computer. To connect to the Internet, you plug the phone line into a port on the back or side of your computer.
External	28.8–56 Kbps	The modem is attached to your computer through a parallel, serial, or USB port. You plug the modem into your computer and the telephone line into your modem.
ISDN	128 Kbps	Requires installing ISDN adapters in your computer. The connection is made through high-speed digital cables installed by the phone computer or a service provider. ISDN stands for Integrated Services Digital Network.
Cable	1.5 Mbps	This type of modem can be an external or internal modem. Through a cable wall outlet, the computer is connected to the cable TV line.
DSL	6.1 Mbps	This type of modem can also be internal or external. It requires a network adapter. DSL stands for digital subscriber line.

To find out whether a modem is installed on your computer, click the Start button and choose Control Panel. In the Control Panel window, choose Phone and Modem Options. You see the Phone and Modem Options dialog box. On the Modems tab, you see a list of modems installed on your computer. If you connect to the Internet by way of a DSL or ISDN line, no modem will be listed.

Book III
Chapter 1

Hooking Up with
the Right Service

Choosing an ISP to Host Your Web Site

If you decide to take the plunge and create a Web site, you need to choose an ISP to host your site. *Hosting* means to put Web sites on a Web server so that people traveling the Internet can find the Web sites. In order for others to find your Web site, it must be hosted on a Web server.

These days, many ISPs host Web sites for their members. Most of them do it at no extra charge or for a small monthly fee. Call your ISP and pop the question, "Can I post my Web site on your Web server?" If your ISP doesn't host Web sites for its members, or if your Web site is too large or too sophisticated for your ISP's Web server to handle, your next task is to find an ISP that offers Web-hosting services. Some outfits offer Web-hosting for free. What's the catch? Usually, you have to carry an advertisement of some kind on your Web site. Sometimes you meet with narrow restrictions as to how large (in megabytes) your Web site can be. What's more, the Web servers at free sites often work slowly, which causes pages to take longer to download.

Paying the extra money each month to host your Web site with the ISP you now use is the way to go if you can afford it. That way, you spare yourself the hassle of signing up with a new ISP. However, if you've never created a Web site and you want to experiment before you decide whether the Web site thing is for you, sign up with a free service. If you get cold feet, you can abandon your Web site without spending any money.

Table 1-2 describes places you can go on the Internet to find ISPs that offer Web-hosting services. Table 1-3 describes where you can go to investigate ISPs that offer Web-hosting services for *free*. You can find hundreds if not thousands of Web-hosting sites by going to the Web pages listed in Table 1-2 and 1-3.

Table 1-2	Web Sites Where You Can Investigate Hosting Services
Web Site	*Address*
HostFinders.com	www.hostfinders.com
HostIndex.com	www.hostindex.com
SMESource.com	www.smesource.com/Hosting/
The List	www.thelist.com

Table 1-3	Web Sites Where You Can Investigate ISPs that Offer Free Hosting
Web Site	*Address*
Free Homepage.com	www.freehomepage.com
Free Webspace.net	www.freewebspace.net

Chapter 2: Managing Your Online Security

In This Chapter

✔ Keeping viruses from infecting your PC

✔ Making sure your kids use the Internet wisely

Many people forget that when you hook up to the Internet, the Internet also hooks up with you. Your computer is suddenly susceptible to virus infections. Graphic images and strange ideas that might not be welcome in your home suddenly appear there. To make sure you use the Internet safely and wisely, this chapter explains how to prevent your computer from being infected with a virus and how to make sure children get all the advantages of the Internet but not the Internet's disadvantages.

Preventing Viruses from Infecting Your Computer

A computer *virus* is a malignant computer program that infects computers without their owners knowing it. Some viruses simply display a text message; others are more virulent and destroy important computer files. In order to be executed, a virus must ride piggyback on another program or document. These days, the majority of viruses are spread in files that are sent by e-mail, although a number of viruses are still spread on floppy disks that are passed from person to person.

If you trade files on a regular basis with others, you owe it to yourself to get antivirus software. The best are VirusScan (by McAfee) and Norton AntiVirus (from Symantec). Either program does a great job of protecting computers from a virus attack. Figure 2-1 shows Norton AntiVirus at work.

The two most important points about any antivirus program are

✦ **Real-time scanning:** Whatever you run or load, the antivirus program should check it before your PC is exposed. With real-time scanning, you only have to check all the files on your PC once every three months or so instead of once every week.

✦ **Automatic and frequent updates:** Seeing as new viruses are invented every day, no antivirus protection is worth a nickel if it can't be updated. McAfee and Symantec provide at least two updates a month. You can update these programs over the Internet.

If you think your computer has been struck by a virus, visit the Microsoft Virus Assistance Center at office.microsoft.com/assistance/9798/ antivirus.aspx. You will find information there about viruses and virus prevention. Another good Web site for learning about viruses is Computer

Virus Myths at `www.vmyths.com`, where you can read about virus hoaxes and virus hoaxsters. Next time someone sends you a panicky e-mail explaining that you were sent a virus, visit the Computer Virus Myths site to see if the virus is really worth panicking over. So far in my experience (he said knocking on wood), every virus I am supposed to have received turned out to be a hoax.

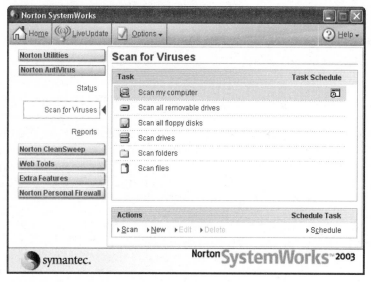

Figure 2-1: I don't fear viruses with Norton AntiVirus on the job.

Maintaining a Kid-Friendly PC

A kid-friendly PC is one that a child or young adult can use to surf the Internet without running into objectionable material. It's no secret that this kind of material is easy to find on the Internet. Pornography, Web sites that espouse violence, and gruesome pictures and images are easy to come by. These pages explain some of the things parents can do to keep their children from finding this stuff.

Supervising kids' access

The best way to keep children from finding objectionable material is to supervise them when they are traveling on the Internet. Put your computer in a common room in the house — in the living room or family room, for example — where you can keep an eye on who is using it. I strongly recommend against letting children keep computers in their bedrooms. Besides giving them the opportunity to get into all kinds of mischief on the Internet, it discourages kids from playing with their friends and developing all the social skills you need for a life that is rewarding and fun.

Using filtering software

Filtering software, also known as *blocking software,* is software that keeps inappropriate material from appearing in a browser window. Here are popular brands of filtering software, along with Web sites where you can learn about the software and even download it:

- **CyberPatrol:** www.cyberpatrol.com
- **Cybersitter:** www.cybersitter.com
- **Net Nanny:** www.netnanny.com
- **SafeSurf:** www.safesurf.com

Some online services have built-in filtering. In America Online, for example, you can click in the keyword box, type **parental control**, and press Enter to find out about filtering.

Screening Web Content with the Content Advisor

Internet Explorer, the browser made by Microsoft, has a feature that prevents (in theory anyway) objectionable material from arriving by way of the Internet. The feature is called the Content Advisor. It works like this: Web site developers rate their Web sites using the four-point scale shown in Table 2-1. Meanwhile, also using the four-point scale, you tell Internet Explorer which Web sites you find objectionable, and those Web sites are not displayed on your computer. The problem with this system is that it relies on Web site developers to install Content Advisor software, rate their Web sites, and rate their Web sites correctly. Not all developers have signed onto the Content Advisor. The ones who have signed on haven't necessarily described their sites accurately on the four-point scale. Still, the Content Advisor is worth a try. Setting it up and using it is quite easy, as I explain here.

Table 2-1		Rating Levels		
Level	*Language*	*Nudity*	*Sex*	*Violence*
0	Inoffensive slang	None	None	None
1	Mild expletives	Revealing attire	Passionate kissing	Fighting
2	Moderate expletives	Partial nudity	Clothed sexual touching	Killing
3	Obscene gestures	Frontal nudity	Nonexplicit sexual touching	Killing with blood and gore
4	Explicit or crude language	Provocative frontal nudity	Explicit sexual activity	Wanton and gratuitous violence

Setting a password and enabling the Content Advisor

To set up the Content Advisor, you have to supply a password, thereby making you its supervisor. If you're very concerned about screening Web content, be sure to provide a password that's hard to guess or crack. To keep your password secure, you should provide one that contains a completely random combination of letters, numbers, and special characters (such as $ and @ signs).

Never lose your password. You need your password to change any of the settings, including setting a new password. Memorize your password or write it down and store it somewhere secure, such as a fire-resistant safe or a safety deposit box at a bank.

Book III
Chapter 2

Managing Your
Online Security

After you decide on your password, follow these steps to get the Content Advisor up and running:

1. **In Internet Explorer, choose Tools⇨Internet Options and click the Content tab.**

You see the dialog box shown in Figure 2-2.

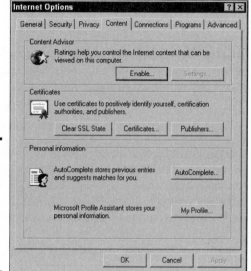

Figure 2-2: Click the Enable button to begin setting up the Content Advisor.

2. **Click the Enable button.**

The first time you attempt to set a password, the Content Advisor dialog box opens and asks you to create a supervisor password. If you have set a password previously and want to change it, skip to the next section, "Changing the Supervisor password."

3. **Click the General tab.**

4. **In the User Options section, select one or both of the following options:**

• **Supervisor Can Type a Password to Allow Users to View Restricted Content:** Select this option if you want the Supervisor password to be used by default.

• **Users Can See Sites That Have No Rating:** If you select this option, the Create Supervisor Password dialog box appears. Enter your password in the Password text box and click OK. This enables the Settings button.

Again, be sure to remember your password. Internet Explorer requires it any time you want to change Content Advisor settings.

5. **Click OK to close the Content Advisor dialog box.**

You can now begin using the Content Advisor with its default settings. If you want to change the Ratings and General options in the Content Advisor dialog box, refer to "Modifying the level of the ratings," later in this chapter.

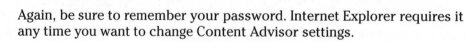

Changing the Supervisor password

If you want to change your Supervisor password, follow these steps:

1. **In Internet Explorer, choose Tools⇨Internet Options and click the Content tab.**

2. **Click the Settings button.**

   The Supervisor Password Required dialog box appears.

3. **Type your existing password in the Supervisor Password Required dialog box and click OK.**

   The Content Advisor dialog box appears.

4. **Click the General tab, and then click the Change Password button to open the Change Supervisor Password dialog box.**

5. **Type your existing password in the Old Password text box, type your new password in the New Password text box, and type your new password again in the Confirm New Password text box.**

6. **Click OK, enter a hint if necessary, and click OK in the dialog box that acknowledges you have changed your password.**

Modifying the level of the ratings

When you first enable the Internet Explorer Content Advisor, the ratings are set to the maximum levels of content screening in all four of the following categories: Violence, Nudity, Sex, and Language. Internet Explorer uses the RSAC (Recreational Software Advisory Council) rating system, which has four levels. Level 0 is the most stringent and Level 4 is the most permissive (refer to Table 2-1).

When you first enable the Content Advisor, all levels are set to the most restrictive (Level 0), by default. To change the level of any of these ratings, follow these steps:

1. **Choose Tools⇨Internet Options; then click the Content tab.**

2. **Click the Settings button, type your password in the Password text box of the Supervisor Password Required dialog box, and then click OK.**

   The Content Advisor dialog box appears, with the Ratings tab displayed. A list box contains the four categories: Language, Nudity, Sex, and Violence.

3. **In the list box of the Content Advisor dialog box, click the category for which you want to set the rating levels.**

4. **Drag the slider control to reset the level for that category.**

5. **Repeat Steps 3 and 4 for each category that you want to reset, and then click the Apply button.**

6. **Click OK when you have made all necessary changes.**

   The Content Advisor dialog box closes, and the new ratings settings are put into effect.

Disabling the Content Advisor

You may want to disable the Content Advisor at some point. (Hey, someday the kids are going to grow up and move away.) Just keep in mind that as soon as you enable the Content Advisor, its Enable button magically turns into a Disable button. To permanently turn off the cyber thought police, click the Content tab of the Internet Options dialog box, and then click the Disable button. Now you're just a password away from disabling the Content Advisor. You can always use the Enable button at a later time if you find the need to use the Content Advisor again. After you have placed a password on the Advisor, you cannot remove it.

CHECK IT OUT

Finding Out Which Web Sites Have Been Visited

In case you want to find out where your children have been surfing on the Internet, here are ways to see lists of recently visited Web sites:

✔ In Internet Explorer, click the History button or press Ctrl+H.

✔ In Netscape Navigator, choose Communicator⇨History or press Ctrl+H.

Chapter 3: America Online

In This Chapter

✓ Installing and signing in to AOL

✓ Reading e-mail and receiving files

✓ Organizing and storing e-mail messages

✓ Sending e-mail and files

✓ Tracking addresses in the Address Book

✓ Surfing the Internet with AOL

America Online (AOL) is an online service for surfing the Internet, sending and receiving e-mail, storing addresses, and doing a few other things besides. The cost of the service is $23.90 (AOL usually offers free service for the first month or two). Chances are if you bought your computer at a big-time electronics store, it comes with the AOL icon on the desktop. Having that icon doesn't mean that you have to subscribe to AOL, but lots of people do. AOL has many fans and many detractors. In general, people who fall on the novice side of computing favor AOL over the hardier, more sophisticated programs for handling the Internet because AOL is easy to use. Starting from one place, you can surf the Internet and trade e-mail messages. AOL's keywords (you'll find out more about them shortly) make it possible to visit Web sites without having to enter cumbersome Web site addresses. This chapter explains how to handle e-mail and surf the Internet with America Online.

Installing AOL

If AOL isn't installed on your computer, you can either install it from a CD or download the program from this address on the Internet: www.aol.com. As part of the installation, you will be asked for a screen name and a password. You will need this name and password each time you log on to AOL.

If you have trouble with the installation or trouble connecting to the Internet with AOL, call 800-827-6364. If you get frustrated and want to cancel the service, call 888-265-8008. You can learn about AOL's cancellation policy by entering the keyword **Cancel** in the Keyword dialog box.

Signing On to AOL

 You must sign on to AOL each time you run the program. To sign on, either double-click the America Online icon on your desktop or click the Start button and choose Programs⇨America Online⇨America Online. You see the Sign On window shown in Figure 3-1. Choose your screen name if you have more than one, enter your password, and click the Sign On button.

Changing and deleting passwords and screen names

AOL makes it easy to change and delete screen names and passwords. (Who doesn't need another Internet personality now and then?) AOL permits you to have as many as seven different screen names. Follow these steps to manage passwords and screen names:

1. **Press Ctrl+K or click the Keyword button on the Quick Start toolbar.**

   The Keywords dialog box appears.

2. **Enter this keyword:** screen names.

3. **Click the Go button.**

   A dialog box for changing and deleting passwords and screen names appears.

4. **Click the appropriate link and answer the questions in the dialog boxes as they appear.**

   Don't worry — this is real simple stuff.

Figure 3-1:
Signing on
to AOL.

A Short Geography Lesson

When you start AOL, you see a window screen like the one in Figure 3-2. I wager that the menu bar and row of buttons along the top of the screen are not foreign to you — they are found in lots of computer programs. From left to right, here are the things that may make the AOL screen seem unusual:

✦ **Quick Start window:** This window is designed to help you do things quickly. It includes buttons found elsewhere in the AOL window. Click its Close button if you don't care to see it. To display it after you have closed it, click the Quick Start button.

✦ **Next and Previous buttons:** Click these buttons to retreat to or go forward to windows either in AOL or on the Internet that you have visited recently.

✦ **URL Address box:** Enter a Web address here and click the Go button to visit a Web site. You can click the down-arrow and select a site from the drop-down list to revisit a site you visited recently.

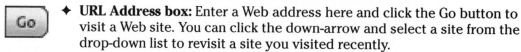
✦ **Search button:** Click the Search button to open a new window and search the Internet.

✦ **Favorites:** Click the Favorites button (or its drop-down arrow) to visit a site you bookmarked because you wanted to visit it again.

Next and Previous buttons   Enter a Web site address   Search the Internet   Favorites

Figure 3-2:
The AOL
screen.

Quick Start window

 When you signed up with AOL, you chose a "Toolset" and "Line Up" for the Welcome screen that appears when you start AOL. If you would like to rethink those choices, click the Change This Screen link in the lower-left corner of the Welcome screen. You will be presented with a series of dialog boxes for constructing a Welcome screen.

Handling Incoming E-Mail

Mark Twain was wrong. He said that nothing is certain except death and taxes. What is just as certain as those inevitabilities is this: Anyone who has an e-mail account will receive ever-increasing amounts of e-mail. Besides reading this mail, the person will have to devise strategies for sorting and organizing it. These topics are covered in the pages that follow.

Reading incoming mail

 When someone sends you e-mail, you hear the words "You've got mail" and a flag rises on the Read button in the upper-left corner of the screen. The number beside this button tells you how many messages are waiting to be read. By moving the pointer over the Read button, you can see a drop-down list with senders' names and message topics. To open your Mailbox and read the mail, click the Read button. You see a Mailbox window similar to the one in Figure 3-3.

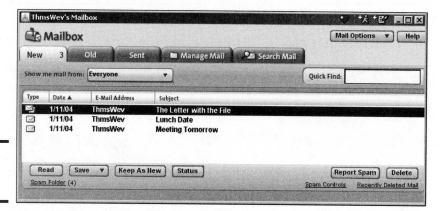

Figure 3-3:
Collecting
the mail.

Here are instructions for reading your mail:

✦ **Reading a message:** Double-click a message or select it and click the
   Read button to open it. The message appears in the Message window, as
   shown in Figure 3-4. After you open a message, it is moved to the Old
   tab. You can read it by opening the Old tab and double-clicking it there
   (click the Keep As New button to move a message from the Old tab back
   to the New tab).

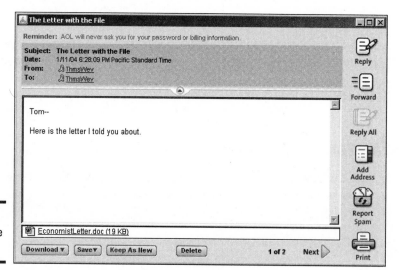

Figure 3-4:
Reading the
mail.

✦ **Deleting a message:** Click the Delete button to remove a message.
   Messages you delete are sent to the Recently Deleted folder. To recover
   a message, open the Recently Deleted folder, select the message, and
   click the Restore button. To open the Recently Deleted folder, open the
   Manage Mail tab and select the folder in the My Mail Folder list.

To find a stray message in the Mailbox window, enter a word you remember
from the message's title or text in the Quick Find box and press the Enter key.

Receiving a file

You can tell when someone has sent you a file because a little page appears behind the standard message icon on the left side of the Mailbox window. The name of the file appears at the bottom of the message window (refer to Figure 3-4).

✦ To download the file now, double-click its name, click Yes when AOL asks if you really want to download it, and select a folder for storing the file in the Download Manager dialog box.

✦ To retrieve the file later on, click the Download button and choose Download Later. When you want to see the file, choose File⇨Download Manager. You see the Download Manager window. Select the file you want to open and click the Finish Download button. You can find the file in your `C:\My Documents` folder.

Managing your e-mail

If you receive e-mail from many different parties, I strongly suggest creating e-mail folders for storing your mail. That way, when you want to find a message from someone, you will know where to find it. Herewith are instructions for creating folders for e-mail and moving e-mail to different folders.

Creating a folder for storing e-mail

To create new folders for e-mail, start by selecting the Manage Mail tab in the Mailbox window. On the left side of this tab is the My Mail Folders list, which lists the folders where your e-mail is stored. Follow these steps to create a new folder:

1. **Click the Saved on My PC folder.**

   All new folders become subfolders of this folder.

2. **Click the Setup Folders button and choose Create Folder.**

   You see the Create New Folder dialog box.

3. **Enter a folder name and click the Save button.**

   Be sure to choose a descriptive name. The name of your new folder appears under the Saved on My PC folder in the folders list.

Moving e-mail messages to different folders

Follow these steps to move an e-mail message to a different folder:

1. **Select the e-mail message.**

2. **Click the Save button and move the pointer over On My PC on the drop-down list.**

   You see a list of folders.

3. **Select the folder you want to move the e-mail to.**

Composing and Sending E-Mail

In order to get invited to parties, you have to issue a few invitations. And in order to get e-mail, you have to send out e-mail. In this section, you will find instructions for composing e-mail messages, replying to or forwarding messages, and sending files.

Writing an e-mail

Follow these steps to compose and send an e-mail message:

1. **Click the Write button or press Ctrl+M.**

   You see the Write Mail window shown in Figure 3-5.

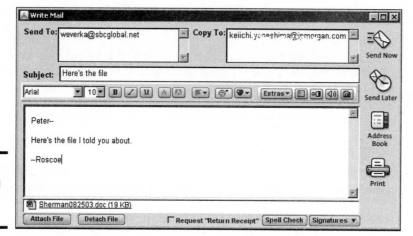

Figure 3-5: Composing an e-mail message.

2. **In the Send To: box, enter the address of the person who is to receive the message.**

   If the address is on file in your Address Book, all you have to do is type the first two or three letters to see a list of e-mail addresses that begin with those two or three letters. Choose a name from the list to enter the whole address.

   To send the same e-mail to more than one person, press Enter to go to the next line of the Send To: box, and enter another address there.

   Enter an address in the Copy To: box if you want to send a copy of the message to someone.

3. **In the Subject: line, enter a descriptive subject for the message.**

4. **Enter the body of the message in the Write box.**

   You can format the message by clicking the Bold or Underline button, for example. However, only people with e-mail software capable of reading formats will see the formatting in your e-mail message.

5. **Click the Send Now button to send the message.**

   Or, to postpone sending it, click the Send Later button. You see the Send Later dialog box. Click the Auto AOL button to schedule a time to send the message. To send the message later on your own, click the Read button to open the Mailbox window. Then click the Manage Mail tab and select the Mail Waiting to Be Sent folder in the My Mail Folders list. Finally, select the message and click the Send button.

Replying to and forwarding messages

Replying to and forwarding messages is a cinch. All you have to do is click the Reply, Forward, or Reply All button in the Message window (refer to Figure 3-4). Immediately, a Write Mail window opens with the sender's e-mail address and subject line already entered. Write a reply or scribble a few words at the top of the forwarded message and click the Send Now or Send Later button.

Sending a file

Follow these steps to send a file to someone else:

1. **Address and compose the message as you normally would.**

2. **Click the Attach File button in the Write Mail window.**

   You will find this button in the lower-left corner of the window. You see the Attached File(s) dialog box.

3. **Select the file or files you want to send and click the Open button.**

   To select more than one file, Ctrl+click the files.

   The name of the file or files you want to send appears on the bottom of the Write Mail window. If you change your mind about sending a file, select it and click the Detach File button.

4. **Click the Send Now or Send Later button.**

Maintaining an Address Book

You can keep street addresses and phone numbers as well as e-mail addresses in the AOL Address Book. Keeping e-mail addresses is worthwhile because you don't have to type an e-mail address to address an e-mail message if the address is listed in the Address Book. AOL fills in addresses from the book automatically.

Choose Mail⇨Address Book to open the Address Book. Here are instructions for doing this, that, and the other thing with addresses:

✦ **Entering a new address:** Click the Add button. You see the Address Card for New Contact dialog box shown in Figure 3-6. Fill in the pertinent information on the different tabs and click the Save button.

✦ **Changing address information:** Select a name and click the Edit button. You see the Address Card for New Contact dialog box. Change the information there and click the Save button.

✦ **Deleting an entry:** Select a name and click the Delete button.

Sending e-mails to groups

Create a group in the Address Book if you need to send the same e-mail to several different people at once. For example, if you're the captain of the softball team, you can compose and address a message about upcoming games to all team members. This spares you the trouble of composing a dozen or more e-mail messages.

Here are instructions for handling group addresses:

✔ **Starting a group:** Click the Add Group button in the Address Book window. You see the Manage Group dialog box. Enter a name for your group. In the Contact List, Ctrl+click to select the names of people you need for the group. Then click the Add button and click Save.

✔ **Changing around the group members:** In the Address Book, group names are shown in boldface text. To change around a group, select its name and click the Edit button. You see the Manage Group dialog box. Select names and click the Add or Remove button to change around the group.

✔ **Sending an e-mail to the group's members:** Select the group in the Address Book, click the Send To button, and choose a sending option on the drop-down list. The Write Mail window appears with the addresses of the group members already entered.

✔ **Deleting a group:** Select the group's name and click the Delete button.

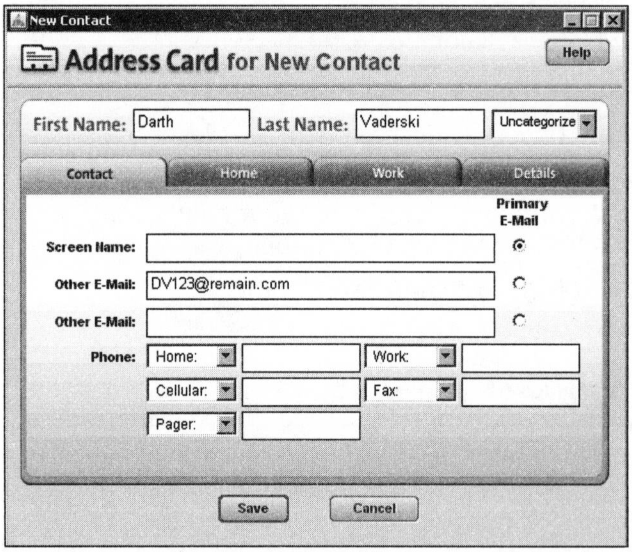

Figure 3-6: Entering an address in the Address Book.

Exploring the Internet in AOL

As well as conventional ways to search the Internet, AOL offers keywords. Instead of typing an unwieldy Web site address, you can enter a keyword. As long as that keyword corresponds to one of AOL's channels, you go to an AOL *channel,* a Web site with many links to the subject in question. For example, entering the keyword "autos" takes you to an AOL-maintained Web site with links to many sites that concern cars.

Exploring the Internet by keyword isn't the big deal it used to be. The Internet is much easier to search and navigate than it was when AOL invented its keyword scheme. AOL subscribers can use Internet Explorer or Netscape Navigator to search the Internet. I recommend doing just that. Those browsers are much easier to use than AOL's, in my opinion.

You, of course, are entitled to your opinion, and to that end, here are instructions for exploring the Internet with AOL:

 ✦ **Entering a keyword:** Click the Keyword button on the Quick Start bar and enter the keyword in the Keywords dialog box, or type the keyword directly into the Web site address box. If the keyword is associated with an AOL channel, you go to the AOL Web site. Choose Keyword⇨ Explore Keywords to see all the AOL keywords.

 ✦ **Surfing the Internet:** Enter an address in the Web site address box and click the Go button.

 ✦ **Searching:** Click the Search button to go to an AOL-maintained site for searching the Internet. (This site is by no means the best place to start an Internet search. Try starting at `www.google.com` instead. Google is the subject of Book III, Chapter 18.)

 ✦ **Bookmarking your favorite Web sites:** When you come across a Web site you want to revisit, bookmark it. Click the Heart button and, in the Favorite Places dialog box, choose Add to Favorites⇨Favorite Places. Next time you want to visit the Web site, click the Favorites button and choose the Web site's name in the Favorites window.

Don't forget to click the Previous or Next button to go backward or forward through Web sites you have visited.

Book III
Chapter 3

America Online

Chapter 4: Browsers and What They Do

In This Chapter

✓ Understanding basic Web concepts

✓ Finding your way around the Web

✓ Using Internet Explorer to navigate the Web

✓ Keeping track of your favorite Web sites

The *World Wide Web* (or *WWW* or just *the Web*) is a system that uses the Internet to link vast quantities of information all over the world. At times, the Web resembles a library, newspaper, bulletin board, and telephone directory — all on a global scale. "The vision I have for the Web," says its inventor, Tim Berners-Lee, "is about anything being potentially connected to anything." Still very much a work in progress, the Web is destined to become the primary repository of human culture.

This chapter explains all you need to know about the basics of the Web and searching the Web. You find out how to launch Internet Explorer, get to know the elements of the screen, and use the browser to begin your travels on the Web. Now boarding Internet Explorer. The next stop in cyberspace is totally up to you!

ABCs of the Web

To start using the World Wide Web, all you need is an Internet connection and a program called a Web browser, such as Internet Explorer or Netscape Navigator. A *Web browser* displays, as individual pages on your computer screen, the various types of information found on the Web and lets you follow the connections — called *hypertext links* — built into Web pages.

Here are some basic Web concepts:

✦ **Hypertext:** A type of electronic document that contains pointers or links to other documents. These links (often called *hyperlinks*) appear in a distinct color or are highlighted when your browser displays the document. When you click a hypertext link, your Web browser displays the document to which the link points, if the document is available.

✦ **Uniform Resource Locator (URL):** The standard format used for hypertext links on the Internet, such as `http://www.microsoft.com`.

✦ **Web site:** A collection of Web pages devoted to a single subject or organization.

✦ **Webmaster:** The person in charge of a Web site.

✦ **Surfing:** The art and vice of bouncing from Web page to Web page in search of whatever.

Ninety-five percent of Web surfers use Internet Explorer, the Web browser that comes with Windows XP.

Web browsers can handle most, but not all, types of information found on the Net. You can add software called plug-ins and ActiveX controls to extend your browser's capabilities.

Uniform Resource Locators (URLs)

One of the key advances that Web technology brought to the Internet is the Uniform Resource Locator, or URL. URLs provide a single, standardized way of describing almost any type of information available in cyberspace. The URL tells you what kind of information it is (such as a Web page or an FTP file), what computer it's stored on, and how to find that computer.

URLs are typically long text strings that consist of three parts:

✦ The document access type followed by a colon and two slashes (`://`)

✦ The host name of the computer on which the information is stored

✦ The path to the file that contains the information

Table 4-1 describes the parts of the following URL:

`http://www.microsoft.com/windows/ie/newuser/default.asp`

Table 4-1	Parts of a URL
Example	*What It Indicates*
`http://`	Indicates a hypertext document (a Web page)
`www.microsoft.com`	Indicates the host computer on which the Web page is stored (www indicates that the site is located on the World Wide Web)
`/windows/ie/newuser/ default.asp`	Indicates the path and filename of the file

Common document access types include the following:

✦ **http:** For hypertext (the Web)

✦ **https:** For hypertext with a secure link

✦ **ftp:** For File Transfer Protocol files

✦ **gopher:** For Gopher files

✦ **mailto:** For e-mail addresses

The following list includes other mysterious things that you see in URLs:

✦ **.html** or **.htm:** The filename extension for a hypertext document; HTML stands for HyperText Markup Language, the set of codes used to build Web pages.

✦ **index.html** or **default.html:** The master page or home page of a Web site (the actual file name depends on the server).

✦ **.txt:** A plain-text document without links or formatting.

✦ **.gif, .jpg, .jpeg, .mpg, .png,** and **.avi:** Pictures, graphics, or video.

✦ **.mp3, .mid (MIDI), .wav, .snd,** and **.au:** Music files. You can even get a Walkman-size unit that accepts and plays these files.

✦ **.zip, .sit, .hqx, .gz, .tar,** and **.z:** Filename extensions for files that have been compressed to save downloading time.

✦ **.class:** A Java applet.

✦ **~george:** As suggested by the tilde (~) character, probably a Unix account belonging to someone with the account name of george.

✦ **www:** Short for World Wide Web.

Finding Your Way around the Web

The Web displays pages of information with hypertext links that take you to other pages. Browsers usually highlight the links to make them easy to spot by using a different color for the item and underlining it. By default, the color of a text hyperlink that you've not yet followed is blue. If you return to a page after clicking hyperlinked text, the hyperlinked text color changes from blue to purple. (As Book III, Chapter 5 explains, you can customize the colors that a Web browser uses to indicate links to pages that you've already visited and links to pages that you have yet to view.)

Some links are just areas you click inside an image or photograph. You can always tell when one of these types of graphics contains a hyperlink and when it doesn't by passing the mouse pointer over the picture. Only graphics with hyperlinks cause your mouse pointer to assume the shape of a pointing hand, as shown in Figure 4-1.

You can bring up a page on your browser in ways other than following a link:

✦ Select a page from your browser's list of bookmarks or favorites.

✦ Type a URL in the address field on your browser's screen and press Enter.

✦ If you have the page stored as a file on a hard drive or CD-ROM on your computer, most browsers let you open it by choosing the File➪Open (or similar) command.

Graphic with hyperlink   Text with hyperlink

Figure 4-1:
Web pages
use both
text
hyperlinks
and
graphics
hyperlinks.

Web page components that appear in your browser can take on other functions, such as the following:

✦ **File items containing text, pictures, movies, or sound:** If your Web browser can handle the file, the browser displays or plays the file. If not, the browser just tells you about the file. If an image or element is missing, the browser displays a broken link icon.

✦ **Search query items that let you type one or more key words:** A Web page displays the results of your search.

✦ **Forms you fill out:** The answers are sent as a long URL when you click Done, Submit, or a similar button on the form.

✦ **Small computer programs called *Java applets:*** You download and run them on your computer.

Getting Started with Internet Explorer

Internet Explorer owes its existence to a single type of document — the *Web page* (also known as an *HTML document*). At first glance, a Web page looks like any other nicely formatted document containing graphics and text. What differentiates a Web page from a regular document? In a Web page, text and graphics elements can be used as hyperlinks. When you click a *hyperlink,* you're transported to another Web page.

Launching Internet Explorer

The Windows desktop includes several doorways to the Internet Explorer browser, as shown in Figure 4-2. Although you could probably hold a contest to find out exactly how many ways Microsoft has provided for starting Internet Explorer, the following three are the most useful:

✦ Double-click the Internet Explorer shortcut on your desktop.

✦ On the Windows taskbar at the bottom of the screen, choose Start⇨All Programs⇨Internet Explorer.

✦ Click the Launch Internet Explorer Browser button on the Quick Launch toolbar located on the taskbar. (If the Quick Launch toolbar is not displayed, right-click the taskbar and choose Toolbars ⇨Quick Launch.)

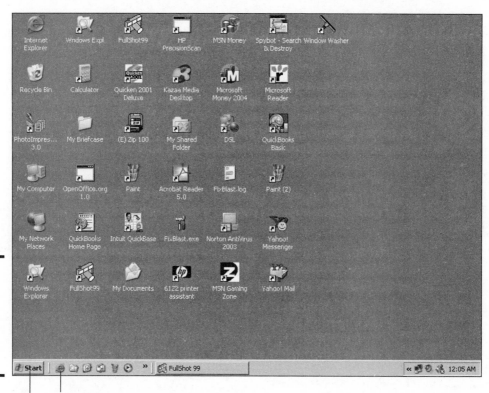

Figure 4-2: You launch Internet Explorer in several different ways.

Launch Internet Explorer browser button

Start button

Book III
Chapter 4

Browsers and
What They Do

Accessing a Web site

After you start Internet Explorer, you can tell it which Web site you want to go to. If you haven't saved the Web site in your Favorites list (see "Keeping Track of Your Favorite Web Sites," later in this chapter), you must type the Web site's URL or choose it from a list of Web sites you've recently viewed.

To access a Web site, follow these steps:

1. **Choose File⇨Open.**

The Open dialog box displays.

2. **In the Open text box, type the URL of the site you want to visit or click the drop-down arrow and select a site from the list.**

3. **Click OK.**

You also can access a Web site by positioning the cursor in the Address box of the Internet Explorer window, typing the URL of the Web site you'd like to go to, and pressing Enter or clicking the Go button.

Elements of the Internet Explorer window

Each of the launch methods covered in the preceding section opens Internet Explorer, as shown in Figure 4-3. Table 4-2 provides a rundown of the various parts of the Internet Explorer screen.

Address bar

Menu bar   Standard buttons toolbar   Links bar

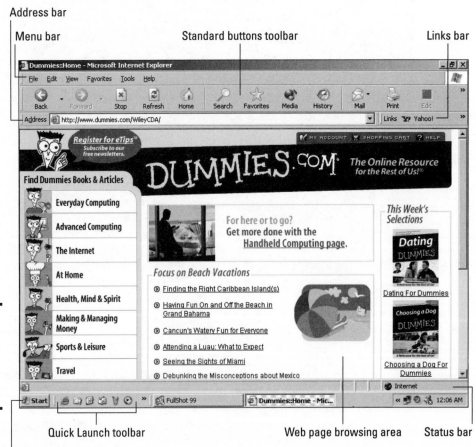

Figure 4-3: The elements of the Internet Explorer window.

Quick Launch toolbar   Web page browsing area   Status bar

Windows taskbar

Table 4-2	Internet Explorer Screen Elements
Part of the Screen	*What It Is*
Address bar	A text box that displays the URL (Web address) of the current Web page, and in which you type the URL that you want to visit. If you click the down arrow on the right of the box, a drop-down list of the addresses you've previously visited appears.
Menu bar	The standard Windows 95/98/XP menu bar with the addition of the Favorites menu.
Standard Buttons toolbar	A set of tools for navigating Web pages and accessing some of the more often used features of Internet Explorer.
Links bar	The choices on the Links bar of the Internet Explorer toolbar contain standard links to various pages on the Microsoft Web site.
Windows taskbar	The standard Windows 95/98/XP taskbar contains the Start button and the Quick Launch toolbar, along with icons for all open programs.
Quick Launch toolbar	A set of tools automatically added to the Windows taskbar when you install Internet Explorer. It provides buttons for launching the browser, minimizing all open windows, viewing channels, and launching Outlook Express.
Web page browsing area	The space where the current Web page actually appears.
Status bar	Provides information on your whereabouts as you travel the Web and also the status of Internet Explorer as it performs its functions.

The Explorer bar

The Explorer bar is a frame that appears on the left side of the Internet Explorer screen when you want to perform a search, work with your Favorites list, or display a history of recently viewed Web pages. Click the Search, Favorites, or History button on the Standard Buttons toolbar to display the Explorer bar and additional options for each of these functions. The contents of the current Web page appear in the area (frame) on the right.

The Explorer bar in Internet Explorer comes in four different flavors:

✦ **Search bar:** The Search bar gives you access to the various search engines that you can use to search the World Wide Web for particular topics. To open the Search bar, click the Search button, choose View⇨Explorer Bar⇨Search, or press Ctrl+E. (See "Searching the Web," later in this chapter.)

✦ **Favorites bar:** The Favorites bar contains links to all the Web pages that you have marked as your favorites. To open the Favorites bar, click the Favorites button, choose View⇨Explorer Bar⇨Favorites, or press Ctrl+I. (See "Viewing pages from the Favorites folder," later in this chapter.)

✦ **Media bar:** The Media bar gives you easy access to buttons that let you play music of your choice, whether it be your favorite radio station or CD. You can also use the rest of the bar to read up on the latest audio and video news.

✦ **History bar:** The History bar gives you access to links of all the Web pages that you've visited in the last 20 days. To open the History bar, click the History button, choose View⇨Explorer Bar⇨History, or press Ctrl+H. (See "Viewing Pages from the History Folder," later in this chapter.)

To remove the Explorer bar from the browsing area when you no longer need access to its links, click the Close button (the X) in the upper-right corner of the Explorer bar.

The toolbars

Internet Explorer includes several varieties of toolbars to help you accomplish tasks quickly. The following list describes these toolbars. (Refer to Figure 4-3 to see where these toolbars are located.)

✦ **Menu bar:** As with all standard Windows menu bars, the Internet Explorer menu bar consists of a group of pull-down menus (File, Edit, View, Favorites, Tools, and Help) that you can click to reveal a list of options and submenus.

✦ **Standard Buttons toolbar:** This toolbar contains the tools that you use most often for navigating and performing tasks, such as the following:

- **Back:** Enables you to return to any Web sites you may have previously visited during your Web session.

- **Forward:** Takes you to any available pages in the History listing.

- **Stop:** Lets you stop a page from loading.

- **Refresh:** Reloads or updates the current Web page.

- **Home:** Displays the Web page you designate as the home page.

- **Search:** Displays or hides the Search Explorer bar.

- **Favorites:** Displays or hides the Favorites Explorer bar.

- **Media:** Displays or hides the Media Explorer bar.

- **History:** Displays or hides the History Explorer bar.

✦ **Address bar:** This bar shows you the URL of the Web page currently displayed in the Internet Explorer browsing area.

As you visit different pages during a Web browsing session, Internet Explorer adds the URL of each site that you visit to the drop-down list attached to the Address bar. To revisit one of the Web pages that you've seen during the session, you can click the drop-down button at the end of the Address box and click its URL or its page icon in the drop-down list.

♦ **Links bar:** This button contains a drop-down list of shortcuts to various Microsoft Web pages — RealPlayer, Customize Links, and various other pages. (If the Links bar is hidden by the Address bar, double-click the word Links to reveal the full Links bar.) You can, however, change the shortcuts listed on the Links bar to reflect the Web pages that you visit most often.

To add a Quick Link button for the Web page that you're currently viewing, drag its Web page icon (the icon that precedes the URL in the Address bar) to the place on the Links bar where you want the Quick Link button to appear. To remove a button from the Links bar, right-click the button and choose Delete from the shortcut menu.

♦ **Discussions bar:** This toolbar appears below the main browsing area when you click the Discuss button on the Standard Buttons toolbar. The Discussions bar contains buttons for taking part in online discussions. You can add your own comments and reply to other people's comments pertaining to the current Web page.

♦ **Quick Launch toolbar:** The Quick Launch toolbar provides one-click access to the Internet Explorer browser and other applications or features. This toolbar, which appears next to the Start button on the Windows taskbar, includes a variety of buttons, depending on the programs you have on your computer.

You can quickly display or hide toolbars by right-clicking the menu bar and selecting the toolbar that you want to display or hide from the shortcut menu. In this shortcut menu, a check mark appears next to toolbars that are currently displayed.

Book III
Chapter 4

Browsers and What They Do

Searching the Web

The World Wide Web holds an enormous wealth of information on almost every subject known to humanity, but you need to know how to get to that information. To help Web surfers like you locate sites containing the information that you're interested in, a number of so-called *search engines* have been designed. Each search engine maintains a slightly different directory of the sites on the World Wide Web (which are mostly maintained and updated by automated programs called *Web crawlers, spiders,* and *robots*).

Starting the search

Internet Explorer gives you access to all the most popular search engines through the Search bar, a special Explorer bar for searching the Web. You can open the Search bar in one of three ways:

♦ Click the Search button on the Standard Buttons toolbar.

♦ Choose View⇨Explorer Bar⇨Search.

♦ Press Ctrl+E.

In this window, you find a text box where you can type a few words to describe the kind of Web page to look for. After you enter the keyword or words (known affectionately as a *search string* in programmers' parlance) to search for in this text box, you begin the search by clicking the Search button.

Internet Explorer then conducts a search for Web sites containing the keywords by using the first search engine (the one listed in the Search bar). If that search engine finds no matches, Internet Explorer then conducts the same search by using the next search engine in its list.

After exhausting the links in the top-ten list, you can display links to the next ten matching pages returned by the search engine by clicking some sort of next button. Note that in some search engines, this button appears as a page number in a list of the next available result pages at the bottom of the Search bar.

After you're convinced that you've seen all the best matches to your search, you can conduct another search with the same search engine by using slightly different terms. You can also switch to another search engine to see what kinds of results it produces by using the same search string.

Limiting your searches

To avoid getting back thousands of irrelevant (or at the very minimum, uninteresting) search results, you need to consider telling the search engines to return links only to sites that contain all the terms you enter in the search string. For example, say that you want to find sites that deal with koi (the ornamental carp that are very popular in Japan) ponds. If you type the search string **koi ponds** in the Find a Web Page Containing text box, the search engines will return links to Web sites with both *koi* and *ponds* (without any reference to the fish) in their descriptions, as well as sites that contain both *koi* and *ponds* in their descriptions. The problem with this approach is that it can give you far too many extraneous results because many search engines search for each term in the search string independently as well as together. It's as though you had asked for Web sites with descriptions containing koi *and/or* ponds.

The easiest way to tell the search engines that you want links to a Web site returned only when *all* the terms in your search string are matched in their descriptions is to enclose all the terms in double quotation marks. In the case of the *koi ponds* search string, you can find more Web sites that deal only with koi ponds (as opposed to frog ponds or other ponds containing just garden plants), by typing **"koi ponds"** in the Find a Web Page Containing text box. Taking this little extra step often brings you fewer, but more useful, results.

Browsing in full screen mode

One of the biggest drawbacks of Web surfing is the amount of scrolling that you have to do to see all the information on a particular Web page. To help minimize the amount of scrolling, Internet Explorer offers a full screen mode that automatically minimizes the space normally occupied by the menu bar, Standard Buttons toolbar, Address bar, and Links bar. In full screen mode, only a version of the Standard Buttons toolbar with small buttons is displayed at the top of the screen, as shown in Figure 4-4.

Figure 4-4:
Press F11 to enter full screen mode and see more of a Web page.

To switch to full screen mode, press F11 or choose View➪Full Screen. To get out of full screen mode and return to the normal view, press F11 again.

Displaying Previously Viewed Web Pages

As you browse different Web sites, Internet Explorer keeps track of your progression through their pages. You can then use the Back and Forward buttons on the toolbar, or the equivalent commands on the View➪Go To submenu, to move back and forth between the pages that you've visited in the current work session.

If you use the Back and Forward buttons on the Standard Buttons toolbar, you get the added benefit of being able to tell in advance which page will be redisplayed when you click the button. Simply position the mouse pointer on the Back or Forward button and hover it there until the title of the Web page appears in a little ToolTip box.

Both the Back and Forward buttons have drop-down lists attached to them. When you display these drop-down lists (by clicking the drop-down arrow to the immediate right of the Back or Forward button), they show a list, in most-recent to least-recent order, of the nine most recent Web pages visited in the work session before (Back) or after (Forward) the current Web page. By using the drop-down list attached to the Back button, you can avoid having to click Back, Back, Back, Back, and so on, to revisit a page that you saw some time ago during the current Web surfing session.

Keeping Track of Your Favorite Web Sites

As you browse the Web with Internet Explorer, you may come across interesting Web sites that you want to revisit later. To make finding a site again easy, you can recall its home page (or any of its other pages) by placing a reference to the page in the Internet Explorer Favorites folder. You can then revisit the page by selecting its title from the Favorites pull-down menu or from the Favorites bar. (See "Viewing pages from the Favorites folder," later in this chapter.)

Adding Web pages to your Favorites folder

To add a Web page to the Favorites folder, follow these steps:

1. **Go to the Web page that you want to add to your Favorites.**

2. **Choose Favorites⇨Add To Favorites.**

   The Add Favorite dialog box opens. The name of the Web page displayed in the title bar of the Internet Explorer browser window also appears in the Name text box.

3. **(Optional) You can edit the Web page title that appears in the Name text box.**

   Keep in mind that this text is listed on the Favorites menu, so you want to make it as descriptive as possible, while, at the same time, keeping it brief.

4. **(Optional) To make the Web page that you're adding to your Favorites available for offline browsing, select the Make Available Offline check box.**

5. **(Optional) To add the favorite to a subfolder of Favorites, click the Create In button to expand the Add Favorite dialog box (if the files and folders aren't already displayed in the list box); then click the icon of the appropriate subfolder (see Figure 4-5) or click the New Folder button to create a new folder in which to add your new favorite.**

6. **Click OK to add the Web page to your Favorites.**

   If you clicked the Make Available Offline check box in Step 4, a synchronization box appears and automatically configures your settings. You're all done!

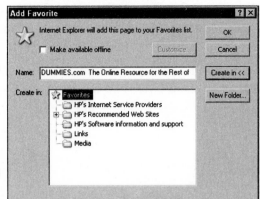

Figure 4-5:
You can
specify the
folder
where you
want to add
your favorite
pages.

Viewing pages from the Favorites folder

The Favorites folder contains hyperlinks to all the Web pages that you've marked during your cyberspace travels on the World Wide Web, as well as all the channels and local folders and files on which you rely. From the Favorites list, you can open Web pages that you want to revisit, go to a channel home page, or open a favorite file with its native application (such as Word 2003 if it's a Word document, or Excel 2003 if it's an Excel workbook).

To display the links in your Favorites folder, you can select the links directly from the Favorites pull-down menu, click the Favorites button on the Standard Buttons toolbar, or press Ctrl+I. When you click the Favorites button or press Ctrl+I, Internet Explorer presents the subfolders and links of your Favorites folder in the Favorites bar (a frame on the left side of the screen). The current Web page appears in a frame on the right.

To display the links in one of the Favorites subfolders, click the folder icon containing the link in the Favorites bar. Then click the desired hyperlink to display a Web page (if it's a Web hyperlink), a list of folders and files (if it's a link to a local disk), or to open a document in its own program (if it's a link to a particular file).

Organizing your favorites

The Organize Favorites dialog box, shown in Figure 4-6 (which you open by choosing Favorites➪Organize Favorites), lets you arrange the links in your Favorites folder (see "Adding Web pages to your Favorites folder," earlier in this chapter), as well as those in your Channels and Links folders.

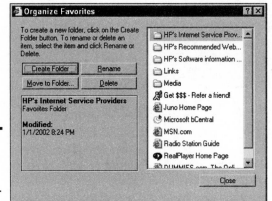

Figure 4-6:
Arrange
your links in
your folders.

Organizing your favorites and links into folders

One of the best methods for organizing favorites is to group them together into folders, maybe even using subfolders within those folders. After you have a folder structure, you can then move the links to your favorite pages into the appropriate folders, renaming them if you so choose.

Use the following options in the Organize Favorites dialog box to group the links in your Favorites and Links folders:

✦ To create a new folder, click the Create Folder button, type a new name for the folder icon, and press Enter.

✦ To move a link to a favorite page, click its icon to highlight it, and then click the Move to Folder button to open the Browse for Folder dialog box. Click the destination folder in the Browse for Folder dialog box and click OK.

✦ To rename a link to a favorite page, click its icon to select it, and then click the Rename button. Edit the description and press Enter.

✦ To delete a link to a favorite page, click its icon, and then click the Delete button. Then click Yes to confirm the deletion.

Don't delete or rename the Links folder in the Organize Favorites dialog box. Internet Explorer needs the Links folder so that it knows what buttons to display on the Links bar.

Organizing your favorites, channels, and links with drag-and-drop

You can also use the drag-and-drop method to reorganize the links to your Favorites and Links folders from the Favorites Explorer bar in Internet Explorer. Click the Favorites button on the Standard Buttons toolbar and perform one of the following actions:

✦ To open a folder to display the folder's contents, click its folder icon in the Favorites bar. Internet Explorer then shows a series of icons for each of the links that it contains. To close a folder and hide its contents, click the folder icon again.

✦ To move an icon to a new position in its folder, drag its icon up or down until you reach the desired position. As you drag, Internet Explorer shows you where the item will be inserted by displaying a heavy horizontal I-beam. The program also shows you where you can't move the icon by displaying the International No symbol.

✦ To move an icon to another (existing) folder, drag its icon to the folder icon. When the folder becomes highlighted, you can drop the icon and it goes into the highlighted folder.

Viewing Pages from the History Folder

The History folder contains a list of links to the Web pages that you visited within the last 20 days (unless you've changed this default setting). These hyperlinks are arranged chronologically from least recent to most recent, grouped by days for the current week, and then by weeks for all days further back.

 To display the links in your History folder, click the History button on the Standard Buttons toolbar or press Ctrl+H. Internet Explorer shows the folders for each Web site that you visited on a particular day or during a particular week in the History bar (a pane on the left side of the screen). The current Web page appears in a pane on the right.

To revisit a Web page in the History folder, click the Web site's folder icon in the History bar to display the links to its pages; then click the hyperlink for the particular page that you want to go to (see Figure 4-7).

Book III Chapter 4

Browsers and What They Do

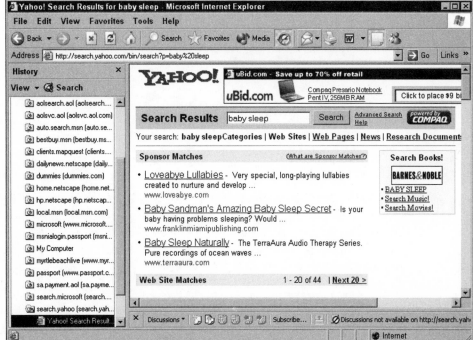

Figure 4-7: Use the History folder to quickly locate sites that you've recently visited.

Using Important Internet Explorer Keyboard Shortcuts

Here are three timesaving key combinations that every IE user should know:

✔ **Ctrl+Enter:** If you type the middle part of an address in the Address bar — say, `wiley` — and then press Ctrl+Enter, IE immediately puts an `http://www.` on the front, and a `.com` on the back. Type **wiley** and press Ctrl+Enter, and IE immediately knows to look for `http://www.wiley.com`.

✔ **Ctrl+F5:** If you think that the Web page is "stuck" — it isn't being updated properly, perhaps because it's been put in the cache on your PC — pressing Ctrl+F5 forces Internet Explorer to go out and get the latest copy of the current page. In theory, the browser even blasts past copies that are cached with your Internet service provider (which can be a real headache if your ISP is slow to update cached pages).

✔ **Shift+click:** When you click a link, sometimes the new page replaces the old window; sometimes the old window stays around and the new one appears in a window of its own. Usually, the person who designs a Web page decides what happens, but you can take over. To force IE to open a Web page in a new window, hold down Shift while you click the link.

Put a sticky note on your monitor with those three key combinations until they become ingrained in your fingers' little gray cells.

Chapter 5: Customizing Your Browser Settings

In This Chapter

✔ Choosing a home page

✔ Adding Active Channels and Active Desktop Items

✔ Working with the cache of Temporary Internet Files

✔ Adjusting History settings

✔ Speeding up your browser

✔ Synchronizing Web pages for offline viewing

✔ Using AutoComplete

*I*n preparation for your extensive travels on the World Wide Web via Internet Explorer, you may need to make some minor adjustments. This chapter is the place to look for information on everything from how to change the way Web pages are displayed on your screen to ways to tweak your browser's performance. This chapter also provides information about adding Active Desktop Items so that the latest and greatest Web information automatically finds its way from cyberspace to your computer desktop, with no World Wide Wait.

Changing Your Home Page

Each time you start the Internet Explorer browser, it opens a specially designated page, which it calls the home page. The home page is also where Internet Explorer goes when you click the Home button on the toolbar.

If your computer isn't connected to the Internet when you click Home, Internet Explorer loads the home page locally from the cache. The *cache* is an area of a computer's hard drive used to store data recently downloaded from the Internet so that the data can be redisplayed quickly. If the page doesn't happen to be in the cache at the time (because you deleted its files before quitting the browser the last time), Internet Explorer gives you an error message and displays an empty Web page called about:blank. To return to your home page, you must go online again and click the Home button.

To change the home page on your computer, follow these steps:

1. **Launch the Internet Explorer browser and go to the Web page that you want to make the new home page.**

2. **Choose Tools⇨Internet Options.**

   The Internet Options dialog box appears. Click the General tab if it isn't already selected.

3. In the Home Page section of the dialog box, click the Use Current button to make the current page your new home page.

You can also type the URL of the page that you want to designate as your home page in the Address text box.

4. Click OK to close the Internet Options dialog box.

After you designate the page of your choice as your home page, you can return that page at anytime by clicking the Home button.

If, for the sake of speed, you want a blank Web page to be used as the home page, click the Use Blank button. Internet Explorer then enters `about:blank` (the name of its standard blank page) in the Address text box. You also can click the Stop button on the navigation bar as soon as Internet Explorer starts loading the page.

Changing the Way Web Pages Look

A Web page, depending on the computer displaying it, can appear in a variety of fonts and colors and can use various characters and symbols for different languages of the world. The combination of the Web browser settings and the design of the individual pages controls how Web pages look in Internet Explorer.

The changes that you make to the Internet Explorer settings only affect the way Web pages look on your screen. You don't have to worry that you're actually changing somebody's Web page.

Changing the text size

You can customize your copy of Internet Explorer so that you get larger, easier-to-read text, or you can choose a smaller font size that lets you see more text at a time on the screen. To change the display size of text in Web pages, follow these steps:

1. Choose View⇨Text Size.

A submenu appears with the following size options: Largest, Larger, Medium, Smaller, and Smallest. The Largest, Larger, Smaller, and Smallest font sizes are all relative to the Medium font size (which is the default size used by Internet Explorer).

2. Choose the Largest or Larger option to make the text on the current Web page appear bigger. Choose the Smaller or Smallest option to make the text appear smaller.

Selecting a different font

Many Web pages do not specify a font for the proportional and fixed-width (or monospaced) text on the Web page, leaving that determination to Internet Explorer. When you first start browsing the Web with Internet

Explorer, it uses Times New Roman to render nonspecifically defined proportional text and Courier New for all fixed-width text. If you prefer other fonts for rendering the proportional and fixed-width text, you can modify one of the Internet Explorer character sets (different styles of the alphabet and other symbols).

To choose other fonts, follow these steps:

1. **Choose Tools⇨Internet Options.**

The Internet Options dialog box appears. Click the General tab if it isn't already selected.

2. **Click the Fonts button.**

The Fonts dialog box opens, as shown in Figure 5-1.

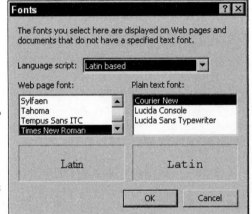

Figure 5-1:
You can change the default fonts via the Fonts dialog box.

3. **To change the font used to render proportional text, choose a font in the Web Page Font list box.**

Your particular choices depend upon which fonts you have installed on the computer.

4. **To change the font used to render fixed-width text, choose a font in the Plain Text Font list box.**

5. **Click OK twice to close the Fonts dialog box and the Internet Options dialog box.**

Changing the text and background colors

If you have problems reading the text on a Web page due to its text color and background, you may be able to modify these colors (assuming that the Web page author hasn't specified his or her own colors). By default, Internet Explorer chooses black for the text color and battleship gray for the background (page) color. To set custom colors for your Web page background and text, follow these steps:

1. **Choose Tools➪Internet Options.**

The Internet Options dialog box appears. Click the General tab if it isn't already selected.

2. **Click the Colors button.**

The Colors dialog box appears, as shown in Figure 5-2. In this dialog box, you can set colors for the text and background as well as the colors for visited and unvisited hyperlinks.

3. **In the Colors section of the Colors dialog box, deselect the Use Windows Colors check box.**

Deselecting this check box enables you to specify your own colors.

4. **To change the text color, click the Text button in the Colors dialog box to open the Color dialog box, and then select a new color from the Basic Colors palette. Then click OK.**

Figure 5-2: You can change the color of Web page text and the background color.

5. **To change the background color of the page, click the Background button in the Colors dialog box to open the Color dialog box, and then select a new color from the Basic Colors palette. Then click OK.**

6. **When you finish setting the text and background colors that you want to use, click OK twice to close the Colors dialog box and the Internet Options dialog box.**

When the Internet Options dialog box closes, Internet Explorer displays the current Web page in the text and background colors that you selected. If it doesn't, this means that the author of this Web page has explicitly set a style for the page, which takes precedence over the browser default settings that you set.

Changing the way your browser displays hyperlinks

Hypertext links (*hyperlinks*) are a special form of text that, when clicked, take you to a new location on the current page or to another page altogether. Traditionally, blue underlined text on-screen indicates the hypertext links that you haven't yet followed. When you follow a hypertext link and later return to the original page, Internet Explorer lets you know that you've followed the link by displaying the same hyperlink in purple underlined text. People often refer to these links as *unvisited* and *visited* links. To modify the color of hypertext links in Internet Explorer, follow these steps:

1. **Choose Tools⇨Internet Options.**

The Internet Options dialog box appears. Click the General tab if it isn't already selected.

2. **Click the Colors button.**

The Colors dialog box appears.

3. **To change the color for visited hyperlinks, click the Visited button and choose a new color from the palette in the Color dialog box. Click OK to close the Color dialog box.**

4. **To change the color for unvisited hyperlinks, click the Unvisited button and choose a new color from the palette in the Color dialog box. Click OK to close the Color dialog box.**

In addition to customizing the visited and unvisited hypertext colors, you can choose to assign a *hover* color (that is, the color that hyper-linked text becomes when you position your mouse pointer over it).

5. **To have text hyperlinks turn a special color whenever your mouse pointer hovers above them, select the Use Hover Color check box.**

If you don't like the default color of red, click the Hover button and choose a new color from the palette in the Color dialog box. Click OK to close the Color dialog box.

6. **When you're finished changing the link colors, click OK twice to close the Colors dialog box and the Internet Options dialog box.**

Customizing Toolbars

Internet Explorer contains several toolbars, which you can customize to your liking. You can change the display size of toolbars, hide toolbars, and add buttons to toolbars. Refer to Book III, Chapter 4 if you need a refresher on the toolbars included with Internet Explorer.

Changing the size of toolbars

You can minimize the amount of space that the toolbar takes up by putting Internet Explorer in full-screen view. To do so, choose View⇨Full Screen or press F11. The full-screen view shrinks the amount of space given to the toolbars — Internet Explorer hides all the toolbars except the Standard Buttons toolbar, which now uses smaller icons.

When Internet Explorer is in full-screen mode, the browser adds an Auto-Hide command to the shortcut menu that appears when you right-click the remaining Standard Buttons toolbar. Selecting the Auto-Hide command causes the entire toolbar to slide up until it's off the screen. To redisplay the toolbar, move the mouse pointer up to the top of the Internet Explorer window. When the mouse pointer rolls over the area where the toolbar would normally be, the toolbar magically (and temporarily) reappears.

To again fix the Standard Buttons toolbar on the screen, choose the Auto-Hide command from the toolbar's shortcut menu. You can also take Internet Explorer out of full-screen mode by pressing F11.

Hiding and unhiding a toolbar

You can hide the Standard Buttons toolbar, the Address bar, or the Links bar. To do so, choose View⇨Toolbars. From the submenu that appears, click to remove the check mark next to the toolbar that you want to hide. You can also right-click any empty area of the toolbar and choose the appropriate name (Standard Buttons, Address bar, or Links) from the toolbar shortcut menu. To display the hidden toolbar again, reverse this procedure.

Adding a button to the toolbar

You can add a button to the Standard Buttons toolbar to make the button's command more accessible. Follow these steps:

1. **Choose View⇨Toolbars⇨Customize or right-click the Standard Buttons toolbar and choose Customize from the shortcut menu.**

   The Customize Toolbar dialog box appears.

2. **In the Available Toolbar Buttons list box, click the button you want to add to the toolbar, and then click Add.**

   Internet Explorer adds the button to the end of the list in the Current Toolbar Buttons list box.

3. **(Optional) To change the position of the newly added button on the toolbar, click the button in the Current Toolbar Buttons list box; then click the Move Up button one or more times.**

4. **Click the Close button to close the Customize Toolbar dialog box.**

Active Channels and Active Desktop Items

Active Channels (also known simply as *channels*) are Web sites that use a technology called *Webcasting*. This technology makes it possible for Internet Explorer to automatically download updated content from the Active Channel's Web site to your computer's *cache* (temporary storage area) on a regular schedule. This enables you to browse the new content even when you're not connected to the Internet (known as *offline viewing*).

Many channels offer a more condensed experience of their online information, known as Active Desktop Items. *Active Desktop Items* are World Wide Web components that appear directly on your Windows desktop and give you immediate access to the information that you want to see without having to browse through Web page after Web page. Active Desktop Items often give you instant access to highlights or headlines of the Web site, which you can click to open into full-screen Web pages.

Adding Active Channels or Active Desktop Items

After initially installing Internet Explorer, you have access to only one Active Desktop Item — the Internet Explorer Channel bar. The Internet Explorer Channel bar provides an easy way to access the Active Channels that you add to your computer as well as to sign up for new channels.

To display this built-in Active Desktop Item, you need to right-click the desktop and choose Active Desktop⇨Show Web Content from the shortcut menu. Of course, if you decide that you want more Active Desktop goodies adorning your desktop, you have to go and get them.

To add additional Active Desktop Items and channels, you need to go online and install them from the Windows Active Desktop Gallery Web page. To connect to this page, follow these steps:

1. **Right-click the desktop.**

   A shortcut menu appears.

2. **Choose Active Desktop⇨Customize My Desktop.**

   The Display Properties dialog box appears with the Web tab selected.

3. **Click the New button to open the New Active Desktop Item dialog box. If the New button is not available (grayed out), select the Show Web Content on My Active Desktop check box, and then click the New button.**

4. **Click Visit Gallery in the New Active Desktop Item dialog box to close both the New Active Desktop Item and the Display Properties dialog boxes.**

   This launches Internet Explorer and opens the Windows Active Desktop Gallery Web page.

5. **Find the specific Active Desktop Item or channel that you want to add, and then click the Add to Active Desktop button.**

6. **Click Yes in the Internet Explorer dialog box to confirm that you want to add the selected Active Desktop Item to your desktop.**

   The Add Item to Active Desktop dialog box appears, listing the name of the item you selected in Step 5.

7. **Click OK to confirm the selected channel.**

   After you click OK, a Downloading dialog box appears, keeping you apprised of the download progress of the Active Channel or Desktop Item that you selected.

If you download a new Active Desktop Item, you need to return to the desktop to check out your new toy. Click the Close box in the title bar of the Internet Explorer window to return to the desktop. If you don't see your new Active Desktop Item right away, right-click the desktop to display the shortcut menu and choose the Refresh command.

Viewing channels with the Channels folder

You can easily display the content of the channels that you add by opening the Favorites Explorer bar in the browser (by clicking the Favorites button on the Standard Buttons toolbar) and clicking the Channels folder icon.

The default channels in the Channels folder are arranged into the following categories (you may see additional channels, depending on your setup):

✦ Microsoft Channel Guide

✦ News and Technology

✦ Sports

✦ Business

✦ Entertainment

✦ Lifestyle and Travel

If you add a channel to a particular category, click its name in the Favorites Explorer bar. When you see the name of the channel whose contents you want to view, click its hyperlink in the Favorites Explorer bar. The channel's opening page then appears in the right frame of Internet Explorer, and hyperlinks to linked channel pages appear in the Favorites Explorer bar (the frame on the left side of Internet Explorer).

To update the contents of the channel that you want to view, right-click the channel's hyperlink and click the Refresh command on the shortcut menu.

Removing an Active Channel or Active Desktop Item

If you decide that you want to remove a channel and its contents from your computer, you can do so via the Favorites Explorer bar. To delete an Active Desktop Item, follow these steps:

1. **Right-click your desktop and choose Active Desktop⇨Customize My Desktop from the shortcut menu.**

The Display Properties dialog box appears.

2. **Click the Web tab, if it isn't already selected.**

3. **Click the item that you want to delete in the View My Active Desktop as a Web page list box and click the Delete button.**

The Active Desktop Item dialog box appears.

4. **Click Yes to confirm that you want to delete this item.**

5. **Click OK to close the Display Properties dialog box.**

Changing the History Settings

When you come across a wonderful Web page, you can save the page to your Favorites list or create a shortcut to the page to make returning there easy (see Book III, Chapter 4 for more details). However, if you forgot to save a Web page to your Favorites list at the time it was displayed in the Internet Explorer browsing window, you can still get back to it by finding its link in the History folder.

By default, the Internet Explorer History folder retains links to the pages that you visited during the last 20 days. But you may want to change the length of time that links remain in your History folder. For example, you can increase the time so that you have access to Web pages visited in the more distant past, or you can decrease the time if you're short on hard drive space. You can also purge the links in the History folder to free up space on your hard drive and restore all hyperlinks to pages that you've visited to their unvisited state (and colors).

To change the History settings, follow these steps:

1. **Choose Tools⇨Internet Options.**

The Internet Options dialog box appears. Click the General tab if it isn't already selected.

2. **In the History section, type a new value in the Days to Keep Pages in History text box or click the up or down arrows to select the desired value.**

3. **Click OK.**

To purge the links in the History folder, follow these steps:

1. **Choose Tools⇨Internet Options.**

The Internet Options dialog box appears. Click the General tab if it isn't already selected.

2. **Click the Clear History button.**

3. **Click OK in the Internet Options alert box that appears, which asks if you want to delete all items from your History folder.**

4. **Click OK to close the Internet Options dialog box.**

Specifying Mail, News, and Internet Call Programs

Internet Explorer can work with other programs to add to its functionality and capabilities. Microsoft has created certain programs that it intends to work so closely with Internet Explorer that it refers to them as *members of the Internet Explorer Suite*.

The auxiliary programs that are included with Internet Explorer as part of the suite depend upon which type of installation you perform:

✦ **Custom:** This installation lets you select which auxiliary programs are installed along with the browser and Outlook Express.

✦ **Minimal:** This installation gives you the Microsoft Internet Connection Wizard along with Internet Explorer.

✦ **Typical:** This installation includes the browser plus Outlook Express, Windows Media Player, and a few multimedia enhancements.

One of the most practical of these many auxiliary programs is Microsoft Outlook Express, which adds e-mail and news-reading capabilities to Internet Explorer. If you do the typical installation and your computer is equipped with sound and video hardware, such as a microphone and video camera, you can use NetMeeting to make Internet calls or set up video conferencing. Even if you don't have such hardware, you can use Chat (originally known as Comic Chat) as part of NetMeeting to participate in online chat sessions.

To see which programs are configured to run from Internet Explorer (such as the Mail, News, and Internet call programs) and, if necessary, change them, follow these steps:

1. **Choose Tools⇨Internet Options; then click the Programs tab (see Figure 5-3).**

2. **To change the program listed in the HTML Editor, E-Mail, Newsgroups, Internet Call, Calendar, or Contact List text boxes, select a new program by using the drop-down list boxes.**

3. **After you finish checking over the programs and making any changes to them, click OK.**

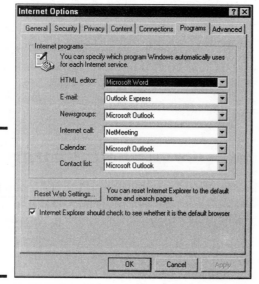

Figure 5-3: Use the Programs tab to view or select programs used with Internet Explorer.

If you have installed another Web browser, such as Netscape Navigator, after installing Internet Explorer, you can click the Reset Web Settings button in this dialog box to restore your original Internet Explorer default settings for search pages and your home page. Clicking this button also restores the prompt to ask you whether you want to make Internet Explorer your default browser each time you launch Microsoft's browser.

Speeding Up the Display of Web Pages

You can speed up the display of Web pages on your computer, but unless you do it by getting a faster connection (with a modem upgrade, a DSL or ISDN line, or a cable modem), the increase in speed comes at the expense of hard drive space or viewing content. You can also dramatically speed up the display of Web pages by turning off the display of most pictures, animations, videos, and sounds. To make this kind of change to Internet Explorer, follow these steps:

1. **Choose Tools⇨Internet Options; then click the Advanced tab.**

2. **In the Multimedia section of the Settings list box, deselect the check boxes of as many of the items as you want to disable to get a sufficient speed boost.**

   These items include Play Videos, Play Sounds, Smart Image Dithering, Show Pictures, and Play Animations.

3. **Click OK to add the new settings and close the Internet Options dialog box.**

Now when you open new Web pages, weird (but fast) generic icons replace the multimedia contents that you've disabled. If you still see graphics on the Web pages that you visit, click the Refresh button on the Internet Explorer toolbar to remove their display.

After disabling the Show Pictures and Play Videos settings, you can still choose to display a particular graphic or play a particular video. Just right-click the icon placeholder and choose Show Picture from its shortcut menu. Internet Explorer then downloads and displays the particular graphic or video that you selected.

To restore the multimedia items that you disabled, click the Advanced tab of the Internet Options dialog box again and click the check boxes to select the desired Multimedia items. Then click OK to save your changes and close the Internet Options dialog box. Remember that you have to use the Refresh button on the Internet Explorer toolbar to see and hear multimedia items on pages that were downloaded to the cache when these items were disabled.

Synchronizing Offline Web Pages

To make sure that you have the most current data from an Active Channel or a Favorites Web site that you've made available for browsing offline, you may want to update the contents of your cache — a process known as *synchronization*. To synchronize individual Active Channels or favorite Web sites, follow these steps:

1. **Choose Tools⇨Synchronize.**

   The Items to Synchronize dialog box appears.

2. **In the Select the Check Box for Any Items You Want to Synchronize list box, make sure that the check box for each offline Web page you want updated is selected. Deselect the check box of any offline Web page you don't want updated.**

3. **Click the Synchronize button.**

Internet Explorer then connects you to the Internet and begins the process of checking each selected offline Web page for updated content, which is then automatically downloaded into your computer's cache. Synchronizing enables you to browse the updated contents (using the Favorites Explorer bar) when you're not connected to the Internet.

If you connect to the Internet over a LAN (local area network) or via a cable modem, DSL, or ISDN connection (you can therefore go online at anytime), you may want to specify when and under what conditions particular offline Web pages are synchronized. To do this, choose Tools⇨Synchronize. Then with the Offline Web Pages folder selected, click the Setup button. When you click this button, Internet Explorer opens the Synchronization Settings dialog box.

The Synchronization Settings dialog box contains three tabs: Logon, On Idle, and Scheduled:

✦ **Logon tab:** Use this tab to select the offline pages that you want synchronized whenever you log onto a networked computer. Select the check boxes for the offline pages to be synchronized when you log onto your computer; then select the When I Log On to My Computer check box.

✦ **On Idle tab:** Use this tab to select the offline pages that you want synchronized whenever your computer is idle for a particular period of time. Select the check boxes for the offline pages to be synchronized when your computer is idle for a particular period, and then select the Synchronize the Selected Items When My Computer Is Idle check box. To specify how long an idle period to use, click the Advanced button and change the settings in the Idle Settings dialog box.

✦ **Scheduled tab:** Use this tab to set up a custom schedule by which selected offline pages are routinely synchronized. To create a new schedule to be used, click the Add button and use the Scheduled Synchronization Wizard to take you through the steps of creating and naming a new custom schedule for certain offline Web pages. To edit the settings for a particular default schedule, click the name of the schedule (such as CNN Desktop Scores Recommended Schedule); then click the Edit button to open a dialog box in which you can modify the current settings (the name of the dialog box and its tabs and options vary depending on the particular synchronization schedule that you're editing).

Customizing Your AutoComplete Settings

The AutoComplete feature makes it easier to fill out addresses, forms, and passwords by providing a drop-down list of suggestions as you type, based on your previous entries. Internet Explorer has added the capability to customize the AutoComplete settings. To customize your AutoComplete settings, follow these steps:

1. **Choose Tools⇨Internet Options and click the Content tab.**

2. **Click the AutoComplete button.**

   The AutoComplete Settings dialog box appears.

3. **Select the check boxes for the items for which you want to use AutoComplete.**

   Select the Web Addresses check box to have AutoComplete suggest URLs for previously visited Web pages. Select the Forms check box if you want AutoComplete to match the field values from the most recently submitted form. Select User Names and Passwords on Forms if you want AutoComplete to retain your user ID and password for sites that require them.

4. **(Optional) To delete the form information that AutoComplete retains, click the Clear Forms button. To delete the list of user IDs and passwords that AutoComplete retains, click the Clear Passwords button.**

   To delete the list of Web addresses that AutoComplete keeps on file, you must click the Clear History button on the General tab of the Internet Options dialog box.

5. **Click OK twice to close both dialog boxes.**

CHECK IT OUT

Stopping Script Debugging

How many times have you run across a pop-up message that asks whether you want to debug a Web page? Debugging is one of the most annoying so-called *features* in Internet Explorer. If there's a bug in a Web page — that is, if the person who created the Web page made a mistake — why would *you* want to fix it? Relax if you're worried that you are at fault for triggering these unwanted Debug messages. You didn't do anything. The messages occur because Internet Explorer can't figure out how to read a Web page. The person who wrote the Web page screwed up. Not you.

Fortunately, it's easy to turn the blasted error messages off, permanently:

1. **Start Internet Explorer.**

2. **Choose Tools⇨Internet Options⇨Advanced.**

   The Internet Options dialog box appears.

3. **Select the Disable Script Debugging check box, in the Browsing section.**

   It's probably not selected, and that's why you see the `Do You Wish to Debug?` messages.

4. **Deselect the Display a Notification About Every Script Error check box.**

   It's probably not selected already, but you should make sure it stays that way.

5. **Click OK.**

   You'll never be asked to debug a script again.

Chapter 6: Printing and Saving Web Information

In This Chapter

✔ Printing the contents of a Web page

✔ Saving a Web page or graphic to your hard drive

✔ Copying a Web graphic to your hard drive

✔ Viewing the HTML contents of a Web page

✔ Turning a Web graphic into your desktop's wallpaper

*W*ith Internet Explorer, you can print and save all or part of a favorite Web page. You can even save an interesting Web graphic or photo and set it as your desktop's wallpaper. To understand what makes a Web page tick, take a look behind the scenes to examine the HTML code used to create the Web page. This chapter provides details on the various aspects of storing and reusing the information that you uncover in your travels with Internet Explorer.

Printing a Web Page

Although you can save a Web page to your hard drive (as you discover how to do in the next section, "Saving a Web Page on Your Computer"), you may prefer to just print its contents. Internet Explorer makes it easy to print the contents of the Web page you're currently browsing. Just remember that a Web page (in spite of its singular name) can produce multiple printed pages due to the amount of information contained on that "page."

When you want to print the contents of the Web page currently displayed in your Internet Explorer browser, you can choose from a couple of methods:

✦ Click the Print button on the Standard Buttons toolbar.

✦ Choose File⇨Print or press Ctrl+P to open the Print dialog box (see Figure 6-1); then click Print or press Enter.

Before you print from Internet Explorer, you should check the page settings. You can change page settings from the Page Setup dialog box (see Figure 6-2), which you open by choosing File⇨Page Setup.

To change the page size, select a new size setting from the Size drop-down list. To change the orientation of the printing from Portrait (vertical) to Landscape (horizontal), click the Landscape option button. To change any or all of the page margins, enter a new value (in inches) in the Left, Right, Top, and Bottom text boxes.

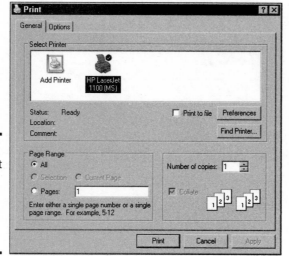

Figure 6-1:
Specify print
settings for
the current
Web page
in the Print
dialog box.

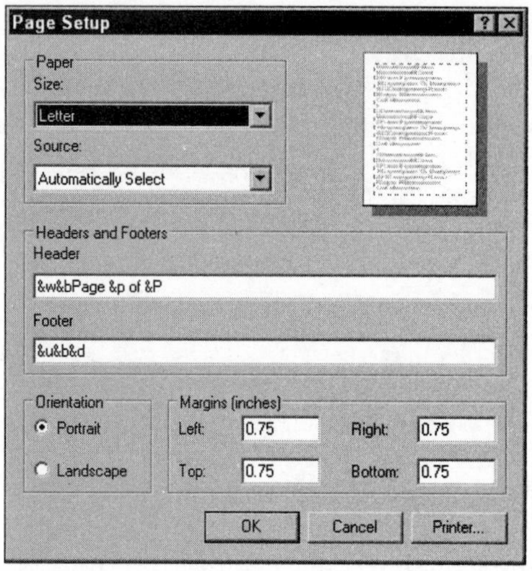

Figure 6-2:
The Page
Setup dialog
box lets you
adjust the
default page
settings.

To change the information that appears at the top of each page as a header or the bottom of each page as a footer, you need to modify the codes in the Header and Footer text boxes. Each of these printing codes begins with an ampersand (&), followed by a single character. You can use any of the printing codes shown in Table 6-1.

Table 6-1	Printing Codes
Printing Code	*What It Prints*
&w	Title of the Web page as it appears in the title bar of the browser window
&u	URL (Web address) of the Web page
&d	Current date using the short date format specified in the Regional Settings control panel (for example: 11/6/04)

Printing Code	What It Prints
&D	Current date using the long date format specified in the Regional Settings control panel (for example: Saturday, November 6, 2004)
&t	Current time as specified in the Regional Settings control panel (for example: 9:41:35 PM)
&T	Current time using a 24-hour clock (for example: 21:41:35)
&p	Page number of the current printout
&P	Total number of pages in the printout
&&	Ampersand character (&) in the header or footer text

When setting up a custom header or footer, you can intersperse the preceding printing codes with standard text. For example, if you want the footer to say something like *Page 2 of 3,* you need to intersperse the codes &p and &P between the words *Page* and *of* in the Footer text box, like this:

```
Page &p of &P
```

All the printing codes and text that you enter in the Header and Footer text boxes in the Page Setup dialog box are automatically left-justified at the top or bottom of the page. To have some of the text or codes right-justified in the header or footer, type the code &b&b immediately before the text and codes that you want to right-justify in the printout. If you want text or codes centered in the text, type &b.

To prevent Internet Explorer from printing a header or footer in the Web page printout, delete all the text and printing codes from the Header and Footer text boxes in the Page Setup dialog box.

**Book III
Chapter 6**

**Printing and Saving
Web Information**

Saving a Web Page on Your Computer

You can save to your computer's hard drive any Web page that you visit. Then you use Internet Explorer to view the page offline. To save a Web page to your hard drive, follow these steps:

1. **Use Internet Explorer to display the Web page that you want to save to your hard drive; then choose File⇨Save As.**

The Save Web Page dialog box opens.

2. **Select the folder on your hard drive where you want to save the Web page.**

The folder name appears in the Save In drop-down list box.

3. **(Optional) If you want to change the filename under which the Web page is saved, you need to edit or replace its current name in the File Name text box.**

4. Click the Save button to close the Save Web Page dialog box.

Internet Explorer downloads the Web page and saves it on your computer's hard drive.

After the Web page is saved on your hard drive, you can view its contents offline by choosing File➪Work Offline, and then opening it from the Internet Explorer Address bar or from the Open dialog box (choose File➪Open or press Ctrl+O).

Saving a Web Graphic on Your Computer

Internet Explorer makes it easy to save any still graphic images in the GIF or JPG (JPEG) graphics file format. (If you want to save a Web graphic as desktop wallpaper, see "Wallpapering Your Desktop with a Web Graphic," later in this chapter.) To save a Web graphic on your computer, follow these steps:

1. Use Internet Explorer to go to the Web page that contains the graphic that you want to save on your computer.

2. Right-click the Web graphic to display its shortcut menu and choose Save Picture As.

The Save Picture dialog box opens.

3. In the Save In drop-down list box, select the folder on your hard drive into which you want to save the graphic.

4. (Optional) If you want to change the filename of the Web graphic, edit or replace its current name in the File Name text box.

5. (Optional) By default, Internet Explorer saves the Web graphic in the GIF graphics file format or JPEG graphics file format (depending on which format the Web designer used).

To save the graphic in the BMP (bitmapped picture) graphics file format — which Windows uses extensively for such things as buttons and desktop backgrounds — choose Bitmap (*.bmp) in the Save As Type drop-down list box.

6. Click Save to close the Save Picture dialog box.

Internet Explorer downloads the Web graphic and saves it on your computer's hard drive.

Copying Web Page Information

When surfing the Internet, you may encounter a Web page that contains information that you want to access offline. In those situations, you can use the Windows Copy and Paste features to incorporate the section of Web page text of interest into a document on your hard drive.

To copy text of a Web page into a local document, follow these steps:

1. **With the Web page displayed in the Internet Explorer browsing window, position the I-beam mouse pointer at the beginning of the text that you want to copy; then click and drag through the characters or rows until all the text you want to copy is selected (highlighted).**

When you drag through the text, all the graphics that appear between or to the side of the paragraphs that you're selecting are highlighted for copying as well. If you don't want to include a particular graphic in your selection, you must copy the text before and after it in separate actions.

If you want to copy everything on the page (including all text and graphics) choose Edit⇨Select All or press Ctrl+A.

2. **Choose Edit⇨Copy or press Ctrl+C.**

The selected text is copied onto the Windows Clipboard.

3. **Switch to the word processor (for example, Microsoft Word), text editor (such as WordPad or Notepad), or e-mail editor (such as Outlook Express) that contains the destination document or e-mail message into which you want to paste the selected text.**

If you prefer, you can close Internet Explorer and launch the word processor, editor, or e-mail program. If you want to copy the selected text into an existing document, open that file with a word processor or text editor. Otherwise, open a new document.

4. **Click the I-beam mouse pointer at the place in the document or e-mail message where you want the selected text to appear, and then choose Edit⇨Paste or press Ctrl+V.**

To copy graphics without surrounding text, you use another copy technique covered in the section, "Saving a Web Graphic on Your Computer," earlier in this chapter.

Depending on the capabilities of the program into which you are pasting the copied Web text, you may find that the copied text retains some or, in rare cases, all of its original formatting (created by using the Web-based computer language HTML). For example, if you copy a section of text formatted in HTML as a bulleted list into a Word document, Word retains the bullets and properly indents the text items.

When copying text from a Web page, you usually copy hyperlinks that the author has included within that text. Some word-processing programs (such as Word) and e-mail editors (such as Outlook Express) retain the correct HTML tags for these hyperlinks, making them functioning links within the destination document. Be forewarned, however, that seldom, if ever, do these hyperlinks work properly when clicked. This problem most often occurs because you don't have the pages to which these links refer copied to your hard drive. You also may end up with extra line breaks or spaces (due to the HTML formatting) when you copy text from a Web page.

When copying information from a table on a Web page, you can retain its tabular format by copying entire rows of the table into Word 2003 documents or Outlook 2003 and Outlook Express e-mail messages. For the best results in copying tables from Web pages, copy the entire table into the Word document or Outlook e-mail message. You can now copy information from a Web table into an Excel 2003 worksheet simply by dragging the copied table cells to the blank worksheet cells and releasing the mouse button!

Viewing the HTML Source of a Web Page

A Web page is no more than a special type of text document that makes extensive use of HTML (HyperText Markup Language) tags to format its contents. If you're a Web page designer (or have any inclination to become one), you can figure out a lot about Web design by viewing the HTML contents of the really cool pages that you visit.

To see the HTML codes behind any Web page displayed in the Internet Explorer browsing window, choose View➪Source. When you select this command, Internet Explorer launches the Windows Notepad utility, which displays a copy of the *HTML source page* (the page containing all the HTML tags and text) for the current Web page, as shown in Figure 6-3.

You can then print the HTML source page by choosing File➪Print within Notepad.

Figure 6-3: The HTML source code appears in the Notepad window.

```
dummies[1] - Notepad
File  Edit  Format  View  Help
<!DOCTYPE HTML PUBLIC "-//W3C//DTD HTML 4.0 Transitional//EN">
<html><head>
<script src="javascript/dummies.js" language="JavaScript"></script>
<script language="JavaScript">
<!--
var lnk = '<LINK REL=STYLESHEET TYPE="text/css" HREF="stylesheet/';
var v = navigator.appVersion;
var a = navigator.appName;
var useNN = false;
if (a.indexof('Netscape')> -1 )
{
        if (v.indexof('3')> -1 | v.indexof('4')> -1)
        {
                useNN = true;
        }
}
lnk += (useNN) ? 'nn_style_scott.css' : 'ie_style_scott.css';
lnk += '">';
document.writeln(lnk);
//-->
</script>
<link rel="STYLESHEET" type="text/css" href="stylesheet/style_scott.css
<title>DUMMIES.com | The Online Resource for the Rest of Us!</title>
</head>
<body bgcolor="#FFFF00" topmargin="0" bottommargin="0" marginwidth="0"
```

Wallpapering Your Desktop with a Web Graphic

Internet Explorer makes it a snap to copy a favorite graphic from a Web page and use the picture as the background for your Windows desktop. To turn a Web graphic into wallpaper for your desktop, follow these steps:

1. **Use Internet Explorer to go to the Web page that contains the graphic that you want to save as wallpaper.**

2. **Right-click the Web graphic to display its shortcut menu and click the Set As Background command.**

As soon as you click Set As Background, Internet Explorer makes the graphic the wallpaper for your desktop and copies the selected graphic onto your hard drive, placing it in the Windows folder. The graphic is given the filename `Internet Explorer Wallpaper.bmp`.

To remove the Web graphic wallpaper, right-click the desktop and select Properties from the shortcut menu that appears. The Display Properties dialog box opens. On the Desktop tab, choose a new graphic or HTML file for the wallpaper in the Background box. If you no longer want any graphic displayed as the wallpaper, select the (None) option at the top of the list.

Book III
Chapter 6

Printing and Saving Web Information

Chapter 7: E-Mail Basics

In This Chapter

✓ Getting up to speed on e-mail basics

✓ Understanding e-mail addresses

*E*lectronic mail, or *e-mail*, is without a doubt the most widely used Internet service. Internet mail is connected to most other e-mail systems, such as those within corporations. That means that after you master Internet e-mail, you can send messages to folks with accounts at most big organizations and educational institutions as well as to folks with accounts at Internet providers and online services. This chapter covers the e-mail basics you need to know, such as how to interpret acronyms and emoticons, how to figure out what your e-mail address is, and how to practice proper e-mail etiquette.

Choosing an E-Mail Program

Chances are, if you purchased this book, you have a choice between two e-mail programs made by the mighty Microsoft Corporation. Your choices are to use Outlook (covered in Book IV, Chapters 7 through 9) or Outlook Express (covered in Book III, Chapters 8 and 9). The programs are similar in that they handle incoming mail the same way and store messages the same way. In both programs, messages are stored in folders and you can move messages from folder to folder to keep track of e-mail. However, Outlook is by far the more sophisticated program. For example, you can schedule tasks and keep a calendar in Outlook.

Unless you are happy with an old-fashioned e-mail program such as Eudora or Netscape Mail, I suggest switching to Outlook or Outlook Express. These programs are very helpful when it comes to sifting through and organizing the barrage of e-mail that most people receive nowadays.

Abbreviations and Acronyms

EUOA! (E-mail users often abbreviate.) People frequently use abbreviations in e-mail messages, instant messages, and chat rooms to help communicate more quickly (and to type less). The abbreviations or acronyms in Table 7-1 can get you started.

Table 7-1	E-Mail Abbreviations and Acronyms
Abbreviation	*What It Means*
AFAIK	As far as I know
AFK	Away from keyboard
BAK	Back at keyboard
BFN	Bye for now
BRB	Be right back
BTW	By the way
CYA	See ya!
FWIW	For what it's worth
GMTA	Great minds think alike
IMHO	In my humble opinion
IMNSHO	In my not-so-humble opinion
L8R	Later
LOL	Laughing out loud
NRN	No response necessary
OIC	Oh, I see
OTOH	On the other hand
ROFL	Rolling on floor, laughing
RSN	Real soon now (not!)
SO	Significant other
TIA	Thanks in advance
TTFN	Ta-ta for now
WB	Welcome back
WRT	With respect to
WTG	Way to go!

E-Mail Addresses

To send e-mail to someone, you need his or her e-mail address. Roughly speaking, mail addresses consist of these elements:

✦ **Mailbox name:** Usually, the username of the person's account.

✦ **@:** The *at* sign.

✦ **Host name:** The name of the host's computer. (See "Host names and domain names," later in this chapter.)

For example, `elvis@gurus.com` is a typical address, where `elvis` is the mailbox name and `gurus.com` is the host name.

Internet mailbox names should *not* contain commas, spaces, or parentheses. Mailbox names can contain letters, numerals, and some punctuation characters, such as periods, hyphens, and underscores. Capitalization normally doesn't matter in e-mail addresses.

The most common situation in which these restrictions cause problems is in numeric CompuServe addresses, which consist of two numbers separated by a comma. When you're converting a CompuServe address to an Internet address, change the comma to a period. For example, the address `71053,2615` becomes `71053.2615@compuserve.com` as an e-mail address. Similarly, some AOL users put spaces in their screen names. You just drop the spaces when you're sending the e-mail. If, for some reason, you must send mail to an address that does include commas, spaces, or parentheses, enclose the address in double quotes.

What's my address?

If you're accessing the Internet through a service provider, your address is most likely

your_login_name@your_provider's_host_name

If you're connected through work or school, your e-mail address is typically

your_login_name@your_computer's_host_name

A host name, however, is sometimes just a department or company name rather than your computer's name. If your login name is `elvis` and your computer is `shamu.strat.gurus.com`, your mail address may look like one of these examples:

```
elvis@shamu.strat.gurus.com
elvis@strat.gurus.com
elvis@gurus.com
```

or even this one:

```
elvis.presley@gurus.com
```

Host names and domain names

Hosts are computers that are directly attached to the Internet. Host names have several parts strung together with periods, like this:

```
ivan.iecc.com
```

You decode a host name from right to left:

✦ The rightmost part of a name is its *top-level domain*, or *TLD* (in the preceding example, `com`). See "Top-level domains," later in this chapter.

✦ To the TLD's left (`iecc`) is the name of the company, school, or organization.

✦ The part to the left of the organization name (`ivan`) identifies the particular computer within the organization.

In large organizations, host names can be further subdivided by site or department. The last two parts of a host name are known as a *domain*. For example, `ivan` is in the `iecc.com` domain, and `iecc.com` is a *domain name*.

For a list of organizations that can register a domain name for you, go to the following URL:

`www.icann.org/registrars/accredited-list.html`

Internet Service Providers often charge substantial additional fees for setting up and supporting a new domain. Shop around.

IP addresses and the DNS

Network software uses the IP address, which is sort of like a phone number, to identify the host. IP addresses are written in four chunks separated by periods, such as

`208.31.42.77`

A system called the *domain name system (DNS)* keeps track of which IP address (or addresses, for popular Internet hosts) goes with which Internet host name. Usually, one computer has one IP address and one Internet host name, although this isn't always true. For example, the Web site at `www.yahoo.com` is so heavily used that a group of computers, each with its own IP address, accept requests for Web pages from that name.

The most important IP addresses to know are the IP addresses of the computers at the Internet provider you use. You may need them in order to set up the software on your computer; if things get fouled up, the IP addresses help the guru who fixes your problem.

Top-level domains

The *top-level domain (TLD),* sometimes called a *zone,* is the last piece of the host name on the Internet (for example, the zone of `gurus.com` is `com`). TLDs come in two main flavors:

✦ Organizational

✦ Geographical

If the TLD is three or more letters long, it's an *organizational name.* Table 7-2 describes the organizational names that have been in use for years.

Table 7-2	Organizational TLDs
TLD	**Description**
com	Commercial organization
edu	Educational institution, usually a college or university
gov	U.S. government body or department
int	International organization (mostly NATO, at the moment)
mil	U.S. military site (can be located anywhere)
net	Networking organization
org	Anything that doesn't fit elsewhere, usually a not-for-profit group

It used to be that most systems using organizational names were in the United States. The com domain has now become a hot property; large corporations and organizations worldwide consider it a prestige Internet address. Address "haves" and "have-nots" are contesting a plan to add additional top-level domain names to those already in use.

If the TLD is two letters long, it's a *geographical name.* The two-letter code specifies a country, such as us for the United States, uk for the United Kingdom, au for Australia, and jp for Japan. The stuff in front of the TLD is specific to that country. Often, the letter group just before the country code mimics the style for U.S. organizational names: com or co for commercial, edu or ac for academic institutions, and gov or go for government, for example.

The us domain — used by schools, cities, and small organizations in the United States — is set up strictly geographically. The two letters just before us specify the state. Other common codes are ci for city, co for county, cc for community colleges, and k12 for schools. The Web site for the city of Cambridge, Massachusetts, for example, is www.ci.cambridge.ma.us.

Port numbers

Internet host computers can run many programs at one time, and they can have simultaneous network connections to lots of other computers. *Port numbers,* which identify particular programs on a computer, keep the different connections straight. For example:

✦ File transfer (FTP) uses port 21.

✦ E-mail uses port 25.

✦ The Web uses port 80.

Typically, your file transfer, e-mail, or newsgroup program automatically selects the correct port to use, so you don't need to know these port numbers. Now and then, you see a port number as part of an Internet address (URL).

URLs versus e-mail addresses

URLs (Uniform Resource Locators) contain the information that your browser software uses to find Web pages on the World Wide Web. URLs look somewhat like e-mail addresses in that both contain a domain name. E-mail addresses almost always contain an @, however, and URLs never do.

URLs that appear in newspapers and magazines sometimes have an extra hyphen added at the end of a line when the URL continues on the next line. If the URL doesn't work as written, try deleting that hyphen.

E-mail addresses usually are not case-sensitive — capitalization doesn't matter — but parts of URLs *are* case-sensitive. Always type URLs exactly as written, including capitalization.

Chapter 8: Sending and Receiving E-Mail with Outlook Express

In This Chapter

✔ Collecting your e-mail

✔ Jazzing up your messages

✔ Sending e-mail — now or later

✔ Printing e-mail messages

*I*f you're using Internet Explorer, you have Outlook Express — Microsoft's friendly e-mail program. If you're not sure how to do something in Outlook Express, don't despair. This chapter tells you what you need to know to get up and running quickly and efficiently with this program. This chapter shows you how to master the basics of composing and sending e-mail, how to get fancy by using color and images in your e-mail, and how to print e-mail messages.

Checking for New Mail

After you start sending messages and giving out your e-mail address, your Inbox will fill up with new mail in no time at all. You need to know not only how to access all the latest tidbits headed your way, but also how to reply to these messages.

Setting Outlook Express to check for mail

Normally, when you launch Outlook Express, the program doesn't automatically tell you when you have new e-mail except when you click the Send/Recv button on the toolbar. If you want, you can have Outlook Express automatically inform you of new e-mail anytime you open the program.

If your computer is not connected to the Internet, Outlook Express dials out, connects, and retrieves your mail at this set interval.

To set this up, follow these steps:

1. **Launch Outlook Express either by clicking the Launch Outlook Express button on the Windows taskbar or by choosing Start⇨Outlook Express.**

You need to launch Outlook Express in this manner because you can't change any of the program's settings from a New Message window.

2. Choose Tools⇨Options on the Outlook Express menu bar.

The Options dialog box appears with the General tab selected.

3. Select the Check for New Messages Every 30 Minute(s) check box and then, in the associated text box, replace 30 with the new number of minutes you desire, or use the spinner buttons to select this interval value.

When you enable the Check for New Messages Every "So Many" Minutes check box, Outlook Express automatically checks your mail server for new messages whenever you launch the program and then continues to check at the specified interval as you work in the program.

4. (Optional) To have Outlook Express play a chime whenever new e-mail messages are downloaded while you're working in the program, select the Play Sound When New Messages Arrive check box.

5. Click Apply.

6. Click OK.

The Options dialog box closes, you return to Outlook Express, and the automatic e-mail checking goes into effect.

After the automatic e-mail checking goes into effect, Outlook Express informs you of the delivery of new e-mail by placing an envelope icon on the Outlook Express status bar (and "dinging" if you enabled the Play Sound When New Messages Arrive check box).

This is very nice for those times when you're spending a great deal of time working in Outlook Express. However, don't expect to get this kind of indicator when browsing the Web with Internet Explorer. The only way to know whether you have any new e-mail when working in this program is by clicking the Mail button on the Internet Explorer toolbar and then choosing the Read Mail command.

Reading e-mail

When you use Outlook Express as your e-mail program, you read the messages that you receive in an area known as the Inbox. To open the Inbox in Outlook Express and read your e-mail messages from Internet Explorer, follow these steps:

1. Open Outlook Express by double-clicking the shortcut on the desktop or by choosing Start⇨Outlook Express.

Alternatively, with the Internet Explorer window active, click the Mail button in the toolbar and then choose Read Mail on the drop-down list that appears.

After you choose the Read Mail command, Outlook Express opens the Inbox — that is, as long as Outlook Express is configured as your e-mail program.

2. **Click the Send/Recv button on the Outlook Express toolbar to download any new messages.**

   As soon as you click the Send/Recv button, Outlook Express opens a connection to your mail server where it checks for any new messages to download for all e-mail accounts on the computer. New messages are then downloaded to your computer and placed in the Outlook Express Inbox.

   Descriptions of any new messages appear in bold in the upper pane of the Inbox, which is divided into six columns: Priority (indicated by the red exclamation point); Attachments (indicated by the paper clip); Flag Status (indicated by the flag); From; Subject; and Received (showing both the date and time that the e-mail message was downloaded to your computer).

   Note that mail messages you haven't yet read are indicated not only by bold type, but also by the presence of a sealed envelope icon in the From column. Mail messages that you've read are indicated by the presence of an opened envelope icon.

3. **To read one of your new messages, click the message in the upper pane of the Inbox.**

   It doesn't matter if your mouse pointer is located in the From, Subject, or Received column when you click the message.

   The message opens and the text appears in the lower pane of the Inbox. The From and Subject information appears on the bar dividing the upper pane from the lower pane.

   If you want the message to open in its own window, rather than in the lower pane of the Inbox, double-click the message.

4. **When you're finished reading your e-mail, click the Close box in the upper-right corner of the Outlook Express Inbox window.**

Replying to a message

Often, you want to reply to a message right away — especially if the e-mail message uses the High Priority (!) icon. Follow these steps:

1. **To reply to the author of the message, click the Reply button. To reply to the author and send copies of the reply to everyone copied on the original message, click the Reply All button instead.**

2. **In the message window, type the text of your reply above the text of the original message, and then send the reply by clicking the Send button.**

Forwarding a message

Sometimes, in addition to or instead of replying to the original message, you need to send a copy of it to someone who was not listed in the To: or Cc: field. To do so, you forward a copy of the original message to new recipients of your choosing. When you forward a message, Outlook Express copies the Subject: field and contents of the original message to a new message, which you then address and send.

**Book III
Chapter 8**

Sending and Receiving E-Mail with Outlook Express

To forward the e-mail message to another e-mail address, click the Forward button on the Outlook Express toolbar and then fill in the recipient information in the To:, and, if applicable, Cc: and Bcc: fields. Add any additional text of your own above that of the original message; then click the Send button to send the forwarded message on its way.

Composing E-Mail Messages

Outlook Express makes it easy to compose and send e-mail messages to anyone in the world who has an e-mail address.

Drafting a message

You can follow these steps to create a new e-mail message:

1. **In Outlook Express, click the Create Mail button on the toolbar.**

   Alternatively, from the Internet Explorer toolbar, click the Mail button and then choose New Message on the drop-down list that appears.

   Whichever method you choose, you see an Outlook Express New Message window.

2. **Type the recipient's e-mail address in the text box of the To: field and click OK.**

   If the recipient is already listed in your Address Book, click the word To: to open the Select Recipients dialog box. Then in the Name list box, click the name of the recipient and click the To:-> button. If you don't want to send the message to anyone else, click OK.

3. **(Optional) Click somewhere in the Cc: field, type the e-mail addresses of everyone you want to add to the list, separated by semicolons (;), and then click OK.**

   When composing a new message, you can send copies of it to as many other recipients (within reason) as you want. To send copies of the message to other recipients, type their e-mail addresses in the Cc: field (if you don't care that they'll see all the other people copied on the message) or in the Bcc: field (if you don't want them to see any of the other people copied on the message). To access the Bcc: field, click the To: or Cc: button and indicate Bcc: in the Select Recipients dialog box.

4. **Click somewhere in the Subject: field and type a brief description of the contents or purpose of the e-mail message.**

   When your message is delivered, the descriptive text that you entered in the Subject: field appears in the Subject column of each recipient's Inbox.

5. **Optional) To boost the priority of the message, click the drop-down list next to the Priority button and choose High Priority, Normal Priority, or Low Priority.**

   In Outlook Express, you can change the priority of the e-mail message from normal to either high or low by using the Priority button. When you make a message either high or low priority, Outlook Express attaches a priority icon to the message that indicates its relative importance. (Keep in mind that whether the recipient sees this icon depends on the e-mail program he or she uses.) The high-priority icon places an exclamation mark in front of the envelope; the low-priority icon adds a downward-pointing arrow.

6. Click the cursor in the body of the message and type the text of the message as you would in any text editor or word processor, ending paragraphs and short lines by pressing Enter.

When composing the text of the message, keep in mind that you can insert text directly into the body of the message from other documents via the Clipboard (using the old Cut, Copy, and Paste commands) or, in the case of text or HTML documents, by choosing Insert⇨Text from File and selecting the name of the file in the Insert Text File dialog box.

7. (Optional) To spell-check the message, click the cursor at the beginning of the message text and click the Spelling button.

When spell-checking the message, Outlook Express flags each word that it can't find in its dictionary and tries its best to suggest an alternative word.

- To replace the unknown word in the text with the word suggested in the Change To text box of the Spelling window, click the Change button or, if it's a word that occurs frequently in the rest of the text, click Change All.

- To ignore the unknown word and have the spell checker continue to scan the rest of the text for possible misspellings, click Ignore or, if it's a word that occurs frequently in the rest of the text, click Ignore All.

8. To send the e-mail message to the recipient(s), click the Send button on the Outlook Express toolbar.

Attaching a file to an e-mail message

In Outlook Express, you can attach files to your e-mail messages to transmit information that you don't want to appear in the body of the message. For example, you may need to send an Excel worksheet to a client in another office.

To attach a file to an e-mail message in Outlook Express, follow these steps:

1. In Outlook Express, click the Create Mail button.

Alternatively, from the Internet Explorer toolbar, click the Mail button and then choose New Message on the drop-down list that appears.

A New Message window appears in Outlook Express.

2. Add the recipient(s) of the e-mail message in the To: or Cc: field(s), the subject of the message in the Subject: field, and any message text explaining the attached files in the body of the message.

3. Click the Attach button on the message window's toolbar to open the Insert Attachment dialog box.

4. **In the Look In drop-down list box, choose the folder that contains the file you want to attach. Click the filename in the main list box, and then click the Attach button.**

   Outlook Express adds an Attach field under the Subject: field displaying the icon(s), filename(s), and size of the file(s) attached to the message.

5. **Click the Send button on the Outlook Express toolbar to send the message to the recipient(s).**

   If you opened a New Message window from Internet Explorer, after sending your message, the Outlook Express window closes, and you return to the Internet Explorer window.

Adding an image to your message

If you want to spice up your message even more, consider adding a graphic.

To insert a graphic in the message that appears in front of your stationery, choose Insert⇨Picture. Use the Browse button in the Picture dialog box to select the graphics file you want to use and then click OK. If the Insert⇨ Picture command isn't available, you are sending messages in plain-text format, which doesn't permit graphics to be sent inside messages. To be able to send your graphic, choose Format⇨Rich Text (HTML).

Formatting Your Messages

Want to send your friends and colleagues a message they'll remember — or at least that they'll find attractive? Then consider experimenting with the Formatting toolbar. This toolbar, which separates the header section of the message from the body window, becomes active as soon as you click the cursor in the body of the message. You can then use its buttons to format the text of your message.

If you don't see this toolbar when you click the message body area, this means that someone has changed the Mail sending format from its default of HTML to Plain Text. (See the next section, "Rich Text (HTML) messages versus Plain Text messages," to see how to change it back.)

Rich Text (HTML) messages versus Plain Text messages

Outlook Express can use one of two file formats for the e-mail messages that you compose. The Rich Text (HTML) format can display all the formatting you see on Web pages on the Internet (including graphics). The Plain Text format can display only text characters (similar to a file opened in the Windows Notepad text-editing utility).

When you first install Outlook Express, it uses the Rich Text (HTML) format for any new e-mail messages that you compose. This setting is fine as long as the e-mail program used by the recipient(s) of the message can deal with HTML formatting. (Many older e-mail programs, especially ones running under the Unix operating system, cannot.)

If you send a message using the Rich Text (HTML) format to someone whose e-mail program can't accept anything but plain text, the message comes to the recipient as plain text with an HTML document attached. That way, he or she can view all the HTML formatting bells and whistles that you added to the original e-mail message by opening the attached document in her Web browser.

To make Plain Text the new default format for Outlook Express, follow these steps:

1. **Launch Outlook Express.**

2. **Choose Tools⇨Options to open the Options dialog box.**

3. **Click the Send tab and then select the Plain Text Settings button in the Mail Sending Format area.**

   If you don't want Outlook Express to put a greater-than symbol (>) in front of each line of the original message when forwarding it to another recipient, click the Plain Text Settings button to open the Plain Text Settings dialog box. Then deselect the Indent the Original Text With check box.

   If you want to change the greater-than symbol (>) to a vertical bar (|) or colon (:), choose the new symbol from the drop-down list to the right.

4. **After making your changes, click OK or press Enter to close the Plain Text Settings dialog box.**

5. **Click OK to close the Options dialog box and put your new settings into effect.**

To change a message you're composing to Rich Text (HTML) format so you can add formatting or a picture to your message, choose Format⇨Rich Text (HTML) in the message window.

Adding bold, italics, underline, and color to your text

The Formatting toolbar in the Outlook Express New Message window makes it easy to add basic HTML formatting to your e-mail message. For example, you can highlight the text that you want to change and then click the Bold, Italics, and Underline buttons to change the way it looks.

In addition to doing basic formatting, you can make your message a little fancier by changing the color of the text. To do so, simply select the text by dragging through it with the mouse pointer and then click the Font Color button on the Formatting toolbar. On the color menu that appears, choose the color that you want the text to be.

Changing the font type and font size

If you really want to make your point, try changing your font type or enlarging its size. To do so, highlight the text you'd like to change, and then choose the type and size you'd like from the two drop-down lists on the left side of the Formatting toolbar.

Sending an E-Mail Message

When you're online (or are about to go online), you can send an e-mail message as soon as you finish writing (and, hopefully, spell-checking). Simply click the Send button in the New Message window (or press Ctrl+Enter or Alt+S) and away it goes, winging its way through cyberspace.

This method doesn't work at all, however, when you're composing an e-mail message while traveling on a plane or train where you may not be able to connect your modem.

For those times when you can't send the message right away, you need to choose File⇨Send Later on the New Message menu bar. When you choose this command, Outlook Express displays an alert box indicating that the message will be placed in your Outbox folder ready to be sent the next time you choose the Send and Receive command. When you click OK, the e-mail message you just composed goes into your Outbox folder. Then the next time you connect to the Internet, you can send all the e-mail messages waiting in the Outbox to their recipients by clicking the Send/Recv button.

Printing a Message

Sometimes, you may need to get a hard copy of a message to share with other less fortunate people who don't have e-mail. To print the contents of an e-mail message, choose File⇨Print and then click OK in the Print dialog box. Now you have your hard copy!

Arranging Your Outlook Express Desktop

Outlook Express, out of the box, does a pretty good job of hiding the more, uh, flamboyant optional parts of the program. To review and add or remove parts to the Outlook Express layout, choose View⇨Layout. You see the Window Layout Properties dialog box, which offers the following choices:

✔ **Contacts:** Choose this option to easily start a new, preaddressed message by double-clicking a contact in the Contacts list. If you have more than a few dozen contacts, this option is probably best left deselected.

✔ **Folders bar:** Deselect this option if you don't want the Folders bar taking up a lot of space.

✔ **Folder list:** With the Folder list on display, getting around in Outlook Express is easier.

✔ **Outlook bar:** This one isn't worth the space it occupies on-screen.

✔ **Status bar:** The strip along the bottom occasionally says something useful.

✔ **Toolbar:** Displays the icons at the top. You need this one.

✔ **Views bar:** This drop-down list is useful if you use custom views.

Make your changes in the Window Layout Properties dialog box and click OK.

Chapter 9: Organizing E-Mail Addresses and Messages

In This Chapter

✔ Organizing e-mail messages into folders

✔ Tracking friends, family, and co-workers in an address book

Getting e-mail is great, but it doesn't take long for you to end up with a disorganized mess. If you don't watch it, your Outlook Express Inbox can end up with hundreds of messages, some of which are still unread and all of which are lumped together in one extensive list. This chapter explains techniques for organizing e-mail.

One of the first things you'll want to do is add the names of all the people with whom you regularly correspond to your Outlook Express Address Book. That way, you'll avoid retyping e-mail addresses each time you want to send a message. Instead, you can simply type the name of your intended recipient. This chapter also explains how to keep an address book in Outlook Express.

Organizing Your Messages with Folders

Outlook Express offers a number of methods for organizing your mail, including a handy little feature known as the Inbox Assistant, which can automatically sort incoming mail according to rules that you set.

Don't forget that the most basic way to organize your e-mail is to sort the messages in the Inbox. To sort all the messages in the Inbox (or any of the other Outlook Express folders, for that matter), click a column heading. For example, if you want to sort the e-mail in your Inbox by subject, click the Subject column heading at the top of the list. And if you want to sort the messages by the date and time received (from most recent to oldest), click the Received column heading at the top of that column.

Clicking the Received column heading once sorts the messages in ascending or descending order according to date. If you click the column heading again, the messages appear in the opposite order.

Creating a new folder

Creating a new folder is easy. Just right-click in the Folders list and choose New Folder from the shortcut menu that appears. Type a name for the folder in the Folder Name text box and click OK. Then click the Inbox icon before clicking the name of the newly created subfolder.

Moving e-mail into a folder

Outlook Express makes easy work of arranging your e-mail messages in folders. To send a bunch of related e-mail messages into a new or existing folder, follow these steps:

 Inbox

1. **Open the Inbox in Outlook Express either by clicking the Mail button in Internet Explorer and then choosing Read Mail on the drop-down list or, if you already have Outlook Express running, by clicking the Inbox icon in the Folders pane.**

2. **Select all the messages that you want to put in the same folder.**

   To select a single message, click it. To select a continuous series of messages, click the first one and hold down the Shift key as you click the last one. To click multiple messages that aren't in a series, hold down Ctrl as you click the description of each one.

3. **After you finish selecting the messages to be moved, choose Edit➪Move to Folder on the Outlook Express menu bar.**

4. **Click the plus sign next to the Local Folders icon; then click the name of the subfolder into which you want to move the selected messages.**

5. **Click the OK button in the Move dialog box to move the messages into the selected folder.**

To verify that the items are in the correct folder, click the big Inbox button with the downward-pointing arrow on the bar at the top of the pane with the messages and then select the subfolder on the pop-up outline.

Organizing your e-mail with the Rule Editor

The Rule Editor can automate the organization of your e-mail by using rules that you create in its Rule Editor dialog box. Outlook Express uses the rules that you create to route e-mail from particular correspondents to particular folders that you've set up.

To create a new rule for systematizing your e-mail, follow these steps:

1. **Launch Outlook Express.**

2. **On the menu bar, choose Tools➪Message Rules➪Mail.**

3. **If you have previously set up mail rules in your copy of Outlook Express, the Message Rules dialog box opens on your screen; click the New button to open the New Mail Rule dialog box.**

   If this is the first time you've opened the Rule Editor to create a mail rule, the New Mail Rule dialog box opens automatically at this point.

4. **In section 1 of the New Mail Rule dialog box, select a check box or boxes for the conditions that must be met by the incoming e-mail.**

5. **In section 2, select a check box or boxes for the action or actions that you want to occur when a message meets the condition(s) you selected in section 1.**

6. **In section 3, click each underlined hyperlink until you have provided all the necessary information that the rule requires.**

   The subsequent dialog boxes that open and the information you are prompted for depend on the options you selected in the New Mail Rule dialog box.

   As an example, assume that you select Where the From Line Contains People in section 1 and Copy It to the Specified Folder in section 2. So in section 3, you click the underlined hyperlink in the Where the From Line Contains People option to open the Select People dialog box. Here, you specify the sender for whom you are establishing the rule. After you type the sender's name, you click the Add button and then OK. The Select People dialog box closes, and you return to the New Mail Rule dialog box. At this point, you click the hyperlink in the Move It to the Specified Folder option in section 3, which opens the Move dialog box. After choosing a folder or clicking the New Folder button to create a new folder, you click OK to exit the Move dialog box. You return to the New Mail Rule dialog box.

7. **(Optional) Type a descriptive name in the Name of the Rule text box to replace the generic name and click OK.**

   The New Mail Rule dialog box closes, and you return to the Message Rules dialog box.

8. **Click the Apply Now button to open the Apply Mail Rules Now dialog box where you choose the folder (most often the Inbox) to which the new rule should be applied.**

9. **Click Close to exit the Apply Rules Now dialog box; then click OK to close the Message Rules dialog box.**

You can set up multiple rules to apply to e-mail messages in the Inbox folder. Just be aware that Outlook Express applies the rules in the order in which they appear on the Mail Rules tab in the Message Rules dialog box. You can use the Move Up and Move Down buttons to rearrange their order.

Deleting and compacting your e-mail

As you get more and more e-mail in your Inbox, you may want to use the File⇨Folder⇨Compact command to compress the messages, thus freeing up valuable disk space. When you have e-mail in all sorts of different folders, you can compact all the messages by choosing File⇨Folder⇨Compact All Folders instead.

Deleted Items   To remove messages from the Inbox without permanently deleting them, select the messages and then press the Delete key. The messages instantly disappear from the Inbox window. However, if you ever need any of these messages again, you can display them by clicking the Deleted Items icon in the pane on the left side of the Outlook Express window.

When you have messages (especially those from blocked senders) that you no longer need to store on your computer's hard drive, you can remove them from the Deleted Items folder permanently by selecting them and choosing Edit⇨Delete. Click Yes in the alert dialog box that tells you that you are about to delete the selected messages forever. (Alternatively, you can simply press the Delete key.)

Normally, Outlook Express deletes all messages from your mail server as soon as they are downloaded to your computer. To keep the original messages on the mail server, giving you not only a backup, but also the means to retrieve the mail from somebody else's computer, follow these steps:

1. **Launch Outlook Express.**

2. **Choose Tools⇨Accounts; then click the "friendly" name for your mail account and click the Properties button.**

3. **Click the Advanced tab; then, in the Delivery section, select the Leave a Copy of the Messages on Server check box.**

   The next time you download messages, these copies will be downloaded to your computer again. Their filenames will be appended with a number to differentiate them from the original copy if it still exists in the same folder.

4. **(Optional) To have the mail left for a set period of time, select the Remove from Server After *xx* Day(s) check box and enter the number of days in the associated text box or use the spinner buttons to select this time period.**

5. **(Optional) To have the messages deleted from the server when you permanently (Ctrl+D) delete them, select the Remove from Server When Deleted from the Deleted Items check box.**

6. **Click OK to close the Properties dialog box; and then click Close to make the Internet Accounts dialog box go away.**

Deleting and renaming folders

If you decide that a folder is no longer useful in your organization scheme, deleting the folder is no problem. Simply highlight the folder, press the Delete key, and the folder is gone. Or you may opt to rename the folder, using a more useful moniker. Click the folder to highlight it, wait a second, and then click again. A rectangular box appears around the folder. Position your cursor inside the box and type your folder's new and improved name.

Adding Entries to Your Address Book

Good news! If you're switching from some other e-mail program, like the one that comes with Netscape Navigator, and you've already created an address book, you can import all those addresses into the Address Book in Outlook

Express. So no retyping required — all you have to do is follow the steps in "Importing addresses from somewhere else."

Creating a new address

You'll want to add all your frequent e-mailees to your Address Book. To add a new recipient, follow these steps:

1. **Open Outlook Express and choose Tools⇨Address Book or click the Addresses button to open the Address Book.**

   Alternatively, you can choose FileÍNewÍContact from the Internet Explorer menu bar.

2. **Click the New Contact button.**

   The Properties dialog box appears, as shown in Figure 9-1.

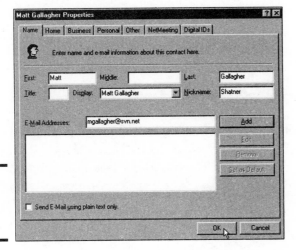

Figure 9-1: The Properties dialog box.

3. **Fill out the Name section with information about the new contact. Then, in the E-Mail Addresses text box, type the recipient's e-mail address and click the Add button.**

   When you click the Add button, Outlook Express adds the address to the list box and designates it as the default e-mail address for the individual you named.

   If the person you're adding to the Address Book has more than one e-mail address (for example, if he maintains an e-mail account with one address at home and an e-mail account with another address at work), you can add the additional e-mail address by repeating this step.

4. **(Optional) Repeat Step 3 to add an additional e-mail address for the same recipient.**

   If you want to make the second e-mail address the default one (that is, the one that Outlook Express automatically uses when you compose a new message to this person), you need to select it in the list box and then click the Set As Default button.

5. **(Optional) If you want, click the other tabs to add more information about your contact.**

   The Home tab enables you to add your contact's street address and phone number(s). The Business tab allows you to add information about your contact's work, and the Personal tab lets you add your contact's birthday, as well as his or her spouse's and children's names (if applicable).

6. **Click OK to close the Properties dialog box and return to the Address Book.**

   Your new contact's Display name appears in the Address Book, followed by the default e-mail address.

7. **Click OK to close the Address Book.**

Importing addresses from somewhere else

To import into the Address Book addresses from an address book created with Eudora, Microsoft Exchange, Microsoft Internet Mail for Windows, Netscape Navigator, or stored in a comma-separated text file, follow these steps:

1. **Choose File⇨Import⇨Other Address Book on the Address Book menu bar.**

   The Address Book Import Tool dialog box appears, as shown in Figure 9-2.

Figure 9-2:
The Address Book Import Tool dialog box.

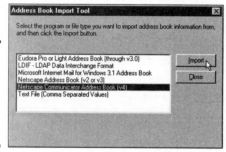

2. **Click the type of address book that you want to import in the list box of the Address Book Import Tool dialog box, and then click the Import button.**

   Outlook Express imports the names and e-mail addresses of all the contacts in the existing address book.

3. **Click Close after all the information is imported.**

   The Address Book Import Tool dialog box closes, and you return to the Address Book dialog box, where the imported contacts now appear.

4. **(Optional) To sort the contacts in the Address Book by their last names, click the Name column head above the first entry. To sort**

the contacts by their e-mail addresses, click the E-Mail Address column head.

5. **Click OK to close the Address Book.**

Finding a recipient's e-mail address

Sometimes, you may know that a person you want to correspond with has an e-mail address, but you don't remember it. Conversely, you know a person's e-mail address but need to look up her telephone number or, heaven forbid, her regular (snail) mail address.

In those situations, you can use the Find People feature in Outlook Express to search a number of different online address directories. You can also use this feature to search for someone you've entered in the Address Book, in the rare instance that the number of contacts in the Address Book is so large that doing this kind of search is significantly faster than scrolling to the person's name.

To look up someone's e-mail address with the Find People feature, follow these steps:

1. **In the Outlook Express window, click the Find button and choose People from the drop-down list.**

   The Find People dialog box appears, as shown in Figure 9-3.

Figure 9-3:
The Find People dialog box.

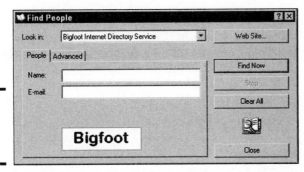

2. **Select the name of the directory that you want to use from the Look In drop-down list.**

3. **Type the name of the person whose e-mail address you want to look up in the Name field; then click the Find Now button.**

   When you click Find Now, Outlook Express searches the directory that you selected for all the people whose names closely or identically match the name you entered. (Of course, you need to be online for this search to occur.) The results of the search then appear in the list box in the lower part of the Find People dialog box, as shown in Figure 9-4.

4. **Scroll through the list to see whether the person is listed with his or her e-mail address.**

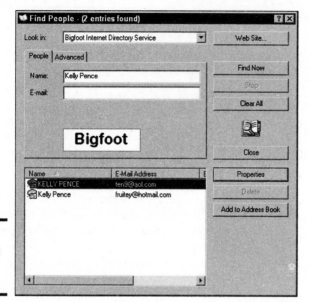

Figure 9-4:
The results of your search.

5. **If you find the person you are searching for in the list, click his or her listing to select it; then click the Add to Address Book button to add the person to your Address Book.**

6. **When you finish searching the various directories, click the X in the upper-right corner of the dialog box to return to the Select Recipients dialog box.**

7. **(Optional) To add the new contact (assuming that your search was successful, which it often won't be) as a recipient in your new e-mail message, click the To:->, Cc:->, or Bcc:-> button before you click OK.**

CHECK IT OUT

Reducing Clutter in Your Contacts List

Outlook Express can be overly paternalistic. Case in point: Whenever you send a message to someone, even if it's a reply to a message that was sent to you, the person you send the message to is automatically added to your Contacts list. More than that, if you add someone to your Windows Messenger Contacts list, and you open Outlook Express with Windows Messenger running, Outlook Express scarfs up the name and puts it in the Contacts list, too.

Follow these steps to keep Outlook Express from adding names to your Contacts list automatically:

1. **Click Tools⇨Options.**

   Outlook Express shows you the Options dialog box.

2. **On the Send tab, deselect the Automatically Put People I Reply to in My Address Book check box.**

3. **Click OK.**

   You probably want to go through your Address Book and get rid of the duplicates. Click Tools⇨Address Book, and be braced for some hard work.

Any time you want to add someone who has sent you a message to your Contacts list, simply right-click the person's name at the top of the message (or in any list of messages, such as the Inbox or the Deleted Items list) and choose Add to Address Book.

Chapter 10: Mailing Lists

In This Chapter

✔ Finding a mailing list

✔ Getting on and off a mailing list

✔ Sending messages to a mailing list

✔ Receiving mailing-list messages

✔ Using filters

✔ Starting your own mailing list

An e-mail *mailing list* offers a way for people with a shared interest to send messages to each other and hold a group conversation. Mailing lists differ from newsgroups in that a separate copy of the mailing list message is e-mailed to each recipient on the list. Mailing lists are generally smaller and more intimate than newsgroups. Lists can be very specific, tend to be less raucous, and are less infested with spam.

Imagine a mailing list that would keep you up to date in an area vital to your work or one that would let you exchange views with people who share your fondest passions. That list probably already exists. This chapter gives you hints on how to find it and how to start it if it doesn't exist.

Addresses Used with Mailing Lists

Each mailing list has its own e-mail address; on most lists, anything sent to that address is remailed to all the people on the list. People on the list respond to messages and create a running conversation. Some lists are *moderated,* which means that a reviewer (moderator) skims messages and decides which to send out.

Every mailing list, in fact, has *two* e-mail addresses:

✦ **List address:** Messages sent to this address are forwarded to all the people who subscribe to the list.

✦ **Administrative address:** Only the list's owner reads messages sent to this address. Use it for messages about subscribing and unsubscribing. Messages to the administrative address often are processed entirely by a computer, called a *mailing list server, list server,* or *MLM* (mailing list manager). In that case, you have to type your message in a specific format, as described throughout this chapter. *Note:* This address may also be called the *request address.*

For matters such as subscribing to or unsubscribing to a list, always send e-mail to the administrative address, not to the list address. If you use the list address, everyone on the list sees your request *except* for the person or computer that needs to act on it. Proper use of the administrative address is the most important thing you need to know about using mailing lists.

You can usually figure out the administrative address if you know the list address:

+ **Manually maintained lists:** Add *request* to the list address. If a manual list is named `unicycles@blivet.com`, for example, the administrative address is almost certainly `unicycles-request@blivet.com`.

+ **Automatically maintained lists:** The administrative address is usually the name of the type of list server program at the host where the list is maintained. Look for the server name in a message header to determine how a list is maintained. The most common list server programs are ListProc, LISTSERV, Mailbase, Lyris, and Majordomo.

+ **Web-based lists:** A number of companies run Web sites that host mailing lists for free in exchange for placing an ad at the end of each message. These firms accept administrative requests at their Web site, and some allow you to read list messages and archives there, too. Popular Web-based list servers include

  ```
  www.coollist.com
  groups.yahoo.com
  www.topica.com
  ```

Some mailing list servers don't care whether your administrative request is in uppercase or lowercase — others may care. In this chapter, we show all commands in uppercase, which generally works with all servers.

Finding a Mailing List

In many cases, the best way to find out about mailing lists is to ask colleagues and friends who share your interests. Many lists are informally maintained and are not indexed anywhere.

Subscribing and Unsubscribing

The way you subscribe and unsubscribe depends on how the list is maintained. Subscribing to a mailing list (unlike subscribing to a magazine) is almost always free.

Lists maintained manually

Send a mail message (such as "Please add me to the unicycles list" or "Please remove me from the unicycles list") to the administrative address. Keep these tips in mind:

✦ Include your real name and complete e-mail address so that the poor list owner doesn't have to pick through your e-mail header.

✦ Because humans read the messages, no fixed form is required.

✦ Be patient. The person maintaining the list is probably a volunteer and may have a life — or be trying to get one.

Lists maintained automatically

To join a list, send an e-mail message to its administrative address with no subject and the following line as the body of the message:

```
SUBSCRIBE listname your-name
```

Replace *listname* with the name of the mailing list, and *your-name* with your actual name. You don't have to include your e-mail address because it's automatically included as your message's return address. For example, George W. Bush would type the following line to subscribe to the leader_support mailing list:

```
SUBSCRIBE leader_support George W. Bush
```

✦ For Mailbase lists, replace SUBSCRIBE with JOIN.

✦ For Majordomo lists, don't include your name.

To get off a list, send e-mail to its administrative address with no subject and the following line as the body of the message:

```
UNSUBSCRIBE listname
```

The command SIGNOFF works with most mailing lists too.

For Mailbase lists, replace UNSUBSCRIBE with LEAVE.

When you're subscribing to a list, be sure to send your message from the e-mail address to which you want list messages mailed. The administrator of the list uses your message's return address as the address he or she adds to the mailing list.

When you first subscribe to a list, you generally receive a welcome message via e-mail. Keep this message! You may want to keep a file of these messages because they tell you what type of server is being used and how to unsubscribe.

Many list servers e-mail you back for confirmation before processing your request. If you plan to unsubscribe from a bunch of lists before going on vacation — a good idea to keep your mailbox from overflowing — be sure to allow enough time to receive and return the confirmation requests.

Web-based lists

You usually join or leave Web-based lists by going to the list company's Web site, although you can often use e-mail, too. Most services ask you to append `-subscribe` or `-unsubscribe` to the list name. For example, send e-mail to `gerbils-subscribe@onelist.com` to join the Gerbils list at ONElist.

Sending Messages to a Mailing List

To send a message to a mailing list, just e-mail it to the list's address. The message is automatically distributed to the list's members.

If you respond to a message with your mail program's Reply button, check to see — before you click Send — whether your reply will be sent to the list address. Edit out the list address if you're replying only to the message's author.

Some lists are moderated — in other words, a human being screens messages before sending them out to everybody else, which can delay messages by as much as a day or two. Mail servers usually send you copies of your own messages to confirm that they were received.

Special Requests to Mailing Lists

Depending on which list server manages a list, various other commands may be available. Read on to find out more about these commands.

Archives

Many mailing lists store their messages for later reference. To find out where these archives are kept, send the following message to the administrative address:

```
INDEX listname
```

Some lists make their archives available on a Web site: Read the message that you received when you joined the list.

Subscriber list

To get a list of (almost) all the people who subscribe to a list, you can send a message to the administrative address. The content of the message depends on the type of server the list uses. See Table 10-1.

Table 10-1	Getting a List of Subscribers
Server	*Message*
ListProc	RECIPIENTS *listname*
LISTSERV	REVIEW *listname*
Mailbase	REVIEW *listname*
Mailserve	SEND/LIST *listname*
Majordomo	WHO *listname*

Privacy

ListProc and LISTSERV mail servers don't give out your name as just described if you send a message to the administrative address. To find out how to hide your name or show it again, see Table 10-2.

Table 10-2	Setting Your Privacy Preference	
Action	*Server*	*Message*
Conceal your name	ListProc LISTSERV	SET *listname* CONCEAL YES SET *listname* CONCEAL
Unconceal your name	ListProc LISTSERV	SET *listname* CONCEAL NO SET *listname* NOCONCEAL

Going on vacation

If you subscribe to a busy mailing list, you probably don't want mailing list messages to flood your inbox while you're on vacation. To stop messages from a list temporarily and continue receiving messages when you get back, see Table 10-3.

Table 10-3	Managing Messages During Your Vacation	
Action	*Server*	*Message*
Stop Messages Temporarily	ListProc LISTSERV	SET *listname* MAIL POSTPONE SET *listname* NOMAIL
Resume receiving messages	ListProc LISTSERV	SET *listname* MAIL ACK or SET *listname* MAIL NOACK or SET *listname* MAIL DIGEST SET *listname* MAIL

Open and Closed Mailing Lists

Most mailing lists are *open,* which means that anyone can send a message to the list. Some lists, however, are closed and accept messages only from subscribers. Other lists accept members by invitation only.

If you belong to a closed list and your e-mail address changes, you must let the list managers know so that they can update their database.

Receiving Digested Mailing Lists

As soon as you join a list, you automatically receive all messages from the list along with the rest of your mail.

Some lists are available in digest form with all the day's messages combined in a table of contents. To get the digest form, send an e-mail message to the list's administrative address with no subject and one of the lines shown in Table 10-4 as the body of the message. Table 10-4 also shows how to undo the digest request.

Table 10-4	Digest Requests	
Action	*Server*	*Message*
Receive digest form	ListProc	SET *listname* MAIL DIGEST
	LISTSERV	SET *listname* DIGEST
	Majordomo	SUBSCRIBE *listname*-digest, UNSUBSCRIBE *listname*
Undo digest request	ListProc	SET *listname* MAIL ACK
	LISTSERV	SET *listname* MAIL
	Majordomo	UNSUBSCRIBE *listname*-digest, SUBSCRIBE *listname*

Using Filters

Joining even one mailing list can overwhelm your e-mail inbox. Some e-mail programs can sort through your incoming mail and put mailing list messages in special mailboxes or folders that you can look at when you have time.

If you use Eudora, choose Tools⇨Filters, click New, select the Incoming check box, and then copy the From line from the mailing list message and paste it into the first `contains` box. (You also can use the second `contains` box if you want to specify another condition.) Then, in the Action section, specify the mailbox to which you want the messages transferred.

If you use Outlook Express, you can use the Rule Editor to organize your incoming e-mail messages. See Book III, Chapter 9 for more information on setting up e-mail rules.

Starting Your Own Mailing List

Maybe you've decided that you've got some extra time on your hands (don't you wish!), and you need a new hobby. Or maybe you want to promote your rock band, create a support group for parents, or share your expertise on a topic. Whatever the reason, starting a mailing list may be just what you need.

Here are some tips for starting a new mailing list:

✦ Before you start a new list, see "Finding a Mailing List," earlier in this chapter, to see whether a list that meets your needs already exists.

✦ You can start a simple manual list with nothing more than an e-mail program that supports distribution lists (such as Outlook Express, Netscape Messenger, or Eudora). When a message comes in, just forward it to the distribution list.

✦ Put manual distribution lists in the Bcc address field if you don't want every message to include all recipients' names in the header. You can put your own address in the To: field, if you want.

✦ You will soon tire of administering your list manually. Some Internet Service Providers let you use their list server, or you can use one of the ad-supported, Web-based services (www.coollist.com, groups.yahoo.com, and www.topica.com are all popular). If someone in your group has a university affiliation, that person may be able to have the list maintained there for free.

✦ Creating a Web page for your list makes it easy to find by using the Internet's search engines.

✦ For public lists, inform the Web sites listed under "Finding a Mailing List" (earlier in this chapter) about your list. Each site has instructions for adding your new mailing list to their collections.

**Book III
Chapter 10**

Mailing Lists

Chapter 11: Chatting Online

In This Chapter

✓ **Chatting online**

✓ **Using Internet Relay Chat (IRC)**

*T*he Internet lets you communicate with people in a more immediate way than sending electronic mail and waiting hours or days for a reply. You can type something, press Enter, and get a reply within seconds — a process called *chatting*. Chatting is generally done in groups that typically include people that you don't know. This chapter dishes the dirt on chatting.

Chatting Online

Online chat lets you communicate with people live, just as you would on the telephone — except that you type what you want to say and read the other person's reply on your computer screen. Here are some things that you need to know about chat:

✦ In chat, a window shows the ongoing conversation. You type in a separate box what you want to send to the individual or group. When you press Enter or click the Send button, your message appears in the conversation window, along with any responses.

✦ Chat differs from e-mail in that you don't have to address each message and wait for a reply. Though sometimes a small lag occurs in chatting, communication is nearly instantaneous — even across the globe.

✦ You're usually limited to a sentence or two in each exchange. Instant messages, described in the next chapter, allow longer expressions.

✦ You can select a group or an individual to chat with, or someone can ask to initiate a private chat with you. Many chat venues exist on the Net, including IRC (Internet Relay Chat), AOL chat rooms (for AOL users only), Web-based chat, and instant messaging systems like ICQ and AIM (AOL Instant Messenger).

✦ Because tens of thousands of people are chatting at any instant of the day or night, the discussions are divided into groups. Different terms exist for chat groups. AOL and ICQ call them *rooms*. IRC (Internet Relay Chat) calls them *channels*.

✦ The chat facilities of the value-added service providers are accessible to only that service's members.

✦ People in chat groups can be unruly and even vicious. The online service providers' chat groups usually are tamer because the service provides some supervision.

◆ You may select a special name — called a *screen name, handle,* or *nickname* — to use when you're chatting. This name can and often does differ from your login name or e-mail address.

Although your special chat name gives you some privacy online, someone could possibly find out your real identity, particularly if your online service or ISP cooperates. Don't go wild out there.

Following group conversations

Get used to following a group conversation if you want to make any sense of chats. Here's a sample of what you may see (screen names and identifying content have been changed):

```
BrtG221: hey Zeb!
Zebra795: Hello
ABE904: Where is everyone from...I am from Virginia
Zebra795: Hi Brt!
HAPY F: how should I know
Zebra795: Hi ABE
HAPY F: <-Virginia
ABE904: Hi Zebra!!!
BrtG221: so StC... what
Zebra795: <-was from Virginia!
ABE904: Hi HAPY ! Didn't see ya
BrtG221: is going on in FL?
HAPY F: HI ABE
Zebra795: Hap's been on all night!
Storm17: Brt...what?...i miss our heart to hearts
HAPY F: on and off
ABE904: Zeb, and wish you were back here!
DDouble6190: im 26 but i like older women
Zebra795: I was over July Fourth!!
Janet5301: Sorry...DD...call me in 10 yrs...
BrtG221: really DD?... where do you live?
BrtG221: lol.. so talk to me Storm..
ABE904: Gee, you didn't call, didn't write...
```

Here are a few tips for getting started:

◆ When you enter a chat group, a conversation is usually already in progress. You can't see what went on before you entered.

◆ Wait a minute or two for a page full of exchanges to appear on-screen so that you can understand some of their context before you start reading, and then determine with whom you want to converse and who you want to ignore.

◆ Start by following the comments from a single screen name. Then follow the people whom that person mentions or who reply to that person. Ignore everything else because the other messages are probably replies to messages that went by before you came in.

◆ A few regulars often dominate the conversation.

◆ The real action often takes place in private, one-on-one side discussions, which you can't see.

Safe chatting guidelines

Here are some guidelines for conducting safe and healthy chats:

✦ Many people in chat groups are totally dishonest about who they are. They lie about their occupation, age, locality, and, yes, even gender. Some think that they're being cute, and others are exploring their own fantasies; a few are really sick.

✦ Be careful about giving out information that enables someone to find you personally, including phone numbers, mailing address, and the schools that your kids attend.

✦ Pick a screen name or handle that's different from your login name; otherwise, you will receive a great deal of unwanted junk e-mail.

✦ Never give out your password to anyone, even if she says that she works for your service provider, the phone company, the FBI, the CIA, or Dummies Press. Never!

✦ If your chat service offers profiles and a person without a profile wants to chat with you, be extra cautious.

✦ If your children use chat, realize that others may try to meet them. Before your kids log on, spend some quality time talking to them about the guidelines.

Internet Relay Chat (IRC)

Internet Relay Chat (IRC) is the Internet's own chat service. IRC is available from most Internet Service Providers. You can even participate in IRC through most online services, although IRC is completely separate from the service's own chat services. You need an *IRC client program* (or just *IRC program*), which is simply another Internet program, like your Web browser or e-mail software. Freeware and shareware IRC programs are available for you to download from the Net. Most Unix systems come with an IRC program. Two of the best shareware IRC programs are mIRC (for Windows) and Ircle (for Macintosh).

You can download updated versions of these programs and get detailed information about installing them from www.irchelp.org. They're also available from TUCOWS (www.tucows.com). Windows XP comes with Windows Messenger. You can download it from www.microsoft.com/downloads.

You use IRC in two main ways:

✦ **Channel:** This is like an ongoing conference call with a bunch of people. After you join a channel, you can read what people are saying on-screen and then add your own comments just by typing them and pressing Enter.

✦ **Direct connection:** This is like a private conversation.

Starting IRC

To start IRC, follow these steps:

1. **Connect to the Internet and run your IRC program.**

If you're on a value-added service, such as AOL, follow its instructions for connecting to the Internet.

2. **Connect to an IRC server.**

See the following section, "Picking a server," to find out how to connect.

3. **Join a channel.**

You're ready to chat! See "IRC channels," later in this chapter, for more about channels.

Picking a server

To use IRC, you connect your IRC program to an *IRC server,* an Internet host computer that serves as a switchboard for IRC conversations. Although dozens of IRC servers are available, many are full most of the time and may refuse your connection. You may have to try several servers, or the same one dozens of times, before you can connect. When you're choosing a server, pick one that's geographically close to you to minimize response lag.

To connect to an IRC server, in mIRC, choose File⇨Options or press Alt+O to display the mIRC Options window; then click the IRC Servers arrow for the drop-down list. Double-click a server on the list to attempt to connect to it. If you choose All as your IRC Servers, one will be selected randomly.

Issuing IRC commands

You control what is happening during your chat session by typing IRC commands. All IRC commands start with the slash character (/). You can type IRC commands in uppercase or lowercase or a mixture — IRC doesn't care. The most important command for you to know gets you out of IRC:

```
/QUIT
```

The second most important command gives you an online summary of the various IRC commands:

```
/HELP
```

Table 11-1 provides some of the most useful IRC commands.

Table 11-1	Useful IRC Commands
Command	*What It Does*
/ADMIN server	Displays information about a server.
/AWAY	Enables you to tell IRC that you will be away for a while. You don't need to leave this type of message; if you do, however, it's displayed to anyone who wants to talk to you.

Command	What It Does
/CLEAR	Clears your screen.
/JOIN *channel*	Joins the *channel* you specify.
/PART	Leaves the current channel.
/LIST	Lists all available channels.
/NICK *thenameyouwant*	Enables you to specify your chat nickname.
/QUERY *nickname*	Starts a private conversation with *nickname*.
/TIME	Displays the date and time in case you can't take your eyes off the screen for even a moment.
/TOPIC *subject*	Changes the topic for the current channel.
/WHO *channel*	Lists all the people on *channel*. If you type /WHO *, you see displayed the names of the people on the channel you're on.

If you use mIRC or Ircle, you can achieve most of the same effects that are controlled by IRC commands by choosing options from the menu bar or clicking icons on the toolbar. These IRC commands work too, however, and some IRC programs don't have menu bar or toolbar equivalents.

IRC channels

The most popular way to use IRC is through *channels*. Most channels have names that start with the # character. Channel names aren't case sensitive. Numbered channels also exist. (When you type a channel number, don't use the # character.)

Thousands of IRC channels are available. You can find an annotated list of some of the best by visiting `www.funet.fi/~irc/channels.html`. Each channel listed there has its own linked home page that tells much more about what that channel offers.

Types of channels

Three types of channels are available in IRC:

✦ **Public:** Everyone can see them, and everyone can join.

✦ **Private:** Everyone can see them, but you can join only by invitation.

✦ **Secret:** They do not show up in the /LIST command, and you can join them only by invitation.

If you're on a private or secret channel, you can invite someone else to join by typing

/INVITE *nickname*

If you get an invitation from someone on a private or secret channel and want to join, just type

/JOIN -INVITE

Some people like to write computer programs that sit on IRC channels and make comments from time to time. These programs are called *bots,* short for *robots.* Some people think that bots are cute; if you don't, just ignore them.

Starting your own channel

Each channel has its own channel operator, or *chanop,* who can control, to some extent, what happens on that channel. You can start your own channel and become its chanop by typing

`/JOIN #unusedchannelname`

As with nicknames, whoever asks for a channel name first gets it. You can keep the name for as long as you're logged on as the chanop. You can let other people be chanops for your channel; just make sure that they're people you can trust. A channel exists as long as anyone is in it; when the last person leaves, the channel winks out of existence.

Filing a complaint

Compared to AOL and CompuServe, IRC is a lawless frontier. Few rules, if any, exist. If things get really bad, you can try to find out the offender's e-mail address by using the `/whois` command — `/whois badmother@iecc.com`, for example. You can then send an e-mail complaint to the postmaster at the same host name — `postmaster@iecc.com`, in this case. Don't expect much help, however.

Getting more info

You can discover much more about IRC from these sources:

✦ **The official IRC home page:** `irchelp.org` (where IRC was invented)

✦ **The New IRC user's page:** `www.newircusers.com`

✦ **The Usenet newsgroup:** `alt.irc`

Chapter 12: Instant Messaging

In This Chapter

✓ **Instant messaging with AOL Instant Messenger**

✓ **Using Yahoo! Messenger**

✓ **Using MSN Messenger to send and receive instant messages**

*I*f you have teenage children, you probably already know what instant messaging is. Instant messaging is something between chatting online and exchanging e-mail messages. What makes instant messaging so popular with teenagers and others is being able to know which of your friends are online at the same time as you and being able to communicate with all of them at once. Instant messaging gives you the opportunity to have an instant online party, or, in a business setting, an instant online meeting.

Instant messaging programs all have a version of the "buddy list," a box that shows which of your friends are online. As soon as the name of someone you want to gossip with appears on the list, well, the dirt gets dished and the party starts flowing. This chapter looks at the three most popular instant messaging programs: AOL Instant Messenger, MSN Messenger, and Yahoo! Messenger.

AOL Instant Messenger

If you're one of the 11 million or so AOL subscribers, you probably already know what Instant Messenger is. If you aren't an AOL subscriber, suffice it to say that it's a tool you'll be addicted to in five minutes flat. AOL Instant Messenger (often called *AIM*) has some really neat features. It can tell you when your chat buddies sign on, even before they send you an online "Hello." If your chat buddies sign off, you know that, too. This software is a breeze to use. What's more, it's free to everybody, even people who don't subscribe to America Online.

Becoming a registered user

Before you can chat with someone using Instant Messenger, you have to install the Instant Messenger software and register yourself as a user with a name nobody else has used. To do that, go the AOL Instant Messenger Web site at this address: www.aim.com. There, click the Download button and complete the form to register yourself.

To log on to Instant Messenger after you've registered, start by clicking the AOL Instant Messenger desktop icon, clicking the Start button and choosing AOL Instant Messenger, or clicking the yellow man icon in the notification area (beside the clock in the lower-right corner of the computer screen).

A logon box appears. Replace <New User> in the Name text box with the online name you registered with, enter your password, and click the Sign In button. You see your buddy list, which looks something like the one in Figure 12-1.

To avoid having to type the password each time you sign on in the future, you can select the Save Password check box. If you want to automatically log in to Instant Messenger each time you sign on to the Internet, select the Auto-Login check box.

Engaging in a chat session

To initiate a session, either double-click a person's name on your Buddy List or click the Send Instant Message, and, in the Instant Message window, type the screen name of the person you want to chat with.

If the person you want to chat with is signed on to Instant Messenger, he or she instantly sees your message on-screen. Your Instant Message window splits into two windows. Type your message in the bottom window and click Send.

To end a chat session, click the Close (X) button in the upper-right corner of the Instant Message window or press Esc.

You can tell which of your buddies is currently signed on by glancing at the Buddy List in your Buddy List window. Click the Online tab in the Buddy List window. The screen names of all those who are currently logged on are displayed there.

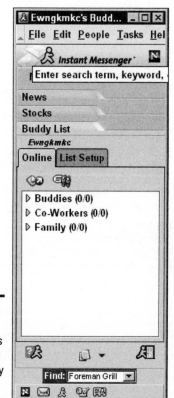

Figure 12-1: The Buddy List appears after you've successfully signed on.

Adding and deleting buddies on your Buddy List

The Buddy List within Instant Messenger is like a phone book listing your buddies' screen names, and you can add buddies to the list. To add a buddy to your Buddy List, follow these steps:

1. **Click the Setup button on the Buddy List window.**

2. **Click a folder to select it as the folder to which you want to add your new buddy.**

3. **Click the Add a Buddy button.**

This creates a *New Buddy* entry within that folder.

4. **Type the Instant Messenger screen name of your buddy and press Enter.**

To delete a buddy from your list, select the name you want to delete, and click the Delete icon.

Yahoo! Messenger

It seems that everyone wants to get into the act. Yahoo! Messenger is Yahoo!'s instant-messaging program. It works much like AOL Instant Messenger and MSN Messenger (described later in this chapter). Do you ever get the impression that the Internet is just a bunch of copycats? To take Yahoo! Messenger for a spin, you must have a Yahoo! ID (it's free) and you must have downloaded the Yahoo! Messenger program:

✦ To get a Yahoo! ID, go to www.yahoo.com, click the Sign In link, and, on the Web page that appears, click the Sign Up Now link.

✦ To download Yahoo! Instant Messenger, go to the Web page at this address: http://messenger.yahoo.com.

Logging on to Yahoo! Messenger

To start running Yahoo! Messenger, either double-click the Yahoo! Messenger icon in the notification area (the lower-right corner of the screen next to the clock), or choose Start⇨Yahoo! Messenger⇨Yahoo! Messenger. You see the Login dialog box, where you enter your Yahoo! ID and password.

Adding and deleting friends

To populate your buddy list with friends old and new, click the Add button. A dialog box offers you the option of searching for people by Yahoo! ID, by e-mail address, or by name. After you find a friend or potential friend, you can add him or her to your friends list.

Engaging in a chat session

Starting up a chat is simple. Just double-click a name in the Friends window. An Instant Message window appears so you can compose your opening volley. Click the Send button to send your words across the Internet.

MSN Messenger

To trade instant messages with MSN Messenger, you need two things: Windows XP and a .NET passport. You need Windows XP because it comes with MSN Messenger software. You need a .NET passport to identify yourself to the Microsoft Network when you go online to instant-message. You can obtain the passport at this Web address: `http://register.passport.com`. To obtain it, you provide information about yourself and select a password. Instant messaging with MSN Messenger is free.

Logging on to MSN Messenger

To start MSN Messenger, double-click the MSN Messenger icon in the lower-right corner of the window (near the clock). You see the MSN Messenger dialog box. Click the Sign In button, enter your e-mail address, enter your password, and click OK. You see the MSN Messenger window shown on the left side of Figure 12-2.

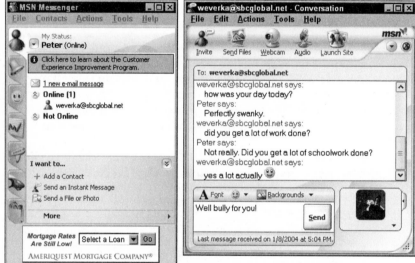

Figure 12-2: The Messenger window (left) and Conversation window (right).

Engaging in a chat session

The names of people on your buddy list who are currently signed on to MSN Messenger appear in boldface. To trade messages with one of these people, double-click his or her name. The Conversation window shown on the right side of Figure 12-2 opens. Enter a message and click the Send button.

To defend your privacy and prevent others from knowing when you are connected to MSN Messenger, choose File⇨My Status⇨Appear Offline. Even if your name is on someone's buddy list, it won't appear there, and your erstwhile friend or bothersome co-worker won't know you are connected.

Adding and deleting buddies

To add a buddy to your list, click the Add a Contact button, and, in the wizard dialog boxes that appear, either select a name from your MSN Messenger dialog box or enter an e-mail address.

Disabling MSN Messenger Automatic Sign-In

When you start Outlook Express, it automatically kicks in MSN Messenger (assuming MSN Messenger wasn't running already). Outlook Express does that so it can show you the status of your Messenger contacts. Of course, as soon as Messenger kicks in, everybody who has you on his or her Messenger Contacts list sees that you've signed in. Many people feel that's an intrusive, time-sapping side-effect of starting Outlook Express. If you agree, it's easy to turn off:

1. **In Outlook Express, choose Tools⇨ Options to open the Options dialog box.**

2. **On the General tab, deselect the Automatically Log On to Windows Messenger check box.**

   Messenger calls it sign in, not log on, but what's a little inconsistency among friends?

3. **Click OK.**

   The next time you start Outlook Express, it will not attempt to start MSN Messenger.

**Book III
Chapter 12**

Instant Messaging

Chapter 13: Keeping Up to Date with News

In This Chapter

✔ Getting started with newsgroups

✔ Posting articles to newsgroups

✔ Reading newsgroups with Google

✔ Participating in newsgroups with Outlook Express

*T*he Internet is chock full of information — you just have to know how to access it. One way that you can delve into some of the most current issues is through newsgroups.

A *newsgroup* is a place on the Internet where people gather to discuss a topic of common interest. A newsgroup resembles an electronic bulletin board on which people post questions or comments, and others respond to these questions and comments. Others then respond to the responses and so on, until a string, or *thread,* of discussion about a topic emerges. At any given time, multiple discussions can be in progress in a particular newsgroup.

Usenet, also known as *network news,* is the worldwide distributed group-discussion system that feeds information to newsgroups. Internet users around the world submit Usenet messages to tens of thousands of news-groups with names such as `rec.gardens.orchids` or `sci.space`. Within a day or so, these messages are delivered to nearly every other Internet host that wants them for anyone to read.

Newsgroup Basics

Reading Usenet is like trying to take a sip of water from a fire hose. Usenet had more than 55,000 different newsgroups the last time I looked. Here are some tips for maintaining your sanity:

✦ Pick a few groups that really interest you, or use an indexing service, such as Google. (See "Reading Newsgroups with Google," later in this chapter.)

✦ Develop a tolerance for the numerous junk-mail messages that infest many groups.

✦ If you feel that you absolutely have to reply to a comment, save the message and sleep on it. If it still seems urgent in the morning, see "Posting articles to newsgroups," later in this chapter.

✦ Don't get into a flame war; however, if ever you do, let the other guy have the last word.

✦ Don't believe everything you read on Usenet.

To read newsgroup postings, you use a *newsreader* program, or you can use your browser to read newsgroup postings on the Google Web site. To configure your newsreader program, ask your Internet Service Provider (ISP) for the name of its *news server,* the program that stores newsgroup postings for you to download.

Newsgroup "netiquette"

Here are some other suggestions for getting along with others in newsgroups:

✦ Don't post to the whole group if you're sending a follow-up intended solely for the author of the original article. Instead, reply via e-mail.

✦ Be sure that each article is appropriate for the group to which you post it.

✦ Don't post a message saying that another message — a spam ad, for example — is inappropriate. The poster probably knows and doesn't care. The first message wasted enough of everyone's time; your response would waste more. Silence is the best answer.

✦ Never criticize someone else's spelling or grammar.

✦ Make your subject line as meaningful as possible. If your reply is tangential to an article, change the subject line to reflect the new topic.

✦ When you're asking a question, use a question mark:

```
Subject: Meaning of Life?
```

✦ Don't post a 2-line follow-up that quotes an entire 100-line article. Edit out most of the quoted material.

✦ Don't *cross-post;* that is, don't post the same article to multiple newsgroups, unless you have a good reason. Be especially careful when you're replying to multiple cross-posted messages; your response may be cross-posted too.

✦ Watch out for *trolls,* messages calculated to provoke a storm of replies. Not every stupid comment needs a response.

✦ Most groups periodically post a list of Frequently Asked Questions (or FAQs). Read the FAQ before asking a question. See "Frequently Asked Questions (FAQs)," later in this chapter.

Newsgroup names

Usenet newsgroups have multipart names separated by dots, such as `comp.dcom.fax`, a data communication discussion group about fax machines. Related groups have related names. Groups about data communication, for example, all start with `comp.dcom`. The first part of a newsgroup name is called its *hierarchy.* In e-mail addresses and Internet host names, the top-level component (`edu`, for example) is on the *right.* In newsgroup names, the top-level component is on the *left.*

Table 13-1 lists the most popular Usenet newsgroup hierarchies.

Table 13-1	Popular Newsgroup Hierarchies
Newsgroup	*Description*
comp	Computer-related topics
humanities	Discussions relating to humanities
misc	Miscellaneous topics that don't fit anywhere else
news	Topics having to do with the Usenet newsgroup system itself; a few newsgroups with valuable general announcements — otherwise, not very interesting
rec	Recreational groups about sports, hobbies, the arts, and other fun endeavors
sci	Science-related topics
soc	Social groups, both social interests and plain socializing
talk	Long arguments, frequently political
alt	Semiofficial "alternative" to the preceding newsgroup hierarchies (which are often called "the big eight"); alt groups range from the extremely useful to the totally weird

In addition to the popular hierarchies in Table 13-1, you can find regional, organizational, and national hierarchies such as ne for New England, ny for New York, uk for the United Kingdom, and ibm for IBM. If you speak another language, you may be interested in hierarchies that serve languages other than English. For example, de is for German, es for Spanish, fj for Japanese, and fr for French.

New hierarchies are being started all the time. Lewis S. Eisen maintains a master list of Usenet hierarchies (619, at last count), at

`www.magma.ca/~leisen/mlnh`

Frequently Asked Questions (FAQs)

Many newsgroups periodically post a list of frequently asked questions and their answers, or *FAQs*. They hope that you read the FAQ before posting a message they have answered dozens of times before, and you should.

MIT collects FAQs from all over Usenet, creating, in effect, an online encyclopedia with the latest information on a vast array of topics that is accessible with your Web browser or via FTP, at this URL:

`ftp://rtfm.mit.edu/pub/usenet-by-hierarchy`

FAQs are often quite authoritative, but sometimes they're just a contributor's opinion. Reader beware!

Posting articles to newsgroups

Standard Usenet dogma is to read a group for a few weeks before posting anything. It's still good advice, although Internet newbies generally aren't big on delayed gratification. Here are some tips on your first posting:

✦ Pick a newsgroup whose subject is one you know something about.

✦ Read the FAQ before you post.

✦ Reply to an article with specific information that you know firsthand or can cite in a reference and that is relevant to the topic being discussed.

✦ Read the entire preceding *thread* (a series of replies to the original article and replies to those replies) to make sure that your point hasn't been raised already.

✦ Edit included text from the original article to the bare minimum.

✦ Keep your reply short, clear, and to the point.

✦ Have your facts straight. Your article should contain more than your opinion.

✦ Check your spelling and grammar.

✦ Stay calm. Don't be inflammatory, use foul language, or call people names.

✦ Avoid Netisms, such as ROFL ("rolling on floor laughing"). If necessary, use — at most — one smiley : -).

✦ Use a local hierarchy for stuff of regional interest. The whole planet does not need to hear about your school's bake sale.

✦ Save your message overnight and reread it before posting.

Some newsgroups are moderated, which means that

✦ Articles are not posted directly as news. Instead, they're e-mailed to a person or program who posts the article only if he, she, or it feels that it's appropriate to the group.

✦ Moderators, because they're unpaid volunteers, do not process items instantaneously, so it can take a day or two for items to be processed.

✦ If you post an article for a moderated group, the news-posting software mails your item to the moderator automatically.

✦ If your article doesn't appear and you really don't know why, post a polite inquiry to the same group.

Remember that Usenet is a public forum. Everything you say there can be read by anyone, anywhere in the world. Worse, every word you post is carefully indexed and archived. However, Google will let you avoid having your material archived if you type **X-No-archive: yes** in the header or first line of the text. If you forget to do this, you can ask Google to remove the message for you or remove the message yourself by using Google's automatic removal tool.

Reading Newsgroups with Google

Google Groups, the area of the Google site that offers newsgroups, is a great place to find answers to problems that you may be having with your computer and its software. You can find a newsgroup for almost every system or program out there, including ones that are obsolete.

Google and Usenet indexes

Usenet has been around almost since the beginning of the Internet and is a bit old and creaky. Google Groups has done much to bring Usenet into the modern Web era. You can use Google Groups to

✦ Do a keyword search for newsgroup articles

✦ Look for newsgroups of interest

✦ Read newsgroup articles

✦ Send e-mail to an article's author

✦ Post a reply article to something you read

✦ Post a newsgroup article on a new topic

Watch out what you post on Usenet newsgroups because anyone can find your posts later by using Google. A simple search for your name displays your e-mail address and a list of every message that you've posted — at least since 1981. If you include your home address, phone number, kids' names, political opinions, dating preferences, personal fantasies, or whatever in any message, that information also is easily retrieved. You have been warned.

Searching Google Groups

The traditional way to read Usenet is to go to a newsgroup and read the recent messages posted there. With tens of thousands of newsgroups, however, this method has become inefficient. Google Groups enables you to search *all* newsgroups by content. To use Google Groups to search all newsgroups by content, follow these steps:

1. **Open your browser and go to** `groups.google.com.`

A list of categories appears.

2. **Click a category or type keywords in the Search text box and click Google Search.**

In the Related Groups area at the top of your search results, you see a list of related newsgroups that include many articles (or contributor's names) with those keywords. The Activity bar to the left of the group name shows how often the groups have been visited. In the Searched Groups For area, you see a list of newsgroups articles that contain your search terms.

3. **Click a group to see a list of specific articles listed by the most recent date, or click an article to read it.**

To see more search results, click the link that says Next or Next 25 Threads.

4. **To save an article, choose File⇨Save As in your browser.**

If you don't find what you want in the search results, change your keywords in the Search text box and click the Google Search button.

If you want to do more advanced searching, check out the Advanced Groups Search. Not only can you search by newsgroup, but you can search by subject, author, message ID, language, and message dates as well.

Replying to an article

You can reply to an article in two ways: by sending a message to the poster's e-mail address or by posting a message to the newsgroup. To reply to a newsgroup article via e-mail, find the person's e-mail address in the article and copy it in the To: field of your favorite e-mail program. (See Part III of Book III for more information on e-mail.) ***Note:*** People often add *nospam* or other text to their e-mail addresses to decrease the amount of spam in their inboxes. Watch for this text to make sure that your message reaches the intended recipient.

To post an article following up on a message, click the Post a Follow-up to This Message link. On the Post a Message page, edit the quoted article to a reasonable size and add your response. You can also edit the list of news-groups to which your article is posted. Click the Preview Message button to preview your reply. You can make changes by clicking the Edit Message button, or you can post the message by clicking Post Message.

Keep in mind that the first time you post a message, you are taken to a reg-istration page where you're asked for your name, e-mail address, and pass-word. Next, you receive a confirmation message. As soon as you reply, you'll be able to post.

Posting a new article

To post a new message to a newsgroup, at the top of the list of threads, click the Post a New Message to *Newsgroup Name* link. On the Post Message page, type your title in the Subject text box. Type the message in the Your Message box. You can also edit the list of newsgroups to which your article is posted. When the message is ready to send, click either the Preview Message or the Post Message–No Preview button.

Reading Newsgroups with Outlook Express

Outlook Express, the e-mail program that comes with Internet Explorer and Windows (see Book III, Chapters 8 and 9), also works as a newsreader. You can receive (by subscribing) copies of all the messages being sent by the participants of the newsgroup, or you can peruse the chitchat (by not sub-scribing to the newsgroup). You must first set up a newsgroup account.

You can add and remove News Server accounts or make an account your default account by choosing Tools⇔Accounts and clicking the News tab of the Internet Accounts dialog box.

Viewing newsgroup messages before you subscribe

To get a feel for a newsgroup by reading some of its messages before actu-ally subscribing to it, follow these steps:

1. **From the Internet Explorer toolbar, click the arrow next to the Mail button and choose Read News.**

   Internet Explorer opens the Outlook Express window for the News server that you selected when you set up your News account.

2. **Click Yes to display a list of all available newsgroups in the Newsgroup Subscriptions dialog box.**

   This process may take a few minutes if your connection speed is slow.

3. **Select a newsgroup in the list box of the Newsgroup Subscriptions dialog box by clicking it.**

   If you want to limit the list of newsgroups, you can enter a term or series of terms used in the newsgroup's title (if you know that kind of thing) in the Display Newsgroups Which Contain text box.

4. **Click the Go To button to download all the messages from the newsgroup into the Outlook Express window.**

   You can read through the newsgroup messages just as you do your own e-mail messages.

5. **(Optional) If you want to reply to a particular message, click the message in the upper pane; then click the Reply button to reply to the author of the message, or click the Reply Group button to reply to the entire group.**

6. **To return to the list of newsgroups on your News server, click the Newsgroups button on the Outlook Express toolbar.**

7. **When you finish perusing the newsgroups of interest, click OK to close the Newsgroup Subscriptions dialog box, and then click the Close button in the Outlook Express window.**

Subscribing to a newsgroup

When you find a newsgroup in which you want to regularly participate, you can subscribe to it as follows:

1. **From the Internet Explorer toolbar, click the Mail button and then choose Read News.**

2. **If you see an alert dialog box telling you that you haven't subscribed to any newsgroups, click Yes.**

   The Newsgroup Subscriptions dialog box opens.

3. **In the list box, click the name of the newsgroup to which you want to subscribe.**

4. **Click the Subscribe button.**

   Outlook Express then adds a newspaper icon in front of the name of the newsgroup to indicate that you are subscribed to it. The program also adds the name of the newsgroup to the Subscribed tab of the Newsgroup Subscriptions dialog box.

5. **Repeat Steps 3 and 4 to subscribe to any other newsgroups of interest.**

6. **When you're finished subscribing, click OK.**

   The Outlook Express window appears, where you now see a list of all the newsgroups to which you have subscribed.

7. **To see the messages in a particular newsgroup, select the newsgroup by clicking its name in the Folders pane. To have Internet Explorer go online and download any new messages for the selected newsgroup, choose Tools⇨Synchronize Newsgroup.**

   The Synchronize Newsgroup dialog box appears.

8. **Select the Get the Following Items check box, and then select the desired option button: All Messages, New Messages Only (the default), or Headers Only; then click OK.**

   After the messages are downloaded, you can get offline and peruse the messages at your leisure.

9. **(Optional) Read and reply to as many of the newsgroup messages as you want. Click the message to display it in the lower pane and then click either the Reply button to reply to the author of the message or the Reply Group button to reply to the entire group.**

10. **When you're finished looking at the newsgroup messages, click the Close button in the upper-right corner of the Outlook Express window.**

After subscribing to a newsgroup, you can click the Mail button on the Internet Explorer toolbar and choose Read News to return to the list of newsgroups in Outlook Express. Remember to click the title of a newsgroup to download its current messages.

Unsubscribing from a newsgroup

Should you decide that you no longer want to participate in a newsgroup to which you're subscribed, you can easily unsubscribe by following these steps:

1. **Click the Newsgroups button on the Outlook Express toolbar.**

   The Newsgroup Subscriptions dialog box appears.

2. **Click the Subscribed tab, and then click the name of the newsgroup to which you want to unsubscribe.**

3. **Click the Unsubscribe button, and then click OK.**

Chapter 14: Getting Started with Web Publishing

In This Chapter

✔ Creating a Web site

✔ Determining what to include on a Web site

✔ Finding space for your Web site

*T*his chapter presents some basic information to help you get started with setting up your own Web site. You discover the basic steps for creating a Web site, what you should include on every Web site (and on every *page* in the site), how to effectively organize the pages in your site, and where to find space for your Web site. In addition, this chapter presents recommendations and guidelines for creating a successful Web site.

Guidelines for Creating a Successful Web Site

When you're planning the content, design, and layout of your Web site, keep the following guidelines in mind so that you create a Web site that people will want to visit over and over again:

✦ **Offer something useful on every page.** Too many Web sites are filled with fluff — pages that don't have any useful content. Avoid creating pages that are just steps along the way to truly useful information. Instead, strive to include something useful on every Web site page.

✦ **Check the competition.** Find out what other Web sites similar to yours have to offer. Don't create a "me, too" Web site that offers nothing but information that is already available elsewhere. Instead, strive for unique information that people can find only on your Web site.

✦ **Make it look good.** No matter how good the information at your Web site is, people will stay away if your site looks as if you spent no more than five minutes on design and layout. Yes, substance is more important than style. But an ugly Web site turns people away, whereas an attractive Web site draws people in.

✦ **Proof it carefully.** If every third word in your Web site is misspelled, people will assume that the information on your Web site is as unreliable as your spelling. If your HTML editor has a spell-check feature, use it and proof your work carefully before you post it to the Web. In fact, you may want to consider having someone else proofread it for you; a fresh pair of eyes can catch things that you may have overlooked.

✦ **Provide links to other sites.** Some of the best pages on the Internet are links to other Web sites that have information about a particular topic. In fact, many of the pages I have bookmarked for my own use are pages of links to topics as diverse as hobby electronics, softball, and backpacking. The time you spend creating a directory of links to other sites with information similar or complementary to your own will be well spent.

✦ **Keep it current.** Internet users won't frequent your site if it contains out-of-date information. Make sure that you frequently update your Web pages with current information. Obviously, some Web pages need to be changed more than others. For example, if you maintain a Web page that lists the team standings for a soccer league, you have to update the page after every game. On the other hand, a page that features medieval verse romances doesn't need to be updated often.

✦ **Publicize it.** Few people will stumble across your Web site by accident. If you want people to visit your Web site, you have to publicize it. Make sure that your site is listed in the major search engines, such as Yahoo! and Lycos. You can also promote your site by putting its address on all your advertisements, correspondence, business cards, e-mail, and so on. For more information about publicizing your site, see Book III, Chapter 17.

Basic Steps for Creating a Web Site

Although you don't have to be obsessively methodical about creating a Web site, it's a good idea to at least follow the three basic steps described in this section.

Step 1: Planning your Web site

Start by making a plan for your Web site. If all you want to do is create a simple, one-page "Here I Am" personal Web site, you don't really need to make a plan. But for a more elaborate Web site, you should plan the content of the site before you start creating actual pages.

One good way to plan a Web site is to sketch a simple diagram on paper showing the various pages that you want to create, with arrows showing the links between the pages. Alternatively, you can create an outline that represents your entire site. You can be as detailed or as vague as you want.

Step 2: Creating your Web pages

You can take several different approaches to creating the pages that will comprise your Web site. If the mere thought of "programming" gives you hives, you can use a simple Web page editor to create your Web pages. Both Microsoft Internet Explorer and Netscape Navigator come with basic Web page editors that enable you to create simple Web pages without any programming. You can also purchase inexpensive programs for creating complete Web sites. One of the best-known Web site development programs is Microsoft FrontPage 2003.

Step 3: Publishing your Web pages

After your Web pages are complete, it's time to publish them on the Internet. First, you have to find a Web server that will host your Web pages. The section "Finding Space for Your Web Site," later in this chapter, gives you ideas for finding a Web server. Next, you copy your Web pages to the Web server. Finally, you can publicize your Web site by cataloging it in the major search services. For more information about these tasks, see Book III, Chapter 17.

What to Include on Every Web Site

Although every Web site is different, you can find certain common elements on most Web sites. The following sections describe the items you should consider including on your Web site.

Home page

Every Web site should include a home page that serves as an entry point into the site. The home page is the first page that most users see when they visit your site (unless you include a cover page, as described in the next section). As a result, devote considerable time and energy to making sure that your home page makes a good first impression. Place an attractive title at the top of the page. Remember that most users have to scroll down to see your entire home page. They see just the top of the page first, so you want to make sure that the title is immediately visible.

After the title, include a site menu that enables users to access the content available on your Web site. You can create a simple text menu or a fancy graphics-based menu in which the user can click different parts of the image to go to different pages. However, if you use this type of menu, called an *image map,* be sure to provide a text menu as an alternative for users who don't want to wait for the image map to download or who have turned off graphic downloads altogether.

 Avoid placing a huge amount of graphics on your home page. Your home page is the first page on your Web site most users see. If it takes more than 10 seconds for your page to load, users may lose patience and skip your page altogether.

Site map

If your site has a lot of pages, you may want to include a site map. A site map is a detailed menu that provides links to every page on the site. By using the site map, a user can bypass intermediate menus and go directly to the pages that interest him or her.

Contact information

Be sure that your site includes information about how to contact you or your company. You can easily include your e-mail address as a link right on the home page. When the user clicks this link, most Web browsers fire up the user's e-mail program and stand ready to compose a message with your e-mail address already filled in the To: field.

If you want to include complete contact information, such as your address and phone number, or if you want to list contact information for several individuals, you may want to place the contact information on a separate page that users can access from the home page.

FAQ

Frequently Asked Questions (FAQ) pages are among the most popular sources of information on the Internet. You can organize your own FAQ page on any topic you want. Just come up with a list of questions and provide the answers. Or solicit answers from readers of your page.

Related links

At some sites, the most popular page is the links page, which provides a list of links to related sites. As the compiler of your own links page, you can do something that search engines such as Yahoo! cannot: You can pick and choose the links you want to include, and you can provide your own commentary about the information contained on each site.

What to Include on Every Page

Although every Web page should contain unique and useful information, all Web pages must contain the following three elements.

Title

Place a title at the top of every page. The title should identify not just the specific contents of the page, but also the Web site itself. A specific title is important because some users may not enter your site through your home page. Instead, they may go directly to one of the content pages in your site.

Navigation links

All the pages of your Web site need a consistent set of navigation links. At the minimum, provide a link to your home page on every page in your site. In addition, you may want to include links to the next and previous pages if your pages have a logical sequential organization.

Author and copyright information

Every page should also include author credits and a copyright notice. Because users can enter your site by going directly to any page, placing the authorship and copyright notices on only the home page is not sufficient.

Organizing the Content

The following sections describe several popular ways to organize the information on your Web site.

Sequential organization

In sequential organization, you simply organize your pages so that they follow one after another, like the pages in a book, as shown in Figure 14-1. On each page, provide navigation links that enable the user to go to the next page, go to the previous page, or return directly to the first page.

Figure 14-1: Sequential organization.

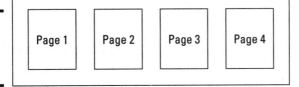

Hierarchical organization

With a hierarchical organization, you organize your Web pages into a hierarchy, categorizing the pages according to subject matter. The topmost page serves as a menu that enables users to access other pages directly (see Figure 14-2).

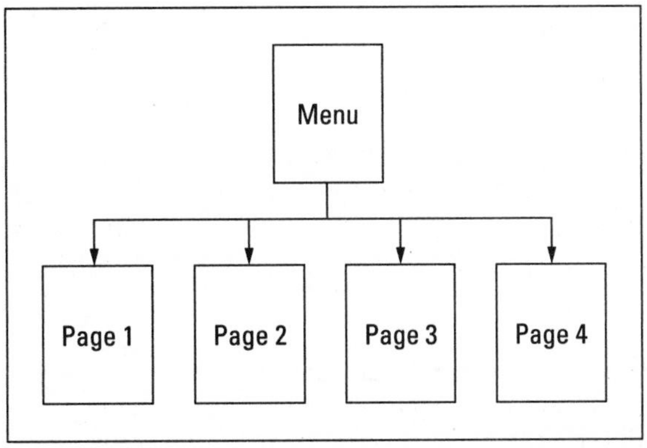

Figure 14-2: Hierarchical organization with one menu level.

On each page, provide a navigation link that returns the user to the menu. You can include more than one level of menu pages, as shown in Figure 14-3. However, don't overdo the menus. Most users are frustrated by Web sites that have unnecessary menus, in which each menu has only two or three choices. When a menu has more than a dozen choices, however, consider splitting the menu into two or more separate menus.

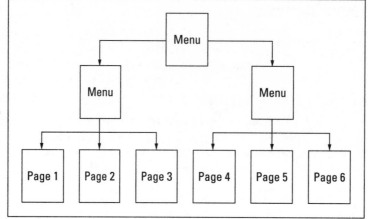

Figure 14-3:
Hierarchical organization with multiple menu levels.

Combination sequential and hierarchical organization

Many Web sites use a combination of sequential and hierarchical organization, in which a menu enables users to access content pages that contain sequential links to one another, as illustrated in Figure 14-4. In a combination organization style, each content page includes a link to the next page in sequence in addition to a link back to the menu page. The menu page contains links to the pages that mark the start of each section of pages.

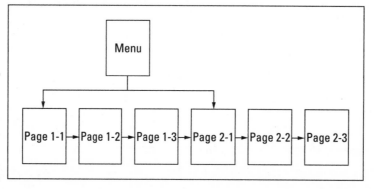

Figure 14-4:
Combination sequential and hierarchical organization.

Troubleshooting Web publishing

The following points summarize the most troublesome aspects of creating high-quality Web pages:

✔ **Different screen sizes:** Some users have 14-inch monitors that are set to 640 x 480 resolution. Others have giant 21-inch monitors that run at 1280 x 1024 (or higher). Your pages look different depending on the display resolution of the user's computer. A good middle-of-the-road approach is to design your pages for 800 x 600 resolution.

✔ **Different connection speeds:** Some users are connected to the Internet over high-speed T3 lines, DSL, or cable modems, which can send megabytes of data in seconds. Others are connected over a phone line at 28.8 Kbps, which downloads large graphics files at a snail's pace. To compensate for lack of speed, some 28.8 Kbps users set up their browsers so that graphics are not automatically downloaded. Keep this fact in mind and don't create pages that are overly dependent on graphics.

Web organization

Some Web sites have pages that are connected with links that defy a strict sequential or hierarchical pattern. In extreme cases, every page in the site is linked to every other page, creating a structure that resembles a web, as shown in Figure 14-5. This is a good style of organization if the total number of pages is limited and you can't predict the sequence in which a user may want to view them.

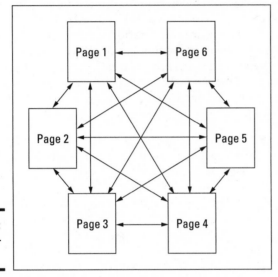

Figure 14-5: Web organization.

Finding Space for Your Web Site

If you don't have a home for your Web site, the following sections give you some ideas for where to find space for your Web pages.

Internet service providers

If you access the Internet through an Internet service provider (ISP), you probably already have space set aside to set up a home page. Most ISPs give each user a small amount of server space for Web pages included in their monthly service. The space may be limited to a few megabytes, but that should be enough to set up several pages. You can probably get additional storage space if you need it for a modest charge. You may also have to pay additional fees for any type of commercial use on your site. Your ISP can give you step-by-step instructions for copying your Web pages to the ISP's Web server.

Online services

Some major online services — CompuServe and America Online among them — let you publish your own Web pages. America Online (AOL), for example, lets you publish your own Web page in the AOL Hometown (hometown.aol.com). Each AOL member is limited to 12MB of storage space. Unfortunately, the domain name you're assigned when using these services may not be easy to remember or type. Write down your domain name and be careful when you're typing it.

Free Web servers

If you can't find a home for your Web page at your Internet service provider or your online service, consider using a free Web server to host your site. The best-known free home page service is Yahoo! GeoCities, which hosts more than 1.2 million home pages. Each free Web site can use up to 15MB of server space. The only limitation is that you must include a banner advertisement at the top of your Web page and a link to the GeoCities home page at the bottom of your page. For more information, go to `www.geocities.com`. Many other free home page services are available, although most cater to specific types of home pages, such as those for artists, churches, chambers of commerce, and so on. To find a good directory of free home page services, go to Yahoo! (`www.yahoo.com`) or Google (`www.google.com`) and search for *Free Web Pages*.

Chapter 15: Elements of Web Page Design

In This Chapter

✔ Discovering the basics of HTML

✔ Inserting headings and formatting text

✔ Creating lists

✔ Specifying page and background settings

This chapter presents a primer on HTML techniques for adding commonly used elements to your Web pages, such as headings, backgrounds, links, tables, and navigation bars. As you read this chapter, keep in mind that you can create Web pages without inserting HTML codes on your own. Microsoft Office FrontPage 2003, Dreamweaver MX 2004, and other popular programs for creating Web pages permit you to use formatting commands to lay out pages, place graphics on pages, and format text. If you aren't comfortable with HTML codes (who is?), seek the aid of a Web site creation program to create your Web site.

HTML Basics

All HTML documents contain the following elements, which define the overall structure of the document:

```
<HTML>
<HEAD>
<TITLE>Your title goes here</TITLE>
</HEAD>
<BODY>
The body of your document goes here.
</BODY>
</HTML>
```

As the preceding example shows, HTML tags are generally used in pairs that enclose portions of your document. The beginning tag, such as <BODY>, signals the start of specific formatting for that section; the closing tag, such as </BODY>, includes a slash before the tag name and signals the end of the formatting for that section. Here is an explanation for each of these tags:

✦ <HTML>: This tag must always appear as the very first thing in an HTML document. It tells the browser that the file is an HTML file.

✦ <HEAD> **and** </HEAD>: These tags enclose the section of the document called the *header*, which contains information that applies to the entire document.

✦ `<TITLE>` **and** `</TITLE>`**:** These tags enclose the document title. Any text that appears within them is used as the title for your HTML document. This is also the text that appears in the browser's title bar.

✦ `<BODY>` **and** `</BODY>`**:** These tags mark the beginning and end of the portion of your document that the browser displays when someone views the page. A lot of stuff typically falls between these tags.

✦ `</HTML>`**:** This tag is always the last tag in your document.

Specifying Font Settings

In the early days of the Web, HTML didn't provide a method that enabled you to precisely control the appearance of type on your Web pages. Now, however, HTML offers several methods for controlling type.

HTML has two tags that let you control font settings: `<FONT>` and `<BASEFONT>`. The `<FONT>` tag enables you to control font settings for an individual block of text, whereas the `<BASEFONT>` tag sets the default font used for an entire document. Both of these tags are immediately followed by one or more *attributes,* which provide specific information for the tag. Here are the most important attributes of the `<FONT>` and `<BASEFONT>` tags:

✦ `FACE`: Sets the typeface.

✦ `SIZE`: Gives the type size on a scale of 1 to 7, where 7 is the largest and 1 is the smallest. The default size is 3.

✦ `COLOR`: Sets the color of the text.

Here is a snippet of HTML that sets the typeface, size, and color used for text:

```
<BODY>
<BASEFONT SIZE="4" COLOR="BLACK" FACE="Times New Roman">
<P>This is normal body text using the font set by the
    BASEFONT tag.
<H1><FONT FACE="Arial">This is a heading</FONT></H1>
<P>After the heading, the text reverts to the BASEFONT
    setting.
</BODY>
```

Following guidelines for Web typography

Typography involves more than just setting a font. Here are some pointers for creating text that is both readable and attractive:

✔ **Don't use too many typefaces on a page.** Two or three different typefaces are plenty.

✔ **Use a serif typeface for body text.** *Serifs* are the little "feet" that appear at the end of each stroke on individual letters. Times New Roman

is an example of a serif typeface. Serifs make large quantities of type easier to read.

✔ **Use either a larger version of the body text typeface or a sans-serif typeface for your headings.** *Sans-serif* typefaces are typefaces that do not have serifs. The best-known sans-serif typeface is Arial.

When you want to force a line to break down to the next line, you can insert the paragraph (<P>) tag at that point. The <P> tag also inserts an extra blank line of space before the new line of text begins. If you don't want to add the extra blank line, you can use the <BR> tag. This tag also forces a line break but doesn't insert any extra space. Neither the <P> tag nor the <BR> tag requires a closing tag.

Figure 15-1 shows how this HTML code would look if it were displayed in Internet Explorer.

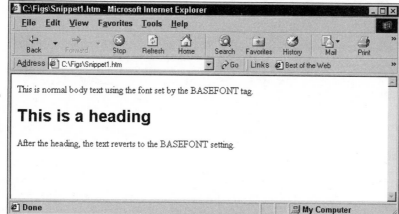

Figure 15-1: The result of HTML text that uses tags to change font settings.

Entering Headings

Don't fill your Web pages with a constant stream of uninterrupted text. Instead, use headings and paragraphs to organize the content on each page. The HTML heading tags make easy work of creating headings that break your text into manageable chunks. You can use up to six levels of headings on your Web pages by using the HTML tags <H1>, <H2>, and so on through <H6>. The following snippet of HTML shows all six heading styles in use:

```
<H1>This is a heading 1</H1>
<H2>This is a heading 2</H2>
<H3>This is a heading 3</H3>
<H4>This is a heading 4</H4>
<H5>This is a heading 5</H5>
<H6>This is a heading 6</H6>
<P>This is a normal text paragraph.
```

Figure 15-2 shows what this HTML code would look like if it were displayed in Internet Explorer.

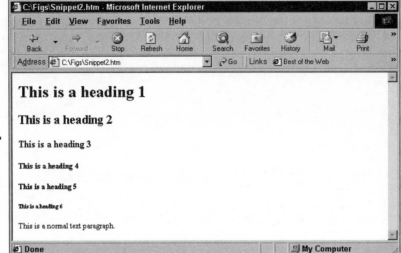

Figure 15-2:
Sample heading text as it would look in Internet Explorer.

Formatting Text

The following subsections show you how to insert formatting commands that control alignment and enable you to add bold, italic, and color to your HTML documents.

Alignment

HTML doesn't give you many options for aligning text. By default, text is left-aligned on the page. But you can use the <CENTER> tag to specify text to be centered, as in this example:

```
<CENTER>This text is centered.</CENTER>
```

Bold

You can use the <B> tag to format your text in boldface type. Add a <B> tag immediately before the text you want to appear in boldface. Then turn the boldface off by adding the </B> end tag, as shown in the following example:

```
This is <B>bold</B> text.
```

Be stingy in your use of the <B> tag. Occasional use of boldface is okay, but if you overuse bold formatting, your text becomes difficult to read.

Italic

You can use the <I> tag to format your text in italic type. Add an <I> tag immediately before the text you want to appear in italic. Then turn the italic typeface off by adding the </I> end tag, as shown in the following example:

```
This is <I>italic</I> text.
```

Occasional use of italic is okay, but try not to overdo it.

Color

You can specify colors in various HTML tags. For example, `<BODY>` has a `BGCOLOR` attribute that lets you specify the background color for your page. The `COLOR` attribute in a `<FONT>` tag sets the text color. Standard HTML defines 14 color names that you can use to set a predefined color: `BLACK`, `SILVER`, `GRAY`, `WHITE`, `MAROON`, `PURPLE`, `FUCHSIA`, `GREEN`, `LIME`, `OLIVE`, `YELLOW`, `NAVY`, `TEAL`, and `AQUA`. The easiest way to set color is to use one of these color names. For example, to create yellow text, you could use a `<FONT>` tag like this:

```
<FONT COLOR="YELLOW">This text is yellow.</FONT>
```

Creating Lists

By using HTML, you can create two basic types of lists for your Web page.

✦ **Bulleted lists:** More formally known as *unordered lists*. In a bulleted list, a bullet character (typically a dot) marks each item in the list.

✦ **Numbered lists:** More formally known as *ordered lists*. A number marks each item in a numbered list. The Web browser takes care of figuring out which number to use for each item in the list.

Bulleted lists

A bulleted, or unordered, list requires these three tags:

✦ `<UL>` marks the beginning of the unordered list.

✦ `<LI>` marks the start of each item in the list. No corresponding `</LI>` tag is needed.

✦ `</UL>` marks the end of the entire list.

Here is a snippet of HTML that sets up a bulleted list:

```
<H3>The Inhabitants of Oz</H3>
<UL>
<LI>The Scarecrow
<LI>The Tin Man
<LI>The Cowardly Lion
<LI>Munchkins
<LI>The Wizard
<LI>The Wicked Witch of the West
<LI>Glenda
</UL>
```

**Book III
Chapter 15**

**Elements of
Web Page Design**

Numbered lists

A numbered, or ordered, list requires these three tags:

✦ <OL> marks the beginning of the ordered list.

✦ <LI> marks the start of each item in the list. No corresponding </LI> tag is needed.

✦ </OL> marks the end of the entire list.

Here is an HTML snippet that creates a numbered list:

```
<H3>Steps for ordering a pizza</H3>
<OL>
<LI>Pick up phone
<LI>Dial number
<LI>Place order
<LI>Hang up phone
</OL>
```

Inserting Horizontal Rules

Horizontal rules are horizontal lines that you can add to create visual breaks on your Web pages. To add a rule to a page, you use the <HR> tag (no closing tag is required). You can control the height, width, and alignment of the rule by using the SIZE, WIDTH, and ALIGN attributes. For example:

```
<HR WIDTH="50%" SIZE="6" ALIGN="CENTER">
```

In this example, the rule is half the width of the page, six pixels in height, and centered on the page.

Many Web designers prefer to use graphic images rather than the <HR> tag to create horizontal rules. Because various Web browsers display the <HR> tag differently, using an image for a rule allows you to precisely control how your rule appears on-screen. To use an image rule, follow these steps:

1. **Type an image rule (<IMG>) tag where you would normally use an <HR> tag to create a horizontal rule:**

    <IMG>

2. **For the source (SRC) attribute within the <IMG> tag, type the name of the graphics file that contains the image rule that you want to use:**

    <IMG SRC="grule1.gif">

3. **Add a WIDTH attribute that specifies the number of pixels you want the rule to span or a percentage of the screen width:**

    <IMG SRC="grule1.gif" WIDTH="100%">

4. **Insert a <BR> tag immediately following the rule to force a line break, like this:**

    <IMG SRC="grule1.gif" WIDTH="100%">

Specifying Page Settings

The following sections explain the importance of page settings — screen size considerations, page length, and page layout — to control how your pages look in a Web browser.

Screen size considerations

Most computer users are used to scrolling up and down to view pages that are longer than the height of the screen. But few users like to scroll left and right to view pages that are too wide. To avoid horizontal scrolling, design your pages so that they fit within the width of the screen.

If you want to target users who run their computers with 800 x 600 screen resolution (which accounts for almost all users now that 15-inch and larger monitors are commonplace), shoot for 780 as the maximum page width.

If your pages consist entirely of text, you don't have to worry about screen size because the user's Web browser automatically adjusts text lines to fit the width of the screen. The only time you have to worry about page width is when you are creating a page that includes elements that have a fixed width, such as tables, images, or frames. The following list explains how to adjust the width for those three elements:

✦ **Tables:** Set the overall width of a table by using the WIDTH attribute in the <TABLE> tag, like this:

```
<TABLE WIDTH="620">
```

✦ **Images:** The size of the image determines how wide the image appears on the page. If the image is too wide, you can change the width by using the WIDTH attribute in the <IMG> tag:

```
<IMG SRC="chick.gif" WIDTH="200">
```

✦ **Frames:** Set the width of side-by-side frames by using the columns (COLS) attribute in the <FRAMESET> tag.

Book III
Chapter 15

Elements of
Web Page Design

Page length

Even though most users don't mind scrolling down to see pages that are longer than the height of the screen, you should still limit the length of your pages. As a general rule, try to limit your pages to two or three times the height of the screen — about the same amount of information that could be printed on a single 8½-x-11-inch sheet of paper.

Page layout

The best way to create an effective design for your Web pages is to set up a basic grid of common elements that will appear in the same or a similar arrangement on all your pages. Figure 15-3 illustrates how these areas may be arranged. The following list indicates some of the elements you may need to include in your Web design grid. (Depending on the content of your site, you may not need to provide all these elements.)

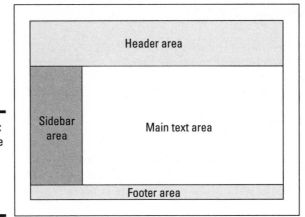

Figure 15-3:
An effective arrange-
ment for
your Web
pages.

✦ **Header area:** The header area appears at the top of each page, indicating the site title, page title, company name, site navigation buttons, and any other elements that you want to place at the top of each page.

✦ **Footer area:** The footer area appears at the bottom of each page, possibly including contact information, a copyright notice, and navigation buttons.

✦ **Main text area:** This area contains the main text and illustrations for each page.

✦ **Sidebar area:** A sidebar occupies a vertical band on the left or right portion of each page. This area can contain elements such as a table of contents or menu for the site.

Working with Backgrounds

When creating Web pages, don't make the mistake of using a garish background image that makes your page almost impossible to read. If you want to use a background image for your pages, choose an image that doesn't interfere with the text and other elements on the page.

Setting the background color

To set the background color of your Web page, follow these steps:

1. **Add the background color (BGCOLOR) attribute to the <BODY> tag.**

2. **Type a color name for the BGCOLOR attribute. For example:**

```
<BODY BGCOLOR="WHITE">
```

For more information about using color, see "Color," earlier in this chapter.

Using a background image

To use a background image for your Web page, follow these steps:

1. **Add the** BACKGROUND **attribute to the** <BODY> **tag.**

2. **Type the name of the image file you want to use for the background as the** BACKGROUND **attribute value, like this:**

```
<BODY BACKGROUND="bgpic.gif">
```

The background image repeats as many times as necessary to fill the page. As a result, the background image file doesn't have to be very large.

Adding Links

Links are an integral part of any Web page. Links let your reader travel to a different location, which can be a part of the same HTML document, a different page located on your Web site, or a page from a different Web site located elsewhere on the Internet. All the user has to do to be transported to a different page is click the link.

Using text links

A *text link* is a portion of text that someone viewing your page can click to jump to another location. To create a text link, follow these steps:

1. **Determine the address of the page that you want the link to jump to.**

2. **Type an** <A> **tag where you want the link to appear on the page.**

In the <A> tag, use an HREF attribute to indicate the address of the page that you want to link to. For example:

```
<A HREF="http://www.dummies.com">
```

3. **After the** <A> **tag, type the text that you want to appear in your document as a link and add a closing** </A> **tag, like this:**

```
<A HREF="http://www.dummies.com">The Official For
    Dummies Web Page</A>
```

The text that appears between <A> and </A> is called the *anchor*. The Web address that appears in the HREF attribute is called the *target*. The anchor text is displayed on the Web page in a special color (usually blue) and is underlined so that the person viewing the page knows that the text is a link.

If the target refers to another page at the same Web site as the page the link appears on, you can use just the filename as the target. Always enclose the filename or URL in quotation marks. For example:

```
<A HREF="emerald7.html">See the Wizard</A>
```

When a user clicks the See the Wizard link, the HTML file named emerald7.html appears on-screen.

Using graphic links

An *image link* is a graphic image that a user can click to jump to another page or a different location on the current page. To create an image link, follow the procedure described in the preceding section, "Using text links." But in Step 3, instead of typing text for the link, type an `<IMG>` tag that contains an `SRC` attribute that identifies the image file to use for the link. For example:

```
<A HREF="emerald7.html"><IMG SRC="emerald.gif"></A>
```

In this example, the graphic image file named `emerald.gif` appears on-screen. If a user clicks it, the browser displays the `emerald7.html` page.

Linking within the same page

To create a link that simply moves the user to another location on the same page, follow these steps:

1. **Assign a name to the section that you want to link to by adding an `<A>` tag with the `NAME` attribute to the first HTML line of that section. Immediately follow the `<A>` tag with an `</A>` end tag.**

2. **Create a text or graphic link to that section, typing the section name preceded by the # symbol in the `HREF` attribute.**

Here is an example of an `<A>` tag that assigns a name to a location in a document:

```
<A NAME="Here"></A>
```

Here is a snippet of HTML that creates a link that jumps to the location named "Here":

```
<A HREF="#Here">Go over there!</A>
```

Chapter 16: Working with Graphics, Sounds, and Videos

In This Chapter

✔ Understanding formats for image, sound, and video files

✔ Working with images and using image maps

✔ Adding background sounds to a Web page

✔ Adding video to a Web page

*T*his chapter presents the techniques for adding graphics, sounds, and video elements to your Web pages. You find out how to add images and image maps to your Web pages, link and embed sound and video files, and use a background sound that plays when your Web page displays.

File Formats for Image, Sound, and Video

You can choose from many different file formats for images, sounds, and videos. Fortunately, you can construct most Web pages using only the formats that we describe in the following sections.

Image file formats

Although dozens of different image file formats exist, only two are widely used for Web page images: GIF and JPEG.

GIF images: GIF, which stands for Graphics Interchange Format, was originally used on the CompuServe online network and is now widely used throughout the Internet. GIF image files have the following characteristics:

✦ GIF images can have a maximum of 256 different colors.

✦ GIF files are compressed to reduce their size. The compression method GIF uses doesn't reduce the image quality.

✦ A GIF image can include a transparent color, which, when displayed in a Web browser, allows the background of the Web page to show through.

✦ GIF images can be interlaced, which allows the Web browser to quickly display a crude version of the image and then display progressively better versions of the image.

✦ GIF supports a simple animation technique that enables you to store several distinct images in the same file. The Web browser displays the animation by displaying the images one after the other in sequence.

The GIF format is the best choice for most Web graphics that were created with drawing or paint programs and that do not contain a large number of different colors. It is ideal for icons, buttons, background textures, bullets, rules, and line art.

A format called PNG (Portable Network Graphics) was developed in 1995 as a successor to the GIF format. PNG (pronounced *ping*) supports all the features of GIF and then some, and supports more colors than GIF. PNG hasn't really caught on, though, so GIF remains the most widely used image format.

JPEG images: JPEG, a format developed by the Joint Photographic Experts Group, is designed for photographic-quality images. It has the following characteristics:

✦ JPEG images can have either 16.7 million or 2 billion colors. Most JPEG images use 16.7 million colors, which provide excellent representation of photographic images.

✦ To reduce image size, JPEG uses a special compression technique that slightly reduces the quality of the image while greatly reducing its size. In most cases, you have to carefully compare the original uncompressed image with the compressed image to see the difference.

✦ JPEG supports progressive images that are similar to GIF interlaced images.

✦ JPEG doesn't support transparent background colors as GIF does.

✦ JPEG doesn't support animation.

Other image file formats: Many other image file formats exist. Here are just a few:

✦ **BMP:** Windows bitmap

✦ **PCX:** Another bitmap format

✦ **TIF:** Tagged Image File

✦ **PIC:** Macintosh picture file

Sound file formats

Following are the most commonly used sound file formats:

✦ **WAV:** The Windows standard for sound recordings. WAV stands for Wave.

✦ **SND:** The Macintosh standard for sound recordings. SND stands for Sound.

✦ **AU:** The Unix standard for sound recordings. AU stands for Audio.

✦ **MID:** MIDI files, which aren't actually sound recordings. MIDI files are music stored in a form that a sound card's synthesizer can play. MIDI stands for Musical Instrument Digital Interface.

Don't confuse sound files with sound you can listen to in real time over the Internet, known as *streaming audio*. The most popular format for streaming audio is RealAudio. RealAudio enables you to listen to a sound as it is being downloaded to your computer, so you don't have to wait for the entire file to be downloaded before you can listen to it. To listen to RealAudio sound, you must first install a RealAudio player in your Web browser. (You can download it from `www.real.com`.)

Video file formats

Three popular formats for video clips are used on the Web:

✦ **AVI:** The Windows video standard. AVI stands for Audio Video Interleaved.

✦ **QuickTime:** The Macintosh video standard. QuickTime files usually have the extension MOV.

✦ **MPEG or MP3:** An independent standard. MPEG stands for Motion Picture Experts Group. MP3 is short for MPEG level 3, an adaptation of MPEG used to send music files over the Net.

Although AVI is known as a Windows video format and QuickTime is a Macintosh format, both formats — as well as MPEG and MP3 — have become cross-platform standards. Both Netscape Navigator and Microsoft Internet Explorer can play AVI, QuickTime, and MPEG videos.

Working with Graphics

You've decided which graphics to include on your Web pages, so what's next? This section shows you how to insert your graphics files and how to use image maps. First, here are some guidelines for using images:

✦ Don't add so many images or such large images that your page takes too long to download.

✦ Use the ALT attribute with the `<IMG>` tag to provide text for users who view your page with images turned off. For example:

```
<IMG SRC="chicken.gif" ALT="Picture of a chicken">
```

✦ Use the HEIGHT and WIDTH attributes with the `<IMG>` tag to preformat your pages for the correct image dimensions.

```
<IMG SRC="chicken.gif" HEIGHT="100" WIDTH="50">
```

✦ Use BORDER="0" in the `<IMG>` tag to eliminate the border that appears around your images (unless you want the borders to appear), like this:

```
<IMG SRC="chicken.gif" BORDER="0">
```

✦ Use transparent GIFs to create images that blend seamlessly with your page background. (See the sidebar, "Using transparent GIF images," later in this chapter.)

✦ If you want to make large image files available for download on your Web site, provide smaller, thumbnail versions of the images that people can preview before deciding whether to download the full-size image.

✦ Keep in mind that many of the images you see displayed on the Web are copyrighted materials that you can't simply copy and use on your own Web site without permission from the copyright holder. Similarly, photographs, artwork, and other images that appear in magazines and books are copyrighted. You can't legally scan copyrighted images and post them on your Web site without the copyright owner's permission.

Inserting a graphic

To insert an image on a Web page, follow these steps:

1. **Obtain an image file that you want to include on your page.**

   If necessary, use a graphics program to convert the file to the format that you want to use (probably GIF or JPEG). Store the image file in the same directory as the HTML document that displays the image. Alternatively, you may prefer to store all images for your Web site together in a separate Images folder.

2. **In the HTML file, add the** `<IMG>` **tag at the point in the document where you want the image to appear. Use the** `SRC` **(source) attribute to provide the name of the image file. For example:**

   ```
   <IMG SRC="image1.gif">
   ```

3. **(Optional) To remove the border around the image, add a** `BORDER` **attribute, as follows:**

   ```
   <IMG SRC="image1.gif" BORDER="0">
   ```

4. **(Optional) To provide text that will be displayed for users who have turned off graphics in their Web browsers, use an** `ALT` **attribute:**

   ```
   <IMG SRC="image1.gif" BORDER="0" ALT="Mountains">
   ```

5. **(Optional) To preformat the Web page with the correct dimensions of the image, use the** `HEIGHT` **and** `WIDTH` **attributes, as follows:**

   ```
   <IMG SRC="image1.gif" BORDER="0" ALT="Mountains"
      HEIGHT="200" WIDTH="100">
   ```

Using image maps

An *image map* is a graphic in which specific regions of the graphic serve as links to other Web pages. For example, if you're creating a Web site about *The Wizard of Oz,* you can use an image map showing the characters to link to pages about these characters.

To create an image map, you must use several HTML tags: `<MAP>` and its companion `</MAP>`, `<AREA>`, and `<IMG>`.

To create an image map, follow these steps:

1. **Find or create a graphic that can serve as an image map.**

   The image should have distinct regions that will serve as the map's links.

2. **Use a graphics program to display the image; then determine the rectangular boundaries of each area of the image that will serve as a**

link. Write down the pixel coordinates of the left, top, right, and bottom edges of these rectangles.

Most graphics programs display these coordinates in the program's status bar as you move the mouse around or when you use the selection tool to select an area. For example, Figure 16-1 shows an area selected in Microsoft Photo Editor.

Figure 16-1: The graphic's coordinates typically appear in the status bar.

Coordinates for selected portion of graphic

For the chicken and egg image, the following coordinates define the rectangular areas for the links:

	Left	*Top*	*Right*	*Bottom*
Egg	0	40	39	79
Chicken	40	0	109	79

3. Type a set of <MAP> and </MAP> tags. In the <MAP> tag, use the NAME attribute to provide a name for the image map, like this:

```
<MAP NAME="IMGMAP1">
</MAP>
```

4. Between the <MAP> and </MAP> tags, type an <AREA> tag for each rectangular area of the image that will serve as a link. In the <AREA> tag, include the following attributes:

```
SHAPE="RECT"
COORDS="start left, start top, end x from left, end x
    from top"
HREF="url"
```

For example:

```
<MAP NAME="IMGMAP1">
    <AREA SHAPE="RECT" COORDS="0,40,39,79"
    HREF="egg.html">
    <AREA SHAPE="RECT" COORDS="40,0,109,79"
    HREF="chick.html">
</MAP>
```

5. Type an `<IMG>` tag. Use the `SRC` attribute to name the image file and the `USEMAP` attribute to provide the name of the image map listed in the `<MAP>` attribute, like this:

```
<IMG SRC="chickegg.gif" USEMAP="#imgmap1">
```

Be sure to type a number sign (#) before the image map name in the `<IMG>` tag's `USEMAP` attribute. But don't use the # symbol when you create the name in the `<MAP>` tag's `NAME` attribute.

Putting it all together, here is a complete HTML document to set up an image map:

```
<BODY>
<H1>Which came first?</H1>
<MAP NAME="IMGMAP1">
    <AREA SHAPE="RECT" COORDS="0,40,39,79" HREF="egg.html">
    <AREA SHAPE="RECT" COORDS="40,0,109,79"
    HREF="chick.html">
</MAP>
<IMG SRC="chickegg.gif" USEMAP="#imgmap1">
</BODY>
```

Figure 16-2 shows how this page appears when displayed.

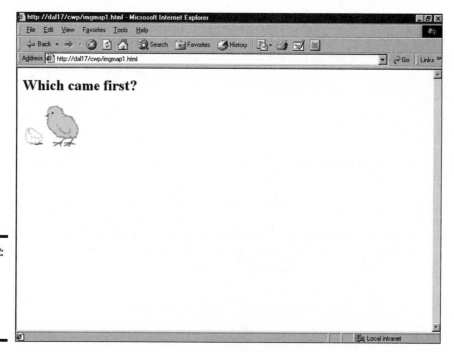

Figure 16-2:
The image map as it appears in a Web browser.

Using transparent GIF images

Most graphics programs can create transparent GIF images, in which one color is designated as transparent. When the image is displayed on your page, the background color of the page shows through the transparent area.

The procedures for setting the transparent color are similar in most graphics programs. The following procedure works for the new version of Microsoft Paint that comes with Windows XP:

1. **Open the GIF file for which you want to create a transparent color.**

2. **In the toolbox, click Select (rectangle shape) to select a rectangular area or click Free-Form Select (star shape) to select a free-form area.**

3. **Drag the pointer to define the area of the picture size.**

4. **Click the button in the bottom-left corner of Paint to apply a transparent background.**

5. **To change the background color, click Pick Color (the eyedropper icon).**

6. **Click the color that you want to use as the image's transparent background color.**

7. **Click Fill with Color and then click the area to change the color.**

8. **Choose File⇨Save to save the file with the transparent color information.**

To use a transparent background color, make sure that the image's background consists of a single color and that the background color doesn't appear elsewhere in the image. You may need to fiddle with your program's painting tools to adjust the background of the image accordingly.

You can use other graphics programs, such as Microsoft PhotoDraw, Adobe Photoshop, or Jasc Software Paint Shop Pro, to create transparent GIF images.

Use the TITLE attribute in the <AREA> tags to create ToolTips that are displayed when the user pauses the mouse pointer briefly over an image map area. For example:

```
<AREA SHAPE="RECT" COORDS="0,40,39,79" HREF="egg.html"
    TITLE="The Egg">
<AREA SHAPE="RECT" COORDS="40,0,109,79" HREF="chick.html"
    TITLE="The Chicken">
```

Remember that some people configure their browsers so that they don't download and display images. Whenever you use an image map, be sure to also provide text links as an alternative to the image map. Otherwise, users who visit your page with images turned off won't be able to navigate your site.

Adding Sounds

You can insert a sound file on a Web page as a link, as an embedded sound, or as a part of the page's background (so that the sound is played automatically whenever the page is displayed). The following sections show you how to use the HTML tags necessary for each method.

Inserting a link to a sound file

The advantage of linking to a sound file is that the sound file is not downloaded to the user's computer until the user clicks the sound file link. To insert a link to a sound file, follow these steps:

1. **Obtain a sound file that you want to link to your Web site and place the sound file in the same directory as the HTML document that will contain the link.**

   Alternatively, you may prefer to store all sound files for your Web site in their own folder.

2. **Add an** `<A>` **tag, some descriptive text, and an** `</A>` **tag to the HTML file as follows:**

   ```
   <A HREF="sound.wav">Click here to play the sound.</A>
   ```

Be sure to type the name of your sound file in the `HREF` attribute.

Embedding a sound file

You can embed a sound on a Web page by using an `<EMBED>` tag:

```
<EMBED SRC="sound.wav">
```

The `SRC` attribute provides the name of the sound file. The Web browser displays the sound controls necessary to enable the user to play the sound.

Using background sounds

A background sound is played automatically whenever a user displays your Web page. To add a background sound to a page, follow these steps:

1. **Obtain a sound file that you want to use as a background sound and place the sound file in the same directory as the HTML file.**

2. **Add a** `<BGSOUND>` **attribute following the** `<BODY>` **tag. Use the** `SRC` **attribute to name the sound file that you want to be played:**

   ```
   <BODY>
   <BGSOUND SRC="music.mid">
   ```

3. **If you want the sound to repeat several times, add the** `LOOP` **attribute like this:**

   ```
   <BGSOUND SRC="music.mid" LOOP="3">
   ```

   You can type any number in the `LOOP` attribute to indicate how many times the sound should be repeated. Or you can type `LOOP="INFINITE"` to play the sound repeatedly as long as the page is displayed.

Some people would rather listen to fingernails dragged across a chalkboard than annoying background sounds that play over and over again. If you want people to visit your site more than once, avoid using `LOOP="INFINITE"`.

Working with Videos

You can insert a video file on a Web page as a link or as an embedded object. The following sections show you each method.

Inserting a link to a video file

To insert a link to a video file, follow these steps:

1. Locate a video file that you want to add a link to on your Web page.

2. Add an <A> tag, some descriptive text, and an </A> tag to the HTML file as follows:

```
<A HREF="movie.avi">Click here to download a movie.</A>
```

Provide the name of the video file in the <A> tag's HREF attribute. When the user clicks the link, the Web browser downloads the file and plays the video.

Embedding a video

Use the <EMBED> tag to embed a video on a Web page. Follow these steps:

1. Locate a video file that you want to embed on a Web page.

2. In the HTML document for the Web page, add an <EMBED> tag specifying the name of the video file in the SRC attribute, like this:

```
<EMBED SRC="movie.avi">
```

3. If you want to change the size of the area used to display the video, add the HEIGHT and WIDTH attributes, like this:

```
<EMBED SRC="movie.avi" HEIGHT="200" WIDTH="200">
```

4. If you want the video to play automatically as soon as it finishes downloading, add AUTOSTART="TRUE" to the <EMBED> tag:

```
<EMBED SRC="movie.avi" AUTOSTART="TRUE">
```

Chapter 17: Publishing on the Web

In This Chapter

✔ Using the Personal Web Server to test your Web pages

✔ Working with Microsoft's Web Publishing Wizard

✔ Using FTP to post your Web files

✔ Telling the world about your site

This chapter presents the procedures that you must follow to make your Web pages available so that others can see them. You find out how to test your Web pages, publish your Web pages with the Web Publishing Wizard, and use FTP to post Web files. Finally, you discover how to announce your site via the major search services.

Previewing Your Web Pages

Before you post your Web pages to a Web server, it's a good idea to test them. You can preview your Web pages from your hard drive with a Web browser by typing **C:\FolderName\filename.html** in the Address bar of the browser. (Note that you need to tailor the directory path to what's on your computer by replacing *Foldername* and *filename.html* with the names of your folder and file. Add any subfolders, too.) Alternatively, you can save the files to a disk, choose File⇨Open from the menu bar in the browser, and then click the Browse button to open the file and view the page. You'll want to preview your page using both Internet Explorer and Netscape Navigator.

Using the Web Publishing Wizard

The Microsoft Web Publishing Wizard simplifies the task of transferring files from your computer to your Web server. The Web Publishing Wizard comes with Internet Explorer 4 and later, Windows 98 or later, and FrontPage 2000 and later.

To set up the Web Publishing Wizard for your Web site and to copy the Web files to your Web server for the first time, follow these steps:

1. In Windows XP, click a document that you want to publish to the Web.

Normally, your document will be in your My Documents folder. If not, go find the document by using Windows Explorer.

2. In the left window pane, click Publish This File to the Web.

The Web Publishing Wizard begins.

3. **Click Next.**

4. **Continue following along with the wizard, changing options and clicking Next as necessary.**

   You're asked about where you want to publish your file and what your e-mail address and password are. See Figure 17-1.

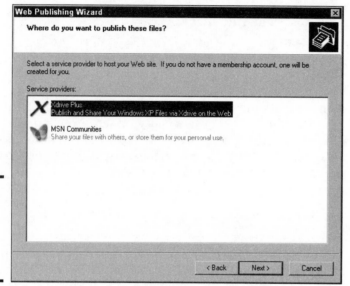

Figure 17-1:
Answer all the Web Publishing Wizard's questions.

5. **Click Finish.**

   Next, you're asked to choose the folder you want the file published in.

6. **Choose the folder (or create a new one), and then continue clicking Next.**

   More than likely, you'll probably save your files in My Webs, which is a folder located in My Documents. If you don't like that location, simply create a new folder.

7. **Click Finish.**

   The Enter Network Password dialog box appears.

8. **Enter the User Name and Password and click OK.**

   Wait a moment while the Web Publishing Wizard connects to the FTP server and transfers your files.

9. **Click OK and celebrate — you're finished!**

The Web Publishing Wizard stores most of the information that it gathers from you the first time you run it so that you don't have to retype everything each time you use the wizard.

Understanding FTP

FTP, or *file transfer protocol,* is a commonly used method of posting your Web files to a Web server. To use FTP in this manner, you need to obtain the following information from your Internet service provider:

✦ **The host name for the FTP server:** This usually, but not always, starts with ftp, as in ftp.*yourwebserver*.com.

✦ **The user ID and password that you must use to sign on to the FTP server:** This is probably the same user ID and password that you use to sign on to your service provider's Web, e-mail, and news servers.

✦ **The name of the directory into which you can copy your Web files:** A directory on an FTP server is similar to a folder in Windows 95/98/XP.

The Windows 95/98/XP FTP Client

If you are a Windows 95/98/XP user, you already have the software you need to access an FTP server. The following procedure describes the steps for transferring files to a Web server using the FTP program that comes with Windows 95/98/XP:

1. **Collect all the files required for your Web site in one folder.**

If you have lots of files — say, 50 or more — you may want to consider using several subfolders to organize the files. Just be sure to keep the folder structure as simple as possible.

2. **Open an MS-DOS command window by choosing Start⇨All Programs⇨ Accessories⇨Command Prompt (see Figure 17-2).**

3. **Use the CD (Change Directory) command to change to the folder that contains the Web files that you want to transfer to the Web server.**

For example, if your Web files are stored in a folder named Webfiles, type the following command:

```
cd \Webfiles
```

**Book III
Chapter 17**

Publishing on the Web

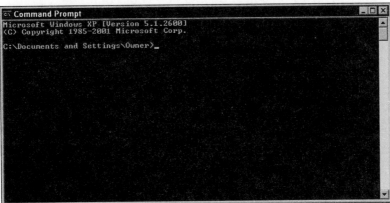

Figure 17-2:
You need
to work in
MS-DOS to
FTP files.

4. **Type** `ftp` **followed by the name of your FTP host, like this:**

```
ftp ftp.yourwebserver.com
```

5. **When prompted, type your user ID and password.**

After you have successfully logged in to the FTP server, you see an FTP prompt that looks like this:

```
ftp>
```

This prompt indicates that you are connected to the FTP server, and the FTP server — not the DOS command prompt on your own computer — processes any commands you type.

6. **Use the** `CD` **command to change to the directory to which you want to copy your files. For example:**

```
cd directory_name
```

Remember that the FTP server processes this command, so it changes the current directory on the FTP server, not on your own computer. The current directory for your own computer is still set to the directory you specified back in Step 3.

7. **Use the following** `MPUT` **command to copy all the files from the current directory on your computer (which you set back in Step 3) to the current directory on the FTP server (which you set in Step 6):**

```
mput *.*
```

You are prompted to copy each file in the directory, like this:

```
mput yourfile.html?
```

8. **Type** Y **and then press Enter to copy the file to the FTP server. Type** N **and then press Enter if you want to skip the file.**

After all the files have been copied, the `FTP>` prompt is displayed again.

9. **Type** exit **to disconnect from the FTP server.**

Windows 95/98/XP and Macintosh use the terms *folders* and *subfolders*. FTP uses the terms *directories* and *subdirectories* to refer to the same concept.

If you have files stored in subfolders on your computer, you must copy those files to the FTP server separately. Just follow these steps:

1. **If needed, use** `MKDIR` **to create the subdirectories on the FTP server.**

For example, to create a subdirectory named `IMAGES`, change to the directory in which you want to create the new subdirectory, and type a command like this:

```
mkdir images
```

2. **Use the** `CD` **command to change to the new directory:**

```
cd images
```

3. Copy files to the new directory by using the MPUT **command.**

You must specify the name of the subfolder that contains the files on your computer in the MPUT command, like this:

```
mput images\*.*
```

You are prompted to copy the files in the IMAGES folder one at a time.

FTP command summary

Table 17-1 lists the FTP commands that you're most likely to use when you store your Web files on an FTP server.

Remember that the FTP> prompt indicates that you're logged on to the FTP server and it's processing your commands.

Table 17-1	Useful FTP Commands
Command	**Description**
exit	Disconnects from the FTP server and exits the FTP program.
cd	Changes the current FTP server directory.
del	Deletes a file on the FTP server.
dir	Displays the names of the files in the current FTP server directory.
copy	Copies a single file from the FTP server to your computer.
mget	Copies multiple files from the FTP server to your computer.
mkdir	Creates a new directory on the FTP server.
mput	Copies multiple files from your computer to the FTP server.
put	Copies a single file from your computer to the FTP server.
rename	Renames a file on the FTP server.
rmdir	Removes (deletes) a directory on the FTP server.

Promoting Your Web Site

Obviously, you want your Web site to be more popular than Britney Spears — and it can be, if you promote it well. Search engines, such as Yahoo!, Lycos, Google, and the rest of them, are always scouring the Internet and recording information about Web pages. Individual search engines work a little differently: Some record information about every word on a Web page and some look only at titles and headings. The search engines store this information in giant databases. When you conduct a search of the Internet, you're really searching a database that the search engine you're using maintains. Obviously, you should do all you can to help search engines find and index your Web site.

Most search engines invite you to submit your Web site for inclusion in their databases. Crawler-based search engines usually request the URL; directory-based engines usually request more information. Table 17-2 lists some search engines to which you can submit your site. You must pay a fee to submit your Web site to search engines whose names are marked with an asterisk in the table.

Table 17-2	Search Engines	
Name	*Type of Search Engine*	*Address*
Altavista	Hybrid using Open Directory	www.altavista.com
AOL Search	Hybrid using Open Directory and Google	http://search. aol.com
Google	Hybrid using Open Directory	www.google.com
Lycos	Hybrid using Open Directory	www.lycos.com
MSN Search*	Hybrid using Looksmart	www.msnsearch.com
Open Directory	Directory	www.dmoz.org
Teoma*	Crawler	www.teoma.com
Yahoo!	Hybrid using Google	www.yahoo.com

* You must pay a fee to submit to these search engines.

Searchengines.com offers a superb explanation of search engines, how they work, and what they are. The Web site is located at this address: www.searchengines.com.

CHECK IT OUT

Other Ways to Publicize a Web Site

Here are some other ways to publicize a Web site:

- ✔ **Include your site in link exchanges and Web rings:** Link exchanges and Web rings are methods of exchanging hyperlinks with other Web sites, as long as you can find an exchange or Web ring that pertains to the topic your Web site covers. A good place to start looking for Web rings is www.webring.com.

- ✔ **Post your Web site on newsgroups:** Place a notice about your Web page on newsgroups where members might be interested in a Web site like yours. If you answer questions or post helpful and informative information to the newsgroup, the participants will appreciate it and probably come visit your site.

- ✔ **Link your site to other sites and hope they reciprocate:** Include a "Links" Web page on your site where hyperlinks to sites similar to yours are listed. Then send an e-mail message to the developer at each Web site to which your Web site is linked and hope that he or she reciprocates.

- ✔ **List your Web site address at the bottom of e-mail messages:** Casually, at the bottom of the e-mail messages you send, enter a link to your Web site. Doing so encourages more people to visit your site.

Chapter 18: Finding Your Way with Google

In This Chapter

✔ Searching the Internet with Google

✔ Mastering advanced search techniques

✔ Taking advantage of the Google toolbar

Google is just about everybody's favorite search engine. A *search engine*, in case you didn't know, is a Web site where you can begin searching the Internet. What makes Google so popular? For one thing, the Google Web page is clean and easy to understand and use. Google is also good at finding material you're looking for. And you can also use Google to look for images, news, and newsgroup discussions.

Basic Search Techniques with Google

Later in this chapter, I explain how you can use Google without visiting the Google Web site by installing the Google toolbar in your browser. Without the toolbar, go to this address to start an Internet search with Google: www.google.com. Starting here, as shown in Figure 18-1, you can select an area to search, and then either enter your search terms directly or click the Advanced Search link on this page to go to the Google Advanced Search page, also shown in Figure 18-1.

Whether you start at the Google main page or the Advanced Search page, you choose an area to search, enter your search terms, and click the Google Search button to conduct your search. These are the different areas you can search:

✦ **Web:** Search for terms on Web pages.

✦ **Images:** Search for graphics on Web pages.

✦ **Groups:** Search newsgroups on usenet. See Book III, Chapter 13 for details.

✦ **Directory:** Google organizes Web sites by content in its directory. You can drill into the directory, starting with broad terms and seeking out ever narrower ones until you reach your goal.

✦ **News:** Google monitors more than 4,000 Web news sites. This is an excellent place to search a news topic in many different newspapers and news sources.

After the search is complete, Google presents you with a list of Web pages with a sentence or two of text from each page. Click the page you want to visit.

Choose an area to search.

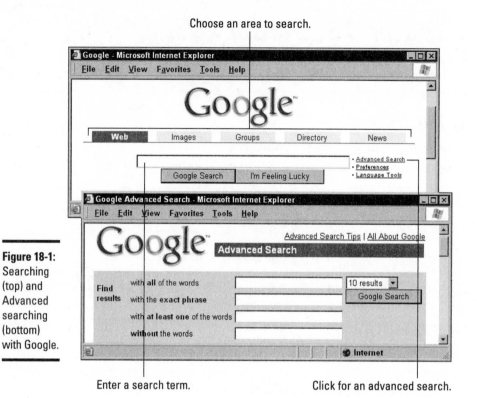

Figure 18-1:
Searching
(top) and
Advanced
searching
(bottom)
with Google.

Enter a search term.

Click for an advanced search.

By clicking a Cached link on the Google search results page, you can go to a copy of the Web page that Google maintains. The advantage of doing this is twofold. First, sometimes these copies still exist after the original Web page has been taken down. Second, your search terms are highlighted in the cached copy. This makes finding the material you're looking for easier.

Conducting a Good Search

The key to a good search is using search terms wisely. Here is some advice for conducting fruitful searches:

✦ **Use precise terms.** As best you can, enter terms as precisely as you can. For example, a search for *Triumph TR6* is more likely to get the results you want than a search for *Triumph*.

✦ **Enter the most meaningful terms first.** If you look for *tours Boston* you'll get a different result list than you get for *Boston tours*. The first focuses on tours of Boston; the second on Boston itself, with tours being secondary.

✦ **The more terms you use, the more specific the results are.** The best way to narrow down a search is to load it down with search terms. For example, *tours Boston south side* focuses on tours of the south side of Boston.

✦ **Use OR searches to tell Google that either of two search terms is okay.** Sometimes an OR search produces better results. For example, searching for *tours Boston OR Cambridge* finds tours of either city. To enter an

OR search on the Advanced Search page, enter the words in the With at Least One text box.

✦ **Search with a specific phrase.** To search for a specific phrase, either enclose it in quotes, or, on the Advanced Search page, enter it in the With Exact Phrase text box. For example, *tours "Paul Revere's House"* finds tours of that specific place.

✦ **Use the plus sign if you need to include common words.** Commonly used words such as "how" and "when" are excluded from searches, but if you want to include them, place a plus sign (+) before the word.

✦ **You can exclude pages from results.** To exclude pages, place a hyphen (-) before the word you want to exclude, or, on the Advanced Search page, enter the word or words to exclude in the Without the Words text box. Excluding words is a great way to cut down on the number of Web pages a search turns up.

You can combine the different search tricks. For example, *tours Boston OR Cambridge -"Paul Revere"* finds Web pages about tours of Boston or Cambridge that do not mention, and presumably do not take visitors to, Paul Revere's house.

By the way, capitalization doesn't matter when you enter search terms. You can save yourself a little time by entering everything in lowercase: *tours boston or cambridge -"paul revere"*.

Advanced Searching Techniques

On the Advanced Search page (refer to Figure 18-1), you can search for Web pages in a certain language, by date of last modification, for search terms by location on Web pages, and in specific Web sites.

Google also offers a handful of advanced search operators. To enter these operators, you enclose them in square brackets ([ ]), with the operator name first, a colon (:), and then the search term that the operator acts upon. For example, *[link: www.Wiley.com]* finds all Web pages with hyperlinks to the Web site at www.Wiley.com. Table 18-1 describes these advanced search operators.

Table 18-1	Advanced Google Search Operators	
Operator	**Example**	**What It Finds**
cache:	[cache: www.wiley.com]	A copy of the Web page that Google stores. As I explain earlier, search terms are highlighted in the cached copy, which makes finding what you are looking for helpful if the Web page is a long one.
define:	[define: osteoporosis]	Provides word definitions from different sources on the Internet. This is an excellent way to look up a word.
intitle:	[intitle: Madagascar]	Finds only pages where the search word is included in the title of the page.

(continued)

Table 18-1 *(continued)*

Operator	Example	What It Finds
link:	[link: www.wiley.com]	Web pages with links to the page in question, but not the page itself. This is a great way to find Web pages whose topics are similar to a certain page.
related:	[related:www.wiley.com]	Finds pages that Google deems similar to the one in the Web page address. I'm not sure how valuable this is, but in any case, no space can appear after the colon with this search operator.

Using the Google Toolbar

If you are a fan of Google, consider using the Google toolbar, as shown in Figure 18-2. This toolbar makes it possible to use the Google search engine without visiting the Google Web page. The toolbar is there at the top of your browser, ready and willing to connect you to Google at a moment's notice.

Figure 18-2:
The Google
toolbar.

Installing the Google toolbar

To install the toolbar, go to the Web site at this address: `http://toolbar.google.com`. Then click the Download Google Toolbar button. You will be asked if you want to disable or enable advanced features. If you enable the advanced features, you can see a page's rank on the Google toolbar when you surf to the page. However, to gather this ranking information, Google tracks users' surfing habits. What the advanced features question really asks is whether you consent to sending information about your surfing behavior to the Google database. Google uses the information to compile data about people's surfing habits.

To turn off the Google toolbar, right-click any empty place on any toolbar and deselect the Google option. To remove the Google toolbar, do it as though you were removing a computer program and start in the Control Panel, as discussed in Book I, Chapter 9.

Using the Google toolbar

The Google toolbar is essentially a way to search with Google without visiting the Google Web site:

✦ **Google menu:** A drop-down list for going directly to Google.com and its various pages.

✦ **Search Terms text box:** A text box for entering search terms.

◆ **Search Web:** A drop-down list for searching for images, news, and so on.

◆ **News:** Click this button to go to the Google News Web site.

◆ **PageRank:** The page ranking (if you enable the advanced features of the toolbar).

◆ **Blocked:** Click this button to keep pop-up ads from appearing at the Web page you are visiting. Click it again to permit pop-up ads.

◆ **AutoFill:** Enables you to fill in address, name, or credit card information automatically on Web forms.

◆ **Blog:** Lets you create a blog (Web log) entry.

◆ **Options:** Presents a way to customize the Google toolbar.

◆ **Highlight:** Click this button to jump from search term to search term on a Web page.

CHECK IT OUT

Making Google the Default Search Engine in Internet Explorer

If you click the Search button in Internet Explorer and start a search in the Search pane, you search using MSN. Personally, I think you should make Google your search engine of choice, and if you agree with me, you can search with Google in Internet Explorer by following these steps:

1. **In Internet Explorer, click the Search button to open the Search pane.**

2. **Click the Customize button.**

   You'll find this button at the top of the Search pane.

3. **In the Custom Search Settings dialog box, select the Use One Search Service option button.**

4. **In the Choose the Search Service menu, choose Google.**

5. **Click OK.**

   From that point on, Google is your default search engine — most of the time. In fact, Microsoft has the game rigged so that anytime you type something Internet Explorer doesn't recognize in the Address bar, Internet Explorer goes to MSN search to find whatever you typed.

Book III
Chapter 18

Finding Your Way
with Google

Chapter 19: Getting Bargains on eBay

In This Chapter

✔ Registering and signing in

✔ Searching for stuff to bid on

✔ Designating favorite searches, categories, and sellers

✔ Getting a winning bid

✔ Closing an auction transaction

Depending on your point of view, eBay is either the world's greatest auction bazaar or the world's greatest rummage sale. At any given time, about a half-million items are being auctioned on eBay. A recent *60 Minutes* story about the online auction house revealed that over 100,000 people earn an income selling items on eBay.

I'm not the kind of person who enjoys shopping, but I visit eBay three or four times a week because I enjoy looking at and occasionally purchasing folk art items. I have purchased about twenty folk art items on eBay in the past three years. Along the way, I became something of an expert on paño arte handkerchief drawings by prisoners in the American southwest, hand-knit sweaters made by the Salish Indians of British Columbia, sandpaper paintings from the nineteenth century, and West African barbershop art. I owe these peculiar fascinations to eBay. It's been a lot of fun.

The problem with eBay is that so many items are up for auction that finding what you're interested in can be difficult. Unless you know how to look for items that interest you or where to find these items, you will soon get lost. This chapter explains how to search eBay and how to maintain a "My eBay" page where you can save searches and the names of sellers you like. You also get strategies for bidding and discover the mechanics of eBay — how to place bids, research sellers, and close a sale.

Registering with eBay

To bid on items at eBay, you must register. Registering costs nothing. Besides being able to bid, registered members get to keep a "My eBay" page for tracking items they are watching or bidding on. Registering also entitles you to a Favorites page where you can save searches, save category names so you can go to categories quickly, and save the names of eBay sellers whose goods you like.

To register, go to this address: www.ebay.com. Then click the Register link and fill in the form. You'll be asked the usual stuff — your name, address, and so on. Remember your password, because you will have to enter it whenever you sign in. For a User ID, don't use your e-mail address. Doing so makes you susceptible to all kinds of junk mail. If you need to change names, passwords, or other personal information, go to the Preferences tab of the My eBay page (the next section in this chapter explains how to open this page).

Occasionally, eBay members get e-mail solicitations that look as though they are from eBay asking for personal information such as addresses and credit card numbers. These solicitations are fraudulent. Registering is the only time eBay asks for personal information. Moreover, eBay does not keep its members' credit card information on file. If you get an e-mail that supposedly comes from eBay and asks you to update your personal information, go to the eBay Security Center at http://pages.ebay.com/security center and report this false solicitation.

Signing In to Your My eBay Page

My eBay

To sign in to eBay, go to www.ebay.com, click the My eBay link, enter your User ID and password, and click the Sign In button. You land in your My eBay page, as shown in Figure 19-1. Every registered member gets one of these pages. Starting here, you can do just about anything a body can do in eBay. To return to your My eBay page at any time, click the My eBay link at the top of the screen.

Start searching.

Figure 19-1:
The My
eBay page.

Select a tab.

The My eBay page offers these tabs for tracking your activity in eBay:

✦ **Bidding/Watching:** A list of items you have placed a bid on, items you are watching, and items you have won. Watching an item means to bookmark it so you can click its name on the Bidding/Watching tab and revisit its Web page. For each item on this tab, eBay tells you its current price, how many bids have been made on it, and how much time remains before the auction closes (if it hasn't already closed).

✦ **Selling:** A list of items you are selling or have sold. Selling items on eBay isn't covered in this book — for more information on selling items, check out *eBay For Dummies*, 4th Edition, by Marsha Collier (published by Wiley Publishing, Inc.).

✦ **Favorites:** Lists of saved searches, category names, and seller names. After you have carefully constructed a search (say, for Elvis 45s), you can save the search and instantly conduct it again by clicking its name on this page. You can also quickly go to item categories or see what your favorite sellers are offering.

✦ **Accounts:** For sellers, so they can track monetary transactions.

✦ **Feedback:** Starting here, you can rate people who have sold you items and see how sellers have rated you. eBay maintains buyer and seller ratings so that buyers can buy with confidence and sellers can sell with confidence.

✦ **Preferences:** Go here to change your personal information — your User ID name, password, and so on.

✦ **All:** For people who like scrolling, this tab has what is on all the other tabs.

Searching for Items of Interest

What are you interested in? Stereo equipment? Antique cowboy clothes? Bank vaults? Everything except guns and body organs is auctioned on eBay. The question is: Where on eBay is it located? Unless the item you want to find has a very specific name — say, a Canon S50 Powershot S-50 — you will have trouble finding it. You can't simply enter "camera" in the Search box, because that means wading through thousands of auctions before finding a camera you want. As an experiment, I just entered **camera** in the search box and got 45,314 auctions pertaining to cameras! You would need a lot of stamina and time to look into that many auctions.

To help you find your diamond in the rough, the following pages explain how to search eBay. All searches begin on the My eBay page (refer to Figure 19-1).

A straight search

As I just explained, a straight search is useful if the item you are looking for has a very specific name. For example, I entered the term **Canon S50 Powershot S-50** in the Search text box, and I found 67 auctions rather than the 45,314 I got when I entered the term **camera**.

eBay offers two ways to conduct a straight search:

Search

✦ **Simple search:** Enter the term in the Search text box on your My eBay page and click the Search button.

✦ **Basic or Advanced search:** Click the Search link on your My eBay page. You see the Search form shown in Figure 19-2. From here, you can fill in a form and conduct a Basic Search or an Advanced Search (by clicking the Advanced Search tab). These forms offer many criteria for narrowing down a search and finding what you want.

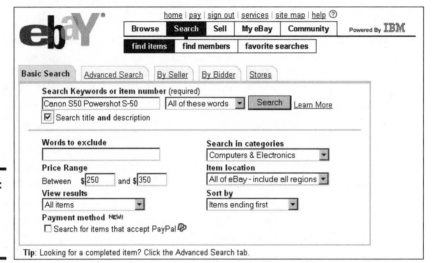

Figure 19-2:
A basic search of eBay auctions.

If you want to get more search results, select the Search Titles and Descriptions check box. This tells eBay to look for your search terms in item descriptions as well as titles.

Browsing eBay categories

eBay auctions are classified by category, subcategory, sub-subcategory, and so on. In the browsing search method, you locate a category or subcategory that describes items you are interested in, you get a list of items in the category or subcategory, and you then click items one at a time to look them over. The browsing technique requires a fair amount of free time. For every gem you discover, you have to look at about 300 pieces of dross. Oh well, browsing can be fun. Follow these steps to browse different eBay categories:

Browse

1. **On your My eBay page, click the Browse link.**

You see the Categories page, as shown in Figure 19-3.

2. **Scroll down to see the complete category and subcategory list.**

3. **Click on a category or subcategory and start browsing different items.**

Want to see detailed category lists with the names of many sub-subcategories? Click the Category Overview link in the Categories window (refer to Figure 19-3). From here, you can select a category and get a detailed list with many, many subcategories. Finding a subcategory like this is a great way to pinpoint what you are interested in.

Select a category.　　　Click to see subcategories.

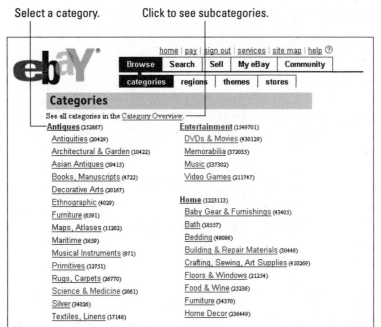

Figure 19-3:
Browsing by
category
and subcat-
egory.

Browsing to and searching a single category

A browse/search permits you to search exclusively in a single eBay category or subcategory. Under this searching method, you browse to the category you are interested in, and then you conduct a search exclusively in
that category. In my experience, this is the most efficient way to search eBay.

In Figure 19-4, for example, I browsed to the Westerns sub-subcategory
(using techniques I describe in the previous section of this chapter). In the
Basic Search form on the left, I entered **Randolph Scott** to search for west-
ern movies starring that golden-haired box office idol of yesteryear. Only 43
items show up in the search.

Book III
Chapter 19

Getting Bargains
on eBay

Enter your search terms.　　　　　　　Browse to a subcategory.

Figure 19-4:
Searching
one
category.

Saving searches, categories, and sellers/stores

After you hang around eBay a while, you will find yourself, depending on your interests, revisiting the same categories, conducting the same searches, and looking at wares offered by the same handful of sellers. Rather than construct the same searches or browse around for the same categories over and over, you can put these searches and categories on the Favorites tab of your My eBay page. Then all you have to do to conduct a search or visit a category is click its name on the Favorites tab. Putting the name of a seller or eBay store on the Favorites tab is a great way to see a sellers' items. I have identified four sellers on eBay who consistently offer items I am interested in. I can see these items merely by clicking a name on the Favorites tab of my My eBay page.

Starting on the Favorites tab of your My eBay page, follow these instructions to be able to quickly visit categories, conduct searches, and see what is being offered by different sellers:

+ **Searches:** On the My Favorite Searches part of the page, click the Add New Search link. You see the Basic Search form. Describe the search and click the Search button. If the search results are to your liking, click the Add to My Favorites Searches link to enter the search on your My eBay page.

+ **Categories:** On the My Favorite Categories part of the page, click the Add/Change Categories link. Then click the names of categories and subcategories till you come to a category you like to visit often. Click the Submit button at the bottom of the page.

+ **Sellers/Stores:** On every auction page is a link called View Seller's Other Items. By clicking this link, you can see a list of other items that the seller is offering. When you find a seller who consistently offers items you find interesting, jot down his or her User ID. Then, starting on the Favorites tab of your My eBay page, click the Add New Seller/Store link. Enter the seller's User ID in the Seller's User ID or Store Name text box and click the Save Favorite button.

You can rearrange the Favorites page by clicking the Move Table Up or Move Table Down button to the right of the My Favorite headings. For example, to move My Favorite Categories to the top of the Favorites page, start clicking the Move Table Up button on the right side of the My Favorite Categories heading.

A Few Rules to Live By

Observe these rules as you bid on eBay items:

+ **Avoid impulse bidding.** Yes, the beanbag chair is being offered at a good price, but do you really need a beanbag chair?

+ **Investigate the price.** Just because an item is being auctioned at eBay doesn't mean that it's a good buy. *Remember:* Many people who auction at eBay are merely reselling items that they purchased at a discount. Sometimes you can purchase these items straight from the manufacturer yourself and buy them cheaply. After all, all kinds of stuff is for sale on the Internet.

✦ **Know what the shipping and handling charges are.** Some sellers who auction items cheaply make up the lost revenue by charging exorbitant fees for shipping and handling.

✦ **Contact the seller if you have any questions.** eBay makes it easy to contact a seller. On the item's eBay page, click the Ask Seller a Question link. A message form appears so you can send an e-mail to the seller. The reply will be sent to the e-mail address you gave eBay when you registered.

✦ **Investigate the seller.** On the item's eBay page, you can click the Read Feedback Reviews link to see a summary of the seller's transactions and ratings, as shown in Figure 19-5. Scroll down the page to see what buyers have said about the seller.

✦ **Ask yourself how difficult the item is to assemble, if it needs assembling.** Not everyone can interpret the complicated directions that come with items you have to put together yourself. Not everyone can wield a screwdriver. Because purchases are delivered by mail, they need assembling more often than other purchases. If you're not good at assembling things, make sure that the items you buy are already assembled.

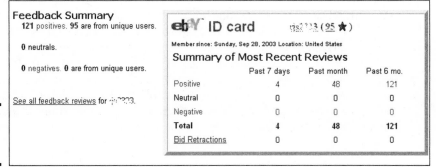

Figure 19-5: Investigating a seller.

Bidding on Items

When you find an item you just gotta have, the next step is to bid on it. Go ahead. Don't be shy. eBay bidding is slightly different from conventional auction bidding, as I explain shortly. I also explain how to place a bid and close a sale.

How bidding works

Each auction page tells you how many days, hours, and minutes are left till closing time. The person who submits the highest bid before closing time, of course, wins the item, but it's not quite that simple. eBay auctions are not live auctions. Because not everyone who wants to bid can be online and signed into eBay at closing time, eBay buyers make what are called maximum bids. Only the bidder knows what his or her maximum bid is. As long as your maximum bid — the maximum amount you are willing to pay for an item — exceeds other buyers' maximum bids, you are the high bidder. But if you make a maximum bid and someone who bid before has made a maximum bid that is higher than yours, you are not the high bidder. Instead the stated price of the item rises to the amount that you submitted in your maximum bid.

Confusing, huh? To see how it works, imagine an auction for a Chippendale mirror. The bidding starts at $50. The bid increment — the amount by which each bid must exceed the previous bid — is $2.50.

Dave, the first bidder, enters a maximum bid of $75. On the auction page, however, the price remains $50. Dave has merely stated how high he is willing to go to win the item. **Remember:** Only Dave knows what his maximum bid is.

The next bidder, Sally, enters a maximum bid of $60, but because her $60 doesn't exceed Dave's maximum bid of $75, eBay informs Sally that she is not the high bidder. Meantime, the price of the item rises to $60, the amount of Sally's maximum bid. If no one else bids, Dave can buy the mirror for $60.

Sally, still keen to own the mirror, enters a maximum bid of $65, but eBay informs Sally that she is still not the highest bidder. At $75, Dave remains the high bidder. The price of the item rises to $65, the amount of Sally's second bid.

Sally just has to have that beautiful Chippendale mirror. She enters a maximum bid of $85. Now she is the high bidder and the stated price of the item is $77.50, Dave's original maximum bid ($75) plus the bid increment ($2.50).

eBay informs Dave by e-mail that he has been outbid. Dave goes to the Bidding/Watching tab of his My eBay page, selects the Chippendale mirror auction, and goes to the Chippendale mirror auction page. He sees that the item now costs $77.50. He has been outbid. He enters a maximum bid of $90. eBay tells Dave that he is the high bidder. The price of the mirror is now $87.50, the amount of Sally's maximum bid ($85) plus the bid increment ($2.50). Dave will win the mirror for $87.50 as long as no one outbids his maximum bid of $90.

Auction sniping

Auction sniping means to outbid competitors at the last possible moment in an eBay auction. If the auction ends at high noon, the successful auction sniper makes the final, highest bid at 11:59.59. If you spend any time on eBay, you are bound to be sniped sooner or later. eBay maintains an article about auction sniping at this address: `http://pages.ebay.com/help/basics/g-sniping.html`

Most people don't have the spare time to be an auction sniper, but several Internet services will do it for you — for a fee, of course. After registering for these services, you tell the service which eBay item you are bidding on, set your price, and let the auction sniper place the bid for you at the last moment. Here are some auction sniping services and the addresses of Web sites where you can find out more about them:

- ✔ **AuctionSniper:** The cost is 1 percent of the auction price, with a minimum fee of $0.25 and a maximum fee of $5. `www.auctionsniper.com`

- ✔ **AuctionStealer:** The cost is $9 to $10 per month, depending on how long you enroll. `http://auctionchief.auctionstealer.com/home.cfm`

- ✔ **Bidnapper:** The cost is between $4 and $6 per month, depending on how long you enroll. `www.bidnapper.com`

- ✔ **HammerSnipe:** The cost is $9 to $10 per month, depending on how long you enroll. `http://hammertap.auctionstealer.com/home.cfm`

Because you never know what the current maximum bid is, you never know whether a maximum bid you submit will make you the high bidder. The maximum bid formula is designed to keep one person from outbidding another by a few dollars at the last minute. It also gives you a chance to participate in auctions without having to be present at your computer while the auction is taking place.

Placing a bid

To place a bid and declare the maximum amount you will pay for an item, click the Place Bid button. You see the Place a Bid window shown in Figure 19-6. Enter your maximum bid and click the Continue button. You see the Submit Your Bid window, where you have a last chance to review your bid before clicking the Submit button.

As soon as you submit a bid, eBay tells you whether you are the high bidder. The item you are bidding on is placed on the Bidding/Watching tab of your My eBay page whether you are the high bidder or not. If someone outbids you, eBay sends you an e-mail telling you as much. The e-mail is sent to the address you entered when you registered. To change this address, go to the Preferences tab of your My eBay page.

Book III
Chapter 19

Getting Bargains
on eBay

Figure 19-6:
Making
a bid.

Strategies for successful bidding

To be a successful bidder, be coy. When you see an item you really like, don't bid on it right away. Click the Watch This Item link to enter the item on your Watch List, a list on the Bidding/Watching tab of your My eBay page. From the Bidding/Watching tab, you can click the item's name and go to its auction page to find out whether others have placed a bid.

Ideally, bids should be placed at the last minute, but forgetting to bid on an item is easy. One strategy for remembering to bid is to enter a low bid in the early going. Each time you are outbid, eBay will send you an e-mail telling you so. The e-mail message will include a link you can click to go directly to the auction page and up your bid.

Setting aside what I just said about being coy, if you really, really want an item, make a large bid for it. This way, you will scare off other bidders and decrease your chances of being sniped.

PayPal

PayPal is an online system for sending and receiving payments by e-mail. Most eBay sellers prefer to receive payments by PayPal. For buyers, PayPal is the most convenient way to pay. Instead of writing checks or dealing with credit card numbers, you can simply give instructions to PayPal for making the transaction. The item will arrive sooner because very little time is spent in the transaction.

PayPal is free to buyers (sellers have to pay a small percentage of the price of the sale). To find out more about PayPal and perhaps subscribe to the service, check out www.paypal.com.

Closing the Sale

When you win an auction, eBay sends you an e-mail telling you how much the item costs including shipping and handling. At that point, it is up to you to pay for the item. If you did your homework, you know how the seller prefers to be paid. You can usually pay by PayPal, by check, or with a credit card.

When the transaction is complete and you have the item in hand, be sure to describe the seller to eBay. You can do so by going to the Feedback tab on your My eBay page. Click the Leave Feedback button to see a list of people who sold you items. Click a seller's name and enter a rating and brief description of the transaction. Other buyers depend on this information to decide whether a seller is trustworthy.

Chapter 20: Planning Your Next Vacation Online

In This Chapter

✔ **Getting directions from the Internet**

✔ **Looking for cheap flights and buying cheap tickets online**

✔ **Booking a room on the Internet**

✔ **Getting ready for a trip abroad**

Most people, however tentatively, are planning their next vacation. You need something to look forward to. About 3:00, when the afternoon starts to wane, lunch is a distant memory, and two or three hours of work are still due at the office, most people dream of being on vacation. Backpacking in the Sierra-Nevada, partying at Mardi-Gras in New Orleans, cruising up the Amazon in a steamer, basking in the sun on a beach in Bali.

This chapter is dedicated to those people who want to make their next vacation the best ever. It describes how to research a destination — how the Internet can help you find out where to stay and what to do while you're away. You find out how to obtain inexpensive airfares, hotel rooms, and rental cars. This chapter also presents Internet resources for traveling abroad.

Researching a Destination

Taping a map to the wall and throwing darts at the map to decide where to go next is one way of travel planning. However, mathematicians have determined that the amount of pleasure you derive from a vacation is directly proportional to the amount of time you spend planning it.

Read on to find out how the Internet can help you plan itineraries, locate attractions on the map, and get directions for driving from here to there. You will also discover how to get up-to-date information about the weather and road conditions where you want to travel.

Deciding where to go and what to see

The hardest decision to make when you are planning a travel itinerary is deciding where to go and what to see when you get there. The following Web sites can help you match your desires and interests with attractions and destinations:

✦ **Arthur Frommer's Budget Travel Online:** This site is the Internet companion to the famous *Frommer's Travel Guides*. Besides travel advice, you can look for hotel accommodations, nightlife, shopping, and dining opportunities in cities the world over. Address: www.frommers.com

✦ **Citysearch.com:** This site currently offers comprehensive guides to several dozen U.S. cities and a handful of cities abroad. The guides are up to date, with detailed information about local restaurants, nightspots, clubs, and shopping. Address: `www.citysearch.com`

✦ **Fodor's Travel Online:** Click the Destinations link to see about traveling in different cities. Not that you will stray from the beaten path, but you will get solid information about the city of your choice. Address: `www.fodors.com`

✦ **Online City Guide:** From this site, you can pinpoint a city in the United States, find a list of hyperlinks with information about the city, and click a link to help plan your vacation. The links are to private Web sites and sometimes are not the greatest, but try your luck. Address: `www.olcg.com`

✦ **Yahoo! Travel Pages:** Starting from this page at Yahoo!, you can begin investigating any number of travel subjects, including eco-tourism, train travel, and hitchhiking. Address: `http://dir.yahoo.com/Recreation/Travel`

Finding out how to get there

The Web sites listed here are meant to keep you from getting lost. These Web sites present online maps and online mapping tools to help you go precisely where you want to go. Still, before you look at the Web sites, consider the advantages of getting lost. Being lost quickens the senses. It makes you acutely aware of your surroundings. It makes you feel alive. Someday, a genius is going to put up a Web site with instructions for helping people get lost.

Meanwhile, visit these Web sites when you are planning your vacation and you want to know where an attraction is and how to get there from your hotel or the airport. These Web sites all permit you to get driving directions from one place to another:

✦ **How far is it?:** As the crow flies, how far is Athens, Georgia, from Athens, Greece? The answer: 5,628 miles (or 9,058 kilometers). This very friendly Web site for crows and travel planners calculates distances in no time at all. Address: `www.indo.com/distance`

✦ **MapBlast!:** Displaying a map is pretty simple, and the tools for zooming in, zooming out, and printing are easy to understand and use. Address: `www.mapblast.com`

✦ **MapQuest:** Another site for creating a map. Enter an address and click the Get Map button to get your map. Address: `www.mapquest.com`

✦ **Maps On Us:** As shown in Figure 20-1, you can enter your starting address and destination address, and this site creates a map for getting from one to the other. Address: `www.mapsonus.com`

✦ **The Subway Navigator:** For several dozen cities around the world, about a dozen in the United States, plan a subway or light train route from one station to the next. Address: `www.subwaynavigator.com`

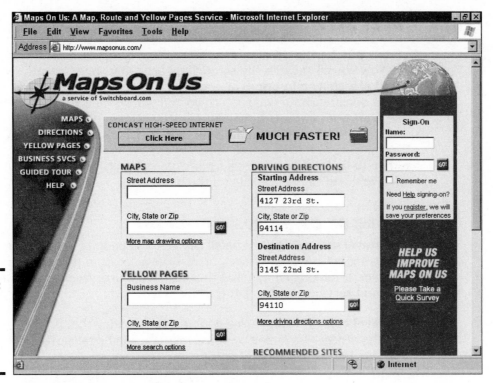

Figure 20-1:
Getting driving directions at Maps On Us.

Weather and road conditions

Ants and mosquitoes can ruin a good picnic, but that's nothing compared to what a vigorous storm can do to a weekend at the beach. Before you leave, check out these Web sites to see whether the roads are passable and what kind of weather you will encounter:

✦ **AccuTraffic:** From here, you can get the latest report about road conditions on American highways. Click the Traffic link and select a state to go the official Web site of the state's Department of Transportation. Weather reports are also available from this site. Address: www.accutraffic.com

✦ **USA Today Online Weather Almanac:** For travel planning, this site offers monthly climate data for cities the world over. Go here to find out what the average monthly high and low temperatures, rainfall, and snowfall are in a vacation spot that you are eyeing. Address: www.usatoday.com/weather/walm0.htm

✦ **The Weather Channel:** While you are deciding whether to pack a sweater or a T-shirt, sunblock or an umbrella, pay a visit to the Weather Channel. By entering a city or zip code, you can find out what meteorologists think the weather will be for the coming week at your destination. Do you remember what Mark Twain said about the weather? He said, "Everybody talks about the meteorology, but nobody does anything about it." Address: www.weather.com

Online Travel Services

As far as purchasing tickets goes, the Internet has put you in the driver's seat. Now you can search the same databases that travel agents search. Instead of looking into prices at one airline or rental car service at a time, you can declare where you want to go and when you want to go there, and make everybody come to you. Your search of the Internet will turn up flights, rental cars, hotel rooms, and railway tickets that meet your travel needs.

Read on to find out how to look for inexpensive airline tickets, hotel rooms, rental cars, and railway tickets on the Internet.

Visiting an all-purpose travel site

These travel sites attempt to be all things to all people. You can book a hotel room, buy an airline ticket, or reserve a car from these sites. The advantage of looking here is that these sites are user-friendly. Compare prices and services, and pick the one you like best.

✦ **1travel.com:** This one has a couple of interesting things you don't find at the others — a currency converter and a list of airports experiencing delays. Address: `www.onetravel.com`

✦ **CheapTickets.com:** This a comprehensive site where you can buy an airline ticket, book a hotel room, or rent a car. Address: `www.cheaptickets.com`

✦ **Expedia.com:** From here, you can buy airline tickets, reserve hotel rooms, and reserve rental cars (see Figure 20-2). So-called wizards make it easy to search for good rates. Address: `www.expedia.com`

Figure 20-2: Look for a cheap flight, a good room, and a trusty rental car at Expedia. com.

✦ **Hotwire.com:** Besides renting cars and booking airline tickets, this site lets you book luxury cruises. Address: www.hotwire.com

✦ **Priceline.com:** Another great site for purchasing airline tickets. You can also rent cars and book hotel reservations here. Address: www.priceline.com

✦ **Travelocity.com:** Besides the usual travel-planning stuff, this is the place to go if your flight dates are flexible and you don't need to search for a ticket on a specific date or time. Select the Search All Dates for Best Fares option button, and you'll get a list of low airfares on different days. Choose a day to travel instead of choosing a ticket. Address: www.travelocity.com

Booking a hotel or motel room

The all-purpose Web sites described earlier in this chapter are the best places to book chain hotels. But if you are looking for something special — a romantic retreat or a cozy hideaway — look to these sites:

✦ **BedandBreakfast.com:** If you are turned off by impersonal hotel chains, this is the site to visit. Address: www.bedandbreakfast.com

✦ **HomeExchange.com:** At this site, you can look into exchanging vacation time at your home with the home of someone in a destination that you want to visit. Address: www.homeexchange.com

✦ **InnSite:** This is a guide to inns and bed and breakfasts in the United States and abroad. This site is slow, perhaps because it indexes 50,000 pages of inn directories. But the wait is worthwhile. Address: www.innsite.com

✦ **Vacation Direct:** Owners list their vacation homes and condos at this site, where you can find descriptions of the vacation rentals and instructions for contacting the owners. Address: www.vacationdirect.com

Of course, you can also go the Web sites of the different hotel chains to book last-minute deals.

Traveling by rail

Traveling by rail offers the pleasures of traveling by car without the hassles. You can get up and stretch your legs. Instead of fast-food restaurants and highway clutter, the picturesque and the seedy roll past the window. Railroads cut through mountain passes and fly above wild rivers. The planet never looked as beautiful as it does from a railroad car.

Here are some Internet resources for traveling by rail:

✦ **Amtrak:** This, of course, is the United States passenger railway service (see Figure 20-3). From this site, you can plan a trip by railroad and purchase tickets. Address: www.amtrak.com

✦ **European Rail Travel:** This site offers planning tips and advice for traveling by rail in Europe. You can get information about the famous Eurail Pass, as well as schedules of all European trains. Address: www.eurorailways.com

✦ **Via Rail Canada:** This is the official site of Rail Canada. Use it to purchase train tickets when traveling in the United States' winsome windswept neighbor to the north. Address: www.viarail.com

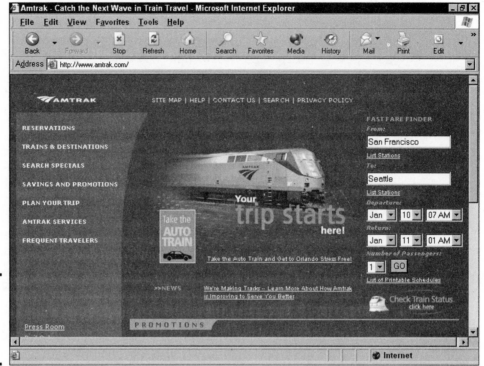

Figure 20-3:
The train is the best way to travel!

Resources for Traveling Abroad

Many people like to travel abroad. When you go to the expense and trouble of traveling, you may want to land in a place where things look different and no one speaks English. That way, you really feel like you've traveled somewhere!

Here are some Internet resources for world travelers:

✦ **Centers for Disease Control — Traveler's Health:** This invaluable Web site offers advice for staying healthy during your vacation. It explains which vaccinations you need and presents health information about specific regions. Address: www.cdc.gov/travel

✦ **Crazy Dog Travel Guide:** This site offers tips, advice, and numerous hyperlinks to help budget travelers all over the world plan their adventures. Address: www.crazydogtravel.com

✦ **Foreign Languages for Travelers:** How do you say "excuse me" in Swedish? You say, "Ursakta," as this Web site so ably points out. What makes this site cool and useful is its sound capabilities. When you click a foreign-language phrase, the Windows Media Player comes on-screen, and you can actually hear the phrase. Address: www.travlang.com/languages

✦ **Lonely Planet Online:** From this superb Web site, you can research different destinations, get travel tips from others, or post a travel question that is bound to get an answer from Lonely Planet's legion of adventurers. Click the Search hyperlink to research a destination abroad or in the United States. Click The Thorn Tree hyperlink to see what others say about a destination or post your own question about it. Address: www.lonelyplanet.com

✦ **Time Out:** This site focuses on nightlife and entertainment in a couple dozen European cities (and a few American and Asian cities as well). Address: www.timeout.com

✦ **The Universal Currency Converter:** One United States dollar will fetch how many Malaysian ringgits? The answer: 3.799 (as of this writing, anyway). Go to this easy-to-use Web site to see what happens when one currency is converted into another. Address: www.xe.net/ucc

✦ **U.S. Customs and Border Protection:** This very helpful Web site explains such matters as how to import a car and why you were charged for what you thought was a duty-free purchase. Address: www.customs.ustreas.gov

✦ **U.S. Department of State — Travel Warnings and Consular Information Sheets:** Here, you will find the visa and entry requirements that Americans must fulfill to travel to every country in the world. You will also find safety statistics, descriptions of medical facilities, and embassy addresses. Address: travel.state.gov/travel_warnings.html

Eccentric Sites for Eccentric Travelers

Finally, here are some eccentric sites for eccentric travelers. One of the drawbacks of getting travel information from the Internet is that much of the information was put there by corporate hotel chains that want to sell you something. These sites are devoted strictly to travel, its spontaneous joys, and its occasional apprehensions:

✦ **Bureau of Atomic Tourism:** This site is dedicated to the promotion of tourist locations worldwide that have witnessed atomic explosions or display exhibits about the development of atomic devices. It's hard to tell how far the creators of this site have thrust their tongues into their cheeks. At any rate, you can see many photos of nuclear devastation and yes, detailed tour schedules and visitor information are available, too. Address: www.atomictourist.com

✦ **Dead Presidents:** Manus Hand, surely one of the most eccentric people on the Internet, has made it his hobby to take photographs of himself at the graves of the presidents of the United States. Writes Mr. Hand, "If you're into dead presidents (and gosh, who isn't?), you came to the right place. By simply clicking your mouse button, you can see pictures of me, Manus Hand, visiting the final resting places of every one of them (save three — I'm still working on it!)." This site is living testimony that any excuse will do when it comes to traveling. Address: http://starship.python.net/crew/manus/Presidents

✦ **Robert Young Pelton's Dangerous Places:** Traveling to dangerous places can be exciting. Traveling vicariously to dangerous places can be exciting as well, as this site demonstrates. Here, you can read tales of dangerous locations and get advice for traveling to dangerous places if you feel like taking the plunge. Address: www.comebackalive.com/df/dplaces.htm

✦ **The World Clock:** You're going to Uzbekistan and you want to arrive fit and refreshed. To do that, however, you have to put yourself on Uzbekistan time three or four days before departure. What time is it in Uzbekistan? You can find out at this Web site. Address: www.timeanddate.com/worldclock

✦ **National Caves Association:** This site is dedicated to spelunkers and their friends who enjoy exploring caves and caverns. Click the Caves & Caverns Directory link to go to the United States map. From there, you can click a state to look into its caves, caverns, and spelunking opportunities. Address: www.cavern.com

✦ **Roadside America:** This is unquestionably one of the very best sites on the World Wide Web. Where to begin? How about the Electronic Map. Click this link to go to a page with links to weird roadside attractions in 50 states (New Jersey, with the Uniroyal Giantess and Palace of Depression, seems to have more than its share). Check out the pet cemetery or the Travel Brain Trauma Center or the Miraculous Virgin Mary Stump. The site is shown in Figure 20-4. Address: www.roadsideamerica.com

Figure 20-4: Go to Roadside America to find out where the roadside attractions are.

✦ **The Walking Connection:** Walking, if you have the time and you are in good company, is the best way to travel. This site is devoted to walking tourism. It offers a message board for walkers, news of upcoming walks, and plenty of advice about good shoes. Address: www.walkingconnection.com

Chapter 21: Researching Investments Online

In This Chapter

✔ Finding investment strategies on the Internet

✔ Researching companies in which you want to invest

✔ Reading the latest news about companies and industries

✔ Investigating a mutual fund or stock on the Internet

*I*n the old days, only the wizards of Wall Street had enough information at their fingertips to evaluate stocks and other investments. A tickertape told them the value of each stock. Expensive newspapers, magazines, and newsletters told them about trends, investments worth buying, and investments worth shunning.

Nowadays, however, anyone with a PC can plug into the Internet and find all kinds of information about investing. Finding out the current value of a stock has become as easy as typing its ticker symbol in a text box. All across the Internet are Web sites that offer investment advice and information. If you are careful and know where to look, you can get your hands on the same information that experts use to play the market. You can read company prospectuses, financial newsletters, and magazines. You can visit a Web site tailor-made to provide a certain kind of information to investors. And the best part is that most of this stuff is free for the taking.

This chapter looks into how the Internet can help you start investing and become a better investor. It demonstrates how to research a company, points the way to financial news services on the Internet, and spells out how to research stocks and mutual funds.

Getting Lessons on How to Invest

Looking before you leap is always the best policy, so before you take the leap and start investing, go on the Internet and discover what investing is all about. Many brokers and banks are eager for you to start investing. For that reason, the Internet is filled with tutorials, online classes, and courses that you can take to learn the ropes.

Can't decide how much of your savings to devote to investments? Don't know what a market index is? Check out these Web sites, which offer online tutorials in investing:

✦ **The Investment FAQ:** Search for investor information by category, or conduct a keyword search. This site, which is shown in Figure 21-1, also offers tours for beginning investors (click the For Beginners hyperlink). Address: `invest-faq.com`

Figure 21-1:
Just the
FAQs,
ma'am:
Searching
for invest-
ment
answers
at the
Investment
FAQ.

✦ **MoneyCentral:** This Microsoft Web site offers general information about planning an investment strategy, as well as late-breaking financial news. Address: `www.moneycentral.com`

✦ **Vanguard Group:** Attend classes at "Vanguard University," and discover the basics of investing and retirement planning. (Click the Personal Investors link.) Address: `www.vanguard.com`

Playing the investment game

Investing isn't a game, of course, but you can make a game of it. These Web sites offer investment games to sharpen your strategies and skills. Here, you can play the game for a few months before graduating to the real thing:

✔ **EduStock:** Read the tutorial, and then test your skill by buying and selling stocks at up-to-date prices. Players start with 100,000 fantasy dollars with which to build a portfolio. You can practice researching stocks and securities from the Web site. Address: `http://library.thinkquest.org/3088`

✔ **Fantasy Stock Market:** Start with the requisite $100,000 in play money, and try to best the other

players in building a healthy portfolio. Players are ranked, and a new game starts each month. You can also research stocks from this Web site. Address: `www.fantasystockmarket.com`

✔ **Investment Challenge:** "The most realistic stock market simulation for students," boast the makers of this site. Here, you start not with $100,000, but with 500,000 fantasy dollars (students always need extra money, don't they?). Different games are designed for middle school, high school, and college students. Address: `www.ichallenge.net`

Researching a Company Online

It goes without saying that before you invest in a company, you owe it to yourself to research it. Has the company undergone a financial setback? Has management experienced a shakeup? What were the company's profits or losses in the last quarter?

To research a company, start by finding the company's Web site on the Internet. You can often make an educated guess as to the company's Web site address by typing **www.*companyname*.com** (where *companyname* is the name of the company) in the Address text box of your browser, pressing the Enter key, and hoping for the best. If that strategy doesn't work, try searching for the company's Web site by using a search engine such as Google (see Book III, Chapter 18 for more about searching the Web with Google).

Next, visit one of these Web sites to track down a company's profile:

✦ **Company News On-Call:** Search by company name in the PR Newswire database for articles published in the past year. Beware, however, because only news about large companies is available here. Address: `www.prnewswire.com/cnoc.html`

✦ **Hoover's Online:** This site provides profiles, revenue reports, balance sheets, and charts on some 8,500 companies (see Figure 21-2). Address: `www.hoovers.com`

Figure 21-2:
Go to
Hoover's
Online to
research
companies.

✦ **OneSource CorpTech:** The focus here is high-tech companies. The site offers company profiles, links to news articles about companies, and stock charts. CorpTech is very good at listing the names of company executives. Give one a call, and see what happens. Address: `www.corptech.com`

✦ **Public Register's Annual Report Service:** This site presents free annual reports from over 3,600 companies. Mind you, the companies themselves provide these reports, so give them a shrewd reading. Address: `www.prars.com`

✦ **U.S. Securities and Exchange Commission:** Publicly traded companies are required to file financial data with the Securities and Exchange Commission (SEC). From the SEC Web site, you can download details about a company's operations, including financial statements, executive pay, and other information. (Click the EDGAR Filers hyperlink.) Address: `www.sec.gov`

Besides visiting the Web sites listed here, try running a conventional Internet search for information about a company. You might find news articles and opinions about the company that way.

Reading the Financial News

It almost goes without saying, but savvy investors stay on top of late-breaking financial news. And keeping abreast of changes in the economy and the political climate isn't a bad idea either. A smart investor gets there first, before the fools rush in.

The Internet offers a daunting number of newspapers, magazines, newsletters, and news organizations that are devoted to financial news and opinions. Visit a few Web sites. Soon you will find a favorite site that focuses on news that matters to the kind of investing you want to do.

Major news services

First, a few mammoth corporate Web sites. Most of these sites — such as ABCNews.com and MSNBC.com — are sponsored by news services that predate the Internet. You won't find eccentric opinions here, but the news stories are trustworthy and the financial advice is as solid (if as plain) as granite:

✦ **ABCNews.com:** This site presents news about financial markets, commentary by experts, and a special section about mutual funds. This is an all-purpose news source. You can also get daily news and news about science and technology here. Address: `www.abcnews.com`

✦ **Bloomberg.com:** Advice for money management, news about financial markets, and columnists can be found here. Address: `www.Bloomberg.com`

✦ **CBS MarketWatch:** As shown in Figure 21-3, this all-purpose site does more than offer financial news. You can get market data, stock quotes, company portfolios, advice for managing your personal finances, and performance charts. Address: cbs.marketwatch.com

Figure 21-3: Whether you want to read the news or investigate a stock, CBS Market-Watch is a good place to start.

**Book III
Chapter 21**

Researching
Investments Online

✦ **MSNBC:** Click the Business link to go to a Web page with business news, stock market news, and news about e-commerce. Address: www.msnbc.com

✦ **TheStreet.com:** This site offers financial news but, better yet, it includes a nice selection of columnists. This is the place to go when you want to gather others' financial opinions. Address: www.thestreet.com

Financial newspapers and magazines

Perhaps financial newspapers and magazines are more to your taste. The online editions of these popular newspapers and magazines are not as comprehensive as the ones you can buy at the newsstand. However, they can still be very valuable:

✦ **Business Week Online:** This site offers news from the financial world, as well as technology and small business news. Address: www.businessweek.com

✦ **The Economist:** *The Economist,* an English financial magazine, is simply the best magazine of its kind in the world. Its cosmopolitan outlook puts to shame some of the narrow-minded, homegrown magazines on the news rack. Read the current issue of this magazine for its world view of economics and business. Address: www.economist.com

✦ **FT.com:** The online version of the *Financial Times* offers market data, news, and analysis. Address: www.ft.com

✦ **Kiplinger Online:** More than a magazine, the online edition of *Kiplinger's Personal Finance Magazine* offers shopping services, advice for buying insurance, and other valuable stuff. Of course, you also get business and market news. Address: www.kiplinger.com

✦ **Money:** The online edition of *Money* magazine provides many news articles and expert opinions. You can also get stock quotes and company profiles here. Address: www.money.cnn.com

✦ **Wall Street Journal:** The online edition of the famous newspaper also presents news summaries and insider information about American businesses. You can also get company reports and stock quotes. Address: www.wsj.com

Online newsletters

The Internet has made it possible for every Tom, Dick, and Harry to post a Web page and call it an investor newsletter. Far be it from me to decide which newsletters are worthy. Instead, you be the judge. Go to the Newsletter Access Web site (www.newsletteraccess.com), and search for a newsletter that whets your appetite. To conduct the search, enter a keyword or browse the different categories.

Researching Mutual Funds and Stocks on the Internet

Mutual funds and stocks are the two most popular kinds of investments. Not coincidentally, numerous Web sites devoted to stocks and mutual funds can be found on the Internet. From these sites, you can check the latest price of a stock or mutual fund. You can also dig deeper to investigate or screen funds and stocks. In the following pages, I unscrew the inscrutable and show you where to go on the Internet to research mutual funds and stocks.

To find out anything about a security on the Internet, you usually have to know its ticker symbol. A *ticker symbol* is an abbreviated company name that is used for tracking the performance of stocks, mutual funds, and bonds. You can usually find these symbols on the statements that you receive from brokers. If you don't know a security's ticker symbol, go to PC Quote (www.pcquote.com) and use the search engine there to find it (look for the Symbol Lookup hyperlink).

No terminology is harder to understand than investment terminology. Do you know what a price/earnings (P/E) ratio is? A short sell? A put? A shot-put? When you get stumped by an investment term, go to the glossary on the Yahoo! Finance Web site at finance.yahoo.com (look under Investing, and click the Glossary hyperlink under Education). The Yahoo! glossary is thorough, well written, and easy to search.

Socially conscious investing

Investing is a bit like casting a vote. When you invest in a company, you endorse its products, its business practices, and its labor practices. For better or worse, your investment helps shape the world in which we live.

On the idea that most people object to child labor, unsafe working conditions, pollution, and unhealthy products, a number of mutual fund managers have taken the lead and established socially conscious mutual funds. These funds do not buy into companies that practice what the managers think is bad business behavior.

To find out more about socially conscious investing and perhaps buy shares of a socially conscious mutual fund, check out the Co-op America Web site (www.coopamerica.org) and the Social Investment Forum (www.socialinvest.org). By the way, studies show that socially conscious mutual funds perform on average as well as other mutual funds.

Researching a mutual fund on the Internet

Mutual funds are the favorite of investors who want to reap the benefits of investing without doing the legwork. A *mutual fund* is a company that buys stocks, bonds, precious metals, and other securities. Investors buy shares in the fund. If the fund managers know their stuff, the securities that the mutual fund owns increase in value — and shares in the fund increase in value as well. Owning shares in a mutual fund is like owning shares of stock in a company. The difference is that a share of a mutual fund represents ownership in many different companies, as well as bonds and other securities.

Many people don't have the time, the expertise, or the inclination to research investment opportunities. For those people, mutual funds are ideal. You can rely on the fund managers' investing know-how. You can buy shares in a mutual fund without speaking to a broker. By definition, a mutual fund is diversified because it owns shares of many different securities, so you don't have to worry about diversification when you invest in a mutual fund.

Before you start dabbling in mutual funds, you need to know how fees are levied, about the different kinds of funds, and about the risks. After you know that, you can start looking for a fund that meets your needs. Here are some Web sites where you can acquire the basics of mutual fund investing:

✦ **Brill's Mutual Funds Interactive:** This is the all-purpose Web site for mutual fund investing. Here, you can read about mutual fund investing or search for funds by name and read about them. Address: www.fundsinteractive.com

✦ **Mutual Fund Investor's Center:** This excellent Web site offers articles about mutual fund investing and ranks mutual funds in various ways. You can also search for mutual funds using different criteria. Address: www.mfea.com

At last count, investors could choose from among 10,000 mutual funds. After you know what you want in a mutual fund, check out these Web sites, where you can search for a mutual fund that fits your investment strategy:

✦ **MoneyCentral Investor:** Enter keywords that describe what you want in a mutual fund. This site, shown in Figure 21-4, also offers charts and performance analyses. Address: `http://moneycentral.msn.com/investor/home.asp`

✦ **Morningstar.com:** The granddaddy of mutual fund analysis, this site offers reports on 7,000 mutual funds. You can get fund profiles, performance reports, financial statements, and news articles. (Click the Funds hyperlink.) Address: `www.morningstar.com`

✦ **SmartMoney.com:** This site offers a sophisticated search engine for pinpointing mutual funds. (Click the Funds hyperlink, and choose the Fund Finder hyperlink.) Address: `www.smartmoney.com`

Figure 21-4: Starting from the Money-Central Investor site, you can locate a mutual fund that fits the bill.

Researching stocks on the Internet

The stock market, it has been said, is 85 percent psychology and 15 percent economics. And that's only half the problem. The other half has to do with its hard-to-understand terminology and the numerous confusing ways to buy and sell stock.

If you decide to forsake mutual funds and jump into the stock market on your own, more power to you. This book cannot possibly delve into everything you need to know to invest in the stock market, but I can point the way to a few Web sites that will help you on the road to riches.

To get general-purpose information about stocks and stock markets, read stock tips, and discover stock-picking strategies, try these sites, which are good starting places:

✦ **DailyStocks.com:** This site provides links to market indexes, news sources, earnings figures, and newsletters. Address: `www.dailystocks.com`

✦ **Wall Street Research Net:** This site offers links to many financial resources, including brokers sites and government data. Address: `stocks.internetnews.com`

When you want to hunker down and examine specific stocks, go to one of these sites (and be sure to read "Researching a Company Online," earlier in this chapter, as well):

✦ **MoneyCentral Investor:** Look under Stocks, and click a hyperlink to find a stock quote, a chart, and analyst ratings. You can also screen stocks from this Web site. Address: `investor.msn.com`

✦ **PCQuote.com:** You can enter a ticker symbol and get stock quotes and charts. This site also presents market news, a "stock pick of the week," and news articles about the markets. Address: `www.pcquote.com`

✦ **Yahoo! Finance:** Enter a ticker symbol and you can get a price chart, news articles about a stock, charts that track its performance, and links to the company's SEC filings. As Figure 21-5 shows, you can also compare the performance of two different stocks against each other. Address: `http://finance.yahoo.com`

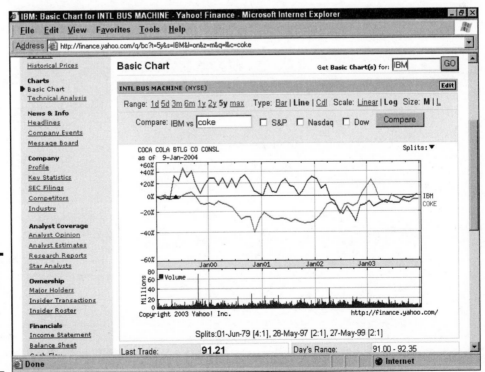

Figure 21-5: Comparing one stock against another at Yahoo! Finance.

Suppose that you want to target a stock but you don't know what it is yet. In other words, you believe that the future is bright for a certain industry and you want to buy shares in companies in that industry. Or you want to buy a certain kind of stock — stock in a foreign corporation, a small cap stock, or a blue-chip stock. Searching for stocks this way is called *screening*. The Reuter's Investor Web site offers stock-screening databases you can search using different variables. (Click the Screening Center hyperlink.) Its address is www.investor.reuters.com.

Chapter 22: Listening to the Music

In This Chapter

✔ The trouble with free file-sharing programs

✔ Looking at different online music stores

Unless you have been living in Outer Mongolia for the past decade, you know that it is possible to download songs and music over the Internet in the form of MP3 files. And you also know that downloading music this way is very controversial because most people download MP3s from Web sites without paying for them. Some believe that downloading music without paying is theft; others think that downloading music on the Internet is no more illegal than trading homemade cassette tapes with friends.

MP3 files, CD burners, and MP3 players (portable computer devices that play MP3 files) have changed the way that people listen to music and the way that music is distributed. As much as the music industry would like to turn back the clock to the days when music was distributed on CDs, it now appears that the MP3 file is here to stay. On the idea that you may as well join them if you can't beat them, music companies have begun licensing their music to online music stores. From these stores, you can legally download music over the Internet. This short chapter explains where these stores are and how you can obtain music from them. It also looks into the controversy surrounding software that permits you to download music for free.

Why Not Get Music for Free?

Back in the 1990s, a free computer program called Napster made it possible to download MP3 files without paying anything. Napster soon became wildly popular with music fans. The program became the most downloaded software in the history of the Internet. Fearing for its profits, the music industry filed lawsuit after lawsuit against Napster and finally succeeded in shutting down the company. But new software programs — Kazaa, Morpheus, Gnutella, and Grokster, among others — soon appeared to take the place of Napster.

These second-generation software programs for downloading MP3 files operate on the peer-to-peer file-sharing model. When you log onto the service, the software takes down your computer's IP address and compiles a list of the audio files on your computer (an *IP address* is a number that identifies each sender and receiver on the Internet). The software then passes your IP address and song list to other computers that are logged on, and these computers also pass along your IP address and list. In this way, your IP address and song list are soon broadcast to literally millions of computers. When you search for an audio file to download, you search IP addresses and song lists that have been passed to your computer. When you give the command to download a file from a list, the software targets the IP address of someone else's computer, locates the audio file on that computer, and downloads the file. If the same file is found on several computers, you download it from several computers at once, which cuts down on the time it takes to download the file. Meanwhile, others download audio files from your computer.

The matter of whether peer-to-peer file-sharing programs are legal is still being argued. Some courts have ruled that the makers of the software are not in violation of the copyright laws because they merely help people share files; they don't distribute the files themselves. The violators, some courts have ruled, are the ones who keep copyrighted material on their computers and give it to others without the people who hold the copyrights being compensated. In 2003, Sony and EMI sued several dozen subscribers to Kazaa on the grounds that they were sharing copyrighted material. The lawsuits sought damages ranging from $100,000 to $150,000 per song!

If you acquire audio files from a program like Kazaa, you run the risk of being sued, although many people are willing to take this risk. At any given time, some three million people are logged onto Kazaa. Your chances of being sued are small. You do, however, take certain risks and expose your computer to certain problems when you run peer-to-peer file-sharing software:

✦ Your computer's IP address is broadcast to millions of people. Sophisticated computer hackers can get into your system if they know your computer's IP address. They can download sensitive material such as credit card numbers.

✦ Ever wonder why these programs are free? They're free because, when you install them on your computer, you also install spyware and adware. *Spyware* is software that tracks where you surf on the Internet and gives the information to advertisers so they can send you ads tailored to your interests. *Adware* is software that makes pop-up advertisements appear on-screen when you browse the Internet. In effect, you pollute your computer when you install these programs. Kazaa is notorious in this regard. It makes your computer run slower.

✦ The quality of the audio files you download runs from very bad to very good, and you never know how bad or good a file is until you download and play it. Some audio files are incomplete. Others are not what they claim to be. Some are inferior recordings.

Finally, there is the ethical problem of downloading copyrighted material that you would normally have to pay for. Many people make a living by earning income or collecting royalties from the sale of music and video that is now being copied freely over the Internet. These people deserve your respect and consideration.

Abiding by the copyright laws

The coming years will see an epic battle between the people who own the copyrights to music and video files and the people who download them from the Internet and copy them from CDs and DVDs. The matter of whether you can legally copy this material to your computer is still unresolved, but one thing is certain: Copying the material and then reselling it is a clear violation of the copyright laws. You can't copy this stuff and package it for resale.

Touring Online Music Stores

The cost of downloading an audio file from an online music store ranges from 79 to 99 cents. This isn't much more than the cost of playing a song on a jukebox. The different stores have different policies as to how many computers you can keep songs on and how many times you can burn a song onto a CD. Table 22-1 compares and contrasts the different stores. Figure 22-1 shows the Napster 2.0 Web site (in 2003, Napster was reincarnated as a legitimate Web site for downloading music).

Table 22-1			Online Music Stores		
Store	*Song Price*	*Songs*	*File Format*	*Album Price (Starting)*	*Web Site*
BuyMusic	79¢	308,000+	WMA	7.95	www.buymusic.com
iTunes	99¢	500,000+	AAC	7.99	www.apple.com/ itunes
MusicMatch	99¢	360,000+	WMA	9.99	www.musicmatch.com
Napster 2.0	99¢	500,000+	WMA	9.95	www.napster.com
RealPlayer	99¢	400,000+	AAC	9.99	www.real.com
Wal-Mart	88¢	200,000+	WMA	9.44	musicdownloads. walmart.com

Book III Chapter 22

Listening to the Music

At the Web sites, you can listen to 30-second song clips before you decide whether to buy a song. Some Web sites charge a $20 to $30 per month subscription fee. WMA stands for Windows Media Audio. WMA files can be played on the Windows Media Player. AAC stands for Advanced Audio Coding. AAC files are meant to be played on Apple computers.

Good luck finding your favorite song.

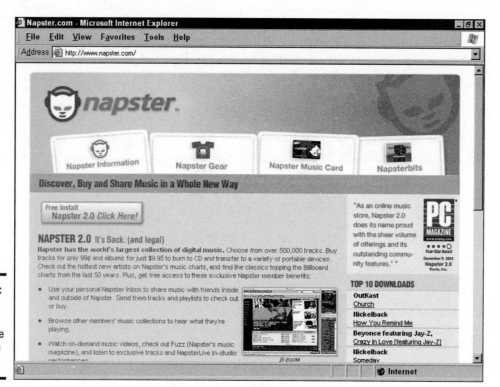

Figure 22-1:
You can download music at the Napster 2.0 Web site.

Book IV

Office 2003 and Money 2004

The 5th Wave   By Rich Tennant

"Get ready, Mona — here come the stats."

Book IV: Office 2003 and Money 2004

Chapter 1: Entering, Editing, and Formatting Text

In This Chapter

↳ **Creating new documents**

↳ **Opening and saving documents**

↳ **Changing text fonts and the size of text**

↳ **Spell checking a document**

This chapter is where you get your feet wet with Microsoft Word. Don't be shy. Walk right to the shore and sink your toes in the water. Don't worry; no one will push you from behind. This chapter explains how to create and open documents, save documents, and change the look of the text. If you aren't the greatest typist or speller, this chapter also tells you how to spell check a document.

Getting Acquainted with Word

Seeing the Word screen for the first time is sort of like trying to find your way through Tokyo's busy *Ikebukuro* subway station. It's intimidating. But when you start using Word, you quickly learn what everything is. To help you get going, Table 1-1 gives you some shorthand descriptions of the different parts of the Word screen. Figure 1-1 shows precisely where these parts of the screen are.

Table 1-1	Parts of the Word Screen
Part of Screen	*What It Is*
Title bar	At the top of the screen, the title bar tells you the name of the document you're working on.
Control menu	Click here to pull down a menu with options for minimizing, maximizing, moving, and closing the window.
Minimize, Restore, Close buttons	These three magic buttons make it very easy to shrink, enlarge, and close the window you are working in.
Menu bar	The list of menu options, from File to Help, that you choose from to give commands.
Task Pane	The pane that appears on the right side of the screen and provides options for opening Word documents and doing other tasks.

(continued)

Part I

Word 2003

Table 1-1 *(continued)*

Part of Screen	*What It Is*
Toolbars	A collection of buttons you click to execute commands. To display or remove toolbars, right-click a toolbar and choose a toolbar name on the shortcut menu.
Scroll bars	The scroll bars help you get from place to place in a document.
View buttons	Click one of these to change your view of a document.
Status bar	The status bar gives you basic information about where you are and what you're doing in a document. It tells you what page and what section you're in, the total number of pages in the document, and where the insertion point is on the page.

To see the Standard toolbar and Formatting toolbar and two separate rows, click the Toolbar Options button and choose Show Buttons on Two Rows. You will find the miniscule Toolbar Options button on the far right side of the Standard or Formatting toolbar.

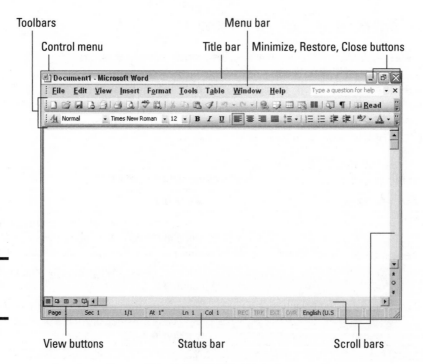

Figure 1-1:
The Word screen.

Creating a New Document

Document is just a fancy word for a letter, report, announcement, or proclamation that you create with Word. When you first start Word, you see a document with the generic name "Document1." Apart from the new document that appears when you start Word, the program offers a bunch of ways to create a brand-new document:

✦ **Starting from a blank document:** Click the New Blank Document button, press Ctrl+N, or click the Blank Document hyperlink in the New Document task pane. Go this route and you get a blank document made from the Normal template. For most occasions, the blank document is a fine place to start.

✦ **Starting with a sophisticated template:** Click the On My Computer hyperlink in the New Document task pane to open the Templates dialog box and choose a template there, as shown in Figure 1-2. You'll find the On My Computer hyperlink under the "Other Templates" in the New Document task pane. If you don't see the task pane, press Ctrl+F1 or choose View⇨Task Pane.

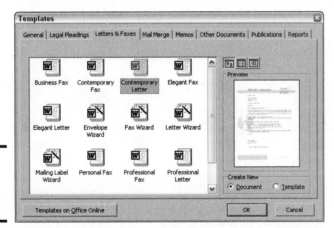

Figure 1-2:
The
Templates
dialog box.

Select a tab in the dialog box, select a template or wizard, and click the OK button. Each template comes with its own sophisticated styles so that you don't have to create fancy layouts yourself (Book IV, Chapter 4 explains styles). A *wizard* is a series of dialog boxes in which you make choices about the kind of document you want. If you are in the market for a fancy document, you can save a lot of time by doing it with a template or wizard because you don't have to do most of the formatting yourself.

✦ **Starting with a template from the Microsoft Web site:** Click the Templates Home Page hyperlink on the New Document task pane to go to Microsoft.com and choose a template there.

Speedy Ways to Open Documents

Rooting around in the Open dialog box to find a document is a bother, so Word offers these handy techniques for opening documents:

+ **File menu:** If you want to open a document you worked on recently, it may be on the File menu. Check it out. Open the File menu and see whether the document you want to open is one of those listed at the bottom of the menu. If it is, click its name or press its number (1 through 4).

+ **Document list in New Document task pane:** The same documents that are listed on the File menu can also be found at the top of the New Document task pane. Click a file there to open it.

+ **My Recent Documents button in the Open dialog box:** Click the My Recent Documents button in the Open dialog box to see a list of the last three dozen documents and folders that you opened. Double-click a document to open it; double-click a folder to see its contents.

 + **My Documents button in the Open dialog box:** Click the My Documents button to see the contents of the My Documents folder. Double-click a document to open it. The My Documents folder is a good place to keep documents you are currently working on. When you're done with a current document, you can move it to a different folder for safekeeping.

+ **Windows Documents menu:** Click the Start button and choose Documents to see a list of the last 15 files you opened (in Word and in other programs). Choose a Word document on the list to open it in Word.

+ **Open the Recent Documents Menu:** Click the Start button, choose My Recent Documents, and select from the last several files you opened. This way, you open a file and a program at the same time.

 To list more than four documents at the bottom of the File menu and the top of the New Document task pane, choose Tools➪Options, select the General tab in the Options dialog box, and enter a number higher than 4 in the Recently Used File List text box.

All about Saving Documents

 Everybody, or nearly everybody, knows how to save a document. All you have to do is press Ctrl+S, click the Save button, or choose File➪Save. The first time you save a document, you are asked to give it a descriptive name and choose the folder where it belongs. Word also offers the File➪Save As command for saving a file under a different name or in a different folder.

Changing the Font and Size of Text

Font is the catchall name for type style and type size. When you change fonts, you choose another style of type or change the size of the letters.

Word offers a whole bunch of different fonts. You can see their names by clicking the down arrow next to the Font drop-down list and scrolling down the list. To change the font:

1. **Select the text or place the cursor where you want the font to change.**

2. **Click the down arrow on the Font drop-down list and select a font name.**

As shown in Figure 1-3, you see the names of fonts, each one dressed up and looking exactly like itself. Word puts all the fonts you've used so far in the document at the top of the Font drop-down list to make it easier for you to find the fonts you use most often.

Figure 1-3: Choosing a font and font size.

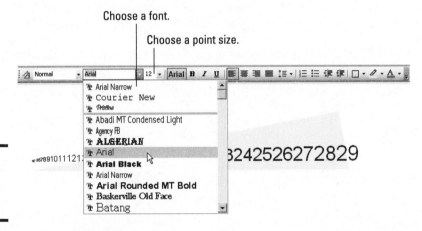

To quickly scroll down the list, press a letter on your keyboard. Press S, for example, to scroll to fonts whose names begin with an S. Fonts with *TT* beside their names are TrueType fonts. Use these fonts if you can because they look the same on-screen as they do when printed on paper.

Type is measured in *points*. A point is $\frac{1}{72}$ of an inch. The larger the point size, the larger the letters. To change the size of letters:

1. **Select the letters or place the cursor where you want the larger or smaller letters to start appearing.**

 2. **Click the down arrow on the Font Size drop-down list and choose a Font size.**

Enter a point size in the Font Size list box if the font sizes on the list don't do the trick.

 You can also change font sizes by selecting the text and pressing Ctrl+Shift+< or Ctrl+Shift+>. Doing so increases or decreases the font size by the next interval on the Font Size drop-down list. Press Ctrl+] or Ctrl+[to increase or decrease the font size by 1 point. To change fonts and font sizes at the same time, choose Format⇨Font and make your choices in the Font dialog box.

Book IV Chapter 1

Entering, Editing, and Formatting Text

What do you do if you look at your screen and discover — to your dismay — that you entered characters iN tHe wRONg casE? You can fix uppercase and lowercase problems by selecting the text you entered incorrectly and pressing Shift+F3. Keep pressing Shift+F3 until the text looks right. Shift+F3 first changes the characters to all lowercase, then to Initial Capitals, then to ALL UPPERCASE, and then back to all lowercase again.

Spell Checking a Document

Don't trust the spell checker — it can't catch all misspelled words. If you mean to type *middle* but type *fiddle* instead, for example, the spell checker won't catch the error because *fiddle* is a legitimate word. The moral is: If you're working on an important document, proofread it carefully. Don't rely on the smell checker to catch all your smelling errors.

The spell checker is great, however, for taking care of the majority of spelling errors. Figure 1-4 demonstrates the two ways to run the spell checker. Red wiggly lines appear under words that Microsoft Word thinks are misspelled. Right-click a misspelled word and choose the correct word on the shortcut menu. Otherwise, go the whole hog and spell or grammar check an entire document or text selection by starting in one of these ways:

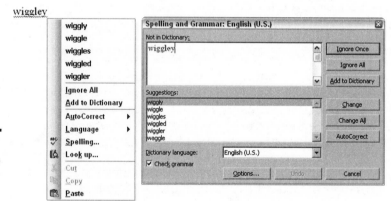

Figure 1-4:
Two ways to fix spelling errors.

 ✦ Click the Spelling and Grammar button.

✦ Choose Tools➪Spelling and Grammar.

✦ Press F7.

The Spelling and Grammar dialog box appears. Options in this dialog box are self-explanatory, except for these beauties:

✦ **Ignore Once:** Ignores the misspelling, but stops on it again if the same misspelled word appears later in the document.

✦ **Ignore All:** Ignores the misspelling wherever it appears in the document. Not only that, the spell checker ignores the misspelling in all your other open documents.

✦ **Add to Dictionary:** Adds the word in the Not in Dictionary box to the words in the dictionary that Microsoft Word deems correct. Click this button the first time that the spell checker stops on your last name to add your last name to the spelling dictionary.

✦ **Change All:** Changes not only this misspelling to the word in the Suggestions box, but also all identical misspellings in the document.

✦ **AutoCorrect:** Adds the suggested spelling correction to the list of words that are corrected automatically as you type them (Book IV, Chapter 2 explains the AutoCorrect mechanism).

✦ **Undo:** Goes back to the last misspelling you corrected and gives you a chance to repent and try again.

✦ **Check Grammar:** Deselect this check box to run the spell checker and ignore what Word thinks are grammatical errors.

You can click outside the Spelling dialog box and fool around in your document, in which case the Ignore button changes names and becomes Resume. Click the Resume button to start the spell check again.

What's with the red and green wiggly lines?

As you must have noticed by now, red wiggly lines appear under words that are misspelled, and green wiggly lines appear under words and sentences that Word thinks are grammatically incorrect. Correct spelling and grammar errors by right-clicking them and choosing an option from the shortcut menu. If the red or green lines annoy you, however, you can remove them from the screen by choosing Tools⇨Options and selecting the Spelling & Grammar tab in the Options dialog box:

✔ **Stop the wiggly lines from appearing:** Deselect the Check Spelling as You Type and the Check Grammar as You Type check boxes.

✔ **Stop the lines from appearing in one document only:** Select the Hide Spelling Errors in This Document or the Hide Grammatical Errors in This Document check boxes.

**Book IV
Chapter 1**

Entering, Editing, and Formatting Text

Chapter 2: Speed Techniques for Using Word

In This Chapter

- ✔ **Changing views of a document**
- ✔ **Splitting the screen**
- ✔ **Selecting text**
- ✔ **Quickly fixing mistakes**
- ✔ **Going here and there in documents**
- ✔ **Entering text quickly**
- ✔ **Finding and replacing text and formats**

Computers are supposed to make your work easier and faster. And if you can cut through all the jargon and technobabble, they can really do that. This chapter explains shortcuts and commands that can help you become a speedy user of Word. Everything in this chapter was put here so that you can get off work earlier and take the slow, scenic route home.

Getting a Better Look at Your Documents

A computer screen can be kind of confining. There you are, staring at the darn thing for hours at a stretch. Do you wish the view were better? The Word screen can't be made to look like the Riviera, but you can examine documents in different ways, zoom in and zoom out, and work in two places at one time in the same document. Better read on.

Viewing documents in different ways

In word processing, you want to focus sometimes on the writing, sometimes on the layout, and sometimes on the organization of your work. To help you stay in focus, Word offers different ways of viewing a document. Figure 2-1 shows what these views are. To change views, click a View button in the lower-left corner of the screen or choose a command from the View menu. Word offers no fewer than six ways to examine documents:

 ✦ **Normal view:** Choose View⇨Normal or click the Normal View button (in the lower-left corner of the screen) when you want to focus on the words. Normal view is best for writing first drafts and proofreading. You can see section breaks clearly in Normal view. You can't, however, see floating graphics in documents.

Figure 2-1:
Clockwise
from upper
left: Normal
view, Web
Layout view,
Outline
view,
Reading
Layout
view, Print
Preview,
and Print
Layout view.

✦ **Web Layout view:** Choose View➪Web Layout or click the Web Layout View button to see what your document would look like as a Web page. Background colors appear. Text is wrapped to the window. Want to see precisely what your document would look like in a Web browser? Choose File➪Web Page Preview. The document opens in your default Web browser (probably Internet Explorer).

✦ **Print Layout view:** Choose View➪Print Layout or click the Print Layout View button to see the big picture. You can see graphics, headers, footers, and even page borders in Print Layout view. This is what your document will look like when it's printed.

✦ **Outline view:** Choose View➪Outline or click the Outline View button to see how your work is organized. In Outline view, you see only the headings in a document and can easily move chunks of a document from place to place. Book IV, Chapter 6 explains outline view.

✦ **Reading Layout view:** Click the Read button on the Standard toolbar, choose View➪Reading Layout, or click the Reading button when you want to focus on the words. The Reading Mode toolbars appear on-screen. Click the Document Map or Thumbnails button to get from heading to heading or page to page. Press Esc or click the Close button to leave Reading Layout view.

✦ **Full Screen view:** Choose View➪Full Screen if you want to get rid of everything except the text you're working on. Click it or press Esc when you want the buttons, menus, and so on to come back. You can give menu commands from the menus on the menu bar in Full Screen view by moving the pointer to the top of the screen to make the menu bar appear.

✦ **Print Preview view:** Choose File➪Print Preview or click the Print Preview button to see what entire pages look like. Use this view to see the big picture and find out whether documents are laid out correctly. By clicking the Multiple Pages button, you can see one, two, or several pages simultaneously.

Zooming in, zooming out

Eyes were not meant to stare at computer screens all day, which makes the Zoom command all the more valuable. Use this command freely and often to enlarge or shrink the text on your screen and preserve your eyes for important things, such as gazing at the horizon. Give this command in one of these ways:

50% ▼

✦ Click the down arrow in the Zoom drop-down list and choose a magnification percentage. You will find the Zoom drop-down list on the Standard toolbar.

✦ Click inside the Zoom drop-down list box, type a percentage of your own, and press the Enter key.

✦ Choose View➪Zoom and, in the Zoom dialog box, choose a setting.

Working in two places in the same document

You can open a window on two different places simultaneously in a document. One reason you might do this: You are writing a long report and want the introduction to support the conclusion, and you also want the conclusion to fulfill all promises made by the introduction. That's difficult to do sometimes, but you can make it easier by opening the document to both places and writing the conclusion and introduction at the same time.

Word offers two methods for opening the same document to two different places: Opening a second window on the document or splitting the screen.

Opening a second window

To open a second window on a document, choose Window➪New Window. Immediately, a second window opens and you see the start of your document.

✦ Select the Window menu and you'll see that it now lists two versions of your document, number 1 and number 2 (the numbers appear after the filename). Choose number 1 to go back to where you were before.

✦ You can move around in either window as you please. Changes you make in either window also appear in the other window. Choose the File➪Save command in either window, and you save all the changes you made in both windows. The important thing to remember here is that you are working on a single document, not two documents.

✦ When you want to close the second or third window, just click its Close Window button. This button is located in the upper-right corner of the screen, below the Close button.

Splitting the screen

Splitting a window means to divide it into north and south halves, as shown in Figure 2-2. In a split screen, two sets of scroll bars appear so that you can travel in one half of the screen without disturbing the other half. In a split screen, you can choose a view for the different halves. For example, choose Outline view for one half and Normal view for the other to see the headings in a document while you write the introduction. Word offers two ways to split the screen:

✦ Move the mouse cursor to the *split box* at the top of the scroll bar on the right. Move it just above the arrow. When the cursor turns into double-arrows, click and drag the gray line down the screen. When you release the mouse button, you have a split screen.

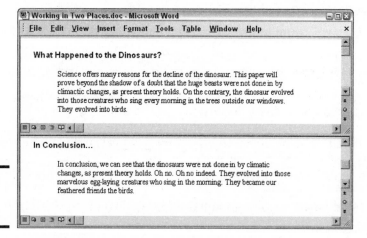

Figure 2-2:
A split
screen.

✦ Choose Window➪Split. A gray line appears on-screen. Roll the mouse down until the gray line is where you want the split to be, and then click. You get two screens split down the middle.

When you tire of this schizophrenic arrangement, choose Window➪Remove Split, drag the gray line to the top or bottom of the screen, or double-click on the line that splits the screen in two.

Selecting Text in Speedy Ways

To move text or copy it from one place to another, you have to select it first. You can also erase a great gob of text merely by selecting it and pressing the Delete key. So it pays to know how to select text. Table 2-1 describes shortcuts for selecting text.

Table 2-1	Shortcuts for Selecting Text
To Select This	*Do This*
A word	Double-click the word.
A line	Click in the left margin next to the line.
Some lines	Drag the mouse over the lines or drag the mouse pointer down the left margin.
A paragraph	Double-click in the left margin next to the paragraph.
A mess of text	Click at the start of the text, hold down the Shift key, and click at the end of the text.
A gob of text	Put the cursor where you want to start selecting, press F8 or double-click EXT (it stands for Extend) on the status bar, and press an arrow key, drag the mouse, or click at the end of the selection.
Yet more text	If you select text and realize you want to select yet more text, double-click EXT on the status bar and start dragging the mouse or pressing arrow keys.
Text with the same formats	Right-click text that is formatted a certain way and choose Select Text with Similar Formatting.
A document	Hold down the Ctrl key and click in the left margin, or triple-click in the left margin, or choose Edit➪Select All, or press Ctrl+A.

If you have a bunch of highlighted text on-screen and you want it to go away but it won't (because you pressed F8 or double-clicked EXT to select it), double-click EXT again.

After you press F8 or double-click EXT, all the keyboard shortcuts for moving the cursor also work for selecting text. For example, press F8 and then press Ctrl+Home to select everything from the cursor to the top of the document. Double-click EXT and press End to select to the end of a line.

Tricks for Editing Text

Following are some tried-and-true techniques for editing faster and better. On these pages, you find out how to take some of the drudgery out of repetitive work, fix errors, fit text on the screen, and view format symbols so that you can tell why text lies where it does on the page.

Undoing a mistake

Fortunately for you, all is not lost if you make a big blunder in Word because the program has a marvelous little tool called the Undo command. This command "remembers" the editorial and formatting changes you made since you opened your document. As long as you catch your error before you do five or six new things, you can "undo" your mistake. Try one of these undo techniques:

+ Choose Edit⇨Undo (or press Ctrl+Z). The name of this command changes on the menu, depending on what you did last. For example, if you just typed a sentence, it says Undo Typing.

+ Click the Undo button to undo your most recent change. If you made your error and went on to do something else before you caught it, click the down arrow next to the Undo button. You see a list of your previous six actions. Click the one you want to undo or, if it isn't on the list, use the scroll bar until you find the error and then click it, as shown in Figure 2-3. However, if you do this, you also undo all the actions on the Undo drop-down list above the one you're undoing.

Figure 2-3:
Fixing a mistake.

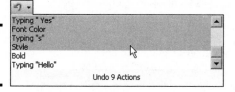

Typing " Yes"
Font Color
Typing "s"
Style
Bold
Typing "Hello"

Undo 9 Actions

Contrary to the Undo command is the Redo command. It redoes the commands you undid. If you've undone a bunch of commands and regret having done so, pull down the Redo drop-down list by clicking its down arrow and then choose the commands you thoughtlessly undid the first time around.

Viewing the hidden format symbols

Sometimes it pays to see the hidden format symbols when you're editing and laying out a document. The symbols show where lines break, where tabs are, where one paragraph starts and another ends, and whether two spaces instead of one appear between words. To see the hidden format symbols, click the Show/Hide ¶ button. Click the button again to hide the symbols. Here's what the hidden symbols look like on-screen:

Symbol	How to Enter
Line break (↵)	Press Shift+Enter
Optional hyphen (¬)	Press Ctrl+hyphen
Paragraph (¶)	Press Enter
Space (·)	Press the spacebar
Tab (→)	Press tab

Repeating an action — and quicker this time

The Edit menu contains a command called Repeat that you can choose to repeat your last action, and it can be a mighty, mighty time-saver. For example, if you just changed a heading style and you want to change another heading in the same way, move the cursor to the next heading and choose Edit⇨Repeat (or press F4 or Ctrl+Y). Rather than go to the trouble of clicking the Style drop-down list and choosing a heading style, all you have to do is choose a simple command or press a key or two.

Moving Around Quickly in Documents

Besides sliding the scroll bar, Word offers a handful of very speedy techniques for jumping around in documents: pressing shortcut keys, browsing in the Select Browse Object menu, using the Go To command, and navigating with the Document Map or thumbnails. Read on to discover how to get there faster, faster, faster.

Keys for getting around quickly

One of the fastest ways to go from place to place is to press the keys and key combinations listed in Table 2-2.

Table 2-2	Keys for Moving Around Documents
Key to Press	*Where It Takes You*
PgUp	Up the length of one screen
PgDn	Down the length of one screen
Ctrl+PgUp	To the previous page in the document
Ctrl+PgDn	To the next page in the document
Ctrl+Home	To the top of the document
Ctrl+End	To the bottom of the document

If pressing Ctrl+PgUp or Ctrl+PgDn doesn't get you to the top or bottom of a page, it's because you clicked the Select Browse Object button at the bottom of the vertical scroll bar, which makes Word go to the next bookmark, comment, heading, or whatever. Click the Select Browse Object button and choose Browse by Page to make these key combinations work again.

Viewing thumbnail pages

In lengthy documents, such as the one shown in Figure 2-4, the best way to get from place to place is to use Thumbnails view. In Thumbnails view, a thumbnail of each page in the document appears in the window pane on the left side of the screen. Each thumbnail is numbered so that you always know which page you are viewing. To quickly move from page to page, use the scroll bar on the left side of the screen. To switch to Thumbnails view, choose View⇨Thumbnails.

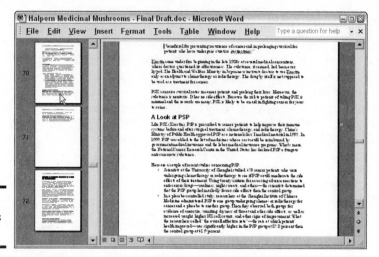

Figure 2-4:
Thumbnails
view.

"Browsing" around a document

A really fast way to move around quickly is to click the Select Browse Object button in the lower-right corner of the screen. When you click this button, Word presents 12 "Browse by" icons. Select the icon that represents the element you want to go to, and Word takes you there immediately.

Going there fast with the Go To command

Another fast way to go from place to place in a document is to use the Edit➪Go To command. Choose this command or press either Ctrl+G or F5 to see the Go To tab of the Find and Replace dialog box. The Go to What dropdown list in this dialog box lists everything that can conceivably be numbered in a Word document, and other things, too. Everything that you can get to with the Select Browse Object button, as well as lines, equations, and objects, can be reached by way of the Go To tab.

Hopping from place to place in the Document Map

Yet another way to hop from place to place is by turning on the document map. To do so, click the Document Map button or choose View➪Document Map. The headings in your document appear along the left side of the screen, as shown in Figure 2-5. Select an item in the Document Map, and Word takes you there in the twinkling of an eye. Right-click the document map and choose a heading level option on the shortcut menu to tell Word which headings to display in the map.

Bookmarks for hopping around

Rather than press PgUp or PgDn or click the scroll bar to thrash around in a long document, you can use bookmarks. Just put a bookmark in an important spot in your document that you'll return to many times. When you want to return to that spot, choose Insert➪Bookmark, double-click the bookmark in the Bookmark dialog box, and click the Close button.

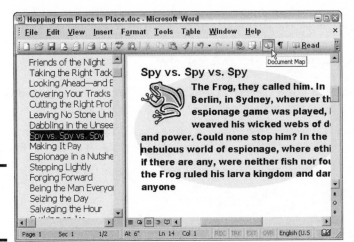

Figure 2-5:
The
Document
Map.

Follow these instructions to handle bookmarks:

✦ **Adding a bookmark:** To place a bookmark in a document, click where you want the bookmark to go, choose Insert⇨Bookmark (or press Ctrl+Shift+F5), type a descriptive name in the Bookmark Name text box, and click the Add button. Bookmarks can't start with numbers or include blank spaces.

✦ **Deleting a bookmark:** To delete a bookmark, select it in the Bookmark dialog box and click the Delete button.

Inserting a Whole File in a Document

One of the beautiful things about word processing is that you can recycle documents. Say that you wrote an essay on the Scissor-Tailed Flycatcher that would fit very nicely in a broader report on North American birds. You can insert the Scissor-Tailed Flycatcher document into your report document by following these steps:

1. **Place the cursor where you want to insert the document.**

2. **Choose Insert⇨File.**

3. **In the Insert File dialog box, find and select the file you want to insert.**

4. **Click the Insert button.**

Finding and Replacing

The Find and Replace commands are some of the most powerful commands in Office. Use them wisely and you can find passages in documents, correct mistakes *en masse,* change words and phrases throughout a document, and even reformat a document. These pages explain how to find errant words and phrases and replace them if you so choose with different words and phrases.

Finding a word, paragraph, or format

You can search for a word in a document, and even search for fonts, special characters, and formats. Here's how:

1. **Choose Edit⇨Find, press Ctrl+F, or click the Select Browse Object button in the lower-right corner of the screen and choose Find.**

   The Find and Replace dialog box appears, as shown in Figure 2-6. In the figure, the More button is clicked so that you can see all the Find options.

Enter a word or phrase

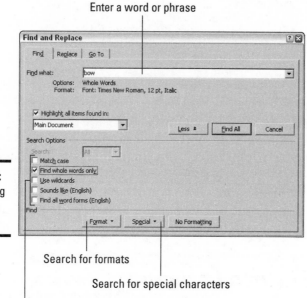

Figure 2-6:
Conducting
a find
operation.

Search for formats

Search for special characters

Choose options for narrowing the search

2. **Enter the word, phrase, or format that you're looking for in the Find What text box (how to search for formats is explained shortly).**

   The words and phrases you looked for recently are on the Find What drop-down list. Open the Find What drop-down list and make a selection from that list if you want.

3. **To search for all instances of the thing you are looking for, check the Highlight All Items Found In check box and make a choice from the drop-down list.**

   If you go this route, Word highlights all instances of the thing you are looking for.

4. **Click the Find Next button if you're looking for a simple word or phrase, or the Find All button to highlight all instances of a word or phrase in your document.**

   Click the More button, if necessary, to open the bottom half of the dialog box and conduct a sophisticated search.

If Word finds what you're looking for, it highlights the thing — or Word highlights all instances of the thing if that is the way you chose to search. To find the next instance of the thing you are looking for, click Find Next again. You can also close the Find and Replace dialog box and click either the Previous Find/Go To or Next Find/Go To button at the bottom of the scroll bar to the right of the screen (or press Ctrl+PgUp or Ctrl+PgDn) to go to the previous or next instance of the thing you're looking for.

By clicking the More button in the Find and Replace dialog box, you can get very selective about what to search for and how to search for it:

✦ **Search:** Open the list and choose a direction for searches.

✦ **Match Case:** Searches for words with upper- and lowercase letters that exactly match those in the Find What text box. With this check box selected, a search for *bow* finds that word, but not *Bow* or *BOW*.

✦ **Find Whole Words Only:** Normally, a search for *bow* yields *elbow*, *bowler*, *bow-wow*, and all other words with the letters *b-o-w* (in that order). Click this option and you get only *bow*.

✦ **Use Wildcards:** Click here if you intend to use wildcards in searches.

✦ **Sounds Like:** Looks for words that sound like the one in the Find What text box. A search for *bow* with this option selected finds *beau*, for example. However, it doesn't find *bough*. This command isn't very reliable.

✦ **Find All Word Forms:** Takes into account verb conjugations and plurals. With this option clicked, you get *bows, bowing,* and *bowed,* as well as *bow.*

To search for words, paragraphs, tab settings, and styles, among other things, that are formatted a certain way, click the Format button and choose an option from the list. You see the familiar dialog box you used in the first place to format the text. In Figure 2-6, Font was chosen on the Format drop-down list and the Find dialog box is ready to search for the word *bow* in Times Roman, 12-point, italicized font. That No Formatting button is there so that you can clear all the formatting from the Find What text box.

Finding and replacing text and formats

The Edit⇨Replace command is a very powerful tool indeed. If you're writing a Russian novel and you decide on page 816 to change the main character's last name from Oblonsky to Oblomov, you can change it on all 816 pages with the Edit⇨Replace command in about half a minute.

But here's the drawback: You never quite know what this command will do. Newspaper editors tell a story about a newspaper that made it a policy to use the word *African-American* instead of *black*. A laudable policy, except that a sleepy editor made the change with the Edit⇨Replace command and didn't review it. Next day, a lead story on the business page read, "After years of running in the red, US Steel has paid all its debts, and now the corporation is running well in the African-American, according to company officials."

Always save your document before you use the Edit⇨Replace command. Then, if you replace text that you shouldn't have replaced, you can close your document without saving it, and then open your document again to get your original document back.

Follow these steps to replace words, phrases, or formats throughout a document:

1. Choose Edit⇨Replace, or press Ctrl+H.

2. Fill in the Find What text box just as you would if you were searching for text or formats.

However, be sure to click the Find Whole Words Only check box if you want to replace one word with another. Depending on which options appear in the dialog box, you might have to click the More button to see all of them. (The previous section, "Finding a word, paragraph, or format," explains how to conduct a search.)

3. In the Replace With text box, enter the text that will replace what is in the Find What text box. If you're replacing a format, enter the format.

4. Either replace everything simultaneously or do it one at a time.

Click one of these buttons:

- Click Replace All to make all replacements in an instant.

- Click Find Next and then either click Replace to make the replacement or Find Next to bypass it.

The sleepy newspaper editor clicked the Replace All button. Do that only if you're very confident and know exactly what you're doing. In fact, one way to keep from making embarrassing replacements is to start by using the Edit⇨Find command. When you land on the first instance of the thing you're searching for, click the Replace tab and tell Word what should replace the thing you found. This way, you can rest assured that you entered the right search criteria and that Word is finding exactly what you want it to find.

CHECK IT OUT

Making Fewer Typing Errors

Most people are clumsy typists. They mistype certain words time and time again. Word's spell checker is great for correcting typos, but you can correct typos literally as you make them with the features described in this section. With AutoCorrect, Word fixes errors for you. Use AutoText to enter whole words or phrases with a simple keystroke or menu selection. The Autoformat As You Type options make text formatting a little bit easier.

As part of its AutoCorrect mechanism, the divine and invisible hand of Word corrects certain typos after you enter them and press the spacebar. Try misspelling *weird* by typing *wierd* to see what

happens. You can have Word correct the typos that you make often, and with a little cunning, you can even use the AutoCorrect feature to enter long company names and hard-to-spell names on the fly. AutoCorrect entries apply to all the Office programs, not just Word.

The AutoCorrect dialog box offers a comprehensive list of words that are autocorrected, as well as options for telling Word what to autocorrect. To open this dialog box, choose Tools⇨AutoCorrect Options. When you have a spare moment, remove the check marks from the AutoCorrect features you don't want, and delete words on the list that you don't want Word to autocorrect.

Most people consistently misspell certain words. You can add the words you misspell often to the list of autocorrected words by right-clicking a misspelling, choosing AutoCorrect on the short-cut menu, and choosing the option that describes how the word is correctly spelled.

If Word makes an autocorrection that you don't care for, move the pointer over the spot where the correction was made. You see the AutoCorrect Options button. By clicking it, you can get a shortcut menu with options for reversing the correction, telling Word never to make the correction again, and opening the AutoCorrect dialog box.

Using the AutoText feature, you can enter long and difficult-to-type words quickly: Put the text and/or graphics that you often use on the Insert⇨AutoText list (Word has already placed a few common entries there). That way, you can enter the long-winded text or a complicated graphic simply by clicking a few menu commands or typing a couple of letters. Addresses, letter-heads, and company logos are ideal candidates for the AutoText list because they take so long to enter.

To create an AutoText entry, type the text or import the graphic, select it, and choose Insert⇨AutoText⇨New (or press Alt+F3). The Create AutoText dialog box appears. Type a name for the text or graphic in the text box and click OK.

Word offers several ways to insert an AutoText entry:

- Start typing the entry's name. Midway through, a bubble appears with the entire entry. Press Enter at that point to insert the whole thing.

- Type the entry's name and then press F3.

- Display the AutoText toolbar, click the All Entries button, select a submenu name, and choose an AutoText entry.

- Choose Insert⇨AutoText, select a submenu name, and choose an AutoText Entry.

To delete an AutoText entry, choose Insert⇨AutoText⇨AutoText to open the AutoCorrect dialog box, select the entry that you want to delete, and click the Delete button.

Finally, Word offers the AutoFormat As You Type feature to make you a better typist. You must have noticed by now that Word occasionally formats text and paragraphs for you. Open a new document, for example, type **The Title** (be sure to capitalize both words), and press Enter twice. Word assigns the Heading 1 style to the words you typed because it assumes that you entered a heading. Now try this: Type **1.**, press the space-bar, type **one**, and press the Enter key. On the next line, Word enters a 2 on the idea that you want to create a numbered list. Try typing **1st**, **2nd**, or **3rd** — Word formats these ordinal numbers like so: 1st, 2nd, 3rd.

Mysterious changes like these are made as part of Word's AutoFormat As You Type options. For the most part, these changes are good, but at some point in your career as a Microsoft Word double-agent, go over these options and choose the ones that are right for you. To check out these options, choose Tools⇨AutoCorrect Options, select the AutoFormat As You Type tab in the AutoCorrect dialog box, and choose which options you want.

**Book IV
Chapter 2**

**Speed Techniques
for Using Word**

Chapter 3: Laying Out Text and Pages

In This Chapter

- ✔ Entering a section break
- ✔ Starting a new page
- ✔ Changing the margins
- ✔ Indenting text
- ✔ Laying out newspaper-style columns
- ✔ Handling bulleted and numbered lists
- ✔ Hyphenating the text
- ✔ Placing watermarks on pages

This chapter explains how to format text and pages. A well-laid-out document says a lot about how much time and thought was put into a document. This chapter presents tips, tricks, and techniques for making pages look just right.

In this chapter, you find out what section breaks are and why they are so important to formatting. You discover how to establish the size of margins, determine how much space appears between lines of text, indent text, handle lists, and hyphenate text, as well as number the pages and handle headers and footers. You will also discover how to lay out pages in newspaper-style columns and put watermarks on pages.

Paragraphs and Formatting

Back in English class, your teacher taught you that a paragraph is a part of a longer composition that presents one idea or, in the case of dialogue, presents the words of one speaker. Your teacher was right, too, but for word-processing purposes, a paragraph is a lot less than that. In word processing, a paragraph is simply what you put on-screen before you press the Enter key. For example, a heading is a paragraph. If you press Enter on a blank line to go to the next line, the blank line is considered a paragraph. If you type **Dear John** at the top of a letter and press Enter, "Dear John" is a paragraph.

It's important to know this because paragraphs have a lot to do with formatting. If you choose the Format➪Paragraph command and monkey around with the paragraph formatting, all your changes affect everything in the paragraph that the cursor is in. To make format changes to a whole paragraph, all you have to do is place the cursor there. You don't have to select the paragraph. And if you want to make format changes to several paragraphs in a row, all you have to do is select those paragraphs first.

Inserting a Section Break for Formatting Purposes

Every document has at least one *section*. That's why "Sec 1" appears on the left side of the status bar at the bottom of the screen. When you want to change page numbering schemes, headers and footers, margin sizes, and the page orientation, you have to create a *section break* to start a new section. Word creates one for you when you create newspaper-style columns or change the size of margins.

Follow these steps to create a new section:

1. Click where you want to insert a section break.

2. Choose Insert⇨Break.

You see the Break dialog box, shown in Figure 3-1.

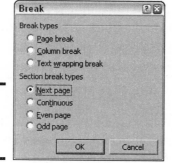

Figure 3-1:
Creating a section break.

3. Under Section Break Types, tell Word which kind of section break you want and then click OK.

All four section break options create a new section, but they do so in different ways:

✦ **Next Page:** Inserts a page break as well as a section break so that the new section can start at the top of a new page (the next one). Select this option to start a new chapter, for example.

✦ **Continuous:** Inserts a section break in the middle of a page. Select this option if, for example, you want to introduce newspaper-style columns in the middle of a page.

✦ **Even Page:** Starts the new section on the next even page. This option is good for two-sided documents in which the headers on the left- and right-side pages are different.

✦ **Odd Page:** Starts the new section on the next odd page. You might choose this option if you have a book in which chapters start on odd pages. (By convention, that's where they start.)

To delete a section break, make sure that you are in Normal view, click the dotted line, and press the Delete key.

Breaking a Line

To break a line of text in the middle before it reaches the right margin without starting a new paragraph, press Shift+Enter. You can also choose Insert⇨Break and select the Text Wrapping Break option button in the Break dialog box. Figure 3-2 shows how you can press Shift+Enter to make lines break better. The paragraphs are identical, but lines in the right-side paragraph were broken to make the text easier to read. Line breaks are marked with the ↵ symbol. To erase line breaks, click the Show/Hide ¶ button to see these symbols; then backspace over them.

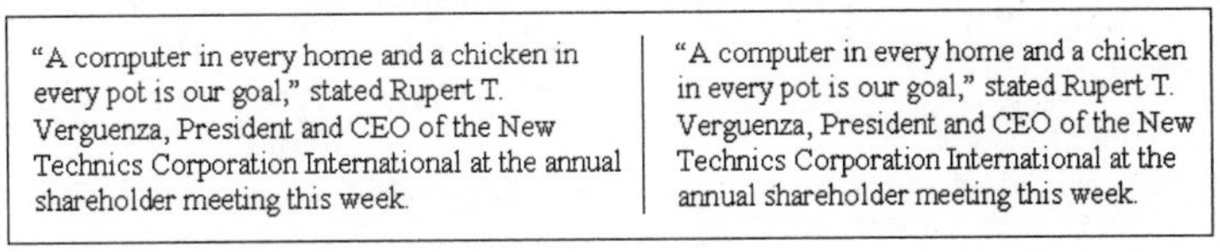

Figure 3-2:
Break lines to make reading easier.

| "A computer in every home and a chicken in every pot is our goal," stated Rupert T. Verguenza, President and CEO of the New Technics Corporation International at the annual shareholder meeting this week. | "A computer in every home and a chicken in every pot is our goal," stated Rupert T. Verguenza, President and CEO of the New Technics Corporation International at the annual shareholder meeting this week. |

Starting a New Page

Word gives you another page so that you can keep going after you fill up one page. But what if you're impatient and want to start a new page right away? Whatever you do, *don't* press Enter again and again until you fill up the page. Instead, create a page break by doing either of the following:

✦ Press Ctrl+Enter.

✦ Choose Insert⇨Break and select the Page Break option in the Break dialog box.

In Normal view, you know when you've inserted a page break because you see the words `Page Break` and a dotted line appear on-screen. In Print Layout view, you can't tell where you inserted a page break. To delete a page break, switch to Normal view, click the words `Page Break`, and press the Delete key. Change views by clicking the View buttons in the lower-left corner of the screen.

Setting Up and Changing the Margins

Margins are the empty spaces along the left, right, top, and bottom edges of a page, as shown in Figure 3-3. Headers and footers fall, respectively, in the

**Book IV
Chapter 3**

Laying Out Text and Pages

top and bottom margins. And you can put graphics, text boxes, and page numbers in the margins as well. Margins serve to frame the text and make it easier to read.

If you change margin settings, indents and page breaks change for good or bad throughout your document. When you start a new document, give a moment's thought to the margins. Changing the size of margins after you have entered the text, clip art, graphics, and whatnot can be disastrous.

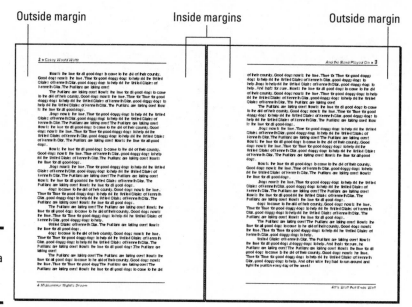

Figure 3-3:
Margins in a
two-sided
document.

 Don't confuse margins with indents. Text is indented from the margin, not from the edge of the page. If you want to change how far text falls from the page edge, indent it. To change margin settings in the middle of a document, you have to create a new section.

To set up or change the margins, start by choosing File➪Page Setup. You see the Page Setup dialog box. The Margins tab offers commands for handling margins:

✦ **Margins:** Enter measurements in the Top, Bottom, Left, and Right boxes to tell Word how much blank space to put along the sides of the page.

✦ **Gutter:** The *gutter* is the part of the paper that the binding eats into when you bind a document. Enter a measurement in the Gutter text box to increase the left or inside margin and make room for the binding. Notice on the pages of this book, for example, that the margin closest to the binding is wider than the outside margin. Select the Top option button in the Gutter Position section if you intend to bind your document from the top, not the left, or inside, of the page. Some legal documents are bound this way.

✦ **Two-sided documents (inside and outside margins):** In a bound document in which text is printed on both sides of the pages, the terms "left margin" and "right margin" are meaningless. What matters instead is in the *inside margin,* the margin in the middle of the page spread next to the bindings, and the *outside margin,* the margin on the outside of the page spread that isn't affected by the bindings (refer to Figure 3-3). Choose Mirror Margins on the Multiple Pages drop-down list and adjust the margins accordingly if you will print on both sides of the paper.

✦ **Apply To:** Choose Whole Document to apply your settings to the entire document, This Section to apply them to a section, or This Point Forward to change margins for the rest of a document. When you choose This Point Forward, Word creates a new section.

Indenting Paragraphs and First Lines

An *indent* is the distance between a margin and the text, not the edge of the page and the text. Word offers a handful of different ways to change the indentation of paragraphs. The fastest way is to use the Increase Indent and Decrease Indent buttons on the Formatting toolbar to move the paragraph away from or toward the left margin:

1. **Click in the paragraph whose indentation you want to change; if you want to change more than one paragraph, select those paragraphs.**

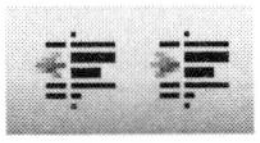

2. **Click the Increase Indent or Decrease Indent button (or press Ctrl+M or Ctrl+Shift+M) as many times as necessary to indent the text.**

You can also change indentations by using the ruler to "eyeball it." This technique requires some dexterity with the mouse, but it allows you to see precisely where paragraphs and the first lines of paragraphs are indented:

1. **Choose View⊏⟩Ruler, if necessary, to put the ruler on-screen.**

2. **Select the paragraph or paragraphs whose indentation you want to change.**

3. **Slide an indent marker with the mouse.**

Figure 3-4 shows where these markers are.

Figure 3-4:
Indenting
with the
ruler.

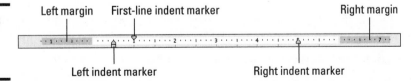

Left margin   First-line indent marker   Right margin

Left indent marker   Right indent marker

• **First-line indent marker:** Drag the down-pointing arrow on the ruler to indent only the first line of the paragraph.

• **Left indent marker:** This one, on the bottom-left side of the ruler, comes in two parts. Drag the arrow that points up (called the hanging indent marker), but not the box underneath it, to move the left margin independently of the first-line indentation. To move the left indentation *and* the first-line indentation relative to the left margin, slide the box. Doing so moves everything on the left side of the ruler.

- **Right indent marker:** Drag this one to move the right side of the paragraph away from or toward the right margin.

If you're not one for "eyeballing it," you can use the Format⇨Paragraph command to indent paragraphs. Choose Format⇨Paragraph or double-click the Left or Right indent marker on the ruler to open the Paragraph dialog box, and then make selections in the Indentation area.

Putting Newspaper-Style Columns in a Document

Columns look great in newsletters and similar documents. And you can pack a lot of words in columns. However, the Columns command is only good for creating columns that will appear on the same page. Running text to the next page with the Columns command can be problematic.

Before you put text in newspaper-style columns, write it. Take care of the spelling, grammar, and everything else first because making text changes to words after they've been arranged in columns is hard. Columns appear only in Page Layout view.

Sometimes it is easier to create columns by creating a table or by text boxes, especially when the columns refer to one another. In a two-column résumé, for example, the left-hand column often lists job titles ("Facsimile Engineer") whose descriptions are found directly across the page in the right-hand column ("I Xeroxed stuff all day long"). Creating a two-column résumé with Word's Format⇨Columns command would be futile because making the columns line up is nearly impossible. Each time you add something to the left-hand column, everything "snakes" — it gets bumped down in the left-hand column and the right-hand column as well.

There are two ways to create columns: with the Columns button on the toolbar and with the Format⇨Columns command. Format⇨Columns gives you considerably more leeway because the Columns button lets you create only columns of equal width. To use the Columns button, follow these steps:

1. **Select the text to be put in columns or simply place the cursor in the document to "columnize" all the text.**

2. **Click the Columns button on the toolbar.**

   A menu drops down so that you can choose how many columns you want.

3. **Click and drag to choose how many columns you want.**

Word creates a new section if you selected text before you columnized it, and you see your columns in Print Layout View. Very likely, they don't look so good. It's hard to get it right the first time. You can drag the column border bars on the ruler to widen or narrow the columns, but it's much easier to choose Format➪Columns and play with options in the Columns dialog box. If you want to start all over, or if you want to start from the beginning with the Columns dialog box, here's how:

1. **Select the text to be put in columns, or put the cursor in the section to be put in columns, or place the cursor at a position in the document where columns are to start appearing.**

2. **Choose Format➪Columns.**

You see the Columns dialog box, as shown in Figure 3-5.

Figure 3-5:
Running text in columns.

3. **Choose options in the Columns dialog box and, as you do so, keep your eye on the Preview box in the lower-right corner.**

Here are the options in the Columns dialog box:

✦ **Preset columns:** Select a Presets box to choose a preset number of columns. Notice that, in some of the boxes, the columns aren't of equal width. Choose One if you want to remove columns from a document.

✦ **Number of Columns:** If a preset column doesn't do the trick, enter the number of columns you want in the Number of Columns text box.

✦ **Line between columns:** A line between columns is mighty elegant and is difficult to do on your own. Select the Line Between check box to run lines between columns.

✦ **Columns width:** If you deselect the Equal Column Width check box, you can make columns of unequal width. Change the width of each column by using the Width text boxes.

✦ **Space between columns:** Enter a measurement in the Spacing text boxes to determine how much space appears between columns.

✦ **Start New Column:** This check box is for putting empty space in a column, perhaps to insert a text box or picture. Place the cursor where you want the empty space to begin, open the Columns dialog box, select this check box, and choose This Point Forward from the Apply To drop-down list. Text below the cursor moves to the next column.

To break a column in the middle and move text to the next column, click where you want the column to break and press Ctrl+Shift+Enter or choose Insert➪Break and select the Column Break radio button.

Numbering the Pages

Word numbers the pages of a document automatically, which is great, but if your document has a title page and table of contents and you want to start numbering pages on the fifth page, or if your document has more than one section, page numbers can turn into a sticky business. The first thing to ask yourself is whether you've included headers or footers in your document. If you have, go to "Putting Headers and Footers on Pages," also in this chapter. It explains how to put page numbers in a header or footer.

Use the Insert➪Page Numbers command to put plain old page numbers on the pages of a document. You see the Page Numbers dialog box, shown in Figure 3-6. This dialog box actually inserts a {Page} field inside a frame in the header or footer. In the Position and Alignment drop-down lists, choose where you want the page number to appear. Deselect the Show Number on First Page check box if you're working on a letter or other type of document that usually doesn't have a number on page 1.

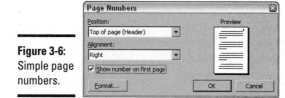

Figure 3-6: Simple page numbers.

Putting Headers and Footers on Pages

A *header* is a little description that appears along the top of a page so that the reader knows what's what, as shown in Figure 3-7. Usually, headers include the page number and a title. A *footer* is the same thing as a header except that it appears along the bottom of the page, as befits its name. To change headers or footers in the middle of a document, you have to create a new section.

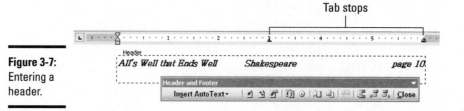

Figure 3-7: Entering a header.

To put a header or a footer in a document, follow these steps:

1. **Choose View⇨Header and Footer.**

If you're in Print Layout view and you've already entered a header or footer, you can edit it by double-clicking the header or footer text.

2. **Type your header in the box, or if you want a footer, click the Switch between Header and Footer button and type your footer.**

While you're typing away in the Header or Footer box, you can call on most of the commands on the Standard and Formatting toolbars. You can change the text's font and font size, click an alignment button, and paste text from the Clipboard. Tabs are set up in headers and footers to make it possible to center, left-align, and right-align text. To center a header or footer, for example, press the Tab key once to go to the Center tab mark and start typing.

3. **Click the Close button.**

To remove a header or footer, choose View⇨Header and Footer or double-click the header or footer in Print Layout view, and then delete the text.

Here are some header and footer features that may be useful to you:

✦ **Inserting a page number:** Click the Insert Page Number button on the Header and Footer toolbar (or press Alt+Shift+P). While you're at it, you can type the words *page* and *of* and click the Insert Number of Pages button to list the total number of pages, like so: page 4 of 16.

✦ **Inserting the date and time:** By clicking the Insert Date and Insert Time button, you can enter the date and time at which the document is printed.

✦ **Changing headers and footers from section to section:** Click the Same As Previous button to change headers and footers (you must first divide the document into sections). Clicking this button again tells Word that you don't want this header or footer to be the same as the header or footer in the previous section of the document. When this button is selected (down), the header or footer is the same, and the Header or Footer box reads Same as Previous, but when you click the button again to deselect it, the words Same as Previous don't appear. You can click the Show Previous or Show Next button to examine the header or footer in the previous or next section and see what the header or footer there is.

✦ **Different headers and footers for odd and even pages:** As explained previously in the section, "Setting Up and Changing the Margins," documents in which text is printing on both sides of the page can have different headers and footers for the left and right side of the page spread (refer to Figure 3-3). Choose File⇨Page Setup or click the Page Setup button on the Header and Footer toolbar to open the Page Setup dialog box. Then, on the Layout tab, select the Different Odd and Even check box. The header and footer boxes now read "Odd" or "Even" to tell you which side of the page spread you're dealing with.

✦ **Removing headers or footers from the first page**: To remove a header or footer from the first page of a document or section, choose File⇨Page Setup or click the Page Setup button on the Header and Footer toolbar. In the Page Setup dialog box, select the Layout tab, select the Different First Page check box, and click OK.

Adjusting the Space Between Lines

To change the spacing between lines, select the lines whose spacing you want to change or simply put the cursor in a paragraph if you're changing the line spacing in a single paragraph (if you're just starting a document, you're ready to go). Then click the down-arrow beside the Line Spacing button and choose an option on the drop-down list.

To take advantage of more line-spacing options, choose Format⇨Paragraph (or select More, the last option on the Line Spacing button drop-down list). Then, in the Paragraph dialog box, select a Line Spacing option:

✦ **At Least:** Choose this one if you want Word to adjust for tall symbols or other unusual text. Word adjusts the lines but makes sure there is, at minimum, the number of points you enter in the At text box between each line.

✦ **Exactly:** Choose this one and enter a number in the At text box if you want a specific amount of space between lines.

✦ **Multiple:** Choose this one and put a number in the At text box to get triple-, quadruple-, quintuple-, or any other number of spaced lines.

To quickly single-space text, click it or select it if you want to change more than one paragraph, and press Ctrl+1. To quickly double-space text, select the text and press Ctrl+2. Press Ctrl+5 to put one and a half lines between lines of text.

Creating Numbered and Bulleted Lists

What is a word-processed document without a list or two? It's like an emperor with no clothes. Numbered lists are invaluable in manuals and books like this one that present a lot of step-by-step procedures. Use bulleted lists when you want to present alternatives to the reader. A *bullet* is a black, filled-in circle or other character.

Simple numbered and bulleted lists

The fastest, cleanest, and most honest way to create a numbered or bulleted list is to enter the text without any concern for numbers or bullets. Just press Enter at the end of each step or bulleted entry. When you're done, select the list and click the Numbering or Bullets button on the Formatting toolbar.

Meanwhile, here are some tricks for handling lists:

✦ **Ending a list:** Press the Enter key twice after typing the last entry in the list. You can also choose Format⇨Bullets and Numbering or right-click the list and choose Bullets and Numbering to open the Bullets and Numbering dialog box, shown in Figure 3-8. From there, click the None option on the Numbered or Bulleted tab and click OK.

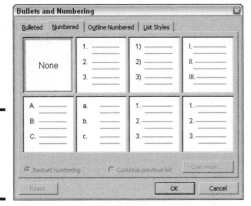

Figure 3-8: The Bullets and Numbering dialog box.

✦ **Picking up where you left off:** Suppose that you want a numbered list to resume where a list you entered earlier ended. In other words, suppose that you left off writing a four-step list, put in a graphic or some paragraphs, and now you want to resume the list at Step 5. Click the Numbering button to start numbering again. The AutoCorrect Options button appears on-screen. Click it and choose Continue Numbering. You can also open the Bullets and Numbering dialog box and select the Continue Previous List option button.

✦ **Starting a new list:** Suppose that you want to start a brand-new list right away. Right-click the number Word entered and choose Restart Numbering on the shortcut menu. You can also open the Bullets and Numbering dialog box (refer to Figure 3-8) and choose Restart numbering.

Book IV
Chapter 3

Laying Out Text
and Pages

Automatic lists and what to do about them

Word creates automatic lists for you whether you like it or not. For example, type the number 1, type a period, press the spacebar, type the first entry in the list, and press Enter to get to the next line and type the second entry. As soon as you press Enter, Word inserts the number 2 and formats the list for you. In the same manner, Word creates bulleted lists when you type an asterisk (*), press the spacebar, type the first entry in the list, and press Enter.

Some people find this kind of behind-the-scenes skullduggery annoying. If you are one such person, either click the AutoCorrect Options button — it appears automatically — and choose Stop Automatically Creating Lists, or else choose Tools⇨AutoCorrect Options, select the AutoFormat As You Type tab in the AutoCorrect dialog box, and deselect the Automatic Numbered Lists and Automatic Bulleted Lists check boxes.

Constructing lists of your own

If you are an individualist and you want numbered and bulleted lists to work your way, start from the Bullets and Numbering dialog box shown in Figure 3-8 (choose Format⇨Bullets and Numbering to get there). On the Bulleted and Numbered tabs, you can choose among different kinds of bullets and different numbering schemes.

If those choices aren't good enough for you, click the Customize button to open the Customize Bulleted List or Customize Numbered List dialog box, shown in Figure 3-9. These dialog boxes offer opportunities for indenting numbers or bullets and the text that follows them in new ways. You can also choose fonts for the numbers and symbols for the bullets. The card shark in Figure 3-9 created bulleted entries for hearts, clubs, spades, and diamonds. Be sure to watch the Preview area of these dialog boxes. It shows exactly what you are doing to your bulleted or numbered lists.

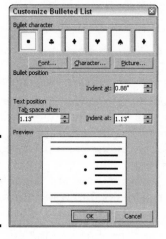 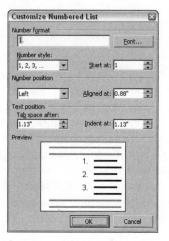

Figure 3-9: Customizing a bulleted or numbered list.

Working with Tabs

Tabs are a throwback to the days of the typewriter, when it was necessary to make tab stops in order to align the next item. Except for making leaders and aligning text in headers and footers, everything you can do with tabs can also be done by creating a table — and it can be done far faster. All you have to do is align the text inside the table and then remove the table borders. Book IV, Chapter 5 explains tables.

A *tab stop* is a point on the ruler around which or against which text is formatted. When you press the Tab key, you advance the text cursor by one tab stop. Tab stops are set at half-inch intervals on the ruler, but you can change that if you want. You can also change the type of tab. By default, tabs are left-aligned, which means that when you enter letters after you press the Tab key, the letters move toward the right in the same way that they move toward the right when text is left-aligned. However, Word also offers right, center, decimal, and bar tabs. Figure 3-10 shows the differences between the tab settings. Notice the symbols on the ruler — they tell you what type of tab you're dealing with.

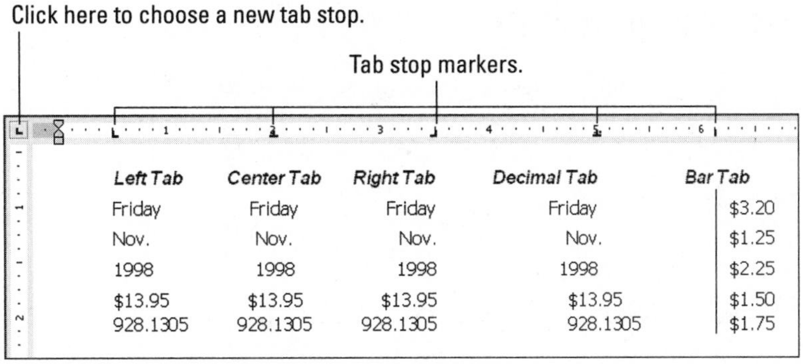

Click here to choose a new tab stop.

Tab stop markers.

Figure 3-10:
The five
kinds of
tab stops.

Left Tab	Center Tab	Right Tab	Decimal Tab	Bar Tab
Friday	Friday	Friday	Friday	$3.20
Nov.	Nov.	Nov.	Nov.	$1.25
1998	1998	1998	1998	$2.25
$13.95	$13.95	$13.95	$13.95	$1.50
928.1305	928.1305	928.1305	928.1305	$1.75

To change tabs or change where tabs appear on the ruler, start by selecting the paragraphs for which you need different tabs. Then click in the box on the left side of the ruler as many times as necessary to choose the kind of tab you want, and click on the ruler where you want the tab to go. You can click as many times as you want and enter more than one kind of tab.

To move a tab, simply drag it to a new location on the ruler. Text that has been aligned with the tab moves as well. To remove a tab, drag it off the ruler. When you remove a tab, the text to which it was aligned is aligned to the next remaining tab stop on the ruler or to the next default tab stop if you didn't create any tab stops of your own.

Sometimes it's hard to tell where tabs were put in the text. To find out, click the Show/Hide ¶ button to see the formatting characters, including the arrows that show where the Tab key was pressed.

Creating a tab leader

In my opinion, the only reason to fool with tabs and tab stops is to create tab leaders like the ones shown in the following figure. A *leader* is a series of punctuation marks — periods in the illustration — that connects text across a page. Leaders are very elegant. For the figure, left-aligned tab stops were used for the characters' names and right-aligned tab stops for the actors' names. Leaders are included so that you can tell precisely who played whom.

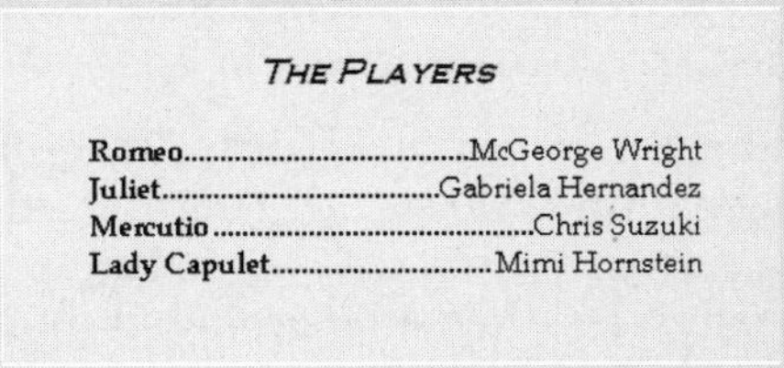

THE PLAYERS

Romeo...McGeorge Wright
Juliet...Gabriela Hernandez
Mercutio ....Chris Suzuki
Lady Capulet...............................Mimi Hornstein

Follow these steps to create tab leaders:

1. Enter the text and, in each line, enter a tab space between the text on the left side and the text on the right side.

2. Select the text and choose Format⇨Tabs to open the Tabs dialog box.

3. Enter a position for the first new tab in the Tab Stop Position text box.

4. Under Leader in the dialog box, select the punctuation symbol you want.

5. Click OK, display the ruler, and drag tab markers to adjust the space between the text on the left and right.

Hyphenating a Document

The first thing you should know about hyphenating the words in a document is that you may not need to do it. Text that hasn't been hyphenated is much easier to read, which is why the majority of text in this book, for example, isn't hyphenated. It has a *ragged right margin,* to borrow typesetter lingo. Hyphenate only when text is trapped in columns or in other narrow places, or when you want a very formal-looking document.

Do not insert a hyphen simply by pressing the hyphen key, because the hyphen will stay there even if the word appears in the middle of a line and doesn't need to be broken in half. Instead, when a big gap appears in the right margin and a word is crying out to be hyphenated, put the cursor where the hyphen needs to go and press Ctrl+- (hyphen). This way, you tell Word to make the hyphen appear only if the word breaks at the end of a line. (To remove a manual hyphen, press the Show/Hide ¶ button so that you can see it; then backspace over it.)

Hyphenating a document automatically

To hyphenate a document automatically:

1. **Choose Tools⇨Language⇨Hyphenation.**

   You see the Hyphenation dialog box, as shown in Figure 3-11.

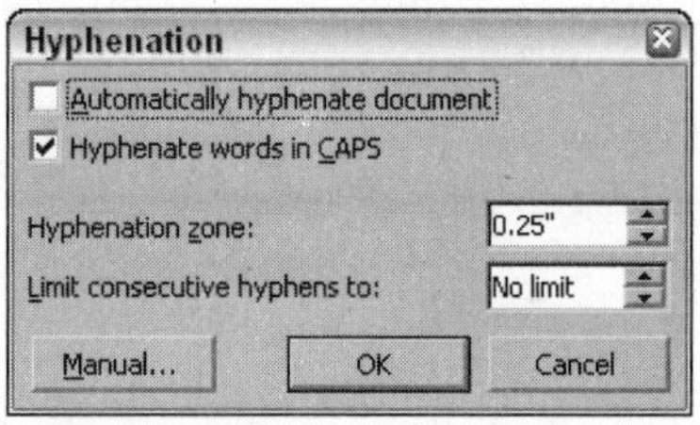

Figure 3-11: Hyphenating the text.

Hyphenation
☐ Automatically hyphenate document
☑ Hyphenate words in CAPS
Hyphenation zone: 0.25"
Limit consecutive hyphens to: No limit
Manual... OK Cancel

2. **Select the Automatically Hyphenate Document check box to let Word do the job.**

   While you're at it, deselect the Hyphenate Words in CAPS check box if you don't care to hyphenate words in uppercase.

   If the text isn't justified — that is, if it's "ragged right" — you can play with the Hyphenation Zone setting (but ragged-right text shouldn't be hyphenated anyway). Words that fall in the zone are hyphenated, so a large zone means a less ragged margin but more ugly hyphens, and a small zone means fewer ugly hyphens but a more ragged right margin.

3. **Having more than two consecutive hyphens on the right margin looks bad, so enter 2 in the Limit Consecutive Hyphens To text box.**

4. **Click OK.**

Hyphenating a document manually

The other way to hyphenate is to see where Word wants to put hyphens, and you can then yea or nay them one at a time:

1. **Select the part of the document you want to hyphenate, or place the cursor where you want hyphens to start appearing.**

2. **Choose Tools⇨Language⇨Hyphenation to display the Hyphenation dialog box (refer to Figure 3-11).**

3. **Click the Manual button.**

   Word displays the Manual Hyphenation dialog box with some hyphenation choices in it. The cursor blinks on the spot where Word suggests putting a hyphen.

4. **Click Yes or No to accept or reject Word's suggestion.**

   Keep accepting or rejecting Word's suggestions. A dialog box appears to tell you when Word has finished hyphenating. To quit hyphenating before Word finishes, click the Cancel button in the Manual Hyphenation dialog box.

Unhyphenating and other hyphenation tasks

More hyphenation esoterica:

✦ To "unhyphenate" a document you hyphenated automatically, choose Tools⇨Language⇨Hyphenation, deselect the Automatically Hyphenate Document check box, and click OK.

✦ To prevent a paragraph from being hyphenated, choose Format⇨ Paragraph, select the Line and Page Breaks tab, and select the Don't Hyphenate check box. (If you can't hyphenate a paragraph, it's probably because this check box was selected unintentionally.)

✦ To hyphenate a single paragraph in the middle of a document — maybe because it's a long quote or some other thing that needs to stand out — select the paragraph and hyphenate it manually by clicking the Manual button in the Hyphenation dialog box.

Decorating a Page with a Border

Word offers a means of decorating title pages, certificates, menus, and similar documents with a page border. Besides lines, you can decorate the sides of a page with stars, pieces of cake, and other artwork. If you want to place a border around a page in the middle of the document, you must create a section break where the page is. Here's how to put borders around a page:

1. **Place the cursor on the page where the border is to appear.**

   Place the cursor on the first page of a document if you want to put a border around only the first page. If your document is divided into sections and you want to put borders around certain pages in a section, place the cursor in the section — either in the first page, if you want the borders to go around it, or in a subsequent page.

2. **Choose Format⇨Borders and Shading.**

3. **Select the Page Border tab in the Borders and Shading dialog box, as shown in Figure 3-12.**

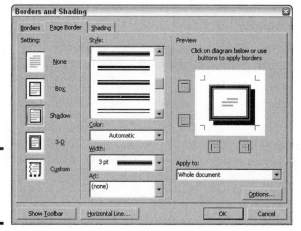

Figure 3-12: Putting borders on pages.

4. **Under Setting, choose which kind of border you want.**

The Custom setting is for putting borders on one, two, or three sides of the page, not four. Use the None setting to remove borders.

5. Under Apply To, tell Word which page or pages in the document get borders.

6. **Select options to construct the border you want and then click OK.**

The Page Border tab offers a bunch of tools for fashioning a border:

✦ **Line for borders:** Under Style, scroll down the list and choose a line for the borders. You will find interesting choices at the bottom of the list. Be sure to look in the Preview window to see what your choices in this dialog box add up to.

✦ **Color for borders:** Open the Color drop-down list and choose a color for the border lines if you want a color border and you have a color printer.

✦ **Width of borders:** If you chose artwork for the borders, use the Width drop-down list to tell Word how wide the lines or artwork should be.

✦ **Artwork for borders:** Open the Art drop-down list and choose a symbol, illustration, star, piece of cake, or other artwork, if that is what you want for the borders. You will find some amusing choices on this long list, including ice cream cones, bats, and umbrellas.

✦ **Borders on different sides of the page:** Use the four buttons in the Preview window to tell Word on which sides of the page you want borders. Click these buttons to remove or add borders, as you wish.

✦ **Distance from edge of page:** Click the Options button and fill in the Border and Shading Options dialog box if you want to get specific about how close the borders can come to the edge of the page or pages.

Dropping in a Drop Cap

A *drop cap* is a large capital letter that "drops" into the text, as shown in Figure 3-13. Drop caps appear at the start of chapters in many books, this book included, and you can find other uses for them, too. In Figure 3-13, one drop cap marks the "A" side of a list of songs on a homemade tape. Follow these steps to create a drop cap:

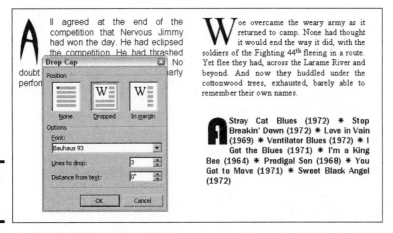

Figure 3-13: Creating a drop cap.

1. **Click anywhere in the paragraph whose first letter you want to "drop."**

   If you want to "drop" more than one letter, select the letters.

2. **Choose Format⇨Drop Cap.**

   You see the Drop Cap dialog box, as shown in Figure 3-13.

3. **Choose which kind of drop cap you want by clicking a box. The None setting is for removing drop caps.**

4. **Choose a font from the Font drop-down list.**

   Choose one that's different from the text in the paragraph. You can come back to this dialog box and get a different font later, if you want.

5. **In the Lines to Drop text box, enter the number of text lines that the letter should "drop on."**

6. **Keep the 0 setting in the Distance from Text text box unless you're dropping an *I, 1,* or other skinny letter or number.**

7. **Click OK.**

You see your drop cap in Print Layout View. The drop cap appears in a text frame. To change the size of the drop cap, choose Format⇨Drop Cap again and play with the settings in the Drop Cap dialog box.

Book IV
Chapter 3

Laying Out Text
and Pages

Putting Watermarks on Pages

A *watermark* is a pale image or set of words that appears behind text on each page in a document. True watermarks are made in the paper mold and can be seen only when the sheet of paper is held up to a light. You can't make true watermarks with Word, but you can make the closest thing to them that can be attained in the debased digital world in which we live. This illustration shows two pages of a letter in which the paper has been "watermarked." Watermarks are one of the easiest formatting tricks to accomplish in Word.

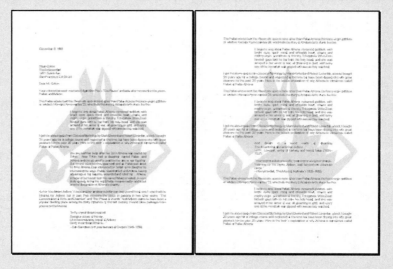

To create a watermark for every page of a document, start by choosing Format⇨Background⇨Printed Watermark. You see the Printed Watermark dialog box. From here, you can create a picture watermark or a text watermark:

- ✔ **Picture watermark:** Select the Picture Watermark option button and then click the Select Picture button. In the Insert Picture dialog box, select a clip art file to use for the watermark and click the Insert button. Back in the Printed Watermark dialog box, choose a size for the clip-art image from the Scale drop-down list. Don't deselect the Washout check box — do so and your image may be too dark and obscure the text.

- ✔ **Text watermark:** Click the Text Watermark option button and type a word or two in the Text text box (or choose an AutoText entry from the drop-down list). Choose a font, size, color, and layout for the words. If you deselect the Semitransparent check box, you do so at your peril because the watermark words may be too dark on the page.

Click OK in the Printed Watermark dialog box to see your watermark. To tinker with it or remove it, choose Format⇨Background⇨Printed Watermark and change the settings in the Printed Watermark dialog box. To remove the watermark, click the No Watermark option button.

Chapter 4: Word Styles

Styles can save a ridiculous amount of time that you would otherwise spend formatting and wrestling with text. And many Word features rely on styles. You can't create a table of contents or use the Document Map unless each heading in your document has been assigned a heading style. Nor can you take advantage of Outline view and the commands on the Outline toolbar, or cross-reference headings or number the headings in a document.

If you want to be stylish, at least where Word is concerned, you have to know about styles.

All about Styles

A *style* is a collection of commands and formats that have been bundled under one name. With styles, you don't have to visit a bunch of dialog boxes to change the formatting of text or paragraphs. Instead, you simply choose a style from the Styles and Formatting task pane or the Style drop-down list. You can be certain that all parts of the document that were assigned the same style look the same. In short, you can fool everybody into thinking your documents were created by a pro.

Which styles are available depends on which template you used to create your document. Each template comes with its own set of styles, and you can create your own styles, too. A simple document created with the Normal template — a document that you created by clicking the New Blank Document button or pressing Ctrl+N — has but a few basic styles, but a document that was created with an advanced template comes with many styles. (Later in this chapter, "Creating Templates" explains templates.)

To see which styles are available in the document you're working on, choose Format⇨Styles and Formatting or click the Styles and Formatting button to open the Styles and Formatting task pane. Want to know which style has been assigned to text or a paragraph? Click the text or paragraph and glance at the Style drop-down list or the Styles and Formatting task pane.

On the Style drop-down list and the task pane, each style name is formatted to give you an idea of what it does when you apply it in your document. Word offers four types of styles:

◆ **Paragraph styles:** Determine the formatting of entire paragraphs. A paragraph style can include these settings: font, paragraph, tab, border, language, and bullets and numbering. Paragraph styles are marked with the paragraph symbol (¶). By far, the majority of styles are paragraph styles.

◆ **Character styles:** Apply to text, not to paragraphs. You select text before you apply a character style. Create a character style for text that is hard to lay out and for foreign-language text. A character style can include these settings: font, border, and language. When you apply a character style to text, the character-style settings override the paragraph-style settings. If the paragraph style calls for a 14-point Arial text but the character style calls for 12-point Times Roman font, the character style wins. Character styles are marked with an underlined *a*.

◆ **Table styles:** Apply to tables (Book IV, Chapter 5 describes creating and formatting tables). Table styles are marked with a grid icon.

◆ **List styles:** Apply to lists (see Book IV, Chapter 3). List styles are marked with a list icon.

The beauty of styles is this: After you modify a style, all paragraphs or text to which the style has been assigned are instantly changed. You don't have to go back and format text and paragraphs throughout your document.

Applying a Style to Text and Paragraphs

Follow these steps to apply a style:

1. **Click the paragraph you want to apply the style to, or, to apply a style to several paragraphs, select all or part of them; if you're applying a character style, select the letters whose formatting you want to change.**

2. **Apply the style.**

As shown in Figure 4-1, Word offers two ways to apply a style:

• Open the Style drop-down list on the Formatting toolbar and select a style. To make all styles in the template appear on the Style drop-down list, hold down the Shift key as you click to open the list.

• Click the Styles and Formatting button to open the Style and Formatting task pane; then select a style there.

Shortcuts for applying styles

Here's a handful of keyboard shortcuts that can be very handy when applying paragraph styles:

✔ Normal: Ctrl+Shift+N

✔ Bulleted List: Ctrl+Shift+L

✔ Heading 1: Ctrl+Alt+1

✔ Heading 2: Ctrl+Alt+2

✔ Heading 3: Ctrl+Alt+3

✔ Next higher heading: Alt+Shift+→

✔ Next lower heading: Alt+Shift+←

Choose a style from the Style menu...   ... or the Styles and Formatting task pane

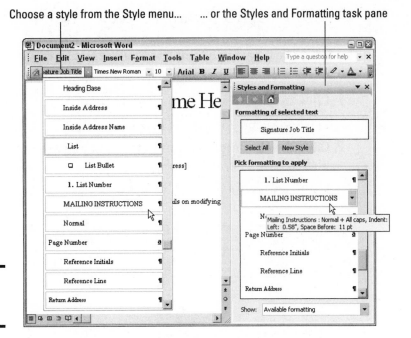

Figure 4-1:
Applying a
style.

Creating a New Style

You can create new styles in two ways: using the New Style dialog box and
directly from the screen. To do a thorough job, use the New Style dialog
box. Styles you create there can be made part of the template you are currently working in and can be copied to other templates (later in this chapter, "Creating Templates" explains templates).

Creating styles directly from the screen

First, you can use the directly-from-the-screen method to create paragraph
styles for a document you're working on:

1. **Click a paragraph whose formatting you would like to turn into a
   style and apply to other paragraphs in your document.**

   Remember, a heading is also a paragraph as far as Word is concerned,
   so if you're creating a style for a heading, click the heading.

2. **Click in the Style drop-down list box and type a name for the style.**

3. **Press the Enter key.**

A style you create this way becomes a part of the document you're working on — it isn't made part of the template from which you created your
document.

Creating styles using the New Style dialog box

If you want to make a style available in documents you will create in the future, make it part of a template and use the New Style dialog box method. Follow these steps:

1. Click the Styles and Formatting button.

The Styles and Formatting task pane opens.

2. Click the New Style button in the task pane to open the New Style dialog box.

Figure 4-2 shows the New Style dialog box.

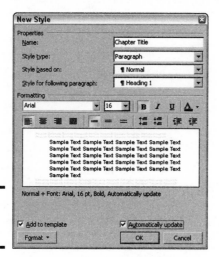

Figure 4-2:
Creating a
new style.

3. Fill in the New Style dialog box.

As you do so, keep your eyes on the Preview box. It shows you what your new style will look like when you apply it to a document.

Here's a rundown of the options in the New Style dialog box:

✦ **Name:** Enter a descriptive name for the style. The name you enter will appear on the Style drop-down list and in the Styles and Formatting task pane.

✦ **Style Type:** On the drop-down list, choose a style type (see "All about Styles," earlier in this chapter, which describes the four style types).

✦ **Style Based On:** If your new style is similar to a style that is already part of the template with which you created your document, choose the style to get a head start on creating the new one. Be warned, however, that if you or someone else changes the based-on style, your new style will inherit those changes and be altered as well.

✦ **Style for Following Paragraph:** Choose a style from the drop-down list if the style you're creating is always followed by an existing style. For example, a new style called "Chapter Title" might always be followed by a style called "Chapter Intro Paragraph." If that were the case, you would choose "Chapter Intro Paragraph" from this drop-down list.

✦ **Formatting:** Choose options from the menus or click buttons to fashion or refine your style (you can also click the Format button to do this).

✦ **Add to Template:** Adds the style to the document's template so that other documents based on the template you are using can also make use of the new style.

✦ **Automatically Update:** Normally, when you make a formatting change to a paragraph, the style assigned to the paragraph does not change at all. By selecting this check box, you tell Word to alter the style itself each time you alter a paragraph to which you've assigned the style. With this check box selected, all paragraphs in the document that were assigned the style are altered each time you change a single paragraph that was assigned the style.

✦ **Format:** This is the important one. Click the button and make a formatting choice. Word takes you to dialog boxes so that you can create or refine the style.

Modifying a Style

What if you decide at the end of an 80-page document that all 35 introductory paragraphs to which you've assigned the "Intro Para" style look funny? If you clicked the Automatically Update check box in the New Style dialog box when you created the style, all you have to do is alter a paragraph to which you assigned the Intro Para style to alter all 35 introductory paragraphs. However, if you decided against updating styles automatically, you can still change the introductory paragraphs throughout your document.

Follow these steps to modify a style that isn't updated automatically:

1. **Click any paragraph, table, or list to which you've assigned the style; if you want to modify a character style, select the characters to which you assigned the style.**

2. **Click the Styles and Formatting button.**

The Styles and Formatting task pane appears. The style you want to modify should be selected in the task pane. If it isn't, select it.

3. **Select the name of the style that needs modifying, open its drop-down list, and choose Modify.**

You see the Modify Style dialog box. Does the dialog box look familiar? That's because it's virtually identical to the New Style dialog box that you used to create the style in the first place (refer to Figure 4-2). The only difference is that you can't choose a style type in the Modify Style dialog box.

4. **Change the settings in the Modify Styles dialog box and click OK.**

The previous section in this chapter explains the settings.

While the Modify Style dialog box is open, you can check the Automatically Update check box if you want future modifications that you make to the style to be applied automatically. This way, when you change a paragraph or text to which the style has been applied, all other paragraphs and text in your document are changed accordingly. Select the Add to Template check box if you want the style change to be made not only in the document you are working on but also in any other documents that you create in the future with this template.

Creating Templates

Every document you create is founded upon a *template*. When you click the New Blank Document button or press Ctrl+N, you create a document founded on the Normal template. And if you click the On My Computer hyperlink in the New Document task pane, you get the chance to open the Templates dialog box and create a complex document from a template of your choice — Contemporary Report, for example, or Brochure, or Elegant Memo.

Each template comes with its own styles and also its own AutoText entries, toolbars, and macros. Suppose that you create a complex document and you want to be able to use its styles, AutoText entries, and so on in other documents. To be able to do that, you can create a template from your document. Here are the ways to create a new template:

✦ **Creating a template from a document:** With your document open, choose File➪Save As. In the Save As dialog box, choose Document Template (`*.dot`) in the Save As Type drop-down list. Then enter a name for your template and click the Save button. The next time you open the Templates dialog box (by selecting the On My Computer hyperlink in the New Document task pane), you will see the name of the template you created on the General tab.

✦ **Assembling styles from other templates:** Create a new template by following the preceding instructions and then copy styles (and AutoText entries, toolbars, and macros as well, if you want) to the new template. To choose a template from which to copy styles, click the Close File button on the left side of the Organizer dialog box, click the Open File button, select the template in the Open dialog box, and click the Open button.

Where templates are stored depends on which version of Windows your computer runs under:

✦ **Windows XP:** Find the Templates folder here:

```
C:\Documents and Settings\Username\Application Data\
    Microsoft\Templates.
```

✦ **Windows NT, 95, 98, 2000, and ME:** Find the Templates folder here:

```
C:\Windows\Profiles\Application Data\Username\
    Application Data\Microsoft\Templates
```
or
```
C:\Windows\Profiles\Application Data\Application Data\
    Microsoft\Templates
```

Suppose that you need to delete styles or rename styles in a template. Follow these steps:

1. **Choose Tools⇨Templates and Add-Ins.**

   The Templates and Add-Ins dialog box appears.

2. **Click the Organizer button to open the Organizer dialog box.**

3. **Click the Close File button on the right side of the dialog box.**

4. **Click the Open File button and, in the Open dialog box, select the template that needs modifying; then click the Open button.**

   The names of items in the template — styles, AutoText entries, toolbars, and macros — appear in the right side of the dialog box. Click a tab, if necessary, to find the item that needs renaming or deleting.

5. **Select the item you want to rename or delete.**

   Follow these steps to rename or delete the item:

   - **Rename an item:** Click the Rename button, enter a new name in the Rename dialog box, and click OK.

   - **Delete an item:** Click the Delete button and then click Yes in the dialog box.

Attaching a Different Template to a Document

It happens in the best of families. You create or are given a document only to discover that the wrong template is attached to it. For times like those, Word gives you the opportunity to switch templates. Follow these steps:

1. **Open the document that needs a new template and choose Tools⇨ Templates and Add-Ins.**

   You see the Templates and Add-Ins dialog box, as shown in Figure 4-3.

2. **Click the Attach button. You see the Attach Template dialog box.**

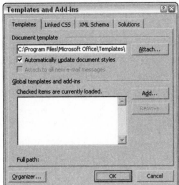

Figure 4-3: Attaching a different template in Word.

3. **Find and select the template you want, and then click the Open button.**

   You return to the Templates and Add-ins dialog box, where the name of the template you chose appears in the Document Template box.

4. **Select the Automatically Update Document Styles check box.**

   Doing so tells Word to apply the styles from the new template to your document.

5. **Click OK.**

Chapter 5: Constructing the Perfect Table

In This Chapter

✔ **Creating a table and working with table formats**

✔ **Entering table data**

✔ **Repeating heading rows on subsequent pages**

✔ **Working with AutoFormats and other fancy elements**

The best way to present a bunch of data at one time is to do it in a table. Provided that the row labels and column headings are descriptive, a table is the easiest way to present information. However, as everyone who has worked on tables knows, tables are a chore. Getting all the columns to fit, making columns and rows the right width and height, and editing the text in a table is not easy. So problematic are tables that Word has devoted an entire menu to constructing them: The Table menu. This chapter explains how to create tables, enter text in tables, change the number and size of columns and rows, and format tables. To start you off on the right foot, this chapter starts with explanations of table jargon.

Talking Table Jargon

As is true of so much else in Computerland, tables have their own jargon. Figure 5-1 describes table jargon. Sorry, but you need to catch up on these terms to construct the perfect table:

✦ **Cell:** The box that is formed where a row and column intersect. Each cell holds one data item.

✦ **Heading row:** The name of the labels along the top row that explain what is in the columns below.

✦ **Row labels:** The labels in the first column that describe what is in each row.

✦ **Borders:** The lines in the table.

✦ **Gridlines:** The gray lines that show where the columns and rows are. Gridlines are not printed — they appear to help you format your table. (Choose Table⇨Show Gridlines or Table⇨Hide Gridlines to display or hide them.) Word prints only the borders, not the gridlines, when you print a table.

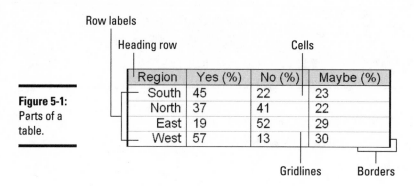

Figure 5-1:
Parts of a
table.

Creating a Table

Word offers no fewer than four ways to create the cells and rows for a table. On your marks, get set, go:

✦ **Insert table button:** Click the Insert Table button, drag out the menu to the number of rows and columns you want, and let go of the mouse button.

✦ **Drawing a table:** Choose Table⇨Draw Table or click the Draw Table button on the Tables and Borders toolbar. The cursor changes into a pencil. Use the pencil to draw the table borders. If you make a mistake, click the Eraser button on the Tables and Border toolbar. The pointer changes into an eraser. Drag it over the parts of the table you regret drawing. When you're finished drawing the table, press Esc or click the Draw Table button to put the pencil away.

✦ **Insert Table dialog box:** The only advantage of the Insert Table dialog box is that it gives you the opportunity to decide how wide to make the table. Choose Table⇨Insert⇨Table. Enter the number of columns and rows you want and click OK.

✦ **Converting text to a table:** Press Tab or enter a comma in the text where you want columns to be divided. For example, if you are turning an address list into a table, put each name and address on one line and press Tab or enter a comma after the first name, the last name, the street address, the city, the state, and the ZIP Code. For this feature to work, each name and address — each line — must have the same number of tab spaces or commas in it. Highlight the tab or comma-separated text you want to convert into a table and choose Table⇨Convert⇨Text to Table. Under Separate Text At in the Convert Text to Table dialog box, choose Tabs or Commas to tell Word how the columns are separated. Then click OK.

Entering the Text and Numbers

After you've created the table, you can start entering text and numbers. All you have to do is click in a cell and start typing. To help you work more quickly, here are some shortcuts for moving the cursor in a table:

Press . . .	. . . To Move the Cursor to the
Tab	Next column in row
Shift+Tab	Previous column in row
Alt+Home	Start of row
Alt+End	End of row
↓	Row below
↑	Row above
Alt+PgUp	Top of column
Alt+PgDn	Bottom of column

If you need to add a row at the bottom of the table to enter more text, place the cursor in the last column of the last row and press the Tab key.

Here's a neat trick for entering data: Enter the heading row and two empty rows, open the Database toolbar, and click the Data Form button. You see a Data Form dialog box like the one shown in Figure 5-2. For each column in the heading row, you can enter the data in a text box. Click the Add New button after you enter the data.

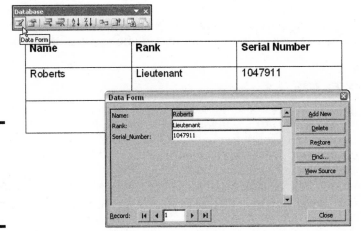

Figure 5-2: Entering table data using the Data Form dialog box.

Aligning Text in Columns and Cells

The easiest way to align text in the columns or cells is to rely on the Align Left, Center, Align Right, and Justify buttons on the Standard toolbar. Select a cell, a column, or columns and click one of those buttons to align the text in a column the same way.

However, if you want to get really fancy, you can use the Align button on the Tables and Borders toolbar. Select the cells that need aligning, click the down arrow to open the Align button drop-down list, and select one of the nine buttons to align text in a new way.

Merging and Splitting Cells and Tables

In the table in Figure 5-3, the cells in rows 2, 4, and 6 have been merged to create three cells for the baseball players' names. Where these rows should have nine cells, they have only one. To merge the cells in a table, select the cells you want to merge and choose Table⇨Merge Cells or click the Merge Cells button on the Tables and Borders toolbar.

1994	1995	1996	1997	1998	1999	2000	2001	2002
Mark McGuire's Home Runs								
53	51	52	58	70	65	32	20	--
Sammy Sosa's Home Runs								
11	38	37	48	64	63	50	64	49
Barry Bonds' Home Runs								
37	33	42	40	37	34	49	73	46

Figure 5-3: Merge cells to create larger cells.

In the same vein, you can split a cell into two or more cells by selecting the cell and choosing Table⇨Split Cells or clicking the Split Cells button on the Tables and Borders toolbar. In the Split Cells dialog box, declare how many columns and rows you want to split the cell into and click OK.

Still in the same vein, you can split a table by placing the cursor in what you want to be the first row of the new table and choosing Table⇨Split Table.

Modifying the Table Layout

Very likely, you created too many or too few rows or columns for your table. Some columns are probably too wide, and others may be too narrow. If that is the case, you have to change the layout of the table by deleting, inserting, and changing the size of columns and rows — in other words, you have to modify the table layout. (Later in this chapter, "Sprucing Up Your Table" explains how to put borders around tables and embellish them in other ways.)

Selecting different parts of a table

Before you can fool with cells, rows, or columns, you have to select them:

✦ **Cells:** To select a cell, click in it. You can select several cells simultaneously by dragging the cursor over them.

✦ **Rows:** Place the cursor in the left margin and click to select one row, or drag to select several rows. You can also select rows by placing the cursor in the row you want to select and then choosing Table⇨ Select⇨Row. To select several rows, select cells in the rows and then choose Table⇨Select⇨Row.

✦ **Columns:** To select a column, move the cursor to the top of the column. When the cursor changes into a fat down-pointing arrow, click once. You can click and drag to select several columns. The other way to select a column is to click anywhere in the column and choose Table⇨Select⇨ Column. To select several columns with this command, select cells in the columns before giving the Select command.

✦ **A table:** To select a table, click in the table and choose Table⇨Select⇨ Table; hold down the Alt key and double-click; or press Alt+5 (the 5 on the numeric keypad, not the one on the main part of the keyboard).

Inserting and deleting columns and rows

Here's the lowdown on inserting and deleting columns and rows:

✦ **Inserting columns:** To insert a blank column, select the column to the right of where you want the new column to go, right-click, and choose Insert Columns. You can also choose Table⇨Insert⇨Columns to the Left (or Columns to the Right). Word inserts the number of columns you select, so, to insert more than one, select more than one column before choosing the Insert Columns command.

✦ **Deleting columns:** To delete columns, select them. Then choose Table⇨ Delete⇨Columns, or right-click and choose Delete Columns. (Pressing the Delete key just deletes the data in the column, leaving blank cells in the column.)

✦ **Inserting rows:** To insert a blank row, select the row below which you want the new one to appear. If you want to insert more than one row, select more than one. Then right-click and choose Insert Rows, or choose Table⇨Insert⇨Rows Above (or Rows Below). You can also insert a row at the end of a table by moving the cursor into the last cell in the last row and pressing the Tab key.

✦ **Deleting rows:** To delete rows, select them and choose Table⇨Delete⇨ Rows, or right-click and choose Delete Rows. (Pressing the Delete key just deletes the data in the row.)

Moving columns and rows

Because there is no elegant way to move a column or row, you should move only one at a time. If you try to move several simultaneously, you open a can of worms that is best left unopened. To move a column or row:

1. **Select the column or row you want to move.**

2. **Right-click in the selection and choose Cut on the shortcut menu.**

The column or row is moved to the Clipboard.

3. **Move the column or row:**

- **Column:** Click in the topmost cell in the column to the right of where you want to move the column. In other words, to make what is now column 4 column 2, cut column 4 and click in the topmost cell of column 2. Then right-click and choose Paste Columns from the shortcut menu.

- **Row:** Move the cursor into the first column of the row below which you want to move your row. In other words, if you're placing the row between what are now rows 6 and 7, put the cursor in row 7. Then right-click and choose Paste Rows on the shortcut menu.

**Book IV
Chapter 5**

**Constructing the
Perfect Table**

Resizing columns and rows

The fastest way to adjust the width of columns and the height of rows is to "eyeball it." To make a column wider or narrower, move the cursor onto a gridline or border between rows or columns. When the cursor changes into a double-headed arrow, start dragging. Tug and pull, tug and pull until the column is the correct width or the row is the correct height. You can also slide the column bars on the ruler or the rows bars on the vertical ruler (if you're in Print Layout View) to change the width of columns and height of rows.

Because resizing columns and rows can be problematic, Word offers these commands on the Table⇨AutoFit submenu for adjusting the width and height of rows and columns:

- ✦ **AutoFit to Contents:** Makes each column wide enough to accommodate its widest entry.

- ✦ **AutoFit to Window:** Stretches the table so that it fits across the page between the left and right margin.

- ✦ **Fixed Column Width**: Fixes the column widths at their current settings.

 ✦ **Distribute Rows Evenly:** Makes all rows the same height as the tallest row. You can also click the Distribute Rows Evenly button on the Tables and Borders toolbar. Select rows before giving this command to make the command affect only those rows.

 ✦ **Distribute Columns Evenly:** Makes all columns the same width. You can also click the Distribute Columns Evenly button. Select columns before giving this command if you want to change the size of a few columns, not all the columns in the table.

Repeating Heading Rows on Subsequent Pages

Making sure that the heading row, sometimes called the header row, appears on a new page if the table breaks across pages is absolutely essential. The header row is the first row in the table, the one that usually describes what each column contains. Without a header row, readers can't tell what the information in a table is or means.

To make the header row (or rows) repeat on the top of each new page, place the cursor in the header row (or select the header rows if you have more than one) and choose Table⇨Heading Rows Repeat. By the way, repeating header rows appear only in Print Layout view, so don't worry if you're in Normal view and you can't see them.

In a top-heavy table, such as the one shown in Figure 5-4, in which the heading row cells contain text and the cells below contain numbers, you can make the entire table narrower by changing the orientation of the text in the heading row. To turn text on its ear, select the cells whose text needs a turn and click the Change Text Direction button on the Tables and Borders toolbar. Keep clicking until the text turns the direction you want.

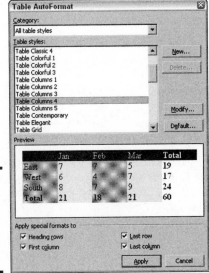

Figure 5-4:
Changing
text
direction.

Sprucing Up Your Table

After you have entered the text, put the rows and columns in place, and made everything the right size, the fun begins. Now you can dress up your table and make it look snazzy.

Almost everything you can do to a document you can also do to a table by selecting parts of the table and then choosing menu commands or clicking buttons. You can change text fonts, align data in the cells in different ways, and even import a graphic into a cell. You can also play with the borders that divide the rows and columns and "shade" columns, rows, and cells by filling them with gray shades or a black background. Read on to find out how to do these tricks and how to center a table or align it with the right page margin.

Formatting a table with Word's AutoFormats

By far the fastest way to get a good-looking table is to let Word do the work for you: Click your table and choose Table⇨Table AutoFormat. You see the Table AutoFormat dialog box, shown in Figure 5-5. Rummage through the Table Styles until you find a table to your liking. The Preview box shows what the different tables look like. (On the Category drop-down list, you can choose an option to put a cap on the number of styles offered in the Table Style list.) Under Apply Special Formats To, select and deselect the check boxes to modify the table format. As you do so, watch the Preview box to see what your choices do.

Figure 5-5:
Lots of
choices in
the Table
AutoFormat
dialog box.

Borders, shading, and color

 Rather than rely on Word's Table⇨Table AutoFormat command, you can draw borders yourself and shade or give color to different parts of a table as well. Figure 5-6 shows these tools. Decorating a table by means of the Tables and Borders toolbar is easier than you might think. Click the Tables and Borders button on the Standard toolbar to display the Tables and Borders toolbar. Then select the part of the table you want to decorate and customize it as follows:

Border Color button

Line Weight menu | Border button and menu

Line Style menu | Shading Color button and menu

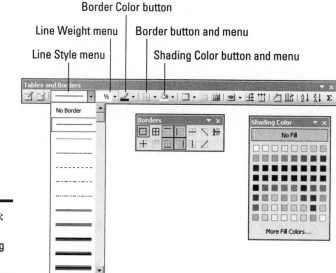

Figure 5-6:
Tools for decorating tables.

✦ **Choosing lines for borders:** Click the down arrow beside the Line Style button and choose a line, dashed line, double line, or wiggly line for the border. (Choose No Border if you don't want a border or you're removing one that is already there.) Then click the down arrow beside the Line Weight button to choose a line width for the border.

 ✦ **Choosing line colors:** Click the down arrow beside the Border Color button and choose one of the colors on the drop-down list. Use the Automatic choice to remove colors and gray shades.

 ✦ **Drawing the border lines:** Click the down arrow beside the Border button and choose one of the border styles on the drop-down list. (Choose No Border to remove borders.) For example, choose Top Border to put a border along the top of the part of the table you selected; choose Inside Border to put the border on the interior lines of the part of the table you selected. You will find the Border button on the Formatting toolbar as well as the Tables and Borders toolbar.

 ✦ **Shading or giving a color background to table cells:** Click the down arrow beside the Shading Color button and choose a color or gray shade on the drop-down list.

After you make a choice from a menu on the Tables and Borders toolbar, the choice you made appears on the button that is used to open the menu. Choose Blue on the Shading Color drop-down list, for example, and the Shading Color button turns blue. If the choice you want to make from a list happens to be the last choice you made, you can click the button instead of opening a drop-down list. To make a blue background show in a table, for example, you can simply click the Shading Color button as long as the Shading Color button is blue.

Chapter 6: Getting Word's Help with Office Chores

In This Chapter

✔ Finding synonyms with the Thesaurus

✔ Commenting on others' work

✔ Tracking revisions to documents

✔ Organizing your work with outlines

✔ Printing on envelopes and labels

✔ Mail merging for form letters and bulk mailing

This chapter is dedicated to the proposition that everyone should get their work done sooner. It explains how Word can be a help in the office, especially when it comes to working on team projects. This chapter also explains *mail merging,* Microsoft's term for generating form letters or labels and envelopes for mass mailings.

Finding the Right Word with the Thesaurus

If you can't seem to find the right word, or if the word is on the tip of your tongue but you can't quite remember it, you can always give the Thesaurus a shot. To find synonyms for a word in your document, start by right-clicking the word and choosing Synonyms on the shortcut menu, as shown in Figure 6-1. With luck, the synonym you're looking for appears on the submenu, and all you have to do is click to enter the synonym in your document. Usually, however, finding a good synonym is a journey, not a Sunday stroll.

To search for a good synonym, click the word in question and press Shift+F7, choose Tools⇨Language⇨Thesaurus, or right-click and choose Synonyms⇨ Thesaurus. The Research task pane opens, as shown in Figure 6-1. Now you're getting somewhere:

✦ **Choosing a synonym:** Move the pointer over the word, open its menu, and choose Insert.

✦ **Finding a synonym for a synonym:** If a synonym intrigues you, click it. The task pane displays a new list of synonyms.

✦ **Searching for antonyms:** If you can't think of the right word, trying typing its antonym and then looking for an antonym in the Research task pane. The task pane sometimes lists antonyms for words.

✦ **Revisit a word list:** Click the Back button as many times as necessary. If you go back too far, you can always click its companion Forward button.

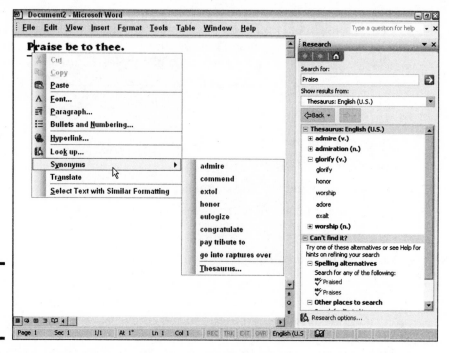

Figure 6-1:
Searching
for
synonyms.

Highlighting Parts of a Document

You can use the Highlight command to mark paragraphs and text that need reviewing later. And on rainy days, you can use it to splash color on your documents and keep yourself amused. Whatever your reasons for highlighting text in a document, follow these steps to do it:

1. If necessary, click the down arrow beside the Highlight button and choose a color.

If the stripe on the bottom of the button is the color you want, just click the button.

2. Drag the cursor over the text you want to highlight.

3. Click the Highlight button again when you're done.

You can also highlight text by selecting it and then clicking the Highlight button to choose a new color from the Highlight drop-down list.

Highlight marks are printed along with the text. To temporarily remove the highlights in a document, choose Tools➪Options, select the View tab in the Options dialog box, and deselect the Highlight check box. To permanently remove highlights, select the document or the text from which you want to remove the highlights, click the down arrow to open the Highlight drop-down list, and select None.

Commenting on a Document

In the old days, comments were scribbled illegibly in the margins of books and documents, but in Word, comments are easy to read. Highlights, a different color for each commenter, appear on-screen where comments have been made in a document, and brackets appear around words and passages as well. As shown in Figure 6-2, you can read a comment in Normal view and Outline view by moving the cursor over bracketed text; in Page Layout view and Web Layout view, comments appear in bubbles. (Choose Tools⇨Options, select the View tab in the Options dialog box, and check the ScreenTips check box if comments don't appear when you move the pointer over them in Normal or Outline view.)

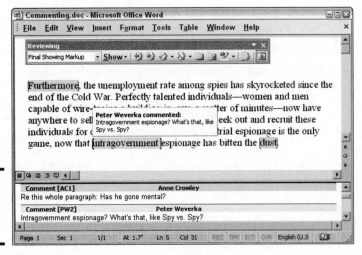

Figure 6-2:
A comment
in Normal
view.

If you're putting together a proposal, you can pass it around the office and invite everyone to comment. If someone makes an especially good comment, you can include it in the main text merely by copying and pasting it. To write a comment:

1. **Select the word or sentence that you want to criticize or praise.**

2. **Choose Insert⇨Comment or click the Insert Comment button on the Reviewing toolbar.**

The Reviewing pane opens at the bottom of the screen with comments that have already been made and the names of the people who made them. You see the Reviewing toolbar as well.

3. **In the Reviewing pane, type your comment in the space provided under the word "Comment" and your name.**

If your name doesn't appear in the Reviewing pane, choose Tools⇨ Options, select the User Information tab, and type your name in the Name text box.

Here are a handful of tasks that deserve comment (if you'll pardon my little pun):

✦ **Seeing and hiding the Reviewing pane:** Click the Reviewing Pane button on the Reviewing toolbar to hide or display the Reviewing pane. You can also click the Show button on the toolbar and choose Reviewing Pane from the menu that appears.

✦ **Seeing and hiding comment brackets:** Click the Show button on the Reviewing toolbar and choose Comments to hide or display the brackets that appear in the text where a comment was made.

✦ **Deleting a comment:** Click a highlighted comment in brackets or a comment in the Reviewing pane and then click the Reject Change/Delete Comment button on the Reviewing toolbar. You can also right-click a comment in your document and choose Delete Comment on the shortcut menu.

✦ **Deleting all the comments in the document:** Click the down arrow beside the Reject Change/Delete Comment button and choose Delete All Comments in Document.

✦ **Deleting comments made by one or two people:** First, isolate comments made by people whose comments you want to delete. To do that, click the Show button on the Reviewing toolbar, choose Reviewers, and, on the submenu, deselect the name of a commenter whose comments you want to keep. Do this as many times as necessary until brackets appear only around the comments you want to delete. Then click the down arrow beside the Reject Change/Delete Comment button and choose Delete All Comments Shown.

✦ **Editing a comment:** Rewrite it in the Reviewing pane. You can right-click a phrase in brackets and choose Edit Comment to open the Reviewing pane to a comment you want to edit.

Showing Revisions to Documents

When many hands go into revising a document, figuring out who made revisions to what is impossible. And more importantly, it's impossible to tell what the first draft looked like. Sometimes it's hard to tell whether the revision work was for the good or the ill.

To help you keep track of changes to documents, Word offers the Tools⇨ Track Changes command. When this command is in effect, all changes to the document are recorded in a different color, with one color for each reviewer. New text is underlined, a vertical line appears in the left margin to show where changes were made, and text that has been deleted either appears in balloons (in Print Layout and Web Layout view) or is crossed out (in Normal and Outline view). By moving the pointer over a change, you can read the name of the person who made it as well as the words that were inserted or deleted. Then you can accept or reject each change. You can also see the original document or a copy with revisions simply by making a choice from a menu.

To give you an idea of what tracking marks look like, Figure 6-3 shows the first two lines of Vladimir Nabokov's autobiography *Speak, Memory* in Normal view, with marks showing where additions were made and text was scratched out.

Vladimir Nabokov, 11/10/1998 3:53:00
AM inserted::

The cradle rocks above an abyss, and ~~Vulgar~~
common sense ~~assures~~ tells us that our existence
is but a brief ~~strip~~ crack of light between two
extremities of ~~complete~~ darkness. Although the
two are identical twins, man, as a rule, ~~maybe we~~
views the prenatal ~~abyss~~one with ~~considerably~~
more calm ~~equanimity~~ than the one he is~~we are~~
heading for (at some forty-five hundred heart
beats an hour).

Figure 6-3:
A document
with
revision
marks.

Marking the changes

To start tracking where editorial changes are made to a document, do one
of the following:

TRK

✦ Double-click TRK on the status bar.

✦ Choose Tools⇨Track Changes (or press Ctrl+Shift+E)

✦ Click the Track Changes button on the Reviewing toolbar.

The Reviewing toolbar appears on-screen. If you're the first author to have
a crack at this document, your changes appear in red. If you are the second
author, they appear in a different color. Word can tell when a new reviewer
has gotten hold of a document and assigns a new color accordingly.

To track formatting changes as well as editorial changes, click the Show
button on the Reviewing toolbar and choose Formatting on the menu. If you
prefer not to see balloons within balloons in Print Layout and Web Layout
view, click the Show button and choose Balloons⇨Never Use Balloons from
the menu that appears.

Marking changes when you forgot to turn on revision marks

Suppose that you write the first draft of a document and someone revises it
but that someone doesn't track revisions. How can you tell where changes
were made? For that matter, suppose that you get hold of a document, you
change it around without turning on revision marks, and now you want to
see what your editorial changes did to the original copy. Here is some good
news: You can see where changes were made, as long as you have a clean
copy of the first draft.

To see where changes were made to the first draft of a document, use the
Tools⇨Compare and Merge Documents command. After you are done com-
paring and merging, revision marks appear where changes were made.
Follow these steps to compare and merge documents:

1. **Open the copy of the document that you or someone else made
changes to.**

In other words, open the second or a subsequent draft.

**Book IV
Chapter 6**

**Getting Word's Help
with Office Chores**

2. **Choose Tools⇨Compare and Merge Documents.**

   You see the Compare and Merge Document dialog box.

3. **Find and select the first-draft file.**

4. **Click the down arrow beside the Merge button and choose an option on the drop-down list:**

   - **Merge:** Makes the changes and revision marks appear in the first draft of the document.

   - **Merge into Current Document:** Makes the changes and revision marks appear in the subsequent draft, that is, in the document you opened in Step 1.

   - **Merge into New Document:** Makes the changes and revision marks appear in a new document.

Compare documents when you want to see where the original and revised documents differ, not what was inserted or deleted. If both reviewers deleted the same paragraph, for example, you won't see the paragraph crossed out; instead, it doesn't appear at all in the compared copy. To compare documents, follow the procedure you use to merge them, but select the Legal Blackline check box in the Compare and Merge Documents dialog box, and then click the Compare button.

Reading and reviewing a document with revision marks

Reading and reviewing a document with revision marks isn't easy. The revision marks can get in the way. Fortunately, Word offers a handful of techniques for dealing with documents that have been scarred by revision marks:

- ✦ **Temporarily remove the revision marks:** Click the Show button on the Reviewing toolbar and deselect the Insertions and Deletions option on the menu. Select the command again when you want to see revision marks.

- ✦ **See what the document would look like if you accepted all revisions:** Open the Display for Review menu on the Reviewing toolbar and choose Final (or choose View⇨Markup).

- ✦ **See what the document would look like if you rejected all revisions:** Open the Display for Review menu and choose Original.

- ✦ **See more clearly where text has been deleted:** Open the Display for Review menu and choose Original Showing Markup. Now a line appears through text that has been deleted. Text that has been deleted does not appear in balloons as it does when you choose Final Showing Markup on the Display for Review menu.

- ✦ **Focus on revisions made by one or two reviewers:** Click the Show button, choose Reviewers, and deselect a reviewer's name on the submenu. Do this as many times as necessary to remove names and be able to see only revisions made by one or two people. Choose All Reviewers on the submenu when you want to see all the revision marks.

Accepting and rejecting changes

Whatever your preference for accepting or rejecting changes, start by selecting a change. To do so, either click it or click the Previous or Next button on the Reviewing toolbar to locate it in your document. With the change selected, do one of the following:

+ **Accept the change:** Click the Accept Change button or right-click and choose Accept on the shortcut menu.

+ **Reject the change:** Click the Reject Change button or right-click and choose Reject on the shortcut menu.

To accept all the changes in a document, click the down arrow beside the Accept Change button and choose Accept All Changes in Document.

Outlines for Organizing Your Work

Outline view is a great way to see at a glance how your document is organized and whether you need to organize it differently. To take advantage of this feature, you must have assigned heading levels to the headings in your document (Book IV, Chapter 4 explains styles.) In Outline view, you can see all the headings in your document. If a section is in the wrong place, you can move it simply by dragging an icon or by pressing one of the buttons on the Outlining toolbar. To change the rank of a heading, simply choose an option on the Outlining toolbar.

Choose View⇨Outline or click the Outline View button in the lower-left corner of the screen to switch to Outline view. Rather than see text, you see the headings in your document, as well as the first line underneath each heading. Now you get a sense of what is in your document and whether it is well organized. By choosing an option from the Show Level drop-down list, you can decide which headings to see on-screen, as Figure 6-4 demonstrates.

Choose which headings to see.

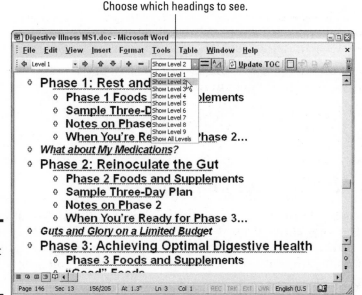

Figure 6-4:
A document in Outline view.

Before you start rearranging your document in Outline view, get a good look at it by taking advantage of buttons and menus on the Outlining toolbar:

✦ **View some or all headings:** Choose an option from the Show Level drop-down list. To see only first-level headings, for example, choose Show Level 1. To see first-, second-, and third-level headings, choose Show Level 3. Choose Show All Levels to see all the headings.

✦ **View heading formats:** Click the Show Formatting button. When this button is selected, you can see how headings were formatted and get a better idea of their ranking in your document.

✦ **View or hide the headings in one section:** To see the headings and text in only one section of a document, select that section by clicking the plus sign beside it; then click the Expand button. To hide the headings and text in a section, select the minus sign beside its name and then click the Collapse button.

✦ **View or hide paragraph text:** Click the Show First Line Only button (or press Alt+Shift+L). When this button is selected, you see only the first line in each paragraph. First lines are followed by an ellipsis (. . .) so that you know that more text follows.

Notice the plus and minus icons next to the headings and the text. A plus icon means that the item has subtext under it. For example, headings almost always have plus icons because text comes after them. A minus icon means that nothing is found below the item in question. For example, body text usually has a minus icon because body text is lowest on the Outline totem pole.

You can do the following tasks with the lists and buttons on the Outlining toolbar:

✦ **Move a section in the document:** To move a section up or down in the document, click the Move Up or Move Down button. You can also drag the plus sign or square icon to a new location. If you want to move the subordinate text and headings along with the section, be sure to click the Collapse button to tuck all the subtext into the heading before you move it.

✦ **Choose a new level for a heading:** Click the heading and choose a new heading level from the Outline Level drop-down list.

✦ **Promote and demote headings:** Click the heading and then click the Promote button or Demote button. For example, you can promote a Level 3 heading to Level 2 by clicking the Promote button. Click the Promote to Heading 1 button to promote any heading to a first-level heading.

Printing an Address on an Envelope

Printing addresses gives correspondence a formal, official look. It makes you look like a big shot. (Later in this chapter, "Churning Out Letters, Labels, and Envelopes for Mass Mailings" explains how to print more than one envelope at a time.) Here's how to print an address and a return address on an envelope:

1. **To save a bit of time, open the document that holds the letter you want to send; then select the name and address of the person you want to send the letter to.**

By doing so, you save yourself from having to type the address again. However, you don't have to open a document to start with.

2. **Choose Tools⇨Letters and Mailings⇨Envelopes and Labels.**

The Envelopes tab of the Envelopes and Labels dialog box appears, as shown in Figure 6-5.

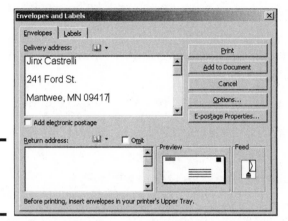

Figure 6-5:
Printing on an envelope.

3. **Enter a name and address in Delivery Address box (the address is already there if you selected it in Step 1).**

Your name and address should appear in the Return Address box. (If they aren't there, enter them for now, but be sure to read the Tip at the end of this section to find out how to put them there automatically.)

4. **Select the Omit check box if you don't want your return address to appear on the envelope.**

5. **Click the Print button.**

Two commands on the Envelopes tab tell Word how your printer handles envelopes and what size your envelopes are.

 Click the envelope icon below the word *Feed* to open the Envelope Options dialog box and choose the right technique for feeding envelopes to your printer. Consult the manual that came with your printer, select one of the Feed Method boxes, click the Face Up or Face Down option button, and open the Feed From drop-down list to tell Word which printer tray the envelope is in or how you intend to stick the envelope in your printer. Click OK when you're done.

 After you've fed the envelope to your printer, click the envelope icon below the word *Preview* — that's right, click the icon — to tell Word what size your envelopes are and whether you want to print bar codes on the envelope.

Book IV
Chapter 6

Getting Word's Help
with Office Chores

To make your name and return address appear automatically in the Envelopes and Labels dialog box, choose Tools⇨Options, select the User Information tab, and enter your name and address in the Mailing Address box.

Printing a Single Address Label (Or a Page of the Same Label)

If you need to print a single label or a sheet of labels that are all the same, you can do it. Before you start printing, however, take note what size and what brand your labels are. You are asked about label brands and sizes when you print labels. (Later in this chapter, "Churning Out Letters, Labels, and Envelopes for Mass Mailings" explains how to print multiple labels as part of a mass mailing.)

Follow these steps to print a single label or a sheet full of identical labels:

1. Choose Tools⇨Letters and Mailings⇨Envelopes and Labels.

You see the Envelopes and Labels dialog box.

2. Select the Labels tab, as shown in Figure 6-6.

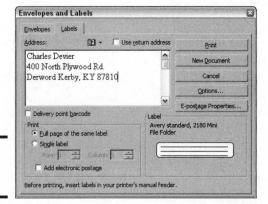

Figure 6-6: Printing labels.

3. Enter the label — the name and address — in the Address box.

If you're printing your return address on labels, check the Use Return Address check box. Your return address appears automatically if you entered it in the Options dialog box by choosing Tools⇨Options and entering it on the User Information tab. If your return address doesn't appear, however, enter it now.

4. Either click the Options button or click the label icon in the Label section to open the Label Options dialog box.

5. In the Printer Information area, select either Dot Matrix or Laser and Ink Jet to say which kind of printer you have; on the Tray drop-down list, choose the option that describes how you will feed labels to your printer.

6. **Open the Label Products drop-down list and choose the brand or type of labels that you have.**

   If your brand is not on the list, you can choose Other/Custom (found at the bottom of the list), click the Details button, and describe your labels in the extremely confusing Address Information dialog box. A better way, however, is to measure your labels and see whether you can find a label of the same size by experimenting with Product Number and Label Information combinations.

7. **In the Product Number drop-down list, select the product number listed on the package that your labels came in.**

   Look in the Label Information area on the right to make sure that the Height, Width, and Page Size measurements match those of the labels you have.

8. **Click OK to return to the Envelopes and Labels dialog box.**

9. **Choose a Print option and click the Print button.**

   Tell Word whether you're printing a single label or a sheet full of labels:

   - **Full Page of the Same Label:** Select this option button if you want to print a pageful of the same label. Likely, you'd choose this option to print a pageful of your own return addresses. Click the New Document button after you make this choice. Word creates a new document with a pageful of labels. Save and print this document.

   - **Single Label:** Select this option button to print one label. Then enter the row and column where the label is and click the Print button.

Churning Out Letters, Labels, and Envelopes for Mass Mailings

Thanks to the miracle of computing, you can churn out form letters, labels, and envelopes for a mass mailing in the privacy of your home or office, just as the big companies do. It's easy, as long as you take the time to prepare the source file. The *source file* is the file that the names and addresses come from. A Word table, an Excel worksheet, a Microsoft Access database table or query, or an Outlook Contacts list or Address Book can serve as the source file.

To generate form letters, labels, or envelopes, you combine the source file with a form letter, label, or envelope document. Word calls this process *merging.* During the merge, names and addresses from the source file are plugged into the appropriate places in the form letter, label, or envelope document. When the merge is complete, you can either save the form letters, labels, or envelopes in a new file or start printing right away.

The following text explains how to prepare the source file and merge addresses from the source file with a document to create form letters, labels, or envelopes. Then you discover how to print the form letters, labels, or envelopes.

Preparing the source file

If you intend to get addresses for your form letters, labels, or envelopes from an Outlook Contact List or Address Book on your computer, you're ready to go. However, if you haven't entered the addresses yet or you are keeping them in a Word table, Access database table, or Access query, make sure that the data is in good working order:

✦ **Word table:** Save the table in its own file and enter a descriptive heading at the top of each column. In the merge, when you tell Word where to plug in address and other data, you will do so by choosing a heading name from the top of a column. In Figure 6-7, for example, the column headings are Last Name, First Name, Street, and so on. (Book IV, Chapter 5 explains how to construct a Word table.)

Figure 6-7:
A source table for a mail merge.

Last Name	First Name	Street	City	State	Zip	Birthday	Sign
Haines	Clyde	1289 Durham Lane	Durban	MA	64901	January 1	Aquarius
Yee	Gladys	1293 Park Ave.	Waddle	OR	98620	May 3	Libra
Harmony	Esther	2601 Estner Rd.	Pecos	TX	34910	April 10	Taurus
Sings	Melinda	2789 23rd St.	Roburgh	NE	68912	June 14	Gemini
Stickenmud	Rupert	119 Scutter Lane	Nyad	CA	94114	August 2	Leo
Hines	Martha	1263 Tick Park	Osterville	MA	03874	March 16	Sagittarius

✦ **Excel table:** Arrange the worksheet in table format with a descriptive heading atop each column. Word will plug in address and other data by choosing heading names.

✦ **Access database table or query:** Make sure that you know the field names in the database table or query where you keep the addresses. During the merge, you will be asked for field names. By the way, if you are comfortable in Access, query a database table for the records you will need. As you will find out shortly, Word offers a technique for choosing only the records you want for your form letters, labels, or envelopes. However, by querying first, you can start off with the records you need and spare yourself from having to choose records in Word.

A Word table or Access table or query can include more than address information. Don't worry about deleting information that isn't required for form letters, labels, and envelopes. As you will find out soon, you get to decide which information to include from the table or query.

Merging the source file with the document

The next step in generating form letters, labels, or envelopes for a mass mailing is to merge the source file with the document. Follow these general steps to do so:

1. **Open a new document if you want to print labels or envelopes en masse; if you want to print form letters, either open a new document or open a letter you have already written and delete the addressee's name, the address, and other parts of the letter that will differ from recipient to recipient.**

2. **Choose Tools⇨Letters and Mailings⇨Mail Merge.**

   The Mail Merge task pane appears, as shown in Figure 6-8. As you complete each step in the Mail Merge Wizard, you will click the Next hyperlink at the bottom of the task pane.

Choose an option.

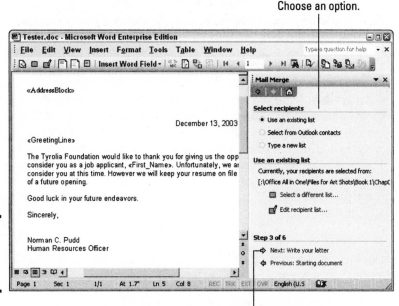

Figure 6-8:
The Mail
Merge task
pane.

Go to the next step.

3. **Under Select Document Type in the task pane, select the Letters, Envelopes, or Labels option button; and, under Step 1 of 6, click the Next: Starting Document hyperlink.**

4. **Under Select Starting Document in the task pane, choose the type of document with which you are dealing; and, under Step 2 of 6, click the Next: Select Recipients hyperlink.**

   Here are your choices in Step 2:

   - **Form letters:** With the Use the Current Document option button already selected, you're ready to go. The text of your form letter already appears on-screen if you followed the directions for opening it or writing it in Step 1. (To use a form letter you have used before, select the Start from Existing Document option button, click the Open button, find and select the letter in the Open dialog box, and click the Open button. Your form letter appears on-screen.)

   - **Labels:** With the Change Document Layout option button already selected, click the Label Options hyperlink under Change Document Layout. You see the Label Options dialog box, where you tell Word what size labels you will print on. See "Printing a Single Address Label (or a Page of the Same Label)," earlier in this chapter, if you need advice for filling out this dialog box. A sheet of sample labels appears on-screen.

**Book IV
Chapter 6**

**Getting Word's Help
with Office Chores**

- **Envelopes**: With the Change Document Layout option button already selected, click the Envelope Options hyperlink under Change Document Layout. You see the Envelope Options dialog box, where, on the Envelope Options and Printing Options tabs, you tell Word what size envelope you will print on. See "Printing an Address on an Envelope" earlier in this chapter, for instructions about filling out these tabs. A sample envelope appears on-screen.

5. **Tell Word what your source file or the source of your address and data information is.**

   The earlier section, "Preparing the source file," explains what a source file is. Your options are as follows:

   - **Addresses from a Word table, Excel table, Access database table, or Access query:** Under Select Recipients, make sure that the Use an Existing List option button is selected and then click the Browse hyperlink under Use an Existing List. You see the Select Data Source dialog box. Locate the Word file or Excel table with the table or the Access database with the table or query, select it, and click the Open button. The Mail Merge Recipients dialog box appears, as shown in Figure 6-9.

Choose the names of recipients.

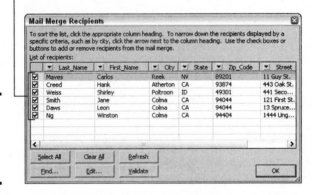

Figure 6-9: Choosing which records to print.

If you select an Access database, you see the Select Table dialog box. Select the table or query you want and click the OK button.

- **Addresses from Microsoft Outlook:** Under Select Recipients, select the Select from Outlook Contacts option button. Then, under Select from Outlook Contacts, click the Choose Contacts Folder hyperlink. The Choose Profile dialog box appears. Click OK in this dialog box. You see the Select Contacts List folder dialog box. Double-click the Contacts folder there. Now you're getting somewhere. You see the Mail Merge Recipients dialog box, with its list of contacts.

6. **In the Mail Merge Recipients dialog box, select the names of people to whom you will send mail; then click OK.**

   To select recipients' names, select or deselect the check boxes on the left side of the dialog box, or else click the Clear All button to remove all the checks and then select recipients' names one at a time.

7. **Click the Next hyperlink in the bottom of the task pane to go to Step 4 of the mail merge.**

8. **Enter the address block on your form letters, labels, or envelopes.**

   The *address block* is the address, including the recipient's name, company, title, street address, city, and ZIP Code. If you're creating form letters, click in the sample letter where the address block will go. If you're printing on envelopes, click in the middle of the envelope where the delivery address will go. Then follow these steps to enter the address block:

   - Either click the Insert Address Block button on the Mail Merge toolbar or click the Address Block hyperlink in the Mail Merge task pane. The Insert Address Block dialog box appears.

   - Choose a format for entering the recipient's name in the address block (watch the Preview window as you do so).

   - Click the Match Fields button. You see the Match Fields dialog box, shown in Figure 6-10.

Match these names with the names from the source file.

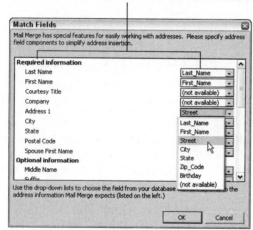

Figure 6-10:
The Match Fields dialog box.

   - Using the drop-down lists on the right side of the dialog box, match the fields in your source file with the address block fields on the left side of the dialog box. In Figure 6-10, for example, the Street field is the equivalent of the Address 1 field on the left side of the dialog box, so Street is being chosen from the drop-down list.

   - Click OK in the Match Fields dialog box and the Insert Block Address dialog box. The <<AddressBlock>> field appears in the document where the address will go. Later, when you merge your document with the data source, real data will appear where the field is now. Think of a field as a kind of placeholder for data.

9. **Click the View Merged Data button on the Mail Merge toolbar to see real data rather than fields.**

   Now you can see clearly whether you entered the address block correctly. If you didn't enter it correctly, click the Match Fields button on the Mail Merge toolbar to open the Match Fields dialog box and make new choices.

10. **Put the finishing touches on your form letters, labels, or envelopes:**

- **Form letters:** Click where the salutation ("Dear John") will go and then click the Insert Greeting Line button on the Mail Merge toolbar or the Greeting Line hyperlink. You see the Greeting Line dialog box, shown in Figure 6-11. Make choices in this dialog box to determine how the letters' salutations will read.

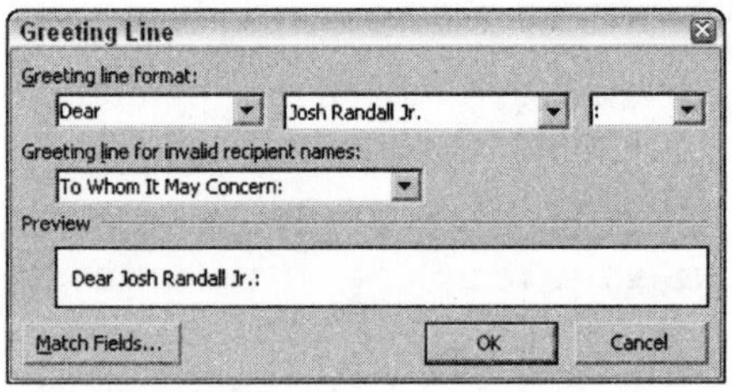

Figure 6-11: Entering the greeting.

The body of your form letter may well include other variable information such as names and birthdays. To enter that stuff, click where variable information goes and then click the Insert Merge Fields button or the More Items hyperlink. The Insert Merge Field dialog box appears and lists fields from the source file. Select a field, click the Insert button, and click the Close button.

If you're editing your form letter and you need to see precisely where the variable information you entered is located, click the Highlight Merge Fields button. The variable information is highlighted in your document.

- **Labels:** Click the Update All Labels button on the bottom of the task pane to enter all recipients' labels in the sample document. (You may have to click the down arrow on the bottom of the task pane several times to see the button.)

To include postal bar codes on labels, click the Postal Bar Code hyperlink in the task pane, make sure that a ZIP Code field is selected in the Insert Postal Bar Code dialog box, and click OK. Postal bar codes help the mail get delivered faster.

- **Envelopes:** If you don't like the fonts or font sizes on the envelope, select an address and change fonts and font sizes with the drop-down lists on the Formatting toolbar.

To enter a return address, click in the upper-right corner and enter it by hand.

To include postal bar codes on envelopes, click below the delivery address, click the Postal Bar Code hyperlink in the task pane, and fill in the Insert Postal Bar Code dialog box.

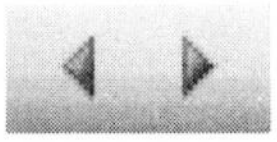

11. **Click the Next Record and Previous Record buttons on the Mail Merge toolbar to skip from recipient to recipient and make sure that you have entered information correctly.**

The items you see on-screen are the same form letters, envelopes, or labels you will see when you have finished printing. (Click the View Merged Data button if you see field names rather than people's names and addresses.)

If an item is incorrect, open the source file and correct it there. When you save the source file, the correction is made in the sample document.

At last — you're ready to print the form letters, labels, or envelopes. Better keep reading.

Printing form letters, labels, and envelopes

After you have gone to the trouble to prepare the data file and merge it with the document, you're ready to print your form letters, labels, or envelopes. Start by loading paper, sheets of labels, or envelopes in your printer:

✦ **Form letters:** Form letters are easiest to print. Just put the paper in the printer.

✦ **Labels:** Load the label sheets in your printer.

✦ **Envelopes**: Not all printers are capable of printing envelopes one after the other. Sorry, but you probably have to consult the dreary manual that came with your printer to find out the correct way to load envelopes.

Now, to print the form letters, labels, or envelopes, save the material in a new document or send it straight to the printer:

✦ **Saving in a new document:** Click the Merge to New Document button on the Mail Merge toolbar (or press Alt+Shift+N) to create a new document for your form letters, labels, or envelopes. You see the Merge to New Document dialog box. Click OK. After Word creates the document, save it and print it. You can go into the document and make changes here and there before printing. In form letters, for example, you can write a sentence or two in different letters to personalize them.

✦ **Printing right away:** Click the Merge to Printer button (or press Alt+Shift+M) to print the form letters, labels, or envelopes without saving them in a document. Click OK in the Merge to Printer dialog box and then negotiate the Print dialog box.

Chapter 7: Getting Acquainted with Outlook

In This Chapter

- ✔ Getting around in Outlook
- ✔ Viewing folders in different ways
- ✔ Searching in folders
- ✔ Deleting items
- ✔ Storing addresses in the Contacts folder

*T*his chapter pulls back the curtain and gives you a first glimpse of Outlook, the e-mailer and personal organizer in the Office suite of programs. Read on to find out once and for all what Outlook does, how to get from folder to folder, and the different ways to view the stuff in folders. You can find advice about keeping folders well organized in this chapter. Finally, this chapter looks at how to maintain an address book in Outlook.

What Is Outlook, Anyway?

Outlook is not in character with the rest of the Office programs. It's a little different — you can tell as soon as you glance at the screen. The familiar Standard and Formatting toolbars are nowhere to be found. Toolbars change altogether when you click a Navigation pane button and go to a different Outlook window.

Outlook can be confusing because the program serves many different purposes. To wit, Outlook is all of these:

- ✦ **An e-mail program:** You can use it to send and receive e-mail messages and files, as well as organize e-mail messages in different folders so that you can keep track of them. (See Book IV, Chapter 8.)

- ✦ **An appointment scheduler:** Outlook is also a calendar for scheduling appointments and meetings. You can tell at a glance when and where you are expected, as well as be alerted to upcoming appointments and meetings. (See Book IV, Chapter 9.)

- ✦ **An address book:** The program can store the addresses, phone numbers, and e-mail addresses of friends, foes, clients, and family members. Looking up this information in the Contact List is easy. (See "Maintaining the Contacts Folder" later in this chapter.)

- ✦ **A task reminder:** Outlook is a means of planning projects. You can tell when deadlines fall and plan your workload accordingly.

- ✦ **A notes receptacle:** The program is a place to jot down notes and reminders.

Outlook is a lot of different things all rolled into one. For that reason, the program can be daunting at first. But hang in there. Soon you will be running roughshod over Outlook and making it suffer on your behalf.

Navigating the Outlook Windows

Figure 7-1 shows the Outlook Today window with the Folder List on display. The Outlook Today window lists calendar appointments, tasks that need doing, and the number of messages in three folders that pertain to e-mail (Inbox, Drafts, and Outbox). Not that it matters especially, but all Outlook jobs are divided among folders, and these folders are all kept in a master folder called Personal Folders.

Folder List

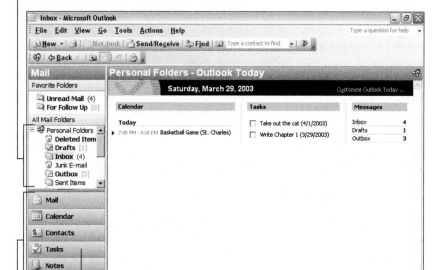

Figure 7-1:
The Outlook
Today
window.

Click here to move to another window.

Navigation pane

Here are the ways to get from window to window in Outlook and undertake a new task:

✦ **Navigation pane:** Click a button — Mail, Calendar, Contacts, Tasks, or Notes — on the Navigation pane to change windows and use Outlook a different way.

✦ **Go menu:** Choose an option on the Go menu — Mail, Calendar, Contacts, Tasks, Notes — to go from window to window. You can also change windows by pressing the Ctrl key and a number from 1 through 5.

✦ **Folder List:** Click the Folder List button to see all the folders in the Personal Folder, and then select a folder (refer to Figure 7-1). For example, to read incoming e-mail messages, select the Inbox folder. The Folder List button is located at the bottom of the Navigation pane. You can also see the Folder List by pressing Ctrl+6 or choosing Go➪Folder List.

 ✦ **Outlook Today button:** No matter where you go in Outlook, you can always click the Outlook Today button to return to the Outlook Today window. You can find this button on the Advanced toolbar.

✦ **Back, Forward, and Up One Level buttons:** Click these buttons to return to a window, revisit a window you retreated from, or climb the hierarchy of personal folders. The three buttons are found on the Advanced toolbar.

By the way, you can open a folder in a new window. To do so, right-click a Navigation pane button and choose Open in New Window. To close a window you opened this way, click its Close button (the *X* in the upper-right corner).

 When you start Outlook, the program opens to the window you were look-ing at when you exited the program. If you were staring at the Inbox when you closed Outlook, for example, you see the Inbox next time you open the program. However, if you prefer to see the Outlook Today window each time you start Outlook, click the Customize Outlook Today button (it's on the right side of the Outlook Today window). Then, in the Outlook Today Options window, select the When Starting, Go Directly to Outlook Today check box and click the Save Changes button.

Choosing what's on the Navigation pane

Click the Configure Buttons button on the Navigation pane to decide which buttons belong on the Navigation pane and which buttons to display. Not everyone needs all the but-tons. Some people, for example, forsake the Tasks and Notes parts of Outlook, so they don't need the Tasks and Notes buttons.

After you click the Configure Buttons button, you can rearrange the Navigation pane like so:

✔ **Remove or add a button:** Select Add or Remove buttons on the shortcut menu and select the name of a button to add or remove.

✔ **Show fewer or more buttons:** Select Show More Buttons or Show Fewer Buttons on the shortcut menu.

✔ **Rearrange the buttons:** Select Navigation Pane Options and, in the Navigation Pane Options dialog box, select button names and click the Move Up or Move Down button.

By the way, you can hide the Navigation pane altogether if the thing gets in your way. To hide (or display) the Navigation pane, choose View➪ Navigation Pane or press Alt+F1.

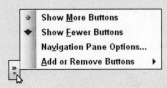

**Book IV
Chapter 7**

**Getting Acquainted
with Outlook**

Getting a Better View of a Folder

Because you spend so much time gazing at folders, you may as well get a good view. To find the items you're looking for and help prioritize your work, Outlook offers different views of each folder. Each option on the menu gives you a different insight into the task at hand. Do one of the following to change views:

✦ Open the Current View drop-down list on the Advanced toolbar and make a choice, as shown in Figure 7-2.

✦ Choose View➪Arrange By➪Current View and an option on the submenu.

✦ Select a Current View option button in the Navigation pane, as shown in Figure 7-2. Current View option buttons are available in the Contacts, Tasks, and Notes folders.

Click here to change views.

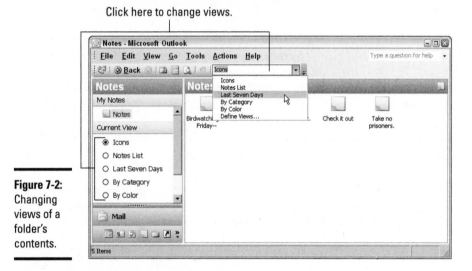

Figure 7-2:
Changing views of a folder's contents.

Finding Items in Folders

If you can't locate an item in a folder by scrolling, changing views, or switching to By Category view, you have to resort to the Find command. Outlook offers two Find commands, a simple Find command that's available on the Standard toolbar, and an Advanced Find command that requires more effort but can yield more exacting results. Keep reading.

The Contacts folder offers a very convenient means of finding stray contact information. In the Find a Contact text box (you can find it on the Standard toolbar), enter a name or an e-mail address and press Enter. If the name or e-mail address can be found, you see the person's Contact information.

Searching in the Find pane

Is it just me, or do others think "pain" instead of "pane" when they hear that the Outlook windows are composed of different panes — the Navigation pane, Reading pane, and so on? As if you aren't already in enough pain, you can follow these steps to conduct simple searches in the Find pane:

1. Click the Find button in any window.

You see a Find pane like the one shown in Figure 7-3.

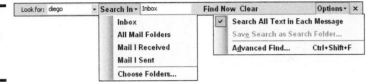

Figure 7-3: Conducting a simple search.

2. If necessary, tell Outlook which folders to search by opening the Search In drop-down list and making a choice.

Choose one of the options on the list or select Choose Folders and pick a folder name in the Select Folder(s) dialog box. You can search more than one folder by opening this dialog box and selecting multiple folders.

In mail folder searches, Outlook searches the text in messages as well as the subject of messages, but if that kind of search produces too many messages to look through, open the Options drop-down list on the Find pane and deselect Search All Text in Each Message (refer to Figure 7-3). This way, Outlook searches messages' subjects only, and fewer messages appear in the search results.

3. Enter what you're searching for in the Look For text box.

4. Click the Find Now button.

If your search doesn't bear fruit, click the Clear button and start all over, or open the Options drop-down list and choose Advanced Find to embark on an advanced search. (The next section explains advanced searching.) Click the Find button or the Close button on the Find pane to remove the Find pane from the screen.

Conducting an advanced search

Run an advanced search when a simple search doesn't do the job, when you want to search using more than one criterion, or when you want to search in several different folders. To start an advanced search, click the Find button (or press Ctrl+Shift+F), open the Options drop-down list on the Find pane (refer to Figure 7-3), and select Advanced Find. You see the Advanced Find window. If your search is a successful one, found items will appear at the bottom of the window, as shown in Figure 7-4. You can double-click to open found items in the search results.

In the Look For drop-down list, choose where you want to search. If the folder isn't on the list, click the Browse button and choose it in the Select Folder(s) dialog box. Then choose options on the three tabs — Contacts, More Choices, and Advanced — in the dialog box. Which options are available depends on which folder you're searching.

Saving a search so that you can run it later

If you find yourself searching for the same stuff repeatedly, save the search criteria in a file. That way, you don't have to enter the search criteria each time you run the search. All you have to do is open the Advanced Find window, choose File⇨ Open Search in the window, and choose a search file in the Open Saved Search dialog box. Searches are saved in special files with the extension `.oss` (Office Saved Searches).

To save a search, start by creating a folder for storing OSS files. After you have conducted a search you want to save, choose File⇨Save Search in the Advanced Save dialog box. You see the Save Search dialog box. Locate the folder where you save searches, enter a descriptive name for the search, and click OK.

Figure 7-4:
Conducting an advanced search.

 The Advanced Find window offers handy commands for dealing with items after you find them. Select the items and choose Edit⇨Move to Folder to move the items into a new folder. Choose Edit⇨Delete to delete the items. Ctrl+click, Shift+click, or choose Edit⇨Select All to select items in the Advanced Find window.

Deleting E-Mail Messages, Contacts, Tasks, and Other Items

Outlook folders are notorious for filling very quickly. E-mail messages, contacts, and tasks soon clog the folders if you spend any time in Outlook. From time to time, go through the e-mail folders, Contacts window, Task window, and Calendar to delete items you no longer need. To delete items, select them and do one of the following:

+ Click the Delete button (or press the Delete key).
+ Choose Edit⇨Delete (or press Ctrl+D).
+ Right-click and choose Delete.

Deleted items — e-mail messages, calendar appointments, contacts, or tasks — land in the Deleted Items folder in case you want to recover them. To delete items once and for all, open the Deleted Items folder and start deleting like a madman.

To spare you the trouble of deleting items twice, once in the original folder and again in the Deleted Items folder, Outlook offers these amenities:

✦ **Empty the Deleted Items folder when you close Outlook:** If you're no fan of the Deleted Items folder and you want to remove deleted items without reviewing them, choose Tools⇨Options, select the Other tab in the Options dialog box, and select Empty the Deleted Items Folder Upon Exiting.

✦ **Empty the Deleted Items folder yourself:** Choose Tools⇨Empty "Deleted Items" Folder to remove all the messages in the Deleted Items folder. You can also right-click the Deleted Items folder in the Folder List and choose Empty "Deleted Items" Folder.

You can search for items and delete them in the Advanced Find window. See "Conducting an advanced search," earlier in this chapter.

Maintaining the Contacts Folder

In pathology, which is the study of diseases and how they are transmitted, a contact is a person who passes on a communicable disease, but in Outlook, a contact is someone about whom you keep information. Information about contacts is kept in the Contacts folder. This folder is a super-powered address book. It has places for storing peoples' names, addresses, phone numbers, e-mail addresses, Web pages, pager numbers, birthdays, anniversaries, nicknames, and other stuff besides. When you address an e-mail message, you can get the address straight from the Contacts folder to be sure that the address is entered correctly. As Book IV, Chapter 6 explains, you can also get addresses from the Contacts folder when you generate form letters, labels, and envelopes for mass-mailings.

Entering a new contact in the Contacts folder

To place someone on the Contacts list, open the Contacts folder and start by doing one of the following:

✦ Click the New button.

✦ Press Ctrl+N (in the Contacts Folder window) or Ctrl+Shift+C.

✦ Choose File⇨New⇨Contact.

You see the Contact form, shown in Figure 7-5. On this form are places for entering just about everything there is to know about a person except his or her love life and secret vices. Enter all the information you care to record, keeping in mind these rules of the road as you go along:

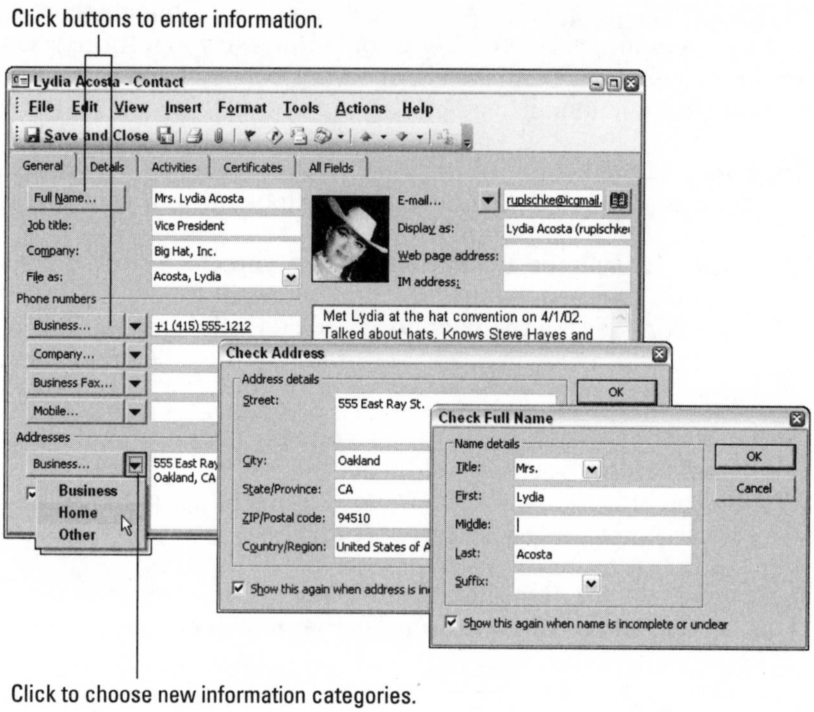

Click buttons to enter information.

Figure 7-5:
A Contact
form.

Click to choose new information categories.

✦ **Full names, addresses, and so on:** Although you may be tempted to simply enter addresses, phone numbers, names, and so on in the text boxes, don't do it! Click the Full Name button on the General tab, for example, to enter a name (refer to Figure 7-5). Click the Business or Home button to enter an address in the Check Address dialog box (refer to Figure 7-5). By clicking the buttons and entering data in dialog boxes, you permit Outlook to separate out the component parts of names, addresses, phone numbers, and so on. As such, Outlook can use names and addresses as a source for mass-mailings and mass e-mailings.

When entering information about a company, not a person, leave the Full Name field blank and enter the company's name in the Company field.

✦ **Information that matters to you:** If the form doesn't appear to have a place for entering a certain kind of information, try clicking a triangle button and choosing a new information category from the drop-down list. Click the triangle button next to the Business button and choose Home, for example, if you want to enter a home address rather than a business address (refer to Figure 7-5).

✦ **File As:** Open the File As drop-down list and choose an option for filing the contact in the Contacts folder. Contacts are filed alphabetically by last name, first name, company name, or combinations of the three. Choose the option that best describes how you expect to find the contact in the Contacts folder.

✦ **Mailing addresses:** If you keep more than one address for a contact, display the address to which you want to send mail and select the This Is the Mailing Address check box. This way, in a mass-mailing, letters are sent to the correct address.

✦ **E-mail addresses:** You can enter three e-mail addresses for each contact (click the triangle button and choose E-mail 2 or E-mail 3 to enter a second or third address). In the Display As text box, Outlook shows you what the To: line of e-mail messages will look like when you send e-mail to a contact. By default, the To: line shows the contact's name followed by his or her e-mail address in parentheses. However, you can enter whatever you wish in the Display As text box, and if entering something different will help you distinguish between e-mail addresses, enter something different. For example, enter Lydia – Personal so that you can tell when you send e-mail to Lydia's personal address as opposed to her business address.

✦ **Photos:** To put a digital photo on a Contact form, click the Add Contact Photo button and, in the Add Contact Picture dialog box, select a picture and click OK.

Be sure to write a few words on the General tab to describe how and where you met the contact. When the time comes to weed out contacts in the Contacts folder list, reading the descriptions will help you decide who gets weeded and who doesn't.

When you're done entering information, click the Save and Close button. If you're in a hurry to enter contact information, click the Save and New button. Doing so opens an empty form so that you can record information about another contact.

Here's a fast way to enter contact information for someone who has sent you an e-mail message: Open the message, right-click the sender's name on the To: line, and choose Add to Outlook Contacts on the shortcut menu. You see the Contact form. Enter more information about the sender if you can and click the Save and Close button.

Changing a contact's information

Changing a contact's information is a chore if you do it by going from field to field on the General and Details tabs of the Contact form. Fortunately for you, there is a faster way to update the information you have about a contact — go to the All Fields tab in the Contact form. As Figure 7-6 shows, this tab lists fields in alphabetical order. Choose an option on the Select From drop-down list, scroll in the form, and update fields as necessary.

**Book IV
Chapter 7**

Getting Acquainted with Outlook

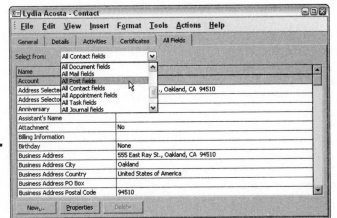

Figure 7-6:
Editing data on the All Fields tab.

Finding a contact

The Contacts folder, which is shown in Figure 7-7, can grow very large, so Outlook offers a number of ways to search it. After you have found the contact you're looking for, double-click it to open the Contact form. Here are some techniques for finding a contact in the Contacts folder:

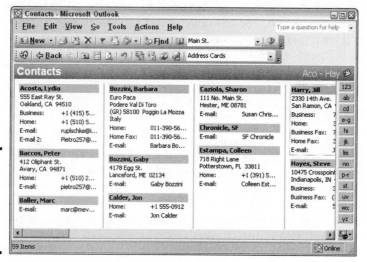

Figure 7-7:
Address Cards view of the Contacts folder.

✦ **The scrollbar:** Click the arrows or drag the scroll box to move through the list.

✦ **Letter buttons:** Click a letter button on the right side of the window to move in the list to a specific letter.

✦ **Change views:** Changing views often helps in the search. Choose a new view from the Current View drop-down list on the Advanced toolbar.

✦ **Find a Contact text box:** Enter a name or e-mail address in this text box and press Enter. The Find a Contact text box is located on the Standard toolbar.

✦ **Find button:** Click the Find button to open the Find pane and look for a contact.

✦ **Search by category:** Categorize contacts as you enter them and switch to By Category view to arrange contacts by category.

CHECK IT OUT

Tracking Your Dealings with a Contact

The Activities tab in the Contacts form is a nifty place to keep track of your comings and goings with a client, friend, or co-worker. E-mail messages you sent to a contact, tasks and journal entries that pertain to a contact, and calendar appointments with a contact can be placed on the Activities tab. To examine your dealings with a contact, all you have to do is open the Activities tab. By double-clicking an item on the tab, you can open an e-mail message, Calendar form, Tasks form, or Journal form and see what's what.

Contacts... Follow these instructions to track your dealings with a contact on the Activities tab of the Contacts form:

✔ **Calendar items, tasks, and journal entries:** On the Appointment, Task, or Journal Entry form you use to set up a calendar appointment, task, or journal entry, click the Contacts button (it's in the lower-left corner) and select a contact in the Select Contacts dialog box. You can select more than one contact by Ctrl+clicking.

✔ **E-mail messages:** As long as the e-mail address on a message is on file somewhere in the Contacts folder, a record of the e-mail message being received or sent is recorded on the Activities tab.

The Activities tab is an excellent place for deleting e-mail messages, because you can see in one place the messages you sent to or received from a client. To delete the messages, select them and press the Delete key.

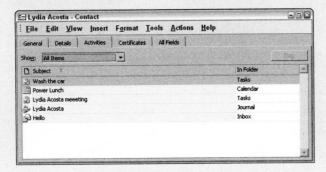

Chapter 8: Handling Your E-Mail

In This Chapter

✓ Addressing, sending, replying to, and forwarding e-mail messages

✓ Creating distribution lists to send messages to groups

✓ Sending files and pictures with e-mail

✓ Understanding HTML and plain-text formats

✓ Receiving e-mail and files over the Internet

✓ Organizing and managing your e-mail

✓ Creating and using different folders to store e-mail

"**N**either snow nor rain nor heat nor gloom of night stays these couriers from the swift completion of their appointed rounds," reads the inscription on the Eighth Avenue New York Post Office Building. E-mailers face a different set of difficulties. Instead of snow, rain, or gloomy nights, they face junk mail blizzards, pesky colleagues, and the occasional co-worker who believes that all e-mail messages should be copied to everyone in the office.

This chapter explains the basics of sending and receiving e-mail, but it also goes a step further to help you organize and manage your e-mail messages. This chapter unscrews the inscrutable. It shows you how to send files and pictures with e-mail messages, make a distribution list so that you can e-mail many people simultaneously, and postpone sending a message. You can also find out how to reorganize e-mail in the Inbox window and be alerted to incoming messages from certain people or from people writing about certain subjects. Finally, this chapter shows how to create different folders for storing and organizing your e-mail.

Addressing and Sending E-Mail Messages

Sorry, you can't send chocolates or locks of hair by e-mail, but you can send words by the bucketful. These pages explain how to send e-mail messages, copies of messages, and blind copies of messages, as well as reply to and forward e-mail.

The basics: Sending an e-mail message

After you get the hang of it, sending an e-mail message is as easy as falling off a turnip truck. The first half of this chapter addresses everything you need to know about sending e-mail messages. Here are the basics:

1. In the Mail folder, click the New button or choose Ctrl+N.

A Message window like the one shown in Figure 8-1 appears.

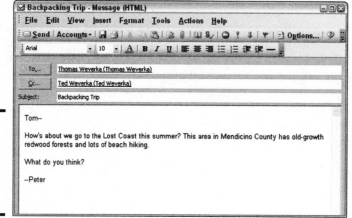

Figure 8-1:
Addressing
and
composing
an e-mail
message.

2. Enter the recipient's e-mail address in the To text box.

The next section in this chapter, "Addressing an e-mail message," explains the numerous ways to address an e-mail message. You can address the same message to more than one person by entering more than one address in the To text box. For that matter, you can send copies of the message and blind copies of the message to others (see "Sending copies and blind copies of messages" later in this chapter).

3. In the Subject text box, enter a descriptive title for the message.

When your message arrives on the other end, the recipient will see the subject first. Enter a descriptive subject that helps the recipient decide whether to read the message right away. After you enter the subject, it appears in the title bar of the Message window.

4. Type the message.

Whatever you do, don't forget to enter the message itself! You can spell-check your message by pressing F7 or by choosing Tools⇨Spelling.

As long as you compose messages in HTML format and the person receiving your e-mail messages has software capable of reading HTML, you can decorate messages to your heart's content (later in this chapter, "All about Message Formats" explains the HTML issue). Experiment with fonts and font sizes. Boldface and underline text. Throw in a bulleted or numbered list. You will find many formatting commands on the Format menu and Formatting toolbar in the Message window.

To choose the default font and font size with which messages are written, choose Tools⇨Options, select the Mail Format tab in the Options dialog box, and click the Fonts button. You see the Fonts dialog box. Click a Choose Font button and, in the dialog box that appears, select a font, font style, and font size.

5. Click the Send button.

As "Postponing Sending a Message" explains later in this chapter, you can put off sending a message. Messages remain in the Outbox folder if you postpone sending them or if Outlook can't send them right away because your computer isn't connected to the Internet.

If you decide in the middle of writing a message to write the rest of it later, choose File⇔Save or press Ctrl+S; then close the Message window. The message will land in the Drafts folder. When you're ready to finish writing the message, open the Drafts folder and double-click your unfinished message to resume writing it.

Copies of e-mail messages you have sent are kept in the Sent Items folder. If you prefer not to keep copies of sent e-mail messages on hand, choose Tools⇔Options and, on the Preferences tab of the Options dialog box, click the E-Mail Options button. You see the E-Mail Options dialog box. Deselect the Save Copies of Messages in Sent Items Folder check box.

Addressing an e-mail message

How do you address an e-mail message in the To text box of the Message window (refer to Figure 8-1)? Let me count the ways:

✦ **Get the address (or addresses) from the Contacts folder:** Click the To (or Cc or Bcc) button to send a message to someone whose name is on file in your Contacts folder. You see the Select Names dialog box, shown in Figure 8-2. Click or Ctrl+click to select the names of people to whom you want to send the message. Then click the To-> button (or Cc-> or Bcc-> button) to enter addresses in the To text box (or Cc or Bcc text boxes) of the Message window. Click OK to return to the Message window. This is the best way to address an e-mail message to several different people.

Select names.

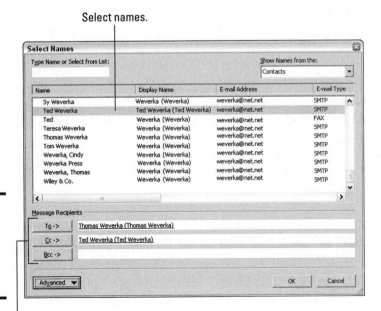

Figure 8-2: Getting addresses from the Contacts folder.

Click a button.

✦ **Type a person's name from the Contacts folder:** Simply type a person's name if the name is on file in the Contacts folder. To send the message to more than one person, enter a comma (,) or semicolon (;) between each name.

✦ **Type the address in the To text box:** If you have entered the address recently or the address is on file in your Contacts folder or Address Book, a pop-up message with the complete address appears. Press Enter to enter the address without your having to type all the letters. To send the message to more than one person, enter a comma (,) or semicolon (;) between each address.

✦ **Reply to a message sent to you:** Select the message in the Inbox folder and click the Reply button. The Message window opens with the address of the person to whom you're replying already entered in the To text box. This is the most reliable way (no typos on your part) to enter an e-mail address. You can also click the Reply to All button to reply to the e-mail addresses of all the people to whom the original message was sent.

Sending copies and blind copies of messages

Sending copies of messages and blind copies of messages is simple enough, but think twice before you do it. In my experience, a dysfunctional office is one where people continuously send copies of messages to one another, to supervisors, to itemize their quarrels or document their work. However, sending copies of messages can clog mailboxes and waste everyone's time.

When you send a copy of a message, the person who receives the message knows that copies have been sent because the names of people to whom copies were sent appear at the top of the e-mail message. But when you send blind copies, the person who receives the message does not know that others received it.

Follow these instructions to send copies and blind copies of messages:

✦ **Send a copy of a message:** Enter e-mail addresses in the Cc text box of the Message window or, in the Select Names dialog box (refer to Figure 8-2), select names and click the Cc->button.

✦ **Send a blind copy of a message:** In the Message window, click the To or Cc button to open the Select Names dialog box (refer to Figure 8-2). Then select the names and click the Bcc-> button, or else enter addresses in the Bcc text box.

People who often send blind copies can make the Bcc text box appear in all Message windows. To do so, choose View⇨Bcc Field in any Message window.

Replying to and forwarding e-mail messages

Replying to and forwarding messages is as easy as pie. For one thing, you don't need to know the recipient's e-mail address to reply to a message. In the Inbox, select the message you want to reply to or forward and do the following:

✦ **Reply to author:** Click the Reply button. The Message window opens with the sender's name already entered in the To box and the original message in the text area below. Write a reply and click the Send button.

✦ **Reply to all parties who received the message:** Click the Reply to All button. The Message window opens with the names of all parties who received the message in the To and Cc boxes and the original message in the text box. Type your reply and click the Send button.

✦ **Forward a message:** Click the Forward button. The Message window opens with the text of the original message. Either enter an e-mail address in the To text box or click the To button to open the Select Names dialog box and select the names of the parties to whom the message will be forwarded. Add a word or two to the original message if you like; then click the Send button.

To find the e-mail address of someone who sent you an e-mail message, double-click the message to display it in the Message window, and then right-click the sender's name in the To box and choose Outlook Properties. The e-mail address appears in the E-Mail Properties dialog box. To add a sender's name to the Contacts folder, right-click the name and choose Add to Outlook Contacts.

By default, the text of the original message appears in the Message window when you click the Reply or Reply to All button to respond to a message. However, Outlook offers the option of not displaying the original text by default. The program also offers different ways of displaying this text. To scope out these options and perhaps select one, choose Tools⇨Options and, on the Preferences tab of the Options dialog box, click the E-Mail Options button. You see the E-Mail Options dialog box. Choose an option on the When Replying to a Message drop-down list to tell Outlook how or whether to display original messages in replies.

Distribution Lists for Sending Messages to Groups

Suppose you're the secretary of the PTA at a school and you regularly send the same e-mail messages to 10 or 12 other board members. Entering e-mail addresses for the 10 or 12 people each time you want to send an e-mail message is a drag. Some would also consider it a violation of privacy to list each person by name in a message. To see why, consider Figure 8-3. Anyone who receives the message shown at the top of the figure can learn the e-mail address of anyone on the To list by right-clicking a name and choosing Outlook Properties. Some people don't want their e-mail addresses spread around this way.

To keep from having to enter so many e-mail addresses, and to keep e-mail addresses private as well, you can create a *distribution list,* a list with different e-mail addresses. To address your e-mail message, you simply enter the name of the distribution list. You don't have to enter 10 or 12 different e-mail addresses. People who receive the message see the name of the distribution list on the To line, not the names of 10 or 12 people, as shown in Figure 8-3.

**Book IV
Chapter 8**

Handling Your E-Mail

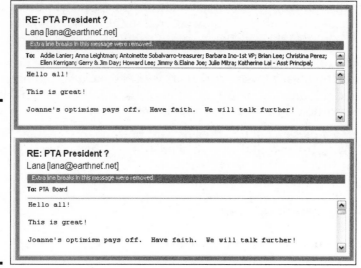

Figure 8-3:
Instead
of entering
many
addresses
(top),
enter a
distribution
list name
(bottom).

Creating a distribution list

Follow these steps to bundle e-mail addresses into a distribution list:

1. **Choose File➪New➪Distribution List or press Ctrl+Shift+L.**

You see the Distribution List window, as shown in Figure 8-4.

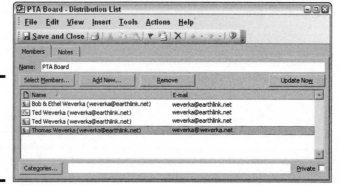

Figure 8-4:
Entering
addresses
for a
distribution
list.

2. **Enter a descriptive name in the Name text box.**

3. **Click the Select Members button to get names and addresses from the Contacts folder.**

You see the Select Members dialog box.

4. **Hold down the Ctrl key and select the name of each person you want to be on the list, click the Members button, and click OK.**

The names you chose appear in the Distribution List window.

5. **To add the names of people who aren't in your Contacts folder, click the Add New button and, in the Add New Member dialog box, enter a name and e-mail address; then click OK.**

6. Click the Save and Close button in the Distribution List dialog box.

You did it — you created a distribution list.

Addressing e-mail to a distribution list

To address an e-mail message to a distribution list, click the New button to open the Message window, click the To button to open the Select Names dialog box, and select the distribution list name. Distribution list names appear in boldface and are marked with a Distribution List icon.

Editing a distribution list

The names of distribution lists appear in the Contacts folder, where they are marked with an icon showing two heads in profile. You can treat the lists like regular contacts. In the Contacts folder, double-click a distribution list name to open the Distribution List window (refer to Figure 8-4). From there, you can add names to the list, remove names from the list, or select new members for the list.

Prioritizing the messages you send

Every day, billions of e-mail messages arrive on peoples' computers, each one begging for the recipient's attention, each one crying out, "Read me first." With this kind of cutthroat competition, how can you give your e-mail messages a competitive advantage? How can you make yours stand out in the crowd?

The best way is to write a descriptive title in the Subject box of the Message window. The subject is the first thing people see in their Inboxes. They decide whether to read a message now, later, or never on the basis of what they see on the Subject line.

Another way to (maybe) get other's attention is to assign a high priority rating to your message. If the recipient reads his or her e-mail with Outlook or Outlook Express, a red exclamation point appears beside the message in the Inbox folder. Conversely, you can assign a low priority to messages as well, in which case a downward-pointing arrow appears next to the message heading in the Inbox folder. However, prioritizing this way is only worthwhile if the recipient runs Outlook or Outlook Express, because other e-mail programs don't know what to make of the exclamation point or the arrow.

 To assign a priority to a message, click the Importance: High or the Importance: Low button in the Message window. In the Inbox folder, click the Sort By: Importance button to arrange messages by their priority ratings.

!	D	0	From	Subject	Received	Size	▽
			Sort by: Importance gh (2 items, 2 unread)				
!	✉		Lana	To the Barricades!	3:35 PM	1 KB	▽
!	✉		Mark	Get the lead out!	3:34 PM	1 KB	▽
			⊟ Importance: Normal (2 items, 2 unread)				
			Marc Ball	"Medicinal Mushrooms" Index	5/31/2002	34 KB	✓
			Becky	Mark's family	5/15/2002	33 KB	✓
			⊟ Importance: Low (2 items, 2 unread)				
↓			Mark	Out to Lunch	3:36 PM	1 KB	▽
↓			Becky	Time To Kill	3:35 PM	1 KB	▽

Inbox

Sending a File along with a Message

Sending a file along with an e-mail message is called "attaching" a file in Outlook lingo. Yes, it can be done. You can send a file or several files along with an e-mail message by following these steps:

1. **With the Message window open, click the Insert File button or choose Insert⇨File.**

   You see the Insert File dialog box.

2. **Locate and select the file that you want to send along with your e-mail message.**

   Ctrl+click filenames to select more than one file.

3. **Click the Insert button.**

   The name of the file (or files) appears in the Attach text box in the Message window. Address the message and type a note to send along with the file. You can right-click a filename in the Attach text box and choose Open on the shortcut menu to open a file you're about to send.

Here's a fast way to attach a file to a message: Find the file in Windows Explorer or My Computer and drag it into the message window. The file's name appears in the Attach box as though you placed it there with the Insert⇨File command.

Including a Picture in an E-mail Message

As shown in Figure 8-5, you can include a picture in the body of an e-mail message, but in order to see it, the recipient's e-mail software must display messages using HTML (HyperText Markup Language). As "All about Message Formats" explains later in this chapter, not everyone has software that displays e-mail by using HTML. People who don't have HTML e-mail software will get the picture anyhow, but it won't appear in the body of the e-mail message; it will arrive as an attached file (see the "Handling Files That Were Sent to You" section, later in this chapter, to find out about receiving files by e-mail). To view the attached file, the recipient has to open it with a graphics software program such as Paint or Windows Picture and Fax Viewer.

Follow these steps to adorn an e-mail message with a picture:

1. **In the Message window, click in the body of the e-mail message where you want the picture to go, and choose Insert⇨Picture.**

   You see the Picture dialog box, shown in Figure 8-5.

2. **Click the Browse button and, in the Picture dialog box, find and select the digital picture you want to send; then click the Open button.**

3. **In the Picture dialog box, click OK.**

   The picture lands in the Message window. Don't worry about the other settings in the Picture dialog box for now. You can fool with them later.

Figure 8-5:
Inserting a
picture in an
e-mail
message.

To change the size of a picture, click to select it and then drag a corner handle. Otherwise, right-click the picture and choose Properties to reopen the Picture dialog box (refer to Figure 8-5) and experiment with these settings:

✦ **Alternate Text:** The description you enter here appears while the picture is loading or, if the recipient has turned off images, appears in place of the image.

✦ **Alignment:** Experiment with these settings to determine where the picture is in relation to the text of the e-mail message.

✦ **Border Thickness:** Determines, in pixels, how thick the border around the picture is. One pixel equals $\frac{1}{72}$ of an inch.

✦ **Horizontal and Vertical:** Determines, in pixels, how much empty space appears between the text and the side, top, or bottom of the picture.

Want to remove a picture from an e-mail message? Select it and press the Delete key.

Postponing Sending a Message

As you probably know, e-mail messages are sent immediately when you click the Send button in the Message window if your computer is connected to the Internet. If it isn't connected, the message lands in the Outbox folder, where it remains until you connect to the Internet.

But suppose you want to postpone sending a message? Outlook offers two techniques for putting off sending a message:

✦ **Moving messages temporarily to the Drafts folder:** Compose your message, click the Save button in the Message window (or press Ctrl+S), and close the Message window. Your e-mail message goes to the Drafts folder. When you're ready to send it, open the Drafts folder, double-click your message to open it, and click the Send button in the Message window.

✦ **Postponing the send date:** Click the Options button in the Message window. You see the Message Options dialog box, the bottom of which is shown in Figure 8-6. Select the Do Not Deliver Before check box, choose a date in the drop-down calendar, and, if you so desire, select a time from the drop-down list. Then click the Close button. In the Message window, click the Send button. Your message goes to the Outbox folder, where it remains until the time arrives to send it.

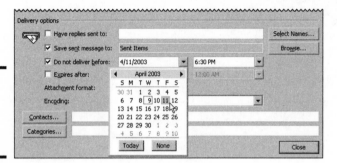

Figure 8-6: Putting off sending an e-mail message.

All about Message Formats

Outlook offers three formats for sending e-mail messages: HTML (HyperText Markup Language), plain text, and rich text. What are the pros and cons of the different formats?

These days, almost all e-mail is transmitted in HTML format, the same format with which Web pages are made. If HTML is the default format you use for creating messages in Outlook — and it is unless you tinkered with the default settings — the e-mail messages you send are, in effect, little Web pages. HTML gives you the most opportunities for formatting text and graphics. In HTML format, you can place pictures in the body of an e-mail message, use a background theme, and do any number of sophisticated formatting tricks.

However, the HTML format has its share of detractors. First, the messages are larger because they include sophisticated formatting instructions, and being larger, they take longer to transmit over the Internet. Some e-mail accounts allocate a fixed amount of disk space for incoming e-mail messages and reject messages when the disk-space allocation is filled. Because they are larger than other e-mail messages, HTML messages fill the disk space quicker. Finally, some e-mail software can't handle HTML messages. In this software, the messages are converted to plain-text format.

In plain text format, only letters and numbers are transmitted. The format does not permit you to format text or align paragraphs in any way, but you can rest assured that the person who receives the message will be able to read it exactly as you wrote it.

The third e-mail message format, rich text, is proprietary to Microsoft e-mailing software. Only people who use Outlook and Outlook Express can see rich text formats. Choosing the rich text format is not recommended.

If formatting text in e-mail messages is important to you, choose the HTML format because more people will be able to read your messages.

When someone sends you an e-mail message, you can tell which format it was transmitted in by looking at the title bar, where the letters HTML, "Plain Text," or "Rich Text" appear in parentheses after the subject of the message. Outlook is smart enough to transmit messages in HTML, plain text, or rich text format when you reply to a message that was sent to you in that format.

Follow these instructions if you need to change the format in which e-mail messages are transmitted:

✦ **Changing the default format:** Choose Tools⇨Options and, in the Options dialog box, select the Mail Format tab. From the Compose in This Message Format drop-down list, choose an option.

✦ **Changing the format for a single e-mail message:** In the Message window, open the Format menu and choose HTML, Plain Text, or Rich Text.

✦ **Always using the plain-text or rich-text format with a contact:** To avoid transmitting in HTML with a contact, start in the Contacts folder, double-click the contact's name, and, in the Contact form, double-click the contact's e-mail address. You see the E-Mail Properties dialog box. In the Internet Format drop-down list, choose Send Plain Text Only or Send Using Outlook Rich Text Format.

Stationery for Decorating E-Mail Messages

Apart from the standard formatting commands, the other way to decorate e-mail messages is to do it with stationery. In Outlook lingo, stationery is a background design meant to give an e-mail message the appearance of having been written on real-life stationery, as shown in Figure 8-7. Some kinds of stationery — Holiday Letter, Party Invitation — are designed for sending certain kinds of notices or invitations. As you choose stationery for your e-mail messages, remember that some people find the stuff extremely annoying.

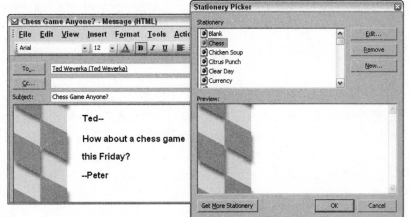

Figure 8-7: Using stationery to adorn e-mail messages.

Follow these steps to choose a stationery for the e-mail messages you send:

1. **Choose Tools⇨Options to open the Options dialog box.**

2. **Select the Mail Format tab.**

3. **Click the Stationery Picker button.**

You see the Stationery Picker dialog box, shown in Figure 8-7.

4. **Click a stationery name to see a preview of it in the Preview box; select the stationery you like and click OK.**

5. **Click OK again in the Options dialog box.**

To quit using stationery in your e-mail, return to the Mail Format tab of the Options dialog box, open the Use This Stationery by Default drop-down list, and choose <None>.

Receiving E-Mail Messages

Let's hope that all the e-mail messages you receive carry good news. These pages explain how to collect your e-mail and all the different ways that Outlook notifies you when e-mail has arrived. You will find several tried-and-true techniques for reading e-mail messages in the Inbox window. Outlook offers a bunch of different ways to rearrange the window as well as the messages inside it.

Getting your e-mail

Here are all the different ways to collect e-mail messages that were sent to you:

✦ **Collecting the e-mail:** Click the Send/Receive button, press F9, or choose Tools⇨Send/Receive⇨Send/Receive All.

✦ **Collecting e-mail from a single account (if you have more than one):** Choose Tools⇨Send/Receive and, on the submenu, choose the name of an e-mail account or group.

✦ **Collect e-mail automatically every few minutes:** Press Ctrl+Alt+S or choose Tools⇨Send/Receive⇨Send/Receive Settings⇨Define Send/Receive Groups. You see the Send/Receive Groups dialog box, the bottom of which is shown in Figure 8-8. Select a group, select a Schedule an Automatic Send/Receive Every check box and enter a minute setting. To temporarily suspend automatic e-mail collections, choose Tools⇨Send/Receive⇨Send/Receive Settings⇨Disable Scheduled Send/Receive.

If you're not on a network or don't have a DSL or cable Internet connection, you shortly see a Connection dialog box. Enter your password, if necessary, and click the Connect button. The Outlook Send/Receive dialog box appears to show you the progress of messages being sent and received.

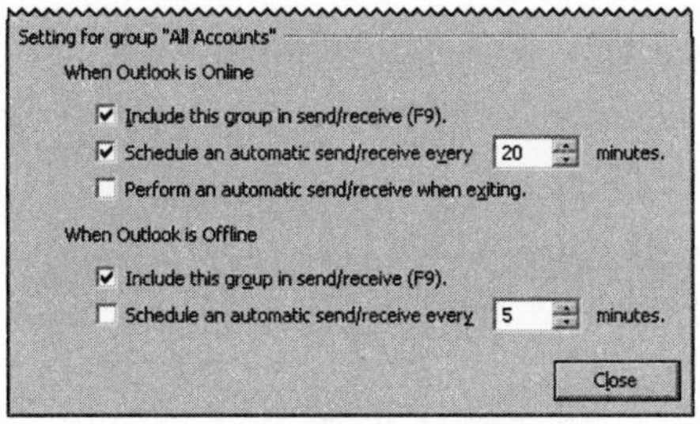

Setting for group "All Accounts"
When Outlook is Online
☑ Include this group in send/receive (F9).
☑ Schedule an automatic send/receive every [20] minutes.
☐ Perform an automatic send/receive when exiting.
When Outlook is Offline
☑ Include this group in send/receive (F9).
☐ Schedule an automatic send/receive every [5] minutes.
[Close]

Figure 8-8:
Entering
Group
settings.

Being notified that e-mail has arrived

Take the e-mail arrival quiz. Winners get the displeasure of knowing that they understand far more than is healthy about Outlook. You can tell when e-mail has arrived in the Inbox folder because

A) You hear this sound: *ding!*

B) The mouse cursor briefly changes to a little envelope.

C) A little envelope appears in the system tray to the left of the Windows clock (and you can double-click the envelope to open the Inbox folder).

D) A pop-up "desktop alert" with the sender's name, the message's subject, and the text of the message appears briefly on your desktop.

E) All of the above.

The answer is E, All of the above, but if four arrival notices strikes you as excessive, you can eliminate one or two. Choose Tools➪Options and, on the Preferences tab of the Options dialog box, click the E-Mail Options button. Then, in the E-Mail Options dialog box, click the Advanced E-Mail Options button. At long last, in the Advanced E-Mail Options dialog box, select or deselect the four When New Items Arrive in My Inbox options. To make desktop alerts stay longer on-screen, click the Desktop Alert Settings button and drag the Duration slider in the Desktop Alert Settings dialog box. While you're at it, click the Preview button to see what the alerts look like.

Reading your e-mail in the Inbox window

Messages arrive in the Inbox window, as shown in Figure 8-9. Unread messages are shown in boldface type and have envelope icons next to their names; messages that you've read (or at least opened to view) are shown in Roman type and appear beside open envelope icons. To read a message, select it and look in the Reading pane or, to focus more closely on a message, double-click it to open it in a Message window, as shown in Figure 8-9. In the Folder List, a number beside the Inbox tells you how many unread messages are in the Inbox folder.

Navigation pane.

Reading pane.

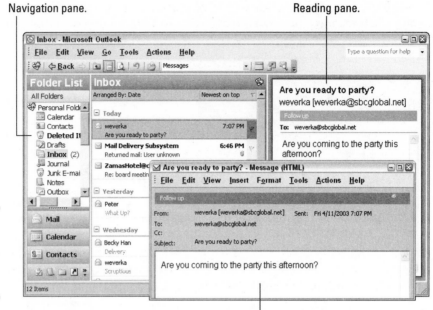

Figure 8-9: Reading messages in the Inbox window.

Double-click a message to read it in a Message window.

Later in this chapter, "Techniques for Organizing E-Mail Messages" explains how to organize messages in the Inbox folder. Meanwhile, here are some simple techniques you can use to unclutter the Inbox folder and make it easier to manage:

✦ **Hiding and displaying the Reading Pane:** Click the Reading Pane button to make the Reading pane appear or disappear. With the Reading pane gone, column headings — From, Subject, Received, Size, and Flagged — appear in the Inbox window, as shown in Figure 8-10. You can click a column heading name to sort messages in different ways. For example, click the From column name to arrange messages by sender name.

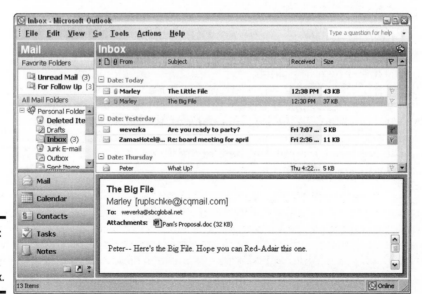

Figure 8-10: Another way to look at the Inbox.

You can eat your cake and have it too by displaying column names *and* the Reading pane, as shown in Figure 8-10. To do so, choose View⇨ Reading Pane⇨Bottom.

✦ **Hiding and displaying the Navigation pane:** Choose View⇨Navigation Pane or press Alt+F1. By hiding the Navigation pane, you get even more room to display messages.

✦ **"Autopreviewing" messages:** Click the AutoPreview button or choose View⇨AutoPreview to read the text of all on-screen messages in small type. The message text appears below the subject heading of each message.

✦ **Changing views:** Choose an option on the Current View menu to reduce the number of messages in the window. For example, you can see only unread messages, or messages that arrived in the past week.

Suppose you open an e-mail message but you regret doing so because you want it to look closed. You want the unopened envelope icon to appear beside the message's name so you know to handle it later on. To make a message in the Inbox window appear as if it has never been opened, right-click it and choose Mark As Unread.

Handling Files That Were Sent to You

You can tell when someone has sent you files along with an e-mail message because the word "Attachments" appears in the Reading pane along with the file names, as shown in Figure 8-11. The word "Attachments" and a file-name appears as well in the Message window. And if columns are on display in the Inbox window (see the previous section of this chapter), a paper-clip icon appears in the Sort By Attachment column to let you know that the e-mail message includes a file or files, as Figure 8-11 also shows.

Attached file.

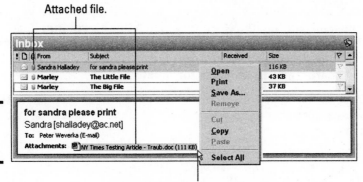

Figure 8-11:
Receiving
a file.

Right-click to handle incoming files.

Files that are sent to you over the Internet land deep inside your computer in a subfolder of the Temporary Internet Files folder. This is the same obscure folder where Web pages you encounter when surfing the Internet are kept. The best way to handle an incoming file is to open it or save it right away to a folder where you can more easily find it when you need it.

To save a file that was sent to you in a new folder:

✦ Right-click the filename and choose Save As, as shown in Figure 8-11.

✦ Choose File⇨Save Attachments⇨*Filename*.

To open a file that was sent to you, do one of the following:

✦ Double-click the filename in the Reading pane or Message window.

✦ Right-click the filename and choose Open, as shown in Figure 8-11.

✦ Right-click the paper-clip icon in the Inbox window and choose View Attachments⇨*Filename*.

Techniques for Organizing E-Mail Messages

If you're one of those unfortunate souls who receives 20, 30, 40 or more e-mail messages daily, you owe it to yourself and your sanity to figure out a way to organize e-mail messages so that you keep the ones you want, you can find e-mail messages easily, and you can quickly eradicate the e-mail messages that don't matter to you. These pages explain the numerous ways to manage and organize e-mail messages. Pick and choose the techniques that work for you, or else try to convince the Postal Service that you are entitled to your own ZIP Code and you should be paid to handle all the e-mail you receive.

In a nutshell, here are all the techniques for organizing e-mail messages:

✦ **Change views in the Inbox window:** Open the Current View drop-down list on the Advanced toolbar and choose Last Seven Days, Unread Messages in This Folder, or another view to shrink the number of e-mail messages in the Inbox window.

✦ **Rearrange, or sort, messages in the Inbox window:** If necessary, click the Reading Pane button to remove the Reading pane and see column heading names in the Inbox window. Then click a column heading name to rearrange, or sort, messages by sender name, subject, receipt date, size, or flagged status. See the section, "Reading your e-mail in the Inbox window," earlier in this chapter, for details.

 ✦ **Delete the messages that you don't need:** Before they clutter the Inbox, delete messages you're sure you don't need as soon as you get them. To delete a message, select it and click the Delete button, press the Delete key, or choose Edit⇨Delete.

✦ **Move messages to different folders:** Create a folder for each project you're involved with and, when an e-mail message about a project arrives, move it to a folder. See "All about E-Mail Folders" later in this chapter.

✦ **Move messages automatically to different folders as they arrive:** See "Earmarking messages as they arrive," later in this chapter.

✦ **Flag messages:** Flag a message with a color-coded flag to let you know to follow up on it. See the following section, "Flagging e-mail messages."

✦ **Have Outlook remind you to reply to a message:** Instruct Outlook to make the Reminder message box appear at a date and time in the future so that you know to reply to a message. See "Being reminded to take care of e-mail messages" later in this chapter.

✦ **Make liberal use of the Find command:** You can always find a stray message with the Find command. (See Book IV, Chapter 7, to know more about finding items in folders.) To quickly find all the messages from one person, right-click an e-mail message from the person and choose Find All⇨Messages from Sender. Choose Find All⇨Related Messages to find messages that are part of the same conversation (the original message and all replies).

Flagging e-mail messages

One way to call attention to e-mail messages is to flag them. As shown in Figure 8-12, you can make color-coded flags appear in the Inbox window. You can use red flags, for example, to mark urgent messages and green flags to mark the not-so-important ones. Which color you flag a message with is up to you. Outlook offers six colors. As Figure 8-12 shows, you can click the Sort By Flag Status button in the Inbox window to arrange messages in color-coded flag order.

Click to flag a message.

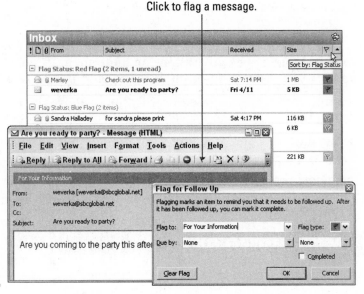

Figure 8-12: Flagging messages so that you can remember to follow up on them.

Follow these instructions to flag an e-mail message:

✦ **Starting in the Message window:** Click the Follow Up button. You see the Flag for Follow Up dialog box, as shown in Figure 8-12. If the color you prefer isn't showing, choose a color from the Flag Type drop-down list. From the Flag To drop-down list, choose follow-up notice, or else type one of your own in the text box. The notice will appear across the top of the e-mail message in the Message window.

✦ **Starting in the Inbox folder:** Select the message and choose Actions⇨ Follow Up and a flag color, or right-click and choose Follow Up and a flag color.

To "unflag" a message, right-click it and choose Follow Up⇨Clear Flag. You can also right-click and choose Follow Up⇨Flag Complete to put a check mark where the flag used to be and remind yourself that you're done with the message. Later in this chapter, "Earmarking messages as they arrive" explains how you can flag messages automatically as messages arrive.

Being reminded to take care of e-mail messages

If you know your way around the Calendar and Tasks windows, you know that the Reminders message box appears when an appointment or meeting is about to take place or a task deadline is about to fall. What you probably don't know, however, is that you can put the Reminders dialog box to work in regard to e-mail messages.

Follow these steps to remind yourself to reply to an e-mail message or simply to prod yourself into considering an e-mail message in the future:

1. **Select the message and choose Actions⇨Follow Up⇨Add Reminder.**

You see the Flag for Follow Up dialog box (refer to Figure 8-12). You can also right-click a message and choose Follow Up⇨Add Reminder to see the dialog box.

2. **On the Flag To drop-down list, choose an option that describes why the e-mail message needs your attention later on, or, if none of the options suits you, enter a description in the Flag To text box.**

The description you choose or enter will appear above the message in the Reading Pane and appear as well in the Reminders message box.

3. **Choose the date and time that you want the Reminders message box to appear.**

The Reminders message box will appear 15 minutes before the date and time you enter. If you enter a date but not a time, Outlook assigns the default time, 5:00 P.M.

4. **Click OK.**

Items flagged this way appear in red text with a red flag. When the reminder falls due, you see the Reminder message box, where you can click the Open Item button to open the e-mail message.

Earmarking messages as they arrive

To help you organize messages better, Outlook gives you the opportunity to mark messages in various ways and even move messages automatically as they arrive to folders apart from the Inbox folder. Being able to move messages immediately to a folder is a great way to keep e-mail concerning different projects separate. If you belong to a newsgroup that sends many messages a day, being able to move those messages instantly into their own folder is a real blessing, because newsgroup messages have a habit of cluttering the Inbox folder.

To earmark messages for special treatment, Outlook has you create so-called *rules*. To create a rule, start by trying out the Create Rule command, and if that doesn't work, test-drive the more powerful Rules Wizard.

Simple rules with the Create Rule command

Use the Create Rule command to be alerted when e-mail arrives from a certain person or the Subject line of a message includes a certain word. You can make the incoming message appear in the New Items Alerts window, play a sound when the message arrives, or move the message automatically to a certain folder.

Follow these steps to create a simple rule:

1. **If you want to be alerted when e-mail arrives from a certain person, find an e-mail message from the person, right-click it, and choose Create Rule; otherwise, right-click any message and choose Create Rule.**

   You see the Create Rule dialog box.

2. **Fill in the dialog box and click OK.**

   These commands are self-explanatory.

Another way to create a simple rule is to choose Tools➪Organize. The Ways to Organize Inbox panel appears. Starting here, you can move messages from a certain person to a folder or color-code messages from a certain person as they arrive.

Creating complex rules with the Rules Wizard

Use the Rules Wizard to create complex rules that earmark messages with words in the message body or earmark messages sent to distribution lists. You can also create a rule to flag messages automatically or delete a conversation (the original message and all replies).

To run the Rules Wizard, click the Rules and Alerts button or choose Tools➪Rules and Alerts. You see the Rules and Alerts dialog box. Click the New Rule button and keep clicking Next in the Rules Wizard dialog boxes as you complete the two steps to create a rule:

✦ **Step 1:** Choose the rule you want to create or how you want to be alerted in the New Item Alerts message box.

✦ **Step 2:** Click a hyperlink to open a dialog box and describe the rule. For example, click the Specific Words link to open the Search Text dialog box and enter the words that earmark a message. Click the Specified link to open the Rules and Alerts dialog box and choose a folder to move the messages to. You must click each link in the Step 2 box to describe the rule.

To edit a rule, double-click it in the Rules and Alerts dialog box and complete Steps 1 and 2 all over again.

All about E-Mail Folders

Where Outlook e-mail is concerned, everything has its place and everything has its folder. E-mail messages land in the Inbox folder when they arrive. Messages you write go to the Outbox folder until you send them. Copies of e-mail messages you send are kept in the Sent folder. And you can create folders of your own for storing e-mail.

If you're one of those unlucky people who receive numerous e-mail messages each day, you owe it to yourself to create folders in which to organize e-mail messages. Create one folder for each project you're working on. That way, you know where to find e-mail messages when you want to reply to or delete them. These pages explain how to move e-mail messages between folders and create folders of your own for storing e-mail.

Moving e-mail messages to different folders

Click to select the message you want to move and use one of these techniques to move an e-mail message to a different folder:

✦ **With the Move To Folder button:** Click the Move To Folder button and, on the drop-down list that appears, select a folder. The Move To Folder button is located on the Standard toolbar to the right of the Print button.

✦ **With the Move To Folder command:** Choose Edit⇨Move to Folder, press Ctrl+Shift+V, or right-click and choose Move to Folder. You see the Move Items dialog box. Select a folder and click OK.

✦ **By dragging:** Click the Folder List button, if necessary, to see all the folders; then drag the e-mail message into a different folder.

Earlier in this chapter, "Earmarking messages as they arrive" explains how to move e-mail messages automatically to folders as they are sent to you.

Creating a new folder for storing e-mail

Follow these steps to create a new folder:

1. **Choose File⇨New⇨Folder.**

You see the Create New Folder dialog box, shown in Figure 8-13. You can also open this dialog box by pressing Ctrl+Shift+E or right-clicking a folder in the Folder List and choosing New Folder.

2. **Select the folder that the new folder will go inside.**

For example, to create a first-level folder, select Personal Folders.

3. **Enter a name for the folder.**

4. **Click OK.**

To delete a folder you created, select it and click the Delete button. To rename a folder, right-click it, choose Rename, and enter a new name.

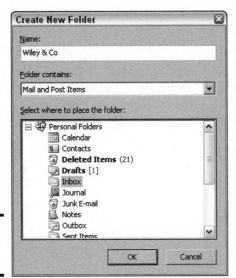

Figure 8-13:
Creating a
new folder.

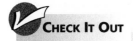

Making Word the E-mail Editor

Fans of Microsoft Word will be glad to know that
you can compose and edit e-mail messages
using Microsoft Word. If you make Word your
e-mail editor, you can do everything to an e-mail
message that you can do to a Word document —
lay out a table, make a bulleted list, or choose a
background theme, for example. All the Word
commands are available to you. That's the good
news. The bad news is that not everyone uses
e-mail software that is capable of displaying the
tables, bulleted lists, themes, and other fancy
doodads you can put in your e-mail messages.
To view this stuff, recipients' e-mail software
must be able to display e-mail messages in HTML
(HyperText Markup Language) or rich text format;
moreover, recipients must have opted to display
their e-mail messages in HTML or rich-text
format.

Here are the two ways to make Word an e-mail
editor:

Compose messages in Word: In
Microsoft Word, click the E-Mail button
(you'll find it on the Standard toolbar) or
choose File⇨Send To⇨Mail Recipient. Text
boxes for addressing the message, entering the

subject, and composing the message appear.
Compose your message and click the Send a
Copy button. (If you change your mind about
composing a message, just click the E-Mail
button to make all the Outlook stuff go away.)

Make Word the default e-mail editor in Outlook:
Choose Tools⇨Options, and, in the Options dialog
box, select the Mail Format tab. Then select the
Use Microsoft Word to Edit E-Mail Messages
check box and click OK. Now when you click the
New button to compose an e-mail message, the
Message window offers every command that
Word offers. If you don't believe me, open the
Table menu or display the Drawing toolbar. You
won't find either of them in a conventional
Outlook window.

If Word is the e-mail editor at your house, you can
choose stationery for your e-mail messages in the
following way: Choose Tools⇨Options in Word
and, on the General tab of the Options dialog box,
click the E-Mail Options button. The E-Mail Options
dialog box opens. On the Personal Stationery tab,
click the Theme button and choose a theme in the
Theme or Stationery dialog box.

Book IV
Chapter 8

Handling Your E-Mail

Chapter 9: Managing Your Time and Schedule

In This Chapter

✔ Understanding how to classify activities

✔ Going to different dates in the Calendar

✔ Scheduling appointments and events

✔ Rescheduling an activity

✔ Getting a better view of your schedule

✔ Customizing the Outlook window

The purpose of the Outlook Calendar is to keep you from arriving a day late and a dollar short. Use the Calendar to schedule meetings and appointments. Use it to make the most of your time. This chapter explains how to go from day to day, week to week, and month to month in the Calendar window. It shows you how to schedule and reschedule appointments and meetings, look at your schedule in different ways, and customize Outlook.

Introducing the Calendar

Use the Calendar to juggle appointments and meetings, remind yourself where you're supposed to be, and get there on time. Surveying your schedule in the Calendar window is easy. Merely by clicking a button, you can tell where you're supposed to be today, any given day, this week, this workweek, this month, or any month. Figure 9-1 shows, for example, someone's schedule during the workweek of April 21 through 25 (a *workweek* comprises Monday through Friday, not Monday through Sunday). All you have to do to find out how busy you are on a particular day, week, or month is gaze at the Calendar window. If someone invites you to a meeting or wants to schedule an appointment, you can open the Calendar and see right away whether your schedule permits you to attend the meeting or make the appointment.

Outlook gives you opportunities to color-code meetings and appointments so that you can tell at a glance what they are all about. Moving a meeting or appointment is simply a matter of dragging it elsewhere in the Calendar window. By double-clicking a meeting or appointment in the Calendar window, you can open a form to find out where the meeting takes place or read notes you jotted down about the meeting. You can even make a bell ring and the Reminder message box appear when a meeting or appointment is forthcoming.

To make the TaskPad, an abbreviated Tasks window, appear beside the Calendar window, choose View➪TaskPad.

Date Navigator.   Click to change views.

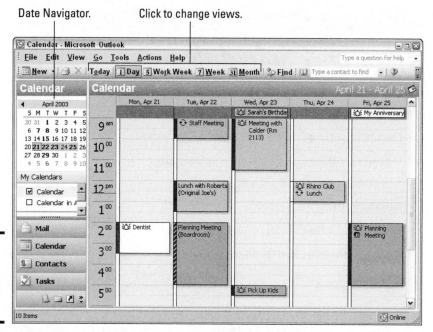

Figure 9-1:
The
Calendar in
Work Week
view.

The Different Kinds of Activities

For scheduling purposes, Outlook makes a distinction between appointments, events, and meetings. Meetings, however, are not everybody's concern. If your computer is connected to a network and the network uses the Microsoft Exchange Server, you can use Outlook to invite colleagues on the network to come to meetings. But if your computer is not on a network, don't bother with meetings. Schedule appointments and events instead. You can schedule the following activities:

✦ **Appointment:** An activity that occupies a certain time period on a certain day. For example, a meeting that takes place between 11 and 12 o'clock is an appointment.

✦ **Recurring appointment:** An appointment that takes place daily, weekly, or monthly on the same day and same time each day, week, or month. A weekly staff meeting is a recurring appointment. The beauty of recurring appointments is that Outlook enters them weeks and months in advance in the Calendar window. You don't have to enter these appointments one at a time.

✦ **Event:** An activity that lasts all day. A trade show, for example, is an event. A birthday is an event. A day spent on vacation is also an event (is it ever!). On the Calendar, events and recurring events appear first.

✦ **Recurring event:** An all-day activity that takes place each week, month, or year. Unromantic users of Outlook are hereby advised to schedule these recurring events in the Calendar: Valentine's Day, their significant other's birthday, and first-date and wedding anniversaries. Thanks to Outlook, no one will ever accuse you again of being coldhearted or indifferent.

✦ **Meeting:** Same as an appointment, except that you can invite others to attend. Scheduling meetings is not covered in this book. See your network administrator for details.

Getting Around in the Calendar Window

Days on which meetings or appointments are scheduled appear in boldface in the *Date Navigator,* the calendar in the upper-left corner of the window (refer to Figure 9-1). Here are all the different ways to go from date to date in the Calendar window:

Today

+ **To today:** Click the Today button on the Standard toolbar.

+ **To a specific day:** Click a day in the Date Navigator. You can also press Ctrl+G and select a day in the Go to Date dialog box. In some views, you can press Alt+PageUp to go to the first day of the month, or Alt+PageDown to go to the last day.

+ **To a different month:** Click an arrow beside the month name in the Date Navigator to go backward or forward by a month. Here's a quick way to go from month to month in the Calendar: Click the month name in the Date Navigator and hold down the mouse button. You see a list of month names. Drag the pointer to the name of the month you want to go to.

Use the scroll bar on the right side of the window to travel from hour to hour in Day view and Work Week view. In Week view and Month view, manipulating the scroll bar takes you from week to week.

Scheduling an Activity

Now that you know how the Calendar works, the next step is to fill the pages of the Calendar with all kinds of busywork. These pages explain how to schedule activities, schedule recurring activities, and magically transform an e-mail message into a Calendar item. You can find many intriguing shortcuts in these pages.

Scheduling an activity: The basics

Follow these basic steps to schedule an appointment, recurring appointment, event, or recurring event:

1. **Select the day in which you want to schedule the activity.**

   If the activity occupies a certain time period, you can select the time period in Day or Work Week view and save yourself the trouble of entering a time period in the Appointment dialog box. To select a time period, drag downward in the Calendar window. To create a half-hour appointment, simply double-click a half hour slot in Day or Work Week view. The Appointment dialog box opens with the Start and End time already entered.

2. **Click the New Appointment button, press Ctrl+N, or choose Actions➪New Appointment.**

   New

   As shown in Figure 9-2, you see a form for naming the activity, stating its starting and ending time, and choosing whether you want to be alerted to its occurrence. When you double-click an appointment or event in the Calendar window, this is the form you see.

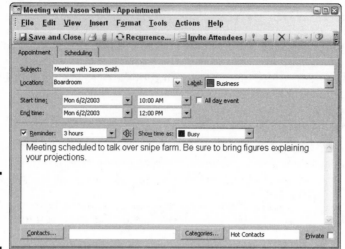

Figure 9-2:
The form for scheduling activities.

3. Enter information in the form.

Table 9-1 explains what all the fields in the Appointment form are. To enter a recurring event or appointment, click the Recurrence button. To enter an event instead of an appointment, select the All Day Event check box.

4. Click the Save and Close button when you're finished describing the appointment or event.

The appointment or event is entered in the Calendar window.

Table 9-1	Appointment Fields
Field	*What to Enter*
Subject	A description of the activity. What you enter will appear in the Calendar window.
Location	Where the activity will take place. You can open the drop-down list and choose from the last 10 locations you entered.
Label	A color from the drop-down list so that you can see at a glance what type of activity it is.
Start Time	When the activity begins. Choose a date and time. In Day or Work Week view, you can enter start and end times before opening the Appointment dialog box by dragging to select time periods in the Calendar window.
End Time	When the activity ends.
All Day Event	When the activity is an event, not an appointment. Select this check box if you are describing an event.
Reminder	If you want to be reminded when the activity is imminent. Select the check box and choose an option from the drop-down list to make the Reminder message box appear before the activity is to begin. In the Calendar window, activities you will be reminded about are marked by the ringing bell icon.
Show Time As	A setting that describes your availability to others on the network. This option is pertinent only if your computer is connected to a network that uses Microsoft Exchange Server and the administrator has activated the Delegate option.

Field	What to Enter
Contacts	The contact name of a person associated with the activity. Click the Contacts button and, in the Select Contacts window, choose a name from your Contacts folder. In this way, you can track your dealings with a contact. The appointment or event will appear on the Activities tab in the person's Contact form.
Categories	A category name for tracking this activity.
Private	When you want others on the network to be able to view this activity on your schedule. This option pertains only if you're connected to a network that uses Microsoft Exchange Server.

Scheduling a recurring appointment or event

To enter a recurring appointment or event, click the Recurrence button in the Appointment form (refer to Figure 9-2). You see the Appointment Recurrence form shown in Figure 9-3. Describe how persistent the activity is and click OK:

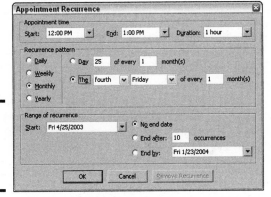

Figure 9-3: My, this appointment is persistent!

+ **Appointment time:** Enter the starting and ending time, if you didn't do so already in the Appointment form.

+ **Recurrence pattern:** Use the options and drop-down lists to describe how often the activity recurs.

+ **Range of recurrence:** Describe when the recurring events will cease recurring. Choose the No End Date option button if the activity occurs *ad infinitum, ad nauseum* (that's Latin for "unto infinity most nauseously").

Using an e-mail message to schedule an appointment

Here's a neat little trick that can save you time when e-mail correspondence has to do with scheduling an appointment. To get a head start on scheduling, drag the e-mail message from the Inbox window over the Calendar button on the Navigation pane. On the theory that you want to schedule an appointment around the information in the e-mail message, the Appointment form appears on-screen. For the subject of the appointment, Outlook enters the subject of the e-mail message. The text of the e-mail message appears on the form as well. Fiddle with the particulars of the appointment and click the Save and Close button.

In the Calendar window, recurring activities are marked by the arrow-chasing-its-tail icon. To change a recurring activity into a one-time activity, click the Recurrence button and, in the Recurrence dialog box, click the Remove Recurrence button.

Scheduling an event

Select the All Day Event check box in the Appointment window (refer to Figure 9-2) to schedule an event, not an appointment. As explained earlier, an event is an activity that lasts all day. Here are some shortcuts for creating events:

✦ In Week view or Month view, double-click the day on which the event is to occur. The Event dialog box opens immediately.

✦ Choose Actions⇨New All Day Event to open the Event dialog box straightaway.

Canceling, Rescheduling, and Altering Activities

Canceling, rescheduling, and altering appointments and events are pretty easy. You can always double-click an activity to open the Appointment or Event form and change the particulars there. And you can take advantage of these shortcuts:

 ✦ **Canceling:** Select an activity and click the Delete button. When you cancel a recurring activity, a dialog box asks whether you want to delete all occurrences of the activity or just the activity on the day you selected. Choose an option and click OK.

✦ **Rescheduling:** Drag the activity to a new location on the schedule. Move the pointer over the left side of the activity and, when you see the four-headed arrow, start dragging.

✦ **Changing start and end times:** In Day or Work Week view, move the pointer over the top or bottom of the activity and start dragging when you see the double arrow.

✦ **Changing the description:** Click in the activity's box and start typing or editing.

Getting a Better Look at Your Schedule

Here are the various and sundry ways to organize and view the activities you so patiently entered in the Calendar window:

✦ **Change Calendar views:** Click one of the five View buttons — Today, Day, Work Week, Week, or Month — to read the fine print or get the bird's-eye view of activities you've scheduled in the Calendar window.

✦ **Change views of the Calendar window:** Open the Current View drop-down list and choose Events, Recurring Appointments, or another view to isolate certain kinds of activities.

✦ **Color-code activities:** Color-coding is a great way to separate the important activities from the not-so-important ones. To change the color of an activity, right-click it, choose Label, and select a color on the submenu.

✦ **Categorize messages:** Assign activities to categories and then arrange activities by category in the Calendar window. To do so, choose By Category in the Current View drop-down list.

Chapter 10: Getting Started in PowerPoint

In This Chapter

✔ Getting familiar with PowerPoint

✔ Starting a new presentation

✔ Making your presentation persuasive

✔ Changing views in the PowerPoint screen

✔ Creating a new slide

✔ Moving and deleting slides

*P*owerPoint presentations are now ubiquitous in the corporate world. It's pretty much impossible to sit through a conference, seminar, or trade show without seeing at least one PowerPoint presentation. PowerPoint has found its way into nearly every office and boardroom. Once upon a time a man — a very unromantic man — proposed to his wife by way of a PowerPoint presentation.

As nice as PowerPoint can be, it has its detractors. If the software isn't used properly, it can come between the speaker and the audience. In an article in the May 28, 2001, *New Yorker* titled "Absolute PowerPoint: Can a Software Package Edit Our Thoughts?," Ian Parker argued that PowerPoint may actually be more of a hindrance than a help in communicating. PowerPoint, Parker wrote, is "a social instrument, turning middle managers into bullet-point dandies." The software, he added, "has a private, interior influence. It edits ideas. . . . It helps you make a case, but also makes its own case about how to organize information, how to look at the world."

To make sure that you use PowerPoint wisely, this chapter offers more than instructions in using the software — it explains how to make your presentations meaningful. Along the way, you discover how to find your way around PowerPoint, create a presentation, change views, insert the slides, and move and delete slides.

Getting Acquainted with PowerPoint

Figure 10-1 shows the PowerPoint window. That thing in the middle is a *slide,* PowerPoint's word for an image that forms part of a presentation. Surrounding the slide are many tools for decorating and adorning slides. When the time comes to show a presentation, you dispense with the tools and make the slide fill the screen, as shown in Figure 10-2. Don't worry about making slides as dazzling as the one in Figures 10-1 and 10-2. PowerPoint offers prefabricated slide designs that take most of the trouble out of decorating the slides.

Slide

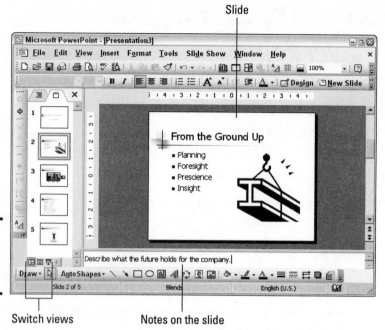

Figure 10-1:
The
PowerPoint
window.

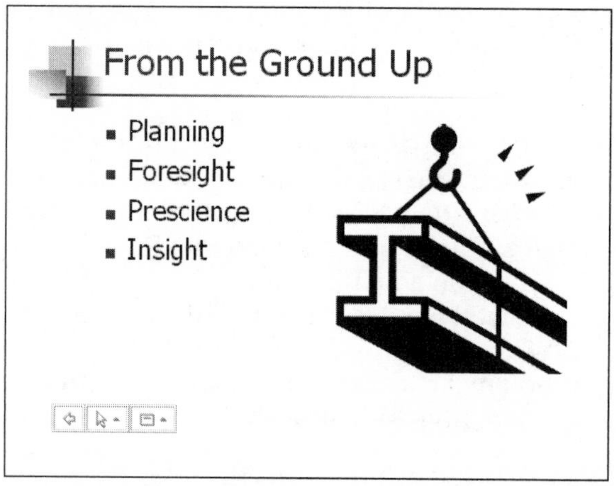

Switch views   Notes on the slide

Figure 10-2:
A slide in
a presen-
tation.

To make PowerPoint do your bidding, you need to know a little jargon:

✦ **Presentation:** All the slides, from start to finish.

✦ **Slides:** The images you create with PowerPoint. During a presentation, slides appear on-screen one after the other. Don't be put off by the word *slide* and dreary memories of sitting through your uncle's slide-show vacation memories. You don't need a slide projector to show these slides. You can now plug a laptop or other computer into special monitors that display PowerPoint slides.

✦ **Speaker notes:** Printed pages that you, the speaker, write and print so that you know what to say during a presentation. Only the speaker sees the speaker notes.

✦ **Handout:** Printed pages that you may give to the audience after a presentation. A handout shows the slides in the presentation. Handouts are also known by the somewhat derogatory term, *leave-behinds*.

Creating a New Presentation

To create a new presentation, start by choosing File➪New (or pressing Ctrl+N). That's all there is to it. The New Presentation task pane appears on the right side of the window. The next step is to choose a look for the slides in the presentation, and PowerPoint offers no fewer than four ways to do that: start with a blank presentation, start from a design template or color scheme, make use of the AutoContent Wizard, or commandeer an existing presentation.

No matter which look you choose for your presentation, you can change your mind and choose a different look later on. To do so, click the Design button or choose Format➪Slide Design and select a new look in the Slide Design task pane. You can choose a new look no matter how far along you are in constructing a presentation.

Starting with a blank presentation

Click the Blank Presentation link in the Slide Design task pane to create a bare-bones presentation. You're on your own. With this technique, you have to fashion a design yourself with the tools on the Drawing toolbar. Don't use this technique unless you know PowerPoint well and have an artistic flair. Why make your own design when you can rely on a design template, one created by a genuine artist?

Starting from a slide design or color scheme

Click the Design button on the Formatting toolbar or the From Design Template link in the task pane to make use of a slide design or color scheme. As shown in Figure 10-3, the Slide Design task pane opens. Scroll through the templates or color schemes, select one, glance at the slide on-screen, and decide which design or color scheme tickles your fancy:

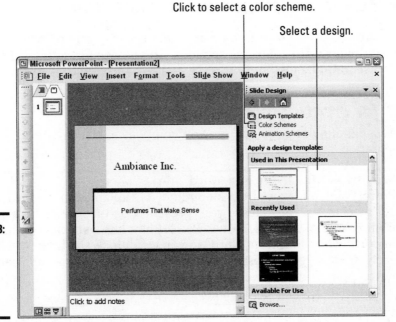

Figure 10-3: Selecting a design template or color scheme.

◆ **Slide design:** Click the Design button or the From Design Template link, if necessary, to see the designs and choose one.

◆ **Color scheme:** Click the Color Schemes link to choose a color scheme. If the Slide Design task pane isn't showing, click the Design button on the Formatting toolbar.

Starting from the AutoContent Wizard

 Click the From AutoContent Wizard link in the New Presentation task pane to create a presentation with the help of the AutoContent Wizard. With this technique, PowerPoint asks questions about the kind of presentation you want. When you're done answering, the program chooses a presentation design for you, complete with generic headings and text, and you enter your own headings and text where the generic stuff is.

Unless you're in a big hurry, don't create a presentation with the AutoContent Wizard. Presentations created this way are invariably cold and impersonal. As explained in "Advice for Building Persuasive Presentations," later in this chapter, a presentation has to be an expression of who you are and what you stand for if it is to be successful. Generic presentations made with the AutoContent Wizard are, by definition, dull and characterless. They are the primary reason that PowerPoint has a bad reputation in some boardrooms and conference halls.

Starting from an Existing Presentation

 If a PowerPoint presentation on your computer or computer network can be used as the starting point for your new presentation, click the From Existing Presentation link in the New Presentation task pane. You see the New from Existing Presentation dialog box. Select the presentation and click the Create New button. The presentation you selected appears in the window. Start tweaking it to your liking.

Advice for Building Persuasive Presentations

In the wrong hands, PowerPoint can make for a very dull presentation. To prevent dullness, the following sections offer advice for building a persuasive presentation, one that brings the audience around to your side.

 ### Tips for creating presentations

Here's a handful of tips to start you on your way as you create a PowerPoint presentation:

◆ **Start by writing the text in Word:** Start in Microsoft Word, not PowerPoint, and work from an outline. As explained in the next section of this chapter, you can see your presentation take shape by working from a Word outline. Moreover, PowerPoint has a special command for importing text files from Word, so you won't lose any time by writing the early drafts of your presentation in Word. In Word, you can clearly see how a presentation develops. You can make sure that your presentation builds to its rightful conclusion.

◆ **When choosing a design, consider the audience:** A presentation to the American Casketmakers Association calls for a mute, quiet design; a presentation to the Cheerleaders of Tomorrow calls for something bright and splashy. Choose a slide design that sets the tone for your presentation and wins the sympathy of the audience.

◆ **Take control from the start:** Spend the first minute introducing yourself to the audience without running PowerPoint (or, if you do run PowerPoint, put a simple slide with your company name or logo on-screen). Make eye contact with the audience. This way, you establish your credibility. You give the audience a chance to get to know you.

◆ **Start from the conclusion:** Try writing the end of the presentation first. A presentation is supposed to build to a rousing conclusion. By writing the end first, you have a target to shoot for. You can make the entire presentation service its conclusion, the point at which your audience says, "Ah-ha! She's right."

◆ **Make clear what you're about:** In the early going, state very clearly what your presentation is about and what you intend to prove with your presentation. In other words, state the conclusion at the beginning as well as the end. This way, your audience will know exactly what you are driving at and be able to judge your presentation according to how well you build your case.

◆ **Personalize the presentation:** Make the presentation a personal one. Tell the audience what *your* personal reason for being there is or why *you* work for the company you work for. Knowing that you have a personal stake in the presentation, the audience is more likely to trust you. The audience will understand that you're not a spokesperson, but a speaker — someone who has come before them to make a case for something that you believe in.

◆ **Tell a story:** Include an anecdote in the presentation. Everybody loves a pertinent and well-delivered story. This piece of advice is akin to the previous one about personalizing your presentation. Typically, a story illustrates a problem for *people* and how *people* solve the problem. Even if your presentation concerns technology or an abstract subject, make it about people. "The people in Shaker Heights needed faster Internet access," not "the data switches in Shaker Heights just weren't performing fast enough."

◆ **Make like a newspaper:** Put a newspaper-style headline at the top of each slide, and think of each slide as a newspaper article. Each slide should address a specific aspect of your subject, and it should do so in a compelling way. How long does it take to read a newspaper article? It depends on how long the article is, of course, but a PowerPoint slide should stay on-screen for roughly the time it takes to explore a single topic the way a newspaper article does.

◆ **Follow the one-slide-per-minute rule:** At the very minimum, a slide should stay on-screen for at least one minute. If you have been given 15 minutes to speak, you are allotted no more than 15 slides for your presentation, according to the rule.

✦ **Beware the bullet point:** Terse bullet points have their place in a presentation, but if you put them there strictly to remind yourself what to say next, you're doing your audience a disfavor. Bullet points can cause drowsiness. They can be a distraction. The audience skims the bullets when it should be listening to you and the argument you're making. (As explained in Book IV, Chapter 11, PowerPoint lets you write speaker notes that the audience doesn't see. If having notes to yourself is what you're after, use the speaker notes, not bullet points in slides.)

✦ **Blank out the screen for dramatic effect:** Show a blank screen when you come to the crux of your presentation and you want the audience's undivided attention. (You can blank out the screen by pressing B, which gives you a black screen, or by pressing W, which gives you a white screen. Press B or W again and a slide reappears). When seeing the blank screen, the audience will focus all attention on you. What you say will have more impact. Sometimes PowerPoint comes between the speaker and the audience. By removing PowerPoint momentarily, you give yourself the chance to talk straight into the heart of your audience.

Want to see just how PowerPoint can suck the life and drama out of a dramatic presentation? Try visiting the Gettysburg PowerPoint Presentation, a rendering of Lincoln's Gettysburg Address in PowerPoint. Yikes! You'll find it here: www.norvig.com/Gettysburg/index.htm.

Start by writing the text

Here's the best piece of advice you will ever get about creating a PowerPoint presentation: Write the text of the presentation before going anywhere near PowerPoint. Focus on the words to begin with. This way, you focus on what you want to communicate, not slide layouts or graphic designs or fonts. If you work in Microsoft Word, you can take advantage of the outline feature to import your outline straight into a PowerPoint presentation.

People enjoy doodling with PowerPoint slides because it distracts them from focusing on what really matters in a presentation — that is, what's meant to be communicated. Building an argument is hard work. People who can afford it pay lawyers and ghostwriters to do the job for them. Building an argument requires thinking long and hard about your topic, putting yourself in the place of an audience member who doesn't know the topic as well as you, and convincing the audience member that you're right. You can do this hard work better in Word, without the carnival atmosphere of PowerPoint to distract you.

In Word, simply write down the text you want to put on each slide. Later, you can copy the text into a PowerPoint presentation. If you're comfortable with Word's outline feature (Book IV, Chapter 6 explains it), write the PowerPoint text in outline form. Moving headings around is easy in Outline view, and, as Book IV, Chapter 11, explains, you can import a Word outline straight into a PowerPoint presentation. After the outline arrives in PowerPoint, you get one slide for each Level 1 heading. Level 1 headings form the titles of the slides, Level 2 headings form first-level bullets, and Level 3 headings form second-level bullets.

Getting a Better View of Your Work

When you work on a presentation, some views are better than others. Figure 10-4 demonstrates different ways of viewing a presentation. To change views, click a View button in the lower-left corner of the window or open the View menu and choose Normal, Slide Sorter, Slide Show, or Notes Page. Click a tab at the top of the task pane in Normal view to see thumbnail slides or outline text. Why choose one view over the other? Here's why:

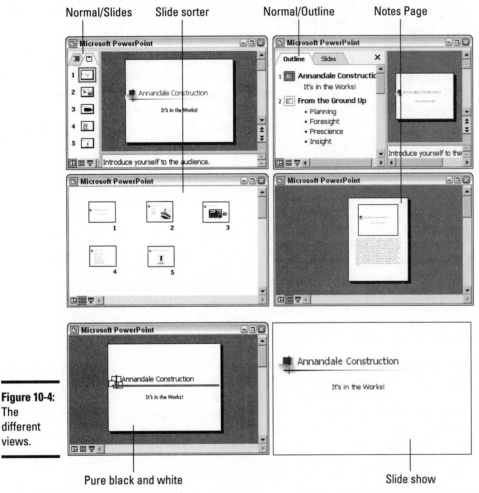

Figure 10-4: The different views.

Book IV
Chapter 10

Getting Started in
PowerPoint

 ✦ **Normal/Outline view for fiddling with the text:** To enter text or read the text in a presentation, switch to Normal view and select the Outline tab (you can find it at the top of the task pane). The words on the slides appear in the task pane. You can select a slide and click a button on the Outlining toolbar to move the slide forward or backward in the presentation.

 ✦ **Normal/Slides view for moving from slide to slide:** Switch to Normal view and click the Slides tab when you want to move around in a presentation or work on a particular slide. Thumbnail slides appear in the task pane. Scroll to and select a slide to make it appear on-screen.

✦ **Slide Sorter view for moving and deleting slides:** In Slide Sorter view, you see thumbnails of all the slides in the presentation. From here, moving slides around is easy, and seeing many slides simultaneously gives you a sense of whether the different slides are consistent with one another.

✦ **Slide Show view for giving the show:** In Slide Show view, you see a single slide. This is what the slide will look like to the audience when you give the presentation. To quit Slide Show view, press the Esc key.

✦ **Notes Page view for reading your speaker notes:** In Notes Page view, you see notes you have written to aid in the presentation, if you've written any. This view is available only on the View menu.

✦ **Grayscale, Black and White:** Sometimes color on slides, not to mention animations and graphics, is a distraction. To strip down slides to their bare essence, click the Color/Grayscale button on the Standard toolbar and choose Grayscale or Pure Black and White on the drop-down list. Pure Black and White is especially useful for focusing on text. These commands do not actually change the color on slides — they change the slides' appearance only on your computer monitor.

You can close the task pane in Normal view if it gets in your way. To close it, click the Close button. To see the task pane again, choose View➪Normal (Restore Panes).

In Normal view, you can make the Outline tab show all the text on slides or just the titles. On the Outlining toolbar, click the Expand All button (or press Alt+Shift+9) to see all the text; click the Collapse All button (or press Alt+Shift+1) to see the titles.

Inserting Slides and Choosing Layouts

After you've written the text for the presentation, it's time to create the slides. To that end, PowerPoint offers *slide layouts,* preformatted slides into which you can plug headings, bulleted lists, graphics, tables, charts, and whatnot. You can also insert a slide by duplicating one you've already made or steal slides from another presentation. Better keep reading.

Inserting a new slide and layout

As shown in Figure 10-5, you choose a slide layout whenever you insert a new slide. Slide layouts appear in the Slide Layout task pane. The first layout is a *title slide* meant for the first slide in presentations; the other slides are known simply as *slides* in PowerPoint-speak (the sidebar, "Slides and title slides," explains the difference between title slides and slides).

Figure 10-5 shows the Title and Text layout. The important thing to remember about these layouts is that you can change them whenever you want, although changing layouts can be problematic, for example, if you entered a graphic or bulleted list on the slide and you choose a layout that doesn't have placeholders for graphics or bulleted lists. To apply a layout to a slide, click the layout in the Slide Layout task pane.

Title slide.   Click new slide.

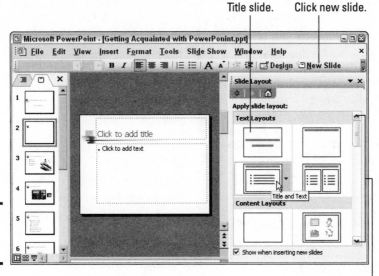

Figure 10-5:
Creating a
new slide.

Choose a slide layout.

Follow these steps to insert a new slide and give it a slide layout:

1. **Select the slide that you want the new slide to go after.**

In Normal view, select the slide on the Slides pane (select the Slides tab, if necessary). In Slide Sorter view, select the slide in the main window.

2. **Click the New Slide button, press Ctrl+M, or choose Insert⇨New Slide.**

A slide appears, as does the Slide Layout task pane (refer to Figure 10-5). The task pane offers 26 slide layouts. Try to find a layout that works for the slide you're creating. If you can't find one, choose the Blank layout and prepare to do a lot of formatting work on your own. In Book IV, Chapter 11, you discover how to plug bulleted lists, graphics, and so on into a slide layout.

3. **Scroll through the layouts and select the one you want.**

Go ahead and experiment. When you select a layout in the task pane, the slide adopts the layout.

Here are a couple of shortcuts for inserting slides in presentations:

✦ Select a slide that's already there, choose Insert⇨Duplicate Slide, and then change the text on the duplicate slide and move it elsewhere.

✦ In Normal view, select a slide and press Enter. Doing so inserts a Title and Text slide (a slide with a placeholder for a heading and a bulleted list) after the slide you selected.

If you mistakenly choose the wrong layout for a slide, you can choose another. Select the slide, choose Format⇨Slide Layout, and choose a different layout in the Slide Layout task pane (refer to Figure 10-5).

Slides and title slides

The Title Slide layout in the Slide Layout task pane (refer to Figure 10-5) is designed for the introductory slide in a presentation. Usually, the first slide is assigned the Title Slide layout. In a presentation that is divided into parts, the Title Slide layout is sometimes assigned to the first slide in each part. This way, the audience knows when one part ends and the next begins.

Whether you choose the Title Slide layout or one of the other slide layouts matters when it comes to formatting slides with a Slide Master. No, "Slide Master" is not the name of a demonic super villain. As explained in Book IV, Chapter 12, a Slide Master presents a way of formatting many slides simultaneously. Slide Masters give you the opportunity to save on formatting work and make sure that slides present a uniform appearance. PowerPoint offers two Slide Masters:

✔ **The Title Master for slides assigned Title Slide layout:** By changing the Title Master slide — by changing its background color or fonts, for example — you change all slides in the presentation that were assigned the Title Slide layout.

✔ **The Slide Master for slides assigned all the other layouts:** By changing the Slide Master, you change all slides *except* those assigned the Title Slide Layout.

The following figure shows the Title Master and Slide Master slide. Choose View⇨Master⇨Slide Master and select the Title Master or Slide Master in the task pane to work over a Master Slide.

Stealing slides from other presentations

Stealing is wrong, of course, except when stealing slides from other PowerPoint presentations. If slides you developed for another presentation will do the trick, don't hesitate to steal them:

1. **Select the slide that you want the new slide or slides to follow.**

2. **Choose Insert⇨Slides from Files to open the Slide Finder dialog box, shown in Figure 10-6.**

3. **Click the Browse button to open the Browse dialog box and select the PowerPoint presentation with the slides you want to steal.**

Slides from the presentation appear in the Slide Finder dialog box.

4. **Select the file you need.**

Click the Insert All button to grab all of them. Otherwise, Ctrl+click to select multiple slides. You can click the unnamed buttons in the dialog box to see the slides in thumbnail or outline form.

5. **Click the Insert button to insert your slides in the presentation you're working on.**

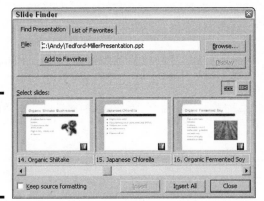

Figure 10-6: Getting slides from another presentation.

Slides that you copy this way adopt the slide design or color background of the presentation you're working on. Be sure to examine the slides to make sure that nothing on the new slides was lost, obscured, mutilated, or spindled by the new design. Dark backgrounds, for example, can sometimes obscure text. To copy slides with their designs intact, select the Keep Source Formatting check box in the Slide Finder dialog box.

Moving and Deleting Slides

As a presentation takes shape, you sometimes have to move a slide forward or backward in the presentation. And sometimes you have to delete a slide. To perform these relatively simple tasks, switch to Slide Sorter or Normal view and do the following:

✦ **Deleting a slide:** Click the slide and then press the Delete key or right-click it and choose Delete Slide.

✦ **Moving a slide:** Click the slide you want to move and drag it to a new position. A vertical line (in Slide Sorter view) or horizontal line (in Normal view) shows where the slide will land when you release the mouse button. With the Outline pane displayed, you can also move a slide by selecting it and clicking the Move Up or Move Down button on the Outlining toolbar.

In my experience, Slide Sorter view is best for moving slides around because you can grab the slides and move them more easily. You can move several slides simultaneously as long as they are next to each other. To select the slides, Ctrl+click them.

**Book IV
Chapter 10**

**Getting Started in
PowerPoint**

Chapter 11: Entering the Text

In This Chapter

- Getting the text from a Word outline
- Fitting text in frames
- Changing the look of text
- Writing the speaker notes
- Presenting lists on slides

It goes without saying, but you can't have much of a PowerPoint presentation without text. This chapter describes everything a mere mortal needs to know about putting the text on slides. It explains text frames, getting the text from a Word document, tending to the appearance of slide text, and putting lists on slides. You also find out what speaker notes are and how they can assist you in giving a presentation.

Entering Text on Slides

After you have decided what your presentation is all about, the next step is to enter the text on the slides. As shown in Figure 11-1, the easiest way to enter text on slides is to click in a text frame and start typing where the placeholder frame is. The other way is to switch to Normal view, select the Outline tab to see the Outline pane, and enter text there. Text you type next to a slide icon in the Outline pane becomes the title of the slide.

On the outline pane   In a text frame

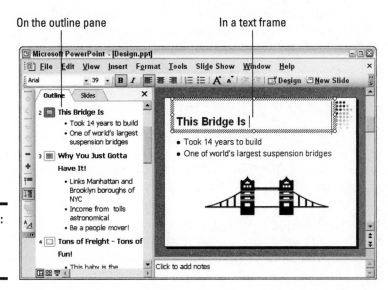

Figure 11-1:
Ways of
entering
text.

To see formatting text in the Outline pane, click the Show Formatting button. When this button is selected, text that is boldfaced, italicized, and underlined in the presentation looks that way in the Outline pane as well.

Making Text Fit in Frames

 When headings, paragraphs, and lists don't fit in a text frame, PowerPoint starts by shrinking the amount of space between lines. Then the program shrinks the text itself. You can tell when PowerPoint has shrunk the text because the AutoFit Options icon appears by the frame when the frame is selected. Click this icon and you get a menu of choices for handling the text, as shown in Figure 11-2.

Figure 11-2:
AutoFit
options.

When text doesn't fit in a frame, the first question to ask yourself is, "Do I want to fool with the integrity of the slide design?" Making the text fit usually means shrinking the text, enlarging the text frame, or compromising the slide design in some way, but audiences notice design inconsistencies. Slides are shown on large screens where design flaws are easy to see. If heading text is shrunk on one slide and the heading frame is enlarged on the next one, the audience may notice the inconsistency and conclude that the presentation is the work of . . . an amateur!

Making text fit in a frame usually means making a compromise. Here are different ways to handle the problem of text not fitting in a frame. Be prepared to click the Undo button (or press Ctrl+Z) as you test these techniques:

✦ **Edit the text:** Usually when text doesn't fit in a frame, the text needs editing. It needs to be made shorter. A slide is not a place for a treatise. The words on the slide are supposed to tell the audience what you're talking about, not provide a full explanation. Editing the text is the only way to make it fit in the frame without compromising the design.

✦ **Enlarge the frame:** Click the AutoFit Options button and choose Stop Fitting Text to Placeholder. Then select the frame and drag the bottom or top selection handle — the round white circle — to enlarge it.

✦ **Increase or decrease the font size:** The easiest way to change font sizes is to select the text and click the Increase Font Size or Decrease Font Size button as many times as necessary to make the text fit within the frame.

✦ **Change the frame's internal margins:** Similarly to the design of a page, text frames have internal margins to keep text from getting too close to the frame border. By shrinking these margins, you can make more room for text. Right-click the text frame and choose Format Placeholder. Then, on the Text Box tab of the Format Placeholder dialog box, enter smaller measurements for the margins.

✦ **Create a new slide for the text:** If you're dealing with a list or paragraph text, the AutoFit Options menu offers two ways to create a new slide. Choose Continue on a New Slide to run the text onto another slide; choose Split Text Between Two Slides to divide the text evenly between two slides. Neither option is recommended, though. If you need to make a new slide, do it on your own, and rethink how to present the material. Inserting a new slide to accommodate a long list throws a presentation off-track.

Making Your Own Text Frames

Intrepid travelers will be glad to know that you don't have to rely solely on the text frames in slide layouts. You can create text frames of your own. And PowerPoint permits you to turn an autoshape into a text frame as well. As Figure 11-3 shows, autoshape text frames are attractive and elegant.

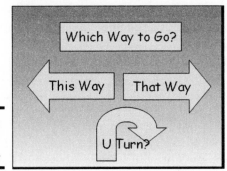

Figure 11-3: Autoshape text frames.

✦ **Text frame:** To insert a text frame of your own, choose Insert➪Text Box or click the Text Box button on the Drawing toolbar. The cursor changes into a cross hair. Click and drag to draw the frame.

AutoShapes▾ ✦ **Autoshape:** To insert an autoshape, click the AutoShapes button on the Drawing toolbar and, on the pop-up menu, choose the kind of shape you want and then the shape itself from the submenu. Drag on the slide to draw the shape.

Click in a text box or autoshape and start typing to enter the text. The Increase Font Size and Decrease Font Size buttons come in very handy when you are trying to make text fit in a text box or autoshape.

Changing the Look of Text

Most of the text-formatting commands that you know and love in Microsoft Word are also available in PowerPoint. These options are available in the Font dialog box, which you can open by choosing Format⇨Font. You can also take advantage of these text-formatting shortcuts:

+ **Changing fonts:** Select the text and choose an option from the Font drop-down list on the Formatting toolbar.

+ **Changing font size:** Select the text and choose an option on the Font Size drop-down list. For your convenience, you can also click the Increase Font Size or Decrease Font Size buttons until the text is just so.

+ **Choosing character styles:** Click the Bold, Italic, Underline, or Shadow button to change the look of the letters.

+ **Changing the color of text:** Select the text, open the Font Color button's menu and select a color.

+ **Changing case:** *Case* refers to whether letters are upper- or lowercase. Press Shift+F3 as many times as necessary until the letters are the right case: Sentence case, lowercase, UPPERCASE, or Title Case. You can also choose Format⇨Change Case and make a choice in the Change Case dialog box.

To quickly change fonts throughout a presentation, PowerPoint offers the Format⇨Replace Fonts command. Going to the Slide Master is another way to change fonts throughout a presentation (see Book IV, Chapter 12).

All about Speaker Notes

Notes, also known as *speaker notes,* are printed pages that you carry to a presentation to remind yourself what to say while each slide is on-screen. Notes are strictly for the speaker. They are not for the unwashed masses. Don't hesitate to write notes to yourself as you put together your presentation. The notes may come in handy when you are delivering your presentation and you run out of things to say. Some people hand out speaker notes after the presentation instead of handouts.

Follow these instructions to enter notes:

+ **In Normal view:** Type the notes in the Notes pane, as shown in Figure 11-4.

+ **In Slide Sorter view:** Select the slide that needs a note, click the Notes button on the Slide Sorter toolbar, and type a note in the Speaker Notes dialog box, as shown in Figure 11-4.

Figure 11-4:
Entering
speaker
notes.

To refer to the notes you have written, follow these instructions:

✦ **Viewing notes on-screen:** Select the slide whose notes need your attention and choose View➪Notes Page. The notes appear on a page along with the slide to which they refer. This is what the page will look like when you print it. Choose 75% or 100% from the Zoom menu to be able to read the notes.

✦ **Printing the notes pages:** Choose File➪Print and, in the Print dialog box, select Notes Pages from the Print What drop-down list. You get one notes page for each slide in your presentation.

Similarly to the Slide Master, PowerPoint offers the Notes Master for laying out notes pages. Choose View➪Master➪Notes Master to see the Notes Master. From the master, you can enter headers and footers for notes pages and decide for yourself which fonts and font sizes to use.

Fans of Microsoft Word will be glad to know that you can save notes and slide thumbnails in a Word file. Choose File➪Send To➪Microsoft Office Word. In the Send to Microsoft Office Word dialog box, select one of the Notes options and click OK. Microsoft Word opens a file with the notes and slides. Save the file and print it.

Making a Numbered or Bulleted List

Everybody knows how to make a numbered or bulleted list: Click the Numbering or Bullets button and start typing. Each time you press Enter, a new bullet or number appears. To make a list out of text you've already entered, select the text and click the Numbering or Bullets button.

So much for conventional numbers and bullets. You will be glad to know that PowerPoint permits you to toy with bullets and numbers to create lists like the ones in Figure 11-5. To create an out-of-the-ordinary list, select the list if you've already entered it and choose Format➪Bullets and Numbering.

**Book IV
Chapter 11**

Entering the Text

In the Bullets and Numbering dialog box, go to the Bulleted or Numbered tab to beautify your list:

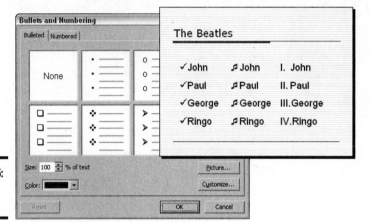

Figure 11-5:
Examples
of lists.

✦ **Bulleted list:** Choose a bullet on the Bulleted tab (this is where the check marks in Figure 11-5 come from). If the choices don't suit you, click the Picture button to open the Picture Bullet dialog box and select small clip-art bullets; or click the Customize button to open the Symbol dialog box and select a symbol for the bullets (this is where the musical notes in Figure 11-5 come from).

✦ **Numbered list:** On the Numbered tab, choose letters, Roman numerals, or another numbering scheme (notice the Roman numerals in Figure 11-5). Enter a number in the Start At text box to resume numbering a list that starts on one slide and continues on another.

✦ **Changing the size of bullets and numbers:** Enter a percentage in the Size % of Text box to change the size of bullets or numbers relative to the text in the list. Entering **200**, for example, makes bullets twice as big as the text.

✦ **Changing the color of bullets and numbers:** Open the Color drop-down list and select a color.

Chapter 12: Advanced Formatting Techniques

In This Chapter

✔ **Fooling with color schemes and slide designs**

✔ **Using Slide Masters to make slides consistent with one another**

✔ **Putting footers on slides**

✔ **Slapping a transition on a slide**

✔ **Placing action buttons on slides**

The purpose of this chapter is to help your slide presentations stand out in a crowd. The chapter explains how to stretch the slide designs and color schemes that come with PowerPoint just a little bit further. You discover how to alter the color schemes and slide designs, get a professional look for your presentations with Slide Masters, handle footers, and make your presentations a little more dramatic with transitions and actions buttons.

Changing or Tweaking a Slide Design or Color Scheme

 Chapter 10 of Book IV explains how you can click the Design button on the Formatting toolbar and choose a new slide design or color scheme from the Slide Design task pane. You can do that no matter how far along you are in constructing your presentation. The new slide design will take over from the old one, even if it means obscuring text or rendering graphics invisible. New slide designs usually change the background of slides. That can have untoward consequences.

Besides changing slide designs or color schemes, you can alter the designs or color schemes themselves by following these instructions:

✦ **Choosing a new background color:** Choose Format⇨Background or right-click a slide in the presentation and choose Background. You see the Background dialog box, shown in Figure 12-1. Open the Background Fill drop-down list and choose a new color or fill effect. Choose Automatic if you want to restore the slide design to its original background color.

✦ **Changing the color scheme:** Click the Design button to display the Slide Design task plane, and then select the Color Schemes link. The Slide Design task pane shows color schemes. If none suits you, click the Edit Color Schemes link. You see the Custom tab of the Edit Color Scheme dialog box. From here, you can select a part of the color scheme, click the Change Color button to open the Background Color dialog box, and select a new color.

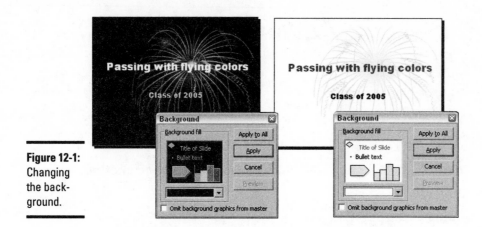

Figure 12-1:
Changing
the back-
ground.

✦ **Changing the fonts:** The only way to change fonts in a slide design is
to go to a master slide. Font changes made to the Slide Master slide
are made to all slides except title slides; font changes made to the Title
Master slide show up on all title slides. Choose View⇨Master⇨Slide
Master to fiddle with master slides. The following section, "Slide Masters
for Consistent Formatting," explains how to handle master slides.

Slide Masters for Consistent Formatting

Consistency is everything in a PowerPoint presentation. The secret to a
good layout is to make sure that the fonts and font sizes on slides are consistent from one slide to the next, that the text boxes for headings are relatively the same size, and that bulleted lists are formatted the same. If the
corner of each slide is to show a company logo, the logo needs to appear in
the same position on each slide.

To make slides consistent with one another, PowerPoint offers the Slide
Masters. A *Slide Master* is similar to a Word template. Formatting changes
made to a Slide Master are made as well to the slides that use the Slide
Master as the basis for their design. Drop a logo or other image in the corner
of a Slide Master, for example, and the logo appears as well on all slides that
are governed by the Slide Master. To put slide numbers, footers, the date —
anything that might appear on every slide in a presentation — on slides,
insert them on a Slide Master.

When you click the New Slide button and choose a layout for a slide, you
make either the Slide Master or the Title Master the basis for your new
slide. The majority of slides are governed by the Slide Master because the
majority of slides are not title slides. Here's the lowdown on the Slide
Master and Title Master:

✦ **Slide Master:** The master for all slides *except* those assigned the Title
Slide layout, the layout designed for the introductory slide. Figure 12-2
shows a Slide Master. It has placeholders for entering a slide number,
the date, and a footer. The placeholder text shows which font and font
size is used for slide titles, first-level bulleted lists, second-level bulleted

lists, and so on. By changing one of these fonts, you change fonts on all slides that the Slide Master governs. Drop a company logo onto this slide, and it will appear on all slides except the title slide.

Select the Slide Master or Title Master.

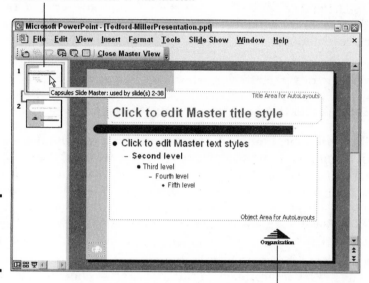

Figure 12-2:
Working with a Slide Master.

This graphic appears on all slides.

✦ **Title Master:** The master for slides assigned the Title Slide layout, the first layout in the Apply Slide Layout task pane. Most presentations have only one title slide, but some people use more than one to mark when a new stage of the presentation is forthcoming. If more than one slide in your presentation has been assigned the Title Slide layout, you can go to the Title Master, make formatting changes to it, and rest assured that your changes will appear on all title slides.

The following pages explain how to change formats on a Slide Master, apply Slide Master formats to slides, and create more than one Slide Master for a presentation.

Changing formats on the Slide Master

Follow these steps to open the Slide Master or Title Master and make formatting changes there:

1. **Choose View⇨Master⇨Slide Master.**

Slide Master thumbnails appear on the task pane (refer to Figure 12-2).

2. **Move the mouse pointer over a thumbnail to see which is the Slide Master and which is the Title Master.**

A ToolTip tells you the name of the slide design you are working on, whether the slide is the Slide Master or the Title Master, and how many slides in the presentation are title slides or normal slides.

3. **Select the Slide Master or the Title Master in the task pane.**

   Which slide you choose depends, of course, on whether you want to alter the appearance of a title slide or the other slides in your presentation.

4. **Change formats on the slide, insert a logo graphic, change the size of text frames, or do whatever it is you want done to slides throughout your presentation.**

   When you're finished doing your masterful work, click the Close Master View button or switch to Normal or Slide Sorter view.

Here are some other things worth knowing when it comes to Slide Masters:

- ✦ **Dealing with placeholder frames:** To remove a placeholder frame, select it and press Delete. Many people, for example, remove the Date Area, Footer Area, or Number Area to make room for a graphic or logo. If you remove a frame but regret doing so, click the Master Layout button or choose Format⇨Master Layout and, in the Master Layout dialog box, select the name of the frame you regret deleting: Title, Text, Date, Slide Number, or Footer.

- ✦ **Working with footers:** To handle the footer along the bottom of slides — the Date Area, Footer Area, and Number Area — choose View⇨Header and Footer. In the misnamed Header and Footer dialog box (misnamed because there are no headers on slides), enter the date, a footer, or slide numbers along the bottom of slides. Later in this chapter, "Handling Footers" takes up this subject in detail.

- ✦ **Getting the original design back:** When you change formats on a Slide Master, you're really tinkering with the slide design itself. Suppose that you regret tinkering with the design and you want the original design back? The only way to start all over with an original slide design is to choose a new design in the Slide Design task pane and immediately choose your original design a second time. Doing so has the effect of washing away all the changes you made on the Slide Master and Title Master of a presentation.

Applying Slide Master formats to formatted slides

If you change formats on an individual slide, PowerPoint assumes that you want the slide to stand out from the crowd, and it breaks the connection between the individual slide and its Slide Master. Thereafter, if you make a change to the Slide Master, the change does not translate to the individual slide whose formats you changed because that slide, PowerPoint reasons, is supposed to stand apart from the rest. Suppose, however, that you want a slide whose formats you changed to adopt the formats of a Slide Master. Follow these steps to reapply the formats on a Slide Master to a rebel slide:

1. Select the slide. To select more than one slide, switch to Slide Sorter view and Ctrl+click the slides.

2. Choose Format⇨Slide Layout to display the Slide Layout task pane.

3. Find the slide layout that you applied originally to the slide or slides, open the layout's drop-down list, and choose Reapply Layout.

Now the formats on the Slide Master, whatever they happen to be, whether you altered them or not, are applied to the slide or slides you selected.

Removing a Slide Master item from one slide

The beauty of Slide Masters is that they permit you to put the same item — a company logo, a slide number, the date — on all the slides in a presentation and rest assured that the items will appear in the same place on each slide. Sometimes, however, Slide Master items get in the way. They occupy valuable space that you need for a chart. They clash with the clip-art illustration on the slide.

PowerPoint offers two ways to remove Slide Master elements from a single slide:

✦ **Removing the footer and all master slide graphics:** Select the slide, choose Format⇨Background, and, in the Background dialog box, select the Omit Background Graphics from Master check box. Then click the Apply button.

✦ **Covering up the item:** With this technique, you block out the item. Click the Rectangle button on the Drawing toolbar and draw a rectangle over the item. Next, open the Fill Color drop-down list on the Drawing toolbar and choose the same color that appears on the slide background. Finally, open the Line Color drop-down list on the Drawing toolbar and choose No Line.

Working with more than one Slide Master

Sometimes a presentation can do with more than one Slide Master. Suppose, for example, that a sales presentation imparts upside and downside information. To help the audience distinguish between optimistic upside slides and their pessimistic downside counterparts, you can create an additional two Slide Masters, a rose-colored one called "Upside" and a murky green one called "Downside." This way, the audience will know immediately which side's views you are presenting when you display a new slide.

To prevent more than one Slide Master from being created, or, for that matter, to create more than one Slide Master if you are unable to create them, choose Tools⇨Options, and, on the Edit tab of the Options dialog box, select or deselect the Multiple Masters check box.

Creating a new Slide Master

To begin with, all slides in a presentation are associated with a single Title Master or Slide Master, but you can follow these steps to create secondary Slide Masters:

1. **Choose View⇨Master⇨Slide Master.**

2. **In the task pane, select the Slide Master thumbnail if you want to create a new Slide Master; select the Title Master thumbnail to create a new Title Master.**

3. **Choose Insert⇨New Slide Master or click the Insert New Slide Master button.**

   To insert a New Title Master, click the Insert New Title Master button. A new Slide Master or Title Master thumbnail appears in the task pane and the master itself appears in the window.

4. Format the new Slide Master.

You can call upon any formatting command you desire. To choose a slide design or color scheme for your new Slide Master, choose Format⇨Slide Design and select the design or color scheme in the Slide Design task pane.

Another way to create a new Slide Master is to duplicate one that is already there and then change the duplicate's formats. In the task pane, select the Slide Master that needs duplicating and choose Insert⇨Duplicate Slide Master. You can then rename the duplicate (described shortly).

Assigning slides to a Slide Master

No slide can serve two masters. When a presentation includes more than one Slide Master or Title Master, you have to tell PowerPoint which master to assign to your slides. Follow these steps to assign a slide or slides to a Slide Master:

1. Select the slide or slides.

2. Click the Design button to open the Slide Design task pane.

3. Under the Used in This Presentation section, select the Slide Master you want to assign the slide or slides, and then choose Apply to Selected Slides from the drop-down list.

Doing this, that, and the other to Slide Masters

Here is some other stuff you may or may not need to know about working with more than one Slide Master:

✦ **Renaming Slide Masters:** A newly made Slide Master is given the boring name "Custom Design," but you can give it a more descriptive name. To do so, select the slide, click the Rename Master button, and enter a new name in the Rename Master dialog box.

✦ **Deleting a Slide Master:** Select the Slide Master and click the Delete Master button. Slides that were assigned the Slide Master you deleted are assigned to the first or only Slide Master in the Slide Master task pane.

Handling Footers

A *footer* is a line of text that appears at the foot, or bottom, of a slide. Figure 12-3 shows a footer and the dialog box for entering footers. Typically, a footer includes the date, a company name, and a slide number. The Slide Master includes frames for entering those very same items. Except for slide numbers, however, putting anything in the footer isn't recommended. Footers crowd slides and distract the audience from gazing at the slide itself.

PowerPoint has a special command, View⇨Header and Footer, for entering the date, a word or two of text, and the slide number in footers. To put other items in footers, do so on your own by going to a Slide Master, drawing a text box, and placing the text box near the bottom of the slide (see "Slide Masters for Consistent Formatting," earlier in this chapter).

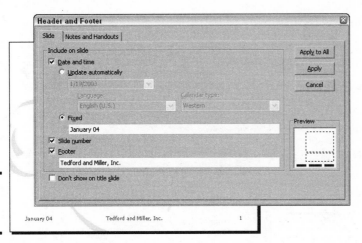

Figure 12-3:
Entering a footer.

To enter a footer with PowerPoint's help, choose View⇨Header and Footer.
You see the Header and Footer dialog box (refer to Figure 12-3) and its self-
explanatory options. Keep your eye on the Preview window. It shows what
your footer will look like.

Here are some things that are worth knowing as you play footsy with
PowerPoint slides:

✦ **Adjusting the position of footer items:** To change where footer items
are on the page, you have to go to a Slide Master. Choose View⇨Master⇨
Slide Master and select the Slide Master or Title Master thumbnail. Then
drag the text frames in the footer to new locations.

✦ **Removing a footer from the first slide:** Choose View⇨Header and
Footer, and, in the Header and Footer dialog box (refer to Figure 12-3),
select the Don't Show on Title Slide check box. To remove a text box
from footers that you placed there yourself, choose View⇨Master⇨Slide
Master, select the Title Master thumbnail, select the item you want to
remove, and press the Delete key.

✦ **Removing the footers from slides:** Select the slides from which you
want to remove footers, choose Format⇨Background, and, in the
Background dialog box, select the Omit Background Graphics from
Master check box. Then click the Apply to All button. However, this
command also removes graphics on the master slide. It removes everything except the title placeholder and text placeholder.

Action Buttons for Going from Slide to Slide

An *action button* is a handy button, usually found in a corner of a slide, that
you may click to go elsewhere in a presentation. Action buttons are especially useful in kiosk-style presentations (Book IV, Chapter 13 explains what
those are). PowerPoint offers action buttons for going to the next slide, the
previous slide, the first or last slide in a presentation, the last slide you
viewed, or a specific slide. Figure 12-4 shows some action buttons and the
dialog box where action buttons are born. Rather than click action buttons,
you can tell PowerPoint to activate them when the mouse pointer moves
over them.

**Book IV
Chapter 12**

**Advanced Formatting
Techniques**

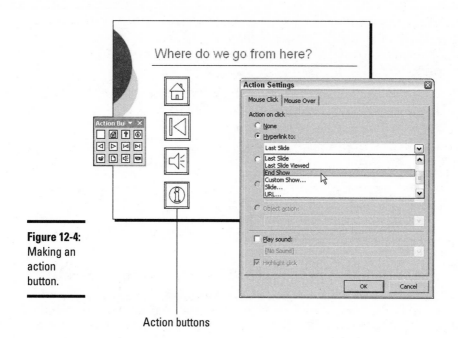

Figure 12-4:
Making an
action
button.

Action buttons

Select the slide that needs action and follow these steps to adorn it with an
action button:

1. **Display the Action Buttons toolbar.**

To do so, either choose Slide Show⇨Action Buttons or click the
AutoShapes button on the Drawing toolbar and choose Action Buttons.

2. **Study the buttons carefully and click the one that best illustrates the
action you want to take.**

The pointer changes to a cross-hair cursor.

3. **Draw the button on the slide.**

To do so, drag the cross-hair cursor in a diagonal fashion. The Action
Settings dialog box (refer to Figure 12-4) appears when you finish
dragging.

4. **Select the Mouse Over tab if you want to activate the button by
moving the mouse pointer over it, not clicking it.**

5. **Select the Hyperlink To option button.**

6. **On the Hyperlink To drop-down list, choose the action you want for
the button.**

7. **Click OK.**

Now to make the button look right and adjust its size and position:

✦ **Choosing a different button:** Sorry, the only way to choose a different
button for an action is to start all over and redraw the button.

✦ **Changing a button's action:** Right-click the button and choose Edit
Hyperlink. In the Action Settings dialog box, choose a new action.

✦ **Changing an action button's appearance:** Double-click the button or right-click it and choose Format AutoShape. You see the Format AutoShape dialog box. On the Colors and Lines tab, choose a color for the button and a line for its border.

✦ **Changing the button's size:** Click the button to display its selection handles. Drag a corner handle — a white circle — to enlarge or shrink the button.

✦ **Changing the button's position:** Click the button to select it. Then drag the button elsewhere.

CHECK IT OUT

Showing Transitions between Slides

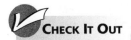 In PowerPoint-speak, a *transition* is a little bit of excitement that occurs as one slide leaves the screen and the next slide climbs aboard. Transitions include the dissolve, the wipe up, and the cover down. Don't worry, you get a chance to test-drive these transitions before you attach them to slides. Follow these steps to show transitions between slides:

1. **Switch to Slide Sorter view.**

2. **Click the Transition button or choose Slide Show⇨Slide Transition to make the Slide Transition task pane appear.**

Flying star icon   Choose a transition

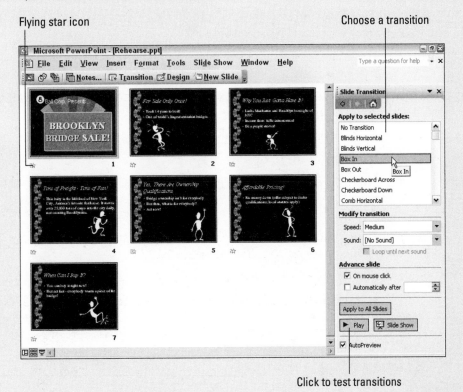

Click to test transitions

**Book IV
Chapter 12**

Advanced Formatting Techniques

CONTINUED

3. Select the slides that need transitions; or, to run transitions throughout your entire presentation, click the Apply to All Slides button or press Ctrl+A.

4. Select a transition in the Apply to Selected Slides list.

As soon as you choose a transition, the slide or slides you selected "transition" — they demonstrate the transition you chose. Click the Play button to see the transition again. Experiment with different transitions until you find Mr. or Ms. Right.

Choose the same transition for all the slides unless your goal is to make a wacky presentation. Transitions already call attention to themselves. Assigning a different transition to each slide has the effect of turning the audience's attention away from you and toward transitions.

5. On the Speed drop-down list, choose a speed for the transition — Slow, Medium, or Fast.

Again, the slides demonstrate how fast or slow these options are.

6. To play a sound during a transition, select the sound from the Sound drop-down list.

These canned sounds can be distracting, however, so choose wisely, or, better yet, don't choose a sound unless you're working on a kiosk presentation.

A flying star icon appears with slides that have been assigned transitions (the star appears as well with slides that have been animated). To remove a transition from slides, select them in Slide Sorter view, click the Transition button, and choose No Transition on the Apply to Selected Slides list in the Slide Transition task pane.

Chapter 13: Giving the Presentation

In This Chapter

↳ **Preparing to give your presentation**

↳ **Printing handouts**

↳ **Showing the presentation slides**

↳ **Setting up a kiosk-style presentation**

At last, the big day has arrived. It's time to give the presentation. "Break a leg," as actors say before they go on stage. These pages explain how to make the last-minute preparations, print handouts, and show the slides. You also discover how to give self-playing, kiosk-style presentations; customize a presentation for different audiences; and put a presentation on a Web page.

Rehearsing Your Presentation

Be sure to rehearse the presentation two or three times. Take note of how long it takes for you to give the presentation. Be sure to take into account time for questions from the audience. You might need to lengthen or shorten the presentation. And before it starts, make sure the machine on which you will give it is hooked up and in working order.

To help you rehearse, PowerPoint offers the Rehearse Timings command. This command keeps count of how long your presentation is and how long each slide is on-screen. When the dress rehearsal is over, you can see in Slide Sorter view how long each slide was on-screen, as shown in Figure 13-1. You can tell whether a slide was on too long and perhaps needs to be divided into two slides. You can tell whether your presentation fits the time you'll be allotted.

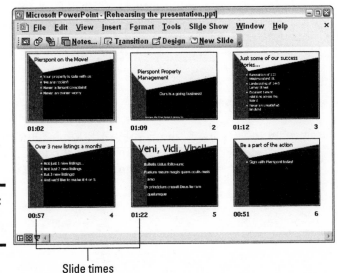

Figure 13-1: Timing the rehearsal.

Slide times

Follow these steps to rehearse a presentation:

1. Choose Slide Show⇨Rehearse Timings.

The first slide appears on-screen, as does the Rehearsal toolbar. You can click the Pause button if during the presentation the dog needs walking or the postman rings twice.

2. Go through your presentation as you expect to on the big day.

When the presentation is over, a dialog box tells you the total time of the presentation and asks whether you want to record how long each slide was on-screen.

3. Click Yes to record the timings; click No to ignore them.

If you click Yes, the timings will appear in Slide Sorter view (refer to Figure 13-1).

Printing Handout Copies of a Presentation

One way to make a slide presentation more memorable is to print copies of it and hand out the copies after the presentation is over. That way, audience members can refer to your presentation or even marvel at it later on. Slides can be printed one, two, three, four, six, or nine to a page.

 Before printing handout copies of the slides in your presentation, tell PowerPoint how many slides to print on a page. Choose View⇨Master⇨ Handout Master. On the Handout Master View toolbar, click the button that corresponds to the number of slides per page you want. While you're looking at the Handout Master, you can enter a header or footer on the handouts.

To print a handout, choose File⇨Print. In the Print dialog box, choose Handouts on the Print What drop-down list. You might want to choose Grayscale on the Color/Grayscale drop-down list even if you have a color printer. Slides, especially those with color backgrounds, are easier to see and examine in grayscale on the printed page.

 As long as the speaker notes you wrote for your slides are suitable for public consumption, you can print speaker notes instead of handouts for your audience. This way, audience members can read explanatory notes as well as see the slides themselves (see Book IV, Chapter 11).

Showing Your Presentation

Compared to the preliminary work, giving a presentation is a piece of cake. To get off to a good start, press the Home key or select the first slide in the presentation. That way, you start at the beginning. Then do the following to show the slides:

✦ **Starting the show:** Choose View⇨Slide Show, press F5, or click the Slide Show button.

 ✦ **Going forward:** To go forward from slide to slide, press the → key, click the mouse button, press N (for Next), press the Page Down key, press the spacebar, right-click and choose Next, or click the Navigation button in the lower-left corner of the screen and choose Next.

✦ **Going backward:** To go backward through the slides, press the ← key, press P (for Previous), press the Page Up key, right-click and choose Previous on the shortcut menu, click the Navigation button in the lower-left corner of the screen and choose Previous, or click the Back button in the lower-left corner of the screen.

✦ **Going to a specific slide:** Either right-click or click the Navigation button, choose Go to Slide, and select the slide from the list. Press the Home key to go to the first slide.

✦ **Ending the show:** Press Esc, right-click, and choose End Show from the shortcut menu, or click the button in the lower-left corner of the screen and choose End Show.

Presentations end with a blank screen and the words, "End of slide show, click to exit." To end presentations without the blank slide, choose Tools⇨Options, select the View tab in the Options dialog box, and deselect the End with Black Slide check box.

Using the Pen for emphasis

To make presentations a little livelier, whip out the Pen and draw on a slide. Draw to underscore bullet points on a slide. Or draw check marks when you hit the key points. To use the Pen, right-click a slide and choose Pointer Options⇨Felt Tip Pen or choose one of the other pens. Now you can draw with the Pen.

Press Esc when you're finished using the Pen (but be careful not to press Esc twice, because the second press tells PowerPoint to end the presentation).

Pen marks are not permanent. At the end of a presentation in which someone has drawn on the screen, PowerPoint asks whether you want to discard or keep your scribblings. You can also choose Pointer Options⇨Eraser, and, with the eraser pointer, click lines you have drawn to erase them.

You can choose different colors for the Pen by right-clicking, choosing Pointer Options⇨Ink Color, and selecting a color on the submenu.

Making the Grade

☑ Looking ahead

☑ Ensuring customer satisfaction

☑ Teamwork, teamwork, teamwork!

**Book IV
Chapter 13**

Giving the Presentation

Giving a Self-Playing, Kiosk-Style Presentation

A kiosk-style presentation is one that plays on its own. You set the works in motion, and it plays over and over on your computer until you or someone else comes along to press the Esc key. To give a kiosk-style presentation, you tell PowerPoint how long to leave each slide on-screen. Then you arrange for the presentation to be shown "kiosk-style."

Deciding how long to keep slides on-screen

Follow these steps to tell PowerPoint how long to keep each slide on-screen:

1. **Switch to Normal view and select the Slides tab.**

2. **Select the first slide in the presentation.**

3. **Choose Slide Show⇨Slide Transition.**

The Slide Transition task pane appears, as shown in Figure 13-2.

Figure 13-2: Setting up a kiosk-style presentation.

Enter the time period.

4. **Deselect the On Mouse Click check box.**

5. **Select the Automatically After check box.**

Select both these check boxes if you want to give the people who view the presentation the option of moving ahead on their own. Whichever comes first, slides advance when the viewer clicks the screen or when each slide's time period comes to an end.

6. **Click the Apply to All Slides button.**

7. Enter how long you want the slide or all the slides to remain on-screen.

How you do this depends on whether you want the slides to stay on-screen the same amount of time:

- **All slides the same time:** Enter a time period in the Automatically After text box and click the Apply to All Slides button again.

- **Each slide a different time:** One by one, select each slide on the Slide tab and enter a time period in the Automatically After text box.

A fast way to enter time periods for individual slides is to rehearse the presentation and save the timings. If you save the timings, the time periods appear in the Automatically After text box. See "Rehearsing Your Presentation," earlier in this chapter.

Making the presentation kiosk-style

Follow these steps to make yours a kiosk-style presentation:

1. Choose Slide Show⇨Set Up Show.

You see the Set Up Show dialog box.

2. Under Show Type, select the Browsed at Kiosk (Full Screen) option.

3. Click OK.

Chapter 14: Up and Running with Excel

In This Chapter

✔ Understanding what a worksheet is

✔ Entering text, as well as numeric, date, and time data

✔ Using the AutoFill command to enter lists and serial data

✔ Formatting text on a worksheet

✔ Setting up data-validation rules

This chapter introduces Excel, the official number cruncher of Office. The purpose of Excel is to track, analyze, and tabulate numbers. Use the program to project profits and losses, formulate a budget, or analyze Elvis sightings in North America. Doing the setup work takes time, but after you enter the numbers and tell Excel how to tabulate them, you're on Easy Street. Excel does the math for you. All you have to do is kick off your shoes, sit back, and see how the numbers stack up.

This chapter explains what a workbook and a worksheet are, and how rows and columns on a worksheet determine where cell addresses are. You also discover tips and tricks for entering data quickly in a worksheet, how to format data, and how to construct data-validation rules to make sure that data is entered accurately.

Getting Acquainted with Excel

If you have spent any time in an Office program, much of the Excel screen will look familiar to you. The buttons on the Formatting toolbar — Bold, the Align button, and the Indent buttons, for example — work the same in Excel as they do in Word. The Font and the Font Size drop-down lists work the same as well. Any command in Excel that has to do with formatting text and numbers works the same in Excel and Word. The commands for opening files, closing files, and creating files are also the same.

An Excel file is called a *workbook*. Each workbook comprises one or more worksheets. A *worksheet*, also known as a *spreadsheet*, is a table where you enter data and data labels. Figure 14-1 shows a worksheet with data about rainfall in different counties. A worksheet works like an accountant's ledger — only it's much easier to use. Notice how the worksheet is divided by gridlines into columns (A, B, C, and so on) and rows (1, 2, 3, and so on). The rectangles where columns and rows intersect are called *cells,* and each cell can hold one data item, a formula for calculating data, or nothing at all. At the bottom of the worksheet are tabs for visiting the other worksheets in the workbook.

Active cell address Formula bar Cells

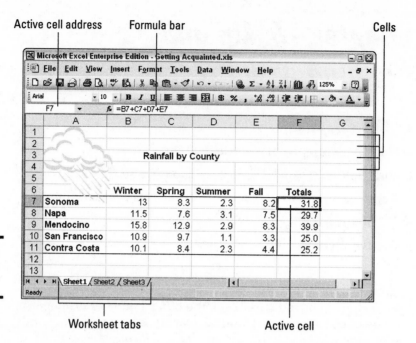

Figure 14-1:
The Excel
screen.

Worksheet tabs Active cell

Each cell has a different cell address. In Figure 14-1, cell B7 holds 13, the amount of rain that fell in Sonoma County in the winter. Meanwhile, as the Formula bar at the top of the screen shows, cell F7 holds the formula =B7+C7+D7+E7, the sum of the numbers in cells — you guessed it — B7, C7, D7, and E7.

The beauty of Excel is that the program does all the calculations and recalculations for you after you enter the data. If you were to change the number in cell B7, Excel would instantly recalculate the total amount of rainfall in Sonoma County in cell F7. People who struggled in math class will be glad to know that you don't have to worry about the math because Excel does it for you. All you have to do is make sure that the data and the formulas are entered correctly.

After you have entered and labeled the data, entered the formulas, and turned your worksheet into a little masterpiece, you can generate charts like the one in Figure 14-2. Do you notice any similarities between the worksheet in Figure 14-1 and the chart in Figure 14-2? The chart is fashioned from data in the worksheet, and it took me exactly six seconds to create that chart. Book IV, Chapter 18 explains charts.

Figure 14-2:
A chart
generated
from the
data in
Figure 14-1.

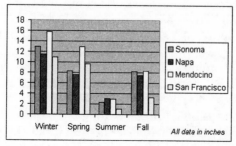

Rows, columns, and cell addresses

Not that anyone except an Enron accountant needs all of them, but an Excel worksheet has 256 columns and 65,536 rows. The rows are numbered, and columns are labeled A to Z, then AA to AZ, then BA to BZ, and so on. The important thing to remember is that each cell has an address whose name comes from a column letter and a row number. The first cell in row 1 is A1, the second cell is B1, and so on. You need to enter cell addresses in formulas to tell Excel which numbers to compute.

To learn a cell's address, either make note of which column and row it lies at the intersection of, or click the cell and glance at the *Formula bar* (refer to Figure 14-1). The left side of the Formula bar lists the address of the *active cell,* the cell you clicked in the worksheet. In Figure 14-1, cell F7 is the active cell.

Workbooks and worksheets

Sheet2

When you open a new Excel file, you open a *workbook,* a file with three worksheets in it. The worksheets are called Sheet1, Sheet2, and Sheet3 (you can change their names and add more worksheets). To get from worksheet to worksheet, click tabs along the bottom of the Excel screen. Why three worksheets? Because you might need more than one worksheet for a single project. Think of a workbook as a stack of worksheets. Besides calculating the numbers in cells across the rows or down the columns of a worksheet, you can make calculations throughout a workbook by using numbers from different worksheets in a calculation.

Entering Data in a Worksheet

Entering data in a worksheet is an irksome activity. Fortunately, Excel offers a few shortcuts to take the sting out of it. These pages explain how to enter data in a worksheet, the different types of data, and how to enter text labels, numbers, dates, and times.

The basics of entering data

What you can enter in a worksheet cell falls in four categories:

+ Text
+ A value (numeric, date, or time)
+ A logical value (True or False)
+ A formula that returns a value, logical value, or text

Still, no matter what type of data you enter, the basic steps are the same:

1. Click the cell where you want to enter the data or text label.

As shown in Figure 14-3, a square appears around the cell to tell you that the cell you clicked is now the active cell. Glance at the left side of the Formula bar if you're not sure which cell you're about to enter data in. The Formula bar lists the cell address.

Enter the data here...   ...or here.

	A	B	C	D	E	F	G
1							
2							
3	Elvis Sightings in North America						
4		Top Five Cities		1999	2000	2001	2002
5			Memphis	23	24		
6			New York	18			
7			New Orleans	44			
8			St. Louis	16			
9			Chicago	16			
10							
11							
12							

Figure 14-3:
Entering
data.

2. Type the data in the cell.

If you find typing in the Formula bar easier, click and start typing there. As soon as you type the first character, you see the Cancel button (an X), the Enter button (a check mark), and the Edit Formula button (an equal sign) on the Formula bar.

3. Press the Enter key to enter the number or label.

Besides pressing the Enter key, you can also press an arrow key (←, ↑, →, ↓) or click the Enter button (the check mark) on the Formula bar.

If you change your mind about entering data, click the Cancel button or press Esc to delete what you entered and start over.

Book IV, Chapter 16 explains how to enter logical values and formulas. The next several pages describe how to enter text labels, numeric values, date values, and time values.

Entering text labels

Sometimes a text entry is too long to fit in a cell. How Excel accommodates text entries that are too wide depends on whether there is data in the cell to the right of the one you entered the text in:

✦ If the cell to the right is empty, Excel lets the text spill into the next cell.

✦ If the cell contains data, the entry gets cut off. Nevertheless, the text you entered is in the cell. Nothing gets lost when it can't be displayed on-screen. You just can't see the text or numbers except by glancing at the Formula bar, where the contents of the cell can be seen in their entirety.

To solve the problem of text that doesn't fit in a cell, widen the column, shorten the text entry, re-orient the text, or wrap the contents of the cell. *Wrapping* means to run the text down to the next line, much the way the text in this paragraph runs to the next line when it reaches the right margin. Excel makes rows taller to accommodate wrapped text in a cell. To wrap

Entering numeric values

When a number is too large to fit in a cell, Excel displays pound signs (###) instead of a number or displays the number in scientific notation. You can always glance at the Formula bar, however, to see the complete number. And you can always widen the column to make the number display in its entirety.

To enter a fraction in a cell, leave a blank space between the whole number and the fraction. For example, to enter 5⅜, type the **5**, press the spacebar, and type **3/8**.

Here's a little trick for entering numbers with decimals quickly. To spare yourself the trouble of pressing the period key (.), you can tell Excel to enter the period automatically. Instead of entering **12.45**, for example, you can simply enter **1245**. Excel enters the period for you: 12.45. To perform this trick, choose Tools➪Options, select the Edit tab in the Options dialog box, choose Fixed Decimal, and, in the Places text box, enter the number of decimal places you want for numbers. Turn off this option when you want to go back to entering numbers the normal way.

Entering date and time values

Dates and times can be used in calculations, but entering a date or time value in a cell can be problematic because these values must be entered in such a way that Excel can recognize them as dates or times, not text.

Entering date values

Enter a date value in one of the following ways:

m/d/yy	7/31/04
m-d-yy	7-31-04
d-mmm-yy	31-Jul-04

After you enter a date this way, Excel converts it to the format it prefers for dates: 7/31/2004. If you don't enter the year, Excel assumes that the date you entered is in the current year. (You can enter fractions as well as dates in cells with the forward slash. However, to make sure that Excel recognizes the entry as a fraction, place a 0 in front of the fraction, if necessary. Excel interprets 3/8 as March 8, but if you enter **0 3/8**, Excel understands you're entering a fraction.)

When it comes to entering two-digit years in dates, the digits 30 through 99 belong to the 20th century (1930–1999), but the digits 00 through 29 belong to the 21st century (2000–2029). For example, 7/31/04 refers to July 31, 2004, not July 31, 1904. To enter a date in 1929 or earlier, enter four digits instead of two to describe the year: **7-31-1929**. To enter a date in 2030 or later, enter four digits instead of two: **7-31-2030**.

Dates entered in these formats are treated as text entries, not date values, and can't be used in calculations:

✦ July 31, 2004

✦ 31 July 2004

To enter a date directly in a formula, enclose the date in quotation marks (and make sure that the cell where the formula is entered has been given the Number format, not the Date format). For example, the formula =today()-"1/1/2003" calculates the number of days that have elapsed since January 1, 2003. Formulas are the subject of Book IV, Chapter 16.

Entering time values

Enter a time value in one of the following ways:

h:mm AM/PM	3:31 AM
h:mm:ss AM/PM	3:31:45 PM

Hours, minutes, and seconds must be separated by colons (:). Unless you enter AM or PM with the time, Excel assumes that you're operating on military time. For example, 3:30 is considered 3:30 in the morning, not 3:30 in the afternoon. Don't enter periods after the letters am or pm (that is, not a.m., p.m.).

Combining date and time values

You can combine dates and time values by entering the date, a blank space, and the time:

✦ 7/31/04 3:31 am

✦ 7-31-04 3:31:45 pm

Here are shortcuts for entering the current time or current date in a cell: Press Ctrl+; (semicolon) to enter the current date; press Ctrl+Shift+; (semicolon) to enter the current time.

Not that you need to know it especially, but Excel converts dates and times to serial values for the purpose of being able to use dates and times in calculations. For example, July 31, 2004 is the number 38199. July 31, 2004 at noon is 38199.5. These serial values represent the number of whole days since January 1, 1904. The portion of the serial value to the right of the decimal point is the time, as a portion of a full day.

Entering Lists and Serial Data with the AutoFill Command

Data that falls in the "serial" category — month names, days of the week, and consecutive numbers and dates, for example — can be entered quickly with the AutoFill command. Believe it or not, Excel recognizes certain kinds of serial data and will enter it for you as part of the AutoFill feature. Instead of laboriously entering this data one piece at a time, you can enter it all at one time by dragging the mouse. Follow these steps to "autofill" cells:

1. **Click the cell that is to be first in the series.**

   For example, if you intend to list the days of the week in consecutive cells, click where the first day is to go.

2. **Enter the first number, date, or list item in the series.**

3. **Move to the adjacent cell and enter the second number, date, or list item in the series.**

   If you want to enter the same number or piece of text in adjacent cells, it isn't necessary to take this step, but Excel needs the first and second items in the case of serial dates and numbers so that it can tell how much to increase or decrease the given amount or time period in each cell. For example, entering **5** and **10** tells Excel to increase the number by 5 each time, so that the next serial entry is 15.

4. **Select the cells or cells you just entered data in.**

   To select a single cell, click it; to select two, drag over the cells. The section in Book IV, Chapter 15 about selecting cells in a worksheet describes all the ways to select cells.

5. **Click the AutoFill handle and start dragging in the direction in which you want the data series to appear on your worksheet.**

   The *AutoFill handle* is the little black square in the lower-right corner of the cell. Finding it can be difficult. Carefully move the mouse pointer over the lower-right corner of the cell and, when you see the mouse pointer change into a black cross, click and start dragging. As you drag, the serial data appears in a ToolTip, as shown in Figure 14-4.

Drag the AutoFill handle.

Q1	Q2	Q3	
			Q4
Monday	Tuesday	Wednesday	
			Thursday
Jan	Feb	March	
			April
1999	2000	2001	
			2002
5	10	15	
			20

Figure 14-4:
Entering
serial data
and text.

The AutoFill Options button appears after you enter the serial data. Click it and choose an option if you want to copy cells or fill the cells without carrying along their formats.

To enter the same number or text in several empty cells, drag over the cells to select them or select each cell by holding down the Ctrl key as you click. Then type a number or some text and press Ctrl+Enter.

Formatting Numbers, Dates, and Time Values

When you enter a number that Excel recognizes as belonging to one of its formats, Excel assigns the number format automatically. Enter **45%**, for example, and Excel assigns the Percent Style format. Enter **$4.25**, and Excel assigns the Currency Style format. Besides assigning formats by hand, however, you can assign them to cells from the get-go and spare yourself the trouble of entering dollar signs, commas, percent signs, and other extraneous punctuation. All you have to do is enter the raw numbers. Excel does the window dressing for you.

Excel offers five number-formatting buttons on the Formatting toolbar — Currency Style, Percent Style, Comma Style, Increase Decimal, and Decrease Decimal. Select cells with numbers in them and click one of these buttons to change the numbers' formatting:

✦ **Currency Style:** Places a dollar sign before the number and gives it two decimal places.

✦ **Percent Style:** Places a percent sign after the number and converts the number to a percentage.

✦ **Comma Style:** Places commas in the number.

✦ **Increase Decimal:** Increases the number of decimal places by one.

✦ **Decrease Decimal:** Decreases the number of decimal places by one.

To format dates and time values as well as numbers, choose Format⇨Cells and make selections on the Number tab of the Format Cells dialog box. Figure 14-5 shows this dialog box. Select a category and choose options to describe how you want numbers or text to appear.

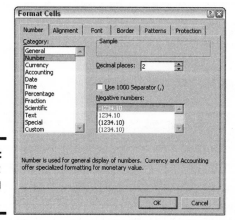

Figure 14-5: The Format Cells dialog box.

To strip formats, including number formats, from the data in cells, choose Edit⇨Clear⇨Formats.

Entering a ZIP Code that starts with a 0 can be problematic because Excel strips the initial 0 from a number if it begins with a 0. To get around that problem, visit the Number tab of the Format Cells dialog box (refer to Figure 14-5), select Special in the Category list, and choose a ZIP Code option.

Formatting Text and Numbers

B *I* U You know the drill. To change the font or font size of text or numbers, select them and make choices from the Font and Font Size drop-down lists on the Formatting toolbar. To boldface, italicize, or underline text or numbers, click the Bold, Italic, or Underline button on the Formatting toolbar. Or, to do a more thorough job of formatting, choose Format➪Cells, select the Font tab in the Format Cells dialog box, and make your choices there.

Sometimes displaying cells slantwise can be a big advantage when your worksheet is a big one. In Figure 14-6, for example, column labels are very long. To pack them in a little, you can display them slantwise and reduce the width of the worksheet considerably. Follow these steps to turn column headings on their ear:

1. **Select the cells you want to slant.**

2. **Choose Format➪Cells or press Ctrl+1.**

You see the Format Cells dialog box.

3. **Select the Alignment tab.**

4. **Drag the marker in the Orientation box or enter an angle in the Degrees text box, and then click OK.**

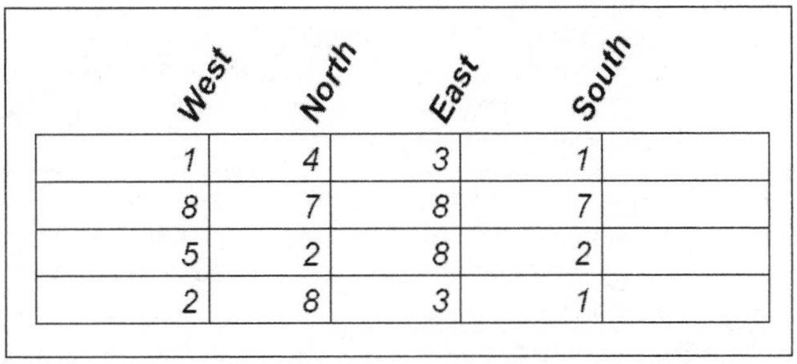

West	North	East	South
1	4	3	1
8	7	8	7
5	2	8	2
2	8	3	1

Figure 14-6:
Turning text
on its ear.

Establishing Data-Validation Rules

By nature, people are prone to enter data incorrectly because the task of entering data is so dull, and this is why data-validation rules are invaluable. A *data-validation rule* is a rule concerning what kind of data can be entered in a cell. When you select a cell that has been given a rule, an input message tells you what to enter, as shown in Figure 14-7. And if you enter the data incorrectly, an error message tells you as much, as shown in Figure 14-7. If the Office Assistant is turned on, the input message comes from the Office Assistant, not a ToolTip.

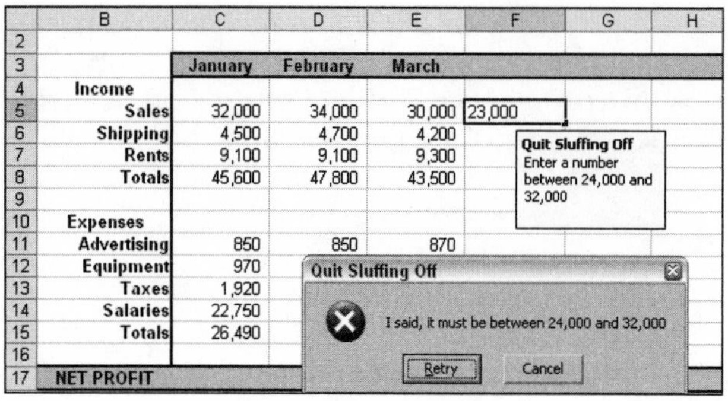

Figure 14-7:
A data-validation rule in action.

Data-validation rules are an excellent defense against sloppy data-entry and that itchy feeling you get when you're in the middle of an irksome task. In a cell that records date entries, you can require dates to fall in a certain time frame. In a cell that records text entries, you can choose an item from a list instead of typing it yourself. In a cell that records numeric entries, you can require the number to fall in a certain range. Table 14-1 describes the different categories of data-validation rules.

Table 14-1	Data-Validation Rule Categories
Rule	*What Can Be Entered*
Any Value	Anything whatsoever. This is the default setting.
Whole Number	Whole numbers (no decimal points allowed). Choose an operator from the Data drop-down list and values to describe the range of numbers that can be entered.
Decimal	Same as the Whole Number rule except that numbers with decimal points are permitted.
List	Items from a list. Enter the list items in cells on a worksheet, either the one you are working in or another. Then reopen the Data Validation dialog box, click the Return to Worksheet button (you will find it on the right side of the Source text box), and select the cells that hold the list. The list items appear in a drop-down list on the worksheet.
Date	Date values. Choose an operator from the Data drop-down list and values to describe the date range. Earlier in this chapter, the "Entering date and time values" section describes the correct way to enter date values.
Time	Time values. Choose an operator from the Data drop-down list and values to describe the date and time range. Earlier in this chapter, "Entering date and time values" describes the correct way to enter a combination of date and time values.
Text Length	A certain number of characters. Choose an operator from the Data drop-down list and values to describe how many characters can be entered.
Custom	A logical value (TRUE or FALSE). Enter a formula that describes what constitutes a true or false data entry.

Follow these steps to establish a data-validation rule:

1. Select the cell or cells that need a rule.

2. Choose Data⇨Validation.

As shown in Figure 14-8, the Data Validation dialog box appears.

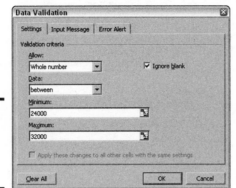

Figure 14-8:
Creating
a data-
validation
rule.

3. On the Allow drop-down list, choose the category of rule you want.

Table 14-1, earlier in this chapter, describes these categories.

4. Enter the criteria for the rule.

What the criteria is depends on what rule category you are working in. Table 14-1 describes how to enter the criteria for rules in each category. You can refer to cells in the worksheet by selecting them.

5. Select the Input Message tab and enter a title and input message.

You can see a title ("Quit Sluffing Off") and input message ("Enter a number between 24,000 and 32,000") in Figure 14-7. The title appears in boldface. Briefly describe what kind of data belongs in the cell or cells you selected.

6. Select the Error Alert tab, choose a style for the symbol on the Message Alert dialog box, enter a title for the dialog box, and enter a warning message.

In the error message in Figure 14-7, the Stop symbol was chosen. The title you enter appears across the top of the dialog box and the message appears beside the symbol.

7. Click OK.

To remove data-validation rules from cells, select the cells, choose Data⇨Validation, and, on the Settings tab of the Data Validation dialog box, click the Clear All button.

CHECK IT OUT

Creating an AutoFill List of Your Own

As you know, Excel is capable of completing lists on its own with the AutoFill feature. You can enter the days of the week or month names simply by entering one day or month and dragging the AutoFill handle to enter the others. Here's some good news: The AutoFill command can also reproduce the names of your co-workers, the roster of a softball team, street names, or any other list you care to enter quickly in a worksheet.

Follow these steps to enter items for a list so that you can enter them in the future by dragging the AutoFill handle:

1. Choose Tools⇨Options to open the Options dialog box.

2. Select the Custom Lists tab.

3. Click the Add button.

4. In the List Entries box, enter items for the list, and enter a comma after each item.

    You can see how it's done by glancing at the Custom Lists box.

5. Click OK.

Chapter 15: Refining Your Worksheet

In This Chapter

✔ Changing and editing worksheet data

✔ Going here and there in a worksheet

✔ Freezing and splitting columns to make data entry easier

✔ Documenting a worksheet with comments

✔ Selecting cells

✔ Copying and moving data

This chapter delves into the workaday world of worksheets (say that three times quickly). It explains how to edit worksheet data and move quickly here and there in a worksheet. You also discover a couple of techniques for entering data quickly, how to select cells, and how to copy and move data in cells.

Editing Worksheet Data

Not everyone enters the data correctly the first time. To edit data you have entered in a cell, do one of the following:

✦ **Double-click the cell.** Doing so places the cursor squarely in the cell, where you can start deleting or entering numbers and text.

✦ **Click the cell and press F2.** This technique also lands the cursor in the cell.

✦ **Click the cell you want to edit.** With this technique, you edit the data on the Formula bar.

If nothing happens when you double-click, or if pressing F2 lands the cursor in the Formula bar, not a cell, somebody has been fooling with Edit settings. Choose Tools⇨Options, select the Edit tab in the Options dialog box, and select the Edit Data Directly in Cell check box.

Moving around in a Worksheet

Going from place to place gets progressively more difficult as a worksheet gets larger. Luckily for you, Excel offers keyboard shortcuts for jumping around. Table 15-1 describes these keyboard shortcuts. (If the keyboard shortcuts in Table 15-1 don't work on your machine, someone has told Excel to adopt the keyboard shortcuts of Lotus 1-2-3, another spreadsheet program. To remedy the problem, choose Tools⇨Options, select the Transition tab in the Options dialog box, and deselect the Transition Navigation Keys option.)

Table 15-1	Keyboard Shortcuts for Getting Around in Worksheets
Press . . .	*To Move the Cursor . . .*
Home	To column A
Ctrl+Home	To cell A1, the first cell in the worksheet
Ctrl+End	To the last cell in the last row with data in it
←, →, ↑, ↓	To the next cell
Ctrl+←, →, ↑, ↓	In one direction toward the nearest cell with data in it or to the first or last cell in the column or row
PgUp *or* PgDn	Up or down one screenful of rows
Alt+PgUp *or* Alt+PgDn	Left or right one screen's worth of columns
Ctrl+PgUp *or* Ctrl+PgDn	Backward or forward through the workbook, from worksheet to worksheet

In addition to pressing keys, you can use these techniques to get from place to place in a worksheet:

✦ **Scroll bars:** Use the vertical and horizontal scroll bars to move to different areas. Drag the scroll box to cover long distances. To cover long distances very quickly, hold down the Shift key as you drag the scroll box on the vertical scroll bar.

✦ **IntelliMouse:** If your computer is equipped with an IntelliMouse, turn the wheel to quickly scroll up and down.

✦ **Name box:** Enter a cell address in the Name box and press Enter to go to the cell. The name box is found to the left of the formula bar. If you named cell ranges in your worksheet (see the section in Book IV, Chapter 16 about naming cell ranges so that you can use them in formulas), you can go to a cell range by choosing its name in the Name box.

✦ **The Go To command:** Choose Edit⇨Go To (or press Ctrl+G or F5) and, in the Go To dialog box, enter a cell address in the Reference box and click OK. Cell addresses you've already visited with the Go To command are already listed in the dialog box, as are cell ranges you named. Click the Special button to open the Go To Special dialog box and visit a formula, comment, or other esoteric item.

✦ **The Find command:** Click the Find button, choose Edit⇨Find, or press Ctrl+F to open the Find dialog box. Enter the data you seek in the Find What box and click the Find Next button.

To scroll to the active cell, press Ctrl+Backspace.

Getting a Better Look at the Worksheet

Especially when you're entering data, it pays to be able to get a good look at the worksheet. You need to know which column and row you are entering data in. These pages explain techniques for changing your view of a worksheet so you always know where you are. Read on to discover how to freeze columns and rows, hide columns and rows, and zoom in and out.

Freezing and splitting columns and rows

Sometimes your adventures in a worksheet take you to a faraway cell address, such as X31 or C39. Out there in the wilderness, it's hard to tell where to enter data because you can't see the data labels in the first column or first row that describe what the data in the worksheet is.

To see one part of a worksheet no matter how far you stray from it, you can split the worksheet or freeze columns and rows on-screen. In Figure 15-1, the worksheet is split so that column A, "Property," always appears on-screen, no matter how far you scroll to the right. Similarly, row 1 also appears on-screen no matter how far you scroll down the worksheet. Notice how the row numbers and column letters are interrupted in Figure 15-1. Because the screen is split, you always know what data to enter in a cell.

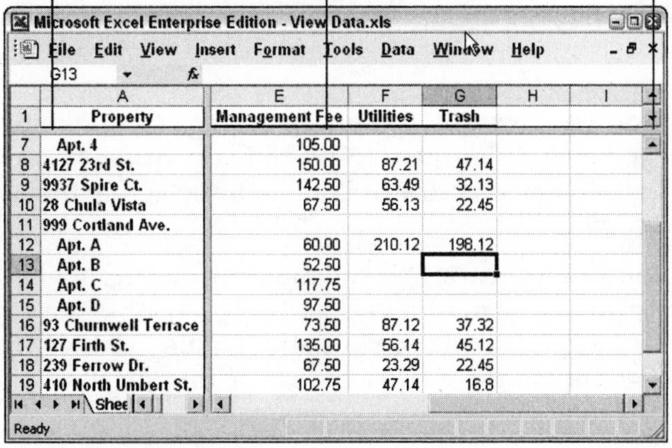

Drag to adjust the split.

Double-click to remove a split line.   Split bar.

Figure 15-1: Splitting a worksheet.

Freezing columns or rows on a worksheet works much like splitting except that lines instead of gray bars appear on-screen to show which columns and rows are frozen.

Follow these steps to split or freeze columns and rows on-screen:

1. **Click the cell directly below the row you want to freeze or split, and click in the column to the right of the column that you want to freeze or split.**

In Figure 15-1, for example, the split occurs at cell B2 (row 2 being below row 1, the row with the column labels, and column B being to the right of column A, the column with the row labels).

2. **Choose Window⇨Freeze Panes or Window⇨Split.**

Gray bars or lines are drawn on-screen to show which row and column have been frozen or split. Move where you will in the worksheet. The column and row you froze stay on-screen.

 The other way to split a worksheet is to grab hold of a *split bar*, the little division markers directly above the vertical scroll bar and directly to the right of the horizontal scroll bar (refer to Figure 15-1). You can tell where split bars are because the pointer turns into a double arrow when it's over a split bar. Click and drag a split bar to split the screen vertically or horizontally.

Choose Window⇨Unfreeze Panes or Window⇨Remove Split when you no longer want a frozen or split worksheet. You can also double-click a split line to remove it from the screen.

 Splitting the worksheet is superior to freezing columns or rows because, for one, you can drag the gray lines to new locations when you split the worksheet, and, moreover, you can remove the horizontal or vertical split by double-clicking it. Double-click the horizontal split line to remove it and divide the worksheet between sides, or double-click the vertical split to remove it and divide the worksheet between top and bottom.

Hiding columns and rows

Another way to take the clutter out of a worksheet is to temporarily hide columns and rows:

✦ **Hiding columns and rows:** Click anywhere in the row or column you want to hide and choose Format⇨Row⇨Hide or Format⇨Column⇨Hide. You can hide more than one row or column by selecting them and then giving a Hide command.

✦ **Unhiding columns and rows:** Select columns to the right and left of the hidden column, or select rows above and below the hidden row, and choose Format⇨Row⇨Unhide or Format⇨Column⇨Unhide. To unhide all columns and rows in the worksheets, click the Select All button (or press Ctrl+A) and give an Unhide command.

 To unhide Row 1 or Column A, choose Edit⇨Go To (or press F5) and, in the Go To dialog box, enter **A1** in the Reference text box and click OK. Then give an Unhide command.

Zooming in and out

 The Zoom commands come in very handy when you're entering data. From the Zoom box on the Standard toolbar, select or enter a percentage and press the Enter key. You can also zoom in or out by choosing View⇨Zoom and making a selection in the Zoom dialog box. Select the data in your work-sheet, choose View➪Zoom, and select the Fit Selection option in the Zoom dialog box to see all the data in a worksheet simultaneously.

If you have an *IntelliMouse,* the supercharged mouse manufactured by the Microsoft Corporation, you can zoom in and out by holding down the Ctrl key and turning the mouse wheel backward or forward. If you want to use the IntelliMouse strictly for zooming, not for scrolling, choose Tools➪ Options, select the General tab in the Options dialog box, and select the Zoom on Roll with IntelliMouse check box.

Comments for Documenting Your Worksheet

It may happen that you return to your worksheet days or months from now and discover to your dismay that you don't know why certain numbers or formulas are there. For that matter, someone else may inherit your work-sheet and be mystified as to what the heck is going on. To take the mystery out of a worksheet, document it by entering comments here and there. As shown in Figure 15-2, a *comment* is a note that describes part of a work-sheet. Each comment is connected to a cell. You can tell where a comment is because a small red triangle appears in the corner of cells that have been commented on. Move the pointer over one of these triangles and you see the comment and the name of the person who entered the comment in a pop-up box.

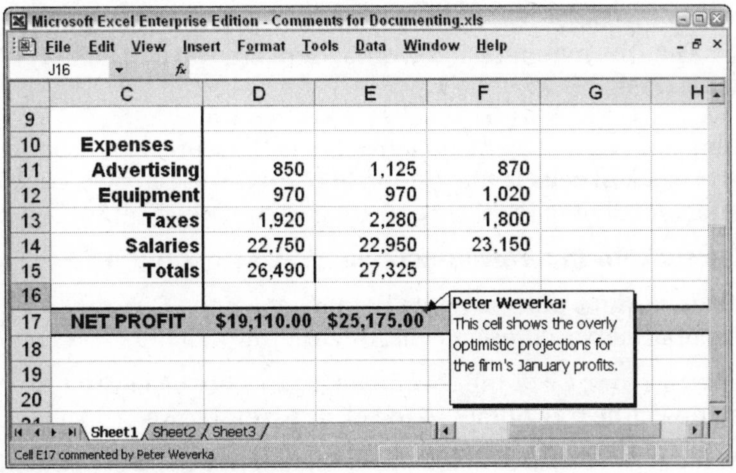

Figure 15-2:
Press
Shift+F2
to enter a
comment.

	C	D	E	F	G	H
9						
10	**Expenses**					
11	**Advertising**	850	1,125	870		
12	**Equipment**	970	970	1,020		
13	**Taxes**	1,920	2,280	1,800		
14	**Salaries**	22,750	22,950	23,150		
15	**Totals**	26,490	27,325			
16						
17	**NET PROFIT**	**$19,110.00**	**$25,175.00**			
18						
19						
20						

Microsoft Excel Enterprise Edition - Comments for Documenting.xls

File Edit View Insert Format Tools Data Window Help

J16

Peter Weverka:
This cell shows the overly optimistic projections for the firm's January profits.

Sheet1 / Sheet2 / Sheet3

Cell E17 commented by Peter Weverka

Book IV
Chapter 15

**Refining Your
Worksheet**

Here's everything a mortal needs to know about comments:

✦ **Entering a comment:** Click the cell that deserves the comment, choose Insert➪Comment (or press Shift+F2), and enter your comment in the pop-up box. Click in a different cell when you're done entering your comment.

✦ **Reading a comment:** Move the pointer over the small red triangle and read the comment in the pop-up box. To search for comments in a workbook, shrink your worksheet to 50 percent, choose Edit➪Go To (or press Ctrl+G), and, in the Go To dialog box, click the Special button. Then, in the Go To Special dialog box, select Comments and click OK. All comments in your worksheet are highlighted.

✦ **Editing a comment:** Select the cell with the comment, choose Insert➪ Edit Comment, and edit the comment in the pop-up box.

✦ **Deleting comments:** Right-click the cell with the comment and choose Delete Comment. To delete several comments, select them and choose Edit➪Clear➪Comments. To delete all the comments in a workbook, use the Edit➪Go To command to highlight all of them; then right-click any highlighted cell with a comment and choose Delete Comment.

If your name doesn't appear in the pop-up box when you enter a comment and you want it to appear there, choose Tools➪Options, select the General tab in the Options dialog box, and enter your name in the User Name text box.

You can print the comments in a worksheet. Choose File➪Page Setup and, on the Sheet tab of the Page Setup dialog box, open the Comments drop-down list and choose At End of Sheet or As Displayed on Sheet.

Selecting Cells in a Worksheet

To format, copy, move, or delete numbers or words in a worksheet, you have to select the numbers and words. Here are ways to select cells and the data inside them:

✦ **A block of cells:** Drag diagonally across the worksheet from one corner of the block of cells to the opposite corner. You can also click in one corner and Shift+click the opposite corner.

✦ **Adjacent cells in a row or column:** Drag across the cells.

✦ **Cells in various places:** While holding down the Ctrl key, click different cells, drag across different cells, or click row numbers and column letters.

✦ **A row or rows:** Click the row number to select an entire row. Click and drag down the row numbers to select several rows.

✦ **A column or columns:** Click the column letter to select an entire column. Click and drag across letters to select several columns.

✦ **Entire worksheet:** Click the Select All button, the square to the left of the heading letters and above the row numbers, press Ctrl+A, or press Ctrl+Shift+Spacebar.

Press Ctrl+Spacebar to select the column that the active cell is in; press Shift+Spacebar to select the row where the active cell is.

You can enter the same data item in several different cells by selecting cells and then entering the data in one cell and pressing Ctrl+Enter. This technique comes in very handy, for example, when you want to enter a placeholder **0** in several different cells.

Deleting, Copying, and Moving Data

To empty cells of their contents, select the cells and then either press the Delete key or right-click and choose Clear Contents.

To copy or move data in a worksheet, use those old standbys, the Cut, Copy, and Paste commands. When you paste the data, click where you want the first cell of the block of cells you're copying or moving to go. Be careful not to overwrite cells with data in them when you copy or move data.

 After you paste data, you see the Paste Options button. Click this button and choose an option from the menu to format the data in different ways.

As for the drag-and-drop method of copying and moving text, you can use it as well. Move the pointer to the edge of the cell block, click when you see the arrow, and start dragging.

 CHECK IT OUT

Your Own Customized Views

After you go to the trouble of freezing the screen or zooming in to a position you're comfortable with, you may as well save your view of the screen as a customized view. That way, you can call upon the customized view whenever you need it. View settings, the window size, the position of the grid on-screen, and cells that are selected can all be saved in a customized view.

To create a customized view, choose View⇨ Custom Views, click the Add button in the Custom Views dialog box, and enter a name for the view in the Add View dialog box. To switch views, choose View⇨Custom Views, select a view, and click the Show button.

 The catch to making customized views is to start by creating a view from the standard screen settings and calling it

Normal or Standard or Ordinary. Without the Normal view, getting back to ordinary screen settings after you switch to a customized view is well-nigh impossible. The only way to do it is to change all the screen settings and undo the work you did to create the customized view in the first place.

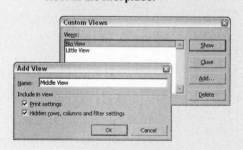

Chapter 16: Formulas and Functions for Crunching Numbers

In This Chapter

- Constructing a formula
- Using cell ranges in formulas
- Naming cell ranges
- Referring to cells in other worksheets
- Copying formulas to other columns and rows
- Using functions in formulas

*F*ormulas are where it's at as far as Excel is concerned. After you know how to construct formulas — and constructing them is pretty easy — you can put Excel to work. You can make the numbers speak to you. You turn a bunch of unruly numbers into meaningful figures and statistics.

This chapter explains what a formula is, how to enter a formula, and how to enter a formula quickly. You also discover how to copy formulas from cell to cell. Finally, this chapter explains how to make use of the hundred or so functions that Excel offers.

How Formulas Work

A *formula,* you may recall from the sleepy hours you spent in the back of math class, is a way to calculate numbers. For example, 2+3=5 is a formula. When you enter a formula in a cell, Excel computes the formula and displays its results in the cell. Click in cell A3 and enter **=2+3**, for example, and Excel displays the number 5 in cell A3.

Referring to cells in formulas

As well as numbers, Excel formulas can refer to the contents of different cells. When a formula refers to a cell, the number in the cell is used to compute the formula. In Figure 16-1, for example, cell A1 contains the number 2; cell A2 contains the number 3; and cell A3 contains the formula =A1+A2. As shown in cell A3, the result of the formula is 5. If you were to change the number in cell A1 from 2 to 3, the result of the formula in cell A3 (=A1+A2) becomes 6, not 5. When a formula refers to a cell and the number in a cell changes, the result of the formula changes as well.

To see the value of using cell references in formulas, consider the worksheet shown in Figure 16-2. The purpose of this worksheet is to track the budget of a school's Parent-Teacher Association. Column C lists income from different sources; column D shows what the PTA members thought income from these sources would be; and column E shows how actual income compares to projected income from the different sources. As the figures in the Actual Income column (column C) are updated, figures in the Over/Under Budget column (column E) and the Total Income row (row 8) change instantaneously. These figures change instantaneously because the formulas refer to the numbers in cells, not to unchanging numbers (known as *constants*).

Formula in Formula bar

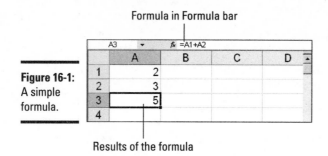

Figure 16-1:
A simple
formula.

Results of the formula

Figure 16-3 shows the formulas used to calculate the data in the worksheet in Figure 16-2. In column E, formulas deduct the numbers in column D from the numbers in column C to show where the PTA over- or under-budgeted for the different sources of income. In row 8, you can see how the SUM function is used to total cells in rows 3 through 7. The end of this chapter explains how to use functions in formulas.

Figure 16-2:
Using
formulas
in a
worksheet.

	A	B	C	D	E
1					
2	Income		Actual Income	Projected Income	Over/Under Budget
3		Book Fair	4,876.40	5,500.00	-623.60
4		Dances	1,476.95	1,800.00	-323.05
5		Fundraising	13,175.00	5,000.00	8,175.00
6		Merchandise Sales	5,888.50	7,000.00	-1,111.50
7		PTA Membership	3,918.00	3,000.00	918.00
8	Total Income		$ 29,334.85	$ 22,300.00	$ 7,034.85

Figure 16-3:
The
formulas
used to
generate the
numbers in
Figure 16-2.

	A	B	C	D	E
1					
2	Income		Actual Income	Projected Income	Over/Under Budget
3		Book Fair	4876.4	5500	=C3-D3
4		Dances	1476.95	1800	=C4-D4
5		Fundraising	13175	5000	=C5-D5
6		Merchandise Sales	5888.5	7000	=C6-D6
7		PTA Membership	3918	3000	=C7-D7
8	Total Income		=SUM(C2:C7)	=SUM(D2:D7)	=SUM(E2:E7)

Excel is remarkably good about updating cell references in formulas when you move cells. To see how good Excel is, consider what happens to cell addresses in formulas when you delete a row in a worksheet. If a formula refers to cell C1 but you delete row B, row C becomes row B, and the value in cell C1 changes addresses from C1 to B1. You would think that references in formulas to cell C1 would be out-of-date, but you would be wrong. Excel automatically adjusts all formulas that refer to cell C1. Those formulas now refer to cell B1 instead.

TIP

To display formulas in worksheet cells instead of the results of formulas, as was done in Figure 16-3, press Ctrl+` (the accent grave, the key above the Tab key on your keyboard). Press Ctrl+` to see formula results again.

Referring to formula results in formulas

Besides referring to cells with numbers in them in a cell, you can refer to formula results in a cell. Consider the worksheet shown in Figure 16-4. The purpose of this worksheet is to track scoring by the players on a basketball team. The Totals column shows the total points each player has scored in the three games. The Average column, using the formula results in the Totals column, determines how much each player has scored on average. The Average column does that by dividing the results in column E by 3, the number of games played.

Averages returned from the formula results in column E.

	A	B	C	D	E	F
1		Game 1	Game 2	Game 3	Totals	Average
2	Jones	4	3	7	14	4.7
3	Sacharsky	2	1	0	3	1.0
4	Mellon	11	13	8	32	10.7
5	Gomez	8	11	6	25	8.3
6	Riley	2	0	0	2	0.7
7	Pealer	3	8	4	15	5.0
8	Subrata	13	18	18	49	16.3
9		43	54	43	140	46.7

Figure 16-4: Using formula results as other formulas.

	A	B	C	D	E	F
1		Game 1	Game 2	Game 3	Totals	Average
2	Jones	4	3	7	=B2+C2+D2	=E2/3
3	Sacharsky	2	1	0	=B3+C3+D3	=E3/3
4	Mellon	11	13	8	=B4+C4+D4	=E4/3
5	Gomez	8	11	6	=B5+C5+D5	=E5/3
6	Riley	2	0	0	=B6+C6+D6	=E6/3
7	Pealer	3	8	4	=B7+C7+D7	=E7/3
8	Subrata	13	18	18	=B8+C8+D8	=E8/3
9		=SUM(B2:B8)	=SUM(C2:C8)	=SUM(D2:D8)	=B9+C9+D9	=E9/3

The order of precedence

When a formula includes more than one operator, the order in which the operators appear in the formula matters a lot. Consider this formula:

    =2+3*4

Does this formula result in 14 (2+[3*4]) or 20 ([2+3]*4)? The answer is 14, because Excel performs multiplication before addition in formulas. In other words, multiplication takes precedence over addition. The order in which calculations are made in a formula that includes different operators is called the *order of precedence*. Be sure to remember the order of precedence when you construct complex formulas with more than one operator:

1. Percent (%)

2. Exponentiation (^)

3. Multiplication (*) and division (/); leftmost operations are calculated first

4. Addition (+) and subtraction (–); leftmost operations are calculated first

5. Concatenation (&)

6. Comparison (=, <, <=, >, >=, <>)

To get around the order of precedence problem, enclose parts of formulas in parentheses. Operations in parentheses are calculated before all other parts of a formula. For example, the formula =2+3*4 equals 20 when it is written this way: =(2+3)*4.

Operators in formulas

Addition, subtraction, and division aren't the only operators you can use in formulas. Table 16-1 explains the arithmetic operators you can use and the key you press to enter each operator. In the table, operators are listed in the order of precedence.

Table 16-1	Arithmetic Operators for Use in Formulas	
Operator	*Symbol*	*Example Formula*
Percent	%	=50%, 50 percent, or 0.5
Exponentiation	^	=50^2, or 50 to the second power, or 2500
Division	/	=E2/3, the number in cell E2 divided by 3
Multiplication	*	=E2*4, the number in cell E2 multiplied by 4
Addition	+	=F1+F2+F3, the sum of the numbers in those cells
Subtraction	–	=G5–8, the number in cell G5 minus 8

Another way to compute a formula is to make use of a function. As "Working with Functions" explains later in this chapter, a function is a built-in formula that comes with Excel. SUM, for example, adds the numbers in cells. AVG finds the average of different numbers.

The Basics of Entering a Formula

No matter what kind of formula you enter, no matter how complex the formula is, follow these basic steps to enter it:

1. **Click the cell where you want to enter the formula.**

2. **Click in the Formula bar.**

3. **Enter an equal sign (=).**

You must be sure to enter the equal sign before you enter a formula. Without it, Excel thinks you're entering text, not a formula.

4. **Enter the formula.**

For example, enter **=B1*.06**. Make sure that you enter all cell addresses correctly. By the way, you can enter lowercase letters in cell references. Excel changes them to uppercase when you finish entering the formula. The next section in this chapter explains how to enter cell addresses quickly in formulas.

5. **Press Enter or click the Enter button (the green check mark).**

The result of the formula appears in the cell.

Warning: Does not compute!

Sometimes you enter a formula, but it doesn't compute and you get an error message, a cryptic three or four letters preceded by a pound sign (#). Here are common error messages and what you can do about them:

- **#DIV/01:** You tried to divide a number by 0 or by an empty cell.

- **#NAME:** You used a cell range name in the formula, but the name hasn't been defined. Sometimes this error occurs because you typed the name incorrectly. (Later in this chapter, "Naming cell ranges so that you can use them in formulas" explains how to name cell ranges.)

- **#N/A:** The formula refers to an empty cell, so no data is available for computing the formula.

Sometimes people enter NA in a cell as a placeholder to signal the fact that data has not been entered yet. Revise the formula or enter a number or formula in the empty cells.

- **#NULL:** The formula refers to a cell range that Excel can't understand. Make sure that the range is entered correctly.

- **#NUM:** An argument you used in your formula is invalid.

- **#REF:** The cell or range of cells that the formula refers to is not there.

- **#VALUE:** The formula includes a function that's used incorrectly, takes an invalid argument, or is misspelled. Make sure that the function uses the right argument and is spelled correctly.

Speed Techniques for Entering Formulas

Entering formulas and making sure that all cell references are correct is a tedious activity, but, fortunately for you, Excel offers a few techniques to make entering formulas easier. Read on to find out how ranges make entering cell references easier and how you can enter cell references in formulas by pointing and clicking. You'll also find instructions here for copying formulas.

Clicking cells to enter cell references

The hardest part about entering a formula is entering the cell references correctly. You have to squint to see which row and column the cell you want to refer to is in. You have to carefully type the right column letter and row number. However, instead of typing a cell reference, you can click the cell you want to refer to in a formula. As soon as you click the cell, Excel enters its address on the Formula bar. What's more, shimmering marquee lights appear around the cell to show you which one you're referring to in the formula.

In the worksheet in Figure 16-5, the user clicked cell F3 instead of entering its address on the Formula bar. The reference F3 appears on the Formula bar and the marquee lights appear around cell F3.

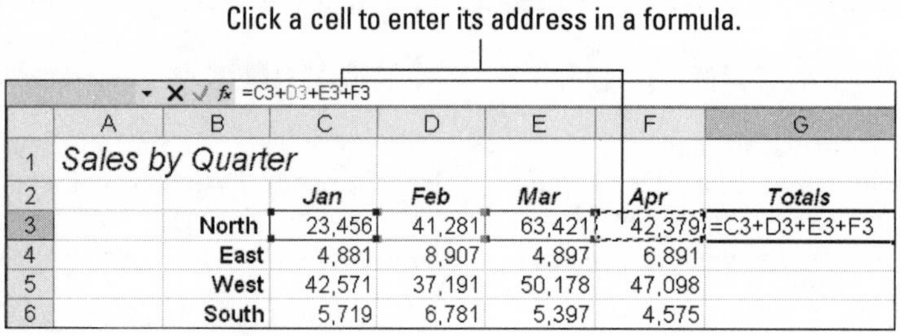

Click a cell to enter its address in a formula.

	A	B	C	D	E	F	G
	▼ X √ *fx* =C3+D3+E3+F3						
1	Sales by Quarter						
2			Jan	Feb	Mar	Apr	Totals
3		North	23,456	41,281	63,421	42,379	=C3+D3+E3+F3
4		East	4,881	8,907	4,897	6,891	
5		West	42,571	37,191	50,178	47,098	
6		South	5,719	6,781	5,397	4,575	

Figure 16-5: Clicking to enter a cell address.

Entering a cell range

A *cell range* is a line or block of cells in a worksheet. Cell ranges come in especially handy where functions are concerned (see "Working with Functions" later in this chapter). To create a cell range, select the cells. In Figure 16-6, the user selected cells C3, D3, E3, and F3 to form cell range C3:F3. The formula in Figure 16-6 uses the SUM function to total the numeric values in cell range C3:F3. Notice the marquee lights around the range C3:F3.

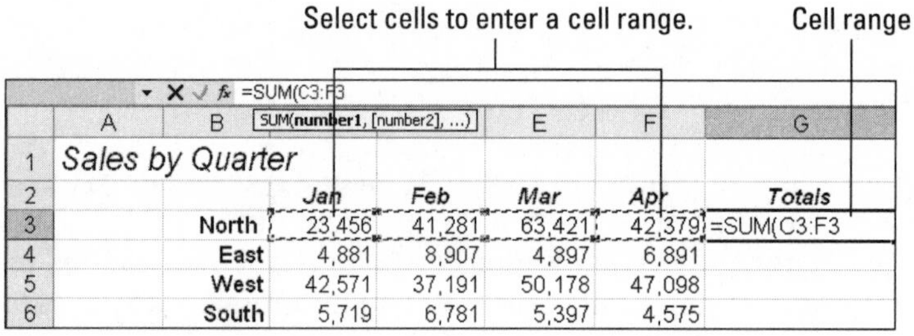

Select cells to enter a cell range.   Cell range

	A	B	C	D	E	F	G
	▼ X √ *fx* =SUM(C3:F3						
			SUM(**number1**, [number2], ...)		E	F	G
1	Sales by Quarter						
2			Jan	Feb	Mar	Apr	Totals
3		North	23,456	41,281	63,421	42,379	=SUM(C3:F3
4		East	4,881	8,907	4,897	6,891	
5		West	42,571	37,191	50,178	47,098	
6		South	5,719	6,781	5,397	4,575	

Figure 16-6: Using a cell range in a formula.

To identify a cell range, Excel lists the outermost cells in the range and places a colon (:) between cell addresses. You can enter cell ranges on your own without selecting cells. To do so, list the first cell in the range, enter a colon, and list the last cell. A cell range comprising cells A1, A2, A3, and A4 has this address A1:A4. A cell range comprising a block of cells from A1 to D4 has this address: A1:D4.

Naming cell ranges so that you can use them in formulas

Whether you type them yourself or drag across cells, entering cell references is a chore. Entering =C1+C2+C3+C4, for example, can cause a finger cramp. Entering =C1:C4 is no piece of cake, either. To take the tedium out of entering cell ranges in formulas, you can name cell ranges. When you want to enter a cell range in a formula, all you have to do is double-click a name in the Paste Name dialog box, as shown in Figure 16-7. Naming cell ranges has an added benefit. You can choose a name from the Name Box drop-down list and go directly to the cell range whose name you choose, as shown in Figure 16-7.

Choose a name to move there.   Double-click to enter the named range in a formula.

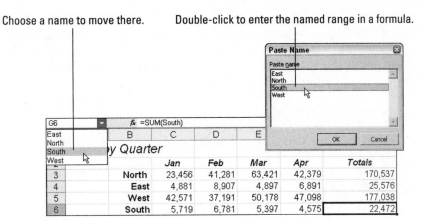

Figure 16-7:
Choosing a named cell range.

Cell range names must begin with a letter, backslash (\), or underscore (_). Select the cells for the range and do either of the following to name a cell range:

✦ Click in the Name Box (you'll find it to the left of the Formula bar), enter a name for the range, and press the Enter key.

✦ Choose Insert⇨Name⇨Define and, in the Define Name dialog box, enter a name and click OK.

To insert a range name in a formula, press F3 or choose Insert⇨Name⇨Paste to open the Paste Name dialog box (refer to Figure 16-7), and then double-click the range name.

Naming cell ranges has one disadvantage, and it's a big one: Excel doesn't adjust the cell references when you copy a formula with a range name from one cell to another. A range name always refers to the same set of cells. Later in this chapter, "Copying Formulas from Cell to Cell" explains how to copy formulas.

Referring to cells in different worksheets

Excel gives you the opportunity to use data from different worksheets in a formula. If one worksheet lists sales figures from January, and the next lists sales figures from February, you can construct a "grand total" formula on either worksheet to tabulate sales in the two-month period. A reference to a cell on a different worksheet is called a *3-D reference*.

Construct the formula as you normally would, but when you want to refer to a cell or cell range in a different worksheet, click a worksheet tab to move to the other worksheet and select the cell or range of cells there. Without returning to the original worksheet, complete your formula in the Formula bar and press Enter. Excel returns you to the original worksheet, where you can see the results of your formula.

Book IV
Chapter 16

Formulas and
Functions for
Crunching Numbers

The only things odd about constructing formulas across worksheets are the cell references. As a glance at the Formula bar tells you, cell addresses in cross-worksheet formulas list the sheet name and an exclamation point (!) as well as the cell address itself. For example, this formula in Worksheet 1 adds the number in cell A4 to the numbers in cells D5 and E5 in Worksheet 2:

```
=A4+Sheet2!D5+Sheet2!E5
```

This formula in Worksheet 2 multiplies the number in cell E18 with the number in cell C15 in Worksheet 1:

```
=E18*Sheet1!C15
```

This formula in Worksheet 2 finds the average of the numbers in the cell range C7:F7 in Worksheet 1:

```
=AVERAGE(Sheet1!C7:F7)
```

Copying Formulas from Cell to Cell

Often in worksheets, the same formula but with different cell references is used across a row or down a column. For example, take the worksheet shown in Figure 16-8. Column F of the worksheet totals the rainfall figures in rows 5 through 9. To enter formulas for totaling the rainfall figures in column F, you could laboriously enter formulas in cells F5, F6, F7, F8, and F9. But a faster way is to enter the formula once in cell F5 and then copy the formula in F5 down the column to cells F6, F7, F8, and F9.

F5	▼	ƒx =B5+C5+D5+E5			
	A	B	C	D	E	F
1						
2			Rainfall by County			
3						
4		Winter	Spring	Summer	Fall	Totals
5	Sonoma	13	8.3	2.3	8.2	31.8
6	Napa	11.5	7.6	3.1	7.5	
7	Mendocino	15.8	12.9	2.9	8.3	
8	San Francisco	10.9	9.7	1.1	3.3	
9	Contra Costa	10.1	8.4	2.3	4.4	+

Figure 16-8: Copying a formula.

Drag the AutoFill handle.

When you copy a formula to a new cell, Excel adjusts the cell references in the formula so that the formula works in the cells to which it has been copied. Astounding! Opportunities to copy formulas abound on most worksheets. And copying formulas is the fastest and safest way to enter formulas in a worksheet.

Follow these steps to copy a formula:

1. **Select the cell with the formula you want to copy.**

2. **Drag the AutoFill handle across the cells to which you'll copy the formula.**

This is the same AutoFill handle you drag to enter serial data (see the section in Book IV, Chapter 14 about entering lists and serial data with the AutoFill command). The AutoFill handle is the small black square in the lower-right corner of the cell. When you move the mouse pointer over it, it changes to a black cross. Figure 16-8 shows a formula being copied.

3. Release the mouse button.

Click in the cells to which you copied the formula and glance at the Formula bar to make sure that the formula was copied correctly.

You can also copy formulas with the Copy and Paste commands. Just make sure that cell references refer correctly to the surrounding cells.

Working with Functions

A *function* is a canned formula that comes with Excel. Excel offers hundreds of functions, some of which are very obscure and fit only for use by rocket scientists or securities analysts. Other functions are very practical. For example, you can use the SUM function to quickly total the numbers in a range of cells. ("Entering a cell range," earlier in this chapter, describes cell ranges.) Instead of entering =C2+C3+C4+C5 on the Formula bar, you can enter =SUM(C2:C5), which tells Excel to total the numbers in cell C2, C3, C4, and C5. To obtain the product of the number in cell G4 and .06, you can use the PRODUCT function and enter =PRODUCT(G4,.06) on the Formula bar. Table 16-2 lists the most common functions.

Table 16-2	Common Functions and Their Use
Function	*Returns*
AVERAGE(*number1,number2, . . .*)	The average of the numbers in the cells listed in the arguments.
COUNT(*value1,value2, . . .*)	The number of cells that contain the numbers listed in the arguments.
MAX(*number1,number2, . . .*)	The largest value in the cells listed in the arguments.
MIN(*number1,number2, . . .*)	The smallest value in the cells listed in the arguments.
PRODUCT(*number1,number2, . . .*)	The product of multiplying the cells listed in the arguments.
STDEV(*number1,number2, . . .*)	An estimate of standard deviation based on the sample cells listed in the argument.
STDEVP(*number1,number2, . . .*)	An estimate of standard deviation based on the entire sample cells listed in the arguments.
SUM(*number1,number2, . . .*)	The total of the numbers in the arguments.
VAR(*number1,number2, . . .*)	An estimate of the variance based on the sample cells listed in the arguments.
VARP(*number1,number2, . . .*)	A variance calculation based on all cells listed in the arguments.

Book IV
Chapter 16

Formulas and Functions for Crunching Numbers

A function takes one or more *arguments* — the cell references or numbers, enclosed in parentheses, that the function acts upon. For example, AVERAGE(B1:B4) returns the average of the numbers in the cell range B1 through B4; PRODUCT(6.5,C4) returns the product of multiplying the number 6.5 by the number in cell C4. When a function requires more than one argument, enter a comma between the arguments.

To get an idea of the numerous functions that Excel offers, click the Insert Function button or choose Insert⇨Function. You see the Insert Function dialog box, shown in Figure 16-9. Choose a function category in the dialog box, select a function name, and read the description. You can click the Help on This Function link to open the Help program and get a thorough description of the function and how it's used.

Choose a category.   Choose a function.

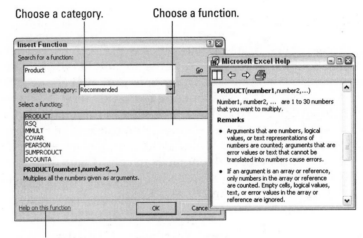

Figure 16-9:
The Insert Function dialog box.

Click to learn more.

Manually entering a function in a formula

If you know a function well, you can enter it yourself in the Formula bar along with the rest of the formula. Be sure to enclose the argument or arguments in parentheses. Don't enter a space between the function's name and the first parenthesis. And please, please, please be sure to start your formula by entering an equal sign (=). Without it, Excel thinks you're entering text.

You can enter function names in lowercase. Excel converts function names to uppercase after you click the Enter button or press Enter to complete the formula. Entering function names in lowercase is recommended because doing so gives you a chance to find out whether you entered a function name correctly. If Excel doesn't convert your function name to uppercase, you made a typing error.

To quickly total the numbers in cells, click the cell where you want the total to appear and then click the AutoSum button on the Standard toolbar. Marquee lights appear around the cells that Excel wants to add up. If these are the cells you want to add up, press Enter immediately. Otherwise, select the cells you want to add up and then press Enter. You can also enter the AVER-AGE, COUNT, MAX, or MIN function and their arguments this way. Click the arrow next to the AutoSum button and choose AVERAGE, COUNT, and so on from the drop-down list.

Getting Excel's help to enter a function

Besides entering a function the conventional way by typing it, you can do it by way of the Function Arguments dialog box, shown in Figure 16-10. The beauty of using this dialog box is that it warns you if you enter arguments incorrectly, and it spares you the trouble of typing the function name without making an error. What's more, the Function Arguments dialog box shows you the results of the formula so that you get an idea whether you're entering the formula correctly.

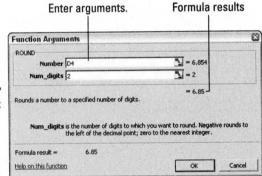

Figure 16-10: The Function Arguments dialog box.

Click the cell where you want to enter a formula, enter an equal sign (=) in the Formula bar, and do one of the following to bring up the Function Arguments dialog box:

✦ Open the Functions drop-down list (it appears on the left side of the Formula bar after you enter the equal sign) and choose a function.

 ✦ Click the Insert Function button or choose Insert⇨Function and, in the Insert Function dialog box (refer to Figure 16-9), find and double-click the name of the function you need for your formula.

 Enter arguments in the spaces provided by the Function Arguments dialog box. To enter cell references or ranges, you can click or select cells in the worksheet. If necessary, click the Go to Worksheet button (you'll find it to the right of an argument text box) to shrink the Function Arguments dialog box and get a better look at your worksheet. Click OK when you have finished fooling with the function.

Chapter 17: Making a Worksheet Easier to Read and Understand

In This Chapter

✔ Aligning numbers and text

✔ Changing the size of columns and rows

✔ Splashing color on a worksheet

✔ Drawing borders between cells and titles

✔ Making worksheets fit well on the page

✔ Printing your worksheet

This short but pithy chapter explains how to dress a worksheet in its Sunday best in case you want to print it and present it to others. It explains how to align numbers and text, as well as insert rows and columns and change the size of rows and columns. You find out how to decorate a worksheet with colors and borders. Finally, this chapter describes everything you need to know to print a worksheet, including how to make it fit on one page and repeat row labels and column names.

Laying Out a Worksheet

Especially if you intend to print your worksheet, you may as well dress it in its Sunday best. And you can do a number of things to make worksheets easier to read and understand. You can change character fonts. You can draw borders around or shade important cells. You can also format the numbers so that readers know, for example, whether they're staring at dollar figures or percentages. This part of the chapter is dedicated to the proposition that a worksheet doesn't have to look drab and solemn.

Aligning numbers and text in columns and rows

To start with, numbers in worksheets are right-aligned in cells, and text is left-aligned. Numbers and text sit squarely on the bottom of cells. You can, however, change the way that data is aligned. For example, you can make data float at the top of cells rather than rest at the bottom, and you can center or justify data in cells. Figure 17-1 illustrates different ways to format text and numbers.

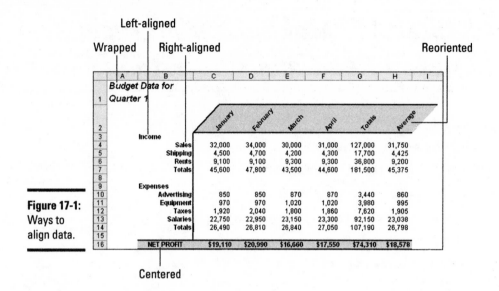

Figure 17-1:
Ways to
align data.

Select the cells whose alignment needs changing and follow these instructions to realign data in the cells:

 ✦ **Changing the horizontal (side-to-side) alignment:** Click an Align or Center button on the Formatting toolbar. You can also choose Format⇨ Cells and, on the Alignment tab of the Format Cells dialog box, choose an option on the Horizontal drop-down list.

 ✦ **Changing the vertical (top-to-bottom) alignment:** Choose Format⇨Cells and, on the Alignment tab of the Format Cells dialog box, choose an option on the Vertical drop-down list. The Distribution option makes all the letters or numbers fit in a cell, even if it means wrapping text to two or more lines.

 ✦ **Reorienting the cells:** Choose Format⇨Cells and, on the Alignment Tab of the Format Cells dialog box, drag the diamond in the Orientation box or enter a number in the Degrees text box.

Merging and centering text across several cells

In the illustration shown here, "Sales Totals by Regional Office" is centered across four cells. Normally, text is left-aligned, but if you want to center it across several cells, drag across the cells to select them and then click the Merge and Center button. Merging also permits you to create large cells that span several columns.

The only way to "unmerge" cells is to select the merged cells, choose Format⇨Cells, and deselect the Merge Cells check box on the Alignment tab of the Format Cells dialog box.

	C	D	E	F
	Sales Totals by Regional Office			
	North	West	East	South

Changing the orientation of text in cells is an elegant solution to the problem of keeping a worksheet from getting too wide. Numbers are usually a few characters wide, but heading labels can be much wider than that. By changing the orientation of a heading label, you make columns narrower and keep worksheets from growing too fat to fit on the page.

Inserting and deleting rows and columns

At some point, everybody has to insert new columns and rows and delete ones that are no longer needed. Make sure before you delete a row or column that you don't delete data that you really need. Do the following to insert and delete rows and columns:

✦ **Deleting rows or columns:** Drag across the row numbers or column letters of the rows or columns you want to delete; then right-click and choose Delete or press the Delete key.

✦ **Inserting rows:** Right-click the row number below where you want the new row to be and choose Insert. For example, to insert a new row above row 11, right-click row 11's number and choose Insert. You can also click in the row below where you want the new row to appear and choose Insert⇨Rows.

✦ **Inserting columns:** Right-click the column letter to the right of where you want the new column to be and choose Insert. You can also click in the worksheet and choose Insert⇨Columns. A fast way to insert several columns is to insert one and keep pressing F4 (the Repeat command) until you've inserted all of them.

After you insert rows or columns, the Paste Options button appears. Click it and choose an option from the drop-down list if you want your new row or column to have the same or different formats as the row or column you selected to start the Insert operation.

To insert more than one row or column at a time, select more than one row number or column letter before giving the Insert command.

Changing the width of columns and height of rows

By default, columns are 8.43 characters wide. To make columns wider, you have to widen them yourself. Rows are 12.75 points high, but Excel makes them higher when you enter letters or numbers that are taller than 12.75 points (72 points equals one inch).

Here are ways to change the height of rows:

✦ **One at a time:** Move the mouse pointer onto the boundary between row numbers and, when the pointer changes to a cross, drag the boundary between rows up or down. A pop-up box tells you how tall the row will be when you release the mouse button. You can also double-click the bottom of a cell border to make the row as tall as its tallest entry.

✦ **Several at a time:** Select the rows and choose Format⇨Row⇨Height. In the Row Height dialog box, enter a measurement and click OK.

Here are ways to make columns wider or narrower:

✦ **One at a time:** Move the mouse pointer onto the boundary between column letters and, when the pointer changes to a cross, drag the border between the columns. A pop-up box tells you what size the column is.

✦ **Several at a time:** Select the columns, choose Format⇨Column⇨Width and, in the Column Width dialog box, enter the number of characters you want to fit in the column. You can also select the columns and drag a column border. Doing so changes the size of all the columns you selected.

Rather than dicker with the width of columns, you can tell Excel to make columns as wide as their widest entries. This way, you can be certain that the data in each cell appears on-screen. To make columns as wide as their widest entries, select the columns and choose Format⇨Column⇨AutoFit Selection. You can also double-click the right border of the columns after you select them.

Decorating a Worksheet with Borders and Colors

The job of gridlines is simply to help you line up numbers and letters in cells. Gridlines aren't printed when you print a worksheet, and because gridlines are not printed, drawing borders on worksheets is absolutely necessary if you intend to print your worksheet. Use borders to steer the reader's eye to the most important parts of a worksheet — the totals, column labels, and heading labels. You can also decorate worksheets with colors. This part of the chapter explains how to put borders and colors on worksheets.

Decorating a worksheet requires clicking buttons on the Drawing toolbar. Click the Drawing button on the Standard toolbar to display the Drawing toolbar.

Choosing an autoformat

Rather than go to the trouble of decorating a worksheet with borders and colors, start by seeing whether one of Excel's autoformats does the trick. An *autoformat* (where do they get these ridiculous names?) is a prefabricated spreadsheet design. Excel offers no less than 19 different autoformats. Trying them on for size takes about a second.

To try on an autoformat, select the data in your worksheet and choose Format⇨AutoFormat. You see the AutoFormat dialog box, shown in Figure 17-2. Scroll through the autoformats and find one that tickles your fancy. Clicking the Options button in the dialog box provides you with a few extra options for tinkering with the worksheet design.

Decorating worksheets with colors

Select the cells that need color and try one of these techniques to splash color on your worksheet:

✦ Click the down arrow beside the Fill Color button and choose a color from the drop-down list. Choose No Fill to remove a color.

✦ Choose Format➪Cells and, on the Patterns tab of the Format Cells dialog box, select a color.

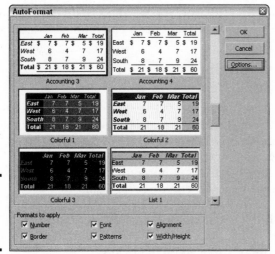

Figure 17-2:
The AutoFormat dialog box.

Slapping borders on worksheet cells

To draw borders on a worksheet, start by selecting the cells around which you want to place borders. Then click the down arrow beside the Borders button (you'll find it on the Formatting toolbar) and choose a border. Usually, you have to wrestle with the Borders buttons until you come up with borders you like. By the way, don't be afraid to click the Undo button and start all over, or select a new set of cells and press F4 to apply the same kind of border a second time.

As shown in Figure 17-3, the Border tab in the Format Cells dialog box offers different lines for borders and colors for borders as well. Choose Format➪ Cells and select the Border tab if you want to try your hand at applying borders by way of the dialog box.

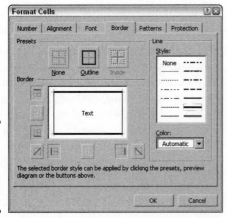

Figure 17-3:
The Borders tab of the Format Cells dialog box.

Printing a Worksheet

Printing a worksheet isn't simply a matter of giving the Print command. A worksheet is a vast piece of computerized sprawl. Most worksheets don't fit neatly on a single page. If you simply click the Print button to print your worksheet, you wind up with page breaks in unexpected places, both on the right side of the page and the bottom. Read on to discover how to print a worksheet so that the people you hand it to can read and understand it easily.

Making a worksheet fit on the page

Unless you tell it otherwise, Excel prints everything from cell A1 to the last cell with data in it in the southeast corner of the worksheet. Usually, it isn't necessary to print all those cells because some of them are blank. And printing an entire worksheet often means breaking the page up in all kinds of awkward places. To keep that from happening, here are some techniques for making a worksheet fit tidily on one or two pages.

 As you experiment with the techniques described here, click the Print Preview button (or Shift+click the Print button) from time to time to see what your worksheet will look like when it's printed.

Printing part of a worksheet

To print part of a worksheet, select the data you want to print and choose File⇨Print Area⇨Set Print Area. This command tells Excel to print only the cells you selected. On the worksheet, a dotted line appears around cells in the print area. To remove the dotted lines from your worksheet, choose File⇨Print Area⇨Clear Print Area.

Adjusting the page breaks

Reading a worksheet is extremely difficult when it's broken awkwardly across pages. To decide for yourself where page breaks occur, choose View⇨Page Break Preview. As shown in Figure 17-4, you switch to Page Break view. In this view, dashed lines show you where Excel wants to break the pages.

Here's everything a body needs to know about page breaks:

✦ **Changing break positions:** In Page Break view, drag a dashed line to adjust the position of a page break. After you drag a dashed line, it ceases being a default page break and becomes a manual page break. Manual page breaks are marked by solid lines, not dashed lines. You can drag them, too. Excel shrinks the numbers and letters on your worksheet if you try to squeeze too much data on a worksheet by dragging a page break.

✦ **Introducing a page break:** Select the cell directly below where you want the horizontal break to occur, and directly to the right of where you want the vertical break to be, and choose Insert⇨Page Break. Drag a page break to adjust its position.

✦ **Removing page breaks:** Select a cell directly below or directly to the right of the page break and choose Insert⇨Remove Page Break. To remove all the page breaks, click the Select All button (or press Ctrl+A) and choose Insert⇨Reset All Page Breaks.

Drag to change page breaks.

Default page break

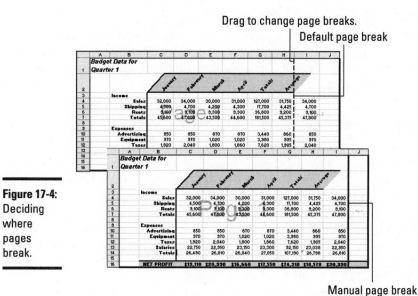

Figure 17-4: Deciding where pages break.

Manual page break

Choose View⇨Normal to return to Normal view after you're done fooling with page breaks. In Normal view, manual page breaks are marked by a dotted line. (If you don't care to see these dotted lines on your worksheet, choose Tools⇨Options, select the View tab in the Options dialog box, and deselect the Page Breaks check box.)

As the next section explains, you can use the Fit To option to scale data and make it small enough to fit on a page. However, the Fit To option and manual page breaks don't get along. Excel cancels manual page breaks if you select the Fit To option.

Scaling data to make it smaller

To scale the number and letters in the worksheet and make them a bit smaller, choose File⇨Page Setup. You see the Page Setup dialog box. On the Page tab, select the Fit To option button. Excel shrinks the data as much as necessary to make it fit on one page. The Fit To option is excellent for shrinking a worksheet that's just a little too big. Click the Print Preview button in the Page Setup dialog box to look at the Preview screen and see whether shrinking your worksheet this way is a help.

Printing a landscape worksheet

If your worksheet is too wide to fit on one page, try turning the page on its side and printing in landscape mode. Choose File⇨Page Setup and, on the Page tab of the page Setup dialog box, select the Landscape option button.

Adjusting the margins

Another way to stuff all the data onto one page is to narrow the margins. Use either of these techniques to adjust the size of the margins:

✦ Choose File⇨Page Setup and, on the Margins tab of the Page Setup dialog box, change the size of the margins.

✦ Click the Print Preview button (or choose File⇨Print Preview) to switch to the Print Preview window. From there, you can drag the margin lines to adjust the size of margins (margin lines are the outermost lines). If you don't see the margin lines, click the Margins button.

Making a worksheet more presentable

Before you print a worksheet, visit the Page Setup dialog box and see what you can do to make your worksheet easier for others to read and understand. To open the Page Setup dialog box, choose File⇨Page Setup or click the Setup button in the Print Preview window. Here are your options:

✦ **Including page numbers on worksheets:** On the Page tab of the Page Setup dialog box, enter **1** in the First Page Number text box. Then, on the Header/Footer tab, choose a Header or Footer option that includes a page number (for example, Page 1 of ?).

✦ **Putting headers and footers on pages:** On the Header/Footer tab of the Page Setup dialog box, choose options from the Header and Footer drop-down lists. You'll find options for listing the file name, page numbers, the date, and your name. By clicking the Custom Header or Custom Footer button, you can open the Header or Footer dialog box and construct a header or footer there. Figure 17-5 shows the Header dialog box.

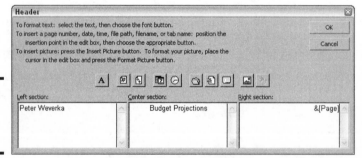

Figure 17-5: Constructing a fancy header.

✦ **Centering worksheet data on the page:** On the Margins tab, choose Horizontally or Vertically to center the worksheet relative to the top or bottom or sides of the page. You can select both check boxes. The preview screen shows what your choices mean in real terms.

✦ **Printing gridlines, column letters, and row numbers:** By default, the gridlines, column letters, and row numbers you know and love in a worksheet aren't printed, but you can print them by selecting the Gridlines and Row and Column Headings check boxes in the Sheet tab of the Page Setup dialog box.

Repeating row labels and column names on each page

If your worksheet is a big one that stretches beyond one page, you owe it to the people who will view your worksheet to repeat row labels and column names from page to page. Without the row labels and column names, no one can tell what the data in the worksheet means. Follow these steps to repeat row labels and column headings from page to page:

1. **Choose File⇨Page Setup.**

You see the Page Setup dialog box.

2. **Select the Sheet tab.**

3. **Select the Row and Column Headings check box.**

4. **To repeat rows, click the Return to Worksheet button next to the Rows to Repeat at Top text box; to repeat columns, click the Return to Worksheet button next to the Columns to Repeat at Left text box.**

The dialog box shrinks so that you can get a better look at your worksheet.

5. **Select the row or column with the labels or names you need.**

You can select more than one row or column, as long as they're next to each other.

6. **Click the Return to Dialog Box button to enlarge the dialog box and see it again.**

The text box now lists a cell range address.

7. **Repeat Steps 4 through 6 to select column names or row labels.**

8. **Click OK to close the Page Setup dialog box.**

Click the Print Preview button to make sure that row labels and column names are indeed repeating from page to page.

To remove row labels and column names, return to the Sheet tab of the Page Setup dialog box and delete the cell references in the Rows to Repeat at Top text box and the Columns to Repeat at Left text box. You can also press Ctrl+F3 and delete Print_Titles in the Define Name dialog box.

**Book IV
Chapter 17**

Making a Worksheet
Easier to Read and
Understand

765

Chapter 18: Seeing Data in Charts

In This Chapter

⮑ **Creating charts with the Chart Wizard**

⮑ **Changing chart types and chart elements**

⮑ **Customizing a chart's appearance**

One of the fastest ways to impress impressionable people is to create a chart from worksheet data. Excel makes it very, very easy to create charts. All you have to do to create a chart is select data and choose a few menu commands. And if you're fickle and don't like the chart you created, you can simply choose another type of chart. And if you're in the mood to do something out of the ordinary with a chart, you can do that, too.

This chapter explains how to create a chart and customize it in various ways to make the chart your very own.

Building Charts from Your Data

Herewith is an explanation of creating a chart. Believe me, creating a chart is easier than you think. All you have to do is paint by numbers. You will also find an explanation here for positioning a chart on the page.

Creating a chart with the Chart Wizard

Figure 18-1 shows an "Elvis Sightings" worksheet and a column chart created from data in the worksheet. You can create charts like these with the Chart Wizard. As you fill in the dialog boxes, you watch your chart take shape. You can always go back to the Chart Wizard dialog boxes and edit your chart, as the rest of this chapter explains in excruciating detail.

Follow these steps to create a chart:

1. Select the data that you want to chart.

Don't select a totals column or row for your chart. The purpose of a chart is to compare and contrast data. Including a totals column or row creates an unrealistic comparison because the totals data is inevitably much, much larger than the other data and you end up with an extra-large pie slice or bar, for example, in your chart.

2. Click the Chart Wizard button or choose Insert⇨Chart.

You see the first of four Chart Wizard dialog boxes, as shown in Figure 18-2.

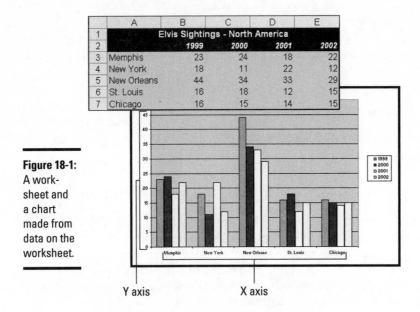

Figure 18-1: A worksheet and a chart made from data on the worksheet.

Y axis   X axis

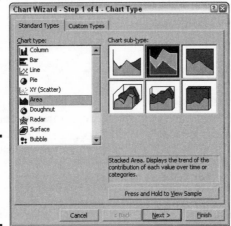

Figure 18-2: The first Chart Wizard dialog box.

3. Clicking the Next button as you go along, construct your chart.

And don't worry about getting it right the first time. Charts usually need a bit of tinkering before they can be made into masterpieces.

You encounter four dialog boxes in your journey to a perfect chart: Chart Type, Chart Source Data, Chart Options, and Chart Location. Keep reading.

The Chart Type dialog box

Choose a chart type. You can click the Press and Hold to View Sample button to see what the data you selected looks like in the chart type you chose. Be sure to scroll to the bottom of the list to look at all the chart types. The Custom Types tab offers some interesting choices.

The Chart Source Data dialog box

From here, you can select source data from your chart, but you already did that in Step 1 if you followed my directions. Choose a Series In option to change the data series on which the chart is plotted. Keep your eye on the sample chart — it shows what your choices mean in real terms.

If you choose the wrong cell range for a data source or you want to choose a different cell range, follow these steps:

1. **Select the Series tab in the Chart Wizard dialog box.**
2. **In the Series box, select the data series that needs replotting.**
3. **Select the Go to Worksheet option button next to the Values text box.**

   The dialog box shrinks so that you can see your worksheet.
4. **Drag to select a different data series in your worksheet.**
5. **Press Esc to return to the Chart Wizard dialog box.**

The Chart Options dialog box

This is where you decide what your chart looks like. There are six tabs in this dialog box:

✦ **Titles:** Enter a title for your chart in the Chart Title text box. If need be, enter descriptive labels for the data being plotted in the Category (X) and Axis, Value (Y) Axis text boxes (pie and doughnut charts don't have axes). However, axes descriptions aren't absolutely necessary. Sometimes including them crowds the chart and makes it smaller. Again, keep your eye on the sample chart to see what your choices mean in real terms.

✦ **Axes:** This is where you tell Excel how to scale the chart. In most cases, Excel recognizes whether it's dealing with category labels or time values, but if the program gets it wrong, select the correct option button.

✦ **Gridlines:** Select check boxes to decide how many vertical and horizontal gridlines you want.

✦ **Legend:** Select an option button to decide where on the chart to place the legend, if the chart needs a legend. The *legend* is the explanatory list of the symbols on the chart.

✦ **Data Labels:** If you so desire, select a check box to attach a data label to one of the data markers in the chart. Keep your eye on the Preview chart. It shows plainly what your choices are. If you choose a data label, choose one, not two or three. Two or three data labels per chart element can congest a chart and make it hard to understand, but if you have to choose two or three, open the Separator drop-down list and choose a punctuation mark for separating the labels.

✦ **Data Table:** Select the Show Data Table option if you want a replica of your Excel worksheet to appear on the page with the chart.

If you make a decision on the Chart Options dialog box that you regret later on, you can return to the Options tab by choosing Chart⊏⊃Chart Options.

The Chart Location dialog box

Choose where to place the new chart, on the worksheet where the data is or on another worksheet in the workbook.

Later in this chapter, "Editing a Chart" explains how to alter different parts of a chart, but if you want to start all over again, you can always do so by revisiting the Chart Wizard dialog boxes. Just select your chart and click the Chart Wizard button.

Adjusting a chart's position on the page

If you opted to place the chart on the same worksheet as the data from which you created the chart, your chart probably needs to be moved down the page. Click the perimeter of the chart to select it and then drag to move the chart elsewhere. While you're at it, select the chart and use one of these techniques to change the chart's size:

✦ Drag a corner handle to make it larger or smaller but keep its proportions.

✦ Drag a corner handle while holding down the Ctrl key to keep the center of the chart in the same position as you change its size.

By default, Excel creates a two-dimensional column chart. If you prefer a different kind of chart to be the default chart, create the kind of chart you like, select it, choose Chart⊏⊃Chart Type, and click the Set As Default Chart button in the Chart Type dialog box.

Editing a Chart

Most charts need to be retooled, kneaded, massaged, and prodded a few times before they are just-so. These pages explain the specifics of editing a chart.

The Chart toolbar appears on-screen after you create a chart (click your chart if you don't see the toolbar, or right-click any toolbar and choose Chart). As the following pages explain, the Chart toolbar comes in handy for fiddling with a chart's appearance.

Choosing a different chart type

So you chose the wrong chart type? It happens in the best of families. To undo the damage, click to select your chart and do one of the following:

✦ Click the arrow beside the Chart Type button and choose a new type from the drop-down list.

✦ Click the Chart Wizard button or choose Insert➪Chart to open the Chart Wizard dialog box (refer to Figure 18-2). On the Standard Types or Custom Types tab, choose a new chart type and click the Finish button.

To select a chart, click its outermost border. If you click inside the chart, you're liable to select a part of the chart — the legend, a data series — rather than the chart itself. You know when you have selected a chart because the black selection handles appear on the chart's corners and sides.

Adding and removing chart elements

Suppose that you construct a chart with the Chart Wizard but discover to your dismay that you forgot to include a title or legend? Suppose that you include a title or legend but regret doing so? Don't despair. With Excel, you always get a second chance. Click to select your chart and follow these steps to add or remove a title, legend, or other element:

1. Click the Chart Wizard button.

You see the Chart Wizard dialog box. Does it look familiar? This is the same dialog box you used to create the chart in the first place.

2. Revisit the different tabs in the Chart Wizard dialog box, and be careful this time to include or exclude chart elements.

3. Click the Finish button.

Earlier in this chapter, "Creating a chart with the Chart Wizard" explains the Chart Wizard.

You can click the Legend button on the Chart toolbar to add or remove the chart's *legend,* the box with explanations as to what everything on the chart is.

If you're in a hurry to remove an element from a chart, simply select it and press the Delete key. If you know which part of a chart you want to alter, select it and choose Chart➪Chart Options. This command opens the third of the four Chart Wizard dialog boxes, the one that pertains to the chart's appearance.

The basics of changing a chart's appearance

A chart is composed of different so-called objects — the legend, the plot area, the different data series, and others. To see for yourself, try clicking part of the chart. Black selection handles appear around the object, or part of the chart, that you clicked. As shown in Figure 18-3, you can open the Chart Objects drop-down list on the Chart toolbar to see a list of all the objects in your chart.

**Book IV
Chapter 18**

Seeing Data in Charts

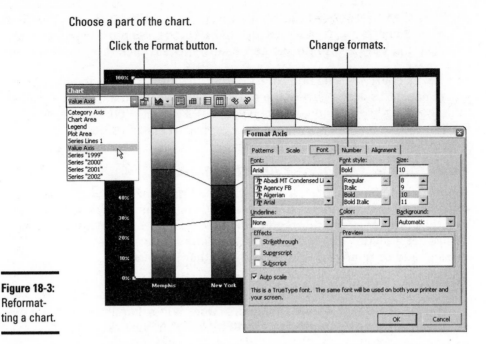

Choose a part of the chart.

Click the Format button.

Change formats.

Figure 18-3:
Reformatting a chart.

To change the size, shape, fonts, or colors of any part of a chart, follow these basic steps:

***1.* Select the part of the chart you want to change by clicking it or by choosing its name on the Chart Objects drop-down list.**

You find this drop-down list on the Charts toolbar.

***2.* Open the Format dialog box (refer to Figure 18-3) to start giving Format commands.**

Excel offers no fewer than five ways to open the Format dialog box:

- Click the Format button on the Chart toolbar.

- Double-click the part of the chart you selected.

- Right-click the part of the chart you selected and choose Format on the shortcut menu.

- Press Ctrl+1.

- Choose Format⇨Selected *object name.*

***3.* Change formats in the Format dialog box.**

Again, which options you get in the dialog box depends on which part of your chart you selected in Step 1. You can find options in the Format dialog box to change the font, color, border, background, and alignment of text.

Choose Edit⇨Undo (or press Ctrl+Z) and start all over if your changes to the chart didn't work out. Usually, you have to wrestle with Format dialog boxes for five minutes or so before the chart starts smelling like a rose.

Seeing as how all parts of a chart are objects, you can select and drag them to new locations. When you see the black selection handles, start dragging. A dotted line shows where the object will land when you release the mouse button.

You can click the By Row or By Column button on the Chart toolbar at any time to experiment with changing the data axes of the chart.

To make one slice in a pie chart stand out from the rest, click to select it, and then drag. Be sure to select a single slice and not the whole pie.

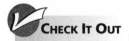

CHECK IT OUT

Decorating a Chart with a Picture

A picture looks mighty nice on the plot area of a chart, especially a column chart. If you have a picture on your computer that would serve well to decorate a chart, you are hereby encouraged to start decorating. Follow these steps to place a picture on the plot area of a chart:

1. Either select the plot area or choose Plot Area on the Chart Objects drop-down list.

2. Click the Format Plot Area button or double-click the plot area.

   You see the Format Plot Area dialog box.

3. Click the Fill Effects button to open the Fill Effects dialog box.

4. Select the Picture tab.

5. Click the Select Picture button to open the Select Picture dialog box.

6. Locate the picture you need, select it, and click the Insert button.

   Try to select a light-colored picture that will serve as a background.

7. Click OK in the Fill Effects dialog box and click OK again in the Format Plot Area dialog box.

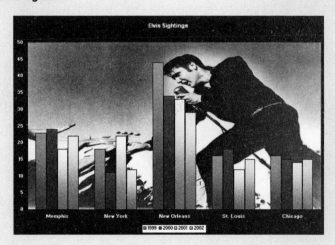

**Book IV
Chapter 18**

Seeing Data in Charts

773

Chapter 19: Introducing Money

In This Chapter

- ✓ Understanding how Money tracks your finances
- ✓ Getting the program started
- ✓ Getting acquainted with the Money windows
- ✓ Deciding what goes on the Home Page

*I*n this chapter, you discover the various ways that Money 2004 can help you stay on top of your finances. You also discover how to start the program, find your way around the Money windows, and choose for yourself what appears on the Home Page, the first page you see when you start Money.

Finding Out How Money Tracks Your Finances

All the personal finance advisors agree that keeping good, accurate records is the first step toward financial security. Before you can start saving for a down payment on a house, you have to know how much you are capable of saving. Before you can tell whether your investments are doing well, you have to track them carefully. If you want to make sound financial decisions, you need to know what your spending habits are and how much income you really have.

Microsoft Money 2004 makes keeping accurate financial records very, very easy. After you use the program for a while, you will know precisely what your account balances are, what your net worth is, and how much your investments — if you have investments — are worth. To find out precisely how much you spend in different areas, all you have to do is generate a chart like the one in Figure 19-1. At tax time, you can run a report that lists and totals all your tax-deductible expenses. With Money, you can print checks, do your banking over the Internet, find out exactly what your spending habits are, compare loans and mortgages, plan for retirement, and track and analyze different kinds of investments. Money 2004, in fact, offers many more techniques for handling and analyzing investments than did its predecessors.

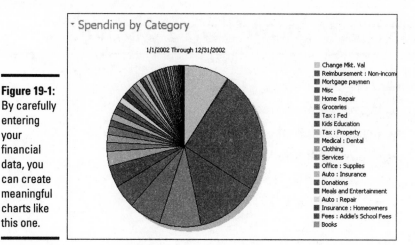

1/1/2002 Through 12/31/2002

- Change Mkt. Val
- Reimbursement : Non-income
- Mortgage paymen
- Misc
- Home Repair
- Groceries
- Tax : Fed
- Kids Education
- Tax : Property
- Medical : Dental
- Clothing
- Services
- Office : Supplies
- Auto : Insurance
- Donations
- Meals and Entertainment
- Auto : Repair
- Insurance : Homeowners
- Fees : Addie's School Fees
- Books

Figure 19-1: By carefully entering your financial data, you can create meaningful charts like this one.

Starting the Program

Starting Money is as easy as falling off a log. You can start the program from the menus or by means of the Microsoft Money shortcut icon on the desktop:

✦ **From the menus:** Click the Start button, choose All Programs, and choose Microsoft Money 2004.

✦ **Microsoft Money shortcut icon:** Double-click the Microsoft Money 2004 shortcut icon on the desktop.

Microsoft Money 2004

When you installed Money, the installation program should have put a Money shortcut icon on the desktop, but if it didn't, you can still create a shortcut icon for starting Money. To do so, follow the standard Windows procedure for creating shortcut icons:

1. **Click the Start button and choose All Programs.**

2. **Locate the Microsoft Money 2004 menu command and right-click it.**

   A shortcut menu appears.

3. **Choose Send To⇨Desktop (Create Shortcut).**

   The shortcut icon appears on the Windows desktop.

A Fast Trip around the Money Windows

When arriving in a foreign city, the first thing most people do, after finding a hotel room and taking a shower, is to go for a stroll. In the following pages, you can stroll very gingerly across the Money screens. Enjoy yourself and take your sweet time. And don't forget to put film in the camera before leaving the hotel.

The Home Page

When you start Money, the first thing you see is the *Home Page,* shown in Figure 19-2. The Home Page is the starting point for all your excursions in

Money. Don't worry — the Home Page is not as complicated as it looks. It offers a peek at different aspects of your finances, buttons that you can click to go to different Money windows, and links to sites on the Internet. If you roll the mouse carefully just about anywhere on the Home page, you find *hyperlinks* — links that you can click to visit a new Money window. Sometimes a little butterfly appears beside the mouse pointer when you move it over a button or hyperlink. That butterfly means that clicking the button or link takes you to a Web site on the Internet.

Notice the Home button in the upper-left corner of the screen. No matter how far you stray from the Home Page, you can always click the Home button (or press Alt+Home) to return to it. The button is always there. Click it if you get homesick.

You can decide for yourself what appears on the Home Page. Later in this chapter, "Personalizing the Home Page" explains how to put what matters most to you on the Home Page.

Going from window to window: The Navigation bar and Navigation buttons

Besides clicking the Home button to return to the Home Page, you can also go from window to window by clicking buttons on the Navigation bar, by making a selection in the Choose a Task drop-down list, or by clicking the Back or Forward button. The Navigation bar and Navigation buttons, as with the Home button, are always available and ready to be clicked. The Choose a Task drop-down list is found on the Home Page.

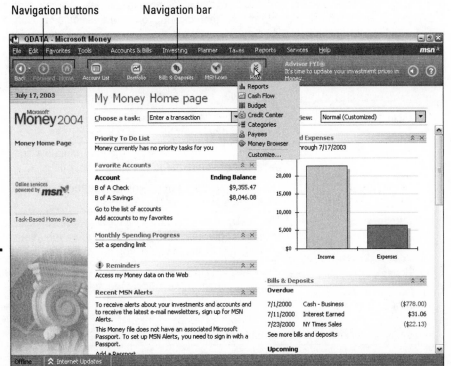

Figure 19-2: The Home Page is the starting point for all activity in Money.

Book IV Chapter 19

Introducing Money

The Navigation bar

Account List is the leftmost button on the Navigation bar; the More button is the rightmost button. By clicking a button, you can visit other windows in Money. By clicking the More button, you make more button choices available on the Navigation bar (refer to Figure 19-2).

Table 19-1 explains where the buttons on the Navigation bar take you. The table is here to show you what happens when you click a button and to give you a glimpse of the different tasks you can do with Money. Try clicking a button to start your own adventures in Money.

Table 19-1	Navigation Bar Buttons and Where They Take You
Clicking This Button	*Takes You To . . .*
Account List	The Bank Accounts window, which lists the name of each account you set up. You can click an account name to go to its account register. Open the Bank Account window when you want to set up an account, enter account transactions, balance an account, or bank online.
Portfolio	The Portfolio window, where you can track stocks, bonds, mutual funds, and other investment holdings. Start here when you want to download security prices from the Internet.
Bills & Deposits	The Bills & Deposits window, where you can record the bills you pay regularly and enlist the Money program's help in paying those bills on time. You can also record automatic deposits in this window.
MSN.com	MSN.com, a Web portal operated by the Microsoft Corporation, where you can get the latest news, search the Internet, or read articles. You can also personalize this Web page and get financial information that pertains to securities you own. Notice that the Web page appears in the Money window, not in your Web browser window. Click the Money button (you will find it next to the Forward navigation button) to return to Money.
Reports	The Reports window, where you can generate reports and charts that show right away where you stand financially.
Cash Flow	The Cash Flow window, where you can forecast what your future income and account balances will be.
Budget	The Budget window, where you can formulate a budget and find out whether you're meeting your budget goals.
Credit Center	The Credit window, where you can generate a credit report and formulate a plan to get out of debt.
Categories	The Set Up Your Categories window, where you create and manage categories, as well as list information about the businesses and people to whom you make payments.
Payees	The Payees window, where you can track the people and businesses to whom you made payments.
Money Browser	The MSN Web portal, where you can check your e-mail (if you have a Hotmail account), read the latest news, or investigate investment opportunities.

Navigation buttons: Back and Forward

The Back and Forward buttons work exactly like the Back and Forward buttons in a Web browser such as Netscape Navigator or Internet Explorer. Click the Back button to return to a window you previously visited; click the Forward button to revisit a window you retreated from.

Next to both the Back and Forward buttons is a little downward-pointing arrow. Click the little arrow and you see a shortcut menu that lists the windows you visited. Click the little arrows beside the Back and Forward buttons early and often. Clicking the arrows and choosing window names is the fastest way to get from place to place in Money.

Personalizing the Home Page

When you start Money 2004, you see the Home Page (refer to Figure 19-2). The Home Page is supposed to give you a quick look at your finances, and if you play your cards right, it can do that. As shown in Figure 19-3, you can change views on the Home Page and peek into a different aspect of your finances by choosing an option from the Choose a View drop-down list. You can, for example, see which bills are due, check account balances, and find out roughly how much in taxes you owe.

Your finances, however, are yours and yours alone, so sooner or later — when you get better acquainted with Money — you need to strip the Home Page of all the stuff that Money has put on it and decide for yourself what goes there.

Choose a view to customize. Change views.

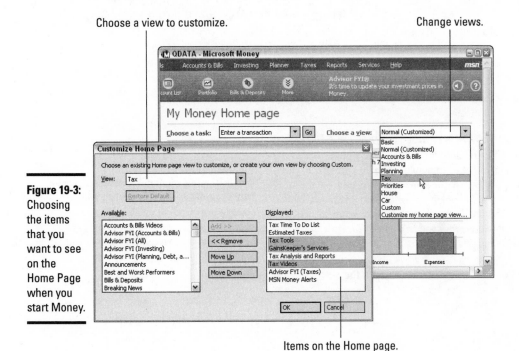

Figure 19-3: Choosing the items that you want to see on the Home Page when you start Money.

Items on the Home page.

To personalize your Home Page, start by following these steps:

1. **Open the Customize Home Page dialog box, shown in Figure 19-3.**

Do one of the following to open this dialog box:

- Open the Choose a View drop-down list and choose the last option, Customize My Home Page View.

- Choose Tools⇨Options, select the Feedback tab in the Options dialog box, and click the Customize button under Home Page Customization.

2. **Choose which view you want to customize from the View drop-down list.**

Do the view names look familiar? They are the same views you can choose from on the Choose a View list on the Home Page (refer to Figure 19-3). Choose Custom if you want to create a Home Page from scratch.

3. **To select which items will be on view, select them one at a time in the Available box and click the Add button.**

4. **To remove an item, select it and click the Remove button.**

5. **To decide the order in which items appear on the Home Page, click the Move Up or Move Down button.**

6. **Click OK when your customized Home Page is just right.**

The fastest way to remove an item from the Home Page is to click the X on the bar to the right of its name. Do that right away to all the advertisements for credit cards and stock-trading companies on the Home Page. Who needs another advertisement? To get rid of all the advertisements on Money screens, choose Tools⇨Options, click the General tab in the Options dialog box, and select the Turn Off Sponsorships and Shopping Links check box.

CHECK IT OUT

Choosing Which Window Appears at Startup

Suppose that you don't care to see the Home Page when you start Money. Maybe you prefer another window, an account register, or the window you were looking at when you closed the program last time around. Follow these steps to choose which window you see when you start the program:

1. Choose Tools⇨Options to open the Options dialog box.

2. Click the General tab.

3. Under Display, open the Start Money with This Page Open drop-down list and choose the window you would like to see. The Last Place Used option opens Money to whichever window was showing when you last closed the program.

4. Click OK.

Chapter 20: Setting Up Your Accounts

In This Chapter

✔ Understanding how accounts and registers record financial activity

✔ Setting up a checking and savings account

✔ Setting up a credit card account

*B*ook IV, Chapter 19 gets you going with Money. In this chapter, you get down to the nitty-gritty and find out how to set up accounts so that you can track financial activity. In this chapter, you discover how to set up savings, checking, and credit card accounts. You also find out about Money files, how to put an account on the Favorites menu, and how to change account names and account types.

Accounts and Registers for Recording Financial Transactions

The first step in tracking your financial activity is to set up an account for each type of item you want to track — a checking account, a savings account, or an IRA, for example. When most people hear the word *account,* they think of savings accounts, checking accounts, and other kinds of bank accounts. However, accounts in Money are a little more than that. For example, you can create a home account for tracking the value of a house. You can also create a credit card account for tracking credit card charges.

When you set up an account, you need to name the kind of account you want. Money offers 17 kinds of accounts. Table 20-1 describes the different kinds of Money accounts and mentions where you can turn to read more about them.

Table 20-1	Microsoft Money's 17 Kinds of Accounts
Account	*What the Account Is For*
Asset	Tracking the value of items that you own — real estate, a truck, a baseball card collection. Asset accounts can be useful for finding out your net worth.
Bank	Recording transactions made to a bank account but not a savings account, checking account, or line of credit.
Car or Other Vehicle	Recording the equity and market value of a car, boat, or other item for which you have taken out a loan.
Cash	Recording cash payments and tracking petty cash accounts.

(continued)

Table 20-1 *(continued)*

Account	What the Account Is For
Checking	Recording activity in a checking account.
Credit Card	Recording credit card purchases, finance charges, and credit card payments.
Employee Stock Option	Tracking stock options you receive from the company you work for.
Home	Tracking how much equity is in a house and determining a house's market value.
Home Equity Line of Credit	Tracking payments and the interest portion of payments on a home equity loan.
Investment	Tracking the value of something you own and intend to sell later for a profit — stocks, bonds, securities, annuities, treasury bills, precious metals, real estate investment trusts (REITs), and unit trusts.
Liability	Tracking debts for which you don't have to pay interest — income taxes that you owe and private loans, for example.
Line of Credit	Recording payments made with a *debit card* — a charge card that debits, or deducts money from, a bank account.
Loan	Tracking debts for which you have to pay interest, such as car loans.
Mortgage	Tracking mortgage payments.
Other	Recording transactions that — you guessed it — don't fit neatly in the other 16 categories.
Retirement	Tracking tax-deferred retirement plans, such as 401(k)s, Keoghs, SEPs (Simplified Employee Pensions), and IRAs.
Savings	Recording activity in a savings account.

Each time you set up an account, Money creates a new register for recording transactions. As all bookkeepers know, a *register* is a place for recording income and expenses, withdrawals, deposits, payments, and the like. Figure 20-1 shows a checking account register for recording checks, deposits, and withdrawals in a checking account.

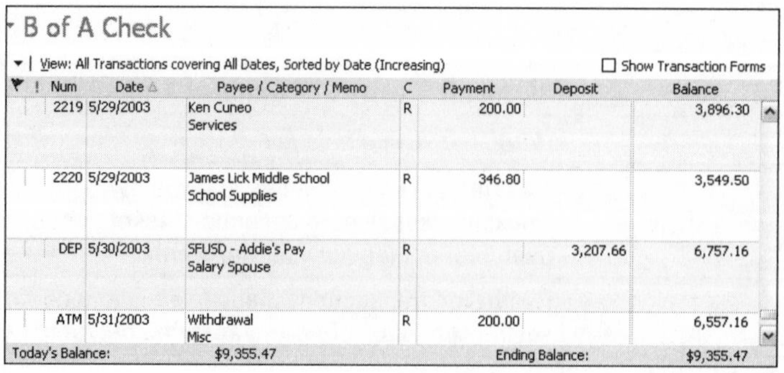

Figure 20-1:
A checking account register.

Registers look different, depending on the type of account you have set up, but all registers have places for recording transaction dates and transaction amounts. Registers also show balances. The *balance* is the amount of money in the account, or, in the case of an asset, liability, or investment account, the value of the thing that you're tracking.

The Basics: Setting Up Checking and Savings Accounts

After you see the big picture and know what an account and a register are, you can create an account. In the next sections, you find out how to set up a checking account, savings account, and credit card account.

Setting up a checking or savings account

Everybody, or just about everybody, has at least one checking and one savings account. Set up an account in Money for each checking and savings account you keep with a bank. Be sure to get out the paperwork before you set up the checking or savings account. You need to know the account number and a few other details.

Follow these steps to set up the account:

1. Choose Accounts & Bills⇨Account Setup.

You land in the Set Up Your Accounts window. This window is the starting point for managing accounts you have set up in Money.

2. Click the Add a New Account hyperlink, the first one listed under "What do you want to do?"

You see the first of several New Account dialog boxes, like the one shown in Figure 20-2. Each dialog box asks a nosy question about your account.

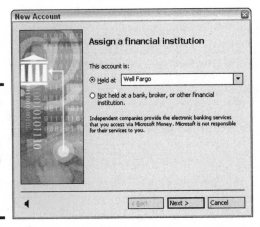

Figure 20-2: To set up a new account, fill out a bunch of dialog boxes like this one.

3. In the Held At text box, type the name of the bank or financial institution in which you keep the account; then click the Next button.

If you have another account with the bank and have set up an account in Money for tracking it, you can enter the bank's name by clicking the down arrow and selecting a bank name from the drop-down list.

4. **In the next dialog box, choose the name of a financial institution.**

   Money needs the name of a bank, credit card company, brokerage house, or other financial institution in case you want to bank online. Information about the institution you choose will be stored in Money in case you want to bank over the Internet.

5. **In the next dialog box, select the type of account you want to create —** **Checking or Savings — and then click the Next button.**

   Table 20-1 explains what the account types are. You can also read their descriptions in the dialog box.

6. **Type a descriptive name for the account and then click the Next** **button.**

   The name you type appears in the Accounts window. Type a descriptive name so that you can distinguish this account from the others you set up in Money.

7. **In the next dialog box, type the account number and click the Next** **button.**

   The dialog box you see next asks for the balance (how much money is in the account).

8. **Enter a figure for the account balance, choose a currency if need be,** **and click the Next button.**

   Knowing the balance isn't as important as you may think — you can change the starting balance after you set up the account by changing the first entry in the account register.

   More power to you if you know the starting balance and you have diligently kept records so that you can enter past transactions and bring the account up-to-date. If you don't know the opening balance, either enter the balance from your last bank statement or make an estimate. Book IV, Chapter 21 explains the ins and outs of starting balances.

9. **Select either I Have No Other Accounts at This Institution or I Have** **Other Accounts at This Institution and click the Next button.**

   This dialog box wants to know whether you keep other accounts at the same bank where you keep this account.

   Clicking I Have No Other Accounts at This Institution takes you to the Finish dialog box.

   Clicking I Have Other Accounts at This Institution takes you to the dialog box for selecting an account type. Follow Steps 5 through 9 again to give Money the lowdown on the next account.

10. **Click the Finish button.**

    At the end of the ordeal, you return to the Set Up Your Accounts window.

Listing contact names, phone numbers, and other account details

Before you put away the paperwork and say good-bye to an account you set up, take a moment to acquaint Money with the details. As Figure 20-3 shows, the program has a special Update Details window for entering a bank's telephone number, an account's minimum balance, and anything else you care to enter.

Enter information about the account.

Figure 20-3:
Keep information about accounts on the Update Details window, where you can get it in a hurry.

The Update Details window is a handy place to store bank telephone numbers and other information. If you lose your passbook, ATM card, or credit card and need to call the bank, for example, you can get the number from the Update Details window. The window also has a check box for making an account appear on the Favorites menu.

Follow these steps to get to the Update Details window and enter the pertinent information or view information about an account you already set up:

1. **Click the Account List button on the Navigation bar to go to the Accounts window.**

   You can also get there by choosing Accounts & Bills⇨Account List.

2. **Click the name of the account whose details you want to enter or see.**

   You go to the account register where activity in the account is recorded.

3. **Click the Change Account Details hyperlink.**

   You can find it on the left side of the window, under "Common Tasks."

   The fastest way to get to the Update Details window is to right-click an account name in the Accounts window and choose See Account Details from the shortcut menu.

4. **Enter or view information about your account in the window.**

5. **Click the Done button if you entered information in the Update Details window.**

Where is the Done button? It's at the bottom of the window. You have to scroll to get there. After you click the Done button, you return to the account register.

Setting Up an Account to Track Credit Card and Line of Credit Transactions

Except for filling out an extra dialog box or two, setting up a credit card or line of credit account works the same way as setting up a checking or savings account. Set up a credit card or line of credit account for each credit card and each line of credit you have. When you set up the account, Money asks how much you owe and whether you want a reminder when the credit card bill or line of credit bill is due.

Get out your last credit card or line of credit statement and follow these steps to set up a credit card or line of credit account:

1. **Place a finger of your right hand on this page and, with your left hand, turn back several pages to "Setting up a checking or savings account."**

2. **Follow Steps 1 through 7 (but not Step 5) of the instructions for setting up a checking or savings account.**

In other words, go to the Set Up Accounts window, click the Add a New Account hyperlink, enter the name of the bank or credit card issuer, select Credit Card or Line of Credit as the account type, enter a descriptive name for the account, and enter the account number.

Those steps bring you to the dialog box shown in Figure 20-4, where Money asks how much you owe. If you resemble the average citizen, you owe the bank or credit card issuer some money. Enter the amount you owe now.

Figure 20-4: In this dialog box, tell Money how much you owe the bank or credit card issuer.

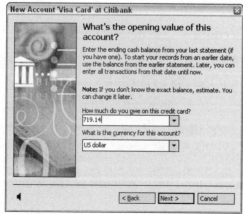

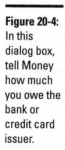

3. Type 0 if the credit card or line of credit is paid in full; otherwise, type how much your last statement says that you owe, and then click the Next button.

4. Select the Credit Card or Charge Card option and click the Next button.

This dialog box asks whether your account will track a credit card or charge card. As the dialog box explains, charge cards have to be paid in full each month, but you can carry debt from month to month with a credit card.

Select the Credit Card option if the account tracks credit card spending or a line of credit. Otherwise, select Charge Card. If yours is a credit card that you don't need to pay in full but you intend to pay off each month, select the Always Pay Entire Balance Each Month check box.

What happens next depends on whether the account tracks a credit card or charge card.

If the account tracks a charge card, skip ahead to Step 6.

If the account tracks a credit card or line of credit, the dialog box that appears asks you to list the interest rate you get charged for carrying debt, as Figure 20-5 shows.

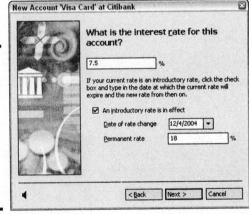

Figure 20-5:
In this dialog box, list the interest rate you get charged for carrying debt on a credit card.

5. Tell Money what rate of interest you are charged for using the credit card, and then click the Next button.

List the interest rate in the first % text box. If the rate is a temporary, introductory rate, select the An Introductory Rate Is in Effect check box and enter the permanent rate and the date that the temporary rate expires. Money needs this information for the Debt Reduction Planner and other features designed to help you manage debt.

6. In the dialog box that follows, type the maximum amount that you can charge on your credit or charge card; then click the Next button.

Your credit card statement lists the most you can borrow on your credit card. Get the figure from your statement.

Book IV
Chapter 20

Setting Up Your
Accounts

7. **Make sure that the first option button, No, Don't AutoBalance This Account, is selected, and then click the Next button.**

This dialog box is kind of misleading. It seems to say that if you pay your credit card bill in full each month, you should select the second radio button, Yes, AutoBalance This Account. But you should do no such thing. Select the second radio button only if you *don't* want to track the charges you run up on your credit card.

8. **If you want the bill to appear on the Bills and Deposits window, make sure that you check the Yes, Remind Me When the Bill Is Due check box. Enter an estimate of how much you owe in an average month; also, enter a date in the Bill Is Due Next On box. Then click the Next button.**

As shown in Figure 20-6, the next dialog box asks whether you want to put the monthly credit card or line of credit payment on the Bill Calendar. If you click Yes, a reminder to pay the bill appears in the Manage Scheduled Bills and Deposits window and in Money Express. The Manage Scheduled Bills and Deposits window reminds you when bills are due. If you want, the notice can also appear on the Home Page, where you can see it each time you start Money.

Figure 20-6:
From this dialog box, you can add the credit card or line of credit payment to the Bill Calendar and maybe pay the bill on time.

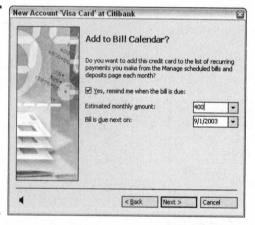

9. **Click Next in the following dialog box, which asks whether you can earn frequent flyer miles with your credit or charge card.**

10. **Select either the I Have No Other Accounts at This Institution button or I Have Other Accounts at This Institution; then click the Next button.**

Selecting I Have No Other Accounts at This Institution takes you to the last dialog box, where you can click the Finish button and be done with it. Selecting I Have Other Accounts at This Institution takes you back to the dialog box for choosing an account type.

11. **Click the Finish button.**

You can ignore the Go to Online Setup button for now. You can set up the online services later if you so choose.

After you set up your credit card or line of credit account, go to the Update Details window and enter the phone number of the credit card issuer or bank. You may need the number, for example, if you must report a lost credit card. In this chapter, "Listing contact names, phone numbers, and other account details" explains how the Update Details window works.

CHECK IT OUT

Selecting Your "Favorite" Accounts

Checking accounts, credit card accounts, and other accounts that you have to dig into on a regular basis are good candidates for "favorite" status. The names of favorite accounts appear on the Favorites menu. All you have to do to open a favorite account is choose Favorites⇨Favorite Accounts and the name of the account. As Book IV, Chapter 19 explains, you can also make your "favorite" accounts appear on the Home Page so that account balances stare you in the face, for good or ill, whenever you start Money. By clicking an account name on the Home Page, you can view the account's register and enter transactions.

Follow these instructions to make an account a favorite account:

✔ Right-click an account name in the Accounts window and choose Favorite (click the Account List button to open the Accounts window).

✔ Choose Favorites⇨Organize Favorites⇨ Accounts and, in the Select Your Favorite Accounts window, check the names of accounts.

✔ Select the Favorite Account check box in the Update Details window.

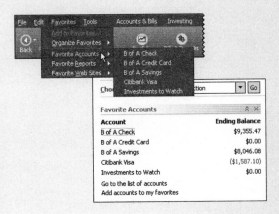

Chapter 21: Recording Your Financial Activity

In This Chapter

✔ Opening an account register

✔ Recording transactions in registers

✔ Recording credit card transactions and payments

✔ Locating and fixing errors in registers

✔ Deleting and voiding transactions

This chapter tackles the four or five things you have to do each time you run the Money program. It explains how to open an account register and how to record deposits, withdrawals, payments, and charges in registers. You also find out how to record a transfer of money between accounts, how to move around in a register, and how to find transactions in large registers. Finally, this chapter describes how to delete and void transactions.

Accomplish the tasks described in this chapter and you are well on your way to becoming an ace user of the Money program.

The Basics: Recording Transactions in Savings and Checking Registers

After you set up an account (the subject of Book IV, Chapter 20), you're ready to start recording transactions in the account's register. A *register* is the place where checks, payments, deposits, charges, and withdrawals are recorded. Figure 21-1 shows a checking account register. As with all registers, this one has places for numbering transactions, recording transaction dates, and viewing balances.

Everybody, or almost everybody, has a savings or checking account, so these accounts are a good place to start. These sections explain how to open an account register and view it in different ways. You also find out how to record deposits, withdrawals, and checks, as well as how to record a transfer of money from one account to another. The basic techniques for recording transactions that you discover here apply to all the accounts you set up in Money — investment accounts, cash accounts, asset accounts, you name it.

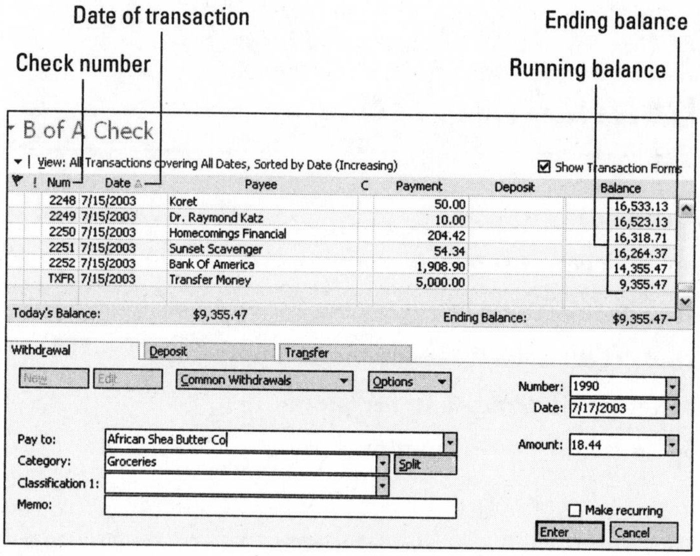

Date of transaction

Ending balance

Check number

Running balance

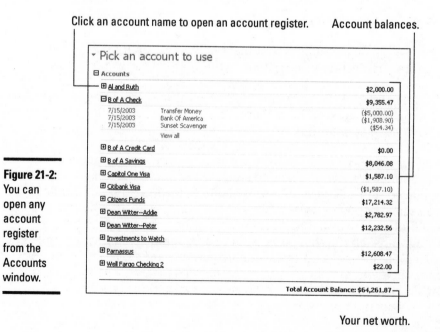

Figure 21-1:
Financial
transactions
are
recorded in
account
registers
like this one.

Opening an account register

The first step to opening an account register is to go to the Accounts window, as shown in Figure 21-2. This window is Account Central as far as Money is concerned. It lists each account you have and how much money is in each account. Negative balances — credit card balances are usually negative because they represent money that you owe — are shown in red and are surrounded by parentheses. At the bottom of the window is your total account balance, the sum of your savings, debts, assets, and liabilities, also known as your *net worth*.

Click an account name to open an account register.   Account balances.

Figure 21-2:
You can
open any
account
register
from the
Accounts
window.

Your net worth.

Account List

You can get to the Accounts window in one of three ways:

✦ Click the Account List button on the Navigation bar.

✦ Choose Accounts & Bills➪Account List.

✦ Press Ctrl+Shift+A.

The Accounts window is a nice place to visit, but when you're in a hurry, you can open an account register without going to the Accounts window first. Here are the various and sundry ways to open an account register:

✦ Click an account name in the Accounts window.

✦ Right-click an account name and choose See Account Register from the shortcut menu.

✦ Choose Favorites➪Favorite Accounts from the menu bar and then click the name of an account, assuming that you opted to make it a favorite. Favorite accounts can also be reached by choosing Accounts & Bills➪Favorite Accounts. As Book IV, Chapter 20 explains, you can also list favorite accounts on the Home Page and open them from there.

Recording checks, deposits, withdrawals, and debit card purchases in registers

At the bottom of the Account Register window is a form for entering transactions in the register, as shown in Figure 21-3. (If you don't see the form, select the Show Transaction Forms check box in the upper-right corner of the window.) To enter a transaction, click a tab — Withdrawal, Deposit, or Transfer — and then fill in the transaction form.

Start by choosing a tab.

Figure 21-3:
Recording a transaction in an account register.

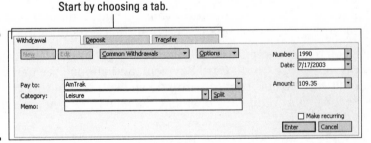

Book IV
Chapter 21

Recording Your
Financial Activity

Which tab you click depends on which type of transaction you want to enter:

✦ **Withdrawal tab:** Taking money out of an account? Stealing from yourself isn't really stealing, but so that you don't feel guilty, let Money know how much you're taking out on this tab. Use this tab when you record check payments and cash withdrawals — any transaction in which money leaves an account.

✦ **Deposit tab:** When you put money into an account, record the transaction on this tab. Record all deposits to an account on this tab. That includes check deposits and deposits made at a cash machine.

✦ **Transfer tab:** Shifting money from one account to another? Click the Transfer tab.

Follow these steps to record a check, deposit, withdrawal, cash-machine withdrawal, or debit card purchase in a register:

1. **Open the register of the account in which you want to record a transaction (see "Opening an account register" earlier in this chapter).**

2. **Click the Withdrawal or Deposit tab.**

   Is money going in or going out of the account? Outgoing money is recorded on the Withdrawal tab; incoming money is recorded on the Deposit tab.

3. **Tell Money what kind of transaction you want to record.**

   In some cases, you have to click the Common Withdrawals or Common Deposits button to describe a transaction.

   • **Cash withdrawal:** Do nothing. You're all set.

   • **ATM cash-machine withdrawal:** Click the Common Withdrawals button and choose ATM. If you have made cash withdrawals before, you can choose an amount on the submenu, but if you haven't withdrawn before or the amount you want to withdraw isn't listed, choose Other Amount. When you are done recording the transaction, the letters ATM (automatic teller machine) will appear in the Number box of the register so that you know that the withdrawal was made at a cash machine.

   • **Check:** Click the Common Withdrawals button and choose Write a Check. Money enters the next available check number in the Number box. If this number is incorrect, enter the correct number.

   • **Check to pay a credit card bill:** Click the Common Withdrawals button, choose Credit Card Payment, and choose the name of the credit card issuer from the drop-down list. Later in this chapter, "Recording a credit card payment" explains this kind of transaction in detail.

   • **Debit card purchase:** Click the Common Withdrawals button and choose Debit Card Purchase. (If you got cash back with your purchase, see "Recording a deposit or debit card purchase with cash back," later in this chapter.)

   • **Cash deposit:** You're all set. Do nothing.

   • **Deposit of a check or checks:** You're all set, unless you want to record a deposit of more than one check or you got cash back after the deposit. See "Splitting deposits and withdrawals that don't fit in one category" and "Recording a deposit or debit card purchase with cash back," later in this chapter.

4. Enter a number in the Number text box, if necessary.

To move from place to place on a transaction form, click elsewhere, or press Tab or Shift+Tab.

Only checks require a number, but you can enter deposit slip and withdrawal slip numbers if you want to track deposits and withdrawals carefully.

Money should have entered the next available check number, but if it didn't, click the down arrow to open the Number drop-down list and then choose Next Check Number. If the number that Money enters is incorrect, enter the correct number.

5. Enter the date in the Date text box, if necessary.

Money puts today's date in the Date text box, so you don't need to do anything if you are recording a transaction you completed today.

6. Enter whom you're paying the money to in the Pay To text box, or whom you received the money from in the From text box.

The Deposit form has a From text box rather than a Pay To text box. You can simply type in the first few letters of a name (if you received or paid money from or to this person or party before) to scroll the list of names and go to the one you want.

For deposits, enter the name of the person or business that wrote you the check or checks you deposited. For withdrawals, enter **Cash** if you withdrew cash from the bank. For ATM withdrawals, Money enters the word *Cash* automatically.

If you've entered this name in the register before, the amount you last paid or received appears in the Amount text box. Not only that, but the category that you assigned to the last transaction with this person or company appears in the Category text box. You may not have to change the amount or category choices. If this transaction is identical to the one you recorded last time, your work is almost done and you can skip to Step 10.

7. Enter the amount of the transaction in the Amount text box.

To enter a round number, you don't have to enter the decimal point or trailing zeroes. In other words, to enter "$21.00," all you have to type is "21." Money adds the zeroes for you.

8. In the Category text box, enter a category (or category and subcategory).

Most of Book IV, Chapter 22 is devoted to the subject of creating and choosing the right categories and subcategories. By assigning categories and subcategories to income and expense transactions, you can discover where you spend your hard-earned money and where it comes from — critical information, especially if you itemize on tax forms.

Expense categories are at the top of the drop-down list. Payments require an expense category. Deposits require an income category, which are found in the middle of the drop-down list.

9. **If you care to, write a few words in the Memo text box to describe the transaction.**

Write a memo if for any reason you may come back to the account register in the future, see the transaction, and not know what it was for.

10. **Click the Enter button or press the Enter key.**

Click the New button if you want to clear the entry form and record another transaction.

How's your view of the register?

Try using the hard-to-find View menu in the Account Register window like a TV remote-control device to change channels when you get bored. As Figure 21-4 shows, you can change views by clicking the little triangle beside the word *View* and making a choice from the drop-down list. No, the views are not especially exciting, but there are worse on TV.

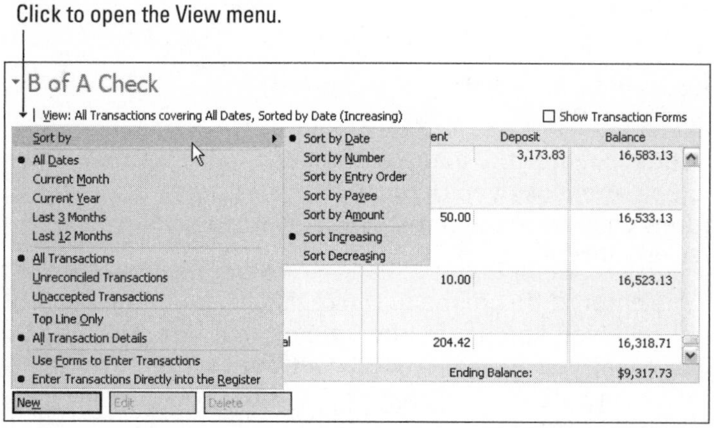

Click to open the View menu.

Figure 21-4:
The View menu offers many different ways to arrange transactions on-screen.

Different kinds of registers offer different kinds of views. However, the options fall into four categories:

✦ **Sort By options:** Options on the Sort By submenu determine the order by which transactions appear in the register. The default is Sort by Date, which arranges transactions in date order, as the way they are arranged on bank statements, but you can also arrange transactions by number, by the order in which *you* entered them, by alphabetical order of the payee's name, or by amount. The last two options on the submenu are for reversing the order of transactions.

✦ **Sort by date options:** Choose an option to show only transactions from the current month, current year, past three months, or past year.

✦ **Number of transaction options:** With the All Transactions option — you guessed it — all transactions appear in the register. However, to make only transactions that have not cleared the bank appear, select the Unreconciled Transactions option. This option is very handy when you are reconciling an account. Book IV, Chapter 23 explains reconciling.

✦ **Amount of detail options:** To see more transactions on-screen, select the Top Line Only option. Only the first line of each transaction is shown. Select the All Transaction Details option to see all parts of transactions, including categories and memo descriptions. Ctrl+T is a toggle key command. Press it to quickly change views.

✦ **Transaction forms options:** Choose the second option, Enter Transactions Directly into the Register, if you prefer doing that to entering transactions on forms. To enter a transaction directly into a register, click the last empty row and choose options from the drop-down lists that appear in the register columns. Some find doing this very inconvenient, but you may like it.

Splitting deposits and withdrawals that don't fit in one category

Suppose that you try to record a transaction in a register but it doesn't fit in a single category. For example, suppose that you write a check to the Old Country Store to buy motor oil, a blouse, and a rocking chair. The transaction doesn't fall neatly in the Automotive, Clothing, or Household: Furnishings categories. And suppose that you deposit two checks at one time, one from your place of work and one from the New Jersey Lottery Commission. To record a transaction like that, you *split* it. Money offers the Split button on the transaction form for that very purpose, and you use it by following these steps:

1. **Record the transaction as you normally would.**

If, like me, you don't have and never have had a good sense of what's normal, follow Steps 1 through 7 under "Recording checks, deposits, withdrawals, and debit card purchases in registers," earlier in this chapter.

To total the checks in a deposit, click the down arrow beside the Amount box and total the checks on the minicalculator. After you click the equals button, the total is entered in the Amount box.

2. **Click the Split button or press Ctrl+S.**

You see the Transaction with Multiple Categories dialog box, shown in Figure 21-5. The Category list is already open so that you can select the first category.

By the way, if you are depositing several checks, you can also click the Common Deposits button and choose Deposit Multiple Items from the menu to open the Transaction with Multiple Categories dialog box.

3. **For the first item that you purchased or deposited, select a category on the first line of the dialog box.**

4. **If you care to, enter a description in the Description text box on the first line.**

5. **In the Amount text box on the first line, enter the cost of the first item or the amount of the first check you deposited.**

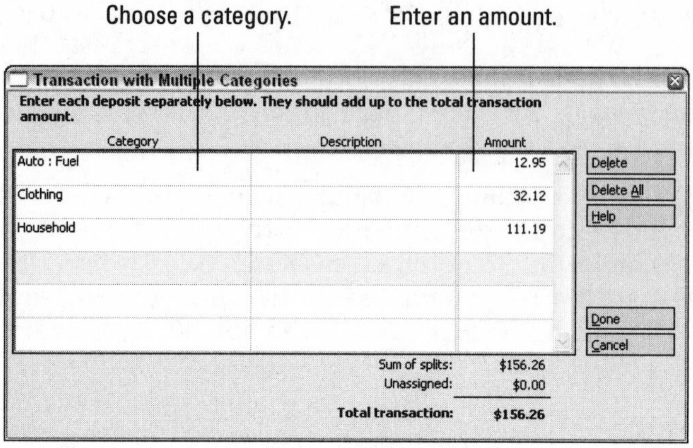

Choose a category.   Enter an amount.

Transaction with Multiple Categories

Enter each deposit separately below. They should add up to the total transaction amount.

Category	Description	Amount	
Auto : Fuel		12.95	Delete
Clothing		32.12	Delete All
Household		111.19	Help

Sum of splits:	$156.26
Unassigned:	$0.00
Total transaction:	**$156.26**

Done   Cancel

Figure 21-5:
Splitting a transaction that doesn't fit into a single category.

6. **Repeat Steps 3 through 5 for each item you purchased or for each check you deposited.**

   When you finish, the Sum of Splits figure should equal the Total Transaction figure, and the Unassigned figure should be 0.00. If the figures don't add up, tinker with the numbers in the Transaction with Multiple Categories dialog box until they do.

7. **Click the Done button to return to the transaction form.**

8. **Make sure that the transaction form is filled out properly; then click the Enter button.**

When a transaction has been split, the words "Split/Multiple Categories" appear in the Category text box of the register, as shown in Figure 21-6. To see how a transaction in a register was divided across categories, click the transaction, click the transaction form, and then click the Split button to open the Transaction with Multiple Categories dialog box.

This transaction was split across several categories.

	Num	Date △	Payee / Category / Memo	C	Payment	Deposit	Balance	
		7/19/2003	Old Country Store Split/Multiple Categories			156.26	9,473.99	

Today's Balance:	$9,473.99		Ending Balance:	$9,473.99

Withdrawal   Deposit   Transfer

New   Edit   Common Deposits ▼   Options ▼   Number: Print
Date: 7/19/2003

From: Old Country Store
Category: Split/Multiple Categories ▼   Split
Memo:
Amount: 156.26
☐ Make recurring
Enter   Cancel

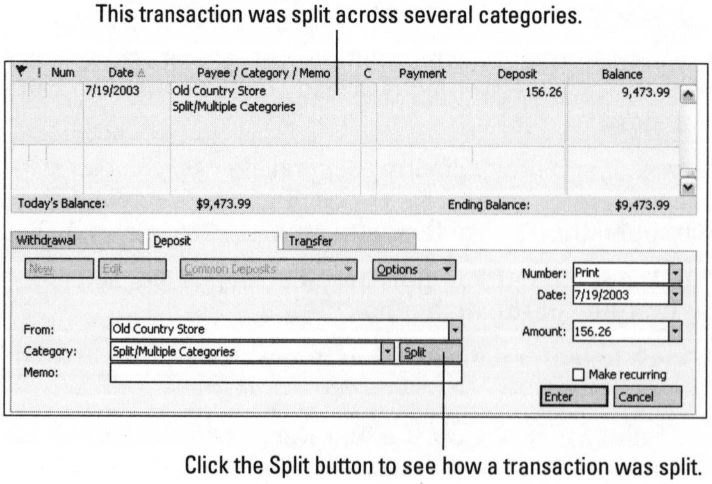

Figure 21-6:
When you split a transaction, the words "Split/ Multiple Categories" appear in the register.

Click the Split button to see how a transaction was split.

Suppose that you split a transaction but regret doing so. Click the transaction; then choose a single category in the Category box. That's all there is to it. Money removes the words "Split/Multiple Categories" and enters the name of the category you chose.

Recording a deposit or debit card purchase with cash back

Suppose that you deposit a check or make a debit card purchase and ask for a little cash back. Who doesn't need a little cash now and then? The problem with recording a cash-back deposit or debit card purchase with extra cash is that the transaction is really two transactions in one. In the case of the debit card purchase, part of the transaction is a debit card purchase and part is a cash withdrawal from a bank account. Likewise with cash-back deposits — part of the transaction is a deposit and part is a cash withdrawal.

Fortunately for you, Money offers special commands for recording these kinds of transactions. Follow these steps to record a cash-back deposit or debit card purchase:

1. **Open the register of the account in which you want to record the deposit or debit card purchase.**

   Earlier in this chapter, "Opening an account register" explains how to do that.

2. **Click the Withdrawal tab to record a cash-back debit card purchase; click the Deposit tab to record a cash-back deposit.**

3. **Click the Common Withdrawals or Common Deposits button.**

   A menu appears with commands for handling special kinds of transactions.

4. **To record a cash-back debit card purchase, select Debit Card Purchase with Cash Back; to record a cash-back deposit, select Deposit With Cash Back.**

   You see one of the dialog boxes shown in Figure 21-7.

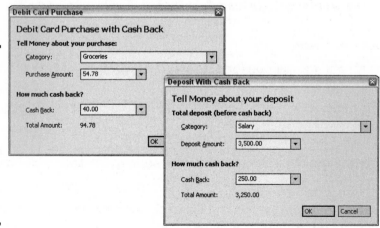

Figure 21-7: In the Cash Back text box, enter how much you withdrew as part of your debit card purchase or deposit.

5. **Enter the amount of the purchase or deposit in the Amount text box.**

6. **In the Category text box, categorize the purchase or deposit.**

7. In the Cash Back text box, enter how much money you took back with the purchase or deposit.

8. Click the OK button.

You return to the account register. Notice, in the Category text box, the words "Split/Multiple Categories." You have entered a split transaction — in this case, a withdrawal of cash as well as a payment or deposit. The amount box shows how much you actually spent or deposited.

If you need to tinker with the figures, click the Split button to open the Transaction with Multiple Categories dialog box (refer to Figure 21-6). From here, you can review the figures one last time or adjust them if need be.

9. Complete the transaction as you normally would and click the Enter button.

To examine a split transaction in a register, select the transaction, click the transaction form, and click the Split button.

Transferring money between accounts

Sometimes, good luck comes your way; you earn a few extra dollars, so you transfer money from your checking account to a savings account or investment account. And sometimes, in a fit of panic, you have to transfer money from a savings account to a checking account to cover a couple of large checks. When you transfer money between real-life bank accounts, record the transfer in your Money account registers as well.

Follow these steps to record a transfer of money from one account to another:

1. Open the register of the account from which you're transferring the money.

In other words, to transfer money from a checking to a savings account, open the checking account register.

2. Click the Transfer tab.

You see the transaction form, shown at the bottom of Figure 21-8.

The fastest way to record a transfer is to click the Common Transfers button and select a transaction from the drop-down list. The menu lists the last five transfers you recorded. If the transfer you want to record is identical to a transfer on the menu, select it.

3. Enter the date that the transfer was made in the Date text box.

4. In the Amount text box, enter the amount of the transfer.

5. Click the down arrow on the To drop-down list and select the account receiving the transferred money.

All the accounts you set up in Money appear on the To drop-down list. The name of the account from which you're transferring the money should already appear in the From text box. Leave the Pay To text box empty when transferring money between bank accounts.

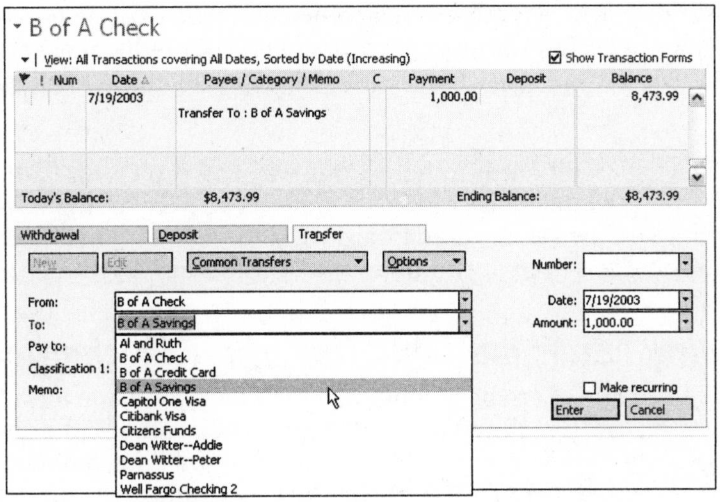

Figure 21-8:
Transferring money between accounts (bottom); what a transfer looks like in a register (top).

6. **Enter a few words to describe the transaction in the Memo text box (optional).**

7. **Click the Enter button or press the Enter key.**

   The top of Figure 21-8 shows what a money transfer looks like in an account register. The transfer is counted as a debit — the amount you transferred is deducted from one account and added to the other.

Transferring is more than meets the eye

It seems odd at first, but Money requires you to transfer funds not only when you transfer funds between bank accounts but also when you contribute to IRAs or other kinds of investments. Think of it this way: If you open an IRA and you write a $1,000 check for a contribution to your IRA, that $1,000 still belongs to you. You haven't really spent it. All you have done is transferred it from one account (checking) to another account (the retirement account with which you track the value of your IRA). Therefore, when you open a new account, you record the initial deposit as a transfer from your checking account to the new account.

You also transfer money between accounts when you pay a credit card bill. Here's how it works: Each time you record a charge in a credit card account, the charge is added to the amount of money that you owe. Suppose that at the end of a month your account shows that you owe $200 because you charged $200 worth of items. To pay the $200 that you owe, you record a check for $200 to the credit card issuer, but in the register, the $200 is shown as a transfer from your checking account to your credit card account. After the transfer is complete, the $200 that you owed is brought to zero. Later in this chapter, "Recording a credit card payment" explains how to pay credit card bills.

Recording Transactions in Credit Card and Line of Credit Accounts

If you slogged through the previous few pages and discovered how to record checking and savings account transactions, you may experience *déjà vu* in the next few pages. Entering credit card and line of credit transactions is mighty similar to recording transactions made in savings and checking accounts.

Besides leaving credit cards at home, one way to keep credit card spending under control is to diligently record charges as you make them. As the amount that you owe in the credit card register gets larger and larger, you will be discouraged from spending so much with your credit card.

Recording credit card and line of credit charges

Credit card and line of credit account registers have a Charge form for recording charges. Figure 21-9 shows a Charge form. As does the Withdrawal form, the Charge form has places for entering a transaction date, amount, payee name, category, and memo. All the drop-down lists and keyboard tricks work the same way on a Charge form as on a Withdrawal form.

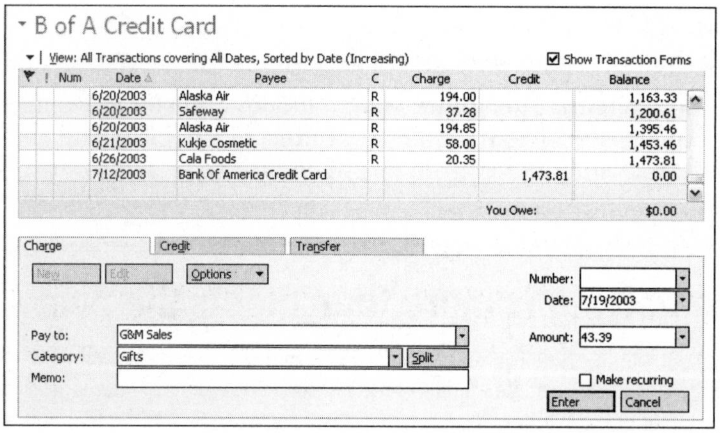

Figure 21-9: Record credit card and line of credit transactions exactly as you would record a check.

▾	B of A Credit Card					
	View: All Transactions covering All Dates, Sorted by Date (Increasing)					☑ Show Transaction Forms
▼ ! Num	Date △	Payee	C	Charge	Credit	Balance
	6/20/2003	Alaska Air	R	194.00		1,163.33
	6/20/2003	Safeway	R	37.28		1,200.61
	6/20/2003	Alaska Air	R	194.85		1,395.46
	6/21/2003	Kukje Cosmetic	R	58.00		1,453.46
	6/26/2003	Cala Foods	R	20.35		1,473.81
	7/12/2003	Bank Of America Credit Card			1,473.81	0.00
				You Owe:		$0.00

Charge | Credit | Transfer

New | Edit | Options ▾

Number: [ ]
Date: 7/19/2003

Pay to: G&M Sales
Category: Gifts | Split
Memo:

Amount: 43.39

☐ Make recurring
Enter | Cancel

To fill in the Charge form, follow these steps:

1. **Open the account register.**

2. **Click the Charge tab.**

3. **Enter a reference number (optional).**

4. **Enter the charge date.**

5. **Enter the business you purchased the item from in the Pay To text box.**

6. **Enter the amount of the charge.**

Don't concern yourself with recording service charges and interest on your credit card. You can do that when you reconcile your account (a topic covered in Book IV, Chapter 23).

7. Select a category.

8. Enter a description (optional).

9. Click the Enter button (or press Enter).

Credit card and line of credit accounts track what you owe, not what you have. Don't forget this all-important detail. In the credit card register shown in Figure 21-9, you can clearly see the words *You Owe* where the words *Ending Balance* appear in a savings or checking account register. In effect, the You Owe number is a negative number. It represents an amount that you will have to pay out of your checking account one of these days.

Recording a credit

If you receive a credit from a bank or credit card issuer, perhaps because you overpaid, disputed a bill, or returned an item you bought, record the credit in the credit card account register. To do so, click the Credit tab and fill in the blanks in the Credit form. The Credit form works exactly like the Charge form (see the preceding section, "Recording credit card and line of credit charges").

Be sure to record the credit in an expense category. Seems odd, doesn't it, to record credits as expenses? But when you recorded the purchase in the register, you assigned it to an expense category. Now that you're getting a refund, assign it to the same expense category so that the amount you spent in the category is accurate on your reports.

Recording a credit card payment

Before you make a credit card or line of credit payment, reconcile the credit card or line of credit account (Book IV, Chapter 23 explains how). Then take note of how much of the debt you intend to pay, and follow these steps to make a payment to the bank or card issuer:

1. Open the register of the account from which you intend to make the payment (see "Opening an account register," earlier in this chapter).

Probably a checking register.

2. Click the Withdrawal tab at the bottom of the register window.

3. Click the Common Withdrawals button, choose Credit Card Payment, and then choose the name of the credit card account where you track the credit card that you want to make a payment on, as shown in Figure 21-10.

The words "Credit Card Payment" and the name of the credit card account appear in the Category text box on the transaction form, as shown at the bottom of Figure 21-10.

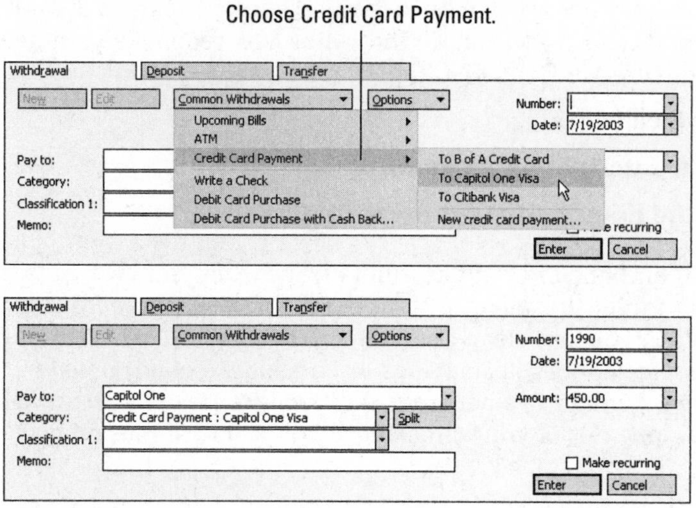

Choose Credit Card Payment.

Figure 21-10:
Paying all
or part of a
credit card
bill.

4. **Enter a check number in the Number text box if the number that appears there isn't correct.**

Remember, you can click the down arrow and choose Next Check Number to enter the next available check number in the text box.

5. **In the Date text box, enter the date that you wrote or will write on the check.**

6. **Enter the amount of the check in the Amount text box.**

Money continues to track what you owe from month to month.

7. **If you care to, write a few descriptive words in the Memo text box.**

8. **Click the Enter button or press Enter.**

The amount you paid is deducted from the checking account. Meanwhile, the You Owe amount in the credit card or line of credit register decreases or is brought to zero. In effect, you have transferred money from your checking account to the account where you track credit card charges. Earlier in this chapter, the sidebar, "Transferring is more than meets the eye," explains the mystery of why you transfer money between accounts to satisfy a credit card debt.

Right-click a credit card payment in a register and choose Go To Account: *Credit Card Name* (or press Ctrl+X) to go to the account register where you track credit card charges.

Fixing Mistakes in Account Registers

Everybody makes mistakes, and absolutely everybody makes mistakes when entering transactions in account registers. Most people do not have an expert typist's nimble fingers or sureness of touch. Therefore, the following sections explain how to find and fix mistakes, how to get from place to place in large registers, how to move transactions from one account to another, and how to delete and void transactions.

Changing, or editing, transactions

All right, so you found the transaction that you entered incorrectly. What do you do now? If you are staring at the transaction in an account register, either double-click it or click it and then click the Edit button on the transaction form. Then go right into the transaction form, fix the mistake in whatever text box or drop-down list it is located in, and click the Enter button.

If you found the error by way of the Tools⇨Find and Replace command, double-click the transaction in the Search Results list. When the Edit Transaction dialog box appears, repair the transaction and click OK.

Suppose, however, that an error was made in numerous places. You misspelled a payee's name. You categorized several transactions incorrectly. In that case, display the errant transactions in the Find and Replace dialog box. Then follow these steps to fix the transactions *en masse:*

1. **Click the Replace button in the Find and Replace dialog box.**

You see the Replace screen, shown in Figure 21-11.

Select the transactions that need replacing.

Figure 21-11:
Use the Replace screen in the Find and Replace dialog box to change several transactions simultaneously.

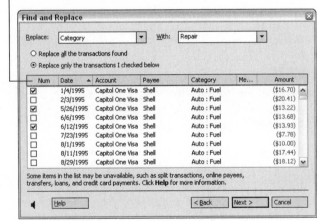

2. **On the Replace drop-down list, choose which part of the transactions needs repairing.**

You can change payee names, category assignments, memo text, or transaction numbers.

3. **In the With text box, either type a new entry or choose one from the drop-down list.**

If you chose Payee or Category on the Replace drop-down list, a list of payees or categories is made available on the With drop-down list.

4. **Select the check boxes next to transactions you want to edit, or select the Replace All the Transactions Found radio button to edit all the transactions in the list.**

5. **Click the Next button.**

A "last chance" dialog box appears and lists all the transactions that will be altered. If you're prudent, look through the list one last time. If you're daring and reckless, click the Finish button right away. You can click the Back button if you get cold feet.

6. Click the Finish button.

Voiding and deleting transactions

To strike a transaction from an account register, either delete or void it. What's the difference? A deleted transaction is erased permanently from your financial records. It may as well have never happened. But a voided transaction stays in the account register, where **VOID** clearly shows that you entered the transaction but voided it later on. What's more, a voided transaction can be "unvoided."

Void a transaction when you want to keep a record of having made it. For example, if you start writing check number 511 but accidentally enter the wrong payee name, void the check instead of deleting it. That way, the account register records what happened to check number 511 and you know that the check wasn't lost or stolen. Likewise, if you stop payment on a check, void it (and explain on the Memo line why you stopped payment).

History records what happened to voided transactions, but deleted transactions are lost forever in the prehistoric murk.

Voiding a transaction

Follow these steps to void a transaction:

1. Select the transaction in the register.

2. Choose Edit⇨Mark As⇨Void.

You can also right-click a transaction and choose Mark As⇨Void or press Ctrl+V to void it.

After a transaction has been voided, **VOID** appears in the balance column of the register, and R (for Reconciled) appears in the C (for Cleared) column to show that the transaction has cleared. Figure 21-12 shows a voided transaction in a register.

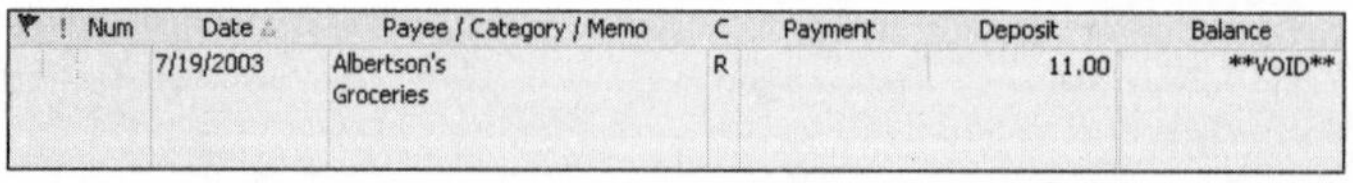

Figure 21-12:
A voided transaction.

!	Num	Date	Payee / Category / Memo	C	Payment	Deposit	Balance
		7/19/2003	Albertson's Groceries	R		11.00	**VOID**

To unvoid a transaction, click it in the register and choose Edit⇨Mark As⇨Void all over again (or right-click and choose Mark As⇨Void). Because voided transactions are reconciled automatically, a dialog box asks whether you're dead sure that you want to change this reconciled transaction. Normally, you click No in this dialog box, because changing a reconciled transaction throws your record and the bank's out of sync. In the case of voiding, however, click the Yes button to make the change. All you're trying to do here is reverse a mistake you made.

Deleting a transaction

Follow these steps to delete a transaction:

1. **Select the transaction in the register.**

2. **Choose Edit⇨Delete, or right-click and choose Delete from the short-cut menu, or press Ctrl+D.**

Sorry, you can't delete a transaction by pressing the Del key.

3. **Click Yes when Money asks whether you really want to go through with it.**

If you try to delete a transaction that is marked as cleared in the register (R appears in the C column), Money warns you that deleting the transaction could upset your account balance and put the account out of sync with bank records. Clicking the No in the dialog box to keep the transaction from being deleted is recommended. Very likely, the transaction was cleared because it appeared on bank records, so it should appear on your records as well. Investigate the matter before deleting the transaction.

Chapter 22: Categorizing Your Spending and Income

In This Chapter

✓ Identifying categories, subcategories, and classifications

✓ Creating your own categories and subcategories

✓ Creating tax-related categories for tax-reporting purposes

✓ Reassigning transactions to different categories

You've probably withdrawn money from an ATM machine, noticed the dwindling account balance, and asked yourself, "Where did the money go?" Or perhaps you balanced a checking account and scratched your head, asking, "Why did I write so many checks?"

Money can help you find out. By assigning each transaction to a category, you can discover a great deal about your spending habits and sources of income. You can generate a report or graph and find out how much you spent on clothing and dining and office supplies. You can find out how much you earned in interest income and how much you earned from different clients. You can even find out how much you are allowed to deduct for income tax purposes.

This chapter explains how to categorize transactions in account registers. You figure out how to choose categories and how to create meaningful categories that work for you. You also explore how to recategorize transactions. You may still have to write the same number of checks, but at least you'll have a better idea why.

Looking at the Ways to Categorize Income and Spending

Money offers four ways to categorize a financial transaction. What are the four ways? You can categorize a transaction by category, subcategory, classification, and tax-related status.

By category

By assigning transactions to categories, you can create neat-looking charts that give you the big picture on your spending, as shown in Figure 22-1. You'll see where all your money is spent and where the money comes from.

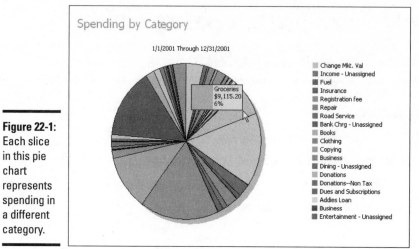

Figure 22-1: Each slice in this pie chart represents spending in a different category.

By subcategory

Divide a category into subcategories when you want to closely examine spending or income. The report in Figure 22-2 shows yearly expenses in five Automobile subcategories: Fuel, Insurance, Registration Fee, Repair, and Road Service. After you have used Money for a while, try running a report like this one to show how much it costs to drive your car for one year.

Figure 22-2: A subcategory report.

By classification

Most people don't need to bother with classifications, but they can be useful for tracking things such as rental properties. As the owner or manager of an apartment building or office building, you need to know precisely how much income the property generates and how much it costs to maintain. The only way to track income and costs, which fall into lots of different expense and income categories and subcategories, is to create a classification.

By tax-related status

By giving a category tax-related status, you can tell Money to include categories and subcategories in tax reports. An accountant may need two or three hours to examine account registers, find all the tax-related transactions, and total them — time that you will be charged for. Money can do it in about six seconds.

Setting Up Your Own Categories and Subcategories

Money gives you a set of generic categories and subcategories so that you can start entering transactions right away. To see the complete list, click the Categories button on the Navigation bar (you may have to click More first) and then choose Categories (or choose Accounts & Bills⇨Categories & Payees or press Ctrl+Shift+C). The list is fine and dandy, but sooner or later you have to give serious thought to which categories and subcategories suit you, especially if you use Money to manage a business or track tax-deductible expenses. If you don't see what you need in the generic lists, create your own!

Sit down and compose a list of all the categories and subcategories you need for your business or personal finances *before* you begin creating categories and subcategories. That way, you get it right from the start and you lower the odds of having to recategorize transactions later on.

Creating a new category

Follow these steps to set up a new category in the New Category dialog box:

1. **Click the Categories button on the Navigation bar, choose Accounts & Bills⇨Categories & Payees, or press Ctrl+Shift+C.**

   Doing so takes you to the Categories window.

2. **If necessary, click the Categories button on the left side of the window to see the Categories list.**

   Figure 22-3 shows the Categories list. While you're viewing the window, you may want to scroll down the list of categories and subcategories and examine the ones already there. Expense categories appear at the top of the list and Income categories appear at the bottom.

Click to change views.

Figure 22-3: Categories and subcategories. Subcategories are indented and appear below their parent categories.

Category	Category Group
Auto	Automobile Expenses
- Fees-License	Unassigned
- Fuel	Automobile Expenses
- Insurance	Automobile Insurance
- Loan	Automobile Expenses
- New Car	Unassigned
- Parking	Unassigned
- Registration fee	Unassigned
- Repair	Unassigned
- Road Service	Unassigned
Babysitting	Unassigned
Backpacking Equipment	Unassigned
Bank Chrg	Bank Charges
- Business checks	Unassigned
- SEP IRA fees	Unassigned
Big Ticket Item	Unassigned
Books	Unassigned
Business Gifts	Unassigned

July 19, 2003

View:
Payees
Categories
Preferred payee names
Classification 1
Classification 2

Common Tasks
Set up tax categories

View: Categories, Subcategories, and Category Groups

Set up your categories

Go to Category | New... | Move... | Modify... | Delete

3. **Click the New button along the bottom of the screen.**

   The New Category dialog box appears.

4. **The Create a New Category? option button is already selected, so click the Next button.**

   The New Category dialog box offers places for entering a category name and category type.

5. **Type a name for the category in the Name text box.**

   The name you enter will appear on the Category drop-down list when you record transactions, so be sure to choose a meaningful name.

6. **Select the Income or Expense option button and click the Next button.**

   All categories fall under the Income or Expense heading. Income categories describe sources of income; expense categories describe how you spend money.

7. **Select a category group from the list.**

   A *category group* is a broad means of defining the category. Money uses category groups to make calculations in the Tax Estimator, Home Worksheet, and other features. When you select a category group, a description appears on the right side of the dialog box.

8. **Click the Finish button.**

   There it is — your new category, alive and kicking in the Categories & Payees window.

Open the View menu in the Categories window and experiment with the different views. In Figure 22-3, Categories, Subcategories, and Their Category Groups was chosen from the View menu. The other options can be useful when you're looking for a category in the list.

Creating a new subcategory

The best way to create a new subcategory is to go straight to the Categories window and start from there. Follow these steps:

1. **Click the Categories button on the Navigation bar, or choose Accounts & Bills⇨Categories & Payees to go to the Categories window.**

2. **If necessary, click the Categories button to view categories.**

   You will find this button on the left side of the window under View.

3. **Select the parent category of the subcategory you want to create.**

   In other words, to create a subcategory of the Education category, scroll to and select Education in the Categories window.

4. **Click the New button.**

   You see the New Category dialog box.

5. **Select the Add a Subcategory to an Existing Category option button; then click Next.**

6. **Enter a name for the subcategory in the Name text box; then click Next.**

7. Select a category group.

Category groups are another one of those bold attempts by Microsoft to do your thinking for you. The Tax Estimator and other features you select can use the group you select in budget projections and tax estimations.

8. Click the Finish button.

Check it out — your new subcategory appears in the Categories window underneath its parent category.

Getting Ready for Tax Time with Tax-Related Categories

Giving a category tax-related status when you create it is one thing. But how do you give an existing category tax-related status? Simply, that's how.

Money offers a special window for handling tax-related categories. In the window, you can select a check box to make sure a category is figured into the tax reports you can generate with Money. And you can assign a category or subcategory to a line item on a tax form. As shown in Figure 22-4, Money offers the Tax Software Report that connects category and subcategory totals to specific income tax forms (W-2, Schedule A, Schedule C, and so on). The Tax Software Report makes filling out income tax forms easier. All you have to do is get the figures from the report and plug them into the right places on the tax forms. However, to make the process work, you have to know more about the tax forms than most people know or care to know.

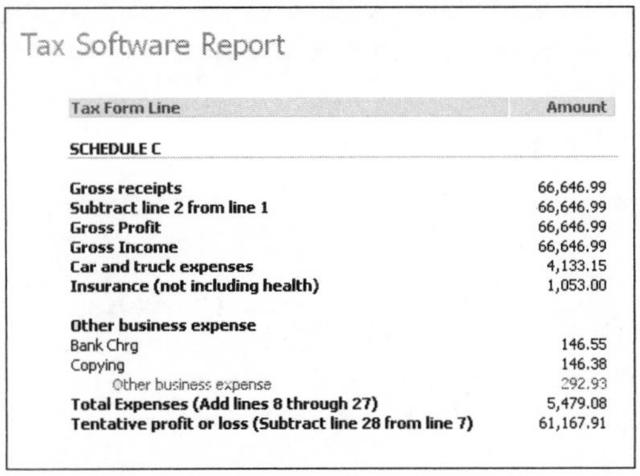

Figure 22-4:
The Tax Software Report presents figures for use in preparing federal income tax returns.

Tax Software Report

Tax Form Line	Amount
SCHEDULE C	
Gross receipts	66,646.99
Subtract line 2 from line 1	66,646.99
Gross Profit	66,646.99
Gross Income	66,646.99
Car and truck expenses	4,133.15
Insurance (not including health)	1,053.00
Other business expense	
Bank Chrg	146.55
Copying	146.38
Other business expense	292.93
Total Expenses (Add lines 8 through 27)	5,479.08
Tentative profit or loss (Subtract line 28 from line 7)	61,167.91

Follow these steps to give an existing category or subcategory tax-related status so that it is figured into tax reports, and, if possible, assign tax forms and line items to a category or subcategory:

1. Click the Categories button on the Navigation bar, or choose Accounts & Bills⇨Categories & Payees to get to the Categories window.

2. Click the Set Up Tax Categories hyperlink.

You can find this hyperlink on the left side of the window under Common Tasks. After you click the link, you see the Categories window, only this time, drop-down lists appear in the lower-right corner so that you can mark categories for tax reports and assign categories to line items on tax forms, as shown in Figure 22-5.

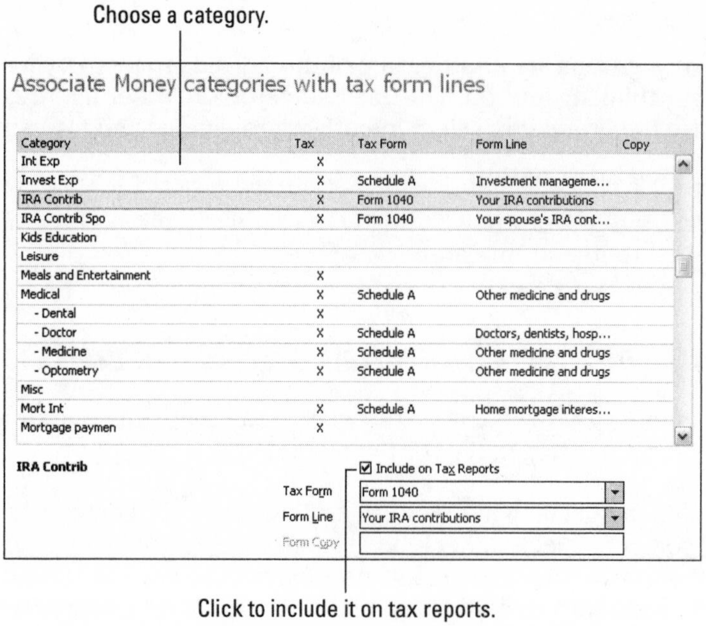

Choose a category.

Figure 22-5: Assigning a tax form and line to a category.

Click to include it on tax reports.

Where possible, the generic categories and subcategories that Money creates automatically are assigned tax forms and form lines. You can see them by scrolling down the list. Tax-related categories show an X in the Tax column. In the Tax Form and Form Line columns, you can see where tax forms and lines have been assigned to categories and subcategories.

3. **Scroll down the list until you find a category or subcategory whose tax status needs changing; then click the category or subcategory to select it.**

4. **Select the Include on Tax Reports check box.**

5. **Click the down-arrow on the Tax Form drop-down list and select a tax form.**

   Being able to tag categories and subcategories to tax forms (such as a W-2, Schedule B, or Form 1040) is a neat idea, but you have to know the tax forms well to pull it off. You have to know, for example, that tax-exempt interest is reported on the Interest Income line of the Schedule B form. Who (besides a tax accountant) knows that?

   If you want to be able to run Tax Software Reports, study your income tax returns from past years to see which forms and form lines to assign to the categories and subcategories that you use. You can also speak to an accountant. Be aware that tax forms change yearly, so what goes on one line one year may go somewhere else the next.

6. **Click the down arrow on the Form Line drop-down list and select the form line on which the income or expense is reported.**

7. **If you use multiple forms (more than one W-2, for example) to report your income, enter the number of forms you use in the Form Copy text box.**

8. **Click the Back button to return to the Categories window.**

TIP

Let others do the work

Don't bother to keep tax records when others do it for you. Employers, for example, keep careful track of their employees' federal income, state income, Social Security, and Medicare tax-deduction information. Why keep those numbers yourself when your employer pays someone to do it? Besides, you have to use your employer's numbers when you file your income tax return.

Similarly, you can track tax-deductible mortgage interest payments, but why bother? At the start of the year, the bank sends you a statement that indicates how much you paid in interest during the previous year. Use Money to keep track of only the tax-related income and expenses that no one tracks for you.

Correcting Transactions Recorded in the Wrong Category

Don't feel foolish if you recorded transactions in the wrong category or subcategory. It happens all the time. Luckily for you, Money offers a special button called Move for reassigning all the transactions in one category to another category. And if you need to reassign only a handful of transactions, you can use the Find and Replace command to reassign transactions one at a time.

WARNING!

The Move button is very powerful indeed. When you use the Move button to reassign all the transactions in one category to another category, you delete the first category as well. For example, suppose that you assigned the Vacation category to a bunch of transactions when you should have assigned the Leisure category. If you use the Move button to move all the Vacation transactions to the Leisure category, you delete the Vacation category from the Categories list as well as move the transactions. Use the Move button only when you want to drop one category altogether and move all its transactions elsewhere.

Another point about the Move button: If you attempt to move transactions in one category to another category and the category you want to move includes subcategories, you lose the subcategory assignments when you make the move. However, you can move subcategory assignments from one subcategory to another subcategory with the Move button.

Moving all transactions from one category to another category

To change category or subcategory assignments throughout your account registers, follow these steps:

1. **Click the Categories button on the Navigation bar, or press Ctrl+Shift+C to go to the Categories window.**

2. If necessary, click the Categories button on the window to make the categories and subcategories appear.

To see the categories and subcategories, you may need to open the View menu and choose Categories and their Subcategories.

3. Scroll down the list and select the name of the category or subcategory whose transactions you want to reassign.

For example, if you erroneously assigned transactions to the Education: Kids subcategory when you should have assigned them to the Childcare category, select the Education: Kids subcategory from the list.

Remember, the category or subcategory you select is deleted from the Categories window after you finish reassigning the transactions. Be sure to examine transactions carefully before you delete anything.

4. Click the Move button.

As shown in Figure 22-6, you see the Move Transactions dialog box. This is where you tell Money where to reassign the transactions in the category or subcategory you chose in Step 3.

Figure 22-6: Use the Move Transactions dialog box to assign transactions to a different category.

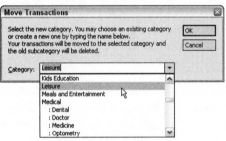

5. In the Category drop-down list, select the category or subcategory to which you want to reassign the transactions.

6. Click OK.

In the Categories list, the category or subcategory you chose in Step 3 has been deleted. Meanwhile, all transactions in your registers that were assigned the old category or subcategory are assigned the one you chose in Step 5.

Reassigning transactions to new categories

Instead of making a wholesale reassignment of one category or subcategory to another, you may decide to examine transactions one at a time and choose which ones need reassigning. To do that, you have to search for transactions in the account registers, examine each transaction, and then either choose a new category or subcategory or move on without moving the transaction.

Here are shorthand instructions for finding and fixing transactions that were assigned the wrong category or subcategory:

1. **Choose Tools➪Find and Replace, or press Ctrl+H.**

You see the Find Transactions dialog box.

2. **Select Category from the In This Field drop-down list; then, from the Find This Text drop-down list, select the category or subcategory whose transactions need reassigning; finally, click the Next button.**

As shown at the top of Figure 22-7, the Search Results list shows transactions assigned to the category you chose. At this point, you can reassign the transactions one at a time or click the Replace button to reassign several transactions simultaneously.

Figure 22-7: Searching for and repairing transactions that were assigned a specific category or subcategory.

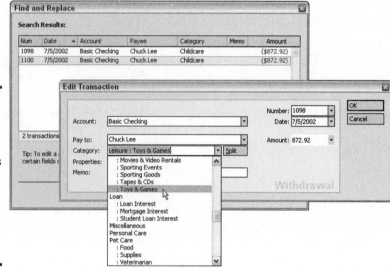

3. **Assign the transactions to new categories:**

- **One at a time.** Double-click a transaction that needs a new category. You see the Edit Transaction dialog box, as shown at the bottom of Figure 22-7. Choose a new category or subcategory from the drop-down list and click OK.

- **Several at one time.** Click the Replace button. You see the Replace screen, shown in Figure 22-8. Select the check box next to each transaction that needs a new category assignment, choose Category from the Replace drop-down list, choose a new category from the With list, and click the Next button. Then click the Finish button on the next screen, which asks, Are you sure?

Check transactions that need reassigning.

Choose category.   Choose a new category.

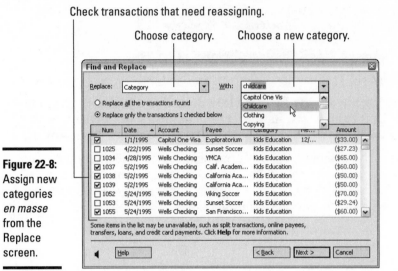

Figure 22-8:
Assign new
categories
en masse
from the
Replace
screen.

By the way, when you reassign a transaction that has been reconciled,
Money beeps and warns you not to change the amount of the transaction you are about to edit. Don't worry about the warning. You're concerned with the category assignment, not the amount of the transaction.

Chapter 23: Reconciling, or Balancing, an Account

In This Chapter

✔ Finding out what reconciling is and how to do it in Money

✔ Reconciling a savings or checking account

✔ Recognizing and fixing reconciliation problems

✔ Forcing an account to balance

*U*ntil they start using Money, many people never *reconcile*, or balance, their checking or savings accounts, not to mention their credit cards. But Money makes balancing an account very easy indeed. No kidding, you can do it in four or five minutes. This chapter explains what reconciling is, how to reconcile the transactions in your records with the bank's records, and what to do if you can't get an account to reconcile.

How Reconciling Works

Reconciling is your opportunity to examine your records closely and make sure that they are accurate. When you reconcile an account, you compare your records to the bank's, fix any discrepancies you find, enter transactions that appear on the statement that you forgot to enter in the register, and click in the C (for Cleared) column next to each transaction that appears both in the register and on the bank statement.

In an account register, transactions that have cleared the bank — transactions that have been reconciled — show an R (for Reconciled) in the C (for Cleared) column, as shown in Figure 23-1. Here, you can see that some transactions have cleared the bank and some are still waiting to clear.

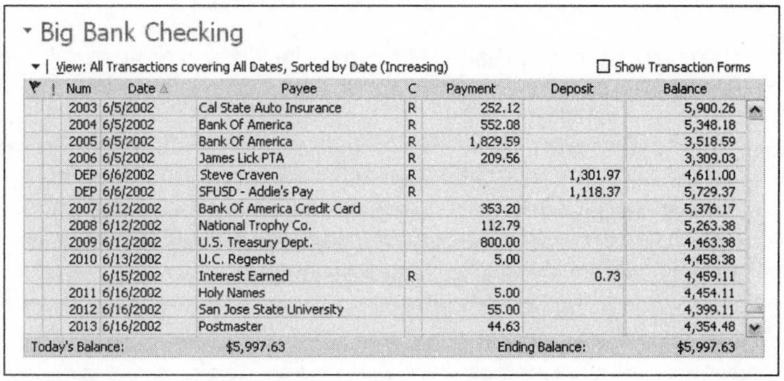

Figure 23-1: An R appears in the C (for Cleared) column when a transaction has cleared the bank.

Big Bank Checking

View: All Transactions covering All Dates, Sorted by Date (Increasing) — ☐ Show Transaction Forms

Num	Date	Payee	C	Payment	Deposit	Balance
2003	6/5/2002	Cal State Auto Insurance	R	252.12		5,900.26
2004	6/5/2002	Bank Of America	R	552.08		5,348.18
2005	6/5/2002	Bank Of America	R	1,829.59		3,518.59
2006	6/5/2002	James Lick PTA	R	209.56		3,309.03
DEP	6/6/2002	Steve Craven	R		1,301.97	4,611.00
DEP	6/6/2002	SFUSD - Addie's Pay	R		1,118.37	5,729.37
2007	6/12/2002	Bank Of America Credit Card		353.20		5,376.17
2008	6/12/2002	National Trophy Co.		112.79		5,263.38
2009	6/12/2002	U.S. Treasury Dept.		800.00		4,463.38
2010	6/13/2002	U.C. Regents		5.00		4,458.38
	6/15/2002	Interest Earned	R		0.73	4,459.11
2011	6/16/2002	Holy Names		5.00		4,454.11
2012	6/16/2002	San Jose State University		55.00		4,399.11
2013	6/16/2002	Postmaster		44.63		4,354.48

Today's Balance: $5,997.63   Ending Balance: $5,997.63

Balancing an Account

Balancing an account is a two-step business. First, you tell the program how much money in interest the account earned (if it earned any) and how much you had to pay the bank for checks, ATM withdrawals, and other services (if you had to pay anything). Then you move ahead to the Balance dialog box, where you make your records jibe with the bank's and click off each transaction that appears both on your bank statement and in the register. Before you begin comparing the register to the bank statement, lay the bank statement flat on your desk. And you may want to put checks in numerical order (if you intend to reconcile a checking account), and your ATM slips in date order (you *have* been saving your ATM slips, haven't you?). With a little luck, you can reconcile without having to glance at checks and ATM slips. But if something goes amiss, you may have to examine the paperwork closely.

Telling Money which transactions cleared the bank

Follow these steps to tell Money which transactions cleared the bank and reconcile an account:

1. **Click the Account List button on the Navigation bar to go to the Accounts window.**

2. **Click the Balance an Account link.**

   You can find this link under Common Tasks on the left side of the window. A link called Balance This Account is also available on account register windows. After you click the link in the Accounts window, you see a list of your accounts that includes the day they were last reconciled.

3. **Click the name of the account you want to balance.**

   You see a Balance dialog box like the one in Figure 23-2. This dialog box is where you enter information from the bank statement. The Starting Balance text box shows the amount of money in the account as of the last time you reconciled it (or the account's opening balance, if you recently opened the account).

What does *reconcile* mean, anyway?

In financial terms, *reconcile* means to compare one set of records to another for the sake of accuracy. When you reconcile an account in Money, you compare the transactions on the statement that the bank or brokerage house sent you to the transactions you entered in the Money register.

If you find a discrepancy between your records and the bank's, you can be pretty sure that the error was made on your side. Not that it doesn't happen, but banks don't err very often when recording financial transactions. Yes, bank lines move too slowly and banks have been known to nickel-and-dime their customers with all kinds of petty charges, but banks are sticklers for accuracy. If you find a discrepancy between your records and the bank's, chances are the error was made on your side, not the bank's.

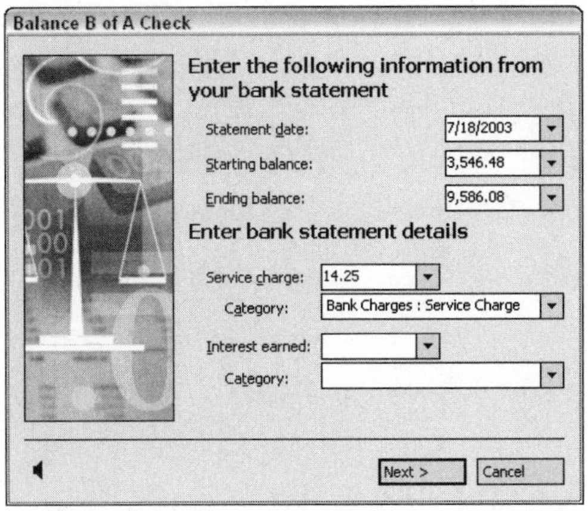

Figure 23-2:
The Balance dialog box, where you tell Money what the bank told you.

Balance B of A Check

Enter the following information from your bank statement

Statement date: 7/18/2003

Starting balance: 3,546.48

Ending balance: 9,586.08

Enter bank statement details

Service charge: 14.25

Category: Bank Charges : Service Charge

Interest earned:

Category:

Next >   Cancel

4. **If necessary, enter the date listed on the bank statement in the Statement Date text box.**

5. **In the Ending Balance text box, enter the closing balance from the bank statement.**

6. **If you have to pay a service charge, enter it in the Service Charge text box, and categorize the service charge as well.**

Banks are like mosquitoes: They like to bite. Banks do it by charging customers all sorts of miscellaneous fees. The fees appear on bank statements. You may get charged for ordering checks, or calling for information, or using an ATM, or sneezing too loudly. Scour the statement for evidence of service charges and enter the sum of those charges in the Service Charge box. For a category, choose Bank Charges: Service Charge, or something similar. (And for more on categorizing, turn to Book IV, Chapter 22.)

7. **In the Interest Earned text box, enter an amount if the account earned any interest, and categorize the interest payment as well.**

You may use the Investment Income: Interest category and subcategory, for example.

Before you click the Next button to move ahead, compare what you entered in this dialog box to what is on your bank statement one last time. Entering numbers incorrectly in this dialog box is one of the primary reasons that people have trouble reconciling their bank accounts.

8. **Click the Next button to move ahead to the Balance Account window, shown in Figure 23-3.**

Only transactions in the register that have not been reconciled appear in the window. Deposits and other transactions that brought money into the account appear at the top of the window; following that are withdrawals and other transactions that record when money was taken out of the account.

If you entered a service charge and/or interest payment in the Balance dialog box (in Steps 6 and 7), the amounts already appear on the window along with a check mark to show that they have been cleared.

Book IV
Chapter 23

Reconciling, or Balancing, an Account

Figure 23-3:
Compare
transactions
in the
register
to the
transactions
on the bank
statement;
click in the
C column
next to each
transaction
that appears
in both
places.

Balance Big Bank Checking							

View: Unreconciled Transactions covering All Dates, Grouped by Deposits, then Checks, t... ☐ Show Transaction Forms

!	Num	Date	Payee	C	Payment	Deposit	Balance
Deposits							
		1/4/2002	SFUSD - Addie's Pay	✓		223.00	31,909.27
	Print	6/19/2002	Walters Inc.			1,000.00	32,909.27
	DEP	6/29/2002	SFUSD - Addie's Pay	✓		3,017.23	35,926.50
Checks							
	1992	5/24/2002	Bridgeport Ranger Station	✓	36.00		35,890.50
	1998	6/1/2002	Capitol One	✓	646.40		35,244.10
	2007	6/12/2002	Bank Of America Credit Card		353.20		34,890.90
	2008	6/12/2002	National Trophy Co.		112.79		34,778.11
	2010	6/13/2002	U.C. Regents	✓	5.00		34,773.11
	2013	6/16/2002	Postmaster	✓	44.63		34,728.48
	2020	6/24/2002	San Jose State University	✓	980.00		33,748.48
	2024	6/26/2002	PG & E		43.34		33,705.14
	2028	7/4/2002	Capitol One		450.00		33,255.14
Other Withdrawals							
	ATM	6/19/2002	Withdrawal	✓	200.00		33,055.14
	ATM	6/25/2002	Withdrawal	✓	100.00		32,955.14
	ATM	6/29/2002	Withdrawal	✓	200.00		32,755.14
		7/4/2002	Old Country Store		156.26		32,598.88
		7/5/2002	Service Charge	✓	14.25		32,584.63

Today's Balance: $32,584.63   Ending Balance: $32,584.63

New   Edit   Delete

Many people think that reconciling accounts is easier when transactions are shown on one line rather than two. To show transactions on one line, open the View menu and choose Top Line Only.

9. Examine your bank statement and click the C column next to each transaction on the statement that also appears in the register.

The left side of the window lists the difference between the ending balance on your bank statement (you listed it in the previous dialog box) and the amount as tabulated by Money. When you click the C column in the register to clear transactions, this amount changes. Gradually, as the account is reconciled, the number changes to 0.00.

To remove a check mark in the C column, click it again. The next section in this chapter explains how you can fix mistakes in the register while you reconcile. The section after that offers strategies for recognizing and fixing reconciliation problems.

If you have trouble finding a transaction in the register, open the View menu and choose Sort⇨Sort by Date or Sort⇨Sort by Number. The Sort by Date command lists transactions in date order, and the Sort by Number command lists them in numerical order in the Num column.

10. Click the Next button when the difference amount is 0.00 and the account is reconciled.

You will find the Next button in the lower-left corner of the window. A Balanced! screen appears and tells you that your account is balanced.

11. Click the Finish button.

Back in the register, all those check marks in the Balance Account window turn to R's in the register. The transactions you clicked off in the Balance Account window have cleared the bank and are reconciled with your records.

If the reconciling business makes you tired or if you find something better to do, click the Postpone button. Later, you can pick up where you left off by clicking the Balance This Account button in the Account window.

Fixing mistakes as you reconcile

Glancing at the bank statement, you discover that you made a mistake when you entered a transaction in a register — you entered the wrong amount or check number. Or perhaps you forgot to enter a transaction altogether. It happens. Cash withdrawals from ATM machines, which usually are made on the spur of the moment, often fail to get recorded in account registers.

Here is how to fix a mistake in a transaction:

1. **Click the transaction that needs correcting.**

If you need to enter a brand-new transaction, go straight to Step 2.

2. **Select the Show Transaction Forms check box.**

As shown in Figure 23-4, a transaction form appears in the window. The form looks and works like the transaction forms you know and love in account registers.

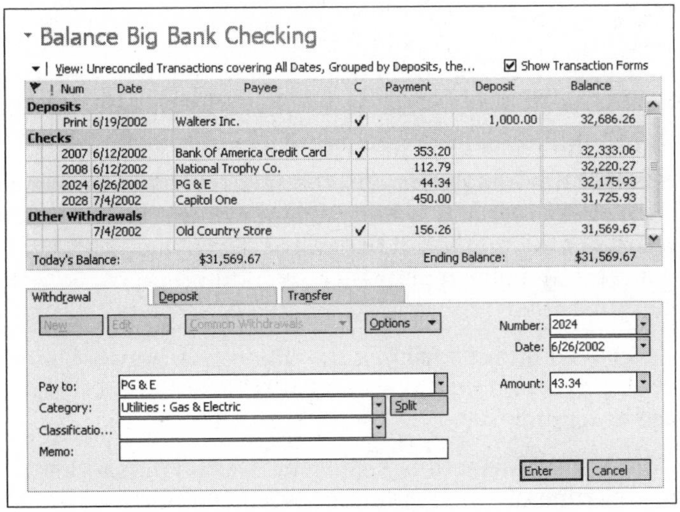

Figure 23-4: Fixing an entry error in the Balance Account window.

3. **Fix the error or enter a new transaction:**

- **New transaction:** Click the New button and enter the transaction.
- **Repair an error:** Enter the correct amount, check number, date, or whatever needs correcting.

4. **Click the Enter button.**

Help! The Darn Thing Won't Reconcile!

Not being able to reconcile a bank account is frustrating. You pore over the bank statement. You examine checks and ATM slips. You gnash your teeth and pull your hair, but still the thing won't reconcile. No matter how hard you try, the Difference figure that lists the difference between the cleared amount and the statement amount cannot be brought to 0.00.

To help you get out of the jam you're in, Money offers techniques for recognizing and fixing reconciliation problems. And Money also has a gizmo called AutoReconcile (which gets its own section later on in this chapter) that may or may not be able to help you reconcile your bank account.

A checklist of things to do if you can't reconcile

If an account won't balance, a number of different things can be wrong. The following sections explain how to recognize and fix reconciliation problems.

✦ **A transaction was not entered:** The primary reason that accounts don't reconcile is because a transaction that is listed on the bank statement has not been entered in the register. ATM withdrawals, for example, are easy to forget and often do not get entered in account registers.

Remedy: Look for a transaction on the bank statement that is equal to the Difference amount on the Balance Account window. If the Difference amount is $35.20, chances are you forgot to record a $35.20 transaction in the register. Look for a $35.20 transaction on the bank statement and, if necessary, click the Show Transaction Forms check box to display a form and enter the transaction. Be sure to enter the date correctly. If the difference is $20.00, $40.00, or another round number, chances are you forgot to enter an ATM withdrawal.

✦ **An amount in the register is incorrect:** Another reason accounts don't reconcile is that amounts were entered incorrectly in the register. This problem is a sticky one and is hard to track down. Look for transposed numbers and numbers entered backward. For example, $32.41 and $34.21 look alike at a glance, but there is a difference of $1.80 between the numbers.

Here's an old accountant's trick: If the difference between what you have and what you should have is evenly divisible by 9, you probably transposed a number.

Remedy: Click the transaction, select the Show Transaction Forms check box, and change the amount on a transaction form.

✦ **A transaction was entered twice:** Look for duplicate transactions in the register to make sure that no transaction was entered twice.

Remedy: Delete one of the transactions by pressing Ctrl+D or right-clicking it and choosing Delete from the shortcut menu.

✦ **A check was entered as a deposit or vice versa:** Making an error like this is easy. Fortunately, detecting it is easy, too.

Remedy: Clear your checks and withdrawals first; then clear your deposits. You'll notice during this process whether a deposit, check, or withdrawal is missing. Click the transaction and then click the Show Transaction Forms check box. On the transaction form, edit the transaction to make it a deposit or a withdrawal. If you feel comfortable doing so, you can also right-click the transaction and choose Change Transaction Type To — Withdrawal or Change Transaction Type To — Deposit.

✦ **The Ending (Statement) balance is incorrect:** If you enter the Ending balance incorrectly in the Balance dialog box (refer to Figure 23-2), you cannot reconcile an account no matter how hard you try.

Remedy: Return to the Balance dialog box (refer to Figure 23-2) and enter a correct Ending Balance figure. To do so, click the Postpone button to return to the Accounts window, click the Balance This Account button, and then click the Next button. You see the Balance dialog box again, where you can enter a correct Ending balance this time. Click Next again to return to the Balance Account window.

✦ **A service charge or interest earned is incorrect:** Besides entering the ending balance incorrectly, you may have entered an incorrect amount in the Service Charge or Interest Earned text box in the Balance dialog box (refer to Figure 23-2). Compare the interest and service charges on your statement to the ones in the Balance Account window to see whether an amount is incorrect.

Remedy: Click the service charge or interest entry in the Balance Account window, select the Show Transaction Forms check box, and enter a correct figure on the transaction form.

✦ **The bank statement was not flipped over:** Don't forget to turn over the bank statement and examine the transactions listed on the other side of the page.

Remedy: Turn the page, note the transactions, and click to put a check mark next to them.

"AutoReconciling" an account

If all else fails, you can try Money's AutoReconcile gizmo to find out why the account won't balance. This contraption scours the register for transactions that it thinks were entered incorrectly and gives you the chance to enter them correctly so that the account can be reconciled. Follow these steps to try it:

1. **Click the Next button.**

Although the account isn't balanced, click the Next button as though it is in balance. You see the Balance dialog box.

2. **Select the second option button, Use AutoReconcile to Help Find the Error.**

If you're in luck and Money can find the error, the Possible Error dialog box appears.

3. **Read the description of the error and click Yes or No to change the transaction in question or to let it stand.**

Forcing an account to balance

If, despite your detective work, you can't find the problem that keeps your account from balancing, you can force the account to balance. Forcing an account to balance means to enter what accountants call an "adjustment

**Book IV
Chapter 23**

Reconciling,
or Balancing,
an Account

825

transaction" — a fictitious transaction, a little white lie that makes the numbers add up. If the difference between what your statement says and what the Balance Account window says is just a few pennies, enter the adjustment transaction and spare yourself the headache of looking for the error. A few pennies here and there never hurt anybody.

The words "Account Adjustment" appear in the register on the Payee line when you force an adjustment transaction. Money gives you the chance to categorize the transaction on your own. After you have torn out your hair trying to discover why an account won't balance, follow these steps to force an adjustment transaction:

1. **Click the Next button in the Balance Account window.**

Click the Next button even though the account has not been reconciled. The Balance dialog box appears. It tells you that the account isn't in balance and asks what you want to do about it.

2. **Select the Automatically Adjust the Account Balance option button.**

3. **Choose a category from the Category drop-down list.**

4. **Click OK.**

Chapter 24: Money for Investors

In This Chapter

✔ Setting up investment, retirement, and employee stock option accounts

✔ Describing the securities in an account

✔ Updating the price of a security

✔ Recording stock and bond transactions

✔ Recording mutual fund transactions

✔ Examining and comparing the investments in a portfolio

The title of this chapter is "Money for Investors," but I hope you didn't come to this part of the book expecting to find 10-, 20-, and 50-dollar bills folded between the pages. No, you have to get money for your investments elsewhere. After you do, though, you can use Microsoft Money to track your investments.

In this chapter, you discover how to record the sale and purchase of mutual fund shares, stock shares, and bonds. You find out how to set up an electronic investment portfolio and examine the investments in the portfolio in different ways. You find out a lot of things, truth be told.

Your Own Electronic Portfolio

A *portfolio* is a collection of investments. After you set up investment and retirement accounts, you can click the Portfolio button and see an electronic version of your portfolio, as shown Figure 24-1. After you have set up a portfolio like this one, recording investment transactions is easy. What's more, the Your Portfolio window is an excellent place to start analyzing your investments.

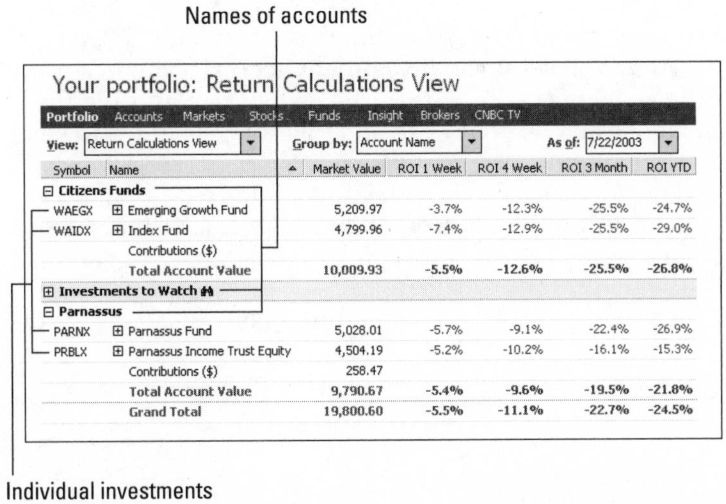

Names of accounts

Figure 24-1: The Your Portfolio window offers many different ways of examining your investments.

Your portfolio: Return Calculations View

| Portfolio | Accounts | Markets | Stocks | Funds | Insight | Brokers | CNBC TV |

View: Return Calculations View   Group by: Account Name   As of: 7/22/2003

Symbol	Name	Market Value	ROI 1 Week	ROI 4 Week	ROI 3 Month	ROI YTD
⊟ **Citizens Funds**						
WAEGX	⊞ Emerging Growth Fund	5,209.97	-3.7%	-12.3%	-25.5%	-24.7%
WAIDX	⊞ Index Fund	4,799.96	-7.4%	-12.9%	-25.5%	-29.0%
	Contributions ($)					
	Total Account Value	10,009.93	-5.5%	-12.6%	-25.5%	-26.8%
⊞ **Investments to Watch** 🔍						
⊟ **Parnassus**						
PARNX	⊞ Parnassus Fund	5,028.01	-5.7%	-9.1%	-22.4%	-26.9%
PRBLX	⊞ Parnassus Income Trust Equity	4,504.19	-5.2%	-10.2%	-16.1%	-15.3%
	Contributions ($)	258.47				
	Total Account Value	9,790.67	-5.4%	-9.6%	-19.5%	-21.8%
	Grand Total	19,800.60	-5.5%	-11.1%	-22.7%	-24.5%

Individual investments

Looking at Figure 24-1, you can see the following:

✦ **The names of the investment or retirement accounts.** Create one investment or retirement account for each statement you receive from a brokerage house, each financial institution you buy certificates of deposit (CDs) or other investments from, and each retirement plan that you participate in. Doing so makes keeping the records easier because you can enter data in the account straight from the brokerage or bank statement and even reconcile your account from the statements that you receive in the mail.

✦ **The names of the individual investments.** After you set up the accounts, you list the names of the securities — the stocks, bonds, mutual funds, CDs, and so on — that belong in the account. You can then record purchases, sales, share reinvestments, capital gains, dividends, stock splits, and so on in the register.

✦ **The grand total value of your investments.** This sum appears at the bottom of the window, along with year-to-date capital gain and return of your investments.

When your portfolio is complete, you can see at a glance the market value and price of each investment. By changing views, you can see how your investments perform, how they have changed in value, and how you have allocated them, among other things. By clicking the Analyze My Portfolio button, you can analyze investments in various ways.

Setting Up Investment, Retirement, and Employee Stock Option Accounts

Before you can analyze your investments, you need to set up an investment account, retirement account, or Employee Stock Option account. This section explains how to do just that.

Setting up an investment account for tracking securities

The first step in tracking investments is to create a new account for each institution, brokerage house, or retirement plan that you trade with or participate in. After you set up an investment account, you describe the securities that the account tracks. Spread the last statement from the bank or brokerage house across your desk and follow these steps to set up an investment account:

1. **Click the Account List button to go to the Account List window.**

2. **Click the Set Up Accounts link.**

You can find this link under Common Tasks.

3. **Click the Add a New Account link.**

   After you click it, the first New Account dialog box appears.

4. **Enter the name of the brokerage house or bank where you keep the account in the text box, or select a name from the drop-down list; then click the Next button.**

   If Money doesn't recognize the name you entered, you see the Confirm Your Name dialog box. Choose a name from the list of financial institutions' names and click Next.

5. **Select the Investment account type and click the Next button.**

6. **In the next dialog box, enter a name for the account.**

   The name you enter will appear in the Account List window after you finish setting up the account. For convenience' sake, you may want to enter the name of the brokerage house where you keep the account.

7. **Click the Taxable or Tax Deferred or Tax Free option button to specify whether the money you track in this account is tax deferred; then click the Next button.**

   Tax deferred means that you don't have to pay income tax on the money that the account generates until you begin withdrawing it at retirement age. Probably the option button to click is Taxable. Most tax-deferred accounts are retirement accounts (how to set up a retirement account is explained shortly).

8. **In the next dialog box, select the No, I'll Do This Later option button; then click Next.**

   A bit later in this chapter, in the section, "Describing the Securities in Investment and Retirement Accounts," I show you how to record security transactions in an Investment account.

9. **In the next dialog box, enter the approximate value of the account in the Investments text box, as shown in Figure 24-2.**

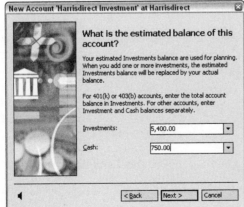

Figure 24-2: Setting up an investment account.

Don't worry about being accurate with these figures — they're used for planning and estimating purposes only. You can get the estimated value of the investments in the account from your most recent statement. Don't include cash in the estimated value of the account if you keep cash as well as investments in the account. If you recently sold a security or made a deposit in the account, it likely includes a bit of cash.

10. **Enter the amount of money in the account in the Cash text box; then click Next.**

    As the dialog box explains, you can estimate the amount of money in the cash account if you want. The amounts you enter in the dialog box are used for planning purposes.

11. **Select the I Have No Other Accounts at This Institution option button and click Next.**

12. **Click the Finish button.**

    Deselect the Go to Online Setup for *Your Brokerage Firm* option button and the last dialog box. That button is for setting up Money so that you can bank online with the brokerage firm.

After you set up the investment account, go to its Details window and enter the name and phone number of your broker. You need that information in case you need to call your broker. You can enter other useful information in the Details window as well. To get to an account's Details window, right-click its name in the Account List window and choose See Account Details.

Setting up a retirement account for tracking retirement savings and investments

Follow these steps to set up an account for tracking the tax-deferred investments you have made for your retirement:

1. **Click the Account List button to go the Account List window.**

2. **Click the Set Up Accounts link.**

Know the tax status of your investment

Don't confuse tax-deferred income with tax-exempt income. The two types of income sound confusingly alike, but they are different in the eyes of the IRS:

✔ **Tax-deferred income:** Income from a tax-deferred account is not taxed until you start withdrawing money from the account. Money placed in an IRA is an example of tax-deferred income.

✔ **Tax-exempt income:** In contrast, you *never* have to pay any tax on tax-exempt income. Most retirement accounts are tax deferred, not tax exempt.

3. Click the Add a New Account link.

You see the first New Account dialog box.

4. Enter the name of the brokerage house or bank where the account is kept or select a name from the drop-down list; then click the Next button.

If Money doesn't recognize the name you entered, choose a brokerage firm from the list in the next dialog box that appears.

5. Select the Retirement account type and click the Next button.

6. In the next dialog box, enter a name for the account and click the Next button.

The name you enter will appear on the Account List window after you finish setting up the account.

7. In the next dialog box, as shown in Figure 24-3, select the type of retirement account you want to set up; then click the Next button.

If you aren't sure what kind of retirement account you are dealing with, you can click an account type in the list box on the left to see its description in the box on the right side of the dialog box.

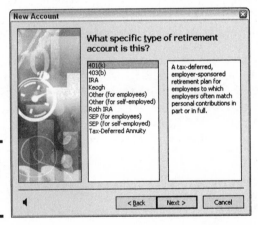

Figure 24-3: Setting up a retirement account.

8. If you track a spouse's or partner's finances with Money, choose the name of the person whose retirement account you want to track; then click the Next button.

Money gets the name or names on the list from the survey you take when you install the program, but if you didn't take the survey, don't worry about it. Enter the name and then fill in the dialog boxes to describe yourself or your spouse or partner.

9. In the next dialog box, select the No, I'll Do This Later option button; then click Next.

Later in this chapter, in the section, "Describing the Securities in Investment and Retirement Accounts," I show you how to record transactions in the account.

10. **In the next dialog box, enter the approximate value of the account in the Investments text box.**

    These figures are used strictly for planning and estimating purposes. You will be given ample opportunities to enter the exact numbers later on. Check your recent statement for the estimated value of the investments in the account. If cash is in the account at present, don't include it in the estimated value.

11. **Enter the amount of money in the account in the Cash text box.**

    As the dialog box explains, you can estimate the amount of money in the cash account if you want.

12. **Select the second option button, I Have No Other Accounts at This Institution, and click Next.**

13. **Click the Finish button.**

Setting up an account to track employee stock options

If you are fortunate enough to work for a company that offers stock options to its employees, you can track the value of that stock with Money. To do so, create an investment account (see "Setting up an investment account for tracking securities," earlier in this chapter), fill in the New Account dialog boxes, and choose Employee Stock Option when you are asked what kind of account you want to set up.

By now you must surely know how to set up an account in Money. Besides the usual questions, you are asked for the date you were granted the stock, how many shares you were granted, and the *strike price* — the closing price of the stock on the day it was given to you. Other than that, the only unusual screen you need to fill out is the one shown in Figure 24-4. This is where you tell Money how quickly or slowly the stock grant becomes yours.

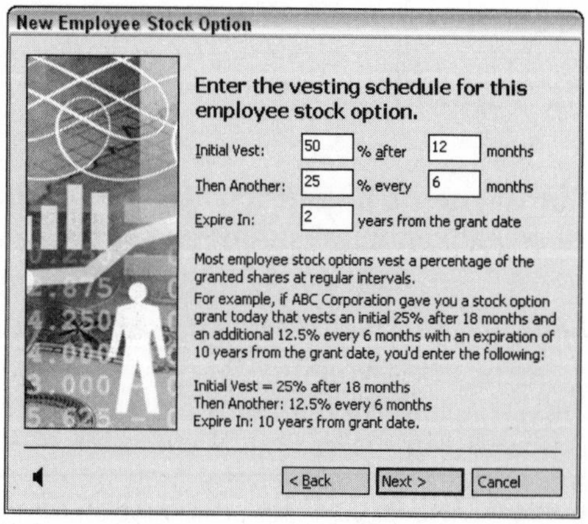

Figure 24-4: Fill in the text boxes to describe how, slowly but surely, you come to own stock in your company.

In most companies, employees are not given stock outright. Instead, they become vested in the stock they own over a period of time. Use the text boxes on the New Employee Stock Option dialog box to describe how your company's plan calls for you to be vested in the stock you were granted.

When you finish setting up the account, open its register. You see future entries that describe when you will receive new stock as part of the vesture. As you update the stock price in this register, it shows the stock's value.

Describing the Securities in Investment and Retirement Accounts

After you set up an investment or retirement account, you must describe each security in the account. *Securities* are the stocks, mutual funds, certificates, bonds, or other financial instruments that the account tracks. Gather the paperwork and follow these steps to describe each security that you own. If you just purchased more shares of a security that you already own and have already described in an investment or retirement account, skip ahead to "Recording a purchase of more stocks or more bonds" or "Recording the sale or purchase of mutual funds" later in this chapter.

1. **Click the Portfolio button on the Navigation bar or choose Investing➪ Portfolio to go to the Your Portfolio window.**

This window is the starting point for handling, managing, and analyzing investments.

2. **Click the Add an Investment link.**

You'll find the link under Common Tasks on the left side of the window. After you click it, the first New Investment dialog box appears.

3. **Click the down arrow to open the Account drop-down list, and choose the investment or retirement account where you track the security; then click Next.**

If no account names appear on the menu, you haven't set up an investment or retirement account yet. The start of this chapter explains how to do that.

4. **In the Investment Name text box, enter the name of the security; then click Next.**

The name you enter will appear in your portfolio. You see the Create New Investment dialog box, shown on the left side of Figure 24-5. In this dialog box, you tell Money what kind of investment you are tracking.

5. **Select an option button to describe the security and then click Next.**

Which dialog box you see next depends on which option button you selected. In Figure 24-5, I chose the Stock option button, so the New Stock dialog box asks me to enter the stock's symbol. Except for bonds, Money asks for your investment's ticker symbol. In the case of a bond, you will be asked for the coupon rate, interest paid, maturity date, and call date.

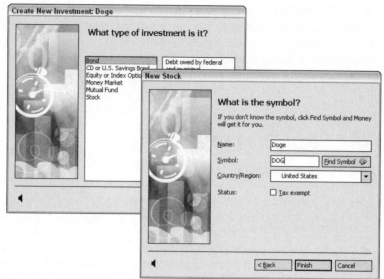

Figure 24-5:
Telling
Money what
kind of
security you
are dealing
with.

6. **Fill in the New dialog box or boxes and then click the Finish button.**

If you can, enter the ticker symbol for your mutual fund, stock, CD, or money market fund in the New dialog box (refer to Figure 24-5). That way, you can update the security's price from the Internet and save a lot of time that you would otherwise spend updating the price by hand. If you don't know the ticker symbol, look for it carefully on your broker-age statement — you can usually find it there. Or try clicking the Find Symbol button to go on the Internet and find the ticker symbol.

7. **In the following dialog box, shown in Figure 24-6, enter in the Quantity text box the number of shares of the security you own.**

For mutual funds and stocks, enter the number of shares you own. If you are describing the purchase of a single CD or bond, enter **1**. For investments such as precious metals, enter the number of ounces or other unit of measurement.

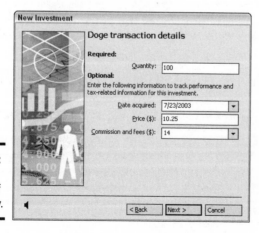

Figure 24-6:
Describing
the value of
the security.

You don't have to fill in the bottom three boxes in the New Investment dialog box, but do so if you intend to track the value of the security from the day you purchased it. By filling in these boxes, you can analyze your investment to see how it has grown or shrunk over time.

8. **In the Date Acquired text box, enter the date that you purchased the security; enter the price per unit you paid in the Price text box; enter the commission, if you paid one, in the Commission/Fee text box; then click the Next button.**

When you enter share prices of stock, you can enter fractions. For example, you can enter 50½ or 10¼. Money converts the entry to a decimal.

For bonds, enter the price of a bond as a percentage of the bond's par value (its face value). For example, if the bond's par value is $1,000 and its price is $950, enter **95** in the Price text box.

If you are tracking the value of this security from the day you bought it, be sure to enter data about your original purchase. You may have bought more shares in the security or sold shares in the past. The value may have gone up or down. You need to enter purchase data as of the date you entered back in the Date Acquired text box.

9. **Click the Finish button if you are done entering securities in the account; if other securities need listing, click the Yes button, click the Next button, and return to Step 3.**

Do not pass Go and do not collect $200.

Repeat the seven steps for each security that the account tracks, and then read on to find out how to update the prices of the securities.

Watch List: Tracking securities you don't own

Suppose that you want to track a stock, mutual fund, money market fund, or other security that you don't own, perhaps to decide whether you want to buy it later. You can do that by placing the security on the Watch List, a special portfolio category that Money maintains for monitoring security prices.

Getting price quotes for securities on the Watch List is a great way to find out from day to day or week to week how a potential investment performs. You can even download index prices in order to compare and contrast the securities you own to the performance of an index.

To add securities to the Watch List, click the Add an Investment link in the Your Portfolio window and describe the investment as you normally would, but choose Investments to Watch from the Account drop-down list. (If you don't see Investments to Watch in the Your Portfolio window, click the See a Different View link and choose Show Watch Accounts from the submenu.)

Next time you download quotes from the Internet, you can see how the investment has performed. Watch List investments appear along with other investments in the Your Portfolio window, where you can study their performance. Right-click a security and choose See Price History to see a chart that shows how well or poorly the security has performed in the past six months.

Book IV
Chapter 24

Money for Investors

Editing an Investment or Retirement Account Transaction

Suppose that you enter a transaction in an investment or retirement account incorrectly. It can happen. And when it does happen, you will be glad to know, you can edit it by using the same techniques you use to edit a transaction in a checking account or savings account — by going into the account register and making the change.

To edit an investment or retirement account transaction, open its account register. Click the Portfolio button on the Navigation bar to go to the Your Portfolio window. Then click the name of the account with the transaction that needs changing to open its account register, find the transaction, click it, and click the Edit button in the transaction form. As shown in Figure 24-7, the transaction form shows the transaction. Now you can edit it to your heart's content.

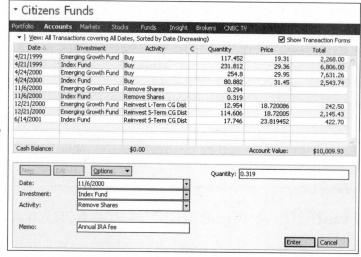

Figure 24-7: Click a transaction and then click the Edit button to change it.

A fast way to open an account register where you track retirement or investment securities is to click the Work with Investments link in the Your Portfolio window and click the name of the security on the submenu that appears.

Updating the Price of a Security

By tracking changes in the value of a security, you can analyze the performance of your investments and the change in the value of your portfolio over time. Follow these steps to manually update the price of a security in your portfolio:

1. Open the Your Portfolio window.

To get there, click the Portfolio button on the Navigation bar.

2. **Click the Update Prices link and choose Update Prices Manually from the submenu, as shown in Figure 24-8.**

   You see the Update Price dialog box, also shown in Figure 24-8.

Choose which security to update.

Choose Update Prices Manually.

Enter its unit price.

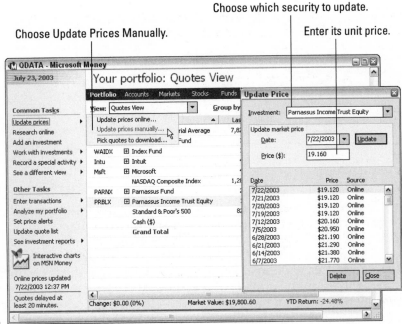

Figure 24-8:
Report changes in the price of a security in the Update Price dialog box.

3. **Click the arrow to open the Investment drop-down list and select the investment whose price you want to update.**

4. **In the Date box, enter the date that the price changed.**

5. **Enter the new price in the Price ($) text box.**

6. **Click the Update button.**

   The new price is entered in the price history list. Note in Figure 24-8 that the Source column says "Online" next to the entries. When you enter a price yourself, the column says "Update," but it says "Online" when you get prices from the Internet.

7. **If you want to record the price history of a security, keep entering new dates and new security prices; otherwise, select a new security from the Investment drop-down list and update its price.**

8. **Click the Close button when you're done.**

Recording Payments to and Disbursements from Brokers

It might seem kind of odd, but when you write a check to a broker or make a contribution to a retirement account, you do so by transferring the money from your checking account to the account where you track your investments or retirement savings. Go ahead and make out the check as you normally would. Enter the brokerage house's name in the Pay To text box, but instead of categorizing the check, choose a Transfer option from the bottom of the Category drop-down list, as shown in Figure 24-9.

Figure 24-9:
Record payments to and disbursements from brokers as money transfers.

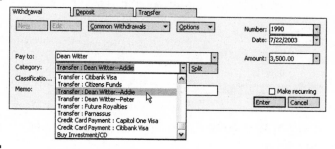

On the other side, in the investment or retirement account, the transfer is recorded as a deposit. The cash in investment and retirement accounts is used to pay for stock, bond, and other security purchases.

Similarly, when you sell or collect interest on a security, the proceeds are recorded as a cash deposit in the Deposit column of the investment or retirement account. Suppose that you decide to take money out of an investment or retirement account. When the check comes from your broker and you deposit it in your bank account, record the transaction as a transfer from your investment or retirement account to your bank account. For example, if you sell a stock and make a $400 dollar profit, record the transaction as a $400 transfer from your investment account to the checking account where you deposit the $400.

You can click the Cash Transactions link (found on the left side of the register window) when you are looking at an investment or retirement account to see money transfers in and out of the account.

Handling Stocks and Bonds

Keeping track of stocks and bonds — especially stocks — is probably the most problematic task you will ever undertake with Money. Merely figuring out what a short sell is, not to mention a margin buy and a stock split, is hard enough to begin with. How can you record these strange events in an investment or retirement account register?

Read on, friend, and you can discover how to record everything from stock sales and purchases to short sells and margin buys.

Recording a purchase of more stocks or more bonds

When you purchase more shares of a stock you already own or more bonds of a type you already own, follow these steps to record the purchase:

1. **Go to the Your Portfolio window.**

   To get there, click the Portfolio button on the Navigation bar or choose Investing⇨Portfolio.

2. **Click the name of the security you want to work with.**

   If you want to see a miniregister with other transactions that pertain to the security, click the plus sign next to the security's name.

3. **Click the Other Tasks link, choose Enter Transactions on the submenu, and then choose Record a Buy.**

   You see the Edit Transaction dialog box, as shown in Figure 24-10.

4. **Click the New button.**

5. **From the Inv. Account drop-down list, choose the account where you track the investment, if necessary.**

   If you selected the right security in Step 2, it isn't necessary.

6. **In the Date text box on the transaction form, enter the date you purchased the stocks or bonds.**

7. **In the Investment box, click the arrow and select the security from the drop-down list.**

   Again, this isn't necessary if you selected the right security in Step 2.

8. **Select Buy from the Activity drop-down list.**

9. **Fill in the rest of the transaction form — the Quantity text box, Commission text box, Price text box, and Transfer From text box.**

   If you need help filling in these boxes, see the "Describing the Securities in Investment and Retirement Accounts" section, earlier in this chapter.

10. **Click the OK button.**

Click to see or remove the mini-register.

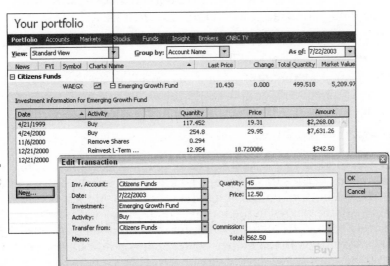

Figure 24-10: Recording the purchase of more stocks or bonds.

Recording the sale of stocks and bonds

Except for the problem of lots, recording the sales of stocks and bonds is pretty simple. A *lot* is a group of securities purchased at the same time for the same price (and also a nephew of Abraham whose wife got turned into a saltshaker, but that's another story). Suppose that you buy 10 shares of Burger Heaven at $10 per share in January, and then buy 10 more shares of the same company at $20 per share in February. In March, you sell 15 shares. How many shares you sell from the $10 lot and the $20 lot is important in determining how much profit you make and how much you have to pay in capital gains taxes. Fortunately, Money offers a wizard for helping you decide which shares to sell.

To see which stock lots you have purchased, click the plus sign to display the miniregister, click the More Investment Data button in the miniregister, and choose View Lots from the pop-up menu.

Follow these steps to record the sale of stocks or bonds:

1. **Go to the Your Portfolio window.**

   To get there, click the Portfolio button on the Navigation bar or choose Investing➪Portfolio.

2. **Select the name of the security you want to work with.**

3. **Click the Other Tasks link, choose Enter Transactions on the submenu, and then choose Record a Sell.**

   You see the Edit Transaction dialog box (refer to Figure 24-10).

4. **Choose the investment account where you track the security, enter the date of the sale, and select the name of the security you sold from the Investment drop-down list.**

   If you selected the right security in Step 2, all you have to do is enter the date.

5. **In the Quantity text box, enter the number of shares or bonds that you sold; enter the price in the Price text box.**

6. **If a commission was charged on the sale, enter the amount of the commission in the Commission text box.**

   Money enters the total amount of the sale in the Total text box. If the figure is incorrect, double-check the Quantity and Price text boxes to make sure that you entered the numbers correctly.

7. **Click the OK button.**

That's all there is to it — unless you purchased the shares in different lots. In that case, you see the What Shares Should I Use? dialog box after you click the OK button. Unless you tell it otherwise, Money assumes that you want to sell the shares in the lot that you purchased first. To do that, simply click the Finish button. But if you want to sell shares from different lots, follow these steps to tell Money which shares you want to sell:

1. **Click the first option, I Would Like to Specify Which Shares to Sell or Transfer, and then click the Next button.**

You see the Allocate Lots dialog box. In this dialog box, you can select shares yourself from the lots, as the following steps demonstrate; you can click the Maximum Gain button to sell lots and pay the most capital gains taxes; or you can click the Minimum Gain button to sell lots.

2. **In the top of the dialog box, click one of the lots from which you sold shares.**

3. **Enter the number of shares you sold from the lot in the Enter Shares to Allocate from Lot Above text box.**

4. **Select another lot and repeat Steps 2 and 3 to tell Money how many shares you sold from it.**

After you're done declaring which shares you sold, the Total Selected and Total to Allocate numbers in the dialog box should be the same.

5. **Click the Finish button.**

Be sure to notify your broker of which shares you want to sell. If you forget to do that, your broker may assume that you want to sell shares beginning with the first lot you purchased.

Recording and reinvesting dividends

Most stocks pay dividends, which means that you have to record dividends as they arrive. And some stocks and mutual funds, rather than pay dividends, give shareholders the opportunity to buy more shares with their dividends as part of a DRIP (dividend reinvestment program). The advantage of reinvesting a dividend is that you often don't have to pay a broker's commission to purchase the new stock.

To record a dividend or the reinvestment of a dividend, start from the Your Portfolio window and click the name of the security that paid a dividend. Then click the Other Tasks link, choose Enter Transactions from the submenu, and choose Record All Details of a Trade. You see the Edit Transaction dialog box (refer to Figure 24-10). Select Dividend or Reinvest Dividend from the Activity drop-down list and do the following:

✦ **Recording a dividend:** In the Total text box, enter the amount of the dividend. Be sure to select the account into which you deposited the dividend from the Transfer To drop-down list. Click Enter when you're done.

✦ **Recording a dividend reinvestment:** Enter the number of shares you purchased with the dividend in the Quantity text box, the price per share in the Price text box, and any commission in the Commission text box. Make sure that the total in the Total text box is correct before you click the OK button.

Recording stock splits, short sells, margin purchases, and other esoterica

The stock market, it seems, has a hundred different ways to trade stock, handle stock sales, and handle stock purchases. I suspect that the brokers like it that way because it makes them appear indispensable. Fortunately, you can use Money to record certain kinds of oddball stock trades and sales.

Stock splits

Occasionally, stock shares are split to lower the price of individual shares and make them more attractive to investors. In a 2-for-1 split, for example, investors are given twice as much stock, but the value of individual stocks is half what it was before, so the owner of 100 shares worth $2,000 now owns 200 shares worth the same amount, $2,000.

Follow these steps to record a stock split:

1. **Starting from the Your Portfolio window, click the Record a Special Activity link and then choose Record a Split from the submenu.**

   You see the Split Shares dialog box.

2. **Click the Investment down arrow and select the stock that was split from the drop-down list.**

3. **Enter the date that the stock was split in the Date text box.**

4. **In the Split the Shares text boxes, enter the ratio of new stocks to old ones.**

   For example, in a 2-for-1 split, enter 2 in the first box and 1 in the second box.

5. **Click OK.**

   In the Your Portfolio window, Money calculates and enters the number of shares you own. The total value of those shares, however, remains the same.

Short sells

A *short sell* is when you believe that a stock will fall in price and you attempt to profit by borrowing shares from a broker, selling them at a high price, and then buying shares when the price drops and using those low-priced shares to replace the ones you borrowed.

Suppose, for example, that you think that ABC Corporation's shares will fall below their current price of $20 a share. You borrow ten shares from your broker and sell those shares for $200. When the price drops to $15 a share, you buy ten shares on your own, pay $150 for them, and give the broker back his or her ten shares. By selling the shares that didn't belong to you first (for $200) and buying them later (for $150), you earn a $50 profit. Of course, if the stock rises in price, you end up paying the broker back out of your own pocket, not from the proceeds of the sale.

How to record brokerage account fees

Brokers charge fees. Not a few of them have been known to nickel-and-dime their customers to death. How do you record brokerage fees in Money? The answer: You record transactions in the investment or retirement account register and select Other Expense from the Activity drop-down list on the transaction tab.

When you select Other Expense, the Category drop-down list appears so that you can categorize the brokerage fee. If the expense is associated with a particular security, select the security from the Investment drop-down list; otherwise, leave the Investment box blank. And make sure that the account from which you paid the fee appears in the Transfer from box.

To record a short sell, fill in the Edit Transaction dialog box as you normally would, but select Short Sell from the Activity drop-down list. Typically, brokers charge interest for the shares you borrow. The interest is reported in the Commission text box.

Return of capital

A *return of capital* is a return of part of the price you paid for stock. Sometimes a return of capital is paid to investors in lieu of a dividend. You'll know when you have been paid a return of capital because your statement tells you so. To record a return of capital, select Return of Capital from the Activity drop-down list in the Edit Transaction dialog box. Enter the amount of the return in the Total text box and select the account where you will stash it from the Transfer to drop-down list.

Margin purchases

Brokers gladly lend money to buy stocks and bonds. Buying a stock or bond with money you borrowed from a broker is called *buying on the margin*.

To record stocks or a bond you purchased on the margin, record it as you would a buy, but select Other Expense from the Activity drop-down list. When you select Other Expense, a category box appears on the transaction form so that you can categorize the expense. Select an expense category from the category drop-down list to describe the interest you had to pay your broker for the loan.

Corporate mergers

When one corporation merges with another and the two swap stocks, you need to record how many shares are being issued for each share of the parent company and the share price that the parent company has to pay for each share of the company that it has swallowed.

When you own stock that is involved in a swap, go to the Your Portfolio window, click the Record a Special Activity link, choose Record a Merger, and fill in the Record a Merger dialog boxes.

Corporate securities spin-off

When a corporation spins off, drops off, or lops off part of itself and you own shares in the corporation, you need to record how many new shares the corporation is issuing for each old share. To do that, go to the Your Portfolio window, click the Record a Special Activity button, and choose Record a Spin-Off from the submenu. Then fill in the Record a Spin-Off dialog boxes.

Handling Mutual Funds

Mutual funds seem to be everybody's favorite investment. A *mutual fund* is an investment company that raises money from shareholders and invests the money in a variety of places, including stocks, bonds, and money market securities. With a mutual fund, you let experts do the work of deciding what to invest in. All you have to do is collect the profits, count them, and hide them under your mattress.

Recording the sale or purchase of mutual funds

You record the sale or purchase of a mutual fund the same way as you record the sale or purchase of stocks and bonds. Earlier in this chapter, the sections "Recording a purchase of more stocks or more bonds" and "Recording the sale of stocks and bonds" explain how.

When you buy shares in the fund, select Buy from the Activity drop-down list; when you sell shares, select (duh) Sell. Be sure to accurately describe the number of shares you purchased or sold in the Quantity text box. And don't forget to enter the price per share correctly in the Price text box, either.

Recording dividends and distributions

From time to time, mutual fund managers send dividend distributions. More than likely, however, dividends are paid in the form of *reinvestments*. Instead of profits that your shares have made coming to you in a check, the profits are used to purchase more shares in the fund. Following are instructions for recording a dividend payment and for recording a mutual fund distribution.

Mutual fund dividend distributions

Follow these steps to record the receipt of mutual fund dividend distributions:

1. **Go to the Your Portfolio window and click the name of the fund from which you received a dividend distribution.**

2. **Click the Other Tasks link, select Enter Transactions from the submenu, and then choose Record All Details of a Trade.**

   You see the Edit Transaction dialog box.

3. **Enter the date that the dividend was disbursed in the Date text box.**

4. **From the Activity drop-down list, select the option that describes the dividend distribution.**

   Look on your mutual fund statement to find out which option to select:

   - **Interest:** An interest distribution
   - **Dividend:** A dividend distribution
   - **S-Term Cap Gains Dist:** A short-term capital gains distribution
   - **Mid-Term Cap Gains Dist:** A mid-term capital gains distribution
   - **L-Term Cap Gains Dist:** A long-term capital gains distribution

5. **Enter the amount of the dividend in the Total text box.**

   The Edit Transaction dialog box should look something like the one in Figure 24-11. Make sure that the account into which you deposited the distribution appears in the Transfer To box.

6. **Click the OK button.**

Figure 24-11: Recording a mutual fund dividend distribution.

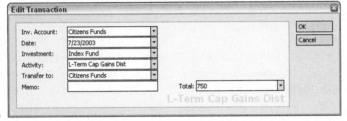

Mutual fund reinvestment distributions

Follow these steps when the profits from a mutual fund are used to purchase more shares in the fund:

1. **In the Your Portfolio window, click the name of the mutual fund.**

2. **Click the Other Tasks link, choose Enter Transactions from the submenu, and then choose Record All Details of a Trade to open the Edit Transaction dialog box.**

3. **Enter the date of the reinvestment in the Date text box.**

4. **From the Activity drop-down list, select the option that describes how the profits were reinvested.**

   Your mutual fund statement tells you which of these options to select:

   - **Reinvest Interest:** A reinvested interest distribution
   - **Reinvest Dividend:** A reinvested dividend distribution
   - **Reinvest S-Term CG Dist:** A reinvested short-term capital gains distribution
   - **Reinvest Mid-Term CG Dist:** A reinvested mid-term capital gains distribution
   - **Reinvest L-Term CG Dist:** A reinvested long-term capital gains distribution

5. **In the Quantity text box, enter the number of shares that the reinvestment purchased.**

6. **In the Price text box, enter the price of shares in the mutual fund.**

7. **If necessary, enter a commission you had to pay in the Commission text box.**

One of the advantages of reinvesting mutual fund profits is *not* having to pay a commission to purchase the shares. Most funds do not require you to pay a commission when you reinvest. If your fund makes you pay a commission, complain about it to the fund manager.

8. **Click the OK button.**

Analyzing and Comparing Investments

The fun begins after you enter the securities and list their prices. Now, starting from the Your Portfolio window, you can examine your investments in different ways. Like peering into the different windows of a house (with the occupants' permission, of course), you can stare into your investments from different angles and see whether you gain any insights that way.

To get to the Your Portfolio window, click the Portfolio button on the Navigation bar or choose Investing⇨Portfolio. Next, choose an option from the View menu. Table 24-1 describes the ten different options from which you can choose. Test them all and see whether you can gain any insights and be a better investor.

Table 24-1	Ways of Examining Investments in the Your Portfolio Window
View Option	*What You See*
Standard View	Securities arranged by account. Choose this view to see in which accounts you keep securities.
Asset Allocation View	Securities arranged by type — stocks first, then mutual funds, CDs, bonds, and so on. Choose this view to see whether you incorrectly placed all your investment eggs in the same basket.
Performance View	Performance data, including how much you have profited or lost on each investment, the gain or loss by percentage, and the annual return by percentage.
Return Calculations View	Return on investment projections for the coming week, four weeks, year, and three-year period. Money makes these calculations based on investment type. Choose this view to see how the wizards at Microsoft think your investments will grow.
Valuation View	Value information about your securities, including their cost bases, appreciation, and increase in value.

View Option	What You See
Quotes View	Market data on each investment, including its latest price, latest change in price, and daily and yearly high and low.
Holdings View	The latest price, number of units you own, and market value of your investment holdings.
Fundamental Data View	Historical price information, including 52-week high and low prices and P/E ratios.
Options View	Stock options in alphabetical order.
Employee Stock Options View	Stocks options you have acquired from your place of employment.
Bonds View	Bonds in your portfolio.

Choose Investing➪Portfolio Analysis to get a very useful report about your investments and how they stand. The report tells you how your investments are allocated, which are performing best and worst, and your risk profile, among other things. You can also choose Investing➪Investment Reports to generate an investment report.

Charting the Performance of an Investment

If you want to press your nose to the glass and get a very, very close look at an investment, double-click its name in the Your Portfolio window. That action takes you to the Price History window, where a chart shows you precisely how well the security is performing, as shown in Figure 24-12.

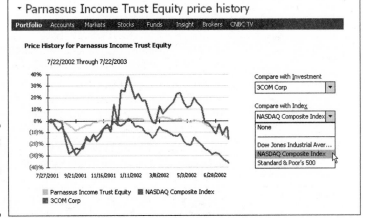

Figure 24-12: Charting the performance of an investment.

Book IV
Chapter 24

Money for Investors

In the Price History window, make selections from the drop-down lists to compare an investment's performance with another investment or with an index. This chart compares the performances of two different stocks and the NASDAQ Composite Index over a one-year period.

Index

Symbols and Numerics

* (asterisk), wildcard character, 106–107
\ (backslash), in Excel range names, 751
: (colon), in Google searches, 535
, (comma)
  adding to Excel values, 732
  e-mail address separator, 664
  in e-mail addresses, 451
$ (dollar sign), adding to Excel values, 732
= (equal sign), in example formulas, 748
% (percent sign), adding to Excel values, 732
# (pound sign)
  in channel names, 483
  in image map names, 522
(pound signs), in Excel cells, 729, 749
? (question mark), wildcard character,
    106–107
; (semicolon), e-mail address separator, 664
/ (slash)
  Excel data entry, 729
  in IRC commands, 482
  through circle, mouse pointer, 29
[ ] (square brackets), in Google searches, 535
_ (underscore), in Excel range names, 751
3-D references, Excel formulas, 751–752
3-D spatial imaging sound cards, 331
3DMark 2001 SE, 334
24-bit sound cards, 301
802.11a standard, 368
802.11b standard, 367–368
802.11g standard, 368–369

A

<A>...</A> tags, 515–516
abbreviations and acronyms, e-mail
    messages, 450
ABCNews.com, 560
abstract visualization of music, 132
AC line wireless networks, 370–371
Accelerated Graphics Port (AGP) slots, 334
accelerator keys, 31
access control, computers, 77–78
access time, hard drives, 319
accessibility options, configuring, 43
Accessories and Utilities, installing, 114
accounts, computer, 43, 78–84

accounts, financial. *See* Money accounts
AccuTrafic, 551
action buttons, PowerPoint slides, 715–717
activating XP, 18–21
Activation Wizard, 20
Active Channels, 424–425, 432–434
Active Desktop layer, 48–49
ad hoc mode, 373
adding values, Excel, 753, 754
Address bar, Internet Explorer, 418
address books
  AOL, 407–408
  Outlook, 655–659
  Outlook Express, 466–470
addressing e-mail messages. *See* e-mail
    addresses
administrative address, mailing lists, 471–472
advanced searches, 107–108
advanced viewfinder cameras, 164
adware, 180
AGP (Accelerated Graphics Port) slots, 334
AIFF format, 247
AirPort base station, 367
album art, displaying, 133
Album folder, 136
albums, ShowBiz, 253
ALIGN attribute, 512
Align to Grid, 54
All Audio folder, 136
All Clips folder, 136
All Programs list, 66
All Programs menu, 44–45
AMD chips *versus* Intel, 310
America Online (AOL). *See* AOL
amount of detail options, 797
Amtrak, 553–554
analog video cameras, 149
antonyms, searching for, 631–632
AOL (America Online), 401–409
AOL Hometown, 505
AOL Instant Messenger, 485–487
Apple Computer, 245, 367
appointments, 684–689
archives, 474, 494
ArcSoft, 251
<AREA> tag, 520–523
arguments, Excel, 754
arrow-shaped mouse pointers, 28

E

G

1

N

S

X

Y

Z

Notes

Notes